RHCSA/RHCE®
Red Hat® Linux® Certification Study Guide, Seventh Edition (Exams EX200 & EX300)

Michael Jang
Alessandro Orsaria

New York   Chicago   San Francisco
Athens   London   Madrid   Mexico City
Milan   New Delhi   Singapore   Sydney   Toronto

Cataloging-in-Publication Data is on file with the Library of Congress

McGraw-Hill Education books are available at special quantity discounts to use as premiums and sales promotions, or for use in corporate training programs. To contact a representative, please visit the Contact Us pages at www.mhprofessional.com.

RHCSA/RHCE® Red Hat® Linux® Certification Study Guide, Seventh Edition (Exams EX200 & EX300)

1234567890   DOC DOC   109876

ISBN: Book p/n 978-0-07-184193-1 and DVD p/n 978-0-07-184195-5
of set 978-0-07-184196-2

MHID: Book p/n 0-07-184193-8 and DVD p/n 0-07-184195-4
of set 0-07-184196-2

Sponsoring Editor *Timothy Green*	**Copy Editor** *Bart Reed*	**Illustration** *Cenveo Publisher Services*
Editorial Supervisor *Jody McKenzie*	**Proofreader** *Lisa McCoy*	**Art Director, Cover** *Jeff Weeks*
Project Editor *LeeAnn Pickrell*	**Indexer** *Rebecca Plunkett*	**Cover Designer** *Jeff Weeks*
Acquisitions Coordinator *Amy Stonebraker*	**Production Supervisor** *James Kussow*	
Technical Editor *Alex Davies*	**Composition** *Cenveo® Publisher Services*	

For the young widows and widowers:
may they find the courage to face their fears,
to navigate their way through the pain,
and to find hope for a brighter future.

Michael Jang (RHCE, LPIC-2, UCP, LCP, Linux+, MCP) is currently a Senior Technical Writer for ForgeRock. His experience with computers goes back to the days of jumbled punch cards. He has written other books on Linux certification, including *LPIC-1 in Depth, Mike Meyers' Linux+ Certification Passport,* and *Sair GNU/Linux Installation and Configuration Exam Cram.* His other Linux books include *Linux Annoyances for Geeks, Linux Patch Management,* and *Mastering Fedora Core Linux 5.* He has also written or contributed to books on Microsoft operating systems, including *MCSE Guide to Microsoft Windows 98* and *Mastering Windows XP Professional, Second Edition.*

Alessandro Orsaria (RHCE, RHCA, CCIE x 2) is an IT professional with more than 15 years' experience in the industry. He has authored articles for technical Linux magazines and is currently employed by a global equity hedge fund as an IT Infrastructure Architect. Alessandro is Red Hat RHCE and RHCA certified and has achieved two Cisco CCIE certifications in Routing & Switching and Datacenter. He holds an MBA from Imperial College of London and a degree in physics.

About the Technical Editor

Alex Davies works for a proprietary trading firm, where he is responsible for Linux systems and manages a team of Linux engineers across Chicago, New York, London, and Singapore. Alex is the author of *MySQL Clustering* and *MySQL High Availability Cookbook.* Earlier in his career he was both RHCE and RHCA certified and received the RHCE of the Year award in 2009 from Red Hat. Alex also holds a degree in economics from the University of Durham.

CONTENTS AT A GLANCE

CONTENTS

ACKNOWLEDGMENTS

I'd like to thank Mark Craig and Jamie Nelson of ForgeRock for supporting my efforts to update this book. I'd also like to thank Alessandro Orsaria for taking on the work required to update this book. We would not have a Seventh Edition without him. Most importantly for me, I'd like to thank my sweet wife, Donna; you are the love of my life.

—Mike Jang

First, I owe a huge debt of gratitude to Mike Jang and Tim Green for giving me the opportunity to work on the Seventh Edition of this book. More people have contributed than I can possibly mention here, but I must thank Conor Kiernan and Neil Jones at Marshall Wace for their encouragement and support. I also owe a lot to Alex, Koti, and Vlad, who helped me in many ways to get where I am today. Last but certainly not least, thank you, Julia, for your patience and sweetness while I was working on this project.

—Alessandro Orsaria

Thanks to all the incredibly hard-working folks at McGraw-Hill—Amy Stonebraker, Tim Green, LeeAnn Pickrell, Jody McKenzie, Bart Reed, and Jim Kussow—for their help in launching a great series and being solid team players.

L inux is thriving. Red Hat is at the forefront of the Linux revolution. And Red Hat Certified System Administrators (RHCSA) and Engineers (RHCE) are making it happen.

Even in the current economic recovery, business, education, and governments are cost conscious. They want control of their operating systems. Linux—even Red Hat Enterprise Linux—saves money. The open-source nature of Linux allows users to control and customize their operating systems to a higher degree than other systems. While there is a price associated with Red Hat Enterprise Linux (RHEL), the cost includes updates and support. With KVM, it's possible to set up a cluster of virtual, independent installations of RHEL (and other operating systems) on a single physical computer. Many companies have already converted rooms full of physical systems into closets of just a few systems, each configured with banks of virtual machines. As an RHCSA and an RHCE, you can join in that revolution.

While there's a cost associated with a supported version of RHEL, you don't need to pay for such support. As we describe shortly, there are trial and developer subscriptions that you can use, along with freely available "rebuilds" of RHEL that are built on the same source code.

on the job **A "rebuild" is software that is built by a third party from the same source code as the original "build." On the other hand, a "clone" is built from different source code.**

Security is another reason to move toward Linux. The U.S. National Security Agency has developed its own patch of the Linux kernel to provide context-based security in a system known as Security-Enhanced Linux (SELinux). RHEL has made SELinux a key part of a layered security strategy.

The RHCSA and RHCE exams are difficult. Available historical data suggests that less than 50 percent of first-time candidates pass the RHCE exam. But do not be intimidated. While there are no guarantees, this book can help you prepare for and pass the RHCSA and RHCE exams. And these same skills can help you in your career as a Linux administrator. Just remember, this book is not intended to be a substitute for the Red Hat prep courses that we describe shortly.

To study for this exam, you should have a network of at least three Linux computers. Because the RHCSA focuses on virtual machines, you're encouraged to use KVM-based systems for two of the computers. After configuring a service, especially a network service, you may find it helpful to check your work from another computer.

Getting Red Hat Enterprise Linux

The Red Hat exams are based on your knowledge of *Red Hat* Enterprise Linux. But here's a significant change. The RHCSA objectives specify a number of points associated with virtual machines. RHEL 7 uses the Kernel-based Virtual Machine (KVM). Red Hat supports KVM as a host only on physical systems with 64-bit CPUs. Therefore, to study for the KVM-related objectives for the RHCSA, you'll need physical hardware that can handle a 64-bit version of RHEL 7. (However, this should not be an issue, unless you run RHEL on a 10-year-old Pentium CPU.)

Also, you should expect to install two or more virtual machines on that 64-bit physical system. Virtual machines work better on systems with multiple CPUs or systems with multicore CPUs. To avoid hardware that slows your studies, you'll want a 64-bit physical system with at least 8GB, but preferably 16GB, of RAM. (We prepared this book on a system with 8GB of RAM.) As the RHCSA objectives list installation and update requirements from the Red Hat Network and other systems, you may want to purchase an RHEL subscription. However, a rebuild distribution is sufficient to study for all the other objectives. If you want a full subscription, which can help you test features associated with the Red Hat Network, the price depends on the hardware and the desired level of technical support.

With Red Hat Enterprise Linux 7, Red Hat has modified its offerings into these categories:

- RHEL Server includes varying levels of support for three different CPU architectures:
    - 64-bit systems based on AMD and Intel CPUs; the cost varies with the number of CPU sockets and supported virtual guests.
    - IBM POWER7 Systems; the cost varies with the number of CPU sockets.
    - IBM System z.
- RHEL Desktop includes varying levels of support suitable for workstations.
- RHEL Developer Suite provides download access to RHEL 7 and several add-on software, but it is limited for development purposes only.
- RHEL add-ons are available in areas such as high availability, resilient storage, load balancing, and more.

We prepared this book with the help of RHEL 7 Server. The RHEL 7 Developer Suite is a moderate cost option that includes the server packages required for the RHCSA and the RHCE exams. While RHEL is released under open-source licenses, that applies just to the source code. Access to the binary packages requires the purchase of a subscription.

One of the advantages of an enterprise-level operating system is stability. When an enterprise upgrades to RHEL 7, it counts on the ability to revise its configuration just once.

Security updates and bug fixes should then be automatic. To that end, Red Hat takes every possible measure to avoid forcing enterprises to revamp their systems just for a minor release such as RHEL 7.1. If an enterprise had to revise its configuration files for any major service for any minor release, the costs associated with Red Hat's enterprise-level operating systems would also rise.

For the same reasons, minor releases do not affect the Red Hat exam objectives. While RHEL 7.2 incorporates bug fixes, collects security updates, and provides new features, it has not changed any of the defaults of any of the configuration files described in the book.

When RHEL 7.3, RHEL 7.4, and so on, are released in future months, we expect a similar result. We've monitored RHEL releases closely for nearly a decade. We've seen no evidence of a change to the exam objectives based just on a minor release. If in doubt, monitor the content of the exam objectives listed at www.redhat.com/en/services/certification/rhcsa and www.redhat.com/en/services/certification/rhce.

If you're just studying for the exams, trial subscriptions are available from the appropriate product page; for example, a link to "Free Evaluation Software" is available at www.redhat.com/rhel/server. An account on the Red Hat Customer Portal is required. While trial subscriptions support updates for 30 days, updates can also be tested using the mirror repositories associated with rebuild distributions. Also, you can download the same operating system (for the trial period) from the same sources as paying Red Hat users.

If you're a student or a member of an educational institution with a .edu e-mail address, academic subscriptions are available. You can also use the RHEL Developer Suite, which includes RHEL 7 and several pieces of add-on software. As of this writing, the cost of a self-support subscription to RHEL Developer Suite ($99) is a significant discount over the standard RHEL Server subscription ($349).

But if you don't have a .edu e-mail address or don't want to purchase RHEL Developer Suite, there are several projects dedicated to "rebuilds" of Red Hat Enterprise Linux. The source code for almost all RHEL RPM packages is released under the Linux General Public License (GPL) or related open-source licenses. This gives anyone the right to build Red Hat Enterprise Linux from the Red Hat–released source code.

The source code is released in Source RPM package format, which means the RPM packages can be built using the **rpmbuild** command. The developers behind rebuild distributions have all revised the source code to remove Red Hat trademarks. Some, such as CentOS 7 and Scientific Linux 7, are freely available; others, such as Oracle Linux, require registration and compliance with certain criteria such as U.S. export control laws.

You can select and download the rebuild that most closely meets your needs. We have tried several of the rebuilds, including those developed by Scientific Linux and Community Enterprise Operating System (CentOS).

The rebuilds of RHEL are freely available. While these rebuilds do make slight modifications to RHEL source code (primarily to remove or replace Red Hat trademarks), we have not seen any difference that would impair your ability to study for the Red Hat exams.

- **Scientific Linux**   It is developed by and includes a lot of intellectual firepower associated with the Fermi National Accelerator Lab, as well as CERN, the lab associated with Tim Berners-Lee, the person most commonly credited with the invention of the World Wide Web.
- **Community Enterprise Linux**   The Community Enterprise Operating System (CentOS) rebuild is developed by the group at www.centos.org. This group probably has the largest community among the rebuilds. In 2014, the CentOS project joined the Red Hat community and is currently supported by Red Hat.

For the exams based on Red Hat Enterprise Linux 7, avoid Fedora Linux. Even though RHEL 7 is based loosely on Fedora 19 and Fedora 20, there are sufficient differences in these releases that may prove confusing for the purpose of an exam. Also, please avoid other Linux distributions because the Red Hat exams are based on Red Hat Enterprise Linux. In many cases, the changes that would be standard on a different Linux distribution would lead to trouble on RHEL 7.

For Instructors and More

We encourage everyone to read this guide for instructors. This book is organized to help you prepare coursework for, or study for, one exam at a time. Because the RHCSA and RHCE are two entirely separate exams, this book is organized to allow you to study for either exam, or both. If you're studying just for the RHCSA, read Chapters 1 through 9. If you're studying just for the RHCE, read Chapters 1 and 2 and Chapters 10 through 17.

Many, perhaps most, candidates have trouble finishing the tasks associated with the RHCSA and RHCE exams in the time allotted. One way to save time during these exams is to keep things simple. While it's important to read over the questions carefully, it's also important not to overdo things. For example, there's no need to configure virtual servers for the RHCSA exam. As suggested by one RHCE-related objective, it's normally sufficient to "configure the service for basic operation."

Every chapter includes some "fill-in-the-blank" questions. While there are no multiple-choice or fill-in-the-blank questions on Red Hat exams, such questions can still help measure student mastery of chapter material. Also, the fill-in-the-blank format puts a premium on the practical experience required on the exam.

In the same fashion, for the RHCE exam, unless directed to do otherwise, keep everything as simple as possible. Configure a firewall that allows access to just the services specified. Simple firewalls are faster to set up, and many security experts suggest that simple firewalls are safer.

As several services are covered in both the RHCSA and RHCE objectives, several services are covered in multiple chapters. For example, the RHCSA objective on firewalls is covered in Chapter 4. The RHCE objective related to the same topic is covered in Chapter 10.

Chapters 1 and 2 are dedicated to helping you set up a system to study for both exams. They also describe the experience associated with both exams in some detail. While they also address the configuration of an FTP server and an HTTP server, they provide instructions on how to configure files from the RHEL 7 DVD as an installation server. With a few tips described in Chapter 7, you'll also be able to set up this installation server as a **yum**-based repository to install software packages for the services associated with the RHCE.

If you're studying for the RHCE exam, you may want to refer to some RHCSA chapters. In fact, the RHCE chapters assume that you've set up KVM-based virtual machines based on the instructions described in Chapter 2, as well as the networked repository configured in Chapter 1, Lab 2, and the repositories described in Chapter 7.

Before an Exam

There is no way to cram for a Red Hat exam. But like athletes warm up before a race, you can "warm up" before a Red Hat exam. Reread each of the objectives associated with the target exam. Review the "Scenario & Solution" tables available toward the end of most chapters. Reflect on the software that has to be installed, the files that need to be configured, and the key commands that you might have trouble remembering otherwise.

Remember, the Red Hat RHCSA and RHCE exams are designed to test candidate qualifications as Linux systems administrators and engineers. If you pass either of these exams, it's not because you've memorized a canned set of answers—it's because you have a set of Linux administrative skills and know how to use them under pressure, whether it be during an exam or in a real-world situation.

In This Book

Some of the key components of this book can be found only on the DVD. Starting in Chapter 2 (Lab 2), the lab questions can be found on the DVD in a format that allows you to read the questions on a test system. The lab answers are still found at the end of each chapter. If you mount the DVD on a Linux system on the /media directory, you'll find the labs in the directories /media/Chapter2, /media/Chapter3, /media/Chapter4, and so on. The DVD also includes the content of the book in electronic format. Chapters are available as PDF files in the same chapter directories as the labs. The PDFs do not include the labs in electronic format. A book PDF has also been provided to allow you to search across chapters.

For more information on the contents of the DVD, see Appendix F.

The RHCSA and the RHCE are separate exams. If you're studying for both exams, this book can help you remember the differences. For example, you'll find coverage of the RHCSA objectives on the Secure Shell (SSH) as a client in Chapters 2 and 4. In contrast, the RHCE objectives related to SSH as a server are covered in Chapter 11.

While this book is organized to serve as an in-depth review for the RHCSA and RHCE exams for both experienced Linux and Unix professionals, it is not intended as a substitute for Red Hat courses—or, more important, real-world experience. Nevertheless, each chapter covers a major aspect of the exam, with an emphasis on the "why" as well as the "how to" of working with and supporting RHEL as a systems administrator or engineer. As the actual RHCSA and RHCE objectives (www.redhat.com/en/services/certification/rhcsa and www.redhat.com/en/services/certification/rhce) change with every release of RHEL (and even sometimes between releases), refer to the noted URL for the latest information.

Red Hat says it's important to have real-world experience to pass their exams, and they're right! However, for the RHCSA and RHCE exams, they do focus on a specific set of Linux administrative skills, as depicted in the respective objectives. This book is intended to help you take advantage of the skills you already have—and more important, to brush up on those areas where you may have a bit less experience.

This book includes relevant information from Red Hat Enterprise Linux 7 (RHEL 7). There are significant changes from Red Hat Enterprise Linux 6. Here are several key differences between RHEL 6 and RHEL 7:

- systemd, a new service manager, provides new features and faster boot times than Upstart and the old SysVinit system.
- The XFS filesystem, which is now the default, supports filesystems up to 500TB in size.
- The firewalld daemon configures a zone-based firewall.
- GNOME 3 is now the default desktop.
- In-place upgrades are available from RHEL 6.

There are many more key features; those that we believe are relevant to the RHCSA and RHCE exams, as defined by the publicly available course outlines, are also included in this book.

While it's a risky practice on production systems, it is fastest to administer RHEL during the exam by logging in to the root user account. The command prompt assumes use of that account. When logged in to the root account, you'll see a command-line prompt similar to the following:

```
[root@server1 root]#
```

As the length of this prompt would lead to a number of broken and wrapped code lines throughout this book, we've normally abbreviated the root account prompt as

```
#
```

Be careful. The hash mark (#) is also used as a comment character in Linux scripts and programs. When logged in as a regular user, you will see a slightly different prompt; for user michael, it would typically look like the following:

```
[michael@server1 michael]$
```

Similarly, we've abbreviated this as

```
$
```

There are a number of command lines and blocks of code interspersed throughout the chapters. Commands embedded within regular text, such as **ls -l**, are shown in bold. User entries and some variables in regular text are also shown in bold.

Sometimes commands exceed the available length of a line. Take this example:

```
# virt-install -n outsider1.example.org -r 1024 --disk
path=/var/lib/libvirt/images/outsider1.example.org.img,size=16
-l ftp://192.168.122.1/pub/inst -x ks=ftp://192.168.122.1/pub/ks1.cfg
```

Unless this command is carefully formatted, line breaks might appear in unfortunate places, such as between the two dashes in front of the **--disk** switch. One way to address this is with the backslash (\), which "escapes" the meaning of the carriage return that follows. (The backslash can also "escape" the meaning of a space, making it easier to work with multiple-word filenames.) Therefore, while the following command appears as if it is on four different lines, the backslashes mean that Linux reads it as one single command:

```
# virt-install -n outsider1.example.org -r 1024 --disk \
> path=/var/lib/libvirt/images/outsider1.example.org.img,size=16 \
> -l ftp://192.168.122.1/pub/inst \
> -x ks=ftp://192.168.122.1/pub/ks1.cfg
```

In some code snippets, we could not use the backslash character to split the output on more than one line. In those cases, we used a continuation arrow, as shown next:

```
5 2 * * 6 root /usr/bin/tar --selinux -czf /tmp/etc-backup-\$(/bin/date ↵
+\%m\%d).tar.gz /etc > /dev/null
```

Sometimes, you'll need to actually type in a command or a response to a question at a command line. In that case, you'll see an instruction such as "Type **y**." Alternatively, some menus require a keypress; for instance, you may be asked to press P to access a password prompt. In that case, the letter *p* is not added to the screen when you press that key. In addition, the A, despite its appearances, is in lowercase. In contrast, A is the uppercase version of that letter.

One area where some publishers have trouble is with the double-dash. Some publishing programs change the double-dash to an "em dash." But that can be a problem. The double-dash is common in many Linux commands. For example, the following command lists all packages currently installed on the local system:

```
# rpm --query --all
```

When we ran this command on our RHEL 7 systems, it listed 1300 packages.

In contrast, the following command lists all files in all packages on the local system:

```
# rpm --query -all
```

When we ran this command on our RHEL 7 system, it listed 143,000 files, a rather different result. So pay attention to the dashes, and rest assured that the team who produced this book took care to make sure that double-dashes are shown as is!

Exam Readiness Checklist

At the end of the introduction, you will find an Exam Readiness Checklist. These tables have been constructed to allow you to cross-reference the official exam objectives with the objectives as they are presented and covered in this book. The checklist also allows you to gauge your level of expertise on each objective at the outset of your studies. This should allow you to check your progress and make sure you spend the time you need on more difficult or unfamiliar sections. References have been provided for the objective exactly as the vendor presents it, the section of the study guide that covers that objective, and a chapter and page reference.

In Every Chapter

For this series, we've created a set of chapter components that calls your attention to important items, reinforces important points, and provides helpful exam-taking hints. Take a look at what you'll find in every chapter:

■ Every chapter begins with the **Certification Objectives**—the skills you need to master in order to pass the section on the exam associated with the chapter topic. The Objective headings identify the objectives within the chapter, so you'll always know an objective when you see it.

■ **Exam Watch** notes call attention to information about, and potential pitfalls in, the exam. These helpful hints are written by authors who have taken the exams and received their certification—who better to tell you what to worry about? They know what you're about to go through!

exam
watch
This book's coverage of the RHCSA and RHCE exam objectives can be found in the front matter for this book, in Tables 2 and 3, starting from page xlii.

■ **Practice Exercises** are interspersed throughout the chapters. These are step-by-step exercises that allow you to get the hands-on experience you need in order to pass the exams. They help you master skills that are likely to be an area of focus on the exam. Don't just read through the exercises; they are hands-on practice that you should be comfortable completing. Learning by doing is an effective way to increase your competency with a product. Remember, the Red Hat exams are entirely "hands on"; there are no multiple-choice questions on these exams.

■ **On the Job** notes describe the issues that come up most often in real-world settings. They provide a valuable perspective on certification- and product-related topics. They point out common mistakes and address questions that have arisen from on-the-job discussions and experience.

■ **Inside the Exam** sidebars highlight some of the most common and confusing problems that students encounter when taking a live exam. Designed to anticipate what the exam will emphasize, they will help ensure you know what you need to know to pass the exam. You can get a leg up on how to respond to those difficult-to-understand labs by focusing extra attention on these sidebars.

■ **Scenario & Solution** sections lay out potential problems and solutions in a quick-to-read format.

■ The **Certification Summary** is a succinct review of the chapter and a restatement of salient skills regarding the exam.

✓ ■ The **Two-Minute Drill** at the end of every chapter is a checklist of the main points of the chapter. It can be used for last-minute review.

Q&A ■ The **Self Test** offers "fill-in-the-blank" questions designed to help test the practical knowledge associated with the certification exams. The answers to these questions, as well as explanations of the answers, can be found at the end of each chapter. By taking the Self Test after completing each chapter, you'll reinforce what you've learned from that chapter. This book does not include multiple-choice questions because Red Hat does not include any such questions on its exams.

■ The **Lab Questions** at the end of the Self Test section offer a unique and challenging question format that requires the reader to understand multiple chapter concepts to answer correctly. These questions are more complex and more comprehensive than the other questions because they test your ability to take all the knowledge you have gained from reading the chapter and apply it to complicated, real-world situations. Starting with Chapter 2, Lab 2, all lab questions are available only on the DVD, consistent with the electronic format associated with the Red Hat exams. Remember, the Red Hat exams contain *only* lab-type questions. If you can answer these questions, you have proven that you know the subject!

Additional Resources

Some readers will want to go further. Perhaps the best way to do so is with Red Hat documentation. Much of what we learned about RHEL 7 comes from the documents available at https://access.redhat.com/documentation/en/red-hat-enterprise-linux/. For our purposes, the following may be the most important of these guides:

■ **Installation Guide**   Although Red Hat exams are given on preconfigured systems, the Installation Guide includes detailed information on Kickstart.

■ **System Administrator's Guide**   The System Administrator's Guide includes Red Hat recommendations on how services can be configured for basic operation.

■ **SELinux User's and Administrator's Guide**   The Security-Enhanced Linux Guide details the options that that can help further secure your SELinux policy.

Some Pointers

Once you've finished reading this book, set aside some time to do a thorough review. You might want to return to the book several times and make use of all the methods it offers for reviewing the material:

■ *Reread all the Exam Watch notes.* Remember that these notes are written by authors who have taken the exam and passed. They know what you should expect—and what you should be on the lookout for.

■ *Review all the Scenario & Solution sections* for quick problem solving.

■ *Retake the Self Tests.* Focus on the labs, as there are no multiple-choice (or even fill-in-the-blank) questions on the Red Hat exams. We've included fill-in-the-blank questions just to test your mastery of the practical material in each chapter.

■ *Complete the exercises.* Did you do the exercises when you read through each chapter? If not, do them! These exercises are designed to cover exam topics, and there's no better way to get to know this material than by practicing. Be sure you understand why you are performing each step in each exercise. If there is something you are not clear on, reread that section in the chapter.

The Red Hat Exam Challenge

This section covers the reasons for pursuing industry-recognized certification, explains the importance of your RHCSA or RHCE certification, and prepares you for taking the actual examination. It gives you a few pointers on how to prepare, what to expect, and what to do on exam day.

This book covers every published exam objective at the time of writing. For the latest objectives, see www.redhat.com/en/services/certification/rhcsa and www.redhat.com/en/services/certification/rhce. Red Hat has also published a syllabus for each of its prep courses for these exams, described shortly. While the published exam objectives are accurate, the prep course syllabi provide additional information. Each Red Hat prep course provides an excellent grounding in systems administration, network administration, security, and more. To that end, this book also includes coverage based on the public syllabi of Red Hat courses RH124, RH134, and RH254, described later.

Nevertheless, this book is not intended to be a substitute for any Red Hat course.

Leaping Ahead of the Competition!

Red Hat's RHCSA and RHCE certification exams are hands-on exams. As such, they are respected throughout the industry as a sign of genuine practical knowledge. If you pass, you will be head and shoulders above the candidate who has passed only a "standard" multiple-choice certification exam.

Red Hat has offered its hands-on exams since 1999. They've evolved over the years. As detailed in Chapter 1, the RHCSA is a 2.5-hour exam, and the RHCE is now a 3.5-hour exam. The requirements are detailed in the Exam Readiness Checklist later in this introduction. While the passing score for these exams is not currently published, it was at one time 70 percent for the relevant Red Hat exams on RHEL 5.

Why a Hands-On Exam?

Most certifications today are based on multiple-choice exams. These types of exams are relatively inexpensive to set up and easy to proctor. Unfortunately, many people without real-world skills are good at taking multiple-choice exams. In some cases, the answers to

INSIDE THE EXAM

The RHCSA and RHCE exams are Red Hat exams. Knowledge of Unix or a Linux distribution such as Ubuntu is certainly helpful, as well as experience with services such as Apache, SMB, NFS, DNS, and SSH. However, it is important to know how to set up, configure, install, and debug these services under Red Hat Enterprise Linux (or rebuild distributions that use the same source code, such as Scientific Linux, CentOS, or Oracle Linux).

these multiple-choice exams are already available online. This results in problems on the job with "certified" engineers who have an image as "paper tigers" and do not have any real-world skills.

In response, Red Hat wanted to develop a certification program that matters. In our opinion, they have succeeded with the RHCSA, the RHCE, and their other advanced certifications.

Linux administrators sometimes have to install Linux on a computer or virtual machine. In fact, the RHCSA includes several objectives on this subject. Depending on the configuration, they may need to install Linux from a central source through a network. Installing Linux is not enough to make it useful. Administrators need to know how to configure Linux: add users, install and configure services, set up firewalls, and more.

Prepare for the RHCSA and RHCE Exams

The topics associated with the RHCSA are independent of the RHCE. Yes, there is some overlap. For example, SELinux is covered on both exams, but the coverage is different. The RHCSA and RHCE certifications are based on separate exams.

The RHCSA is the entry-level Red Hat certification. While you can take the RHCE exam first, Red Hat won't award you an RHCE unless you've also passed the RHCSA exam. Some candidates take both exams on the same day. As discussed in Chapter 1, Red Hat has also publicly stated that their exams are now "presented electronically." Therefore, this book includes (most) labs and sample exams in electronic format on the DVD that accompanies this book.

Work with Red Hat Enterprise Linux. Install it on a computer that you don't need for any other purpose. Configure the services described in this book. Find different ways to secure each service. Test the results from systems both inside and outside a network.

As you read this book, you'll have the opportunity to install RHEL several times. Courtesy of virtualization, you can install RHEL over a network. Then you can work with the different network services. Test each service as you configure it, preferably from another computer on your network. Testing your work becomes especially important when verifying the security features that are required, whether on an exam or in a production network.

Red Hat Certification Program

Red Hat offers several courses that can help you prepare for the RHCSA and RHCE. Most of these courses are four or five days long. In some cases, the courses are offered electronically.

These aren't the only Red Hat courses available; there are a number of others related to the Red Hat Certified Architect (RHCA), Red Hat Certified Virtualization Administrator (RHCVA), as well as several Certificates of Expertise in specific areas such as server hardening and performance tuning. But study this first; the RHCSA and RHCE are prerequisites for more advanced certifications such as the RHCA.

Should You Take an RHCSA/RHCE Course?

This book is *not* intended as a substitute for any particular Red Hat RHCSA or RHCE prep course. However, the topics in this book are based in part on the topics listed in the course outlines provided at www.redhat.com/en/services/training/all-courses-exams. By design, these topics may help Linux users qualify as real-world administrators and can also be used as such. Red Hat can change these topics and course outlines at any time, so monitor www.redhat.com for the latest updates. Table 1 describes those courses associated with the RHCSA and RHCE exams.

TABLE 1	Red Hat RHCSA/RHCE-Related Courses

Course	Description
RH124	System Administration I: Core system administration skills
RH124L	The hands-on labs of course RH124, available online
RH134	System Administration II: Command line skills for Linux administrators (RH135 without the RHCSA exam)
RH134L	The hands-on labs of course RH134, available online
RH135	System Administration II with the RHCSA exam
RH199	RHCSA rapid-track course for experienced administrators
RH200	RH199 + RHCSA exam
EX200	Just the RHCSA exam
RH254	System Administration III: Advanced security and service configuration
RH254L	The hands-on labs of course RH254, available online
RH255	System Administration III with the RHCE exam
RH299	Red Hat Certification lab, a rapid-track course for experienced administrators
RH300	RH299 + RHCSA and RHCE exams
EX300	The RHCE exam

The courses given by Red Hat are excellent. The Red Hat instructors who teach these courses are highly skilled. If you have the resources, it is the best way to prepare for the RHCSA and RHCE exams. If you feel the need for classroom instruction, read this book and then take the appropriate course.

If you're not sure you're ready for the course or book, read Chapter 1. It includes a rapid overview of the requirements associated with the Red Hat RHCSA and RHCE certifications. If you find the material in Chapter 1 to be overwhelming, consider one of the books noted near the start of the chapter, or one of the other lower-level Red Hat courses. In addition, Chapter 1 includes a lab that prompts you to examine the requirements of the Linux Professional Institute for its Level 1 certification (LPIC-1). Linux geeks like yourself who are ready to study for the Red Hat exams often take the LPIC-1 exams first.

Alternatively, you may already be familiar with the material in this book. You may have the breadth and depth of knowledge required to pass the RHCSA and RHCE exams. In that case, use this book as a refresher to help you focus on the skills and techniques needed to pass both exams.

Signing Up for the RHCSA/RHCE Course and/or Exam

Red Hat provides convenient web-based registration systems for the courses and tests. To sign up for any of the Red Hat courses or exams, navigate to www.redhat.com, click the link for Services & Support | All Courses and Exams, and select the desired course or exam. As shown back in Table 1, exams may be taken independently from a course. For example, the RHCSA and RHCE exams are associated with exam codes EX200 and EX300, respectively. Exams may also be taken as part of an online or instructor-led course. Alternatively, contact Red Hat Enrollment Central at training@redhat.com or (866) 626-2994.

Discounts may be available for a limited time for candidates who have been previously .certified as an RHCSA or RHCE. Current discounts are shown at https://www.redhat.com/en/services/training/specials/.

Before signing up, read current Red Hat policies, available at www.redhat.com/en/services/training/student-center/. Be aware, Red Hat has sometimes canceled courses for low attendance.

Final Preparations

The Red Hat exams are grueling. Once you have the skills, the most important thing you can take to the exam is a clear head. If you're tired or frantic, you may miss the easy solutions that are often available. Get the sleep you need the night before the exam. Eat a good breakfast. Bring snacks that can keep your mind in top condition.

INSIDE THE EXAM

The RHCSA and RHCE certifications are associated with two separate exams. However, the RHCE topics generally require skills more advanced than the RHCSA. As they are separate exams, we've cited the associated objectives separately. Watch for updates at www.redhat.com/en/services/certification/rhcsa and www.redhat.com/en/services/certification/rhce.

The RHCSA exam is two and a half hours long. The RHCE exam is three and a half hours long. In many cases, Red Hat makes it possible for candidates to take both exams in the same day. While it's a terrific convenience for those who have to travel to Red Hat exam facilities (in over 50 cities just in North America), taking the two exams in the same day is like running two world-class marathons. This is an advanced book, not designed for beginners to Unix or Linux. The former "prerequisite skills" have been incorporated in the body of the RHCSA requirements. Accordingly, we've only covered the tools associated with these prerequisites briefly—mostly in Chapters 1 and 3. If you need more time to learn these prerequisite skills, consider attending the RH124 course; alternatively, read the reference books we've cited in Chapter 1.

The RHCSA Exam

| TABLE 2 | RHCSA Exam Readiness Checklist |

RHCSA Exam Readiness Checklist

Certification Objective	Study Guide Coverage	Ch #	Pg #
Category: Understand and Use Essential Tools			
Access a shell prompt and issue commands with correct syntax	Shells, Standard Command-Line Tools	3	118, 122
Use input-output redirection (>, >>, |, 2>, etc.)	Shells	3	118
Use **grep** and regular expressions to analyze text	The Management of Text Files	3	131
Access remote systems using SSH	Administration with the Secure Shell and Secure Copy	2	95

TABLE 2   RHCSA Exam Readiness Checklist (*Continued*)

RHCSA Exam Readiness Checklist

Certification Objective	Study Guide Coverage	Ch #	Pg #
Log in and switch users in multiuser targets	User and Shell Configuration	8	416
Archive, compress, unpack, and uncompress files using **tar**, **star**, **gzip**, and **bzip2**	Elementary System Administration Commands	9	444
Create and edit text files	The Management of Text Files	3	131
Create, delete, copy, and move files and directories	Standard Command-Line Tools	3	122
Create hard and soft links	Standard Command-Line Tools	3	122
List, set, and change standard ugo/rwx permissions	Basic File Permissions	4	178
Locate, read, and use system documentation, including **man**, **info**, and files in /usr/share/doc	Local Online Documentation	3	142
Category: Operate Running Systems			
Boot, reboot, and shut down a system normally	Bootloaders and GRUB 2, Between GRUB 2 and Login	5	245, 259
Boot systems into different targets manually	Bootloaders and GRUB 2	5	245
Interrupt the boot process in order to gain access to a system	Bootloaders and GRUB 2	5	245
Identify CPU/memory-intensive processes, adjust process priority with **renice**, and **kill** processes	Elementary System Administration Commands	9	444
Locate and interpret system log files and journals	Local Log File Analysis	9	464
Access a virtual machine's console	Configure a Virtual Machine on KVM	2	68
Start and stop virtual machines	Configure a Virtual Machine on KVM	2	68
Start, stop, and check the status of network services	Network Configuration and Troubleshooting	3	154
Securely transfer files between systems	Administration with the Secure Shell and Secure Copy	2	95
Category: Configure Local Storage			
List, create, and delete partitions on MBR and GPT disks	Storage Management and Partitions	6	287

TABLE 2　　RHCSA Exam Readiness Checklist (*Continued*)

RHCSA Exam Readiness Checklist

Certification Objective	Study Guide Coverage	Ch #	Pg #
Create and remove physical volumes, assign physical volumes to volume groups, and create and delete logical volumes	Logical Volume Management (LVM)	6	313
Configure systems to mount file systems at boot by Universally Unique ID (UUID) or label	Filesystem Management	6	320
Add new partitions and logical volumes, and swap to a system non-destructively	Filesystem Management	6	320
Category: Create and Configure File Systems			
Create, mount, unmount, and use vfat, ext4, and xfs filesystems	Storage Management and Partitions, Filesystem Formats, Filesystem Management	6	287, 305, 320
Mount and unmount CIFS and NFS network filesystems	Filesystem Management	6	320
Extend existing logical volumes	Logical Volume Management (LVM)	6	313
Create and configure set-GID directories for collaboration	Special Groups	8	432
Create and manage access control lists (ACLs)	Access Control Lists and More	4	186
Diagnose and correct file permission problems	Basic File Permissions	4	178
Category: Deploy, Configure, and Maintain Systems			
Configure networking and hostname resolution statically or dynamically	Network Configuration and Troubleshooting	3	154
Schedule tasks using **at** and **cron**	Automate System Administration: **cron** and **at**	9	456
Start and stop services and configure services to start automatically at boot	Control by Target	5	270
Configure systems to boot into a specific target automatically	Between GRUB 2 and Login	5	270
Install Red Hat Enterprise Linux automatically using Kickstart	Automated Installation Options	2	80
Configure a physical machine to host virtual guests	Configure KVM for Red Hat	2	56
Install Red Hat Enterprise Linux systems as virtual guests	Configure a Virtual Machine on KVM	2	68

TABLE 2   RHCSA Exam Readiness Checklist (*Continued*)

RHCSA Exam Readiness Checklist

Certification Objective	Study Guide Coverage	Ch #	Pg #
Configure systems to launch virtual machines at boot	Configure a Virtual Machine on KVM	2	68
Configure network services to start automatically at boot	Control by Target	5	270
Configure a system to use time services	Time Synchronization	5	274
Install and update software packages from Red Hat Network, a remote repository, or from the local file system	The Red Hat Package Manager, Dependencies and the **yum** Command, More Package Management Tools	7	344, 357, 379
Update the kernel package appropriately to ensure a bootable system	The Red Hat Package Manager	7	344
Modify the system bootloader	Bootloaders and GRUB 2	5	245
Category: Manage Users and Groups			
Create, delete, and modify local user accounts	User Account Management	8	397
Change passwords and adjust password aging for local user accounts	User Account Management	8	397
Create, delete, and modify local groups and group memberships	User Account Management	8	397
Configure a system to use an existing authentication service for user and group information	Users and Network Authentication	8	421
Category: Manage Security			
Configure firewall settings using **firewall-config, firewall-cmd,** or **iptables**	Basic Firewall Control	4	195
Configure key-based authentication for SSH	Securing SSH with Key-Based Authentication	4	207
Set enforcing and permissive modes for SELinux	A Security-Enhanced Linux Primer	4	213
List and identify SELinux file and process context	A Security-Enhanced Linux Primer	4	213
Restore default file contexts	A Security-Enhanced Linux Primer	4	213
Use boolean settings to modify system SELinux settings	A Security-Enhanced Linux Primer	4	213
Diagnose and address routine SELinux policy violations	A Security-Enhanced Linux Primer	4	213

The RHCE Exam

TABLE 3   RHCE Exam Readiness Checklist

RHCE Exam Readiness Checklist

Certification Objective	Study Guide Coverage	Ch #	Pg #
Category: System Configuration and Management			
Use network teaming or bonding to configure aggregated network links between two Red Hat Enterprise Linux systems	Network Interface Bonding and Teaming	12	606
Configure IPv6 addresses and perform basic IPv6 troubleshooting	An Introduction to IPv6	12	602
Route IP traffic and create static routes	IP Routes	12	598
Use firewalld and associated mechanisms such as rich rules, zones, and custom rules to implement packet filtering and configure network address translation (NAT)	Firewalls and Network Address Translation	10	487
Use /proc/sys and sysctl to modify and set kernel run-time parameters	Kernel Run-time Parameters	12	595
Configure system to authenticate using Kerberos	Authentication with Kerberos	12	613
Configure a system as either an iSCSI target or initiator that persistently mounts an iSCSI target	iSCSI Targets and Initiators	13	660
Produce and deliver reports on system utilization (processor, memory, disk, and network)	Set Up System Utilization Reports	12	590
Use shell scripting to automate system maintenance tasks	Automate System Maintenance	12	581
Category: Network Services **(The following six objectives apply to all network services)**			
Install the packages needed to provide the service	All RHCE chapters	10–17	479–842
Configure SELinux to support the service	Security-Enhanced Linux, other chapters for each service	11, 13–17	541, 631–842
Use SELinux port labeling to allow services to use nonstandard ports	Security-Enhanced Linux, other chapters for each service	11, 13–17	541, 631–842

TABLE 3	RHCE Exam Readiness Checklist (*Continued*)

RHCE Exam Readiness Checklist

Certification Objective	Study Guide Coverage	Ch #	Pg #
Configure the service to start when the system is booted	A Security and Configuration Checklist, other chapters for each service	11, 13–17	541, 631–842
Configure the service for basic operation	All RHCE chapters	10–17	479–842
Configure host-based and user-based security for the service	All RHCE chapters	10–17	479–842
Subcategory: HTTP/HTTPS			
Configure a virtual host	Regular and Secure Virtual Hosts	14	706
Configure private directories	Specialized Apache Directories	14	700
Deploy a basic CGI application	Deploy a Basic CGI Application	14	719
Configure group-managed content	Specialized Apache Directories	14	700
Configure TLS security	Regular and Secure Virtual Hosts	14	706
Subcategory: DNS			
Configure a caching-only name server	Minimal DNS Server Configurations	13	634
Troubleshoot DNS client issues	Minimal DNS Server Configurations	13	634
Subcategory: NFS			
Provide network shares to specific clients	The Network File System (NFS) Server, Test an NFS Client	16	774, 790
Provide network shares suitable to group collaboration	The Network File System (NFS) Server	16	774
Use Kerberos to control access to NFS network shares	NFS with Kerberos	16	792
Subcategory: SMB			
Provide network shares to specific clients	Samba Services, Samba as a Client, Samba Troubleshooting	15	734, 757, 761

TABLE 3	RHCE Exam Readiness Checklist (*Continued*)

RHCE Exam Readiness Checklist

Certification Objective	Study Guide Coverage	Ch #	Pg #
Provide network shares suitable to group collaboration	Samba Services, Samba Troubleshooting	15	734, 761
Subcategory: SMTP			
Configure a system to forward all e-mail to a central mail server	The Configuration of Postfix	13	650
Subcategory: SSH			
Configure key-based authentication	Securing SSH with Key-Based Authentication	4	207
Configure additional options described in documentation	The Secure Shell Server	11	552
Subcategory: NTP			
Synchronize time using other NTP peers	The Network Time Service	13	666
Category: Database Services			
Install and configure MariaDB	Introduction to MariaDB, Secure MariaDB	17	808, 826
Back up and restore a database	Database Backup and Recovery	17	831
Create a simple database schema	Database Management	17	815
Perform simple SQL queries against a database	Simple SQL Queries	17	819

Chapter 1

Prepare for Red Hat Hands-on Certifications

The Red Hat exams are an advanced challenge. This book covers the Red Hat Certified System Administrator (RHCSA) exam in Chapters 1 to 9, and it provides the foundation for those who want to earn the Red Hat Certified Engineer (RHCE) certification in the subsequent chapters. Red Hat offers several courses to help prepare for these exams, as described in the front matter and in this chapter.

The focus of this chapter is installation, to create a common version of Red Hat Enterprise Linux (RHEL) as a test bed for future chapters. It assumes and describes hardware required to implement Red Hat's default virtualization solution, the Kernel-based Virtual Machine (KVM). As rebuild distributions such as the Community Enterprise Operating System (CentOS) and Scientific Linux are essentially identical to RHEL, you should be able to use those solutions too. Just about the only differences between a rebuild and RHEL are the trademarks and the access to repositories, which will be described in Chapter 7.

Those of you familiar with earlier versions of the Red Hat requirements may remember the changes to the Red Hat exams during the past years. After the release of RHEL 6, Red Hat discontinued the RHCT exam and replaced it with the RHCSA. Although the RHCSA is, in many ways, similar to the RHCT, there are significant differences. Most RHCSA objectives were covered on the former RHCT exam. However, the RHCSA is not easier than the RHCT; it is just a prerequisite to the RHCE. The RHCSA also includes a number of requirements that were formerly part of the RHCE objectives.

Red Hat suggests that candidates for the RHCSA have one to three years of experience with the bash shell, user administration, system monitoring, basic networking, software updates, and more. Details are described in the introduction to this book.

If you're new to Linux or Unix, this book may not be enough for you. It's not possible to provide sufficient detail, at least in a way that can be understood by newcomers to Linux and other Unix-based operating systems. If after reading this book, you find gaps in your knowledge, please refer to one of the following guides:

- *Linux Administration: A Beginner's Guide,* Seventh Edition, by Wale Soyinka (McGraw-Hill, 2016), provides a detailed step-by-step guide to this operating system.

- *Security Strategies in Linux Platforms and Applications*, by Michael Jang (Jones & Bartlett, 2010), gives you a detailed look at how you can secure your Linux system and networks in every possible way.

- *LPIC-1 in Depth*, by Michael Jang (Course Technology PTR, 2009), covers the certification many Linux professionals qualify for prior to working on the RHCSA and RHCE.

Before installing Red Hat Enterprise Linux (RHEL), you need the right hardware. The installation of RHEL 7 is supported only on systems with 64-bit CPUs. This is not a problem if you have a server with the latest Intel or AMD processor model, but may be an issue if you want to install RHEL 7 on a machine running a 10-year-old Pentium CPU. Details are discussed in the chapter. As such, while the RHCSA and RHCE exams are, by and large, not hardware exams, some basic hardware knowledge is a fundamental requirement for any Linux administrator. As for the operating system itself, you can purchase a subscription to RHEL, or you can use one of the "rebuild" distributions where the distribution is built by third parties from source code publicly released by Red Hat.

If you're experienced with other Unix-type operating systems such as Solaris, AIX, and HP-UX, prepare to leave some defaults at the door. There are even significant differences between the Ubuntu and Red Hat distributions. When Red Hat developed its Linux distribution, the company made some choices that differed from other Unix implementations. When one of the authors of this *Study Guide* took Red Hat's RH300 course, some students with these backgrounds had difficulties with the course and the RHCE exam.

For the purpose of this book, we'll be running most commands as the Linux administrative user, root. Logging in as the root user is normally discouraged unless you're administering a computer. However, since the RHCSA and RHCE exams test your administrative skills, it's appropriate to run commands in this book as the root user. Of course, you will also need to know how to set up regular users with partial or full administrative privileges.

INSIDE THE EXAM

A Virtual Host

The RHCSA assumes that you know how to "configure a physical machine to host virtual guests." In other words, you need to be able to prepare a system to house VMs where other instances of RHEL (or even other operating systems such as Microsoft Windows) can be installed.

As this is RHEL, this is based on the Red Hat default VM system, KVM. Because appropriate rebuild distributions such as CentOS and Scientific Linux use the same source code, they also use KVM. In this chapter, not only will you install RHEL, but also you will install those packages that support KVM.

Default File Sharing Configuration Services

In the previous version of the RHCSA exam, candidates were expected to know how to "configure a system to run a default configuration HTTP server" and "configure a system to run a default configuration FTP server." Although those requirements have been removed from the RHCSA objectives on RHEL 7, we think that they are still valuable skills for your preparation, especially if you want to set up a remote HTTP or FTP software repository for a lab environment. Hence, in this chapter we have briefly illustrated the configuration of a simple HTTP and FTP server.

The default Red Hat solutions for these services are the Apache web server and the Very Secure FTP Daemon (vsftpd) server. Although these services can be complex, the steps required to set up these servers to share files are fairly simple. In fact, no changes are required to the default configuration files for these services. Some of the related steps described in this chapter depend on skills presented in future chapters.

(Continued)

The original release of the RHCSA objectives was worded slightly differently: "Deploy file sharing services with HTTP/FTP." We believe this provided a significant clue to Red Hat's original intent with these objectives. To that end, you'll examine how to set up these services as file servers, based on their default configurations.

Using Other Versions of Red Hat

For the purpose of this chapter, you can install RHEL 7 using a paid subscription or from a demonstration DVD. You can also use one of the rebuild distributions. However, whereas RHEL 7 is based in part on the work done by many open-source contributors, it's also based on both the Fedora 19 and 20 releases. Don't use Fedora to study for the Red Hat exams. If you use Fedora 19 or 20, some configuration settings may differ from RHEL 7. Later versions of Fedora are likely to have features not found in RHEL 7.

CERTIFICATION OBJECTIVE 1.01

The RHCSA and RHCE Exams

Red Hat first started giving certification exams in 1999. Since that time, its exams have evolved. The former RHCT was a complete subset of the RHCE. Today, the RHCSA covers topics separate from but closely related to the RHCE.

In addition, Red Hat has focused the exams more on hands-on configuration. Multiple choice questions were removed from the exam in 2003. More recently, in 2009, it simplified the exam by removing the requirement to install Linux on a "bare-metal" system. (However, the changes implemented in 2011 suggest that you need to know how to install Linux over a network on a VM.) In addition, there is no longer a separate troubleshooting portion of the exam. For more information, see http://www.redhat.com/certification/faq.

exam
watch

Red Hat provides "pre-assessment" tests for Red Hat RHCSA and RHCE Exam Prep courses. They correspond to the RH134 and RH254 courses, respectively. These tests are available through http://www.redhat.com/en/services/training/skills-assessment. Red Hat requires contact information before providing those pre-assessment tests.

The Exam Experience

Red Hat's certification tests are hands-on exams. As a result of this, they are respected throughout the industry as a sign of genuine practical knowledge. When you pass a Red Hat exam, you will stand head and shoulders above the candidate who has passed only a "standard" multiple choice certification exam.

When time starts, you'll be faced with a live system. You'll be given actual configuration problems associated with the items listed in the exam objectives for each certification, shown at http://www.redhat.com/en/services/certification/rhcsa and http://www.redhat .com/en/services/certification/rhce. Naturally, this book is dedicated to helping you gain the skills described on those web pages.

While you won't have Internet access during the exam, you will have access to online documentation such as man and info pages, as well as documentation in the /usr/share/doc/ directories, assuming appropriate packages are installed.

In addition, Red Hat provides the exam in electronic format. Although the basic instructions may be in a local language such as English, the RHCSA and RHCE exams are available in 12 different languages: English, Simplified Chinese, Traditional Chinese, Dutch, French, Italian, Japanese, Korean, Portuguese, Russian, Spanish, and Turkish. If one of these alternatives is desired, you should contact Red Hat training to be sure, at training@redhat.com or 1-866-626-2994.

Red Hat also has prep courses for both exams. The outlines for those courses are available from http://www.redhat.com. Although this book is not intended as a substitute for such courses, it is consistent with their outlines. This book covers the objectives associated with each of these exams.

e**x**a**m**

ⓦ a t c h   **This book's coverage of the items listed in the RHCSA and RHCE exam objectives can be found in the front matter for this book, in Table 2, page xlii.**

The RHCSA Exam

The RHCSA exam allows you to demonstrate your ability to configure live physical and virtual systems for networking, security, custom filesystems, package updates, user management, and more. In essence, the RHCSA exam covers those skills required to configure and administer a Linux workstation in the enterprise.

The RHCSA exam lasts two and a half hours. When you sit down to take the exam, you'll have tasks to perform on a live RHEL system. Any changes that are made must survive a reboot. When you've completed the given tasks, the person grading the exam will see if the system is configured to meet the requirements. For example, if you're told to "create, delete, and modify local user accounts," it doesn't matter if the associated configuration file has been modified with the **vi** editor or the graphical User Manager tool. As long as you don't cheat, it's the results that count.

The RHCE Exam

The RHCE exam tests your ability to configure live physical and virtual servers, running network services such as Apache, MariaDB, the Network File System (NFS), Samba, iSCSI targets, and more. It also tests your ability to handle complex configuration options associated with Security Enhanced Linux (SELinux), firewalls, networking, and more. In essence, if you pass the RHCE exam, hiring managers will know that you're qualified to help manage their enterprises of Linux systems.

The RHCE exam lasts three and a half hours. When you sit down to take the exam, you'll be given tasks to perform on a live RHEL system. As with the RHCSA, any changes that are made must survive a reboot. Usually, there are different ways to complete a task. For example, you can use BIND or Unbound to set up a caching name server. The choice is up to you; it's the result that matter, rather than how you actually got there.

The topics in the Red Hat preparation courses in a few areas go beyond those listed in the Red Hat Exam Prep guide. Although such topics are not currently part of the exam, they may be included in future versions of the Red Hat exams.

If You're Studying "Just" for the RHCSA Exam

Red Hat has been known to make minor changes to the requirements on occasion. Future changes may be based on topics covered in the Red Hat RHCSA Rapid Track course, RH199/RH200. So if you're not planning to take the RHCSA within the next few months, watch the outline for that course. It may, in effect, be a preview of where Red Hat wants to take the RHCSA exam in the future.

Evolving Requirements

Changes happen to the requirements for the Red Hat exams. You can see that in the differences between the old RHCT exam and the RHCSA. You can see that in the changes to the exam format, where bare-metal installations are no longer required. In fact, that change happened over two years into the life of RHEL 5. Changes happened in the first month after RHEL 6 was released. So when you're preparing for the RHCSA or RHCE exam, watch the associated exam objectives carefully.

CERTIFICATION OBJECTIVE 1.02

Basic Hardware Requirements

Now it's time to explore in detail the hardware that Red Hat Enterprise Linux can handle. Although some manufacturers now include their own Linux hardware drivers, most Linux hardware support comes from third parties, starting with the work of volunteers. Fortunately, there is a vast community of Linux users, many of whom produce drivers for Linux and distribute them freely on the Internet. If a certain piece of hardware is popular, you can be certain that Linux support for that piece of hardware will pop up somewhere on the Internet and will be incorporated into various Linux distributions, including Red Hat Enterprise Linux.

Hardware Compatibility

RHEL 7 can be installed only on 64-bit systems. Fortunately, most PCs and servers sold today are 64-bit systems. Even the lowly Intel i3 CPU can handle 64-bit operating systems. There are even 64-bit versions of the Intel Atom CPU common on netbook systems. Similar comparisons can be made for CPUs from Advanced Micro Devices.

Be careful when purchasing a new computer to use with Linux. Though Linux has come a long way the last few years, and you should have little problem installing it on most modern servers or PCs, you shouldn't assume Linux will install or run flawlessly on *any* computer, especially if the system in question is a state-of-the-art laptop computer. Laptops are often designed with proprietary configurations that work with Linux only after some reverse engineering. For example, when one of the authors of this book installed RHEL 7 on a brand-name laptop built in 2014, he had to do a bit of extra work to make the graphics card work with RHEL 7.

The architecture of a server or PC defines the components it uses as well as the way those components are connected. In other words, the architecture describes much more than just the CPU. It includes standards for other hardware such as memory, data paths such as computer buses, general system design, and more. All software is written for a specific computer architecture.

Even when a manufacturer creates a device for a CPU platform, it may not work with Linux. Therefore, it's important to know the basic architecture of a computer. But strictly speaking, if you want hardware compatible with and supported by Red Hat, consult the hardware compatibility list at https://hardware.redhat.com.

Architectures

Although RHEL 7 has been built for a variety of architectures, you can focus on the Intel/AMD 64-bit or x86_64 architecture for the RHCSA and RHCE exams. As of this writing, these exams are offered only on computers with such CPUs, so you need not worry about special architecture-specific issues such as specialty bootloaders or custom proprietary drivers. Nevertheless, customized Red Hat distributions are available for a variety of platforms.

You can install RHEL 7 on systems with a wide variety of CPUs. Red Hat supports three different basic 64-bit CPU architectures:

- Intel/AMD64 (x86_64)
- IBM POWER7
- IBM System z

To identify the architecture of a system, run the following command:

```
# uname -p
```

If you're planning to configure VMs on RHEL 7, be sure to choose a system that supports hardware-assisted virtualization, along with Basic Input/Output System (BIOS) or Universal Extensible Firmware Interface (UEFI) menu options that allow you to activate hardware-assisted virtualization. A configuration that supports hardware-assisted virtualization will have either the **vmx** (Intel) or **svm** (AMD) flags in the /proc/cpuinfo file.

on the **🛈 o b**   **If you're not sure about a system, look at the processor specifications on the vendor's website, and check that the processor comes with extensions for hardware-assisted virtualization.**

RAM Requirements

Although it's possible to run RHEL 7 on less, the RAM memory requirements are driven by the needs of the Red Hat installer. For basic Intel/AMD-based 64-bit architectures, Red

Hat officially requires 1GB of RAM. However, the graphical installer runs with a minimum of 512MB.

Of course, actual memory requirements depend on the load from every program that may be run simultaneously on a system. That can also include the memory requirements of any VMs that you might run on a physical RHEL 7 system. There is no practical maximum RAM because, theoretically, you could run 64TB of RAM on RHEL 7. But that's just theory. The maximum RAM supported on RHEL 7 for 64-bit Intel/AMD-based systems is 3TB, and since RHEL 7.1 the limit has been increased to 6TB.

on the
Ϙ o b
If you're setting up Linux as a server, RAM requirements increase with the number of applications that may need to run simultaneously. The same may be true if you're running several different VMs on a single system. However, administrators typically "overcommit" RAM on VMs configured with different functionality. VMs can also transparently share memory pages to further improve efficiency.

Hard Drive Options

Before a computer can load Linux, the BIOS or UEFI has to recognize the active primary partition on the hard drive. This partition should include the Linux boot files. The BIOS or UEFI can then set up and initialize that hard drive, and then load Linux boot files from that active primary partition. You should know the following about hard drives and Linux:

■ The number of drives that can be installed on modern computers has increased. On commodity hardware it's relatively easy to get 16 or 24 Serial Advanced Technology Attachment (SATA) or Serial Attached SCSI (SAS) internal drives on a system.

■ You need both a UEFI firmware and a GPT-partitioned disk to boot from a drive larger than 2TB. UEFI is a firmware interface that is meant to replace the traditional BIOS, and today is available on many PCs on the market. The GUID Partition Table (GPT) is a partitioning format that supports drives larger than 2TB, but you also require a UEFI firmware (rather than a traditional BIOS firmware) to boot from such device.

■ You can install RHEL 7 on a storage area network (SAN) volume. RHEL 7 supports more than 10,000 multipath devices.

Networking

As Linux was originally designed as a clone of Unix, it retains the advantages of Unix as a network operating system. However, not every network component works with Linux. A number of manufacturers of wireless network devices have not built Linux drivers. In most such cases, Linux developers have been working furiously to develop appropriate drivers and to get those drivers incorporated into the major distributions, including RHEL.

Virtual Machine Options

Virtualization makes it relatively easy to set up a large number of systems, so it can help you configure machines, each dedicated to a specific service. To that end, virtualization can be classified into different categories. Some solutions can belong to more than one category. As an example, VMware ESXi is a bare-metal, hypervisor-based virtualization solution that supports hardware-assisted virtualization and provides optional paravirtual drivers to be installed on the guest OS.

- **Application level vs. VM level** Systems such as Wine Is Not an Emulator (Wine) support the installation of a single application. In this case, Wine allows an application designed for Microsoft Windows to be installed on Linux. On the other end, VM-level virtualization emulates a number of complete computer systems for the installation of separate guest OSs.

- **Hosted vs. bare-metal hypervisor** Applications such as VMware Player and VirtualBox are hosted hypervisors because they run on a conventional operating system such as Microsoft Windows 8. Conversely, bare-metal virtualization systems, such as VMware ESXi and Citrix XenServer, include a minimal operating system dedicated to VM operations.

- **Paravirtualization vs. full virtualization** Full virtualization allows a guest OS to run unmodified on a hypervisor, whereas paravirtualization requires specialized drivers to be installed in the guest OS.

The KVM solution configured with RHEL 7 is known as a hypervisor—a VM monitor that supports the running of multiple operating systems concurrently on the same CPU. KVM replaces the previous default in RHEL 5, Xen.

on the
job

KVM has replaced Xen in many open-source distributions. XenServer is owned by Citrix.

Another virtualization approach that is attracting a lot of interest is Linux containers, such as those provided by the Red Hat Enterprise Linux Atomic Host project. This solution is not hypervisor based but rather relies on the process and filesystem isolation techniques available in the Linux kernel (that is, cgroups and namespaces) to run multiple isolated Linux systems on the same physical host.

CERTIFICATION OBJECTIVE 1.03

Get Red Hat Enterprise Linux

The RHCSA and RHCE exams are based on your knowledge of RHEL. To get an official copy of RHEL, you'll need a subscription. In some cases, trial subscriptions are available. However, if you don't need the same "look and feel" of RHEL to prepare for an exam, third-party rebuilds are available. As such, "rebuilds" use the same source code as RHEL, and except for the trademarks and the connection to the Red Hat Customer Portal, they're essentially functionally identical to RHEL.

Once you either purchase a subscription or get approved for an evaluation copy, you'll be able to download RHEL 7 from the Red Hat Customer Portal at https://access.redhat .com/downloads. Downloads are available for the operating system in a format appropriate for a DVD. There's also a download available for a network boot CD. You'll even be able to download files with the source code for associated packages. These downloads are in ISO image format, with an **.iso** extension. Such files can be burned to appropriate media, using standard tools such as K3b, Brasero, and even corresponding tools on Microsoft systems. Alternatively, you can set up a VM where the virtual CD/DVD drive hardware points directly to the ISO file, as discussed in Chapter 2. Unless you purchase an actual boxed subscription, the burning or other use of these ISO files is your responsibility.

Be aware, some of the installation options described in this part of the chapter have been subdivided into different sections. For example, the ways you can configure partitions are spread across multiple sections.

Purchase a Subscription

Different subscriptions are available for desktops, workstations, and servers. While the RHCSA is focused on workstations, it also does require the configuration of SSH and NTP services. Of course, the RHCE also requires the configuration of a variety of network services. Therefore, ideally most readers would need a server subscription.

A variety of server subscriptions are available, depending on the number of CPU sockets and virtual guests, and on the support level. A system associated with a standard RHEL subscription is limited to two CPU sockets and two virtual nodes. Each socket can have a multicore CPU. Significant discounts for academic users are available.

Red Hat also offers a "Red Hat Linux Development Suite" subscription, currently priced at $99 in the United States. This subscription provides download access to RHEL and several types of add-on software, but it is limited to development use only. According to the Red Hat legal agreement for Subscription Services, "development purposes" means that the software can also be used for testing.

Get an Evaluation Copy

Red Hat currently offers a 30-day unsupported evaluation option for RHEL. Red Hat requires some personal information from such users. Once approved by Red Hat, you'll get instructions on how to download the distribution. However, Red Hat provides evaluation subscriptions "for the sole purpose of evaluating the suitability of the Subscription Services for your future purchase, [...] and not for Production Purposes, Development Purposes or any other purpose."

Third-party Rebuilds

You don't have to pay for operating system support to prepare for Red Hat exams. To comply with the Linux General Public License (GPL), Red Hat releases the source code for just about every RHEL package. However, the GPL only requires that Red Hat makes the source code available to its customers. Red Hat does not have to make the binary packages compiled from that source code publicly available.

o n t h e

Üo b

The description in this book of the GPL, trademark law, and Red Hat legal agreement for Subscription Services is not a legal opinion and is not intended as legal advice.

Under trademark law, Red Hat can prevent others from releasing software with its trademarks, such as the Red Hat logo. Nevertheless, the GPL gives anyone the right to compile that source code. If they make changes, all they need to do is release their changes under the same license. And several "third parties" have taken this opportunity to remove the trademarks from the released source code and have compiled that software into their own rebuilds, functionally equivalent to RHEL.

The RHEL source code, which used to be available at ftp://ftp.redhat.com for earlier releases, has now been moved to https://git.centos.org/project/rpms. However, the building of a distribution, even from source code, is a tricky process. But once complete, the rebuild has the same functionality as RHEL. Although it is true that rebuild distributions don't have a connection to and can't get updates from the Red Hat Customer Portal, this is not part of the Red Hat Exam Prep guide. And the developers behind rebuild distributions also use the source code associated with new RHEL packages to keep their repositories up to date. Here are two options for rebuild distributions:

- **Community Enterprise Operating System (CentOS)** The rebuild known as CentOS includes a number of experienced developers who have been working with RHEL source code since the release of RHEL 3 back in 2002. In 2014, the CentOS project joined the Red Hat community. The current board of the project includes members from Red Hat as well as from the original CentOS core team. For more information, see http://www.centos.org.

- **Scientific Linux** This distribution is developed and supported by experts from the U.S. Government's Fermilab and the European Organization for Nuclear Research, known by its French acronym, CERN. The people associated with these organizations are among the smartest scientists around. For more information, see http://www.scientificlinux.org.

Check the Download

For downloads from the Red Hat Subscription Manager portal, Red Hat provides checksums based on the 256-bit Secure Hash Algorithm (SHA256). You can check these ISO files against the given checksum numbers with the **sha256sum** command. For example, the following command calculates the SHA256 checksum for the initial RHEL 7 DVD:

```
# sha256sum rhel-server-7.0-x86_64 dvd.iso
```

Although it's a good sign when a downloaded ISO image passes these tests, such a result is not a guarantee that the burned DVD will be free of errors.

CERTIFICATION OBJECTIVE 1.04

Installation Requirements

According to the Red Hat certification blog, Red Hat provides "pre-installed systems" for its exams. So you won't start from scratch, at least for the host physical system, but you'll still need to set up practice systems. The RHCSA objectives suggest that you need to do so with a network installation. On a pre-installed system, given the other requirements, that means that you need to know how to set up network installations on KVM-based VMs.

The installation requirements described in this section are suited to the creation of an environment for practice labs. That environment may also work as a baseline for other RHEL systems. On many real networks, new virtual systems are created or cloned from that baseline. Those new systems are then dedicated for a single service.

When you create a physical host for test VMs, make sure to have enough room available for the host physical system and the guest VMs. This section suggests that you create three VMs for test purposes. For such purposes, 80GB of free space on a physical system would be sufficient. With some careful planning, you may be able to live with a smaller amount of free space and just two VMs. For more information on how to configure RHEL 7 on a VM, see Chapter 2.

You Won't Start from Scratch

Before installing RHEL 7, it may be helpful to review what is known about the latest RHCSA and RHCE exams. As described in the Red Hat blog announcement at http://redhatcertification.wordpress.com/, Red Hat now provides the following:

- Pre-installed systems
- Questions presented "electronically"

In other words, when seated for an exam, you'll see an installed copy of RHEL 7 on the test system, with questions in some electronic format. No public information is available on the format of the questions. This book will assume the most basic format for Red Hat exam questions—text files available in the root administrative user's home directory, /root.

The Advantages of Network Installation

Network installation means you don't have to use a full DVD on every system when installing RHEL 7. It means that every system is installed from the same set of installation packages, which are available on a remote software repository over the network. Network installations are usually faster than those from physical DVDs.

Network installations become especially powerful when combined with Kickstart files and the Pre-boot eXecution Environment (PXE). In that configuration, all you need to do to install RHEL 7 is boot a system, automatically download the appropriate Kickstart file, and—voila!—after a few minutes, you'll have a complete RHEL 7 installation.

o n   t h e
ⓘ o b **It is important to understand how you plan to configure VMs before setting up a physical host system. Although we describe basic information about the VMs in this chapter, you won't set up the actual KVM-based VMs until Chapter 2.**

Red Hat and Virtual Machines

The objectives associated with the RHCSA suggest that you need to know how to "configure a physical machine to host virtual guests." It also suggests that you need to know how to perform a number of tasks with VMs as well as "install Red Hat Enterprise Linux automatically using Kickstart." That's consistent with the use of Kickstart files to set up RHEL 7 on a KVM-based VM.

One of the advantages of a VM is how it supports the use of an ISO file on a virtual CD/DVD drive. Files accessed from that virtual drive are not slowed by the mechanical speed of physical CD/DVD media. Therefore, virtual CD/DVD drives might be as fast as network access from a host system.

Virtual and Physical Systems

Virtual systems can't stand alone. They require some connection to a physical system. Even a "bare-metal" virtualization solution such as Citrix XenServer was built from or otherwise relies on a specialized version of the Linux kernel, which acts as the operating system on the physical host.

However, it's possible to install a substantial number of virtual systems on a single physical system. If those systems are dedicated to different services, they'll load the physical system at different times. Such loads make it possible to "overcommit" the RAM and other resources of the physical system.

For our purposes, there is no real difference whether the installation is performed on a physical or a virtual system. The software functions in the same way. As long as IP forwarding is enabled on the physical host system, networking on the virtual system works in the same way as well.

A Pre-installed Environment for Practice Labs

The baseline RHEL 7 system configured in this chapter is relatively simple. It starts with a 16GB virtual disk. Part of that disk will be organized as shown in Table 1-1. Some of the space will be configured as regular partitions. The remaining space on the hard drive will be left empty for potential configuration during the lab exercises as logical volumes.

Two additional virtual disks of 1GB each are included to facilitate the post-installation configuration of a logical volume. The 16GB hard disk and 10GB root partition are arbitrary sizes that provide plenty of room for RHEL 7 software. If space is limited on your system, you might go as low as 8GB for a virtual disk or skip full disk allocation, as long as swap space is also appropriately limited. Swap space in Linux is used as an extension of local RAM, especially when that resource runs short.

The baseline minimum installation of RHEL 7 does not include a GUI. Although it is fairly easy to install the package groups associated with the GUI after installation is

Location	Size
/boot	500MB
/	10GB
/home	1024MB
Swap	1024MB

TABLE 1-1

Filesystem
Mount Points

complete, that process requires the installation of several hundred megabytes' worth of packages. And that takes time. Since Red Hat provides a pre-installed system to reduce the time required for the exam, it is reasonable to suggest that the system provided by Red Hat includes the GUI. And the default GUI for Red Hat systems is the GNOME Desktop Environment.

on the
Job

GNOME was initially an acronym within an acronym. It stood for the GNU Network Object Model Environment. GNU is itself a recursive acronym because it stands for GNU's Not Unix. Linux is filled with similar recursive acronyms, such as PHP: Hypertext Preprocessor (PHP).

The amount of RAM to allocate is more complex, especially on a VM. For the purpose of this book, we've configured VMs with 1GB of RAM to comfortably enable GUI-based illustrations of the RHEL installation process. If text-mode installations are acceptable, you can run RHEL 7 in 512MB of RAM, or possibly even less. Since different VMs rarely use all the RAM simultaneously, it's possible to "overcommit" RAM; for example, it may be possible to set up three VMs, with 1GB of RAM each, on a physical host system with less than 3GB of physical RAM. Some RAM on the VMs will remain unused, available to the physical host system.

System Roles

Ideally, you can set up several systems, each dedicated to different roles. A network with a dedicated DNS (Domain Name Service) server, a dedicated DHCP (Dynamic Host Configuration Protocol) server, a dedicated Samba file sharing server, and so on is more secure. In that situation, a security breach in one system does not affect any other services.

However, that's not practical, especially during the Red Hat exams. Table 1-2 lists the roles appropriate for each of the three systems described in Lab 1.

TABLE 1-2	System	Roles
Roles for Test Systems	server1	Main server to practice with the labs in this book, configured as server1.example.com on the 192.168.122.0/24 network. This book assumes a fixed IP address of 192.168.122.50.
	tester1	Secure shell server that supports remote access, configured as tester1.example.com on the 192.168.122.0/24 network. May include servers for client testing, such as the Domain Name Service (DNS). This book assumes a fixed IP address of 192.168.122.150.
	outsider1	Workstation on a third IP address, configured as outsider1.example.org. Some services should not be accessible from that workstation. This book assumes a fixed IP address of 192.168.100.100.

There's also another implicit fourth system in this network—the physical host for the virtual machines. We will configure some services used by the other nodes (such as the files required to install the other VMs) on this machine later in this chapter. When multiple networks are configured, that host will have virtual network adapters that connect to each network. For this book, we've set up a system named maui.example.com. The following excerpts from the **ip address show** command display the virbr0 and virbr1 adapters, with connections to both networks:

```
4: virbr0 <BROADCAST,MULTICAST,UP,LOWER_UP> mtu 1500 qdisc noqueue↵
state UP
    link/ether 9e:56:d5:f3:75:51 brd ff:ff:ff:ff:ff:ff
    inet 192.168.122.1/24 brd 192.168.122.255 scope global vibr0
      valid_lft forever preferred_lft forever
5: virbr1 <BROADCAST,MULTICAST,UP,LOWER_UP> mtu 1500 qdisc noqueue↵
state UP
    link/ether 86:23:b8:b8:04:70 brd ff:ff:ff:ff:ff:ff
    inet 192.168.100.1/24 brd 192.168.100.255 scope global vibr1
      valid_lft forever preferred_lft forever
```

Of course, you can change the names and IP addresses associated with each of these systems. They are just the defaults to be used in this book. The server1.example.com system is the designated exam system, which will be used for exercises that address actual Red Hat exam requirements. For convenience, we have also set up some RHCE services on the physical host system.

The tester1 system can be used to verify the configuration on the server1 system. For example, if you've configured two virtual websites with different names, you should be able to access both websites from the tester1 system. The Red Hat exams assume that you may connect a system as a client to servers such as Samba and LDAP. They also assume that a DNS server is configured with appropriate hostnames and IP addresses. Although the configuration of some services such as Kerberos is beyond the scope of the RHCSA/RHCE exams, they can be used during the exams by the other systems as clients.

Finally, the outsider1 system is essentially a random system from an external network such as the Internet. Appropriate security settings mean that some services on the server1 machine won't be accessible to outsider1. Before following these recommendations, read Chapter 2. This chapter is focused on the configuration of a physical host system.

CERTIFICATION OBJECTIVE 1.05

Installation Options

Even most beginner Linux users can install RHEL 7 from a CD/DVD. Although this section addresses some of the options associated with installation, it is focused on the creation of that baseline system that can be used to set up other custom RHEL 7 systems.

In addition, the installation process is an opportunity to learn more about RHEL 7, not only boot media, but the logical volumes that can be configured after installation is complete. However, because pre-installed physical systems are now the norm for Red Hat exams, detailed discussions of logical volumes have been consolidated in Chapter 6.

The steps described in this section assume that you're installing directly from the RHEL 7 Binary DVD, or from a USB drive that contains the RHEL 7 Binary DVD image, as explained in the next section.

Boot Media

When you are installing RHEL 7, the simplest option is to boot it from the RHEL 7 DVD. But that's not the only available installation option. In essence, five methods are available to start the RHEL 7 installation process:

- Boot from a RHEL 7 Binary DVD.
- Boot from a USB drive containing the RHEL 7 Binary DVD image.
- Boot from a minimal RHEL Boot CD.
- Boot from a USB key containing a minimal RHEL Boot CD image.
- Boot from a Kickstart server using a PXE network boot card.

The last three options generally assume that you're going to install RHEL over a network. The installation and boot media are available from the Red Hat Customer Portal for users with a subscription. They are also be available from servers associated with rebuild distributions.

Nevertheless, if you need to create a boot USB drive containing the full RHEL 7 DVD image or a flash key with the minimal boot CD, download the appropriate ISO file from the Red Hat Customer Portal. Then, you can write that image to the USB device. If that USB device is located on /dev/sdc, you'd write the image with the following command:

```
# dd if=name-of-image.iso of=/dev/sdc bs=512k
```

Be careful—if /dev/sdc is a drive with data, these commands will overwrite all data on that drive.

on the

Job

Know how to create the right boot disk for your system. If you have a problem, the installation boot CD or USB drive can also serve as a rescue disk. At the boot prompt, a Troubleshooting option will eventually bring you to a Rescue a Red Hat Enterprise Linux System menu, which can start a rescue mode to mount appropriate volumes and recover specific files or directories.

CD/DVD or Boot USB Starts Installation

Now you can boot a target system from the installation DVD or a USB drive. After a few files are opened and decompressed, a RHEL installation screen should appear with at least the following three options:

- Install Red Hat Enterprise Linux 7.0
- Test this media & install Red Hat Enterprise Linux 7.0
- Troubleshooting

The first option should work for most users. If you want to check the integrity of the installation media before starting the installation process, select the second option.

Two modes are associated with the Red Hat installation program (also known as "Anaconda"): text mode and graphical mode. Although the graphical mode is the recommended method, you would be automatically redirected to text mode if the installation program does not properly detect your video card.

You can also force installation in text mode if you wish. To do so, highlight the Install Red Hat Enterprise Linux 7.0 option and press the TAB key. When you do, the following options are revealed on that screen, on one line:

```
> vmlinuz initrd=initrd.img inst.stage2=hd:LABEL=RHEL-7.0\x20Server.x86_64↵
quiet
```

To force installation in text mode, add **inst.text** to the end of this line.

Basic Installation Steps

The basic RHEL installation is straightforward and should already be well understood by any Red Hat certification candidate. Most of the steps are described here for reference; it's useful to remember this process as you work on advanced configuration situations such as the Kickstart files described in Chapter 2.

The order of these steps vary depending on whether they're run directly from the CD/DVD or over a network. Variations occur depending on whether there's a previous version of Linux and Linux-formatted partitions on the local system. For this section, the following assumptions are made:

- Installation based on the RHEL 7 Binary DVD, or from a USB drive that contains the RHEL 7 Binary DVD image
- At least 512MB of RAM
- RHEL 7 as the only operating system on the local computer

However, dual-boot situations are acceptable. In fact, one of the authors of this book usually works on an Intel Core i7 laptop system in a triple-boot configuration where RHEL 7 coexists with Windows 7 and Ubuntu 14.04. If you're installing the system on a dedicated physical computer or a VM, the basic steps are the same. As a physical host is required for VMs, we assume you'll be first installing RHEL 7 on a physical system.

The most efficient way—and therefore (in our opinion) the most likely way—to install Red Hat Enterprise Linux is via a text or graphical installation from a remote server. For that purpose, Lab 2 configures an FTP server with the RHEL 7 installation files. Alternatively, it's possible to set up those installation files on an HTTP server such as the Apache web server, as discussed later in this chapter.

The sequence of steps for the installation process varies, depending on whether you're installing from the DVD or the network installation CD, as well as whether you're installing in text or graphical mode. It also may vary if you're using a rebuild distribution of RHEL 7. So be flexible when reading the following instructions:

1. Boot your computer from the RHEL DVD, or a boot USB drive that contains a copy of the DVD ISO image. Three options are normally shown:
   - Install Red Hat Enterprise Linux 7.0
   - Test this media & install Red Hat Enterprise Linux 7.0
   - Troubleshooting
2. Figure 1-1 illustrates the options from the Scientific Linux 7.0 DVD. Select the first option and press ENTER.
3. Select a language to use during the installation process, as shown in Figure 1-2. English is the default; over 50 options are available.

FIGURE 1-1

The installation
boot screen

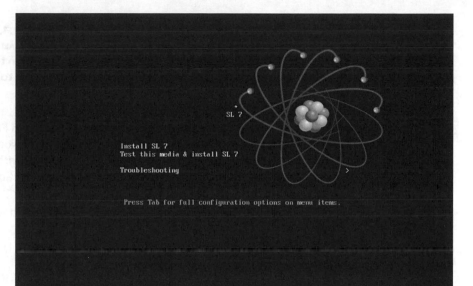

FIGURE 1-2

Select a language
for installation

If you encounter problems, examine the messages in the first, third, fourth, and fifth consoles; to do so, press CTRL-ALT-F1, CTRL-ALT-F3, CTRL-ALT-F4, **or** CTRL-ALT-F5. **A command line is available by pressing** CTRL-ALT-F2. **To return to the GUI screen, press** CTRL-ALT-F6. **If in text-mode installation, you can return to that screen by pressing** ALT-F1.

4. The next screen is the Installation Summary screen, shown in Figure 1-3. From this interface you can review and edit all installation settings. As you can see in Figure 1-3, one item in the Installation Summary screen is marked with a "warning" symbol. This indicates that you must configure the corresponding section before being able to proceed with the installation.

5. From the Installation Summary screen, review the date and time zone of the local system, and make appropriate changes if necessary.

6. Similarly, you can review the keyboard configuration and the language settings if needed.

FIGURE 1-3   The Installation Summary screen

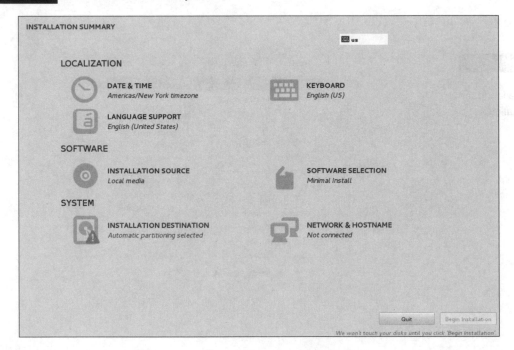

7. The next option in the Installation Summary screen relates to the installation media. Because you are installing from a local DVD or USB drive, leave this setting as "Local media." For network installations, you would need to specify the location of an installation source. For example, to point to the FTP server that you will configure in Lab 2, select the "On the network" installation option, specify the ftp:// URL locator from the drop-down menu, and type the IP address and path of the installation source, such as 192.168.122.1/pub/inst.

8. Review the Network & Hostname settings in the Installation Summary screen, as shown in Figure 1-4. The left panel lists the network interfaces detected by the installation program. Select the interface you want to activate, and move the switch at the top-right corner to the ON position.

9. Click the Configure button to choose how you want IP addressing to be configured. You will see the window shown in Figure 1-5. Your options are to enable support as a DHCP client for IPv4 and/or IPv6 addresses, or to manually enter a static IP address. (If the network DHCP server, such as a home router, does not support IPv6, select Ignore in the drop-down menu under IPv6 Settings.) For a physical system on a home network, Automatic (DHCP) should work if your home router provides DHCP services. For the three systems listed in Table 1-2, fixed IPv4 addresses should be set up. If you are not sure what to do, this is an excellent time to plan a network as described in Lab 1.

FIGURE 1-4   The Network & Hostname configuration screen

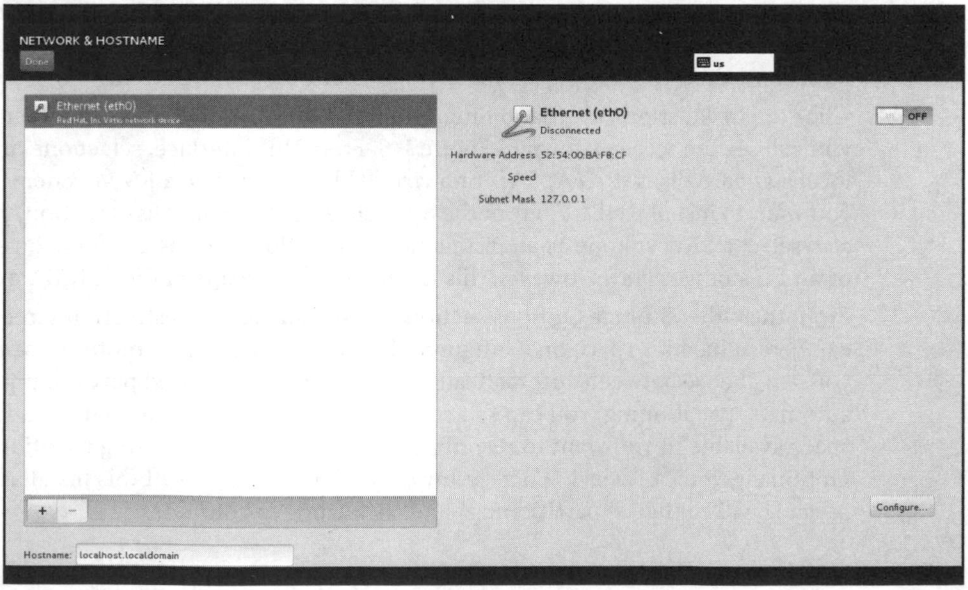

IPv4 network
settings

10. In the input field shown at the bottom left in Figure 1-4, set a hostname for the local system. If you are installing one of the virtual systems listed in Table 1-2, the hostname is indicated in the table (for example, server1.example.com). Once you have completed your configuration changes, click the Done button.

11. Click the Installation Destination item from the Installation Summary screen, and you will see the screen shown in Figure 1-6. From this interface, select one or more local standard disks (SATA, SAS, or a virtual block device on a KVM system) where you want to install RHEL 7. From the Specialized & Network Disks section, you can also select a SAN volume as an installation destination, such as a volume on an iSCSI or an FC storage array. However, this is outside of the scope of the RHCSA exam.

12. From the Other Storage Options section of the Installation Destination screen, you can determine how space on configured disk drives, local and remote, is used. Here, you can choose between automatically and manually configured partitioning. For automatic partitioning, you can select the checkbox "I would like to make additional space available" if you want to reconfigure space from other existing partitions. Optionally, you can select "Encrypt my data." For the purpose of this installation, select "I will configure partitioning" and click Done to continue.

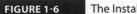

FIGURE 1-6   The Installation Destination screen

> INSTALLATION DESTINATION
>
> Done
>
> us
>
> **Device Selection**
> Select the device(s) you'd like to install to. They will be left untouched until you click on the main menu's "Begin Installation" button.
>
> **Local Standard Disks**
>
> 16.38 GB
>
> **Virtio Block Device**
> vda / 969.23 KB free
>
> *Disks left unselected here will not be touched.*
>
> **Specialized & Network Disks**
>
> Add a disk...
>
> *Disks left unselected here will not be touched.*
>
> **Other Storage Options**
> **Partitioning**
> ○ Automatically configure partitioning.   ○ I will configure partitioning.
> ☐ I would like to make additional space available.
> **Encryption**
> ☐ Encrypt my data. *You'll set a passphrase later.*

The Installation Perspective on Partitions

Once a partition is created, you can configure Linux to mount a partition on that directory. Alternatively, that partition can be designated as a RAID device or as part of a logical volume.

To define a partition, you may need some background on naming conventions, the configuration of different filesystems, uses of swap space, logical volumes, and RAID arrays. This is just an overview. Detailed information is available in Chapter 6, including tasks that may be required during the Red Hat exams and on real systems.

Naming Conventions

Linux has a simple naming standard for disk partitions: three letters followed by a number. The first letter identifies the type of drive (*s* is for SATA or SAS, and *v* is for virtual disks on KVM-based VMs). The second letter is *d* for disk, and the third letter represents the relative position of that disk, starting with *a*. For example, the first SATA drive is sda, followed by sdb, sdc, and sdd.

The number that follows is based on the relative position of the partition. Two partitioning schemes are available on modern PCs: the traditional Master Boot Record (MBR) and the newer GUID Partition Table (GPT) scheme.

In the MBR scheme, partitions can be one of three types: primary, extended, or logical. Primary partitions can contain the boot files for an operating system. Hard drives can also be configured with one extended partition, which can then contain a number of logical partitions.

Hard disks are limited to four primary partitions. When four partitions are not enough, an extended partition can be substituted for the last primary partition. That extended partition can then be subdivided into logical partitions. So when planning a partition layout, make sure that extended partition is big enough. Although it's possible to create more, you should not create more than 12 logical partitions on any individual SATA, SAS, or virtual hard drive.

The GPT partitioning scheme does not have such limitations and by default can support up to 128 partitions.

Each partition is associated with a Linux device file. At least that is straightforward; for example, the device filename associated with the third partition on the first SATA drive is /dev/sda3.

A volume is a generic name for a formatted segment of space that can be used to contain data. Volumes can be partitions, RAID arrays, or those logical volumes associated with Logical Volume Management (LVM). A filesystem exists inside a volume and provides the ability to store files. Filesystems handle the conversion of blocks on the volumes to files. For example, Red Hat uses the XFS filesystem as the default format for its volumes. The standard way to access data in Linux is to first mount that filesystem onto a directory. For example, when the /dev/sda1 partition is formatted to the XFS filesystem, it can then be mounted on a directory such as /boot. It is common to say something like, "The /dev/sda1 filesystem is mounted on the /boot mount point." For more information, see Chapter 6.

Separate Filesystem Volumes

Normally, you should create several volumes for RHEL 7. Even in the default configuration, RHEL is configured with at least three volumes—a top-level root directory (/), a /boot directory, and Linux swap space. Additional volumes may be suitable for directories such as /home, /opt, /tmp, and /var. They're also suitable for any custom directories such as for websites, dedicated groups of users, and more.

Although it's important to configure the /boot directory on a regular partition, other directories can readily be configured on logical volumes or RAID arrays.

Dividing the space from available hard drives in this manner keeps system, application, and user files isolated from each other. This helps protect the disk space used by system services and various applications. Files cannot grow across volumes. For example, an application such as a web server that uses huge amounts of disk space can't crowd out space needed by another service. Another advantage is that if a bad spot develops on the hard drive, the risk to your data is reduced, as is recovery time. Stability is improved.

While there are many advantages to creating more volumes, it isn't always the best solution. When hard drive space is limited, the number of partitions should be kept to a minimum. For example, if you have a 10GB hard drive and want to install 5GB of packages, having dedicated /var and /home volumes could lead to a situation where disk space runs out far too quickly.

Linux Swap Space

Linux swap space is normally configured either on a dedicated partition or a logical volume. Such space is used to extend the amount of effective RAM on a system as virtual memory for currently running programs. But normally you should not just buy extra RAM and eliminate swap space. Linux moves infrequently used programs and data to swap space even if you have gigabytes of free RAM.

The way Red Hat recommends to assign swap space is based on the amount of RAM on a system. For systems of up to 2GB, the recommended swap space size is twice the amount of installed RAM. Between 2GB and 8GB, it's equal to the amount of RAM. Above 8GB, it's half the amount of RAM. But those are not "hard and fast" rules. Workstations with several gigabytes of RAM frequently use very little swap space. However, certain application workloads may need a big swap partition, such as applications that use large tmpfs filesystems (tmpfs is a temporary filesystem stored in RAM that relies on swap space as a backing store if the server is under memory pressure). In any case, the default installation configures swap space not in a dedicated partition, but as a logical volume.

Basic Information on Logical Volumes

The creation of a logical volume from a partition requires the following steps. Details on these concepts as well as the actual commands required to execute these steps are described in Chapter 6. Some of these steps are run automatically if you create a logical volume during the installation process.

- The partition should be labeled as a Linux LVM volume.
- The labeled partition can then be initialized as a physical volume.
- One or more physical volumes can be combined as a volume group.
- A volume group can be subdivided into logical volumes.
- A logical volume can then be formatted to a Linux filesystem or as swap space.
- The formatted logical volume can be mounted on a directory or as swap space.

Basic Information on RAID Arrays

RAID was an explicit requirement on the RHCT/RHCE exams up to the release of RHEL 6. Because it is no longer found in either the RHCSA/RHCE objectives or the outlines of the prep courses for these certifications, you can relax a bit on that topic. In any case, the RAID configured on RHEL 7 is software RAID. The acronym, Redundant Array of Independent Disks, is somewhat misleading because software RAID is usually based on independent partitions. Redundancy comes from the use of partitions from different physical hard drives.

Partition Creation Exercise

Now we return to the installation process. If you followed the steps described so far in this chapter and the system has sufficient RAM, you should see the Manual Partitioning screen shown in Figure 1-7.

At this screen, the drop-down menu gives you the opportunity to configure filesystems on standard partitions, on LVM volumes, on thin-provisioned LVM volumes, and on BTRFS volumes. The /boot mount point will be always configured on a standard partition, regardless of the partition scheme settings you have selected in this screen.

1. Select Standard Partition from the partitioning scheme drop-down menu. LVM will be discussed in Chapter 6. BTRFS is also an available option, but it's outside of the scope of the RHCSA exam.

FIGURE 1-7   Partition configuration from the Manual Partitioning screen

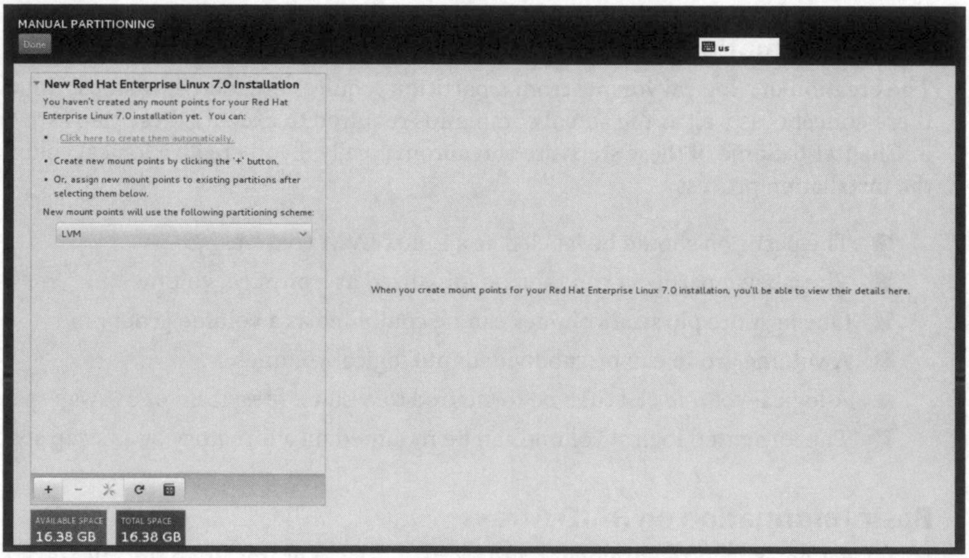

FIGURE 1-8

Adding a mount point

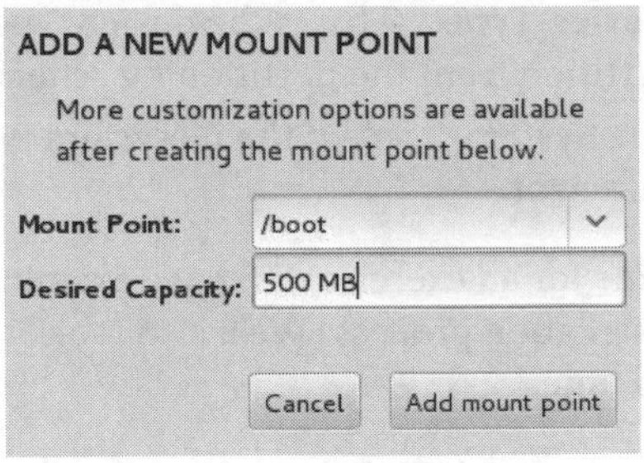

ADD A NEW MOUNT POINT

More customization options are available after creating the mount point below.

Mount Point: /boot

Desired Capacity: 500 MB

Cancel   Add mount point

2. Configure standard mount points as described earlier in Table 1-1. Larger partitions are acceptable if you have the space. They would be necessary if you're creating the physical host system that will contain the VMs. At the bottom left of the screen, the + button supports the creation of a new mount point, as shown in Figure 1-8.

3. Back in the Manual Partitioning screen, you should now see the settings shown in Figure 1-9. This window supports a number of choices:

- **Mount Point**   This is the directory (such as /boot) whose files will be stored on the partition.

- **Label**   You can provide an optional label.

- **Desired Capacity**   Indicate the desired capacity of the partition in MB; in this case, the partitions to be configured for this baseline system are defined in Table 1-1.

FIGURE 1-9   Configuration for the /boot partition

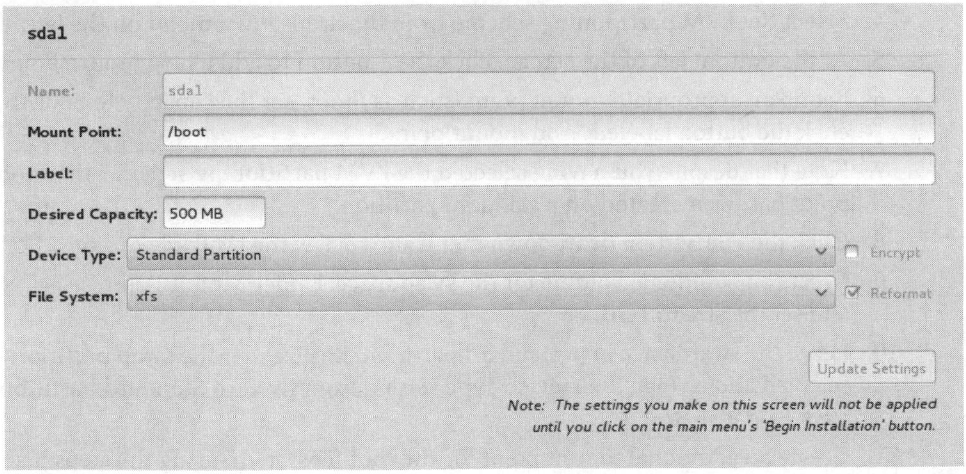

sda1

Name: sda1

Mount Point: /boot

Label:

Desired Capacity: 500 MB

Device Type: Standard Partition   ☐ Encrypt

File System: xfs   ☑ Reformat

Update Settings

Note: The settings you make on this screen will not be applied until you click on the main menu's 'Begin Installation' button.

- ■ **Device Type** This is the device type, which you previously set to Standard Partition from the partitioning scheme menu.
- ■ **File System** Select the filesystem type; in this case, the default xfs filesystem is sufficient.

Now it's time for an exercise. First, we examine how to create and configure partitions during the installation process. We'll also look at how to allocate a filesystem to a partition or a logical volume.

Partitioning During Installation

This exercise is based on changes that you would make to an installation of RHEL 7, in progress, so be sure to take care. However, it is easy to recover from mistakes because you can click the Reload Storage Configuration button to discard any configuration changes. This exercise starts with the Manual Partitioning screen shown in Figure 1-7 and continues with the screens shown in Figures 1-8 and 1-9. In addition, it assumes sufficient RAM (512MB) to work with the graphical installation.

1. Click the Reload Storage Configuration button (second-to-last button at the bottom left in Figure 1-7) to discard all the configuration changes you have made. If you're starting with one or more blank hard disks, no partitions will be configured.

2. If no space is available, delete the configured partitions using the – button at the bottom left of the screen.

3. Create a custom layout.

4. Select the LVM partitioning scheme from the drop-down menu on the left.

5. At the bottom left of the screen, click the + button to add a new mount point.

6. Set up an appropriate mount point, such as /boot, set the capacity to 500MB, and click the button labeled "Add mount point."

7. Note that despite you having selected the LVM partitioning scheme, the /boot mount point has been created on a standard partition.

8. Click the File System drop-down menu and review the available options.

9. Create an additional volume for the swap space. Under Mount Point, select "swap" and set the size to 1GB.

10. Leave the swap space on a standard partition. Ensure that the swap partition is selected and change the Device Type setting from LVM to Standard Partition. Then click Update Settings.

11. Create an additional mount point for the root filesystem, using the steps just described. Select / in the Mount Point input box and set the size to 10GB. If you are

installing RHEL on a physical system, you may want to adjust this setting based on the total disk space available.

12. Ensure that the / mount point is selected. What is the free space available on the volume group?

13. You will now extend the volume group to take all the space available on the disk. Click the Modify button next to the Volume Group menu and review the settings. Set the Size policy to "As large as possible" and click Save.

14. Click Update Settings again. What is the free space available on the volume group?

15. Repeat the preceding step to create a mount point for the /home filesystem and set the size to 1GB. If you are installing RHEL on a physical system, you may want to adjust the size of the partition based on the total disk space available. If you wish to use all the remaining disk space for this mount point, leave the Desired Capacity setting blank and click Update Settings.

Now that the exercise is complete, the partition configuration should reflect at least the minimums shown in Table 1-1. One version is shown in Figure 1-10. If a mistake is made, highlight a partition and edit its configuration settings. Do not be concerned with small errors; modest variations in size are not relevant in practice—and the Red Hat exams reflect what happens in practice.

FIGURE 1-10

Sample partition configuration

DATA

/home   1 GB >
rhel-home

SYSTEM

/boot   500 MB
vda1

/   10 GB
rhel-root

swap   1 GB
vda2

FIGURE 1-11

Configure the
bootloader

SELECTED DISKS

Boot	Description	Name	Capacity	Free
✓	Virtio Block Device (None)	vda	16.38 GB	969.23 KB

Do not install bootloader   Remove

1 disk; 16.38 GB capacity; 969.23 KB free space (unpartitioned and in filesystems)

Close

To complete this part of the process, click Done. You will see a Summary of Changes screen. This is your last chance to cancel before proceeding. Assuming you're satisfied, click Accept Changes to continue.

Return to the Installation Destination screen, and at the bottom click the "Full disk summary and bootloader" link. The standard Linux bootloader is GRUB 2, the GRand Unified Bootloader version 2. The settings shown in Figure 1-11 are reasonable defaults. In most cases, no changes are required.

on the !job **The terms "boot loader" and "bootloader" are interchangeable. Both are frequently found in Red Hat documentation.**

Wow, Look at All That Software!

Over 4300 packages are available just from the RHEL 7 installation DVD. That number does not include a number of packages available only through other subscription channels on the Red Hat Customer Portal. With so many packages, it's important to organize them into groups. After configuring the GRUB 2 bootloader, click Software Selection from the Installation Summary screen. You'll see the options shown in Figure 1-12, which allow you to configure the local system to a desired functionality. The selection depends on your objective. If you're installing on a production physical system to set up KVM-based

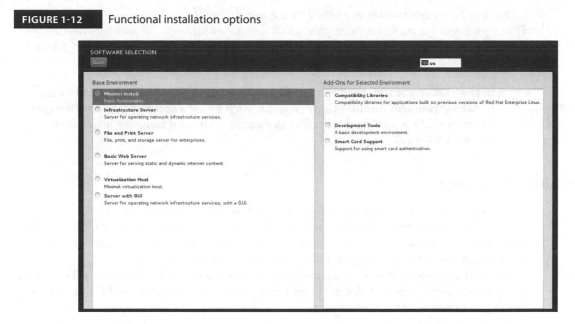

FIGURE 1-12 Functional installation options

virtualization, select Virtualization Host. If you're setting up virtual guests (or other dedicated physical servers), select Server with GUI. During a Red Hat exam, you'll be installing most additional software after basic operating system installation is complete. Other options are listed in Table 1-3. Depending on the rebuild distribution, the options may vary significantly.

TABLE 1-3 Installation Software Categories

Category	Description
Minimal Install	Includes a minimal list of packages for the operating system
Infrastructure Server	Installs basic packages for Red Hat as a server
File and Print Server	Configures a system with Samba, NFS, and CUPS
Basic Web Server	Sets up a system with the Apache web server
Virtualization Host	Configures a system for running virtual machines using the KVM hypervisor
Server with GUI	Same as the Infrastructure Server, plus a GUI

For a truly secure baseline in a production environment, consider the minimal installation. Fewer packages means fewer vulnerabilities. You can then add just the packages needed for the desired functionality. Any software that isn't installed can't be exploited by a "black hat" hacker.

on the **! Job**

In the security world, the term "white hat" hackers refers to good people who break systems for nonmalicious reasons, such as for a security penetration test. The term "black hat" hackers refers to people who want to break into other systems with evil intent.

Baseline Packages

In this section, you'll get a basic overview of what's available during the RHEL 7 installation process. During the exams, you may refer to one of these package groups with the Red Hat Add/Remove Software tool. You can also find a list of available package groups with the **yum group list** command. More information is available in Chapter 7.

Red Hat package groups are organized logically. It's important to choose only the package groups you need. Fewer installed packages means more room for personal files, as well as the log files needed to monitor systems.

Package Groups

This section includes the briefest possible overview of each of the package groups available during the RHEL installation process. As you can see from Figure 1-12, there are high-level groups in the left panel ("environments"), such as Infrastructure Server, and package groups in the right panel ("add-ons"), such as Development Tools. Some add-ons in the right panel are separated by a horizontal line. The add-ons below the line are common to all environment groups, whereas the add-ons above the line are available only to the environment group you have selected.

The details of the RPMs associated with each package group are stored in an XML file. To review that file, go to the RHEL installation DVD and read the *-comps-Server-x86_64.xml file in the /repodata directory.

For an example of the details within a package group, open the file *-comps-Server-x86_64 .xml file with an editor of your choice, and look for the line containing the string "Server with GUI." After scrolling down a few lines, you will find the content listed in Figure 1-13.

As you can see from Figure 1-13, the Server with GUI group is a collection of other groups. In RHEL there is a distinction between regular groups, which include standard software packages, and environment groups (such as Server with GUI), which are collections of regular groups.

Whereas the groups listed in the **<grouplist>** section are all mandatory, those listed under **<optionlist>** are optional, and correspond to the add-ons listed on the right panel in the Software Selection screen.

FIGURE 1-13

Package group
details for "Server
with GUI"

```
<grouplist>
  <groupid>base</groupid>
  <groupid>core</groupid>
  <groupid>desktop-debugging</groupid>
  <groupid>dial-up</groupid>
  <groupid>fonts</groupid>
  <groupid>gnome-desktop</groupid>
  <groupid>guest-agents</groupid>
  <groupid>guest-desktop-agents</groupid>
  <groupid>input-methods</groupid>
  <groupid>internet-browser</groupid>
  <groupid>multimedia</groupid>
  <groupid>print-client</groupid>
  <groupid>x11</groupid>
</grouplist>
<optionlist>
  <groupid>backup-server</groupid>
  <groupid>directory-server</groupid>
  <groupid>dns-server</groupid>
  <groupid>file-server</groupid>
  <groupid>ftp-server</groupid>
  <groupid>ha</groupid>
  <groupid>hardware-monitoring</groupid>
```
:

Take some time studying this screen. Examine the packages within each package group. You'll learn about the kinds of packages that are installed by default. If you don't add them during the installation process, it isn't the end of the world. You can still add them with the **rpm** and **yum** commands or the GNOME Software tool described in Chapter 7.

If the XML file is too confusing, just make a note of the name of a package group. From that name, you can find a list of associated packages after installation is complete. For example, the following command identifies mandatory, default, and optional packages for the **base** package group:

```
$ yum group info base
```

For the purpose of this installation, select Server with GUI from the Software Selection screen shown in Figure 1-12. In addition, for the physical host system configured for KVM-based VMs, make sure that the Virtualization add-ons are selected.

Once the add-ons for the desired packages are selected, click Done and then click Begin Installation. Anaconda then proceeds to the installation process.

During the Installation

After the installation of the software packages is initiated, you will see the screen shown in Figure 1-14. From this interface, you can set a password for the root user and optionally create a user account.

Click the Root Password option and enter a password for the root administrative user twice. Although not required at this stage, you can create a regular user for the system.

FIGURE 1-14 Installing the RPM packages

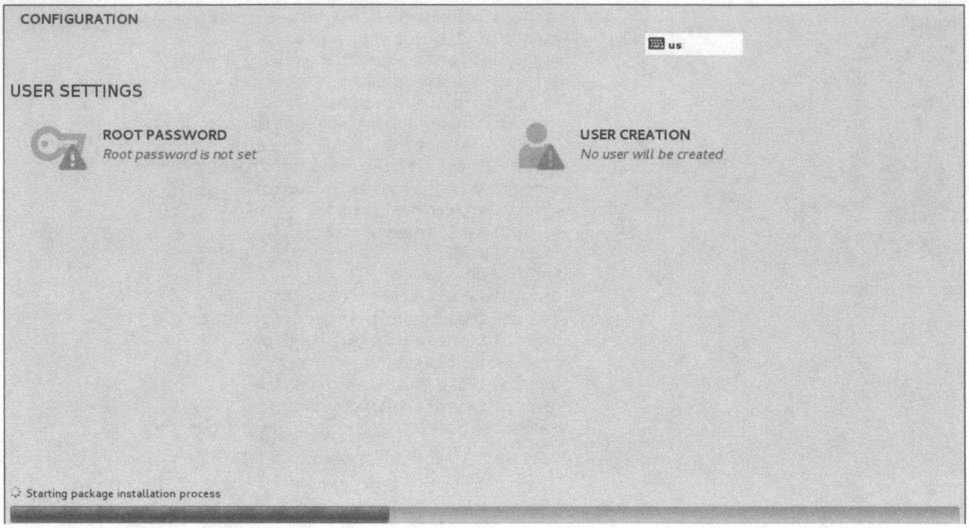

If you click User Creation, a window opens that can help you customize user details, as discussed in Chapter 8. Set up a local user and then click Done to continue.

When the installation is complete, you'll see a final message to that effect, with an option to reboot the system. If you've installed RHEL 7 on a physical system, don't forget to eject or remove the boot disk and/or the installation DVD. In most installations, RHEL 7 will start the Firstboot application discussed later in this chapter.

CERTIFICATION OBJECTIVE 1.06

System Setup Options

Baseline configurations are important. Once a baseline is configured, you can clone it to set up as many systems as needed. On a real network, a good baseline can be used to create systems dedicated to specific services. To enable remote access, it will have a Secure Shell (SSH) server, configured with a regular user.

For the boot process, RHEL 7 includes systemd, which replaces the SysVinit-based Upstart system available on RHEL 6. It determines the consoles, services, and displays, as well as the target units that are activated when a system is booted. Some systems use remote authentication, configured to connect to remote servers for username and password verification. Although these systems are covered in other chapters, enough information is provided in this section to set up a baseline system.

Initial Setup and Firstboot

In most cases, the first time RHEL 7 boots, two applications start: the Initial Setup screen, followed by Firstboot. The following steps assume a GUI-based RHEL 7 installation:

1. At the initial setup screen, accept a license agreement. The agreement varies depending on whether this is RHEL 7 or a rebuild distribution.
2. If you did not create a regular user account during the installation process, you can do so from the Initial Setup screen.
3. Click Finish Configuration.
4. The next screen allows you to enable and customize the configuration of Kdump, a service that collects data associated with kernel crashes. This is not covered in the RHCSA requirements, so leave the default settings and click Forward.
5. On a RHEL 7 system, you're prompted to connect the system to Red Hat Subscription Management (RHSM). To register, you'll need an RHSM account, with an available subscription. Complete this step and click Forward to continue.
6. On the next screen, review your language and keyboard settings, along with the date and time for the local system. Make desired changes and click Next to continue.

Default Security Settings

When RHEL 7 is installed, there are default settings associated with SELinux and the zone-based firewall. For more information on SELinux security options, see Chapters 4, 10, and others.

First, SELinux is enabled in enforcing mode by default. You can confirm the setting with the **sestatus** command, which should lead to the following output:

```
SELinux status:                 enabled
SELinuxfs mount:                /sys/fs/selinux
SELinux root directory:         /etc/selinux
Loaded policy name:             targeted
Current mode:                   enforcing
Mode from config file:          enforcing
Policy MLS status:              enabled
Policy deny_unknown status:     allowed
Max kernel policy version:      28
```

You'll learn more about SELinux and the RHCSA exam in Chapter 4. If you go for the RHCE, you'll also learn to configure SELinux from Chapter 10 onward to support a wide variety of services.

If you want detailed information about the current firewall configuration for the default zone, run the following command:

```
firewall-cmd --list-all
```

This command lists the network interfaces in the default firewall zone, along with the allowed inbound services.

In the list of allowed services you should see at least the Secure Shell (SSH) service, which supports remote administration of the local system. If there's a good network connection, you'll be able to connect remotely to this system. If the local IP address is 192.168.122.50, you can connect remotely to Michael's user account with the following command:

```
# ssh michael@192.168.122.50
```

The SSH server can be configured to enhance security even further. For more information, see Chapter 11.

Special Setup Options for Virtual Machines

On a physical host running the KVM hypervisor, you may notice additional firewall rules. For example, if you run **iptables -L** to list firewall rules, you should see the following additional rules, which accept traffic over the default subnet attached to the virtual machines:

```
Chain FORWARD (policy ACCEPT)
target     prot opt source               destination
ACCEPT     all  --  anywhere             192.168.122.0/24      ↵
cstate RELATED,ESTABLISHED
ACCEPT     all  --  192.168.122.0/24     anywhere
```

These rules work for IPv4 networking with the help of IP forwarding, as shown in the /proc/sys/net/ipv4/ip_forward virtual file. If the content of this file is set to 1, IPv4 forwarding is active. When IP forwarding is active, the host acts as a router, forwarding traffic from one interface to another.

On stand-alone hosts, IPv4 forwarding is disabled by default. However, on physical hosts running the KVM hypervisor, IP forwarding is enabled to allow routing between VM network segments and the external network.

If you have installed the Virtualization Hypervisor add-on, this setting should be enabled. To be sure, check the content of /proc/sys/net/ipv4/ip_forward. You could set it to 1, but that is not enough because it won't persist a system reboot. To permanently activate IP forwarding, open the /etc/sysctl.conf file and add the following line:

```
net.ipv4.ip_forward=1
```

To implement the changes immediately on the local system, run the following command:

```
# sysctl -p
```

For more information on the related /proc filesystem, see the RHCE section on Kernel run-time parameters in Chapter 12.

CERTIFICATION OBJECTIVE 1.07

Configure Default File Sharing Services

The RHEL 6 version of the RHCSA objectives included two additional objectives:

■ Configure a system to run a default configuration HTTP server
■ Configure a system to run a default configuration FTP server

Even though you won't be tested on these objectives, we believe the related skills can help you set up a lab to prepare for the certification exam.

The default HTTP server is the Apache web server. The corresponding default FTP server is vsFTP. These systems include basic functionality in their default installations.

You'll confirm the operation of the default installation. Next, you'll take this process one step further to set up these services to share files, specifically the files copied from the installation DVD.

It is fairly simple to configure these services for file sharing. You do not need to change the main configuration files. Assuming SELinux is enabled (as it should be during the exams), the basic steps are as follows:

■ Mount and copy the contents of the RHEL 7 installation DVD to the appropriate directory.
■ Make sure the contents of the noted directory are configured with the right SELinux contexts.
■ Configure the noted service to point to the specified directory and to start when the system is booted.

Naturally, the steps vary by service. The details described in this chapter are rudimentary and may not be sufficient if the related commands and services are new to you. For more information on the **mount** command, see Chapter 6. For more information on SELinux, see Chapter 4. For more information on the Apache web server, see Chapter 14.

Mount and Copy the Installation DVD

The **mount** command is used to connect a device such as a partition or a DVD drive on a specified directory. For example, the following command mounts the standard DVD drive onto the /media directory:

```
# mount /dev/cdrom /media
```

If the DVD is properly configured, it should automatically find the appropriate filesystem format from the /etc/filesystems file. In this case, the DVD media is formatted to the iso9660 standard. If there's a problem, you'd see the following error message:

```
mount: you must specify the filesystem type
```

Alternatively, you can mount an ISO file on a directory, without wasting a physical DVD. For example, you could mount the RHEL 7 DVD ISO file with the following command:

```
# mount -o loop rhel-server-7.0-x86_64-dvd.iso /media
```

Next, copy the contents of the DVD to a directory configured on the file server of your choice (FTP or HTTP). For example, the following command copies all files in archive (**-a**) mode recursively. When you include the dot at the end of the /media directory, you're including all hidden files in the copy command.

```
# cp -a /media/. /path/to/dir
```

Set Up a Default Configuration Apache Server

The Apache web server uses the /var/www/html directory as the repository for its default website. You can configure subdirectories for file sharing. Do make sure port 80 is open in any existing firewall.

The steps required to configure Apache as a RHEL installation server are similar to those required to configure vsFTP. In Exercise 1-2, you'll take the steps required to configure Apache as an installation server. But first, you need to make sure Apache is installed with the following command:

```
# yum -y install httpd
```

If the command is successful, you will find the main Apache configuration file, httpd.conf, in the /etc/httpd/conf/ directory. To make sure the default installation works, first start the Apache service with the following command:

```
# systemctl start httpd
```

FIGURE 1-15	Proof of a working default Apache server

Next, use a browser on the system where Apache is installed and navigate to the localhost IP address with the following URL: http://127.0.0.1/. An example is shown in Figure 1-15.

If port 80 is open in an existing local firewall, this page should be accessible from remote systems as well. In addition, you'll need to make sure Apache starts automatically the next time RHEL 7 is booted. One way to do so is with the following command:

```
# systemctl enable httpd
```

For more information on how services such as Apache are controlled during the boot process, see Chapter 11. Although that is an RHCE chapter, the **systemctl** command shown here is simple.

EXERCISE 1-2

Configure Apache as an Installation Server

In this exercise, you'll install and configure the Apache web server as a file server, suited for RHEL 7 installations. You'll need either a copy of the RHEL 7 DVD or the associated file in ISO format. In this exercise, you'll take the steps needed to create an appropriate directory, copy the installation files, set an appropriate SELinux context, open port 80 in any existing firewall, and restart the Apache service. Here are the basic steps (detailed Apache configuration is discussed in Chapter 14):

1. Mount the RHEL 7 DVD on an empty directory. You might use one of the following two commands. Whereas the first mounts an actual physical CD or DVD, the second mounts the ISO file:

   ```
   # mount /dev/cdrom /media
   # mount -o loop rhel-server-7.0-x86_64-dvd.iso /media
   ```

2. Create an appropriate directory for the installation files. Since the standard directory for Apache web server files is /var/www/html, it's simplest to create a subdirectory there with the following command:

   ```
   # mkdir /var/www/html/inst
   ```

3. Copy the files from the mounted DVD to the new directory:

   ```
   # cp -a /media/. /var/www/html/inst/
   ```

4. Make sure the files have the right SELinux context with the **chcon** command. The **-R** switch applies the changes recursively through the copied installation files. The **--reference=/var/www/html** switch applies the default SELinux context from that directory.

   ```
   # chcon -R --reference=/var/www/html /var/www/html/inst
   ```

5. Open port 80, the default associated with the Apache web server. To do so from the command line, just run the following commands. You'll learn to configure firewalls in more detail in Chapters 4 and 10.

   ```
   # firewall-cmd --permanent --add-service=http
   # firewall-cmd --reload
   ```

6. Make sure the Apache web server is running and is enabled to start at boot with the following commands:

   ```
   # systemctl restart httpd
   # systemctl enable httpd
   ```

Browsing the files from the RHEL 7 DVD

The Apache web server should now be ready for use as a file server, sharing the installation files from the RHEL 7 DVD. To confirm, point your browser to the IP address for the server and to the inst/ subdirectory. If that IP address is 192.168.122.1, you'd navigate to

```
http://192.168.122.1/inst
```

If successful, you'll see a page of clickable and downloadable files, as shown in Figure 1-16.

Share Copied Files via FTP Server

The Red Hat implementation of the vsFTP server includes the /var/ftp/pub directory for published files. For the purpose of the installation files, you can create the /var/ftp/pub/inst directory. To make the system compatible with SELinux, you'll then change the security contexts of each of those files with one command. When you then start or restart the vsFTP server, it will be ready for use as an installation server. The process is documented in Lab 2.

Assuming an appropriate connection to remote repositories using RHSM or from a rebuild distribution, you can make sure the latest version of the vsFTP server is installed with the following command:

```
# yum install vsftpd
```

If successful, you can find the main vsFTP configuration file, vsftpd.conf, in the /etc/vsftpd directory, as well as the main data directory in /var/ftp/pub. Make sure to start the vsFTP service with the following command:

```
# systemctl start vsftpd
```

As web browsers can access FTP servers, you can confirm the default FTP server configuration on the local system by navigating to ftp://127.0.0.1/. The default result in the Firefox web browser is shown in Figure 1-17. The pub/ directory shown is actually the /var/ftp/pub directory.

Note the security associated with the vsFTP server. Click the Up To Higher Level Directory hyperlink. The current directory does not change. Users who connect to this FTP server are unable to see, much less download, files from anything above the /var/ftp directory.

FIGURE 1-17 Access to the default FTP server

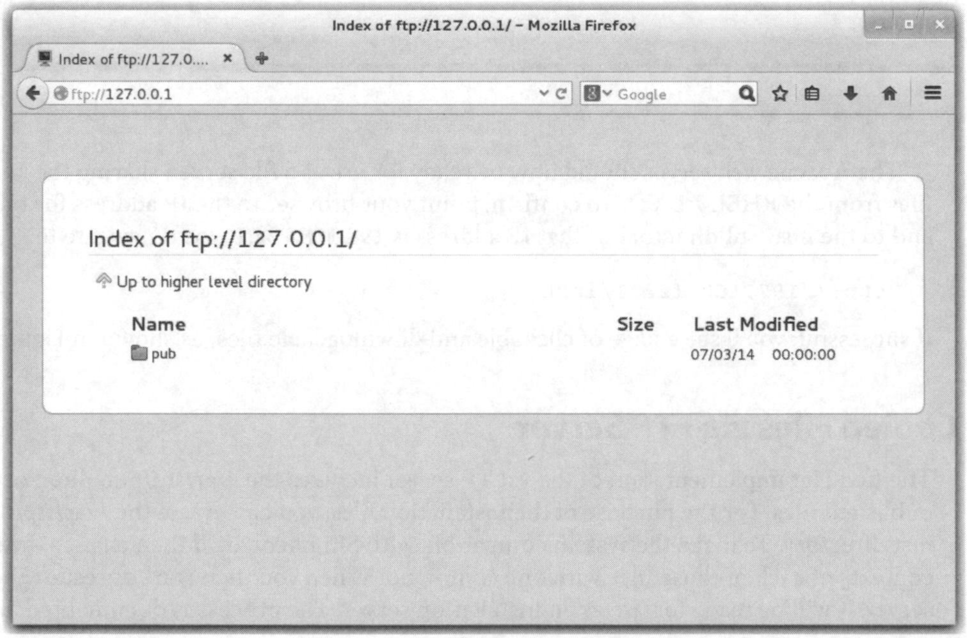

To grant access to the FTP service from remote systems, run the following commands:

```
# firewall-cmd --permanent --add-service=ftp
# firewall-cmd --reload
```

In addition, you'll need to make sure the vsFTP server starts automatically the next time RHEL 7 is booted. One way to do so is with the following command:

```
# systemctl enable vsftpd
```

The *d* at the end of vsFTP refers to its daemon. For more information on how services such as vsFTP are controlled during the boot process, see Chapter 11. Although that is an RHCE chapter, it should not be hard to remember this one **systemctl** command.

CERTIFICATION SUMMARY

The RHCSA and RHCE exams are not for beginners. This chapter helps you install a basic RHEL system, with the packages and settings suitable for the remainder of this book. Both exams are practical, hands-on exams. When you sit for either exam, you'll be faced with a live RHEL system with a series of problems to solve and systems to configure. The RHCSA covers core system administration skills.

RHEL 7 supports only the use of a 64-bit system. Also, you're required to configure RHEL 7 as a virtual host for the RHCSA.

With a subscription to the RHSM, you can download RHEL installation ISO files from the associated account. Since RHEL software is released under open-source licenses, third parties such as CentOS and Scientific Linux have used that source code without Red Hat trademarks. You can also use such rebuild distributions to study for the RHCSA and RHCE exams.

It will be helpful to create multiple installations of RHEL 7 to practice the skills you'll learn in later chapters. To that end, we recommend the configuration of three systems. Although many users don't have three spare physical computers to dedicate to their studies, VMs make it possible to set up these systems on a single physical computer.

Because the installation of RHEL 7 is relatively easy even for newer Linux users, not every detail is covered in this chapter. After installation comes the Initial Setup and Firstboot applications. However, this varies depending on whether you've installed a GUI.

TWO-MINUTE DRILL

Here are some of the key points from the certification objectives in Chapter 1.

The RHCSA and RHCE Exams

❑ The RHCSA is a separate exam from the RHCE.

❑ Red Hat exams are all "hands-on"; there are no multiple choice questions.

❑ If you're studying for the RHCSA, focus on Chapters 1–9. If you're studying for the RHCE, although you're responsible for the information in the entire book, focus on Chapters 1–2 and 10–17.

Basic Hardware Requirements

❑ Although RHEL 7 can be installed on a variety of platforms, you'll need hardware with 64-bit CPUs and hardware-assisted virtualization for the Red Hat exams.

❑ Red Hat supports RHEL 7 installations on systems with at least 1GB of RAM. Less is possible, especially on systems without a GUI. You need, at a minimum, 512MB of RAM to start the GUI installation program.

❑ RHEL 7 can be installed on local or a variety of storage network devices.

Get Red Hat Enterprise Linux

❑ The Red Hat exams use Red Hat Enterprise Linux.

❑ Production and development subscriptions of RHEL 7 are available.

❑ Since Red Hat releases the source code for RHEL 7, third parties are free to "rebuild" the distribution from the Red Hat source code (except for the trademarks).

❑ Third-party rebuilds of RHEL 7 are functionally identical, except for access to Red Hat Subscription Management.

❑ Reputable third-party rebuilds are available from CentOS and Scientific Linux.

Installation Requirements

❑ Red Hat has stated that exams are presented on "pre-installed systems" with questions presented "electronically."

❑ The RHCSA requires the configuration of a physical machine as a virtual host.

❑ The native RHEL 7 VM solution is KVM.

❑ It's useful to set up multiple VMs to simulate network communications.

Installation Options

❑ You can start the installation process from a variety of boot media.

❑ RHEL 7 can be installed from DVD, from a local drive, from an NFS directory, from an Apache web server, or from an FTP server.

❑ RHEL 7 should be configured on separate volumes for at least the top-level root directory (/), the /boot directory, and Linux swap space.

❑ RHEL 7 includes installation package groups in a number of categories.

System Setup Options

❑ The first post-installation steps involve the Initial Setup and Firstboot applications.

❑ SELinux and zone-based firewalls are enabled by default.

Configure Default File Sharing Services

❑ Although not strictly required by the RHCSA exam objectives, it is convenient to deploy HTTP and FTP servers to practice with RHEL installations over the network.

❑ The default services associated with the HTTP/FTP protocols are the Apache web server and the vsFTP server.

❑ One way to deploy a default HTTP or FTP server is to configure it with the installation files from the RHEL DVD.

SELF TEST

The following questions will help you measure your understanding of the material presented in this chapter. Because there are no multiple choice questions on the Red Hat exams, there are no multiple choice questions in this book. These questions exclusively test your understanding of the chapter. It is okay if you have another way of performing a task. Getting results, not memorizing trivia, is what counts on the Red Hat exams.

The RHCSA and RHCE Exams

1. How many multiple choice questions are there on the RHCE exam? And on the RHCSA exam?

   _____

Basic Hardware Requirements

2. Assuming Intel-based PC hardware, what's the default virtualization technology for RHEL 7?

   _____

3. Which Intel/AMD CPU architectures can be used on RHEL 7?

   _____

Get Red Hat Enterprise Linux

4. Name one third-party distribution based on RHEL 7 source code.

   _____

Installation Requirements

5. How much time is allocated for installation during the RHCSA and RHCE exams?

   _____

Installation Options

6. Name two different options for installation media that will boot the RHEL 7 installation program.

_____

_____

7. Name three types of volumes that can be configured and formatted during the RHEL 7 installation process to store data.

_____

_____

_____

8. Say you've mounted the RHEL 7 DVD on the /media directory. There's an XML file on that DVD with a database of packages and package groups. In what directory can you find that XML file?

_____

System Setup Options

9. What application is started after the Initial Setup screen?

_____

10. What service is allowed through the default firewall?

_____

Configure Default File Sharing Services

11. What is the standard directory for file sharing for the RHEL 7 implementation of the vsFTP server?

_____

12. What is the standard directory for HTML files on the Apache web server?

_____

LAB QUESTIONS

The first lab is fairly elementary, designed to get you thinking in terms of networks and networking. The second lab should help you configure an installation server. The third lab suggests that you look at the requirements associated with the Linux Professional Institute for a different perspective on system administration.

Lab 1

In this lab, you'll plan the network configuration for the systems required to complete the practice labs in the rest of the book. You have three computers configured with RHEL 7. Two of these computers are to be configured on one domain, example.com. These computers will have short hostnames: server1 and tester1. The third computer is to be configured on a second domain, example.org, with a short hostname of outsider1.

If these systems are configured as guests on a KVM virtual host, IP forwarding will make it possible for these systems to communicate, even though they're set up on different networks. Alternatively, one of the computers in the example.com domain, server1, may be configured with two network cards. The focus will be on IPv4 addressing.

- Systems on the example.com domain will be configured on the 192.168.122.0/24 network.
- Systems on the example.org domain will be configured on the 192.168.100.0/24 network.

Ideally, you should set up the server1.example.com system as a server with GUI. The basic instructions described in this chapter should suffice because it will be up to you to install and configure required services after installation is complete. It will be the primary system you use for practice. You'll install RHEL 7 on this system in Chapter 2, and you'll clone it for different chapters as well as the sample exams at the end of this book.

The tester1.example.com system will be a system that allows remote access only from the SSH service. In some cases, services not necessarily required for certification may be configured on the physical host or on the outsider1.example.org network. That will allow you to test clients that are required for certification.

Lab 2

This lab assumes you've downloaded the DVD-based ISO for RHEL 7 or a rebuild such as CentOS or Scientific Linux. The DVD-based ISO is important because it will serve two purposes. It will be the installation repository used earlier in this chapter as well as the package repository to be configured in Chapter 7. This lab simply includes those commands required to configure the noted files on the vsFTP server.

Although the Red Hat exams are given on a pre-installed system, the associated requirements do suggest that you need to know how to install systems over a network as well as configure Kickstart installations. Also, because you don't have Internet access during the exam, you won't have access to Red Hat Subscription Management or any other Internet repository.

1. Create a directory for your installation files. With the following command, create the /var/ftp/pub/inst directory. (If you get an error message, vsFTP may not be properly installed.)

```
# mkdir /var/ftp/pub/inst
```

2. Insert the RHEL 7 installation DVD into its drive. If not automatically mounted, do so with a command such as **mount /dev/cdrom /media**. (If all you have are the ISO files, say in the Downloads/ subdirectory, substitute **mount -ro loop Downloads/*rhel*.iso* /media**.)

3. Copy the required files from the RHEL 7 installation DVD. Use the **cp -a /*source*/. /var/ftp/ pub/inst** command, where *source* is the mount directory (such as /media/).

4. Make sure there's nothing blocking access to your vsFTP server. Use a tool such as the **firewall-cmd** configuration tool to open up ports for the FTP services on the local system, as illustrated in the following commands. For more information on firewalls and SELinux, see Chapter 4.

   ```
   # firewall-cmd --permanent --add-service=ftp
   # firewall-cmd --reload
   ```

5. If SELinux is enabled on the local system, run the following command to apply appropriate SELinux contexts to the files on the new directory:

   ```
   # chcon -R -t public content t /var/ftp/
   ```

6. Now activate the FTP server with the following command:

   ```
   # systemctl restart vsftpd
   # systemctl enable vsftpd
   ```

7. Test the result. On a remote system, you should be able to use the Firefox web browser to connect to the local FTP server, using its IP address. Once connected, you'll be able to find the installation files in the pub/inst/ subdirectory.

Lab 3

The Red Hat exams are an advanced challenge. In this lab, you'll examine the Red Hat exam prerequisites from a slightly different perspective. If you're uncertain about your readiness for this exam, the Linux Professional Institute has Level 1 exams that test basic skills in more detail. In addition, they cover a number of related commands that we believe are implied prerequisites for the Red Hat certifications.

To that end, examine the detailed objectives associated with the noted exams 101 and 102. Links to those objectives are available from www.lpi.org. If you're comfortable with most of the files, terms, and utilities listed in the objectives for those exams, you're ready to start your studies for the Red Hat exams.

A

SELF TEST ANSWERS

The RHCSA and RHCE Exams

1. There are no multiple choice questions on any Red Hat exams. It has been more than a decade since the Red Hat exams had a multiple choice component. The Red Hat exams are entirely "hands-on" experiences.

Basic Hardware Requirements

2. The default virtualization technology for RHEL 7 is KVM. Although there are many excellent virtualization technologies available, KVM is the default option supported by Red Hat on RHEL 7.

3. To install RHEL 7, you need a system with one or more 64-bit CPUs.

Get Red Hat Enterprise Linux

4. There are several different distributions available built on RHEL 7 source code. The most common options are CentOS, Oracle Linux, and Scientific Linux. There may be additional correct answers.

Installation Requirements

5. There is no correct answer to this question. Although the Red Hat exams are now presented on pre-installed systems, it's possible that you'll have to install RHEL 7 on a VM within an existing RHEL 7 installation.

Installation Options

6. Options for installation boot media for RHEL 7 include a CD, a DVD, and a USB drive.

7. You can configure and format regular partitions, RAID arrays, and logical volumes during the installation process to store data.

8. You can find the specified XML file under the noted conditions in the /media/repodata directory.

System Setup Options

9. Firstboot is started after the Initial Setup screen.

10. The default RHEL 7 firewall allows access to the Secure Shell service (SSH for short).

Configure Default File Sharing Services

11. The standard directory for file sharing for the RHEL 7 implementation of the vsFTP server is /var/ftp/pub.

12. The standard directory for HTML files for the RHEL 7 implementation of the Apache web server is /var/www/html.

LAB ANSWERS

Lab 1

When configuring a network connected to the Internet, you'll want to allow access to some systems and deny it to others. To that end, this lab provides a framework for the systems you'll want to set up to study for the RHCSA/RHCE exams.

As the RHCSA is in many ways an exercise in configuring a workstation, it may seem less important to set up a network to study for that exam. However, there are server elements to that exam, such as the configuration of NFS clients, so networks can't be neglected for the RHCSA.

With the development of VMs, the cost of hardware should be less of a handicap even for home users who are studying for the Red Hat exams. RHCSA specifically requires the configuration of VMs, so this should be practiced even if physical hardware is available.

Although dynamic IPv4 addresses are used for most workstations, static IPv4 addresses are more appropriate in many cases, including services such as DNS, FTP, Web, and e-mail.

Three systems is a suggested minimum because the rules associated with firewalls are typically not applied to a local system and you will need to be able to test services from a client that is both permitted and denied; the second system is a remote client that should have access to local server services, and the third should not.

Of course, "real-life" networks are much more complex—and you are welcome to set up a network with more systems.

In Chapter 2, when you install RHEL 7 systems on KVM-based virtual machines, you will want to clone one system to support configuration from a baseline. And, in fact, that's what happens in many enterprises. VMs make it practical to dedicate one or more RHEL 7 systems to a specific service, such as the Apache web server.

Lab 2

During the Red Hat exams, you won't have access to the Internet. However, many installations and updates require Internet access to download software packages.

When you configure the files from the RHEL 7 installation DVD on a remote system, you're configuring an effective substitute for the purpose of installation of additional packages. In addition, those files support network installation, which is still an RHCSA requirement.

The steps described are associated with the configuration of the vsFTP server, protected by SELinux. Do not fear SELinux. As suggested by the steps in this lab, the configuration of the vsFTP server is fairly simple. Although the use of SELinux may seem intimidating to the RHCSA candidate, it is a requirement. The commands described in this lab show how you can live with SELinux on a vsFTP server. Chapter 4 will explain how you can make life with SELinux work for you in a number of other situations.

Lab 3

This lab may seem odd given that it references the requirements for a different Linux certification. However, many Linux administrators take the exams of the Linux Professional Institute (LPI) seriously. LPI creates excellent certifications. Many Linux administrators study for and pass the LPIC Level 1 exams. Passing the LPIC 101 and 102 exams provides an excellent foundation for the RHCSA and RHCE exams.

If you feel the need to get more of a grounding in Linux, refer to some of the books described at the beginning of this chapter.

The Red Hat exams are an advanced challenge. Some of the requirements for the RHCSA and RHCE exams may seem intimidating. It's okay if some of them seem beyond your capabilities at the moment, because that is the reason you are reading this book. However, if you're uncomfortable with basic command-line tools such as **ls**, **cd**, and **cp**, you might need more of a grounding in Linux first. Many candidates are successfully able to fill in the gaps in their knowledge with some self-study and practice.

Chapter 2

Virtual Machines and Automated Installations

The management of virtual machines (VMs) and Kickstart installations are required RHCSA skills. In other words, you need to be prepared to install RHEL 7 on a VM over a network, manually, and with the help of Kickstart.

Chapter 1 covered the basics of the installation process. It assumed that you could also set up virtualization during the installation process. But it's possible that you'll need to install and configure KVM after installation is complete.

Kickstart is the Red Hat system for automated installations. It works from a text file that provides answers to the RHEL 7 installation program. With those answers, the RHEL 7 installation program can work automatically, without further intervention.

Once installation is complete on the systems used for test, study, and service, you'll want to be able to administer them remotely. Not only is an understanding of SSH connections an RHCSA requirement, but also it's an excellent skill in the real world. The references to menu options in this book are based on the GNOME desktop environment. If you're using a different desktop environment, such as KDE, the steps are somewhat different.

CERTIFICATION OBJECTIVE 2.01

Configure KVM for Red Hat

In Chapter 1, you configured a physical 64-bit RHEL 7 system with the packages required to set up VMs. If all else fails, that configuration can help you set up multiple installations of RHEL 7. But if you're faced with a RHEL installation without the needed packages, what do you do?

With the right packages, you can set up KVM modules, get access to VM configuration commands, and set up detailed configuration for a group of VMs. Some of the commands described in this section are, in a way, previews of future chapters. For example, the tools associated with updates are covered in Chapter 7. But first, it's important to discuss why anyone would want to use a VM when physical hardware is so much more tangible.

INSIDE THE EXAM

Manage Virtual Machines

The RHCSA objectives suggest that you need to know how to

- Access a virtual machine's console
- Start and stop virtual machines
- Configure systems to launch virtual machines at boot

- Install Red Hat Enterprise Linux systems as virtual guests

It's reasonably safe to assume the VMs in question are based on Red Hat's default VM solution, KVM. In Chapter 1, you set up that solution during the installation process on a

64-bit system; however, you may also need to install the associated packages on a live system during an exam. In addition, there is the Virtual Machine Manager graphical console used by Red Hat to manage such VMs. Of course, that Virtual Machine Manager is a front end to the management API provided by the libvirt library. It can also be used to install and configure a system to be started automatically during the boot process.

Although the Red Hat exam blog noted in Chapter 1 suggests that you'll take an exam on a "pre-installed" system, that doesn't preclude installations on VMs. Therefore, in this chapter, you'll learn how to set up an installation of RHEL 7 on KVM.

Kickstart Installations

The RHCSA objectives state that you need to know how to

- Install Red Hat Enterprise Linux automatically using Kickstart

To that end, every RHEL installation includes a sample Kickstart file, based on the given installation. In this chapter, you'll learn

how to use that file to automate the installation process. It's a bit trickier than it sounds, because the sample Kickstart file must be modified first, beyond unique settings for different systems. But once it's configured, you'll be able to set up as many installations of RHEL as you need using that baseline Kickstart file.

Access Remote Systems and Transfer Files Securely

The RHCSA objectives state that you need to know how to

- Access remote systems using SSH
- Securely transfer files between systems

If systems administrators had to be in physical contact with every system, half of their lives would be spent en route from system to system. With tools such as the Secure Shell (SSH), administrators have the ability to do their work remotely and transfer files securely. Although SSH is automatically installed in a standard configuration in RHEL 7, custom configuration options such as key-based authentication will be covered later in the book.

Why Virtual Machines

It seems like everyone wants to get into the VM game. And they should. Enterprises had once dedicated different physical systems for every service. Actually, to ensure reliability, they may have dedicated two or more systems for each of those services. Sure, it's possible to configure multiple services on a single system. In fact, you might do so on the Red Hat exams. But in enterprises that are concerned about security, systems are frequently dedicated to individual services, to reduce the risk if one system or service is compromised.

With appropriately configured systems, each service can be configured on its own dedicated VM. You might find 10 VMs all installed on a single physical host system. As different services typically use RAM and CPU cycles at different times, it's often reasonable to "overcommit" the RAM and CPU on the local physical system. For example, on a system with 256GB of RAM, it's often reasonable to allocate 16GB each to 20 VMs configured on that system.

In practice, an administrator might replace 20 physical machines on an older network with two physical systems. Each of the 20 VMs would be installed on a shared storage volume, formatted with a clustered filesystem such as GFS2, and mounted on each physical system. Of course, those two physical systems require some powerful hardware. But the savings otherwise are immense, not only in overall hardware costs, but also in facilities, energy consumption, and more.

If You Have to Install KVM

If you have to install any sort of software on RHEL 7, the GNOME Software tool can be a great help. Log in to the GUI as a regular user. To open it from the GUI, click Applications | System Tools | Software. As long as there's an appropriate connection to repositories such as the RHN or those associated with third parties, it'll take a few moments to search. In the left pane, click the arrow next to Virtualization. The four virtualization package groups should appear. Click the Virtualization Hypervisor package group and then the first package in that group to see a screen similar to that shown in Figure 2-1.

FIGURE 2-1

Add/Remove
Software tool

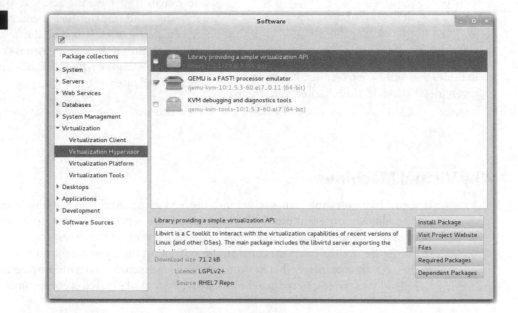

	Package	Description
TABLE 2-1	qemu-kvm	The main KVM package
	libvirt	The libvirtd service to manage hypervisors
Packages	libvirt-client	The virsh command and clients API to manage virtual machines
Associated with	virt-install	Command-line tools for creating VMs
Virtualization	virt-manager	GUI VM administration tool
	virt-top	Command to display virtualization statistics
	virt-viewer	Graphical console to connect to VMs

All you need to do to install KVM is select appropriate packages from the Virtualization Hypervisor, Virtualization Client, and Virtualization Platform package groups. If you don't remember the list shown in Table 2-1, just install the latest version of all virtualization packages.

That's just seven packages! Of course, in most configurations, they'll pull in other packages as dependencies. But that's all you really need to configure VMs on a physical RHEL 7 system. Although the Virtualization Tools group does not have any mandatory packages, it includes software that may be helpful in real life, such as tools that can help read and manage the VM disk images. If you want to display the content of a VM disk or manage VM partitions and filesystems from the hypervisor host, the libguestfs-tools package is what you need.

Installation with the GNOME Software tool is fairly simple. Just select (or deselect) the desired packages and click Apply. If there are dependent packages that also require installation, you'll be prompted with the full list of those packages. Of course, from the command-line interface, you can install these packages one at a time with the **yum install** *packagename* command. As an alternative, install the Virtualization Host and Virtualization Client groups, as shown here:

```
# yum group install "Virtualization Host" "Virtualization Client"
```

You will learn more about yum and package groups in Chapter 7.

The Right KVM Modules

In most cases, installation of the right packages is good enough. Appropriate kernel modules should be loaded automatically. Before KVM can work, the associated kernel modules must be loaded. Run the following command:

```
# lsmod | grep kvm
```

If KVM modules are properly loaded, you'll see one of the following two sets of modules:

```
kvm_intel       138567  0
kvm             441119  1 kvm_intel
```

or

```
kvm_amd         59887   0
kvm             261575  1 kvm_amd
```

As the module names suggest, the output depends on the CPU manufacturer. If you don't get this output, first make sure the hardware is suitable. And as suggested in Chapter 1, make sure the **svm** or **vmx** flag is listed in the contents of the **/proc/cpuinfo** file. Otherwise, additional configuration may be required in the system BIOS or UEFI menu. Some menus include specific options for hardware virtualization, which should be enabled.

If one of the noted flags exists in the **/proc/cpuinfo** file, the next step is to try loading the applicable modules. The simplest method is with the **modprobe** command. The following command should also load the dependent KVM module. If the system has an AMD processor, replace **kvm_intel** with **kvm_amd**:

```
# modprobe kvm_intel
```

Configure the Virtual Machine Manager

The Virtual Machine Manager is part of the **virt-manager** package. And you can start it in a GUI with the command of the same name. Alternatively, in the GNOME desktop click Applications | System Tools | Virtual Machine Manager. It opens the Virtual Machine Manager window shown in Figure 2-2.

FIGURE 2-2   Virtual Machine Manager

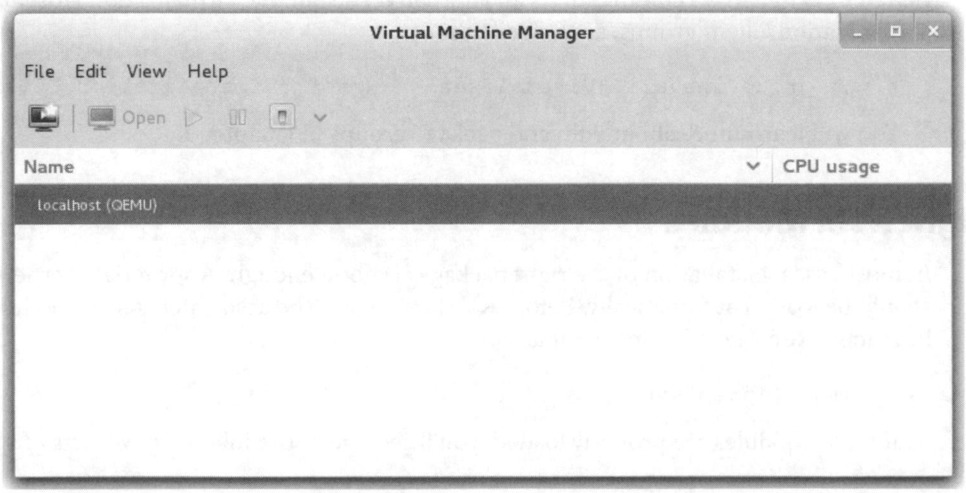

If desired, the KVM-based VMs can be configured and administered remotely. All you need to do is connect to the remote hypervisor. To do so, click File | Add Connection. This opens an Add Connection window that allows you to select the following:

- A Linux container or a hypervisor, normally KVM or Xen. (Xen was the default hypervisor on RHEL 5, but has not been supported since RHEL 6.)
- A connection, which may be local or remote, using a connection method such as SSH.

Remote connections can be given with the hostname or IP address of the remote system.

Configuration by Hypervisor

Each hypervisor can be configured in some detail. Right-click the localhost (QEMU) hypervisor and select Details in the pop-up menu that appears. This opens a details window named after the host of the local system, as shown in Figure 2-3.

FIGURE 2-3   VM host details

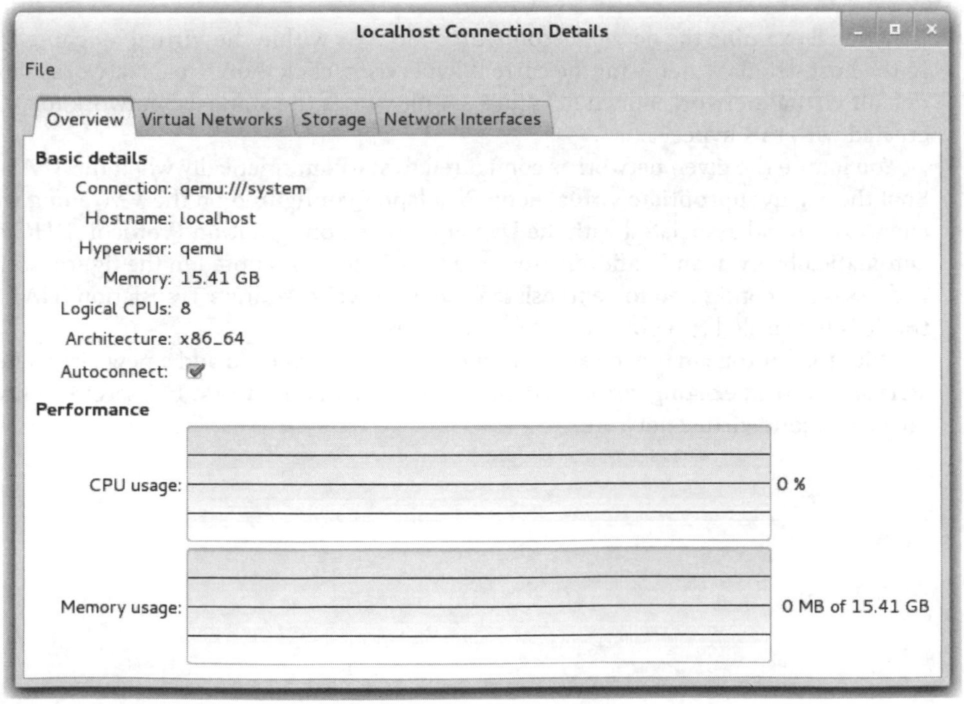

Setting	Description
Connection	Universal Resource Identifier (URI) for the hypervisor.
Hostname	Hostname for the VM host.
Hypervisor	QEMU is used by KVM.
Memory	Available RAM from the physical system for VMs.
Logical CPUs	Available logical CPUs; this is a quad-core system with hyper-threading enabled, which gives eight logical CPUs.
Architecture	CPU architecture.
Autoconnect	Indicates whether to automatically connect to the hypervisor during the boot process.

As shown in Table 2-2, the Overview tab lists the basics of the VM configuration. For the next section, stay in the host details window for the current hypervisor.

Virtual Networks on a Hypervisor

Now you'll examine the networks configured for VMs within the Virtual Machine Manager. In the host details window for the current hypervisor, click the Virtual Networks tab. The default virtual network shown in Figure 2-4 illustrates the standard network for VMs created with this hypervisor.

You'll note the given network is configured to start automatically when the VM is booted. So if there's an appropriate virtual network adapter configured on the VM, along with a client command associated with the Dynamic Host Configuration Protocol (DHCP), it's automatically given an IP address from the noted range. As noted in the figure, assigned addresses are configured to be translated using Network Address Translation (NAT) when traffic is forwarded to a physical network adapter.

With the buttons in the lower-left part of the screen, you can add a new virtual network, start and stop an existing virtual network, and delete that network. In Exercise 2-1, you'll create a second virtual network.

FIGURE 2-4   VM network details

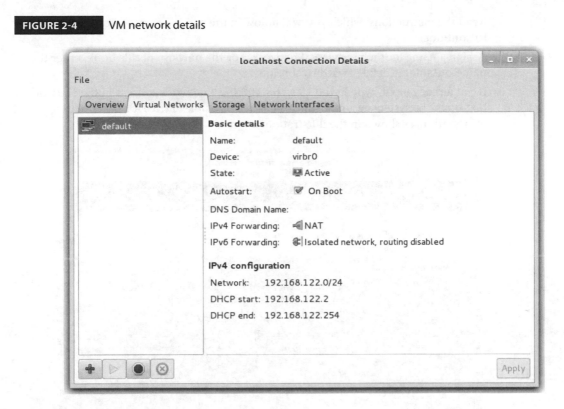

EXERCISE 2-1

Create a Second Virtual Network

In this exercise, you'll create a second virtual network on the standard KVM hypervisor in the GUI Virtual Machine Manager. This exercise requires a RHEL 7 system configured as a Virtualization Host, as discussed early in this chapter.

1. If you do not have the details window open, right-click the standard localhost (QEMU) hypervisor. In the pop-up menu that appears, select Details.

2. In the Host Details window that appears with the name of the local system, select the Virtual Networks tab.

3. Click the plus sign in the lower-left corner of the Virtual Networks tab to open the Create a New Virtual Network Wizard.

4. Read the instructions, which you will follow in the coming steps. Click Forward to continue.

5. Assign a name for the new virtual network. For the purpose of this book, enter the name **outsider**. Click Forward to continue.

6. If not already input, type in the **192.168.100.0/24** network address in the Network text box. The system automatically calculates plausible entries for other network information, as shown in the illustration.

Create a new virtual network

Defining IPv4 addresses

You will need to choose an **IPv4** address space for the virtual network.

☑ Enable IPv4 network address space definition

Network: `192.168.100.0/24`

💡 **Hint:** The network should be chosen from one of the IPv4 private address ranges. eg 10.0.0.0/8, 172.16.0.0/12, or 192.168.0.0/16

Gateway: 192.168.100.1

Network Type: Private

☑ Enable DHCPv4

Start: `192.168.100.128`

End: `192.168.100.254`

☐ Enable Static Route Definition

to Network: [ ]

via Gateway: [ ]

[Cancel] [Back] [Forward]

---

on the job

Take care to avoid IP address conflicts with existing hardware on the local network, such as with routers and wireless access points. For example, if a cable modem uses IP address 192.168.100.1 on its interface, the noted 192.168.100.0/24 network on the hypervisor would make that cable modem inaccessible from the Linux host. If you have such hardware, change the network address shown in the illustration.

7. Now you can select the range of IP addresses within the configured network that can be assigned to a DHCP client. Per Table 1-2 in Chapter 1, you'll configure a static IP address for the **outsider1.example.org** system on this network. As long as the noted 192.168.100.100 IP address is outside the range of DHCP-assignable IP addresses, no changes are required. Make any needed changes and click Forward to continue.

8. Optionally, you can define an IPv6 address range. IPv6 is part of the RHCE objectives and will be covered in Chapter 12. Click Forward to continue.

9. Now you'll want a system that forwards network packets to the physical network, if only because that's how systems on this network communicate with systems on different virtual networks, possibly on different virtual hosts. The destination can be Any Physical Device, in NAT mode, to help hide these systems from remote hosts. Unless you want to limit routing from VMs to a specific physical network card, the defaults under Forwarding to Physical Network should work. The options are covered later in this chapter, in the discussion of the Network Interfaces tab. Make appropriate selections and click Forward to continue.

10. Review the summary of what has been configured. If you are satisfied, click Finish. The outsider network will now be available for use by new VM systems and network cards.

Virtual Storage on a Hypervisor

Now you'll examine the virtual storage configured for VMs within the Virtual Machine Manager. In the host details window for the current hypervisor, click the Storage tab. The default filesystem directory shown in Figure 2-5 configures the /var/lib/libvirt/images directory for virtual images. Such images are essentially huge files of reserved space used as hard drives for VMs.

Those huge files can easily overwhelm many systems. One way to get control over such files is to dedicate a partition or logical volume to that /var/lib/libvirt/images directory.

Because you may have already dedicated the largest amount of free space to a partition for your /home directory, you can create dedicated storage in that area. As an example, the user "michael" can have a /home/michael/KVM directory to contain his VM files used for virtual hard drives.

The following commands will create the appropriate directory as a regular user, log in as the root user, set the appropriate SELinux contexts, remove the /var/lib/libvirt/images directory, and re-create that directory as a link to the appropriate user directory:

```
$ mkdir /home/michael/KVM
$ su - root
# semanage fcontext -a -t virt_image_t '/home/michael/KVM(/.*)?'
# restorecon /home/michael/KVM
# rmdir /var/lib/libvirt/images
# ln -s /home/michael/KVM /var/lib/libvirt/images
```

FIGURE 2-5   VM storage details

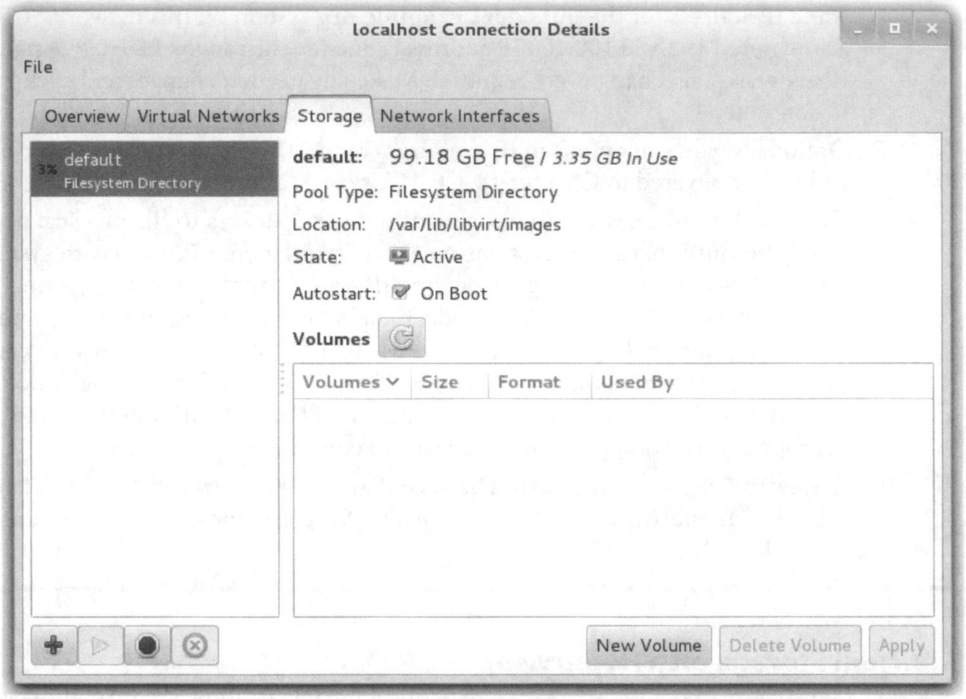

One advantage of this setup is that it retains the default SELinux settings for the /var /lib/libvirt/images directory, as defined in the file_contexts file in the /etc/selinux/targeted /contexts/files directory. In other words, this configuration survives a relabel of SELinux, as explained in Chapter 4.

Network Interfaces on a Hypervisor

Now you'll examine the network interfaces configured for VMs within the Virtual Machine Manager. In the host details window for the current hypervisor, click the Network Interfaces tab. The network interface device shown in Figure 2-6 specifies only the loopback interface. You may see other interfaces, such as an Ethernet adapter, if this is installed on your system.

If the local system connects via an Ethernet network card or wireless adapter, the default configuration should be sufficient. A properly configured VM should have access to

FIGURE 2-6   VM network cards

external networks, given the firewall and IP forwarding configuration options described in Chapter 1. In RHEL 7, each virtual network is associated to a virtual switch, such as virbr0. Virtual switches operate in NAT mode by default when traffic is forwarded outside the physical host.

In the same fashion as with the Virtual Network and Storage tabs, you can configure another network interface by clicking the plus sign in the lower-left corner of the Network Interfaces tab. It opens a Configure Network Interfaces window that can help you configure one of four different types of network interfaces:

- ■ **Bridge**   Bridges a physical and a virtual interface
- ■ **Bond**   Combines two or more interfaces in a single logical interface for redundancy
- ■ **Ethernet**   Configures an interface
- ■ **VLAN**   Configures an interface with IEEE 802.1Q VLAN tagging

Configure a Virtual Machine on KVM

The process for configuring a VM on KVM is straightforward, especially from the Virtual Machine Manager. In essence, all you have to do is right-click the QEMU hypervisor, click New, and follow the prompts that appear. However, because it's important to understand the process in detail, you'll read about it, step by step. New VMs can be configured not only from the GUI, but also from the command-line interface. As is common for Linux services, the resulting VM configuration is stored as a text file.

Configure a Virtual Machine on KVM

To follow along with this section, open the Virtual Machine Manager in the GUI. Another way to do so is from a GUI-based command line (by running the **virt-manager** command). If prompted, enter the root administrative password. If the localhost (QEMU) hypervisor is shown as not connected, right-click it and select Connect in the pop-up menu that appears. With the following steps, you'll set up the VM associated with the server1.example.com system discussed in Chapter 1. Now to set up a new VM, take the following steps:

1. Right-click the localhost (QEMU) hypervisor. In the pop-up menu that appears, click New to open the New VM window shown in Figure 2-7.

FIGURE 2-7

Create a new VM

New VM

Create a new virtual machine
Step 1 of 5

Enter your virtual machine details

Name: server1.example.com

Connection: localhost (QEMU/KVM)

Choose how you would like to install the operating system

- ● Local install media (ISO image or CDROM)
- ○ Network Install (HTTP, FTP, or NFS)
- ○ Network Boot (PXE)
- ○ Import existing disk image

Cancel   Back   Forward

2. Type in a name for the new VM; to match the discussion in the remainder of this book, you should name this VM **server1.example.com**.

3. Now select whether the installation media is available on local install media (ISO image or CD-ROM) or from a network installation server. That server may be associated with the HTTP, NFS, or FTP protocol. Select the Local Install Media option and click Forward to continue. (In Lab 1, you'll rerun this process with the Network Install option.)

4. If the media is available in a local CD/DVD drive, an option for such will be available, as shown in Figure 2-8. But for the purpose of these steps, select Use ISO Image and click Browse to navigate to the location of the RHEL 7 DVD or Network Boot ISO image. In addition, you'll need to use the OS Type and Version drop-down text boxes to select an operating system type and distribution, as shown.

5. Choose the amount of RAM memory and number of CPUs to allocate to the VM. Be aware of the minimums described earlier in this chapter and Chapter 1 for RHEL 7. As shown in Figure 2-9, in smaller print, you'll see information about available RAM and CPUs. Make appropriate selections and click Forward to continue.

FIGURE 2-8

Virtual machine media installation options

Virtual machine
RAM and CPU
selection

New VM

Create a new virtual machine
Step 3 of 5

Choose Memory and CPU settings

Memory (RAM): | 1024 | − | + | MB

Up to 15775 MB available on the host

CPUs: | 2 | − | +

Up to 8 available

Cancel   Back   Forward

6. Now you'll set up the hard drive for the VM, in the screen shown in Figure 2-10. Although it's possible to set it up in dedicated physical volumes, the standard is to set up big files as virtual hard drives. While the default location for such files is the /var /lib/libvirt/images directory, it can be changed, as discussed earlier in this chapter. On an exam, it's likely that you'll have more than sufficient room in the /var/lib/libvirt /images directory. The Select Managed or Other Existing Storage option supports the creation of a virtual hard drive in a different preconfigured storage pool.

7. Make sure the virtual drive is 16GB and the Allocate Entire Disk Now option is selected and click Forward to continue.

8. In the next window, confirm the options selected so far. Click Advanced Options to open the selections shown in Figure 2-11.

   You may have options to select one of the available virtual networks. If you performed Exercise 2-1, the "outsider" virtual network, associated to the IP subnet 192.168.100.0/24, should also be available.

9. The system may take a little time to create the VM, including the large file that will serve as the virtual hard drive. When complete, the Virtual Machine Manager should automatically start the system from the RHEL 7 installation DVD in a console window.

FIGURE 2-10

Create a virtual
hard drive

FIGURE 2-11

Review the
configuration
options

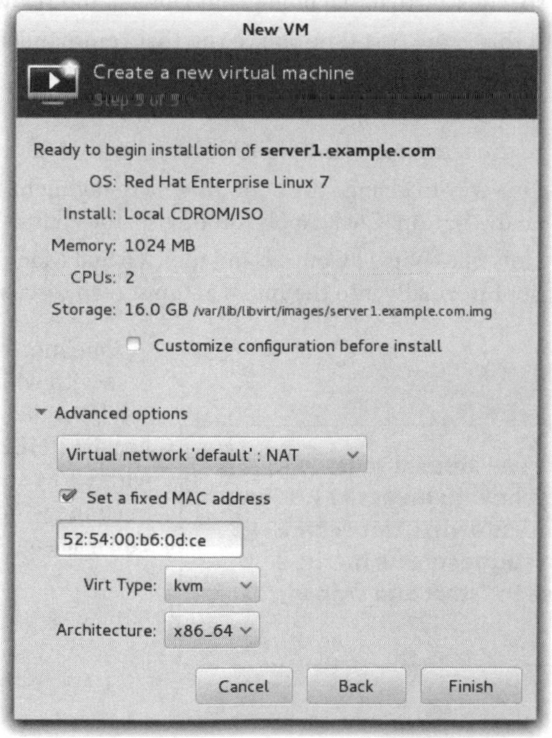

10. If the new system doesn't start automatically, that VM should be listed in the Virtual Machine Manager shown back in Figure 2-2. You should then be able to highlight the new VM (in this case, named server1.example.org) and click Open.

11. You should now be able to proceed with the installation of RHEL 7 in the VM as discussed in Chapter 1.

12. If you reboot the VM, the installation program "ejects" the DVD. If you want to reconnect the DVD later, you have to click View | Details, select the IDE CDROM 1 option, click Disconnect, and then click Connect. In the Choose Media window that appears, select the appropriate file with the DVD ISO image or CD-ROM for physical media.

13. Be aware that when you select software to install, this system is a virtual guest, not a virtual host configured in Chapter 1. There is no need to add any virtualization packages to the installation. Select Server with GUI without specifying any of the optional add-ons, and click Done.

14. When the installation is complete, click Reboot. If the system tries to boot from the DVD drive again, you'll need to change the boot order between the DVD and the hard drive. If the system boots directly from the hard drive, you're done!

15. If the system tries to boot from the DVD, you need to shut down the system. To do so, click Virtual Machine | Shut Down | Shut Down.

16. If this is the first time you've run that command sequence, the Virtual Machine Manager prompts for confirmation. Click Yes.

17. Now click View | Details.

18. In the left pane, select Boot Options, as shown in Figure 2-12.

19. One way to change the boot order is to highlight CDROM and then click the down-arrow button. Click Apply; otherwise, the changes won't be recorded.

20. Now click View | Console and then Virtual Machine | Run. The system should now boot normally into the Initial Setup screen discussed in Chapter 1.

e**x**a m
ⓦatch   **The steps discussed in this section describe how to meet the RHCSA objective to "access a virtual machine's console." It also suggests one method that you can use to "start and stop virtual machines."**

One more reason for the use of VMs is the ease with which additional virtual hard drives can be added. The process varies by VM solution. For the RHEL 7 default Virtual Machine Manager with KVM solution, you can do so from the machine window by clicking View | Details. You'll see an Add Hardware option in this screen.

FIGURE 2-12   Boot options in the VM

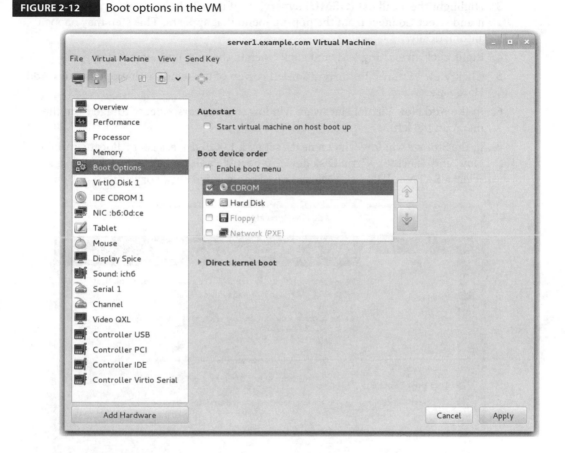

Add Virtual Hard Drives

In this exercise, you'll create an additional virtual hard drive on a KVM-based VM. We assume there's an existing KVM VM for that purpose, along with the use of the GUI Virtual Machine Manager.

1. Open the Virtual Machine Manager. From the command line in a GUI, run the **virt-manager** command.

2. If prompted, enter the root administrative password and click Authenticate.

3. Highlight the localhost (QEMU) hypervisor. If it isn't already connected, right-click it and select Connect from the pop-up menu that appears. This step may happen automatically.

4. Right-click an existing VM, and click Open in the pop-up menu that appears.

5. Click View | Details. In the bottom-left corner of the window that opens, click Add Hardware.

6. In the Add New Virtual Hardware window that appears, select Storage from the menu on the left.

7. In the Storage window (shown next), set up a 1.0GB drive, select Allocate Entire Disk Now, and select the Virtio Disk device type in default cache mode. (You can also select a SATA or IDE disk.) Make desired choices and click Forward to continue.

8. You may see a confirmation of selected settings. If satisfied, click Finish to create the new virtual hard drive.

9. Repeat previous steps to create a second 1GB hard drive.

10. The next time you boot this system, run the **fdisk -l** command from the root account. It should confirm appropriate information about the configured hard drive devices.

FIGURE 2-13   The configuration file for a KVM virtual machine

```
<domain type='kvm'>
  <name>server1.example.com</name>
  <uuid>7782a007-60eb-4292-b731-8b2b60594933</uuid>
  <memory unit='KiB'>1048576</memory>
  <currentMemory unit='KiB'>1048576</currentMemory>
  <vcpu placement='static'>2</vcpu>
  <os>
    <type arch='x86_64' machine='pc-i440fx-rhel7.0.0'>hvm</type>
    <boot dev='hd'/>
    <bootmenu enable='no'/>
  </os>
  <features>
    <acpi/>
    <apic/>
    <pae/>
  </features>
  <clock offset='utc'/>
  <on_poweroff>destroy</on_poweroff>
  <on_reboot>restart</on_reboot>
  <on_crash>restart</on_crash>
  <devices>
    <emulator>/usr/libexec/qemu-kvm</emulator>
    <disk type='file' device='disk'>
      <driver name='qemu' type='raw' cache='none'/>
      <source file='/var/lib/libvirt/images/server1.example.com.img'/>
      <target dev='vda' bus='virtio'/>
      <address type='pci' domain='0x0000' bus='0x00' slot='0x06' function='0x0'/>
    </disk>
    <disk type='file' device='disk'>
      <driver name='qemu' type='raw' cache='none'/>
      <source file='/var/lib/libvirt/images/server1.example.com-1.img'/>
      <target dev='hda' bus='ide'/>
      <address type='drive' controller='0' bus='0' target='0' unit='0'/>
    </disk>
```

KVM Configuration Files

KVM-based VMs are normally configured in two different directories: /etc/libvirt and /var/lib/libvirt. When a KVM VM is configured, it is set up in files in XML format in the /etc/libvirt/qemu directory. For example, Figure 2-13 shows a relevant excerpt of the configuration file for the main VM we used to help prepare this book (server1.example.com.xml).

Important parameters for the VM are labeled. For example, the amount of memory is shown in KiB (1 KiB = 1024 bytes), two virtual CPUs are allocated, KVM is the emulator, the disk can be found in the server1.example.com.img file in the /var/lib/libvirt/images directory, and so on.

Although you can edit this configuration file directly, changes aren't implemented until the **libvirtd** service is restarted with a command such as **systemctl restart libvirtd**.

Control Virtual Machines from the Command Line

Of course, command-line tools can be used to create, clone, convert, and install VMs on RHEL 7. The key commands to that end are **virt-install**, **virsh**, and **virt-clone**. The **virsh** command is an especially useful way to address two different RHCSA objectives.

The virt-install Command

You can perform the same steps as was done earlier in this chapter using the Virtual Machine Manager. All you need is the **virt-install** command. The command with the **--help** switch shows all the options for the required information described earlier. Look at the command help screen and compare with the example shown in Figure 2-14.

For many, that's simpler than configuring the GUI Virtual Machine Manager. The Creating Domain message at the end of Figure 2-14 starts a console window with a graphical view of the given installation program. If you get a "cannot open display" error, ensure that you have opened a GNOME Desktop session as root.

If you make a mistake with the **virt-install** command, you can abort the process by pressing CTRL-C. But be aware that the newly created VM is still running. And there's now a configuration file and virtual disk for that VM. If you try to rerun the **virt-install** command with the same name for the VM, an error message will appear. Therefore, if you want to use the same name for the VM, take the following steps:

1. Stop the VM just created. If it's the tester1.example.com system shown in Figure 2-14, you can do so with the following command:

```
# virsh destroy tester1.example.com
```

FIGURE 2-14

Configure a VM with the virt-install command

```
[root@Maui ~]# virt-install --name=tester1.example.com \
> --ram=1024 --vcpus=2 \
> --disk path=/var/lib/libvirt/images/tester1.example.com.img,size=16 \
> --graphics=spice \
> --location=ftp://192.168.122.1/pub/inst \
> --os-type=linux \
> --os-variant=rhel7

Starting install...
Retrieving file .treeinfo...                          |  4.2 kB    00:00 !!!
Retrieving file vmlinuz...                            |  9.3 MB    00:00 !!!
Retrieving file initrd.img...                         |   68 MB    00:00 !!!
Allocating 'tester1.example.com.img'                  |   16 GB    00:00
Creating domain...                                    |    0 B     00:00
Domain installation still in progress. You can reconnect to
the console to complete the installation process.
```

2. Delete the associated XML configuration file in the /etc/libvirt/qemu directory and the virtual disk file, normally created in the /var/lib/libvirt/images directory. However, this is not necessary if you want to reuse the file.

```
# virsh undefine tester1.example.com --remove-all-storage
```

3. Now you'll be able to run the **virt-install** command again with the same name for the VM.

The virt-install Command and Kickstart

For Kickstart installations described later in this chapter, the **virt-install** command can be used to cite a Kickstart configuration file. For that purpose, you'll need to understand some of the key switches associated with the **virt-install** command, as shown in Table 2-3.

For example, the following **virt-install** command will install a system named outsider1.example.org automatically using a Kickstart file named ks1.cfg from the FTP server on the noted IP address, with 1GB of RAM, and an outsider1.example.org.img virtual disk.

```
# virt-install -n outsider1.example.org -r 1024 --disk \
path=/var/lib/libvirt/images/outsider1.example.org.img,size=16 \
-l ftp://192.168.122.1/pub/inst \
-x ks=ftp://192.168.122.1/pub/ks1.cfg
```

This command contains a number of switches. Most of the switches shown are described in the examples listed in the man page for the **virt-install** command. You may note additional command options, which are helpful but are not required for RHEL 7 installation. However,

	Switch	Description
TABLE 2-3	-n (--name)	Sets the name for the VM.
	--vcpus	Configures the number of virtual CPUs.
Command Switches for virt-install	-r (--ram)	Configures the amount of RAM in MB.
	--disk	Defines the virtual disk; often used with **path=/var/lib/libvirt/images/**_virt_**.img,size=**_size_in_GB_.
	-l (--location)	Specifies the directory or URL with the installation files (equivalent to --**location**).
	--graphics	Specifies the graphical display settings of the guest; valid options are **vnc**, **spice**, and **none**.
	-x (--extra-args=)	Includes extra data, such as the URL of a Kickstart file.

they are required to look for the given Kickstart file. Remember the format for the extra arguments, with the quotes, which may also be expressed as follows:

```
--extra-args="ks=ftp://192.168.122.1/pub/ks1.cfg"
```

The virsh Command

The **virsh** command starts a front end to existing KVM VMs. When run alone, it moves from a regular command line to the following prompt:

```
virsh #
```

From that prompt, run the **help** command. It includes access to a number of commands, some of which are listed in Table 2-4. Not all of those commands shown in the output to the **help** screen are active for KVM. Those **virsh** commands that are usable can also be run directly from the bash shell prompt; for example, the **virsh list --all** command lists all configured VMs, whether or not they're currently running. In the context of KVM, an instance of an operating system running on a VM is a *domain*. Domain names are referenced by different **virsh** commands.

Take a look at the output to the **virsh list --all** command on our system:

```
Id Name                        State
---------------------------------------
 - server1.example.com   shut off
 - tester1.example.com   shut off
```

With the right **virsh** commands, you can meet two RHCSA objectives. First, the following command starts the noted server1.example.com system:

```
# virsh start server1.example.com
```

TABLE 2-4	virsh Command	Description
Selected Commands at the virsh Prompt	autostart <domain>	Configures a domain to be started during the host system boot process
	capabilities	Lists the abilities of the local hypervisor
	edit <domain>	Edits the XML configuration file for the domain
	list --all	Lists all domains
	start <domain>	Boots the given domain
	shutdown <domain>	Gracefully shuts down the given domain

The **virsh shutdown** command gracefully shut downs the operating system and powers off a VM:

```
# virsh shutdown server1.example.com
```

To immediately power off a virtual machine, you'd have to run a somewhat more severe command:

```
# virsh destroy server1.example.com
```

The **virsh destroy** command is functionally equivalent to disconnecting the power cord on a physical system. As that can lead to different problems, it's best to stop a VM by running the **poweroff** command from within the VM.

Even on the most protected systems, power failures happen. Kernel updates still require a system reboot. In those cases, it's helpful to automate the start of VMs on a virtual host during the boot process.

To start and stop a VM, you can run the virsh start *vmname* **and** virsh destroy *vmname* **commands, where** *vmname* **is the domain name of the VM, as shown in the output to the** virsh list --all **command.**

In addition, the **virsh** command is the most straightforward way to make sure a VM is started the next time a system is booted. For example, the following command configures the noted tester1.example.com system to start during the boot process of the host system:

```
# virsh autostart tester1.example.com
```

Once the boot process is complete for both the host and the VM, you'll be able to use commands such as **ssh** to connect to that VM system normally. However, from the physical host GUI, you'll still have to start the Virtual Machine Manager and connect to the associated hypervisor to actually access the virtual console for that tester1.example.com system.

The command creates a soft linked file in the /etc/libvirt/qemu/autostart directory. To reverse the process, either run the command

```
# virsh autostart --disable tester1.example.com
```

or delete the soft linked file named after the target VM from that directory.

The virt-clone Command

The **virt-clone** command can be used to clone an existing VM. Before starting the process, make sure the system to be cloned is shut down. It's straightforward; one example where a **tester1 .example.com** system is created from a **server1 .example.com** system is shown in Figure 2-15.

To configure a VM to start automatically when a system is booted, you can run the virsh autostart *vmname* **command, where** *vmname* **is the name of the VM, as shown in the output to the** virsh list --all **command.**

FIGURE 2-15

Cloning a virtual
machine

```
[root@Maui ~]# virt-clone --original=server1.example.com \
> --name=tester1.example.com \
> --file=/var/lib/libvirt/images/tester1.example.com.img \
> --file=/var/lib/libvirt/images/tester1.example.com-1.img \
> --file=/var/lib/libvirt/images/tester1.example.com-2.img
Allocating 'tester1.example.com.img'                    |  16 GB     00:46
Allocating 'tester1.example.com-1.img'                  | 1.0 GB     00:00
Allocating 'tester1.example.com-2.img'                  | 1.0 GB     00:00

Clone 'tester1.example.com' created successfully.
[root@Maui ~]#
```

Note that you must specify a path to a virtual disk using the **--file** switch for every disk of the original virtual machine that you want to clone. In this case, server1.example.com has three virtual drives because we added two new drives in Exercise 2-2.

Once the process is complete, not only will you find the noted hard drive images in the specified directories, but also you'll find a new XML configuration file for that VM in the /etc/libvirt/qemu directory.

The first time you boot a cloned machine, it may be best to boot it into the rescue target. The rescue target does not start most services, including networking (for more information, see Chapter 5). In that case, you'll be able to modify any networking settings, such as the hostname and IP address, before starting that cloned machine on a production network. In addition, you'll want to make sure that the hardware (MAC) address for the related network card is different from that of the source guest to avoid conflicts with the original network card.

Although that process may not be difficult for one or two VMs, imagine setting up a few dozen VMs, each later configured for different services. That situation would be helped by more automation. To that end, Red Hat provides a system known as Kickstart.

CERTIFICATION OBJECTIVE 2.03

Automated Installation Options

Kickstart is Red Hat's solution for an automated installation of RHEL. Think of each of the steps performed during the installation process as questions. With Kickstart, each of those questions can be answered automatically with one text file. With Kickstart, you can set up identical systems very quickly. To that end, Kickstart files are useful for quick deployment and distribution of Linux systems.

In addition, the installation process is an opportunity to learn more about RHEL 7—not only the boot media, but the partitions and logical volumes that can be configured after installation is complete. With the advent of VMs, it isn't difficult to set up an automated installation on a new VM with the help of Kickstart.

The steps described in this section assume a connection to the FTP server with RHEL 7 installation files created and configured in Lab 2 of Chapter 1.

Kickstart Concepts

One of the problems with a Kickstart-based installation is that it does not include the custom settings created after the basic installation was complete. Although it's possible to include those settings based on post-installation scripts, that's beyond the scope of the RHCSA exam.

There are two methods for creating the required Kickstart configuration file:

- Start with the anaconda-ks.cfg file from the root user's home directory, /root.
- Use the graphical Kickstart Configurator, accessible via the **system-config-kickstart** command.

The first option lets you use the Kickstart template file created for the local system by Anaconda: anaconda-ks.cfg in the /root directory. The second option, the Kickstart Configurator, is discussed in detail later in this chapter.

It's relatively easy to customize the anaconda-ks.cfg file for different systems. Shortly, you'll see how to customize that file as needed for different hard disk sizes, hostnames, IP addresses, and more.

Set Up Local Access to Kickstart

Once the Kickstart file is configured, you can set it up on local media such as a USB key, a CD, a spare partition, or even a floppy drive. (Don't laugh; many VM systems, including KVM, make it easy to use virtual floppy drives.) To do so, follow these basic steps:

1. Configure and edit the anaconda-ks.cfg file as desired. We'll describe this process in more detail shortly.

2. Mount the desired local media. You may need to run a command such as **fdisk -l** as the root user to identify the appropriate device file. If the drive doesn't mount automatically, you can then mount the drive with a command such as **mount /dev/sdb1 /mnt**.

3. Copy the Kickstart file to ks.cfg on the mounted local media. (Other names are okay; ks.cfg is just the most common filename for this purpose in Red Hat documentation.)

4. Make sure the ks.cfg file has at least read permissions for all users. If SELinux is active on the local system, the contexts should normally match that of other files in the same directory. For more information, see Chapter 4.

   Be aware that a Kickstart configuration file on an FTP server may be a security risk. It's almost like the DNA of a system. If a black hat hacker gets hold of that file, he could use it to set up a copy of your systems and see how to break into and compromise your data. Because this file normally contains a root administrative password, you should change the password as soon as the system is booted for the first time.

on the **!** **Job**
Be careful with the Kickstart configuration file. Unless direct root logins are disabled, the file includes the root administrative password. Even if that password is encrypted, a black hat hacker with the right tools and a copy of that Kickstart configuration file can run a dictionary attack and decrypt that password if it is not secure enough.

You should now be ready to use the Kickstart media on a different system. You'll get to try this again shortly in an exercise.

5. Now try to access the Kickstart file on the local media. Boot the RHEL 7 installation CD/DVD. When the first menu appears, highlight Install Red Hat Enterprise Linux 7.0 and press TAB. Commands to Anaconda should appear, similar to the following, and a cursor should appear at the end of that line:

```
> vmlinuz initrd=initrd.img inst.stage2=hd:LABEL=RHEL-7.0↵
\x20Server.x86_64 quiet
```

6. Add information for the location of the Kickstart file to the end of the line. For example, the following addition locates that file on the first partition of the second hard drive, which may be a USB drive:

```
ks=hd:sdb1:/ks.cfg
```

Alternatively, if the kickstart file is on the boot CD, try adding the following command:

```
ks=cdrom:/ks.cfg
```

Alternatively, if the kickstart file is on the first floppy drive, enter the following:

```
ks=hd:fd0:/ks.cfg
```

There may be some trial and error with this method. Yes, device files are generally assigned in sequence (sda, sdb, sdc, and so on). However, unless you boot Linux with the given storage media, there is no certainty about which device file is assigned to a specific drive.

Set Up Network Access to Kickstart

The process of setting up a Kickstart file from local media can be time consuming, especially if you have to go from system to system to load that file. In many cases, it's more efficient to set up the Kickstart file on a network server. One logical location is the same network server used for the installation files. For example, based on the FTP server created in Chapter 1, Lab 2, assume there's a ks.cfg file in the FTP server's /var/ftp/pub directory. SELinux contexts should match that of that directory, which can be confirmed with the following commands:

```
# ls -Zd /var/ftp/pub
# ls -Z /var/ftp/pub
```

Once an appropriate ks.cfg file is in the /var/ftp/pub directory, you can access it by adding the following directive to the end of the **vmlinuz** line described earlier in Step 5:

```
ks=ftp://192.168.122.1/pub/ks.cfg
```

Similar options are possible for a Kickstart file on an NFS and an HTTP server, as follows:

```
ks=nfs:192.168.122.1:/ks.cfg
ks=http://192.168.122.1/ks.cfg
```

If there's an operational DNS server on the local network, you can substitute the hostname or fully qualified domain name of the target server for the IP address.

on the
Òob
To ease the process of creating a Kickstart-based installation server, see the Cobbler project at http://cobbler.github.com. Cobbler uses profiles and small blocks of code (called "snippets") to dynamically generate Kickstart files and automate network installations.

Sample Kickstart File

We've based this section on the anaconda-ks.cfg file created when we installed RHEL 7 inside a KVM-based VM with a number of added comments. Although you're welcome to use it as a sample file, be sure to customize it for your hardware and network. This section just scratches the surface of what you can do with a Kickstart file; your version of this file may vary.

e x a m

w a t c h
Unlike what's available for many other Red Hat packages, the Kickstart documentation available within an installed RHEL 7 system is somewhat sparse. In other words, you can't really rely on man pages or files in the /usr/share/doc directory for

Kickstart help during an exam. If you're uncertain about specific commands to include in the Kickstart file, the Kickstart Configurator described later in this chapter can help.

Although most of the options are self-explanatory, we've interspersed our explanation of each command within the file. This file illustrates just a small portion of the available commands. For more information on each command (and options) in this file, read the latest RHEL 7 Installation Guide, which is available online at https://access.redhat.com /documentation.

Follow these ground rules and guidelines when setting up a Kickstart file:

- In general, retain the order of the directives. However, some variation is allowable depending on whether the installation is from local media or over a network.
- You do not need to use all the options.
- If you leave out a required option, the user will be prompted for the answer.
- Don't be afraid to make a change; for example, partition-related directives are commented out by default.
- Line wrapping in the file is acceptable.

on the job
If you leave out an option, the installation process will stop at that point. This is an easy way to see if a Kickstart file is properly configured. However, because some Kickstart options change the partitions on a hard drive, even tests can be dangerous. Therefore, it's best to test a Kickstart file on a test system—or even better, an experimental VM.

The following is the code from one of our anaconda-ks.cfg files. The first line tells us that this file was created for RHEL 7:

```
#version=RHEL7
```

Next, the **auth** command sets up the Shadow Password Suite (**--enableshadow**) and the SHA 512-bit encryption algorithm for password encryption (**--passalgo=sha512**). A password encrypted to the SHA512 algorithm starts with a **$6**:

```
authconfig --enableshadow --passalgo=sha512
```

The next command is simple; it starts the installation process from the first DVD/CD drive on the system:

```
cdrom
```

The next step is to specify the source of the installation files. To use RHEL 7 DVDs, leave the existing **cdrom** entry. To install from an NFS server, specify the URI as follows. If there's a reliable DNS server for the local network, you can substitute the hostname for the IP address.

```
nfs --server=192.168.122.1 --dir=/inst
```

You can also configure a connection to an FTP or HTTP server by substituting one of the commands shown here. The directories specified are based on the FTP and HTTP installation servers created in Chapter 1:

```
url --url http://192.168.122.1/inst
```

or

```
url --url ftp://192.168.122.1/pub/inst
```

If the ISO file that represents the RHEL 7 DVD exists on a local hard drive partition, you can specify that as well. For example, the following directive points to ISO CDs or DVDs on the /dev/sda10 partition:

```
harddrive --partition=/dev/sda10 --dir=/tmp/michael/
```

The **firstboot --enable** runs the setup agent during the first installation. If you want to avoid the Firstboot process, you can also replace this line with the **firstboot --disabled** directive. As there's no way to set up a Kickstart file with answers to the Firstboot prompts, that **--disabled** directive helps automate the Kickstart process.

```
firstboot --disabled
```

The **ignoredisk** directive that follows specifies volumes only on the noted vda drive. Of course, this works only if there is a specified virtual drive on the target VM. (It's possible to specify SAS or SCSI drives on such VMs, which would conflict with these directives.)

```
# ignoredisk --only-use=vda
```

The **lang** command sets the language to use during the installation process. It matters if the installation stops due to a missing command in this file. The **keyboard** command is self-explanatory—it specifies the keyboard layout to configure on this computer.

```
keyboard --vckeymap=us --xlayouts='us'
lang en_US.UTF-8
```

The required **network** command is simplest if there's a DHCP server for the local network: **network --device eth0 --bootproto dhcp**. In contrast, the following two lines configure static IP address information, with the noted network mask (**--netmask**), gateway address (**--gateway**), DNS server (**--nameserver**), and computer name (**--hostname**).

```
network --bootproto static --device=eth0 --gateway=192.168.122.1↵
--ip=192.168.122.150 --netmask=255.255.255.0 --noipv6↵
--nameserver==192.168.122.1 --activate
network --hostname tester1.example.com
```

Please note that all static networking information for the **network** command *must* be on *one* line. Line wrapping, if the options exceed the space in a text editor, is acceptable. If you're setting up this file for a different system, don't forget to change the IP address and hostname information accordingly. Be aware, if you did not configure networking during the installation process, it won't be written to the subject anaconda-ks.cfg file. Given the complexity of the **network** directive, you could either use the Kickstart Configurator to help set up that directive or configure networking after installation is complete.

As the password for the root user is part of the RHEL 7 installation process, the Kickstart configuration file can specify that password in encrypted format. Although encryption is not required, it can at least delay a black hat hacker who might break into a system after installation is complete. Because the associated cryptographic hash function is the same as is used for the /etc/shadow file, you can copy the desired password from that file.

```
rootpw --iscrypted $6$5UrLfXTk$CsCW0nQytrUuvycuLT317/
```

The **timezone** command is associated with a long list of time zones. They're documented in the tzdata package. For a full list, run the **rpm -ql tzdata** command. By default, Red Hat sets the hardware clock to the equivalent of Greenwich Mean Time with the **--isUtc** switch. That setting supports automated changes for daylight saving time. The following setting can be found as a subdirectory and file in the /usr/share/zoneinfo directory:

```
timezone America/Los_Angeles --isUtc
```

The **user** directive can be included to create a user during the boot process. It requires a username, an encrypted password, and optionally a list of groups the user should belong to and the GECOS information for the user (typically his full name). In the following example, the encrypted password is omitted for brevity:

```
user --groups=wheel name=michael --password=... --iscrypted --gecos="MJ"
```

As for security, the **firewall** directive can optionally be added. When coupled with **--service=ssh**, it specifies the services that are allowed through the firewall:

```
firewall --service=ssh
```

The **selinux** directive is also optional and can be set to **--enforcing**, **--permissive**, or **--disabled**. The default is **--enforcing**:

```
selinux --enforcing
```

The default bootloader is GRUB 2. It should normally be installed on the space between the Master Boot Record (MBR) of a hard drive and the first partition. You can include a **--boot-drive** switch to specify the drive with the bootloader and an **--append** switch to specify parameters for the kernel:

```
bootloader --location=mbr --boot-drive=vda
```

As suggested by the comments that follow, it's first important to clear some existing sets of partitions. First, the **clearpart --all --initlabel --drives=vda** directive clears all partitions on the vda virtual hard drive. If it hasn't been used before, **--initlabel** initializes that drive:

```
clearpart --all --initlabel --drives=vda
```

Changes are required in the partition (**part**) directives that follow. They should specify the directory, filesystem format (**--fstype**), and **--size** in MB:

```
part /boot --fstype="xfs" --size=500
part swap --fstype="swap" --size=1000
part / --fstype="xfs" --size=10000
part /home --fstype="xfs" --size=1000
```

Be aware, your version of an anaconda-ks.cfg file may include an **--onpart** directive that specifies partition device files such as /dev/vda1. That would lead to an error unless the noted partitions already exist. So if you see any **--onpart** directives, it's simplest to delete them. Otherwise, you'd have to create those partitions before starting the installation process, and that can be tricky.

Although other partition options may be used for RAID arrays and logical volumes, the implicit focus of the Red Hat exams is to set up such volumes after installation is complete. If you want to try out other options such as logical volumes, create your own Kickstart file. It's best if you set it up from a different VM installation. Just be aware, the Kickstart file can configure physical volumes (PVs), volume groups (VGs), and logical volumes (LVs), in that order (and the order is important), similar to what's shown here:

```
part pv.01 --fstype="lvmpv" --ondisk=vda --size=11008
part /boot --fstype="xfs" --ondisk=vda --size=500
part swap --fstype="swap" --ondisk=vda --size=1000
volgroup rhel --pesize=4096 pv.01
logvol / --fstype="xfs" --size=10000 --name=root --vgname=rhel
logvol /home --fstype="xfs" --size=1000 -name=home --vgname=rhel
```

For more information on how LVs are configured, see Chapter 8.

The default version of the Kickstart file may contain a **repo** directive. It would point to the FTP network installation source from Chapter 1, Lab 2, and should be deleted from or commented out of the Kickstart file as follows:

```
#repo --name="Red Hat Enterprise Linux" ↵
--baseurl=ftp://192.168.122.1/pub/inst --cost=100
```

To make sure the system actually completes the installation process, this is the place to include a directive such as **reboot**, **shutdown**, **halt**, or **poweroff**. If you're reusing an existing KVM-based VM, it may be necessary to shut off the system to change the boot media from the CD/DVD to the hard drive. Therefore, you may prefer to use the following directive:

```
shutdown
```

What follows is a list of package groups that are installed through this Kickstart configuration file. These names correspond to the names you can find in the *-comps-Server.x86_64.xml file in the RHEL 7 DVD /repodata directory described in Chapter 1. Because the list is long, the following is just an excerpt of package groups (which start with @) and package names:

```
%packages
@base
@core
...
@print-client
@x11
%end
```

After the package groups are installed, you can specify post-installation commands after the following directive. For example, you could set up custom configuration files. However, the **%post** directive and anything that follows is not required.

```
%post
```

Finally, use the **ksvalidator** utility to verify the syntax of the Kickstart file. An example is shown here:

```
# ksvalidator ks.cfg
The following problem occurred on line 32 of the kickstart file:

Unknown command: vogroup
```

EXERCISE 2-3

Create and Use a Sample Kickstart File

In this exercise, you will use the anaconda-ks.cfg file to duplicate the installation from one computer to another with identical hardware. This exercise installs all the exact same packages with the same partition configuration on the second computer. Additionally, this exercise even configures the SELinux context for that Kickstart file.

Because the objective is to install the same packages as the current installation, no changes are required to packages or package groups from the default anaconda-ks.cfg file in the /root directory. This assumes access to a network installation source such as that created in Lab 2 of Chapter 1.

The steps in this exercise assume sufficient space and resources for at least two different KVM-based VMs, as discussed in Chapter 1:

1. Review the /root/anaconda-ks.cfg file on server1.example.com. Copy it to ks.cfg.

2. If there's an existing **network** directive in the file, modify it to point to an IP address of 192.168.122.150, with a hostname of tester1.example.com. If a system with that hostname and IP address already exists, use a different hostname and IP address on the same network. It is okay if such a directive doesn't already exist; networking can be configured after installation is complete, using the techniques discussed in Chapter 3.

3. Make sure the directives associated with drives and partitions in the ks.cfg file are active and they are not commented out. Pay attention to the **clearpart** directive; it should normally be set to --**all** to erase all partitions and --**initlabel** to initialize newly created disks. If there's more than one hard drive attached to the VM, the --**drives**=vda switch can focus on the first virtual drive on a KVM-based VM.

4. Remove the **cdrom** directive if present. Review the location of the installation server, associated with the **url** or **nfs** directive. This lab assumes it's an FTP server accessible on IP address 192.168.122.1, in the pub/inst/ subdirectory. If it's a different IP address and directory, substitute accordingly.

   ```
   url --url ftp://192.168.122.1/pub/inst
   ```

5. Make sure the following directive is included just before the **%packages** directive at the end of the file:

   ```
   shutdown
   ```

6. Use the **ksvalidator** utility to check the syntax of the Kickstart file. If no errors are reported, proceed to the next step:

   ```
   ksvalidator ks.cfg
   ```

7. Copy the ks.cfg file to the base directory of the installation server; if it's the vsFTP server, that directory is /var/ftp/pub. Make sure that file is readable for all users (by default it is accessible only by root with permissions 600). For example, you could use the following command:

```
# chmod +r /var/ftp/pub/ks.cfg
```

8. Assuming that the base directory is /var/ftp/pub, modify the SELinux context of that file with the following command:

```
# restorecon /var/ftp/pub/ks.cfg
```

9. Make sure any existing firewalls do not block the communication port associated with the installation server. For detailed information, see Chapter 4. The simplest way to do so is to open the ftp service with the **firewall-cmd** command:

```
# firewall-cmd --permanent --add-service=ftp
# firewall-cmd --reload
```

10. Create a KVM-based virtual machine on the local host so that it has sufficient hard drive space. Boot that VM using the RHEL 7 DVD.

11. At the Red Hat Installation menu, highlight the first option and press TAB. It will display the startup directives toward the bottom of the screen. At the end of that line, add the following directive:

```
ks=ftp://192.168.122.1/pub/ks.cfg
```

If the Kickstart file is on a different server or on local media, substitute accordingly.

You should now see the system installation creating the same basic setup as the first system. If the installation process stops before rebooting, then there's some problem with the Kickstart file, most likely a case of insufficient information.

The Kickstart Configurator

Even users who prefer to work at the command line can learn from the Red Hat GUI tool known as the Kickstart Configurator. It includes most (but not all) of the basic options associated with setting up a Kickstart configuration file. You can install it with the following command:

```
# yum install system-config-kickstart
```

As a GUI tool associated with the installation process, this command typically includes a number of dependencies.

Those of you sensitive to properly written English may object to the term "Kickstart Configurator," but it is the name given by Red Hat to the noted GUI configuration tool.

on the
!
ʊ o b

Now that you understand the basics of what goes into a Kickstart file, it's time to solidify your understanding through the graphical Kickstart Configurator. It can help you learn more about how to configure the Kickstart file. Once the right packages are installed, it can be opened from a GUI command line with the **system-config-kickstart** command. To start it with the default configuration for the local system, cite the anaconda-ks.cfg file as follows:

```
# system-config-kickstart /root/anaconda-ks.cfg
```

This should open the Kickstart Configurator shown in Figure 2-16. (Of course, it's probably a good idea to back up the anaconda-ks.cfg file first.)

on the
!
ʊ o b
Before starting the Kickstart Configurator, it's best to make sure there's an active connection to a remote RHEL 7 repository through the RHN.

FIGURE 2-16   The Kickstart Configurator

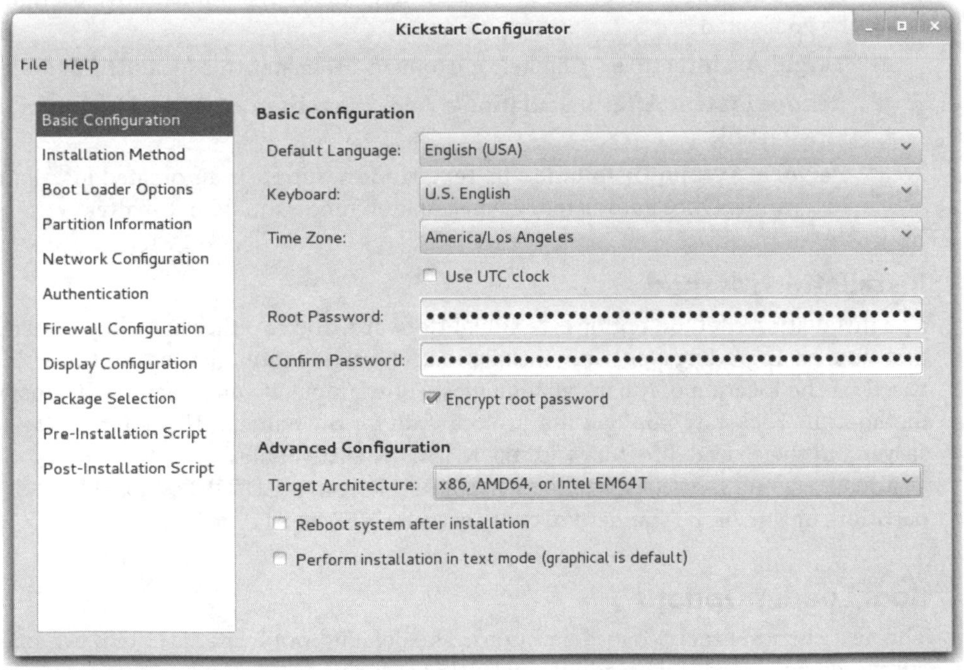

The screen shown in Figure 2-16 illustrates a number of basic installation steps. If you've already installed RHEL, all of these steps should look familiar.

A number of other options appear in the left pane, each associated with different Kickstart commands. To learn more about Kickstart, experiment with some of these settings. Use the File | Save command to save these settings with the filename of your choice, which you can then review in a text editor. Alternatively, you can choose File | Preview to see the effect of different settings on the Kickstart file.

The following sections provide a brief overview of each option shown in the left pane. A detailed understanding of the Kickstart Configurator can also help you understand the installation process.

Basic Configuration

In the Basic Configuration screen, you can assign settings for the following components:

- **Default Language** Specifies the default language for the installation and operating system.
- **Keyboard** Sets the default keyboard; normally associated with language.
- **Time Zone** Customizes the local time zone and specifies whether the hardware clock is set to UTC, which is essentially the same as Greenwich Mean Time.
- **Root Password** Specifies the password for the root administrative user; may be encrypted.
- **Target Architecture** Can help customize a Kickstart file for different systems.
- **Reboot System After Installation** Adds the **reboot** command to the end of the kickstart file.
- **Perform System Installation in Text Mode** Supports automated installation in text mode. Once automated, the installation mode should not matter.

Installation Method

The Installation Method options are straightforward. You're either installing Linux for the first time or upgrading a previous installation. The installation method, and your entries, are based on the location of the installation files. For example, if you select an NFS installation method, the Kickstart Configurator prompts you for the name or IP address of the NFS server and the shared directory with the RHEL installation files.

You can set up the Kickstart file to install RHEL from a CD/DVD, a local hard drive partition, or one of the standard network servers: NFS, HTTP, or FTP.

Boot Loader Options

The next section lists boot loader options. The default boot loader is GRUB, which supports encrypted passwords for an additional level of security during the boot process.

Linux boot loaders are normally installed on the MBR. If you're dual-booting Linux and Microsoft Windows with GRUB, you *can* set up the Windows boot loader (or an alternative third-party boot loader) to point to GRUB on the first sector of the Linux partition with the /boot directory.

Partition Information

The Partition Information section determines how this installation configures the hard disks on the affected computers. Although it supports the configuration of standard and RAID partitions, it does not yet support the configuration of LVM groups. The Clear Master Boot Record option allows you to wipe the MBR from an older hard disk that might have a problem there; it includes the **zerombr** command in the Kickstart file.

on the

Job

Don't use the zerombr **option if you want to keep an alternative bootloader on the MBR such as the Microsoft Windows Bootmgr.**

You can remove partitions depending on whether they've been created on a Linux filesystem. If you're using a new hard drive, it's important to initialize the disk label as well. Click the Add button; it opens the Partition Options dialog box.

Network Configuration

The Network Configuration section enables you to set up IP addressing on the network cards on a target computer. You can customize static IP addressing for a specific computer, or configure the use of a DHCP server. Just click Add Network Device and explore the Network Device Information window.

Authentication

The Authentication section lets you set up two forms of security for user passwords: Shadow Passwords, which encrypts user passwords in the /etc/shadow file, and the encryption hash for those passwords. If you have a fingerprint scanner installed, you can select the corresponding check box to enable a fingerprint reader. This enables two-factor authentication by requesting users to provide their credentials at logon and scan on the fingerprint reader.

This section also allows you to set up authentication information for various protocols:

- **NIS** Network Information Service is used to connect to a login authentication database on a network with Unix and Linux computers.
- **LDAP** In this context, the Lightweight Directory Access Protocol is a directory service that can be used as an alternative login authentication database.

- **Kerberos 5**   The MIT system for strong cryptography is used to authenticate users on a network.
- **Hesiod**   Hesiod is a network database that can be used to store user account and password information.
- **SMB**   Samba connects to a Microsoft Windows–style network for login authentication.
- **Name Switch Cache**   Associated with NIS for looking up user accounts and groups.

Firewall Configuration

The Firewall Configuration section allows you to configure a default firewall for the subject computer. On most systems, you'll want to keep the number of trusted services to a minimum. However, in a situation such as the Red Hat exams, you may be asked to set up a multitude of services on a single system, which would require the configuration of a multitude of trusted services on a firewall.

In this section, you can also configure basic SELinux settings. The Active and Disabled options are straightforward; the Warn option corresponds to a permissive implementation of SELinux. For more information, see Chapter 4.

Display Configuration

The Display Configuration section supports the installation of a basic Linux GUI. The actual installation depends on those packages and package groups selected in the next section. Although there is a lot of debate on the superiority of GUI- versus text-based administrative tools, text-based tools are more stable. For this reason (and more), many Linux administrators don't even install a GUI. However, if you're installing Linux on a series of workstations, as might be done with a series of Kickstart files, it's likely that most of the users won't be administrators.

In addition, you can disable or enable the Setup Agent, also known as the Firstboot process. For a completely automated installation, the Setup Agent should be disabled.

Package Selection

The Package Selection section allows you to choose the package groups that are installed through this Kickstart file. As noted earlier, the associated screens are blank if there's no current connection to a remote repository such as updates from the RHN. At the time of writing, you would get the same problem if you used a local installation source. In that case, you need to manually edit the file generated by Kickstart Configurator and add the required package selection.

Installation Scripts

You can add pre-installation and post-installation scripts to the Kickstart file. Post-installation scripts are more common, and they can help configure other parts of a Linux operating system in a common way. For example, if you wanted to install a directory with employee benefits information, you could add a post-installation script that adds the appropriate **cp** commands to copy files from a network server.

CERTIFICATION OBJECTIVE 2.04

Administration with the Secure Shell and Secure Copy

Red Hat Enterprise Linux installs the Secure Shell (SSH) packages by default. The RHCSA requirement with respect to SSH is simple; you need to know how to use it to access remote systems. In addition, you also need to know how to securely transfer files between systems. Therefore, in this section, you'll examine how to use the **ssh** and **scp** commands to access remote systems and transfer files.

As suggested earlier, the stage is already set by the default installation of SSH on standard installations of RHEL 7. Although firewalls are enabled by default, the standard RHEL 7 firewall leaves TCP port 22 open for SSH access. Related configuration files are stored in the /etc/ssh directory. SSH server configuration is part of the RHCE requirements. Related client commands such as **ssh**, **scp**, and **sftp** are covered in this section.

The Secure Shell daemon is secure because it encrypts messages. In other words, users who are listening on a network can't read the data sent between SSH clients and servers. And that's important on a public network such as the Internet. RHEL incorporates SSH version 2, which supports multiple key-exchange methods and is incompatible with the older SSH version 1. Key-based authentication for SSH is covered in Chapter 4. If you're studying for the RHCE objectives on SSH, read Chapter 11.

Configure an SSH Client

The main SSH client configuration file is /etc/ssh/ssh_config. Individual users can have custom SSH client configurations in their ~/.ssh/config files. Four directives are included by default. First, the **Host *** directive applies the other directives to all connections:

```
Host *
```

This is followed by a directive that supports authentication using the Generic Security Services Application Programming Interface (GSSAPI) for client/server authentication. This provides support for Kerberos authentication:

```
GSSAPIAuthentication yes
```

This next directive supports remote access to GUI applications. X11 is a legacy reference to the X Window System server used on Linux.

```
ForwardX11Trusted yes
```

The next directives allow the client to set several environmental variables. The details are normally trivial between two Red Hat Enterprise Linux systems.

```
SendEnv LANG LC_CTYPE LC_NUMERIC LC_TIME LC_COLLATE LC_MONETARY LC_MESSAGES
SendEnv LC_PAPER LC_NAME LC_ADDRESS LC_TELEPHONE LC_MEASUREMENT
SendEnv LC_IDENTIFICATION LC_ALL LC_LANGUAGE
SendEnv XMODIFIERS
```

This sets the stage for command-line access of remote systems.

Command-Line Access

This section is based on standard access with the **ssh** command. To access a remote system, you need the username and password on that remote system. By default, direct ssh-based access to the root account is enabled. For example, the following command opens a shell using that account on the noted server1 system:

```
$ ssh root@server1.example.com
```

on the **!** ob

If you get an error such as "Name or service not known" when you attempt to access a remote host via SSH, that indicates that the system cannot resolve the hostname to an IP address. We will configure name resolution in Chapter 3. In the meantime, to log in to server1.example.com via SSH, use its IP address 192.168.122.50.

The following command works in the same way:

```
$ ssh -l root server1.example.com
```

Without the username, the **ssh** command assumes that you're logging in remotely as the username on the local system. For example, if you were to run the command

```
$ ssh server1.example.com
```

from the user michael account, the **ssh** command assumes that you're trying to log in to the server1.example.com system as user michael. The first time the command is run between systems, it presents something similar to the following message:

```
$ ssh server1.example.com
The authenticity of host 'server1.example.com (192.168.122.50)'
can't be established.
ECDSA key fingerprint is b6:80:5d:8c:1d:ab:18:ab:46:15:c5:c8:e3:ea:9f:1c.
Are you sure you want to continue connecting (yes/no)? yes

Warning: Permanently added 'server1.example.com,192.168.122.50'
(ECDSA) to the list of known hosts.
michael@server1.example.com's password:
```

Once connected via **ssh**, you can do anything on the remote system that's supported by your user privileges on that machine. For example, you can even shut down the remote system gracefully with the **poweroff** command. After executing that command, you'll typically have a couple of seconds to exit out of the remote system with the **exit** command.

More SSH Command-Line Tools

If you prefer to access the remote system with an FTP-like client, the **sftp** command is for you. Although the **-l** switch doesn't have the same meaning of the **ssh** command, it still can be used to log in to the account of any user on the remote system. Whereas regular FTP communication proceeds in clear text, communication with the **sftp** command can be used to transfer files in encrypted format.

Alternatively, if you just want to transfer files over an encrypted connection, the **scp** command can help. For example, we created some of the screenshots for this book on the test VMs configured in Chapters 1 and 2. To transmit one of those screenshots to one of our systems, we used a command similar to the following, which copied the F02-20.tif file from the local directory to the remote system with the noted hostname, in the /home/michael /RHbook/Chapter2 directory:

```
# scp F02-20.tif michael@server1:/home/michael/RHbook/Chapter2/
```

Unless key-based authentication has been configured (as discussed in Chapter 4), the command prompts for the password of the user michael on the system named server1. Once the password is confirmed, the **scp** command transfers the F02-20.tif file in encrypted format to the noted directory on the remote system named server1.

Graphical Secure Shell Access

The **ssh** command can be used to forward the output of a GUI application over a network. As strange as it sounds, it works if the local system runs an X server while you call remote GUI client applications from remote systems.

Remote GUI access
via SSH

```
                                    alex@server1:~
File  Edit  View  Search  Terminal  Help
[alex@Maui ~]$ ssh -X server1.example.com
alex@server1.example.com's password:
Last login: Tue Feb  3 21:15:14 2015 from redcloud.example.com
[alex@server1 ~]$ gnome-system-monitor
```

| | System Monitor (on server1.example.com) | | | | |

| Processes | Resources | File Systems |

Device	Directory ⌄	Type	Total	Available	Used	
/dev/mapp /	xfs	10.5 GB	7.3 GB	3.1 GB		29 %
/dev/vda1 /boot	xfs	520.8 MB	396.6 MB	124.2 MB		23 %
/dev/mapp /home	xfs	1.0 GB	1.0 GB	37.4 MB		3 %

By default, both the SSH server and client configuration files are set up to support X11 communication over a network. All you need to do is connect to the remote system with the **-X** switch (or **-Y**, to use trusted X11 forwarding, which bypasses some security extension controls). For example, you could use the command sequence shown in Figure 2-17 to monitor the remote system.

CERTIFICATION OBJECTIVE 2.05

Consider Adding These Command-Line Tools

You may want to consider adding several command-line tools to help administer various Linux systems. These tools will be used later in this book to make sure various servers are actually operational. Although it's best to test services such as Postfix with actual e-mail clients (for instance, Evolution and Thunderbird), command tools like **telnet**, **nmap**, and **mutt** can be used to check these services remotely from a command-line interface. For exam purposes, you can use these tools to test, diagnose, and solve system issues in the time that it would take to download a complex tool such as Evolution. Although the **ssh** command can help access GUI tools remotely, communication with such tools can be time consuming.

For administrative purposes, tools of interest include the following:

- Use **telnet** and **nmap** to verify remote access to open ports.
- Use **mutt** as an e-mail client to verify the functionality of an e-mail server.
- Use **elinks** as a web browser to make sure web services are accessible.
- Use **lftp** to access FTP servers with command completion.

Checking Ports with telnet

The **telnet** command is a surprisingly powerful tool. Anyone who is aware of the security implications of clear-text clients may hesitate to use **telnet**. People who use **telnet** to log in to remote servers do transmit their usernames, passwords, and other commands in clear text. Anyone with a protocol analyzer such as Wireshark can read that data fairly easily.

However, **telnet** can do more. When run locally, it can verify the operation of a service. For example, the following command verifies the operation of vsFTP on the local system:

```
$ telnet localhost 21
Trying 127.0.0.1...
Connected to localhost.
Escape character is '^]'.
220 (vsFTPd 3.0.2)
```

The "Escape character" is CTRL-] (the CTRL key and the right square bracket pressed simultaneously). Pressing this key combination from the noted screen brings up the **telnet>** prompt. From there, you can exit with the **quit** command.

```
^]
telnet> quit
```

In most cases, you don't even need to execute the Escape character to quit; just type in the **quit** command.

If vsFTP is not running or had been configured to communicate on a port other than 21, you'd get the following response:

```
Trying 127.0.0.1...
telnet: connect to address 127.0.0.1: Connection refused
```

If there's no firewall, you'd get the same result from a remote system. If a firewall is blocking communications over port 21, however, you may get a message similar to the following:

```
telnet: connect to address 192.168.122.50: No route to host
```

Some services such as the Postfix e-mail server are by default configured to accept connections only from the local system. In that case, with or without a firewall, you'd get the "connection refused" message when trying to connect from a remote system.

Checking Ports with nmap

The **nmap** command is a powerful port-scanning tool. As such, the website of the nmap developers states that "when used improperly, nmap can (in rare cases) get you sued, fired, expelled, jailed, or banned by your ISP." Nevertheless, it is included in the standard RHEL 7 repositories. As such, it is supported by Red Hat for legal use. It's a quick way to get a view of the services that are open locally and remotely. For example, the **nmap localhost** command shown in Figure 2-18 detects and reveals those services that are running on the local system.

But in contrast, when the port scanner is run from a remote system, it looks like only one port is open. That shows the effect of the firewall on the server.

```
Starting Nmap 6.40 ( http://nmap.org ) at 2015-02-02 09:52 PST
Nmap scan report for server1.example.com (192.168.122.50)
Host is up (0.027s latency).
Not shown: 999 filtered ports
PORT   STATE SERVICE
22/tcp open  ssh
```

Configure an E-mail Client

The configuration process for a GUI e-mail client should be trivial for any candidate for Red Hat certification. However, the same may not necessarily be true for command-line clients, and they're useful for testing the functionality of standard e-mail server services such as Postfix and Sendmail. For example, once a server is configured for Post Office Protocol

FIGURE 2-18

Applying a port scanner locally

```
[root@server1 ~]# nmap localhost

Starting Nmap 6.40 ( http://nmap.org ) at 2015-02-03 21:36 GMT
mass_dns: warning: Unable to determine any DNS servers. Reverse DNS is disabled.
 Try using --system-dns or specify valid servers with --dns-servers
Nmap scan report for localhost (127.0.0.1)
Host is up (0.0000070s latency).
Other addresses for localhost (not scanned): 127.0.0.1
Not shown: 997 closed ports
PORT    STATE SERVICE
22/tcp  open  ssh
25/tcp  open  smtp
111/tcp open  rpcbind

Nmap done: 1 IP address (1 host up) scanned in 2.40 seconds
[root@server1 ~]#
```

(POP) e-mail—even e-mail that is delivered using the near-ubiquitous version 3 (POP3)—it can be checked with the following command:

```
# mutt -f pop://username@host
```

Since GUI e-mail clients should be trivial for readers, the remainder of this section is focused on the use of command-line e-mail clients.

Command-Line Mail

One way to test a local mail system is with the built-in command line **mail** utility. It provides a simple text-based interface. The system keeps each user's mail in /var/mail directory files associated with each username. Users who read messages with the **mail** utility can also reply, forward, or delete associated messages.

You can certainly use any of the other mail readers, such as **mutt**, or the e-mail managers associated with different GUI web browsers to test your system. Other mail readers store messages in different directories. Mail readers such as **mutt** and **mail** can be used to send messages if a Simple Mail Transfer Protocol (SMTP) server is active for the local system.

There are two basic methods for using **mail**. First, you can enter the subject and then the text of the message. When done, press CTRL-D. The message is sent, and the **mail** utility returns to the command line. Here's an example:

```
$ mail michael
Subject: Test Message
Text of the message
EOT
$
```

Alternatively, you can redirect a file as the text of an e-mail to another user. For example, the following command sends a copy of /etc/hosts to the root user on server1, with the Subject name of "hosts file":

```
$ mail -s 'hosts file' < /etc/hosts root@server1.example.com
```

Reading Mail Messages

By default, the **mail** system doesn't open for a user unless there is actual e-mail in the appropriate file. Once the mail system is open, the user will see a list of new and already read messages. If you've opened the **mail** system for an account, you can enter the number of the message and press ENTER. If you press ENTER with no argument, the mail utility assumes you want to read the next unread message. To delete a mail message, use the **d** command after reading the message, or use **d#** to delete the message numbered #.

Alternatively, mail messages can be read from the user-specified file in the local /var/mail directory. Files in this directory are named for the associated username.

The Use of Text and Graphical Browsers

Linux includes a variety of graphical browsers. Access of regular and secure websites is available through their associated protocols, the Hypertext Transfer Protocol (HTTP), and its secure cousin, Hypertext Transfer Protocol, Secure (HTTPS). The use of graphical browsers should be trivial for any serious user of Linux.

You may not always have access to the GUI, especially when working from a remote system. In any case, text-based browsers work more quickly. The standard text-based browser for Red Hat is ELinks. Once the package is installed, you can use it from the command line to open the website of your choice. For example, Figure 2-19 illustrates the result of the **elinks http://www.google.com** command.

To exit from ELinks, press the ESC key to access the menu bar, and then press F | x and accept the prompt to exit from the browser. As an alternative, the Q key can be used as a shortcut.

If you configure a web server, the easiest way to make sure it works is with a simple-text home page. No HTML coding is required. For example, we could add the following text to home.html:

```
This is my home page
```

FIGURE 2-19   The ELinks browser

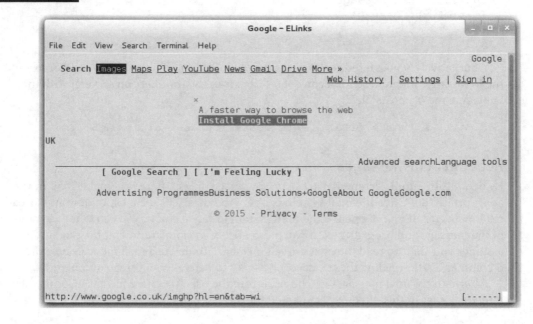

We could then run the **elinks home.html** command to view this text in the ELinks browser. If you've set up an Apache file server on the /var/www/html/inst directory as discussed in Chapter 1, you can also use **elinks** to review the files copied to that server with the following command:

```
$ elinks http://192.168.122.1/inst
```

Using lftp to Access URLs

The original FTP client software was a basic command-line, text-oriented client application that offered a simple but efficient interface. Most web browsers offer a graphical interface and can also be used as an FTP client.

Any FTP client allows you to view the directory tree and files. Using **ftp** as a client is easy. You could use the **ftp** command to connect to a server such as ftp.redhat.com with the following command:

```
# ftp ftp.redhat.com
```

However, that client asks for a username and password. You could enter username **anonymous** and your e-mail address as a password to access the Red Hat FTP server. But if you accidentally enter a real username and password, that data is sent in clear text, available to anyone who happens to be using the right network analyzer applications on the network. Strangely enough, the **ftp** command client is not installed on standard RHEL 7 installations.

That's one reason why **lftp** is better. It automatically attempts an anonymous login, without prompting for a username or password. It also supports command completion, which can especially help you access files and directories with longer names.

Sure, there are risks with most FTP clients as they transmit data in clear text, but as long as usage of this command is limited to public servers with anonymous access, the risk is minimal. After all, if you use **lftp** to download Linux packages from public servers, it's not like you're putting any private information at risk. To be sure, there are other security risks with such clients, but Red Hat developers are constantly working to keep that client up to date.

If the risks are acceptable, the **lftp** command can be used to log in to an FTP server where usernames and passwords are enabled. User michael could log in to such a server with the following command:

```
$ lftp ftp.example.org -u michael
```

The **lftp** client can handle a number of different commands, as shown in Figure 2-20. Some of these commands are described in Table 2-5.

Almost all commands from the FTP prompt are run at the remote host, similar to a Telnet session. You can run regular shell commands from that prompt; just start the command with an exclamation point (!).

This is only a subset of the commands available through **lftp**. If you don't remember something, the command **help** *cmd* yields a brief description of the specified command.

FIGURE 2-20

Commands in lftp

```
[root@Maui ~]# lftp ftp.redhat.com
lftp ftp.redhat.com:~> help
  !<shell-command>                        (commands)
  alias [<name> [<value>]]                attach [PID]
  bookmark [SUBCMD]                       cache [SUBCMD]
  cat [-b] <files>                        cd <rdir>
  chmod [OPTS] mode file...               close [-a]
  [re]cls [opts] [path/][pattern]         debug [<level>|off] [-o <file>]
  du [options] <dirs>                     exit [<code>|bg]
  get [OPTS] <rfile> [-o <lfile>]         glob [OPTS] <cmd> <args>
  help [<cmd>]                            history -w file|-r file|-c|-l [cnt]
  jobs [-v] [<job_no...>]                 kill all|<job_no>
  lcd <ldir>                              lftp [OPTS] <site>
  ln [-s] <file1> <file2>                 ls [<args>]
  mget [OPTS] <files>                     mirror [OPTS] [remote [local]]
  mkdir [-p] <dirs>                       module name [args]
  more <files>                            mput [OPTS] <files>
  mrm <files>                             mv <file1> <file2>
  [re]nlist [<args>]                      open [OPTS] <site>
  pget [OPTS] <rfile> [-o <lfile>]        put [OPTS] <lfile> [-o <rfile>]
  pwd [-p]                                queue [OPTS] [<cmd>]
  quote <cmd>                             repeat [OPTS] [delay] [command]
  rm [-r] [-f] <files>                    rmdir [-f] <dirs>
  scache [<session_no>]                   set [OPT] [<var> [<val>]]
  site <site-cmd>                         source <file>
  torrent [-O <dir>] <file|URL>...        user <user|URL> [<pass>]
  wait [<jobno>]                          zcat <files>
  zmore <files>
lftp ftp.redhat.com:~> ▌
```

TABLE 2-5

Standard lftp
Client Commands

Command	Description
cd	Changes the current working directory at the remote host
ls	Lists files at the remote host
get	Retrieves one file from the remote host
mget	Retrieves many files from the remote host with wildcards or full filenames
put	Uploads one file from your computer to the remote host
mput	Uploads a group of files to the remote host
pwd	Lists the current working directory on the remote host
quit	Ends the FTP session
!ls	Lists files on your host computer in the current directory
lcd	Changes the local host directory for upload/download
!pwd	Lists the current working directory on the local host computer

CERTIFICATION SUMMARY

Given the importance of virtualization in today's computing environment, it's no surprise that Red Hat has made KVM part of the requirements associated with the RHCSA. Assuming a valid connection to appropriate repositories, installation of KVM-related packages is fairly easy. You may need to use a command such as **modprobe kvm** to make sure appropriate modules are loaded. The Virtual Machine Manager can then be used to set up VMs using KVM on an RHEL 7 system. You can also use commands such as **virt-install**, **virt-clone**, and **virsh** to install, clone, and manage those VMs.

You can automate your entire installation with Kickstart. Every RHEL system has a Kickstart template file in the /root directory, which you can modify and use to install RHEL on other systems automatically. Alternatively, you can use the GUI Kickstart Configurator to create an appropriate Kickstart file.

With all of these systems, remote access is a must. The SSH command can help set up remote encrypted communications between Linux systems. The RHCSA requires that you know how to use an SSH client and to securely transfer files between systems. The **ssh** command can be used to log in to remote systems; the **ssh -X** command can even be used to access remote GUI applications. The **scp** command can copy files remotely over an encrypted connection.

When you are reviewing and troubleshooting RHEL services, it can be helpful to have some command-line tools at your disposal. The **telnet** command can connect to remote services on selected ports. The **nmap** command can be used as a port scanner. The **mutt** command can check the functionality of an e-mail server. The **elinks** command can be used as a command-line browser. Finally, the **lftp** command is an excellent FTP client that supports command completion.

✓ TWO-MINUTE DRILL

The following are some of the key points from the certification objectives in Chapter 2.

Configure KVM for Red Hat

❑ Packages required for KVM are part of the Virtualization package groups.

❑ KVM-based VMs can be configured with the Virtual Machine Manager.

❑ The kernel modules required for KVM include **kvm** and **kvm_intel** or **kvm_amd**.

Configure a Virtual Machine on KVM

❑ The default storage directory for KVM-based VMs is /var/lib/libvirt/images.

❑ VM configuration files are stored in various /etc/libvirt subdirectories.

❑ VM consoles are accessible with the Virtual Machine Manager, which you can start in the GUI with the **virt-manager** command.

❑ VMs can be installed, cloned, and configured with the **virt-install**, **virt-clone**, and **virsh** commands.

❑ The **virsh list --all** command lists all configured VMs.

❑ The **virsh autostart** *vmname* command configures the VM domain named *vmname* to start automatically when the host system is booted.

❑ The **virsh start** *vmname* command starts the boot process for the VM domain named *vmname*.

❑ The **virsh destroy** *vmname* command in effect cuts power to the VM domain named *vmname*.

Automated Installation Options

❑ Installation of a system is documented in the /root/anaconda-ks.cfg Kickstart text file.

❑ The Kickstart file can be modified directly or with the Kickstart Configurator tool.

❑ Kickstart files can be called from local media or network servers.

Administration with the Secure Shell and Secure Copy

❑ SSH is installed by default on RHEL 7. It's even accessible through default firewalls.

❑ The **ssh** command can be used to access remote systems securely. It can even enable access to remote GUI utilities.

❑ Related commands include **sftp** and **scp**.

Consider Adding These Command-Line Tools

❑ Administrators may sometimes only have the command line to verify access to servers.

❑ The **telnet** and **nmap** commands can be used to verify remote access to open ports.

❑ The **mutt** e-mail client can be used to verify the functionality of an e-mail server.

❑ The **elinks** console web browser can verify the working of a web server.

❑ The **lftp** client can be used to verify access to FTP servers with the benefit of command completion.

SELF TEST

The following questions will help measure your understanding of the material presented in this chapter. As no multiple choice questions appear on the Red Hat exams, no multiple choice questions appear in this book. These questions exclusively test your understanding of the chapter. Getting results, not memorizing trivia, is what counts on the Red Hat exams. There may be more than one answer to many of these questions.

Configure KVM for Red Hat

1. Name one kernel module associated with KVM.

   _____

2. What is the name of the tool that can configure KVM-based VMs in the GUI?

   _____

Configure a Virtual Machine on KVM

3. What command starts the Virtual Machine Manager in the GUI?

   _____

4. In what directory are default virtual disks stored by the Virtual Machine Manager?

   _____

5. What command can be used to create a new VM?

   _____

Automated Installation Options

6. What command starts the GUI-based Kickstart configuration tool?

   _____

7. What's the name of the file in the /root directory that documents how RHEL was installed?

   _____

8. What directive in the Kickstart configuration file is related to networking?

   _____

9.   If the installation FTP server is located at ftp://server1.example.com/pub/inst, what directive in the Kickstart configuration file points to that server?

   _____

10.   What directive in the Kickstart configuration file would shut down a system after installation is complete?

   _____

Administration with the Secure Shell and Secure Copy

11.   What **ssh** command switch enables access to remote GUI utilities?

   _____

12.   What command initiates a secure copy of the file /etc/hosts from the system server1.example.com to the /tmp directory on the local host?

   _____

Consider Adding These Command-Line Tools

13.   What command would you use to see if a server is running on port 25 on a system with IP address 192.168.122.1?

   _____

14.   What command can be used to verify active and available (from your client) services on a remote system with IP address 192.168.122.1?

   _____

LAB QUESTIONS

Several of these labs involve installation exercises. You should do these exercises on test machines only. The instructions in some of these labs delete all of the data on a system.

   Red Hat presents its exams electronically. For that reason, most of the labs in this and future chapters are available from the DVD that accompanies the book in the Chapter2/ subdirectory. In case you haven't yet set up RHEL 7 on a system, the first lab is presented here in the book.

Lab 1

In this lab, you will install RHEL to create a basic server on a KVM-based VM. You will need sufficient room for one hard disk of at least 16GB (with sufficient space for 11GB of data plus a swap partition, assuming at least 512MB of spare RAM for the VM). You'll also need room for an additional two virtual hard drives of 1GB each (18GB total).

The steps in this lab assume an installation on a KVM-based VM. To start the process, open a GUI and run the **virt-manager** command. If it doesn't happen automatically, right-click the Localhost (QEMU) option and click Connect in the pop-up menu that appears. Enter the root administrative password if prompted to do so. Once connected, you can then right-click the same option and then click New. This starts the wizard that helps configure a VM.

If you're configuring the actual VMs to be used in future chapters, this will be the server1.example .com system discussed in Chapter 1.

Ideally, there will be sufficient space on your main machine for at least four different virtual systems of the given size. That includes the three systems specified in Chapter 1, plus one spare. In other words, a logical volume or partition with 75GB of free space would be (barely) sufficient.

The steps described in this lab are general. By this time, you should have some experience with the installation of RHEL 7. In any case, the exact steps vary with the type of installation and the boot media:

1. Start with the RHEL 7 network boot CD or the installation DVD.

2. Based on the steps discussed in Chapter 1, start the installation process for RHEL 7.

3. From the Installation Summary screen, select Installation Source and point the system to the FTP-based installation server created in Chapter 1. If you followed the directions in that chapter, the server will be on ftp://192.168.122.1/pub/inst.

4. From the Installation Summary screen, click Installation Destination and select custom partitioning.

5. Create the first partition of about 500MB of disk space, formatted to the xfs filesystem, and assign it to the /boot directory.

6. Create the next partition with 1GB of disk space (or more, if space is available), reserved for swap space.

7. Create a third partition with about 10GB disk space, formatted to the xfs filesystem, and assign it to the top-level root directory, /.

8. Create another partition with about 1GB of disk space and assign it to the /home directory.

9. From the Installation Summary screen, set up the local system on a network configured on the KVM hypervisor. The default is the 192.168.122.0/24 network; for the server1.example.com system, this will be on IP address 192.168.122.50 and gateway 192.168.122.1. Configure the hostname **server1.example.com**.

10. From the Installation Summary screen, click Software Selection and then select Server with GUI. Installation of virtualization packages within a VM is not required.

11. Continue with the installation process, using your best judgment.

12. Reboot when prompted and log in as the root user. Run the **poweroff** command when you're ready to finish this lab.

SELF TEST ANSWERS

Configure KVM for Red Hat

1. Three kernel modules are associated with KVM: kvm, kvm_intel, and kvm_amd.

2. The tool that can configure KVM-based VMs in the GUI is the Virtual Machine Manager.

Configure a Virtual Machine on KVM

3. The command that starts the Virtual Machine Manager in the GUI is **virt-manager**.

4. The directory with default virtual disks for the Virtual Machine Manager is /var/lib/libvirt/images.

5. The command that can be used to create a new VM is **virt-install**.

Automated Installation Options

6. The command that starts the GUI-based Kickstart configuration tool is **system-config-kickstart**.

7. The name of the Kickstart file in the /root directory that documents how RHEL was installed is anaconda-ks.cfg.

8. The directive in the Kickstart configuration file related to networking is **network**.

9. The directive that points to the given FTP installation server is **url --url ftp://server1.example.com/pub/inst**.

10. The directive in the Kickstart configuration file that would shut down a system after installation is complete is **shutdown**.

Administration with the Secure Shell and Secure Copy

11. The **ssh** command switch that enables access to remote GUI utilities is **-X**. The **-Y** switch is also an acceptable answer.

12. The required command to securely copy /etc/hosts from server1 to /tmp on the local host is **scp server1.example.com:/etc/hosts /tmp/**.

Consider Adding These Command-Line Tools

13. The command that you would use to see if a server is running on port 25 on a system with IP address 192.168.122.1 is **telnet 192.168.122.1 25**.

14. The command that can be used to verify active and available services on a remote system with IP address 192.168.122.1 is **nmap 192.168.122.1**.

LAB ANSWERS

Lab 1

Although there is nothing truly difficult about this lab, it should increase your confidence with VMs based on KVM. Once it's complete, you should be able to log in to the VM as the root administrative user and run the following checks on the system:

1. Check mounted filesystems, along with the space available. The following commands should confirm those filesystems that are mounted, along with the free space available on the associated volumes:

   ```
   # mount
   # df -m
   ```

2. Assuming you have a good connection to the Internet and a subscription to the Red Hat Portal, make sure the system is up to date. If you're using a rebuild distribution, access to their public repositories is acceptable. In either case, run the following command to make sure the local system is up to date:

   ```
   # yum update
   ```

   This lab confirms your ability to "install Red Hat Enterprise Linux systems as virtual guests."

Lab 2

Remember, this and all future labs in this book can be found on the DVD that comes with this book. Labs 2 through 8 can be found in the Chapter2/ subdirectory of that DVD.

One of the issues with system cloning is how it includes the hardware MAC address of any network cards. Such conflicts can lead to problems on a network. So not only would you have to change the IP address, but you may also need to ensure that a unique hardware address is assigned to the given virtual network adapter. Because of such issues, KVM normally sets up a different hardware MAC address for a cloned system. For example, if the original system had an eth0 network card with one hardware address, the cloned system would have a network card with a different hardware address.

If this seems like too much trouble, feel free to delete the cloned system. After all, there is no reference to VM cloning in the RHCSA requirements. However, it may be helpful to have a different backup system. And that's an excellent opportunity to practice the skills gained in Lab 4 with Kickstart installations.

Lab 3

The purpose of this lab is to show you the command-line method for configuring a KVM-based VM. If you haven't yet set up the four different VMs suggested in Chapter 1 (three VMs and a backup), this is an excellent opportunity to do so. One way to do this is with the **virt-install** command. Specify the following information:

- Allocated RAM (**--ram**) in megabytes, which should be at least 512.
- The path to the virtual disk file (**--disk**), which could be the same as that virtual disk created in Lab 2, and its size in gigabytes, if that file doesn't already exist.
- The URL (**--location**) for the FTP installation server created in Chapter 1, Lab 2. Alternatively, you could use the HTTP installation server also discussed in Chapter 1.
- The OS type (**--os-type=***linux*) and variant (**--os-variant=***rhel7*).

You can now complete this installation normally or run a variation of that installation in Lab 5.

Lab 4

If you're not experienced with Kickstart configuration, some trial and error may be required. But it's best to run into problems now and not during a Red Hat exam or on the job. If you're able to set up a Kickstart file that can be used to install a system without intervention, you're ready to address this challenge on the RHCSA exam.

One common problem relates to virtual disks that have just been created. They must be initialized first; that's the purpose of the **--initlabel** switch to the **clearpart** directive.

Lab 5

If you've recently run a Kickstart installation for the first time, it's best to do it again. If you practice now, it means you'll be able to set up a Kickstart installation faster during an exam. And that's just the beginning. Imagine the confidence you'll have if your boss needs a couple of dozen VMs with the same software and volumes. Assuming the only differences are hostname and network settings, you'll be able to accomplish this task fairly quickly.

If you can set up a Kickstart installation from the command line with the **virt-install** command, it'll be a lot easier to set it on a remote virtual host. You'll be able to configure new systems from remote locations, thus increasing your value in the workplace.

If you haven't yet set up the four VMs suggested in Chapter 1 (three as test systems, one as a backup), this is your opportunity to do so.

To use a Kickstart file with **virt-install**, you'll need to use regular command switches. As you're not allowed to bring this book into an exam, try to perform this lab without referring to the main body of this chapter. You'll be able to refer to the man page for the **virt-install** command for all of the important switches.

Be sure to put the **ks=** directive along with the URL of the Kickstart file within quotes. Success is the installation of a new system.

Lab 6

This lab is designed to increase your understanding of the use of the **ssh** command as a client. The encryption performed should be transparent, and will not affect any commands used through an SSH connection to administer remote systems.

Lab 7

This lab is somewhat critical with respect to several different RHCSA objectives. Once you understand the process, the actual tasks are deceptively simple. After completing this lab, you should have confidence in your abilities to do the following:

- Start and stop virtual machines.
- Configure systems to launch virtual machines at boot.

The lab also suggests one method for remotely accessing a VM.

Lab 8

This lab is designed to increase your familiarity with two important network troubleshooting tools, **telnet** and **nmap**. Network administrators with some Linux experience may prefer other tools. If you're familiar with other tools such as **nc**, great. It's the results that matter.

Chapter 3

Fundamental Command-Line Skills

The Red Hat exams are an advanced challenge. This chapter covers RHCSA requirements that were formerly listed as prerequisites for the now-obsolete RHCT certification. Many of these requirements specify basic command-line tools associated with entry-level certifications such as those offered by the Linux Professional Institute.

Command-line skills are no longer listed as prerequisites, but they are required to achieve the exam objectives. As most candidates for the RHCSA exam should already be familiar with these command-line tools, this chapter covers the related topics with minimum detail. If after reading this chapter you feel the need for more guidance about these topics, the excellent beginning Linux books described in Chapter 1 can help.

Linux gurus should recognize that we've "oversimplified" a number of explanations to keep this chapter as short as possible. However, because most IT professionals are specialists, you may feel a bit uncertain about a few topics in this chapter. That is okay. In fact, it's natural that many experienced Linux administrators don't frequently use every command. Many candidates are successfully able to fill in the gaps in their knowledge with some self-study and practice.

INSIDE THE EXAM

Shells

The related RHCSA exam objective is pretty generic:

- Access a shell prompt and issue commands with correct syntax

The default shell for Linux is bash, the "Bourne-Again shell." In fact, the original release of the RHCSA objectives specified the use of bash. Although many Linux gurus use one of the many other shells available, in the exam it is extremely likely you will be faced with bash.

Whatever shell you prefer, you need to know how to get to a shell prompt and run regular commands from that prompt. Some basic commands are described in some of the other objectives. It's fairly easy to open a shell prompt from a console and within the GUI.

Pipelines and Redirection

Data into and out of a shell is often thought of in Linux as a stream of information. One basic Linux skill is the ability to redirect

such streams. As described in the RHCSA requirements, that's the ability to

- Use input/output redirection (>, >>, |, 2>, etc.)

The operators in parentheses can redirect the streams from command output, command error, data files, and more.

File and Directory Management

Now that you have access to a command line, file and directory management is next. With related commands, you can navigate around the Linux directory tree, as well as perform all the tasks suggested in the related objectives:

- Create, delete, copy, and move files and directories
- Create hard and soft links

The Analysis of Text Output

Most Linux configuration files are text files. It is important to understand and analyze the flow of text as it is sent through the shell. Tools such as the **grep** command can help you focus on needed information. In this chapter, you will examine how to meet the following objective:

■ Use grep and regular expressions to analyze text

The Variety of Local Documentation

Internet access is not available during the Red Hat exams, but that's okay. Google is not your only friend. Linux has some excellent documentation installed with most packages. Command manuals are also available. The following objective is straightforward; it describes the commands and directory associated with most Linux online documentation:

■ Locate, read, and use system documentation including man, info, and files in /usr/share/doc

The objectives include an interesting remark:

■ Note: Red Hat may use applications during the exam that are not included in Red Hat Enterprise Linux for the purpose of evaluating candidate's abilities to meet this objective.

Most Linux developers follow the basic parameters just described for system documentation. Does Red Hat's "note" mean they will "hide" some key information in a man page or a file in the /usr/share/doc directory? The wording suggests you need to be prepared for such a scenario.

The Use of Text Editors

To configure Linux, you need to know how to edit text files. And for those newer to Linux, that requires a different paradigm. Although word processors such as OpenOffice.org Writer and Microsoft Word can save files in text format, a mistake with a key configuration file can render a Linux system unbootable, and these editors can inject hidden data or otherwise cause problems when used for simple text editing. Therefore, you need to know how to handle the following objective with standard non-GUI utilities:

■ Create and edit text files

The Management of Network Services

Although there are excellent GUI tools to help manage network services, mistakes are too easy to make with such tools. Command-line tools can help you understand and manage network services directly or through associated configuration files. The associated objective is

■ Start, stop, and check the status of network services

Of course, this objective requires a basic understanding of IP networking.

The Configuration of Networking and Name Resolution

Name resolution depends on databases of hostnames or fully qualified domain names (FQDNs) such as server1.example.com and IP

(Continued)

addresses such as 192.168.122.50. The sources from which Linux obtains name resolution information are usually the local /etc/hosts database of hostnames and IP addresses, as well as available databases of Domain Name Service (DNS) servers. That is an interpretation of the following RHCSA objective:

■ Configure networking and hostname resolution statically or dynamically

When the RHCSA was first released, this was depicted as two objectives. Although these objectives are no longer officially in effect, they do provide more information on what it means to configure networking and hostname resolution:

■ Manage network devices: understand basic IP networking/routing, configure IP addresses/default route statically or dynamically

■ Manage name resolution: set local hostname, configure /etc/hosts, configure to use existing DNS server

While network troubleshooting is no longer a part of the entry-level Red Hat exam, the way you address problems with respect to network configuration and hostname resolution can help you better understand how networks operate.

CERTIFICATION OBJECTIVE 3.01

Shells

A *shell* is a user interface. A text-based shell is also used as a command-line interpreter. In Linux, the shell is the interpreter that allows you to interact with the operating system using various commands. With the right file permissions, you can set up commands in scripts to run as needed, even in the middle of the night. Linux shells can process commands in various sequences, depending on how you manage the input and output of each command. The way commands are interpreted is in part determined by variables and parameters associated with each shell.

The default shell in Linux is bash, also known as the Bourne-Again Shell. The focus of commands in this book is based on how they're used in bash. However, a number of other shells are available that are popular with many users. As long as the appropriate RPMs are installed, users can start any of these shells. If desired, you can change the default shell for individual users in the /etc/passwd file.

Other Shells

Users can choose between four command-line shells in RHEL 7. Although bash is the default, long-time Linux and Unix users may prefer something else:

- **bash** The default Bourne-Again shell, based on the command-line interpreter originally developed by Stephen Bourne.
- **ksh** The Korn shell, developed by David Korn at Bell Labs in the 1980s, to incorporate the best features of the Bourne and C shell.
- **tcsh** An enhanced version of the Unix C shell.
- **zsh** A sophisticated shell, similar to the Korn shell.

These shells are located in the /bin directory. If a user prefers one of these options as their default shell, it's easy to change. The most direct method is to change the default shell in the /etc/passwd file. For example, the line that applies to one of the authors' regular accounts is

```
michael:x:1000:1000:Michael Jang:/home/michael:/bin/bash
```

As an example, to change the default shell to ksh, change /bin/bash to /bin/ksh. You also need to install the corresponding RPM package for the Korn shell. Package management will be covered in Chapter 7.

e x a m

ⓦ a t c h   **Even though it should be trivial for most Linux users, a part of one RHCSA objective is to "access a shell prompt." You should now know how to set up access to different shell prompts.**

Virtual Terminals

If you have access to the console of a RHEL system, you can use six virtual terminals to open six independent login sessions. However, only one virtual terminal is activated by default. The other login prompts are launched dynamically when you switch to an unused terminal. Virtual terminals are defined by the logind.conf file in the /etc/systemd directory. Take a look at that file. You'll see an option named NAutoVTs, which defines the maximum number of virtual terminals that can be activated. Virtual terminals are associated with device files /dev/tty1 through /dev/tty6. When a GUI is configured, it takes /dev/tty1. It's possible to configure more virtual terminals, limited by those allowed for the root administrative user in the /etc/securetty file.

Normally, to change between virtual terminals, press ALT and the function key associated with that terminal. For example, the ALT-F2 key combination moves to the second terminal. However, in the RHEL GUI, the ALT-F*n* key combinations are used to provide other functionalities, such as to start the Run Application tool via ALT-F2. Therefore, you'll need to press CTRL-ALT-F*n* to move to the *n*th virtual console from the GUI.

FIGURE 3-1

A first GUI login
console

At a text console login, you'd see the following prompt, which depends a bit on the
release of RHEL, the version number of the kernel, and the system hostname:

```
Red Hat Enterprise Linux Server
Kernel 3.10.0-123.el7.x86_64 on an x86_64

server1 login:
```

The graphical login, which requires the installation of the GNOME Display Manager
(GDM), is more intuitive, as shown in Figure 3-1.

GUI Shell Interfaces

Once you are logged in to the GUI, access to the bash shell is easy. If you're in the default
GNOME desktop environment, click Applications | Utilities | Terminal. Traditionally,
administrators have worked from the console. But in many cases, working on the command
line from the GUI can be helpful, especially with the windows that can be placed side by
side. A right-click on a GUI terminal screen supports opening of additional terminals in
different windows or in tabs. It also supports copy and paste as needed.

The screenshots of the command line taken for this book are from the GUI-based
command line, in part because dark text on a white screen is easier to read.

Differences Between Regular and Administrative Users

What you can do at the command line depends on the privileges associated with the login account. Two basic prompts are available. The following is an example of what you might see when logged in as a regular user:

```
[michael@server1 ~]$
```

Note how it includes the username, the hostname of the local system, the current directory, and a $ prompt. The $ prompt is the standard for regular users. As noted in the introduction to the book, examples of commands run from a regular user account just show the following:

```
$
```

In contrast, take a look at a prompt for the root administrative user on the same system. It should look familiar. Except for the name of the account, the only consistent difference is the prompt.

```
[root@server1 ~]#
```

In this book, examples of commands run from the root administrative account just show the following:

```
#
```

Besides ownership and permissions, other differences between regular and administrative accounts are discussed in Chapter 8.

Text Streams and Command Redirection

Linux uses three basic data streams. Data goes in, data comes out, and errors are sent in a different direction. These streams are known as standard input (stdin), standard output (stdout), and standard error (stderr). Normally, input comes from the keyboard, whereas standard output and standard error go out to the screen terminal. In the following example, when you run **cat** *filename,* the contents of that file are sent to the screen as standard output (as are any errors):

```
# cat filename
```

You can redirect each of these streams to or from a file. For example, if you have a program named database and a datafile with a lot of data, the contents of that datafile can be sent to the database program with a left redirection arrow (<). As shown here, datafile is taken as standard input:

```
# database < datafile
```

Standard input can come from the left side of a command as well. For example, if you need to scroll through the boot messages, you can combine the **dmesg** and **less** commands with a pipe:

```
# dmesg | less
```

The output from **dmesg** is redirected as standard input to **less**, which then allows you to scroll through that output as if it were a separate file.

Standard output is just as easy to redirect. For example, the following command uses the right redirection arrow (>) to send the standard output of the **ls** command to the file named filelist:

```
# ls > filelist
```

You can add standard output to the end of an existing file with a double redirection arrow with a command such as **ls >> filelist**.

If you want to save the error messages of a program into a file, redirect the error stream from it with a command such as the following:

```
# program 2> err-list
```

Sometimes you may want to discard all errors. This can be achieved by redirecting the error stream to the special device file /dev/null:

```
# program 2> /dev/null
```

Another useful redirection operator is the ampersand and right arrow (&>), which sends both the standard output and error to a file or device. An example is shown here:

```
# program &> output-and-error
```

CERTIFICATION OBJECTIVE 3.02

Standard Command-Line Tools

While newer Linux users may prefer to use the GUI, the most efficient way to administer Linux is from the command-line interface. Although excellent GUI tools are available, the look and feel of those tools varies widely by distribution. In contrast, if you know the standard command-line tools, you'll be able to find your way around every Linux distribution.

Remember, in any bash session you can go through the history of previous commands, using the UP- and DOWN-ARROW keys, and CTRL-R to make a search. You can also take advantage of text completion, which allows you to use the TAB key almost as a wildcard to complete a command, a filename, or a variable (if the text begins with the $ character).

exam
watch　　　**This section covers only the** **command. Nevertheless, it allows you to**
most basic of commands available in Linux. **"issue commands with correct syntax," as**
It describes only a few capabilities of each **described in the RHCSA objectives.**

Almost all Linux commands include options (or "switches") and arguments. Command options allow you to change the behavior of a command and are usually prepended by one or two dashes (such as **ls -a** or **ls --all**). Arguments specify files, devices, or other targets that a command should act on. Only a few commands are covered in this chapter. If you're less familiar with some of them, use their man pages. Study the command options. Try them out! Only with practice, practice, and more practice can you really understand the power behind some of these commands.

Two basic groups of commands are used to manage Linux files. One group helps you get around Linux files and directories. The other group actually does something creative with the files. Those commands will be covered in the next sections, but first we'll review some basic filesystem concepts.

File and Directory Concepts

As noted previously, everything in Linux can be reduced to a file. Directories are special types of files that serve as containers for other files. To navigate and find important files, you need some basic commands and concepts to tell you where you are and how to move from directory to directory. The most important command is **pwd**; a variable that always leads to a user's home directory is the tilde (~); and the concept that describes where you are in the Linux directory tree is the path. Closely related are the directories searched when a command is typed in, which is based on the environment variable known as the PATH. Once these concepts are understood, you can navigate between directories with the **cd** command.

pwd

At the command-line interface, the current directory may be in either the top-level root (/) directory or a subdirectory. The **pwd** command identifies the current directory.

Try it out. It'll give you a directory name relative to the top-level root directory (/). With this information in hand, you can move to a different directory if needed. Incidentally, **pwd** is short for print working directory (which has nothing to do with modern printers, but respects the days when output was printed on a teletype). For example, when the user michael runs that command in his home directory, he gets the following output:

```
/home/michael
```

The Tilde (~)

Upon a standard login, every Linux user is taken to a home directory. The tilde (~) can be used to represent the home directory of any currently active user. For example, when user john logs in, he's taken to his home directory, /home/john. In contrast, the home directory of the root administrative user is /root.

Thus, the effect of the **cd ~** command depends on your username. For example, if you've logged in as user mj, the **cd ~** command navigates to the /home/mj directory. If you've logged in as the root user, this command navigates to the /root directory. You can list the contents of your home directory from anywhere in the directory tree with the **ls ~** command. The **cd** and **ls** commands are described shortly. When you log in as the root administrative user and run the **ls** command, you should see the following:

```
anaconda-ks.cfg  initial-setup-ks.cfg
```

Incidentally, these files describe what happened during the installation process, the packages that were installed, and the users and groups added to the local system. The **anaconda-ks.cfg** command is important for automated Kickstart installations, as described in Chapter 2.

Directory Paths

You need to know two path concepts when working with Linux directories: absolute paths and relative paths. An absolute path describes the complete directory structure in terms of the top-level directory, root (/). A relative path is based on the current directory. Relative paths do not include the slash in front.

The difference between an absolute path and a relative one is important. Especially when you're running a command absolute paths are essential. Otherwise, commands referencing a wrong directory may lead to unintended consequences. For example, say you're in the top-level root directory, and you have backed up the /home directory using its relative path to the root (/). If you happen to be in the /home directory when restoring that backup, the files for user michael, for example, would be restored to the /home/home/michael directory.

In contrast, if the /home directory was backed up using the absolute path, the current working directory doesn't matter when you are restoring these files. That backup will be restored to the correct directories.

Environment PATHs

Strictly speaking, when running a command, you should cite the full path to that command. For example, since the **ls** command is in the /bin directory, users should actually run the **/bin/ls** command to list files in the current directory. With the benefit of the PATH, an environment variable, that's not required. A shell, such as bash, automatically searches through the directories listed in a user's PATH for the command that user just typed at the command line. Environment variables are constant from console to console.

To determine the PATH for the current user account, run the **echo $PATH** command. You should see a series of directories in the output. The differences between the PATH for a regular user and one for a root user have narrowed in RHEL 7:

```
$ echo $PATH
/usr/local/bin:/bin:/usr/bin:/usr/local/sbin:↵
/usr/sbin:/home/michael/.local/bin:/home/michael/bin

# echo $PATH
/usr/local/sbin:/usr/local/bin:/sbin:/bin:/usr/sbin:/usr/bin:/root/bin
```

The directories in the PATH for regular users and the root administrative user are slightly different. But the differences matter because the directories are searched in order. For example, the **system-config-keyboard** command is available from both the /usr/bin and /usr/sbin directories. As you can see from the default PATH for regular and root users, the version that is run varies because of the differences in the PATH.

The PATH is determined globally by current settings in the /etc/profile file or by scripts in the /etc/profile.d directory. You might notice differences between the PATH as configured for User ID (UID) 0 and all other users. UID 0 corresponds to the root administrative user.

As well as the global settings, the PATH for individual users can be customized with an appropriate entry in that user's home directory, in the hidden files named ~/.bash_profile or ~/.profile.

cd

It's easy to change directories in Linux. Just use **cd** and cite the absolute path of the desired directory. If you use the relative path, just remember that the destination depends on the present working directory.

By default, the **cd** command by itself navigates to your home directory. The tilde is not required for that command. Another common shortcut is two consecutive dots (..) to represent the directory that is one level up in the hierarchy. Thus, **cd ..** moves to the parent directory of the current working directory.

File Lists and ls

Now that you've reviewed those commands that can navigate from one directory to another, it's time to see what files exist in a directory—and that's the province of the **ls** command.

The Linux **ls** command, with the right switches, can be quite powerful. The right kind of **ls** can tell you everything about a file, such as last modification time, last access time, and size. It can help you organize the listing of files in just about any desired order. Important variations on this command include **ls -a** to reveal hidden files, **ls -l** for long listings, **ls -t** for a list sorted by modification time, and **ls -i** for inode numbers (inodes are internal data structures in a filesystem that store information about a file). Other useful command options are **-r**, to reverse the listing order, and **-R**, to list the contents of all subdirectories recursively.

You can combine switches; we often use the **ls -ltr** command to display a recursive long listing with the most recently changed files last. The **-d** switch, when combined with others, can give you more information on the current directory, or on a directory that you have passed as an argument to the **ls** command.

One important feature that returns SELinux contexts is the **ls -Z** command. Take a look at the output in Figure 3-2. The system_u, object_r, var_t, and s0 output demonstrates the current SELinux contexts of the noted files. During the RHCSA exam (and RHCE as well), you'll be expected to configure a system with SELinux enabled. Starting with Chapter 4, this book covers how SELinux can be configured for every service that's installed.

FIGURE 3-2

Current SELinux contexts

```
[root@server1 ~]# \ls -Z /var/
drwxr-xr-x. root root system_u:object_r:acct_data_t:s0 account
drwxr-xr-x. root root system_u:object_r:var_t:s0       adm
drwxr-xr-x. root root system_u:object_r:var_t:s0       cache
drwxr-xr-x. root root system_u:object_r:kdump_crash_t:s0 crash
drwxr-xr-x. root root system_u:object_r:var_t:s0       db
drwxr-xr-x. root root system_u:object_r:var_t:s0       empty
drwxr-xr-x. root root system_u:object_r:public_content_t:s0 ftp
drwxr-xr-x. root root system_u:object_r:games_data_t:s0 games
drwx--x--x. gdm  gdm  system_u:object_r:xserver_log_t:s0 gdm
drwxr-xr-x. root root system_u:object_r:var_t:s0       gopher
drwxr-xr-x. root root system_u:object_r:var_t:s0       kerberos
drwxr-xr-x. root root system_u:object_r:var_lib_t:s0   lib
drwxr-xr-x. root root system_u:object_r:var_t:s0       local
lrwxrwxrwx. root root system_u:object_r:var_lock_t:s0  lock -> ../run/lock
drwxr-xr-x. root root system_u:object_r:var_log_t:s0   log
lrwxrwxrwx. root root system_u:object_r:mail_spool_t:s0 mail -> spool/mail
drwxr-xr-x. root root system_u:object_r:var_t:s0       nis
drwxr-xr-x. root root system_u:object_r:var_t:s0       opt
drwxr-xr-x. root root system_u:object_r:var_t:s0       preserve
lrwxrwxrwx. root root system_u:object_r:var_run_t:s0   run -> ../run
drwxr-xr-x. root root system_u:object_r:var_spool_t:s0 spool
drwxrwxrwt. root root system_u:object_r:tmp_t:s0       tmp
drwxr-xr-x. root root system_u:object_r:var_t:s0       var
drwxr-xr-x. root root system_u:object_r:httpd_sys_content_t:s0 www
drwxr-xr-x. root root system_u:object_r:var_yp_t:s0    yp
[root@server1 ~]#
```

File-Creation Commands

Two commands are used to create new files: **touch** and **cp**. Alternatively, you can let a text editor such as vi create a new file. Of course, although the **ln**, **mv**, and **rm** commands don't create files, they do manage them in related ways.

touch

Perhaps the simplest way to create a new file is with the **touch** command. For example, the **touch abc** command creates an empty file named abc in the local directory. The **touch** command is also used to change the time of the last modification of a file. For example, try the following three commands:

```
# ls -l /etc/passwd
# touch /etc/passwd
# ls -l /etc/passwd
```

Note the timestamps listed with the output of each **ls -l** command, and compare them with the current date and time returned by **date**. After you run the **touch** command, the timestamp of /etc/passwd is updated to the current date and time.

cp

The **cp** (copy) command allows you to take the contents of one file and place a copy with the same or different name in the directory of your choice. For example, the **cp** *file1 file2* command takes the contents of *file1* and saves the contents on *file2* in the current directory. One of the dangers of **cp** is that it can easily overwrite files in different directories, without prompting you to make sure that's what you really wanted to do.

Another usage of the cp command is with multiple file sources to be copied into a single destination directory. In this case the syntax is **cp** *file1 file2 ... dir*.

The **cp** command, with the **-a** switch, supports recursive changes and preserves all file attributes, such as permissions, ownerships, and timestamps. For example, the following command copies all subdirectories of the noted directory, along with associated files, into /mnt/backup:

```
# cp -a /home/michael/. /mnt/backup/
```

mv

Although there isn't a "rename" command in Linux, you can use **mv**. The **mv** command puts a different label on a file. For example, the **mv** *file1 file2* command changes the name of *file1* to *file2*. Unless you're moving the file to a different filesystem, everything about the file, including the inode number, remains the same. The **mv** command works with directories too.

ln

Linked files allow users to refer to the same file using different names. When linked files are devices, they may represent more common names, such as /dev/cdrom. File links can be hard or soft.

Hard links are directory entries that point to the same inode. They must be created within the same filesystem. You could delete a hard-linked file in one directory, and it would still exist in the other directory (files are only deleted when the number of dentry records pointing to them hit 0, which is tracked via a counter per file). For example, the following command creates a hard link from the actual Samba configuration file to smb.conf in the local directory:

```
# ln /etc/samba/smb.conf smb.conf
```

On the other hand, a soft link serves as a redirect; when you open a file created with a soft link, the link redirects you to the original file. If you delete the original file, the file is lost. Although the soft link is still there, it has nowhere to go. The following command is an example of how you can create a soft-linked file:

```
# ln -s /etc/samba/smb.conf smb.conf
```

rm

The **rm** command is somewhat dangerous. At the Linux command line, there is no trash bin. So if you delete a file with the **rm** command, it's at best difficult to recover that file.

The **rm** command is powerful. For example, when we downloaded the source files for the Linux kernel, several thousand files were included in the /root/rpmbuild/BUILD /kernel-3.10.0-123.el7 directory. Obviously, it's not practical to delete those files one by one. Therefore, the **rm** command includes some powerful switches. The following command removes all of those files in one go:

```
# rm -rf /root/rpmbuild/BUILD/kernel-3.10.0-123.el7
```

The **-r** switch works recursively, and the **-f** switch overrides any safety precautions, such as the **-i** switch shown in the output to the **alias** command for the root administrative user. It's still quite a dangerous command. For example, a simple typing mistake such as putting a space between the first forward slash and the directory name, as shown here, would first delete every file starting with the top-level root directory (/) before looking for the root/rpmbuild/BUILD/kernel-3.10.0-123.el7 subdirectory:

```
# rm -rf / root/rpmbuild/BUILD/kernel-3.10.0-123.el7
```

This would delete every file on the system, including any mount points.

Directory Creation and Deletion

The **mkdir** and **rmdir** commands are used to create and delete directories. The ways these commands are used depend on the already-discussed concepts of absolute and relative paths. For example, the following command creates the test subdirectory to the current directory. If you're currently in the /home/michael directory, the full path would be /home/michael/test.

```
# mkdir test
```

Alternatively, the following command creates the /test directory:

```
# mkdir /test
```

If desired, you can use the following command to create a series of directories:

```
# mkdir -p test1/test2/test3
```

That command is equivalent to the following commands:

```
# mkdir test1
# mkdir test1/test2
# mkdir test1/test2/test3
```

Conversely, the **rmdir** command deletes a directory only if it's empty. If you're cleaning up after the previous **mkdir** commands, the **-p** switch is useful there as well. The following command deletes the noted directory and subdirectories, as long as all of the directories are otherwise empty:

```
# rmdir -p test1/test2/test3
```

alias

The **alias** command can be used to simplify a few commands. For the root administrative user, the default aliases provide a bit of safety. To see the aliases for the current user, run the **alias** command. The following output shows the default Red Hat aliases for the root user:

```
alias cp='cp -i'
alias egrep='egrep --color=auto'
alias fgrep='fgrep -color=auto'
alias grep='grep --color=auto'
alias l.='ls -d .* --color=auto'
alias ll='ls -l --color=auto'
alias ls='ls --color=auto'
alias mv='mv -i'
alias rm='rm -i'
alias which='alias | /usr/bin/which --tty-only --read-alias ↵
--show-dot --show-tilde'
```

TABLE 3-1

Wildcards in the
Shell

Wildcard	Description
*	Any number of characters (or no characters at all). For example, the **ls ab*** command would return the following filenames, assuming they exist in the current directory: ab, abc, abcd.
?	One single character. For example, the **ls ab?** command would return the following filenames, assuming they exist in the current directory: abc, abd, abe.
[]	A range of options. For example, the **ls ab[123]** command would return the following filenames, assuming they exist in the current directory: ab1, ab2, ab3. Alternatively, the **ls ab[X-Z]** command would return the following filenames, assuming they exist in the current directory: abX, abY, abZ.

Some of these aliases help protect key files from mistakes. The **-i** switch prompts the user for confirmation before a file is deleted or overwritten with the **cp**, **mv**, or **rm** command. Just be aware, the **-f** switch supersedes the **-i** for the noted commands.

Wildcards

Sometimes you may not know the exact name of the file or the exact search term. That is when a wildcard is handy, especially with the commands described throughout the book. Three basic wildcards are shown in Table 3-1.

on the
ᶦ o b

The use of wildcards is sometimes known in the Linux world as *globbing*.

File Searches

Most users who study Linux for a while become familiar with key files. For example, named.conf is the key configuration file for the standard DNS (Domain Name Service) servers, based on the Berkeley Internet Name Domain (BIND). But not many people remember that a sample named.conf file, with all kinds of useful configuration hints, can be found in the /usr/share/doc/bind-*/sample/etc directory.

To that end, there are two basic commands for file searches: **find** and **locate**.

find

The **find** command searches through directories and subdirectories for a desired file. For example, if you wanted to find the directory with the named.conf DNS sample configuration file, you could use the following command, which would start the search in the root directory:

```
# find / -name named.conf
```

But the speed of that search depends on the memory and disk speed available on the local system. Alternatively, if you know that this file is located in the /usr subdirectory tree, you could start in that directory with the following command:

```
# find /usr -name named.conf
```

That command should now find the desired file more quickly.

locate

If this is all too time consuming, RHEL allows you to set up a database of installed files and directories. Searches with the **locate** command are almost instantaneous—and **locate** searches don't require the full filename. The drawback is that the **locate** command database is normally updated only once each day, as documented in the **/etc/cron.daily/mlocate** script.

As daily jobs are run only once every 24 hours, that's not good enough, especially during a 2.5-hour exam. Fortunately, the noted script can be executed directly from the command-line interface by the root administrative user. Just type in the full path to the file as if it were a command:

e x a m

ⓦatch **When you take Red Hat exams, you can run** updatedb **or the noted** mlocate **script early on to find needed files more quickly later on without delay.**

```
# /etc/cron.daily/mlocate
```

CERTIFICATION OBJECTIVE 3.03

The Management of Text Files

Linux and Unix are typically managed through a series of text files. Linux administrators do not normally use graphical editors to manage these configuration files. Editors such as OpenOffice.org Writer or Microsoft Word normally either save files in a binary format or change the encoding of plain-text files. Unless text files are preserved in their original format, changes that are made can render a Linux system unbootable.

Linux commands have been set up to manage text files as streams of data. You've seen tools such as redirection arrows and pipes. However, that data can be overwhelming without tools that can sort through that data. Even before files are edited, it's important to know how to read these files at the command-line interface.

Commands to Read Text Streams

Previously, you reviewed commands such as **cd**, **ls**, and **pwd** that can help you get around Linux files. With commands such as **find** and **locate**, you reviewed how to identify the location of desired files.

Now it's time to start reading, copying, and moving the files around. Most Linux configuration files are text files. Linux editors are text editors. Linux commands are designed to read text files. To identify the types of files in the current directory, try the **file *** command.

cat

The most basic command for reading files is **cat**. The **cat** *filename* command scrolls the text within the *filename* file. It also works with multiple filenames; it concatenates the filenames that you might list as one continuous output to your screen. You can redirect the output to the filename of your choice, as described in the section "Text Streams and Command Redirection."

less and more

Larger files demand command utilities that can help you scroll through the file text at your leisure. These utilities are known as *pagers,* and the most common are **more** and **less**. With the **more** *filename* command, you can scroll through the text of a file, from start to finish, one screen at a time. With the **less** *filename* command, you can scroll in both directions through the same text with the PAGE UP, PAGE DOWN, and arrow keys. Both commands support vi-style searches.

As the **less** and **more** commands do not change files, they're an excellent way to scroll through and search for items in a large text file such as an error log. For example, to search through the basic /var/log/messages file, run the following command:

```
# less /var/log/messages
```

You'll then be able to scroll up and down the log file for important information. You can use the forward slash and question mark to search forward or backward through the file. For example, once you've run the command just shown, you'll be taken to a screen similar to that shown in Figure 3-3.

FIGURE 3-3

The less pager and
/var/log/messages

```
Dec 28 09:36:31 server1 NetworkManager: DHCPREQUEST on eth0 to 255.255.255.255 p
ort 67 (xid=0x14b16e00)
Dec 28 09:36:31 server1 NetworkManager[829]: <info> (eth0): DHCPv4 state changed
 nbi -> preinit
Dec 28 09:36:31 server1 dhclient[1707]: DHCPACK from 192.168.122.1 (xid=0x14b16e
00)
Dec 28 09:36:31 server1 NetworkManager: DHCPACK from 192.168.122.1 (xid=0x14b16e
00)
Dec 28 09:36:31 server1 dhclient[1707]: bound to 192.168.122.225 -- renewal in 1
441 seconds.
Dec 28 09:36:31 server1 NetworkManager: bound to 192.168.122.225 -- renewal in 1
441 seconds.
Dec 28 09:36:31 server1 NetworkManager[829]: <info> (eth0): DHCPv4 state changed
 preinit -> reboot
Dec 28 09:36:31 server1 NetworkManager[829]: <info>    address 192.168.122.225
Dec 28 09:36:31 server1 NetworkManager[829]: <info>    plen 24 (255.255.255.0)
Dec 28 09:36:31 server1 NetworkManager[829]: <info>    gateway 192.168.122.1
Dec 28 09:36:31 server1 NetworkManager[829]: <info>    server identifier 192.168.
122.1
Dec 28 09:36:31 server1 NetworkManager[829]: <info>    lease time 3600
Dec 28 09:36:31 server1 NetworkManager[829]: <info>    hostname 'server1'
Dec 28 09:36:31 server1 NetworkManager[829]: <info>    nameserver '192.168.122.1'
Dec 28 09:36:31 server1 NetworkManager[829]: <info> Activation (eth0) Stage 5 of
:
```

To search forward in the file for the term "IPv4 tunneling," type the following in the pager:

```
/IPv4 tunneling
```

To search in the reverse direction, substitute a **?** for the /.

The **less** command has one more feature unavailable to commands such as **more** and **cat**: it can read text files compressed in gzip format, normally shown with the .gz extension. For example, the man pages associated with many standard commands that are run in the shell can be found in the /usr/share/man/man1 directory. All of the files in this directory are compressed in .gz format. Nevertheless, the **less** command can read those files.

And that points to the operation of the **man** command. In other words, these two commands are functionally equivalent:

```
# man cat
# less /usr/share/man/man1/cat.1.gz
```

head and tail

The **head** and **tail** commands are separate tools that work in essentially the same way. By default, the **head** *filename* command looks at the first 10 lines of a file; the **tail** *filename* command looks at the last 10 lines of a file. You can specify the number of lines shown with the **-n***xy* switch. For example, the **tail -n 15 /etc/passwd** command lists the last 15 lines of the /etc/passwd file.

The **tail** command can be especially useful for problems in progress. For example, if there's an ongoing problem with failed login attempts, the following command monitors the noted file and displays new lines on the screen as new log entries are recorded:

```
# tail -f /var/log/secure
```

Commands to Process Text Streams

A text stream is the movement of data. For example, the **cat** *filename* command streams the data from the *filename* file to the terminal. When these files get large, it's convenient to have commands that can filter and otherwise process these streams of text.

Linux includes simple commands to help you search, check, or sort the contents of a file. In addition, there are special files that contain others; some of these container files are known colloquially as "tarballs."

on the
job

> **Tarballs are a common way to distribute Linux packages. Packages are normally distributed in a compressed format, with a .tar.gz or .tgz file extension, consolidated as a package in a single file.**

sort

You can sort the contents of a file in a number of ways. By default, the **sort** command sorts the contents in alphabetical order, depending on the first letter in each line. For example, the **sort /etc/passwd** command would sort all users (including those associated with specific services and such) by username.

grep

The **grep** command uses a search term to look through a file. It returns the full line that contains the search term. For example, **grep 'Michael Jang' /etc/passwd** looks for the name of this author in the /etc/passwd file.

You can use regular expressions within a **grep** command. Regular expressions provide a powerful way to specify complex search patterns. Some of the characters that have a special meaning inside a regular expression are shown in Table 3-2. If you want a metacharacter to lose its special meaning and be taken literally, precede it by a blackslash (\).

The **grep** command supports some useful switches. To make the search case-insensitive, you can pass the **-i** option to the command line. The **-E** option enables the use of extended regular expression syntax. Another interesting switch is **-v**, which reverses the matching logic—that is, it tells **grep** to select only the lines that do *not* match a regular expression.

As an example, suppose you want to select only the lines from /etc/nsswitch.conf that are not blank and do not contain a comment (that is, they do not start with the # character). This can be achieved by running the following command:

```
# grep -v '^$' /etc/nsswitch.conf | grep -v '^#'
```

TABLE 3-2	Special Characters in Regular Expressions

Metacharacter	Description
.	Any single character. Often used with the * multiplier to indicate any number of characters.
[]	Match any single character included within the square brackets. For example, the command **grep 'jo[ah]n' /etc/passwd** would return all lines in /etc/passwd that contain the string *joan* or *john*.
?	Match the preceding element zero or one time. For example, the command **grep -E 'ann?a' /etc/passwd** would return all lines in /etc/passwd that contain the string *ana* or *anna*.
+	Match the preceding element one or more times. For example, the command **grep -E 'j[a-z]+n' /etc/passwd** would return all lines in /etc/passwd that contain the letters *j* and *n*, with one or more lowercase letters in between. Therefore, this regular expression would match strings such as *joan*, *john*, and also *jason* and *jonathan*.
*	Match the preceding element zero or more times. For example, the command **grep 'jo[a-z]*n' /etc/passwd** would return all lines in /etc/passwd that contain the string *jo* followed by zero or more lowercase letters and terminated by the character *n*. Therefore, the previous regular expression would match strings such as *jon*, *joan*, or *john*.
^	Match the beginning of a line. For example, the command **grep '^bin' /etc/passwd** would return all lines in /etc/passwd that start with the sequence of characters *bin*.
$	Match the end of a line. For example, the command **grep '/bin/[kz]sh$' /etc/passwd** would return all lines in /etc/passwd that terminate with the sequence of characters */bin/ksh* or */bin/zsh* (that is, all records corresponding to the users who have set Korn or Zsh as their default shells).

Note how the first **grep** command selects all the lines that are not blank (the regular expression that matches a blank line is ^$—that is, start of line and immediately end of line). Then, the output is piped to a second **grep** command, which excludes all the lines that start with a hash character.

The same result can be obtained with a single instance of **grep** and the **-e** switch, which allows you to specify multiple search patterns on the same command:

```
# grep -v -e '^$' -e '^#' /etc/nsswitch.conf
```

For more information on regular expressions, type **man 7 regex**.

diff

One useful option to find the difference between files is the **diff** command. If you've just used a tool such as the Network Manager Connections Editor described later in this chapter, it'll modify a file such as ifcfg-eth0 in the /etc/sysconfig/network-scripts directory.

If you've backed up that ifcfg-eth0 file, the **diff** command can identify the differences between the two files. For example, the following command identifies the differences between the ifcfg-eth0 file in the /root and the /etc/sysconfig/network-scripts directories:

```
# diff /root/ifcfg-eth0 /etc/sysconfig/network-scripts/ifcfg-eth0
```

wc

The **wc** command, short for word count, can return the number of lines, words, and characters in a file. The **wc** options are straightforward; for example, **wc -w** *filename* returns the number of words in that file.

sed

The **sed** command, short for stream editor, allows you to search for and change specified words or even text streams in a file. For example, the following command exchanges the first instance of the word "Windows" with "Linux" in each line of the file opsys and writes the result to the file newopsys:

```
# sed 's/Windows/Linux/' opsys > newopsys
```

However, this may not be enough. If there's more than one instance of "Windows" in a line in the opsys file, it does not change the second instance of that word. But you can fix this by adding a "global" suffix:

```
# sed 's/Windows/Linux/g' opsys > newopsys
```

The following example would make sure that all Samba shares configured with the **writable = yes** directive are reversed:

```
# sed 's/writable = yes/writable = no/g' /etc/samba/smb.conf > ~/smb.conf
```

Of course, you should then review the results in the /root/smb.conf file before overwriting the original /etc/samba/smb.conf file.

awk

The **awk** command, named for its developers (Aho, Weinberger, and Kernighan), rather than a command, is more of a full programming language. It can identify lines with a keyword and read out the text from a specified column in that line. A common example is with the /etc/passwd file. For example, the following command will read out the fourth field in /etc/passwd (the group ID) of every user with a listing of "mike":

```
# awk -F : '/mike/ {print $4}' /etc/passwd
```

Edit Text Files at the Console

The original version of the RHCSA objectives specified the use of the vim editor. Strictly speaking, it doesn't matter what text editor you use to edit text files. However, we believe that you need to know how to use the vim editor, and apparently some at Red Hat agree. The vim editor is short for "vi, improved." When installed, the vim editor can be started with the **vi** command. Hereafter, we refer to that text editor as vi.

We believe every administrator needs at least a basic knowledge of vi. Although emacs would also be a valid choice, vi may help you save a broken system. If you ever have to restore a critical configuration file using emergency boot media, vi may be the only editor you'll have available.

While RHEL 7 also includes access to the more intuitive nano editor, a knowledge of vi commands can help you in searching and editing key sections of text files more quickly. Although the RHEL rescue media supports more console-based editors, vi is one of the most feature-rich and efficient editors available on Linux.

You should know how to use the two basic modes of vi: command and insert. When you use vi to open a file, it opens in command mode. Some of the commands start insert mode. Opening a file is easy: just use the **vi** *filename* command. An example of vi with the /etc/nsswitch.conf file is shown in Figure 3-4.

The following is only the briefest of introductions to the vi editor. For more information, you can consult a number of the books available on the topic, as well as a tutorial that you can start through the **vimtutor** command.

FIGURE 3-4

The vi editor with /etc/nsswitch.conf

```
passwd:     files sss
shadow:     files sss
group:      files sss
#initgroups: files

#hosts:     db files nisplus nis dns
hosts:      files dns myhostname

# Example - obey only what nisplus tells us...
#services:  nisplus [NOTFOUND=return] files
#networks:  nisplus [NOTFOUND=return] files
#protocols: nisplus [NOTFOUND=return] files
#rpc:       nisplus [NOTFOUND=return] files
#ethers:    nisplus [NOTFOUND=return] files
#netmasks:  nisplus [NOTFOUND=return] files

bootparams: nisplus [NOTFOUND=return] files

ethers:     files
netmasks:   files
networks:   files
protocols:  files
rpc:        files
```

vi Command Mode

In command mode, you can do everything to a text file except edit it. The options in command mode are broad and varied, and they are the subject of a number of book-length texts. In summary, options in vi command mode fall into seven categories:

- **Open**   To open a file in the vi editor from the command-line interface, run the **vi** *filename* command.
- **Search**   For a forward search, start with a backslash (**/**), followed by the search term. Remember, Linux is case sensitive, so if you're searching for "Michael" in /etc/passwd, use the **/Michael** (not **/michael**) command. For a reverse search, start with a question mark (**?**).
- **Write**   To save your changes, use the **w** command. You can combine commands; for example, **:wq** writes the file and exits vi.
- **Close**   To leave vi, use the **:q** command.
- **Abandon**   If you want to abandon any changes, use the **:q!** command.
- **Edit**   You can use a number of commands to edit files through vi, such as **x**, which deletes the currently highlighted character, **dw**, which deletes the currently highlighted word, and **dd**, which deletes the current line. Remember, **yy** copies the current line into a buffer, **p** places text from a buffer, and **u** restores text from a previous change.
- **Insert**   A number of commands allow you to start insert mode, including **i** to start inserting text at the current position of the editor and **o** to open up a new line immediately below the current position of the cursor.

Basic Text Editing

In modern Linux systems, editing files with vi is easy. Just use the normal navigation keys (arrow keys, PAGE UP, and PAGE DOWN), and then one of the basic commands such as **i** or **o** to start vi's insert mode, and type your changes directly into the file.

When you're finished with insert mode, press the ESC key to return to command mode. You can then save your changes, or abandon them and exit vi.

on the
ⓘob

There are several specialized variations on the vi **command. Three are** vipw, vigw, **and** visudo, **which edit /etc/passwd, /etc/group, and /etc/sudoers, respectively. The** vipw -s **and** vigr -s **commands edit the /etc/shadow and /etc/gshadow files, respectively.**

Using vi to Create a New User

In this exercise, you'll create a new user by editing the /etc/passwd file with the vi text editor. Although there are other ways to create new Linux users, this exercise helps you verify your skills with vi and at the command-line interface.

1. Open a Linux command-line interface. Log in as the root user, and type the **vipw** command. This command uses the vi editor to open /etc/passwd.

2. Navigate to the end of the file. There are several ways to do this in command mode, including the DOWN ARROW key, the PAGE DOWN key, and the **G** command.

3. Identify a line associated with a regular user. If you've just created a new user, it should be the last line in the file, with UID numbers of 1000 and above. If a regular user does not yet exist, identify the first line, which should be associated with the root administrative user, with the number 0 in the third and fourth column.

4. Make one copy of this line. If you're already comfortable with vi, you should know that you can copy an entire line to the buffer with the **yy** command. This "yanks" the line into the buffer. You can then restore or put in that line as many times as desired with the **p** command.

5. Change the username, user ID, group ID, user comment, and home directory for the new user. For detailed information on each entry, see Chapter 8. For example, in the following illustration, this corresponds to tweedle, 1001, 1001, Tweedle Dee, and /home/tweedle. Make sure the username also corresponds to the home directory.

```
rpc:x:32:32:Rpcbind Daemon:/var/lib/rpcbind:/sbin/nologin
rpcuser:x:29:29:RPC Service User:/var/lib/nfs:/sbin/nologin
nfsnobody:x:65534:65534:Anonymous NFS User:/var/lib/nfs:/sbin/nologin
named:x:25:25:Named:/var/named:/sbin/nologin
oprofile:x:16:16:Special user account to be used by OProfile:/var/lib/oprofile:/
sbin/nologin
tcpdump:x:72:72::/:/sbin/nologin
usbmuxd:x:113:113:usbmuxd user:/:/sbin/nologin
colord:x:998:996:User for colord:/var/lib/colord:/sbin/nologin
abrt:x:173:173::/etc/abrt:/sbin/nologin
chrony:x:997:995::/var/lib/chrony:/sbin/nologin
libstoragemgmt:x:996:994:daemon account for libstoragemgmt:/var/run/lsm:/sbin/no
login
qemu:x:107:107:qemu user:/:/sbin/nologin
radvd:x:75:75:radvd user:/:/sbin/nologin
rtkit:x:172:172:RealtimeKit:/proc:/sbin/nologin
saslauth:x:995:76:"Saslauthd user":/run/saslauthd:/sbin/nologin
ntp:x:38:38::/etc/ntp:/sbin/nologin
pulse:x:171:171:PulseAudio System Daemon:/var/run/pulse:/sbin/nologin
gdm:x:42:42::/var/lib/gdm:/sbin/nologin
gnome-initial-setup:x:993:991::/run/gnome-initial-setup/:/sbin/nologin
michael:x:1000:1000:Michael Jang:/home/michael:/bin/bash
tweedle:x:1001:1001:Tweedle Dee:/home/tweedle:/bin/bash
```

6. Return to command mode by pressing the ESC key. Save the file with the **:w** command, and then exit with the **:q** command. (You can combine the two commands in vi; the next time you make a change and want to save and exit, run the **:wq** command.)

7. You should see the following message:

```
You have modified /etc/passwd.
You may need to modify /etc/shadow for consistency.
Please use the command 'vipw -s' to do so.
```

That message can be ignored because the next step adds appropriate information to the /etc/shadow file. However, you don't need to modify /etc/shadow directly.

8. As the root user, run the **passwd** *newuser* command. Assign the password of your choice to the new user. For this example, the new user is tweedle.

9. The process is not yet complete; every user needs a group. To that end, run the **vigr** command. Repeat the earlier steps that copied an appropriate line from near the end of the file. Note that group names and group ID numbers normally are identical to their usernames and user ID numbers.

10. All you need to change for the new entry is the group name and group ID number. Based on the information shown in the previous illustration, this would be a group name of tweedle and a group number of 1001.

11. Repeat the aforementioned **:wq** command to close vi and save the change.

12. Pay attention to the following message:

```
You have modified /etc/group.
You may need to modify /etc/gshadow for consistency.
Please use the command 'vigr -s' to do so.
```

13. As suggested, run the **vigr -s** command to open the /etc/gshadow file. You'll note that there's less information in this file. Once a copy is made of an appropriate line, all you'll need to do is change the group name.

14. Repeat the aforementioned **:wq** command to close vi and save the change. Actually, you'll get a message that suggests that the file is read-only. You'd have to run the **:wq!** in this case to write to this "read-only" file, overriding current settings.

15. Additional steps are required to properly set up the new user related to that user's home directory and standard files from the /etc/skel directory. For more information, see Chapter 8.

If You Don't Like vi

By default, when you run commands such as **edquota** and **crontab**, associated quota and cron job configuration files are opened in the vi editor. If you absolutely hate vi, the default editor can be changed with the following command:

```
# export EDITOR=/bin/nano
```

To change the default editor for all users, add the preceding line to the /etc/environment configuration file. You don't absolutely have to use the vi editor to change /etc/environment; instead, the following appends the noted command to the end of the /etc/environment file:

```
# echo 'export EDITOR=/bin/nano' >> /etc/environment
```

Because the nano editor is fairly intuitive, as shown in Figure 3-5, instructions will not be provided in this book. The full manual is available from www.nano-editor.org/dist/v2.3/nano.html.

Similar changes can be made if you prefer a different editor, such as emacs.

Edit Text Files in the GUI

No question, the Red Hat exams have become friendlier for users of the GUI. The gedit text editor was even included for a short time in the RHCSA objectives. More traditional Linux administrators may have been horrified. (The gedit editor has since been deleted from the objectives.)

FIGURE 3-5

The nano editor with /etc/nsswitch.conf

```
GNU nano 2.3.1              File: /etc/nsswitch.conf

#
# /etc/nsswitch.conf
#
# An example Name Service Switch config file. This file should be
# sorted with the most-used services at the beginning.
#
# The entry '[NOTFOUND=return]' means that the search for an
# entry should stop if the search in the previous entry turned
# up nothing. Note that if the search failed due to some other reason
# (like no NIS server responding) then the search continues with the
# next entry.
#
# Valid entries include:
#
#       nisplus                 Use NIS+ (NIS version 3)
#       nis                     Use NIS (NIS version 2), also called YP
#       dns                     Use DNS (Domain Name Service)
#       files                   Use the local files
#       db                      Use the local database (.db) files
                        [ Read 64 lines ]
^G Get Help   ^O WriteOut   ^R Read File  ^Y Prev Page  ^K Cut Text   ^C Cur Pos
^X Exit       ^J Justify    ^W Where Is   ^V Next Page  ^U UnCut Text ^T To Spell
```

If the gedit editor is not installed in your system, run the **yum install gedit** command. Once gedit is installed, you can start it by clicking Applications | Accessories | gedit. Because it is an intuitive GUI text editor, its use is trivial. Don't obsess about editors; they are just tools on exams and in real life.

However, if you're editing configuration files on remote systems, it's possible that you won't have access to gedit on that system, especially if the GUI hasn't been installed there. Of course, you can install the GUI and use X forwarding on any Red Hat system. But many administrators set up VMs without the GUI to save space and reduce security risks.

CERTIFICATION OBJECTIVE 3.04

Local Online Documentation

Although there's no Internet access allowed during Red Hat exams, there is a lot of documentation available already installed on a RHEL 7 system. It starts with the man pages, which document the options and settings associated with most commands and many configuration files. It continues with the info documents. Although fewer commands and files have such documents, when available, they do provide even more information.

Many packages include extensive documentation in the /usr/share/doc directory. Just apply the **ls** command to that directory. Every subdirectory there includes information about the capabilities of each associated package.

When You Need Help

The first thing we usually do when we need help with a command is to run it by itself. If more information is required, the command prompts with a request for more information, including a variety of options. As an example, look at the output to the following command:

```
$ yum
```

If that approach doesn't work, generally some amount of help is available with the **-h** or the **--help** switch. Sometimes a mistake leads to some hints; the output to the following command suggests legal options to the **cd** command:

```
$ cd -h
bash: cd: -h: invalid option
cd: usage: cd [-L|[-P [-e]]] [dir]
```

FIGURE 3-6

Help with the ls
command

```
[alex@server1 ~]$ ls --help
Usage: ls [OPTION]... [FILE]...
List information about the FILEs (the current directory by default).
Sort entries alphabetically if none of -cftuvSUX nor --sort is specified.

Mandatory arguments to long options are mandatory for short options too.
  -a, --all                  do not ignore entries starting with .
  -A, --almost-all           do not list implied . and ..
      --author               with -l, print the author of each file
  -b, --escape               print C-style escapes for nongraphic characters
      --block-size=SIZE      scale sizes by SIZE before printing them; e.g.,
                               '--block-size=M' prints sizes in units of
                               1,048,576 bytes; see SIZE format below
  -B, --ignore-backups       do not list implied entries ending with ~
  -c                         with -lt: sort by, and show, ctime (time of last
                               modification of file status information);
                               with -l: show ctime and sort by name;
                               otherwise: sort by ctime, newest first
  -C                         list entries by columns
      --color[=WHEN]         colorize the output; WHEN can be 'never', 'auto',
                               or 'always' (the default); more info below
  -d, --directory            list directories themselves, not their contents
  -D, --dired                generate output designed for Emacs' dired mode
  -f                         do not sort, enable -aU, disable -ls --color
```

Sometimes the **-h** switch is more helpful; take a look at the output to the **fdisk -h** command. But the **-h** option doesn't always show a help message; in that case, the **--help** switch may serve that purpose. Look at Figure 3-6 as an example, which displays the output to the **ls --help** command.

A Variety of man Pages

Few people can remember every switch to every command. That's one reason why command documentation is so important. Most Linux commands are documented in a format known as the man page. If you run the **man** command by itself, RHEL returns the following message:

```
What manual page do you want?
```

For example, say you need to set up a physical volume but have forgotten the switches associated with the **lvextend** command. To browse the man page for that command, run **man lvextend**. As with many other commands, there's an EXAMPLES section, like that shown in Figure 3-7. If you've run the **lvextend** command before, that section may help jog your memory.

Such man pages are available for most configuration files and commands. However, there may be more. So what if you're not sure about the name of the man page? In that case, the **whatis** and **apropos** commands can help. For example, to find the man pages with "nfs" in the title, run the following command:

```
# whatis nfs
```

FIGURE 3-7

Examples from
the lvextend man
page

```
        --use-policies
                Resizes  the  logical volume according to configured policy. See
                lvm.conf(5) for some details.

    Examples
                Extends the size of the logical volume "vg01/lvol10" by 54MiB on physi-
                cal volume /dev/sdk3. This is only possible if /dev/sdk3 is a member of
                volume group vg01 and there are enough free physical extents in it:

        lvextend -L +54 /dev/vg01/lvol10 /dev/sdk3

                Extends the size of logical volume "vg01/lvol01" by the amount of  free
                space  on  physical  volume /dev/sdk3. This is equivalent to specifying
                "-l +100%PVS" on the command line:

        lvextend /dev/vg01/lvol01 /dev/sdk3

                Extends a logical volume "vg01/lvol01" by 16MiB using physical  extents
                /dev/sda:8-9 and /dev/sdb:8-9 for allocation of extents:

        lvextend -L+16M vg01/lvol01 /dev/sda:8-9 /dev/sdb:8-9

    SEE ALSO
                fsadm(8),  lvm(8), lvm.conf(5), lvcreate(8), lvconvert(8), lvreduce(8),
                lvresize(8), lvchange(8)
```

If you want to find the man pages with nfs in the description, the following command can identify related commands:

```
# apropos nfs
```

However, if you've just installed a service such as httpd, associated with the Apache web server, commands such as **whatis httpd** and **apropos apachectl** probably won't provide any information. These commands work from a database in the /var/cache/man directory. You can update that database with the man-db.cron job in the /etc/cron.daily directory. As that script is already executable, the following command updates the database of man pages:

```
# /etc/cron.daily/man-db.cron
```

If you encounter a situation, such as during a Red Hat exam, where the associated man page is not installed, there are at least three possible reasons. The associated functional software package may not be installed. The RPM package named man-pages may also not be installed. In some cases, there is a package specifically dedicated to documentation that must be installed separately. For example, there's a system-config-users-doc package that includes GUI-based documentation for the User Manager configuration tool. There's also an httpd-manual package installed separately from the Apache web server.

In some cases, multiple man pages are available. Take a look at the following output to the **whatis smbpasswd** command:

```
smbpasswd               (5)  - The Samba encrypted password file
smbpasswd               (8)  - change a user's SMB password
```

The numbers (5) and (8) are associated with different sections of man pages. If you're interested in details, they're shown in the output to the **man man** command. The man page shown by default is the man page associated with the **smbpasswd** command. In this case, if you want the man page for the smbpasswd encrypted password file, run the following command:

```
$ man 5 smbpasswd
```

To exit from a man page, press **q**.

The info Manuals

The list of available info manuals is somewhat limited. However, the coverage of some topics (for example, the bash shell) is usually more extensive than a corresponding man page. For a full list of info documents, run the **ls /usr/share/info** command. When an info manual is not available, a request defaults to the associated man page.

To learn more about the bash shell, run the **pinfo bash** command. **pinfo** has a user interface similar to the Lynx web browser and it is a more user-friendly alternative to the traditional **info** command. As shown in Figure 3-8, info manuals are organized into sections. To access a section, move the cursor to the asterisked entry and press ENTER.

To exit from an info page, press **q**.

FIGURE 3-8	

A sample info manual

```
File: bash.info,  Node: Top,  Next: Introduction,  Prev: (dir),  Up: (dir)

    This manual is meant as a brief introduction to features found in
Bash.  The Bash manual page should be used as the definitive reference
on shell behavior.

* Menu:

* Introduction::              An introduction to the shell.
* Definitions::               Some definitions used in the rest of this
                              manual.
* Basic Shell Features::      The shell "building blocks".
* Shell Builtin Commands::    Commands that are a part of the shell.
* Shell Variables::           Variables used or set by Bash.
* Bash Features::             Features found only in Bash.
* Job Control::               What job control is and how Bash allows you
                              to use it.
* Command Line Editing::      Chapter describing the command line
                              editing features.
* Using History Interactively:: Command History Expansion
* Installing Bash::           How to build and install Bash on your system.
* Reporting Bugs::            How to report bugs in Bash.
* Major Differences From The Bourne Shell::    A terse list of the differences
Viewing line 39/44, 88%
```

Detailed Documentation in /usr/share/doc

The list of documentation available in the /usr/share/doc directory seems impressive. But the quality of the documentation depends on the work of its developers. The subdirectories include the name and version number of the installed package. Some of these subdirectories include just one file, normally named COPYING, which specifies the license under which the given software was released. For example, most of the system-config-* packages include a copy of the GNU GPL in the COPYING file in the associated /usr/share/doc directory.

Sometimes, the documentation directory includes useful examples. For example, the sudo-*/ subdirectory includes sample configuration files and directives for administrative control, which can be helpful when you're configuring administrators with different privileges.

The documentation may include entire manuals in HTML format. For an example, take a look at the pam-*/ subdirectory, which includes an entire online manual for the Pluggable Authentication Modules (PAM) system discussed in Chapter 10.

CERTIFICATION OBJECTIVE 3.05

A Networking Primer

TCP/IP is a series of protocols organized in layers, known as a protocol suite. It was developed for Unix and eventually adopted as the standard for communication on the Internet. IP addresses help you communicate across a network. A number of TCP/IP tools and configurations are available to help you manage a network.

As with the previous sections in this chapter, the statements here are oversimplifications. So if you find this section overwhelming and/or incomplete, read the references cited in Chapter 1. Linux is built for networking, and there is no practical way to pass any Red Hat exam unless you understand networking in some detail.

Although the focus of current networks is still on IP version 4 addressing, some organizations have mandated a move toward IP version 6 (IPv6) networks. The focus of this section is on IPv4, whereas IPv6 will be covered in Chapter 12. However, most of the configuration files and tools that are used for IPv4 also apply to IPv6.

IPv4 Networks

Every computer that communicates on a network needs its own IP address. Some addresses are assigned permanently to a particular computer; these are known as *static* addresses. Others are leased from a DHCP server for a limited amount of time; these are known as *dynamic* IP addresses.

	Class	IP Range	Note
TABLE 3-3	A	1.1.1.0–127.255.255.255	Allows networks of up to 16,777,214 hosts
IP Address Classes	B	128.0.0.0–191.255.255.255	Allows networks of up to 65,534 hosts
	C	192.0.0.0–223.255.255.255	Allows networks of up to 254 computers
	D	224.0.0.0–239.255.255.255	Reserved for multicasts
	E	240.0.0.0–255.255.255.255	Reserved for experimental use

IPv4 addresses are 32-bit binary numbers and are usually expressed in "dot-decimal" notation (such as 192.168.122.50), with each decimal octet representing 8 bits. An IP address is made up of two parts: a network (or subnet) address and a host part. Until the publication of RFC 1517 in 1993 by the Internet Engineering Task Force (www.ietf.org), IP addresses were categorized into different classes, which defined the size of the network and the host part of the address.

Today, IP addresses are usually analyzed using a classless logic. The subnet mask, rather than the address class, is used to determine the network and host parts of an IP address. The old classful addressing scheme introduced by RFC 791 is shown Table 3-3. Some concepts of RFC 791 still remain in practice today; as an example, the IP range 224.0.0.0–239.255.255.255 is used for multicast addresses.

In addition, a number of private IP addresses are not to be assigned to any computer that is directly connected to the Internet. The most common private network ranges are defined in RFC 1918 and are associated with network addresses 10.0.0.0–10.255.255.255, 172.168.16.0–172.168.31.255, and 192.168.0.0–192.168.255.255. In addition, network addresses 127.0.0.0 through 127.255.255.255 are used for loopback communication on a local host.

Networks and Routing

As we have discussed in the previous section, an IP address has two parts: a network prefix and a host identifier. To determine the network and the host part, IP addresses are associated with a subnet mask (also known as netmask or prefix). This is a 32-bit number made of a sequence of binary ones followed by zeros.

The subnet mask can be represented in the same dot-decimal notation used for IPv4 addresses. For example, 255.255.255.0 is a subnet mask made of 24 binary ones and 8 zeros. An alternative notation is known as Classless Inter-Domain Routing (CIDR) notation and consists of a slash character (/) followed by a number that indicates the amount of one bits in the netmask. As an example, the subnet mask 255.255.255.0 can be written as /24 in CIDR notation.

Given an IP address and a subnet mask, all you have to do to determine the network portion of the IP address is provide a logical AND between the IP address and the netmask. For example, given the IP address 192.168.122.50 with netmask /24, the first three bytes of the address (192.168.122) represent the network part, whereas the last byte (50) is the host identifier.

Three key IP addresses define a network: the network address, the broadcast address, and the subnet mask. The network address is always the first IP address in a range; the broadcast address is always the last address in the same range. The subnet mask, as you have seen, helps your computer define the network and the host portion of an IP address. You can assign IP addresses between the network and broadcast addresses (not including these addresses) to any computer on the network.

As an example, let's define the range of addresses for a private network. Start with the private network address 192.168.122.0 and a subnet mask of 255.255.255.0. Based on these two addresses, the broadcast address is 192.168.122.255, and the range of IP addresses that you can assign on that particular network is 192.168.122.1 through 192.168.122.254. That subnet mask is also defined by the number of associated bits, 24. In other words, the given network can be represented by 192.168.122.0/24.

IP addresses are assigned to network interfaces. A host with multiple network interfaces that forwards traffic across different networks is called a *router*. IP hosts separated by other groups of IP hosts by a router must be located in different networks.

Related to networking and netmasks is the concept of the gateway. It's an IP address that defines the junction between the local network and other networks. Although that gateway IP address is part of the local network, that address is assigned to a router with an IP address on a different network, such as the public Internet. The gateway IP address is normally configured in the routing table for the local system, as defined by the **ip route** command described in the following section.

Tools and Commands

A substantial number of tools are available to manage the TCP/IP protocol suite on your Linux computer. In the previous versions of Red Hat Enterprise Linux, some of the most important network management commands were **ifconfig**, **arp**, **netstat**, and **route**. Those commands have been deprecated. The **ip** tool supports more advanced features. To ease the transition to the **ip** tool, Table 3-4 provides a list of the deprecated commands, along with their equivalent **ip** commands.

on the
job

By default, Red Hat Enterprise Linux 7 names network interfaces based on their physical location (enoX and emX for onboard network interfaces, and enpXsY and pXpY for PCI slots). RHEL 7 will use the traditional enumeration method of eth0, eth1, ... only as a fallback choice. Hence, you may find the first onboard network interface to be named *eno1*, while an interface located on PCI bus 3, slot 0 would be named *enp3s0*.

TABLE 3-4	The ifconfig, arp, and netstat Commands with Their Equivalent ip Commands

Obsolete Command	Equivalent Command in RHEL 7	Description
ifconfig	ip [-s] link ip addr	Shows the link status and IP address information for all network interfaces
ifconfig eth0 192.168.122.150 ↵ netmask 255.255.255.0	ip addr add ↵ 192.168.122.150/24 dev eth0	Assigns an IP address and netmask to the eth0 interface
arp	ip neigh	Shows the ARP table
route netstat -r	ip route	Displays the routing table
netstat -tulpna	ss -tupna	Shows all listening and non-listening sockets, along with the program to which they belong

Other important network commands are **ping** and **traceroute**, which are often used to diagnose and troubleshoot network problems.

But these are just the tools. In the next section, you'll examine the Red Hat files that determine the commands that are called upon to configure networks automatically during the boot process.

ping and traceroute

The **ping** command allows you to test connectivity. It can be applied locally, within a network, and across networks on the Internet. For the purpose of this section, assume your IP address is 192.168.122.50 and the gateway address on the local network is 192.168.122.1. If you're having problems connecting to a host try the following **ping** commands in order. The first step is to test the integrity of TCP/IP on your computer:

```
# ping 127.0.0.1
```

Normally, **ping** works continuously on Linux; you'll need to press CTRL-C to stop this command. If you need to verify a proper connection to a LAN, **ping** the IP address of the local network card:

```
# ping 192.168.122.50
```

If that works, **ping** the address of another computer on your network. Then start tracing the route to the Internet. **ping** the address for the network gateway (in this case,

192.168.122.1). If possible, **ping** the address of the network's connection to the Internet, which would be on the other side of the gateway. It may be the public IP address of your router on the Internet. Finally, **ping** the address of a computer that you know is active on the Internet.

You can substitute hostnames such as www.google.com for an IP address. If the hostname doesn't work, there is likely a problem with the database of hostnames and IP addresses, more commonly known as a Domain Name Service (DNS). It could also indicate a problem with the /etc/hosts configuration file.

The **traceroute** command automates the process just described by tracking the route path to a destination. For example, the following command finds the path to the IP address 192.168.20.5:

```
# traceroute -n 192.168.20.5
traceroute to 192.168.20.5 (192.168.20.5), 30 hops max, 60 byte
packets
 1  192.168.122.1  0.204 ms  0.152 ms  0.148 ms
 2  192.168.1.1  1.826 ms  2.413 ms  4.050 ms
 3  192.168.20.5  2.292 ms  2.630 ms  2.554 ms
```

Look at the **-n** option in this command. This tells **traceroute** to display IP addresses rather than hostnames. The command also shows the round trip time (RTT) to reach each hop along the path. By default, three different probes are sent for each hop.

Please note that some **traceroute** command options require root privileges. Another command that serves the same purpose and is not subjected to this limitation is **tracepath**.

on the

job

By default, traceroute **relies on UDP probe packets with an increasing time-to-live (TTL) value in the IP header in order to find the route path to a given destination. Sometimes, a firewall along the path may block UDP packets. In that case, you may try to run** traceroute **with the** -I **or** -T **option to enable ICMP or TCP probe packets, respectively.**

Review Current Network Adapters with ip

The **ip** command can display the current state of active network adapters. It also can be used to assign network addresses and more. Run the **ip link show** command to review the link status of the active network adapters on the system. Optionally, include the **-s** switch if you want to display statistics about network performance.

To review IP address information, try the **ip address show** command, which gives the same output of **ip link show**, but it also includes IP addresses and their properties. The

ip address show eth0 command listed next reflects the current configuration of the first Ethernet network adapter:

```
# ip addr show eth0
2: eth0: <BROADCAST,MULTICAST,UP,LOWER_UP> mtu 1500 qdisc pfifo_fast state ↵
UP qlen 1000
    link/ether 52:54:00:40:1e:6a brd ff:ff:ff:ff:ff:ff
    inet 192.168.122.50/24 brd 192.168.122.255 scope global eth0
       valid_lft forever preferred_lft forever
    inet6 fe80::2e0:4cff:fee3:d106/64 scope link
       valid_lft forever preferred_lft forever
```

The **ip** command is flexible. For example, the **ip a s** command is functionally equivalent to **ip addr show** or **ip address show**.

Configure a Network Adapter with ip

You can also use **ip** to assign IP address information. For example, the following command adds the noted IP address and network mask to the eth0 network adapter:

```
# ip addr add 192.168.122.150/24 dev eth0
```

The first argument, **192.168.122.150/24**, specifies the new IP address and netmask. The next argument, **dev eth0**, tells you which device is being configured. To make sure the change worked, run the **ip addr show eth0** command again.

With the right options, the **ip** command can modify additional network settings. Some of these options are shown in Table 3-5.

TABLE 3-5   ip Command Options

Command	Description
ip link set dev *device* up	Activates the specified interface.
ip link set dev *device* down	Deactivates the specified interface.
ip addr flush dev *device*	Removes all IP addresses from the specified interface.
ip link set dev *device* txqlen *N*	Changes the length of the transmit queue for the specified interface.
ip link set dev *device* mtu *N*	Sets the maximum transmission unit as *N*, in bytes.
ip link set dev *device* promisc on	Activates promiscuous mode. This allows the network adapter to read all packets received, not just the packets addressed to the host. Can be used to analyze the network for problems or to try to decipher messages between other hosts.
ip link set dev *device* promisc off	Deactivates promiscuous mode.

Of course, you'll want to make sure the changes survive a reboot, whether it be for the exam or for a server that you want to administer remotely. That depends on appropriate changes to configuration files in the /etc/sysconfig/network-scripts directory, described shortly. Also, any changes made with the **ip** command are, by definition, temporary.

Activate and Deactivate Network Adapters

It's possible to use the **ip** command to activate and deactivate network adapters. For example, the following commands deactivate and reactivate the first Ethernet adapter:

```
# ip link set dev eth0 down
# ip link set dev eth0 up
```

However, a couple of more intuitive scripts are designed to control network adapters: **ifup** and **ifdown**. Unlike the **ip** command, they call appropriate configuration files and scripts in the /etc/sysconfig/network-scripts directory.

For example, the **ifup eth0** command activates the Ethernet network adapter named eth0, based on the ifcfg-eth0 configuration file and the ifup-eth script in the /etc/sysconfig/network-scripts directory.

ip as a Diagnostic Tool

The Address Resolution Protocol (ARP) associates the hardware address of a network interface (MAC) with an IP address. The **ip neigh** command displays a table of hardware and IP addresses on the local computer. This command can help detect problems such as duplicate addresses on the network. Such problems may happen with improperly configured systems or cloned virtual machines. If needed, the **ip neigh** command can set or modify ARP table entries manually. As hardware addresses are not routable, an ARP table is limited to the local network. Here's a sample output from the command, showing all ARP entries in the local database:

```
# ip neigh show
192.168.122.150 dev eth0 lladdr 52:a5:cb:54:52:a2 REACHABLE
192.168.100.100 dev eth0 lladdr 00:a0:c5:e2:49:02 STALE
192.168.122.1 dev eth0 lladdr 00:0e:2e:6d:9e:67 REACHABLE
```

The first column in the output lists known IP addresses on the LAN, followed by the interface to which the neighbor is attached, and its link layer address (MAC address). The last entry shows whether or not the neighbor's hardware address is reachable. A STALE entry may indicate that its ARP cache timeout has expired since a packet was last seen from that host. If the ARP table is empty, no recent connections exist to other systems on the local network.

Routing Tables with ip route

The **ip** command is versatile. One important version of this command, **ip route**, displays routing tables. It's functionally equivalent to the deprecated **route** command. When run with the **-r** switch (**ip -r route**), this command looks to /etc/hosts files and DNS servers to display hostnames rather than numeric IP addresses.

The routing table for the local system normally includes a reference to the default gateway address. For example, look at the following output to the **ip route** command:

```
default via 192.168.122.1 dev eth0  proto static  metric 1024
192.168.122.0/24 dev eth0  proto kernel  scope link  src 192.168.122.50
```

The deprecated **netstat -nr** command should display the same table. For this routing table, the gateway IP address is 192.168.122.1. Any network packets with a destination other than the 192.168.122.0 network are sent through the gateway address (in other words, the layer 2 address for this gateway is looked up and put in the frame as the destination MAC address). The system at the gateway address, usually a router, forwards that packet to the next router according to its routing table until it gets to a router that is directly connected to the destination.

Dynamically Configure IP Addresses with dhclient

Although the name of the command has changed from time to time, the functionality has remained the same. The **dhclient** command, used with the device name of a network card, such as **eth0**, calls a Dynamic Host Configuration Protocol (DHCP) server for an IP address and more:

```
# dhclient eth0
```

Generally, the network options configured through a DHCP server include the IP address, the network mask, the gateway address for access to external networks, and the IP address of any DNS servers for that network.

In other words, the **dhclient eth0** command not only assigns IP address information in the way done with the **ip** command described earlier, but it also sets up the default route for the routing table shown with the **ip route** command. In addition, it adds the IP address of the DNS server to the /etc/resolv.conf configuration file.

Display Network Connections with ss

The **ss** command replaces the deprecated **netstat** tool to display network connections. With the right combination of command switches, it can show listening and nonlistening TCP and UDP sockets. One command we like to use is

```
# ss -tuna4
```

FIGURE 3-9

Output from the
ss -tuna4 command

```
[root@server1 ~]# ss -tuna4
Netid  State    Recv-Q Send-Q    Local Address:Port      Peer Address:Port
tcp    UNCONN   0      0                    *:68                 *:*
tcp    UNCONN   0      0                    *:111                *:*
tcp    UNCONN   0      0                    *:123                *:*
tcp    UNCONN   0      0            127.0.0.1:323                *:*
tcp    UNCONN   0      0                    *:609                *:*
tcp    UNCONN   0      0                    *:43630              *:*
tcp    UNCONN   0      0            127.0.0.1:659                *:*
tcp    UNCONN   0      0                    *:45931              *:*
tcp    UNCONN   0      0                    *:5353               *:*
tcp    UNCONN   0      0                    *:61050              *:*
tcp    LISTEN   0      100          127.0.0.1:25                 *:*
tcp    LISTEN   0      128                  *:52991              *:*
tcp    LISTEN   0      128                  *:111                *:*
tcp    LISTEN   0      128                  *:22                 *:*
tcp    LISTEN   0      128          127.0.0.1:631                *:*
tcp    ESTAB    0      0       192.168.122.50:22     192.168.122.1:43910
[root@server1 ~]#
```

where the command shows all (**-a**) network sockets using IPv4 (**-4**) and both the TCP (**-t**) and UDP (**-u**) protocols in numeric (**-n**) format. If the **-p** switch is specified, **ss** will also show the PID of the process using each socket. Figure 3-9 illustrates the output on the baseline server.

At the end of the output, note the peer address of 192.168.122.1:43910. The 43910 port number is just the source port on the remote server. The corresponding local address of 192.168.122.50:22 specifies a port number of 22 (the local SSH service) for a connection from 192.168.122.1. You may also see a second entry with the same port number, which identifies the associated SSH daemon listening for connections. Other lines in this output identify other listening services.

CERTIFICATION OBJECTIVE 3.06

Network Configuration and Troubleshooting

Now that you've reviewed the basics of IP addressing and associated commands, it's time to look at the configuration files. These configuration files determine whether networking is started during the boot process. If networking is activated, these files also determine whether addresses and routes are configured statically as documented or dynamically with the help of commands such as **dhclient**.

Basic network configuration only confirms that systems can communicate through their IP addresses. But that is not enough. Whether you're pointing to systems such as server1.example.com or URLs such as www.mheducation.com, network configuration is not enough if hostname resolution is not working.

on the !ob **Some of the most common causes of network problems are physical in nature. This section assumes you've checked all network connections. On a VM, that means making sure the virtual network card wasn't accidentally deleted on the VM or on the physical host.**

Network Configuration Files

If there's trouble with a network configuration, one thing to check is the current status of the network. To do so, run the following command:

```
# systemctl status network
```

RHEL 7 uses a service known as the Network Manager to monitor and manage network settings. Using the **nmcli** command-line tool, you can interact with Network Manager and display the current status of network devices:

```
# nmcli dev status
```

The command should list configured and active devices. If a key device such as eth0 is not listed as connected, your network connection is probably down or the device is unconfigured. Key configuration files are located in the /etc/sysconfig/network-scripts directory.

Sometimes mistakes happen. If you've deactivated an adapter or just lost a wireless connection, try something simple: restart networking. The following command restarts networking with current configuration files:

```
# systemctl restart network
```

on the !ob **Always use** systemctl **to execute the network script. Never run the RHEL 7 /etc/init.d/network script directly because it may fail to execute cleanly.**

If a simple restart of networking services doesn't work, then it's time to get into the files. The /etc/sysconfig/network-scripts directory is where Red Hat Enterprise Linux stores and retrieves networking information. With available Red Hat configuration tools, you don't have to touch these files, but it's good to know they're there. A few representative files are shown in Table 3-6.

/etc/sysconfig/network

If you run the **ip addr show** command and see no output, that means all network devices are currently inactive. The first thing to check in that case is the contents of the

TABLE 3-6	Files in the /etc/sysconfig/network-scripts Directory

File in /etc/sysconfig/network-scripts	Description
ifcfg-lo	Configures the loopback device, a virtual device that is used for network communication within the local host.
ifcfg-*	Each installed network adapter, such as em1, gets its own ifcfg-* script. For example, eth0 is given file ifcfg-eth0. This file includes the IP address information required to identify this adapter on a network.
network-functions	This script contains functions used by other network scripts to bring network interfaces up and down.
ifup-* and ifdown-*	These scripts activate and deactivate their assigned protocols. For example, **ifup-ppp** brings up a PPP device, usually a telephone modem.

/etc/sysconfig/network configuration file. It's a pretty simple file and usually contains one or two configuration lines. On systems that are configured to retrieve addressing information via DHCP, this file is usually empty.

If the /etc/sysconfig/network file contains the setting **NETWORKING=no**, then the /etc/init.d/network script doesn't activate any network devices. One other network-related directive that may appear is **GATEWAY**, if it's the same IP address for all network devices. Otherwise, that configuration is supported either by the **dhclient** command or set up in the IP address information for a specific network device, in the /etc/sysconfig/network-scripts directory.

/etc/sysconfig/network-scripts/ifcfg-lo

Speaking of the /etc/sysconfig/network-scripts directory, perhaps the foundation of networking is the loopback address. That information is configured in the ifcfg-lo file in that directory. The contents of the file can help you understand how files in that directory are used for network devices. By default, you should see the following entries in that file, starting with the name of the loopback device:

```
DEVICE=lo
```

It's followed by the IP address (**IPADDR**), network mask (**NETMASK**), and the network IP address (**NETWORK**), along with the corresponding broadcast address (**BROADCAST**):

```
IPADDR=127.0.0.1
NETMASK=255.0.0.0
NETWORK=127.0.0.0
BROADCAST=127.255.255.255
```

The next entries specify whether the device is activated during the boot process and the common name of the device:

```
ONBOOT=yes
NAME=loopback
```

/etc/sysconfig/network-scripts/ifcfg-eth0

What you see in the ifcfg-eth0 file depends on how that first Ethernet network adapter was configured. For example, look at the situation where networking was set up only for the purposes of installation. If you did not configure networking when setting the hostname during the GUI installation process, networking will not be configured on the system. In that case, the ifcfg-eth0 file would contain at least the following two directives:

```
HWADDR="F0:DE:F3:06:C6:DB"
TYPE=Ethernet
```

Of course, if networking were not configured during the installation process, there's no reason for the interface to be activated during the boot sequence:

```
ONBOOT="no"
```

By default, RHEL 7 uses a service known as the Network Manager to manage network settings. To make sure it's running, execute the **systemctl status NetworkManager** command. Network Manager includes **nmcli**, a command-line tool to control the status of the service and apply network configuration changes.

Rather than modifying the configuration via **nmcli**, you can change a device configuration file directly. For that purpose, the configuration file shown in Figure 3-10 provides a guide.

Most of these directives are straightforward. They define the device as an Ethernet network card with name eth0, using a defined IP address, a netmask, a default gateway, and a DNS server. Of course, if you prefer to use a DHCP server, the static network address

FIGURE 3-10

A manual
configuration
of eth0

```
HWADDR="00:50:56:40:1E:6A"
TYPE="Ethernet"
BOOTPROTO="none"
NAME="eth0"
UUID="394f6436-5524-4154-b26e-6649b4d29027"
ONBOOT="yes"
IPADDR0="192.168.122.50"
PREFIX0=24
GATEWAY0="192.168.122.1"
DEFROUTE="yes"
DNS1="192.168.122.1"
~
~
~
~
```

information specified in the last five lines of the file would be omitted, and the following directive would be changed:

```
BOOTPROTO=dhcp
```

After saving the file, you still have to notify Network Manager of the changes. This is achieved by running the following commands (**con** is short for **connection**):

```
# nmcli con reload
# nmcli con down eth0
# nmcli con up eth0
```

Shortly, you'll see how to use Network Manager's command-line tool to modify the configuration of a network device.

Other /etc/sysconfig/network-scripts Files

Most of the files in the /etc/sysconfig/network-scripts directory are actually scripts. In other words, they are executable files based on a series of text commands. Most of those scripts are based on the **ifup** and **ifdown** commands, customized for the network device type. If there's a special route to be configured, the configuration settings get their own special file in this directory, with a name like route-eth0. That special route would specify the gateway to a remote network address/network mask pair. One example based on the systems described in Chapter 1 might include the following directive:

```
192.168.100.0/24 via 192.168.122.1
```

Network Configuration Tools

Red Hat includes several tools that can be used to configure network devices in RHEL 7. The first is the Network Manager command-line tool, **nmcli**. If you prefer a text-based graphical tool, **nmtui** can be started from a virtual terminal. As an alternative, the Network Manager Connections Editor is a GTK+ 3 application that you can start from a GUI command line with the **nm-connection-editor** command. The GNOME shell also includes a graphical utility that can be opened by clicking Applications | Sundry | Network Connections.

All the tools mentioned interact with Network Manager, a system service that is responsible for managing network devices.

The nmcli Configuration Tool

Network Manager can store different profiles, also known as *connections*, for the same network interface. This allows you to switch from one profile to another. For example, you may have a home profile and a work profile for a laptop Ethernet adapter and switch between the two depending on the network to which you are attached.

You can display all the configured connections in Network Manager by running the following command:

```
# nmcli con show
NAME   UUID                                   TYPE           DEVICE
eth0   394f6436-5524-4154-b26e-6649b4d29027   802-3-ethernet eth0
```

To show how **nmcli** can be used to set up a different connection profile, let's create a new connection for eth0:

```
# nmcli con add con-name "eth0-work" type ethernet ifname eth0
```

Then, a static IP address and default gateway can be configured, as shown here:

```
# nmcli con mod "eth0-work" ipv4.addresses ↵
"192.168.20.100/24 192.168.20.1"
```

You can run **nmcli con show** *connection-id* to display the current settings for a connection. Additional properties can be modified from the Network Manager command-line tool. For example, to add a DNS server to the eth-work connection, run

```
# nmcli con mod "eth0-work" +ipv4.dns 192.168.20.1
```

Finally, to switch to the new connection profile, run

```
# nmcli con up "eth0-work"
```

A connection can be prevented from starting automatically at boot with the following command:

```
# nmcli con mod "eth0-work" connection.autoconnect no
```

The nmtui Configuration Tool

As suggested by the name, this tool provides a text-based user interface and can be started from a command-line terminal. Just run the **nmtui** command. With a console tool, you'd need to press TAB to switch between options, and the SPACEBAR or the ENTER key to select the highlighted option.

Press the DOWN ARROW key until Quit is highlighted, and then press ENTER. For now, make a backup of the ifcfg-eth0 file from the /etc/sysconfig/network-scripts directory. Based on the **diff** command, Figure 3-11 compares the contents of an eth0 card that uses the DHCP protocol, as configured during the installation process, with a card that uses static IP addressing, configured with the **nmtui** tool.

The directives shown in Figure 3-11 are described in Table 3-7.

FIGURE 3-11

The differences
between static and
dynamic network
configuration

```
[root@server1 ~]# diff ifcfg-eth0 /etc/sysconfig/network-scripts/ifcfg-eth0
2c2
< BOOTPROTO=dhcp
---
> BOOTPROTO=none
8a9,13
> IPADDR0=192.168.122.50
> PREFIX0=24
> GATEWAY0=192.168.122.1
> DNS1=192.168.122.1
> DOMAIN=example.com
10,11d14
< PEERDNS=yes
< PEERROUTES=yes
[root@server1 ~]# █
```

TABLE 3-7   Network Configuration Directives in the /etc/sysconfig/network-scripts Directory

Directive	Description
DEVICE	Network device; eth0 is the first Ethernet network interface.
NAME	Name of the interface connection profile used by Network Manager.
UUID	Universal Unique Identifier for the device.
HWADDR	Hardware (MAC) address for the network device.
TYPE	Network type; should be set to "Ethernet" for an Ethernet device.
ONBOOT	Directive that specifies whether the network device is started during the boot process.
BOOTPROTO	May be set to "none" for static configuration or "dhcp" to acquire IP addresses from a DHCP server.
IPADDR0	Static IP address; additional IP addresses can be specified with the variables IPADDR1, IPADDR2, ...
PREFIX	Network mask in CIDR format (i.e., /24)
GATEWAY0	IP address of the default gateway.
DEFROUTE	Binary directive to set the interface as the default route.
DNS1	IP address of the first DNS server.
DOMAIN	Specifies the domain search list in /etc/resolv.conf.
PEERDNS	Binary directive allowing the modification of /etc/resolv.conf.
IPV6INIT	Binary directive that enables the use of IPv6 addressing.
USERCTL	Binary directive to allow users to control a network device.
IPV4_FAILURE_FATAL	Binary directive; if set to "no", when connecting to IPv6 networks, allows the IPv6 configuration to complete if the IPv4 configuration fails.

EXERCISE 3-2

Configure a Network Card

In this exercise, you'll configure the first Ethernet network card with the Network Manager text-based user interface tool. All you need is a command-line interface. It doesn't matter whether the command line is in the GUI or a virtual terminal. To configure a network card, take the following steps:

1. Back up a copy of the current configuration file for the first Ethernet card. Normally, it's ifcfg-eth0 in the /etc/sysconfig/network-scripts directory. For other interface names such as em1, substitute accordingly. (Hint: use the **cp** and not the **mv** command.)

2. Run the **nmtui** command.

3. In the menu that appears, Edit a Connection should be highlighted. If necessary, press the ARROW or TAB keys until it is. Then press ENTER.

4. In the screen that appears, the first Ethernet network card should be highlighted. When it is, press ENTER.

5. In the Edit Connection window shown here, the Automatic option may be selected under IPv4 Configuration. If so, highlight it and press ENTER; then select Manual.

6. Highlight the Show option at the right of IPv4 Configuration and press ENTER. This will expand the current IPv4 settings.

7. Enter the IP address information for the system. The settings shown in the window are based on the settings described in Chapter 1 for the server1.example.com system. When complete, highlight OK and press ENTER.

8. You're taken back to the device screen. Make sure Quit is highlighted and press ENTER.

9. Deactivate and then reactivate the first Ethernet card with the **ifdown eth0** and **ifup eth0** commands, and check the result with the **ip addr show eth0** and **ip route** commands. The configuration of the network card and the associated routing table should reflect the new settings.

10. To restore the original configuration, restore the ifcfg-eth0 file to the /etc/sysconfig/network-scripts directory and restart the network with the **systemctl restart network** command.

The Network Manager Connections Editor

Now you'll work with the default graphical network management tool for RHEL 7, the Network Manager Connections Editor tool. With the number of users on multiple network connections, the Network Manager is designed to make that switching between, say, a wireless and an Ethernet connection as seamless as possible. But that's something more applicable to portable systems, as opposed to servers. For our purposes, all you need to know is how to configure a network card with that tool.

The Network Manager Connections Editor is not really new, because it has been in use in Fedora for several years. It only runs in the GUI. To start it, you can run the **nm-connection-editor** command. This opens the Network Connections tool shown in Figure 3-12.

FIGURE 3-12

The Network Manager Connections Editor

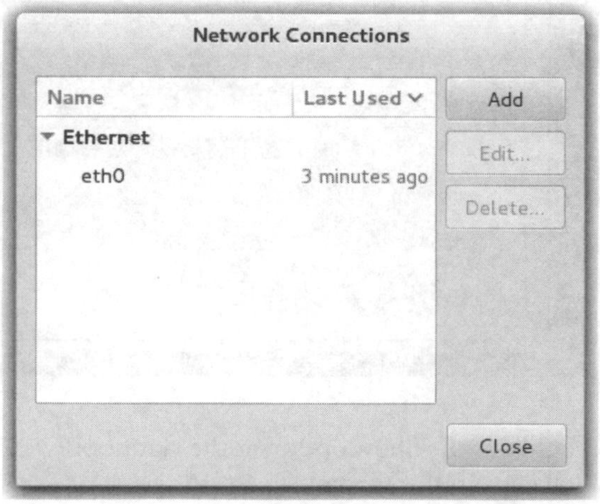

FIGURE 3-13

Editing an Ethernet
connection in the
Network Manager
Connections Editor

Editing eth0

Connection name: eth0

General | Ethernet | 802.1x Security | DCB | IPv4 Settings | IPv6 Settings

Method: Automatic (DHCP)

Addresses

Address	Netmask	Gateway	Add
			Delete

Additional DNS servers:

Additional search domains:

DHCP client ID:

☐ Require IPv4 addressing for this connection to complete

Routes...

Cancel | Save...

As you can see from the figure, the tool lists the connection profile for the first Ethernet
network interface. It also supports the configuration of other types of networks, including
wireless, mobile broadband cards (such as those used to connect to 3G and 4G networks),
and Digital Subscriber Line (DSL) connections. On a regular server, the focus is on reliable
connections, and that is still based on a standard wired Ethernet device.

Highlight the connection profile of the first Ethernet device (eth0) and click Edit; then
select the IPv4 Settings tab. It'll open the window shown in Figure 3-13. Unless previously
configured, it assumes that the network interface will receive its configuration settings from
a DHCP server.

Click the Method drop-down text box. Although it supports the configuration of a network
card in several different ways, the only one of interest in this case is Manual. Select that option,
and the Addresses section of the window should no longer be blanked out. Now add the

IP address information for the system. Based on the server1.example.com system described in Chapter 1, here are the appropriate options:

- **IP address** 192.168.122.50
- **Network mask** 255.255.255.0 (24 in CIDR notation is an acceptable equivalent in this field)
- **Gateway address** 192.168.122.1
- **DNS server** 192.168.122.1
- **Search domains** example.com
- **Require IPv4 Addressing for This Connection to Complete** Deselected

If properly entered, the configuration associated with the first Ethernet card is titled with the connection name listed in Figure 3-13. For that configuration, the settings are saved in the ifcfg-eth0 file in the /etc/sysconfig/network-scripts directory.

Configure Name Resolution

The final piece in network configuration is typically name resolution. In other words, does the local system have the information required to translate domain names such as mheducation.com to IP addresses such as 198.45.24.143?

Name resolution was easy when Unix was first being developed. When the predecessor to the Internet was first put into use, the worldwide computer network had four hosts, one computer at each of four different universities. It was easy to set up a static file with a list of each of their names and corresponding addresses. That file has evolved into what is known in Linux as /etc/hosts.

But now the Internet is more complex. Although you could try to set up a database of every domain name and IP address on the Internet in the /etc/hosts file, that would take almost forever and would not be a scalable solution. That's why most users set up connections to DNS (Domain Name Service) servers. On RHEL 7, that's still documented in the /etc/resolv.conf configuration file. As an RHCE, you need to know how to configure a caching-only DNS server; that subject is covered in Chapter 13. DNS server configuration is not an RHCSA requirement.

On smaller networks, some administrators set up the /etc/hosts file as a database for the name of each system and IP address on the local network. If desired, administrators could even set up a few IP addresses of domains on the Internet, although this setup would break if any of those Internet domains made DNS changes on their own.

But if you've configured a connection to a DNS server and systems in /etc/hosts, what's searched first? That's the purpose of the /etc/nsswitch.conf configuration file, which specifies the search order for various name-service databases, including hostnames.

Hostname Configuration Files

RHEL 7 includes at least four hostname configuration files of interest: /etc/hostname, /etc/hosts, /etc/resolv.conf, and /etc/nsswitch.conf. These four files, taken together, contain the local hostname, the local database of hostnames and IP addresses, the IP address of one or more DNS servers, and the order in which these databases are considered.

/etc/nsswitch.conf

The /etc/nsswitch.conf file specifies database search priorities for everything from authentication to name services. As the name server switch file, it includes the following entry, which determines what database is searched first:

```
hosts: files dns
```

When a system gets a request to search for a hostname such as outsider1.example.org, the preceding directive means the /etc/hosts file is searched first. If that name is not found in /etc/hosts, the next step is to search available configured DNS servers, normally using those configured in the /etc/resolv.conf file.

The resolver library also uses information in the /etc/host.conf file. The entry in this file is simply

```
multi on
```

which tells the system to return all IP addresses in /etc/hosts that are mapped to the same hostname, instead of returning only the first entry.

/etc/hosts

The /etc/hosts file is a static database of hostnames/FQDNs and IP addresses. It's suitable for small, relatively static networks. However, it can be a pain for networks where there are frequent changes. Every time a system is added or removed, you'll have to change this file—not only on the local system, but also on every other system on that network.

It's well suited to the local network systems created in Chapter 1. A simple version of the file might include the following entries:

```
127.0.0.1 localhost localhost.localdomain localhost4 localhost4.localdomain4
::1 localhost localhost.localdomain localhost6 localhost6.localdomain6
192.168.122.50 server1.example.com server1
192.168.122.150 tester1.example.com tester1
192.168.100.100 outsider1.example.org outsider1
```

In some cases, you may want to set up multiple entries for an IP address. For example, the following entries could be added to specify the IP addresses for web and FTP servers:

```
192.168.122.50 www.example.com
192.168.122.150 ftp.example.com
```

/etc/resolv.conf

The standard file for documenting the location of DNS servers is still /etc/resolv.conf. Typically, it'll have one or two entries, similar to the following:

```
search example.com
nameserver 192.168.122.1
```

The **search** directive appends the example.com domain name to searches for simple hostnames. The **nameserver** directive specifies the IP address of the configured DNS server. If in doubt about whether the DNS server is operational, run one of the following commands:

```
# dig @192.168.122.1 mheducation.com
# host mheducation.com 192.168.122.1
```

If needed, substitute the IP address associated with the **nameserver** directive in your /etc/resolv.conf file. You can specify up to three **nameserver** directives in this file.

on the **Job**

It may not be wise to edit the /etc/resolv.conf file directly. If you have configured DNS servers with another tool such as nmcli**, the Connections Editor, or with a DNS1 directive in a device configuration file, the Network Manager will overwrite any changes you make when directly editing that file unless you override this behavior with PEERDNS in the ifcfg file.**

Hostname Configuration Options

During the boot process, the network service looks to the /etc/hostname file to define the value of the local hostname. The hostname should be set as a FQDN such as tester1.example.com. As suggested earlier, it's a simple file, where the hostname is documented with a directive such as the following:

```
tester1.example.com
```

Of course, you can modify the value of the hostname with the **hostname** *newname* command. However, this change is only temporary and is not reflected in the /etc/hostname file. To make the change persistent, use the **hostnamectl set-hostname** *newname* command.

SCENARIO & SOLUTION	
Networking is down.	Check physical connections. Run **ip link show** to check active interfaces. Run the **systemctl status network** command.
Unable to access remote systems.	Use the **ping** and **traceroute** commands to test access to local and then remote IP addresses.
Current network settings lead to conflicts.	Check network device configuration in the /etc/sysconfig/network-scripts files. Review settings with the Network Manager Connections Editor.
Network settings not consistent.	Check network device configuration in the /etc/sysconfig/network-scripts files. Review settings with the Network Manager Connections Editor. The scenario suggests a desire for a static network configuration, so review accordingly.
Hostname is not recognized.	Review /etc/hostname, run the **hostname** command, and review /etc/hosts for consistency.
Remote hostnames not recognized.	Review /etc/hosts and /etc/nsswitch.conf. Check /etc/resolv.conf for an appropriate DNS server IP address. Run the **dig** command to test the DNS resolution.

CERTIFICATION SUMMARY

The focus of this chapter is two-fold. It covered the basic command-line tools formerly associated with Red Hat exam prerequisites. As those objectives have been incorporated into the main body of the RHCSA, they have been combined with network configuration to allow you to practice these command-line tools.

The command line starts with a shell, an interpreter that allows you to interact with the operating system using various commands. Although no shell is specified in the objectives, the default shell in most Linux distributions, including RHEL 7, is bash. You can start a command-line prompt at one of the default consoles or at a terminal in the GUI. At the bash prompt, you can manage the files and directories through which Linux is configured and organized. As Linux configuration files are by and large in text format, they can be set up, searched, and modified with a variety of commands. Linux text files can be analyzed as streams of data that can be interpreted and processed. To edit a text file, you need a text editor such as vim or gedit.

Documentation online within Linux is extensive. It starts with command switches such as **-h** and **--help**, which provide hints on what goes with a command. It continues with man and info pages. Many packages include extensive documentation files in the /usr/share/info directory. In many, perhaps most, cases, you do not need Internet access to find the hints needed.

Linux is inherently a network operating system. Network devices such as eth0 can be configured with both IPv4 and IPv6 addresses. Network review and configuration commands include **ip**, **ifup**, **ifdown**, and **dhclient**. Additional related commands include **ss**, **ping**, and **traceroute**. Associated configuration files start with /etc/sysconfig/network. Individual devices are configured in the /etc/sysconfig/network-scripts directory. Network devices can also be configured with the **nmcli** and **nmtui** commands at the console and the Network Manager Connections Editor.

✓ TWO-MINUTE DRILL

Here are some of the key points from the certification objectives in Chapter 3.

Shells

❑ The default Linux shell is bash.

❑ Six command-line virtual terminals are available by default; if the GUI is installed, it takes over the first virtual terminal.

❑ You can open multiple command-line terminals in the GUI.

❑ Shells work with three data streams: stdin, stdout, and stderr. To that end, command redirection means streams of data can be managed with operators such as >, >>, <, |, and 2>.

Standard Command-Line Tools

❑ Everything in Linux can be reduced to a file.

❑ Commands such as **pwd** and **cd** can help navigate directories.

❑ Concepts such as directory paths, the PATH, and the tilde (~) can help you understand and use commands at the shell.

❑ Basic commands allow you to find needed files and read file contents. These commands include **ls**, **find**, and **locate**.

❑ File creation (and deletion) commands include **touch**, **cp**, **ln**, **mv**, and **rm**; corresponding directory creation and deletion commands are **mkdir** and **rmdir**.

❑ Commands can be customized with the **alias** command.

The Management of Text Files

❑ Linux is managed through a series of text configuration files.

❑ Text files can be read as streams of data with commands such as **cat**, **less**, **more**, **head**, and **tail**.

❑ New files can be created, copied, moved, linked, and deleted with the **touch**, **cp**, **mv**, **ln**, and **rm** commands. Commands can be customized with the **alias** command.

❑ File filters such as the **sort**, **grep**, **wc**, **sed**, and **awk** commands support the processing of text streams.

❑ Understanding text editors is a critical skill. An earlier version of the RHCSA objectives specified the use of vim and gedit.

Local Online Documentation

❑ If you need a hint for a command, try it by itself; alternatively, try the **-h** and **--help** switches.

❑ Command man pages often include examples; **whatis** and **apropos** can search for man pages on different topics.

❑ If an info manual is available for a command or file, you'll find it in the /usr/share/info directory.

❑ Many packages include extensive documentation and examples in the /usr/share/doc directory.

A Networking Primer

❑ IPv4 addresses have 32 bits. There are five classes of IPv4 addresses and three different sets of private IPv4 addresses suitable for setting up TCP/IP on a private LAN.

❑ The subnet mask (also known as netmask or prefix) is used to find the network and host parts of an IP address.

❑ Tools such as **ping**, **traceroute**, **tracepath**, **ip**, and **ss** can help you diagnose problems on the LAN.

❑ Name resolution configuration files such as /etc/resolv.conf determine how a system finds the right IP address; the /etc/resolv.conf file may be configured from a DHCP server with the **dhclient** command or by Network Manager.

Network Configuration and Troubleshooting

❑ Individual network devices are configured in the /etc/sysconfig/network-scripts directory.

❑ Network configuration tools include the console-based **nmcli** and **nmtui** commands as well as the Network Manager Connections Editor.

❑ Name resolution configuration files include /etc/nsswitch.conf, /etc/hosts, and /etc/resolv.conf.

SELF TEST

The following questions will help you measure your understanding of the material presented in this chapter. As there are no multiple choice questions on the Red Hat exams, there are no multiple choice questions in this book. These questions exclusively test your understanding of the chapter. Getting results, not memorizing trivia, is what counts on the Red Hat exams.

Shells

1. What is the name of the default Linux shell?

   _____

2. From the GUI, what key combination moves to virtual console 3?

   _____

Standard Command-Line Tools

3. What single command creates the /abc/def/ghi/jkl series of directories?

   _____

4. What symbol represents the home directory of the current user?

   _____

The Management of Text Files

5. What command lists the last 10 lines of the /var/log/messages file?

   _____

6. What command returns lines with the term Linux from the /var/log/dmesg file?

   _____

Local Online Documentation

7. What command searches the database of man pages for manuals that reference the **passwd** command and configuration file?

_____

8. If there are man pages for the hypothetical **abcde** command and file, in sections 5 and 8, type in the command that is sure to call up the man pages from section 5.

_____

A Networking Primer

9. In IPv4 addressing, with a network address of 192.168.100.0 and a broadcast address of 192.168.100.255, what is the range of assignable IP addresses?

_____

10. Given the addresses described in Question 9, what command assigns IPv4 address 192.168.100.100 to network device eth0?

_____

Network Configuration and Troubleshooting

11. What is the full path to the configuration file with the hostname of the local system?

_____

12. What is the default full path to the configuration file associated with the eth0 Ethernet adapter for the local system?

_____

LAB QUESTIONS

Several of these labs involve configuration exercises. You should do these exercises on test machines only. It's assumed that you're running these exercises on virtual machines such as KVM.

Red Hat presents its exams electronically. For that reason, the labs in this and future chapters are available from the DVD that accompanies the book in the Chapter3/ subdirectory in .doc, .html, and .txt formats. In case you haven't yet set up RHEL 7 on a system, refer to Chapter 1 for installation instructions.

The answers for each lab follow the Self Test answers for the fill-in-the-blank questions.

SELF TEST ANSWERS

Shells

1. The default Linux shell is bash, also known as the Bourne-Again shell.

2. From the GUI, the key combination that moves to virtual console 3 is CTRL-ALT-F3.

Standard Command-Line Tools

3. The single command that creates the /abc/def/ghi/jkl series of directories is **mkdir -p /abc/def/ghi/jkl**.

4. The symbol that represents the home directory of the current user is the tilde (~).

The Management of Text Files

5. The command that lists the last 10 lines of the /var/log/messages file is **tail -n 10 /var/log/messages**. Because 10 lines is the default, **tail /var/log/messages** is also acceptable.

6. The command that returns lines with the term Linux from the /var/log/dmesg file is **grep Linux /var/log/dmesg**. Other variations are acceptable, such as **cat /var/log/dmesg | grep Linux**.

Local Online Documentation

7. The command that searches the database of man pages for manuals that reference the **passwd** command and configuration file is **whatis passwd**. The **apropos** and **man -k** commands go further because they list man pages with the text "passwd" in the command or the description.

8. The command that calls up the man page from section 5 for the hypothetical **abcde** command and file is **man 5 abcde**.

A Networking Primer

9. The range of assignable IP addresses in the noted IPv4 network is 192.168.100.1 through 192.168.100.254.

10. Given the addresses described in Question 9, the command that assigns IPv4 address 192.168.100.100 to network device eth0 is **ip addr add 192.168.100.100/24 dev eth0**.

Network Configuration and Troubleshooting

11. The full path to the configuration file with the hostname of the local system is /etc/hostname.

12. The full path to the configuration file associated with the first Ethernet adapter for the local system is /etc/sysconfig/network-scripts/ifcfg-eth0. If you use different connection profiles in Network Manager, you would find a file for each connection profile within the /etc/sysconfig/network-scripts directory.

LAB ANSWERS

Lab 1

This lab tested the situation where networking was deactivated with the most innocuous of settings, the NETWORKING directive in the /etc/sysconfig/network file. When set to no, that setting deactivates networking on a system. Nothing else is changed; the IP address information for specific network cards is still correct. Sure, you could still activate networking through other means, but if **NETWORKING=no** is in the noted file, such changes would not survive a reboot.

The script used in this lab saved the original copy of /etc/sysconfig/network in the /root/backup directory. Now that the lab is complete, you may restore that file to its original location. Be aware, the immutable flag has been applied to the copied file; to delete it from the /root/backup directory, you'd first have to remove the immutable flag with the **chattr -i** command.

Lab 2

This lab sets up an invalid IP address configuration for the first Ethernet adapter, eth0. The standard for the systems configured in Chapter 1 is based on the 192.168.122.0/24 network. The configuration file in the /etc/sysconfig/network-scripts directory may go by a slightly different name, depending on how that adapter was configured. The original file from that directory was moved to the /root/backup directory. If your efforts in re-creating that configuration file fail, restore the original configuration file from that /root/backup directory.

Be aware, the immutable flag has been applied to the copied file; to delete it from the /root/backup directory, you'd first have to remove the immutable flag with the **chattr -i** command. In fact, before Lab 3 works, you'll have to run the following command:

```
# chattr -i /root/backup/*
```

Lab 3

This lab deactivates the first Ethernet device on the system and works if that device has the default eth0 device filename.

Lab 4

In this lab, you set up the /etc/hosts file on each of the systems described in Chapter 1. Except for the local system settings added by the Network Manager, the data in /etc/hosts on all three systems may be identical. Specifically, that file should include the following entries:

```
192.168.122.50   server1.example.com server1
192.168.122.150  tester1.example.com tester1
192.168.100.100  outsider1.example.org outsider1
```

It doesn't matter that the systems are on different IP networks. As long as there's a routing path between systems, the data in each /etc/hosts file will work. Also, duplication with data inserted by the Network Manager is not a problem, as long as the data is consistent. In fact, it's possible to set up multiple names for an IP address; for example, if we set up a web server on the 192.168.122.50 system, we could add the following entry to /etc/hosts:

```
192.168.122.50   www.example.com
```

Labs 5 and 6

Be sure to learn the common settings associated with directives in the configuration file, such as HWADDR, BOOTPROTO, and DNS1.

Chapter 4

RHCSA-Level
Security Options

L inux security starts with a concept known as discretionary access control (DAC). This includes the permissions and ownership associated with files and directories. With specialized bits, including access control lists (ACLs), permissions can be more granular than the simple user/group/other categories. These ACLs support permissions given to specific users or groups, overriding standard permissions and allowing more fine-grained access rules for a given file or directory.

Also in the realm of security is the firewall. In this chapter, you'll examine both the iptables service (which was the default firewall in RHEL 6) and the new firewalld daemon, which provides support for different trust zones. You will learn how to allow or block services through firewalld using the **firewall-config** graphical utility and the **firewall-cmd** command tool.

A service that is installed on most Linux systems is SSH. As it is a very common service for logging in to a machine, "black hat" hackers everywhere want to find a weakness in SSH. So this chapter also describes how you can improve security by using key-based authentication for SSH.

Further protection can be provided by a different kind of security known as mandatory access control (MAC). The RHEL 7 MAC implementation is known as Security-Enhanced Linux (SELinux). Red Hat expects you to work with SELinux enabled during exams. In this chapter, you will examine how to set enforcing modes, change file contexts, use boolean settings, and diagnose SELinux policy violations.

If you're starting with the default installation created during the installation process, you may need to install additional packages during this chapter. If a remote repository is available, take the name of the package and apply the **yum install** command to it. For example, to review the GUI-based firewall configuration tool, you'll need to install it with the following command:

```
# yum install firewall-config
```

For more information on the package install process, see Chapter 7.

INSIDE THE EXAM

Basic File Permissions

Security in Linux starts with the permissions given to files. As everything in Linux can be defined as a file, it's an excellent start. In any case, the related objectives, once understood, are fairly straightforward:

- List, set, and change standard ugo/rwx permissions
- Diagnose and correct file permissions problems

Standard permissions for Linux files are defined for users, groups, and others, which leads to the *ugo*. Those permissions are read, write, and execute, which define the *rwx*. Such permissions are defined as discretionary access control, to contrast with the mandatory access control system known as SELinux, also discussed in this chapter.

Access Control Lists

ACLs can be configured to override and extend basic file permissions. For example, with ACLs, you can set up a file in your home directory that can be read by a limited number of other users and groups. The related RHCSA objective is

 Create and manage access control lists (ACLs)

Firewall Control

As configured in Linux, a firewall can block traffic on all but a few network ports. It also can be used to regulate traffic in a number of other ways, but that is the province of the RHCE exam. The related RHCSA objective is

- Configure firewall settings using firewall-config, firewall-cmd, or iptables

The Secure Shell Server

As suggested in the introduction, there's a special focus on the SSH service. The related RHCSA objective is

- Configure key-based authentication for SSH

With key-based authentication, you'll be able to log in to remote systems by using private/public key pairs. Password transmission over the network would no longer be required. The 1024 or more bits associated with such authentication are a lot harder to crack than a password transmitted over a network.

Security-Enhanced Linux

There's no way around it. On the Red Hat exams, you're expected to work with SELinux.

It's not clear whether you can even pass the Red Hat exams unless at least some services are configured with SELinux in mind. To help exam candidates understand what's needed, Red Hat has broken down SELinux-related objectives. The first objective is fundamental to SELinux, as it relates to the three modes available for SELinux on a system (enforcing /permissive/disabled):

- Set enforcing and permissive modes for SELinux

The next objective requires that you understand the SELinux contexts defined for different files and processes. Although the associated commands are straightforward, the available contexts are as broad as the number of services available on Linux:

- List and identify SELinux file and process contexts

As you experiment with different SELinux contexts, mistakes happen. You may not remember the default contexts associated with important directories. But with the right commands, you don't have to remember everything; as suggested by the following objective, it's relatively easy to restore the default:

- Restore default file contexts

The next objective may seem complex. But the boolean settings associated with SELinux have descriptive names. Excellent tools are available to further clarify the boolean contexts that are available. In essence, this means that to run a certain service under SELinux, all you need to do is turn on one or more

(Continued)

boolean settings (rather than having to modify the SELinux policy rules directly):

■ Use boolean settings to modify system SELinux settings

Once SELinux is operational, you should monitor the system for policy violations. A violation may be the result of a misconfiguration or an unauthorized intrusion attempt. Hence, to get the most out of SELinux, you should know how to audit for policy violations and be able to address common problems. The related RHCSA objective is

■ Diagnose and address routine SELinux policy violations

CERTIFICATION OBJECTIVE 4.01

Basic File Permissions

The basic security of a Linux computer is based on file permissions. Default file permissions are set through the **umask** command. Special permissions can be configured to give all users and/or groups additional privileges. These are known as the super user ID (SUID), super group ID (SGID), and sticky permission bits. Ownership is based on the default user and group IDs of the person who created a file. The management of permissions and ownership involves commands such as **chmod**, **chown**, and **chgrp**. Before exploring these commands, it's important to understand the permissions and ownership associated with a file.

File Permissions and Ownership

Linux file permissions and ownership are straightforward. As suggested by the related RHCSA objective, they're read, write, and execute, classified by the user, the group, and all other users. However, the effect of permissions on directories is more subtle. Table 4-1 shows the exact meaning of each permission bit.

TABLE 4-1			
Permissions on Files and Directories	**Permission**	**On a File**	**On a Directory**
	read (r)	Permission to read the file	Permission to list the contents of the directory
	write (w)	Permission to write (change) the file	Permission to create and remove files in a directory
	execute (x)	Permission to run the file as a program	Permission to access the files in the directory

Position	Description
1	Type of file; - = regular file, *d* = directory, *b* = device, *l* = symbolic link
234	Permissions granted to the owner of the file
567	Permissions granted to the group owner of the file
890	Permissions granted to all other users on the Linux system

TABLE 4-2

Description of File Permissions

Consider the following output from **ls -l /sbin/fdisk**:

```
-rwxr-xr-x. 1 root root 182424 Mar 28  2014 /sbin/fdisk
```

The permissions are shown on the left side of the listing. Ten characters are shown. The first character determines whether it's a regular or a special file. The remaining nine characters are grouped in threes, applicable to the file owner (user), the group owner, and everyone else on that Linux system. The letters are straightforward: *r* = read, *w* = write, *x* = execute. These permissions are described in Table 4-2.

It's common for the user and group owners of a file to have the same name. In this case, the root user is a member of the root group. But they don't have to have the same name. For example, directories designed for collaboration between users may be owned by a special group. As discussed in Chapter 8, that involves groups with several regular users as members.

Keep in mind that permissions granted to the group take precedence over permissions granted to all other users. Similarly, permissions granted to the owner take precedence over all other permissions categories. Thus, in the following example, although everyone else has full permissions to the file, the members of the group "mike" have not been granted any permissions, and as such they won't be able to read, modify, or execute the file:

```
$ ls -l setup.sh
-rwx---rwx. 1 root mike 127 Dec 13 07:21 setup.sh
```

There's a relatively new element with permissions—and it's subtle. Notice the dot after the last x in the output to the **ls -l setup.sh** command? It specifies that the file has a SELinux security context. If you've configured ACL permissions on a file, that dot is replaced by a plus sign (+). But that symbol doesn't override SELinux control.

You need to consider another type of permission: the special permission bits. Not only are these the SUID and SGID bits, but also another special permission known as the sticky bit. The effects of the special permission bits on files and directories are shown in Table 4-3.

An example of the SUID bit is associated with the **passwd** command in the /usr/bin directory. The **ls -l** command on that file leads to the following output:

```
-rwsr-xr-x. 1 root root 27832 Jan 30 2014 /usr/bin/passwd
```

TABLE 4-3	Special Permission Bits	
Special Permission	**On an Executable File**	**On a Directory**
SUID	When the file is executed, the effective user ID of the process is that of the file.	No effect.
SGID	When the file is executed, the effective group ID of the process is that of the file.	Give files created in the directory the same group ownership as that of the directory.
Sticky bit	No effect.	Files in a directory can be renamed or removed only by their owners.

The **s** in the execute bit for the user owner of the file is the SUID bit. It means the file can be executed by other users with the authority of the file owner, the root administrative user. But that doesn't mean that any user can change other user's passwords. Access to the **passwd** command is further regulated by Pluggable Authentication Modules (PAM), as described in Chapter 10. This is an RHCE skill. An example of the SGID bit can be found with the **ssh-agent** command, also in the /usr/bin directory. It has the SGID bit to properly store passphrases. The **ls -l** command on that file displays the following output:

```
---x--s--x. 1 root nobody 145312 Mar 19  2014 /usr/bin/ssh-agent
```

The **s** in the execute bit for the group owner of the file (group nobody) is the SGID bit.

Finally, an example of the sticky bit can be found in the permissions of the /tmp directory. It means that users can copy their files to that directory, but no one else can remove those files, apart from their respective owners (which is the "sticky"). The **ls -ld** command on that directory shows the following output:

```
drwxrwxrwt. 22 root root 4096 Dec 15 17:15 /tmp
```

The **t** in the execute bit for other users is the sticky bit. Note that without the sticky bit, everyone will be able to remove everyone else's files in /tmp because write permissions have been granted to all users on that directory.

The Loophole in Write Permissions

It's easy to remove write permissions from a file. For example, if you wanted to make the license.txt file "read-only," the following command removes write permissions from that file:

```
$ chmod a-w license.txt
```

The user who owns the file can still make changes, however. It won't work in GUI text editors such as gedit. It won't even work in the nano text editor. But if a change is made in the vi text editor, the user who owns that file can override a lack of write permissions with the bang character, which looks like an exclamation point (!). In other words, while in the vi editor, the user who owns the file can run the following command to override the lack of write permissions:

```
w!
```

Although this may seem surprising, in practice the **w!** command of the vi editor is not bypassing the Linux file permission system. The **w!** command overwrites a file—that is, it deletes the existing file and creates a new one with the same name. As you can see from Table 4-1, the permission bit that grants the privilege to create and delete files is the write permission on the parent directory, not the write permission on the file itself. Hence, if a user has write permission on a directory, she can overwrite the files in it, regardless of the write permission bits set on files.

Commands to Change Permissions and Ownership

Key commands that can help you manage the permissions and ownership of a file are **chmod**, **chown**, and **chgrp**. In the following subsections, you'll examine how to use those commands to change permissions along with the user and group that owns a specific file, or even a series of files.

One tip that can help you change the permissions on a series of files is to use the **-R** switch. It is the recursive switch for all three of these commands. In other words, if you specify the **-R** switch with any of the noted commands on a directory, it applies the changes recursively. The changes are applied to all files in that directory, including all subdirectories. *Recursion* means that the changes are also applied to files in each subdirectory, and so on.

The chmod Command

The **chmod** command uses the numeric value of permissions associated with the owner, group, and others. In Linux, permissions are assigned the following numeric values: $r = 4$, $w = 2$, and $x = 1$. In numerical format, permissions are represented by an octal number, where each digit is associated with a different group of permissions. For example, the permission number 640 means that the owner is assigned permission 6 (read and write), whereas the group has permission 4 (read), and everyone else has no permissions. The **chown** and **chgrp** commands adjust the user and group owners associated with the cited file.

The **chmod** command is flexible. You don't always have to use numbers. For example, the following command sets execute permissions for the user owner of the Ch3Lab1 file:

```
# chmod u+x Ch3Lab1
```

Note how the **u** and the **x** follow the ugo/rwx format specified in the associated RHCSA objective. To interpret, this command adds (with the plus sign) for the user owner of the file (with the **u**) execute permissions (with the **x**).

These symbols can be combined. For example, the following command disables (with the minus sign) write permissions (with the **w**) for the group owner (with the **g**) and all other users (with the **o**) on the local file named special:

```
# chmod go-w special
```

Rather than adding or removing permissions with the + and – operators, you can set the exact mode of a permission group using the equal operator (=). As an example, the following command changes the group permissions of the file named special to read and write, and clears the execute permission if it was set:

```
# chmod g=rw special
```

While you can use all three group permission types in the **chmod** command, it's not necessary. As described in the labs in Chapter 3, the following command makes the noted file executable by all users:

```
# chmod +x Ch3Lab2
```

For the SUID, SGID, and sticky bits, some special options are available. If you choose to use numeric bits, those special bits are assigned numeric values as well, where SUID = 4, SGID = 2, and sticky bit = 1. For example, the following command configures the SUID bit (with the first "4" digit in permission mode). It includes rwx permissions for the user owner (with the "7"), rw permissions for the group owner (with the "6"), and r permission for other users (with the last "4") on the file named testfile:

```
# chmod 4764 testfile
```

If you'd rather use the ugo/rwx format, the following command activates the SGID bit for the local testscript file:

```
# chmod g+s testscript
```

And the following command turns on the sticky bit for the /test directory:

```
# chmod o+t /test
```

For the **chmod** command, changes don't have to be made by the root administrative user. The user owner of a file is allowed to change the permissions associated with her files.

The chown Command

The **chown** command can be used to modify the user who owns a file. For example, take a look at the ownership for the first figure that we created for this chapter, based on the **ls -l** command:

```
-rw-r--r--. 1 michael examprep 855502 Oct 25 14:07 F04-01.tif
```

The user owner of this file is michael; the group owner of this file is examprep. The following **chown** command changes the user owner to user elizabeth:

```
# chown elizabeth F04-01.tif
```

You can do more with **chown**; for example, the following command changes both the user and group owner of the noted file to user donna and group supervisors, assuming that user and group already exists:

```
# chown donna.supervisors F04-01.tif
```

Only the root administrative user can change the user owner of a file, whereas group ownership can be modified by root and also by the user who owns the file.

The chgrp Command

You can change the group owner of a file with the **chgrp** command. For example, the following command changes the group owner of the noted F04-01.tif file to the group named project (assuming it exists):

```
# chgrp project F04-01.tif
```

Special File Attributes

Just beyond regular rwx/ugo permissions are file attributes. Such attributes can help you control what anyone can do with different files. Whereas the **lsattr** command lists current file attributes, the **chattr** command can help you change those attributes. For example, the following command protects /etc/fstab from accidental deletion, even by the root administrative user:

```
# chattr +i /etc/fstab
```

With that attribute, if you try to delete the file as the root administrative user, you'll get the following response:

```
# rm /etc/fstab
rm: remove regular file '/etc/fstab'? y
rm: cannot remove '/etc/fstab': Operation not permitted
```

The **lsattr** command shows an active immutable attribute on /etc/fstab:

```
# lsattr /etc/fstab
----i----------- /etc/fstab
```

Of course, the root administrative user can unset that attribute with the following command. Nevertheless, the initial refusal to delete the file should at least give pause to that administrator before changes are made:

```
# chattr -i /etc/fstab
```

TABLE 4-4	Attribute	Description
File Attributes	append only (**a**)	Prevents deletion, but allows appending to a file—for example, if you've run **chattr +a tester**, **cat /etc/fstab >> tester** would add the contents of /etc/fstab to the end of the tester file. However, the command **cat /etc/fstab > tester** would fail.
	no dump (**d**)	Disallows backups of the configured file with the **dump** command.
	extent format (**e**)	Set with the ext4 filesystem; an attribute that may not be removed.
	immutable (**i**)	Prevents deletion or any other kind of change to a file.

Several key attributes are described in Table 4-4. Other attributes, such as **c** (compressed), **s** (secure deletion), and **u** (undeletable), don't work for files stored in the ext4 and XFS filesystems. The extent format attribute is associated with ext4 systems.

Basic User and Group Concepts

Linux, like Unix, is configured with users and groups. Everyone who uses Linux is set up with a username, even if it's just "guest." There's even a standard user named "nobody." Take a look at /etc/passwd. One version of this file is shown in Figure 4-1.

As shown, all kinds of usernames are listed in the /etc/passwd file. Even a number of Linux services such as mail, news, ftp, and apache have their own usernames. In any case,

FIGURE 4-1

The /etc/passwd file

```
rpcuser:x:29:29:RPC Service User:/var/lib/nfs:/sbin/nologin
nfsnobody:x:65534:65534:Anonymous NFS User:/var/lib/nfs:/sbin/nologin
named:x:25:25:Named:/var/named:/sbin/nologin
oprofile:x:16:16:Special user account to be used by OProfile:/var/lib/oprofile:/
sbin/nologin
tcpdump:x:72:72::/:/sbin/nologin
usbmuxd:x:113:113:usbmuxd user:/:/sbin/nologin
colord:x:998:996:User for colord:/var/lib/colord:/sbin/nologin
abrt:x:173:173::/etc/abrt:/sbin/nologin
chrony:x:997:995::/var/lib/chrony:/sbin/nologin
libstoragemgmt:x:996:994:daemon account for libstoragemgmt:/var/run/lsm:/sbin/no
login
qemu:x:107:107:qemu user:/:/sbin/nologin
radvd:x:75:75:radvd user:/:/sbin/nologin
rtkit:x:172:172:RealtimeKit:/proc:/sbin/nologin
saslauth:x:995:76:"Saslauthd user":/run/saslauthd:/sbin/nologin
ntp:x:38:38::/etc/ntp:/sbin/nologin
unbound:x:994:993:Unbound DNS resolver:/etc/unbound:/sbin/nologin
pulse:x:171:171:PulseAudio System Daemon:/var/run/pulse:/sbin/nologin
gdm:x:42:42::/var/lib/gdm:/sbin/nologin
gnome-initial-setup:x:993:991::/run/gnome-initial-setup/:/sbin/nologin
alex:x:1000:1000:Alessandro Orsaria:/home/alex:/bin/bash
michael:x:1001:1001:Michael Jang:/home/michael:/bin/bash
```

the /etc/passwd file follows a specific format, described in more detail in Chapter 8. For now, note that the only regular users shown in this file are alex and michael; their user IDs (UID) and group IDs (GID) are, respectively, 1000 and 1001; and their home directories match their usernames. The next user gets UID and GID 1002, and so on.

This matching of UIDs and GIDs is based on the Red Hat user private group scheme. Now run the **ls -l /home** command. The output should be similar to the following:

```
drwx------. 4 alex    alex     4096 Dec 15 16:12 alex
drwx------. 4 michael michael  4096 Dec 16 14:00 michael
```

Pay attention to the permissions. Based on the rwx/ugo concepts described earlier in this chapter, only the named user owner has access to the files in his or her home directory.

The umask

The way **umask** works in Red Hat Enterprise Linux may be surprising, especially if you're coming from a different Unix-style environment. You cannot configure **umask** to allow the automatic creation of new files with executable permissions. This promotes security: if fewer files have executable permissions, fewer files are available for a "black hat" hacker to use to run programs to break through your system.

Every time you create a new file, the default permissions are based on the value of **umask**. When you type the **umask** command, the command returns a four-digit octal number such as 0002. If a bit of the umask is set, then the corresponding permission is disabled in newly created files and directories. As an example, a umask of 0245 would cause newly created directories to have 0532 octal permissions, which is equivalent to the following permission string

```
r-x-wx-w-.
```

In the past, the value of **umask** affected the value of all permissions on a file. For example, if the value of **umask** was 000, the default permissions for any file created by that user were once 777 − 000 = 777, which corresponds to read, write, and execute permissions for all users. They're now 666, since regular new files can no longer get executable permissions. Directories, on the other hand, require executable permissions so that any file contained therein can be accessed.

The Default umask

With that in mind, the default **umask** is driven by the /etc/profile and /etc/bashrc files, specifically the following stanza, which drives a value for **umask** depending on the value of the UID:

```
if [ $UID -gt 199 ] && [ "`id -gn`" = "`id -un`" ]; then
    umask 002
else
    umask 022
fi
```

In other words, the **umask** for user accounts with UIDs of 200 and above is 002. In contrast, the **umask** for UIDs below 200 is 022. In RHEL 7, service users such as adm, postfix, and apache have lower UIDs; this affects primarily the permissions of the log files created for such services. Of course, the root administrative user has the lowest UID of 0. By default, files created for such users have 644 permissions; directories created for such users have 755 permissions.

In contrast, regular users have a UID of 1000 and above. Files created by such users normally have 664 permissions. Directories created by such users normally have 775 permissions. Users can override the default settings by appending an **umask** command in their ~/.bashrc or ~/.bash_profile.

CERTIFICATION OBJECTIVE 4.02

Access Control Lists and More

There was a time when users had read access to the files of all other users. By default, however, users have permissions only in their own directories. With ACLs, you can give selected users read, write, and execute permissions to selected files in your home directory. This provides a second level of discretionary access control, a method that supports overriding of standard ugo/rwx permissions.

Strictly speaking, regular ugo/rwx permissions are the first level of discretionary access control. In other words, ACLs start with the ownership and permissions described earlier in this chapter. You'll see how that's displayed with ACL commands shortly.

To configure ACLs, you'll need to mount the appropriate filesystem with the **acl** option. Next, you'll need to set up execute permissions on the associated directories. Only then can you configure ACLs with desired permissions for appropriate users.

ACLs are supported on ext4 and XFS filesystems, as well as on the Network File System (NFS) version 4.

The getfacl Command

Assuming the acl package is installed, you should have access to the **getfacl** command, which displays the current ACLs of a file. For example, the following command displays the current permissions and ACLs for the anaconda-ks.cfg file in the /root directory:

```
[root@server1 ~]# getfacl anaconda-ks.cfg
# file: anaconda-ks.cfg
# owner: root
```

```
# group: root
user::rw-
group::---
other::---
```

Run the **ls -l /root/anaconda-ks.cfg** command. You should recognize every element of the output shown here: as no ACLs are set in the anaconda-ks.cfg file, the **getfacl** command displays only standard permissions and ownership. The ACLs that you'll add shortly are over and above the permissions shown here. But first, you may need to make a filesystem friendly to that second level of ACLs.

Make a Filesystem ACL Friendly

RHEL 7 uses the XFS filesystem. When you create an XFS or an ext2/ext3/ext4 filesystem on RHEL 7, ACLs are enabled by default. On the other hand, ext2, ext3, and ext4 filesystems created on older versions of Red Hat may not automatically have ACL support enabled.

To verify whether an ext2/ext3/ext4 filesystem has the acl **mount option enabled by default on a partition device such as /dev/sda1, run the command** tune2fs -l /dev/sda1**. Remember, XFS filesystems and all ext filesystems created on RHEL 7 have ACL support enabled by default. Hence, mounting a filesystem with the acl option would be required only on ext filesystems created on older versions of Red Hat Enterprise Linux or on ext2/ext3/ext4 filesystems where the** acl **option has been explicitly removed.**

If you want to enable ACL support on a filesystem that does not have the **acl** mount option configured, you can remount the existing partition appropriately. For example, we can remount the /home partition with ACL using the following command:

```
# mount -o remount -o acl /home
```

To make sure this is the way /home is mounted on the next reboot, edit /etc/fstab. Based on the previous command, the associated line might read as follows if /home is formatted with ext4:

```
/dev/sda3     /home     ext4     defaults,acl     1,2
```

Once the change is made to /etc/fstab, you can activate it with the following command:

```
# mount -o remount /home
```

To confirm that the /home directory is mounted with the **acl** option, run the **mount** command alone, without switches or options. You should see **acl** in the output, similar to what's shown here:

```
/dev/sda3 on /home type ext4 (rw,acl)
```

Now you can start working with ACL commands to set access control lists on desired files and directories.

Manage ACLs on a File

Now with a properly mounted filesystem and appropriate permissions, you can manage ACLs on a system. To review the current ACLs, run the **getfacl** *filename* command. For this example, we've created a text file named TheAnswers in the /home/examprep directory. The following is the output from the **getfacl /home/examprep/TheAnswers** command:

```
# file home/examprep/TheAnswers
# owner: examprep
# group: proctors
user::rw-
group::r--
other::---
```

Note that the file TheAnswers is owned by user examprep and group proctors. That user owner has read and write permissions; that group owner has read permissions to that file. In other words, whereas the examprep user can read and change this file, user members of the proctors group can read it.

Now if you were the examprep user or the root user on this system, you could assign ACLs for the file named TheAnswers for me (user michael) with the **setfacl** command. For example, the following command gives michael read, write, and execute permissions to that file:

```
# setfacl -m u:michael:rwx /home/examprep/TheAnswers
```

This command modifies the ACLs for the noted file, modifying (**-m**) the ACLs for user michael, giving that user read, write, and execute permissions to that file. To confirm, run the **getfacl** command on that file, as shown in Figure 4-2.

FIGURE 4-2

The ACLs of a file

```
[root@server1 ~]# getfacl /home/examprep/TheAnswers
getfacl: Removing leading '/' from absolute path names
# file: home/examprep/TheAnswers
# owner: examprep
# group: examprep
user::rw-
user:michael:rwx
group::r--
mask::rwx
other::r--

[root@server1 ~]#
```

But when we tried to access that file from michael's user account, it didn't work. Actually, if we try to access the file with the vi text editor, it suggests that /home/examprep/ TheAnswers is a new file. Then it refuses to save any changes we might make to that file.

Before files from the /home/examprep directory are accessible, the administrative user will need to either change the permissions or the ACL settings associated with that directory. Before we get to modifying discretionary access controls on a directory, let's explore some different **setfacl** command options.

Despite the name, the **setfacl** command can be used to remove such ACL privileges with the **-x** switch. For example, the following command deletes the previously configured rwx permissions for user michael:

```
# setfacl -x u:michael /home/examprep/TheAnswers
```

In addition, the **setfacl** command can be used with groups; for example, if the teachers group exists, the following command would give read privileges to users who are members of that group:

```
# setfacl -m g:teachers:r /home/examprep/TheAnswers
```

You can also use the **setfacl** command to remove all permissions from a named user. For example, the following command denies access to the /home/examprep directory for the user michael:

```
# setfacl -m u:michael:- /home/examprep
```

If you want to see how ACLs work, don't remove the ACL privileges on the TheAnswers file, at least not yet. Alternatively, if you want to start over, the following command, with the **-b** switch, removes all ACL entries on the noted file:

```
# setfacl -b /home/examprep/TheAnswers
```

Some of the switches available for the **setfacl** command are shown in Table 4-5.

	Switch	Description
TABLE 4-5 Description of File Permissions	-b (--remove-all)	Removes all ACL entries; retains standard ugo/rwx permissions
	-k	Deletes default ACL entries
	-m	Modifies the ACL of a file, normally with a specific user (u) or group (g)
	-n (--mask)	Omits the recalculation of the mask entry
	-R	Applies changes recursively
	-x	Removes a specific ACL entry

One slightly dangerous option relates to other users. For example, the command

```
# setfacl -m o:rwx /home/examprep/TheAnswers
```

allows other users read, write, and execute permissions for the TheAnswers file. It does so by changing the primary permissions for the file, as shown in the output to the **ls -l /home/examprep/TheAnswers** command. The **-b** and the **-x** switches don't remove such changes; you'd have to use the following command:

```
# setfacl -m o:- /home/examprep/TheAnswers
```

Configure a Directory for ACLs

There are several ways to set up a directory for file sharing with ACLs. First, you could set the regular execute bit for all other users. One way to do so on the noted directory is with the following command:

```
# chmod 701 /home/examprep
```

It is a minimal way to provide access to files in a directory. Users other than examprep and root can't list the files in that directory. They have to know that the file TheAnswers actually exists to access that file.

However, with the execute bit set for other users, any user can access files in the /home/examprep directory for which she has permission. That should raise a security flag. Any user? Even though the file is hidden, do you ever want to give real privileges to anything to all users? Sure, ACLs have been set for only the TheAnswers file in that /home/examprep directory, but that's one layer of security that you've taken down voluntarily.

The right approach is to apply the **setfacl** command to the /home/examprep directory. The safest way to set up sharing is to set ACL execute permissions just for the user michael account on the noted directory, with the following command:

```
# setfacl -m u:michael:x /home/examprep
```

As the examprep user is the owner of the /home/examprep directory, that user can also run the noted **setfacl** command.

Sometimes, you may want to apply such ACLs to all files in a directory. In that case, the **-R** switch can be used to apply changes recursively; for example, the following command allows user michael to have read and execute permissions on all files in the /home/examprep directory as well as any subdirectories that may exist:

```
# setfacl -R -m u:michael:rx /home/examprep
```

There are two methods available to unset these options. First, you could apply the **-x** switch to the previous command, omitting the permission settings:

```
# setfacl -R -x u:michael /home/examprep
```

Alternatively, you could use the **-b** switch; however, that would erase the ACLs configured for all users on the noted directory (and with the **-R** switch, applicable subdirectories):

```
# setfacl -R -b /home/examprep
```

Configure Default ACLs

Directories can also contain one or more *default* ACLs. The concept of a default ACL is similar to a regular ACL entry, with the difference that a default ACL does not have any effect on the current directory permissions, but it is inherited by the files created within the directory.

As an example, if you want all new files and directories in /home/examprep to inherit an ACL that grants read and execute permissions to the user michael, you can run the following command:

```
# setfacl -d -m u:michael:rx /home/examprep
```

The **-d** option in the preceding command specifies that the current operation applies to a default ACL. The **getfacl** command can display standard and default ACLs on the noted directory:

```
# getfacl /home/examprep
getfacl: Removing leading '/' from absolute path names
# file: home/examprep
# owner: examprep
# group: examprep
user::rwx
user:michael:--x
group::---
mask::--x
other::---
default:user::rwx
default:user:michael:r-x
default:group::---
default:mask::r-x
default:other::---
```

ACLs and Masks

The mask associated with an ACL limits the permissions available on a file for named users and groups, and for the group owner. The mask shown in Figure 4-2 is rwx, which means there are no limits. If it were set to r, then the only permissions that could be granted with a command such as **setfacl** is read. To change the mask on the TheAnswers file to read-only, run the following command:

```
# setfacl -m mask:r-- /home/examprep/TheAnswers
```

Now review the result with the **getfacl /home/examprep/TheAnswers** command. Pay attention to the entry for a specific user. Based on the ACL privileges given to user michael earlier, you'll see a difference with Figure 4-2:

```
user:michael:rwx    #effective:r--
```

In other words, with a mask of **r--**, you can try to provide other users with all the privileges in the world. But all that can be set with that mask is read privileges.

on the !job   **The mask has an effect only on the group owner and on named users and groups. It does not have any effect on the user owner of the file and on the "other" permission group.**

EXERCISE 4-1

Use ACLs to Deny a User

In this exercise, you'll set up ACLs to deny access to the loopback configuration file to a regular user. That is the ifcfg-lo file in the /etc/sysconfig/network-scripts directory. This exercise assumes that you've configured a regular user. Because we've configured user michael on our systems, that is the regular user listed in this exercise. Substitute accordingly. To deny such access, take the following steps:

1. Back up a copy of the current configuration file for the loopback device. It's the ifcfg-lo file in the /etc/sysconfig/network-scripts directory. (Hint: use the **cp** and not the **mv** command.)

2. Execute the **setfacl -m u:michael:- /etc/sysconfig/network-scripts/ifcfg-lo** command.

3. Review the results. Run the **getfacl** command on both copies of the file, in the /etc/sysconfig/network-scripts and backup directories. What are the differences?

4. Log in as the target user. From the root administrative account, one method to do so is with the **su - michael** command.

5. Try to read the /etc/sysconfig/network-scripts/ifcfg-lo file in the vi text editor or even with the **cat** command. What happens?

6. Repeat the preceding step with the file in the backup directory. What happens?

7. Now run the **cp** command from the backup of the ifcfg-lo file, and overwrite the current version in the /etc/sysconfig/network-scripts file. (Don't use the **mv** command for this purpose.) You would need to return as the root user to do so.

8. Try the **getfacl /etc/sysconfig/network-scripts/ifcfg-lo** command again. Are you surprised at the result?

9. There are two ways to restore the original ACL configuration for the ifcfg-lo file. First, apply the **setfacl -b** command on the file. Did that work? Confirm with the **getfacl** command. If any other related commands have been applied, it may or may not have worked.

10. Another way to restore the original ACL of a file is to restore the backup by first deleting the changed file in the /etc/sysconfig/network-scripts directory and then by copying the file from the backup directory.

11. However, if you run Step 10, you may also need to restore the SELinux contexts of the file with the following command:

```
restorecon -F /etc/sysconfig/network-scripts/ifcfg-lo
```

More information on the **restorecon** command is available later in this chapter.

NFS Shares and ACLs

Although there's no evidence that the Red Hat exams cover NFS-based ACLs, it is a feature that Linux administrators should know. As such, the description in this section just provides examples and is far from complete. For more information, refer to the nfs4_acl man page, which is installed by the nfs4-acl-tools RPM package.

Frequently, the /home directory is taken from a shared NFS volume. In fact, NFS-based ACLs are more fine-grained than standard ACLs. This feature was introduced with NFS version 4, the standard for RHEL 7. To that end, the **nfs4_getfacl** command can display the ACLs associated with files on a shared directory. Based on the ACLs previously given, Figure 4-3 shows the output to the **nfs4_getfacl** command.

The output is in the format

```
type:flags:principal:permissions
```

```
[michael@server1 ~]$ nfs4_getfacl /test/examprep/
A::OWNER@:rwaDxtTcCy
A::michael@localdomain:xtcy
A::GROUP@:tcy
A::EVERYONE@:tcy
[michael@server1 ~]$ nfs4_getfacl /test/examprep/TheAnswers
D::OWNER@:x
A::OWNER@:rwatTcCy
A::michael@localdomain:rwaxtcy
A::GROUP@:rtcy
A::EVERYONE@:rtcy
[michael@server1 ~]$ █
```

where the settings are delineated by the colon. Briefly, the two types shown either allow (**A**) or deny (**D**) the noted principal (a user or group) the specified permissions. No flags are shown in Figure 4-3, which can provide relatively fine-grained control. The principal may be a regular user or group, in lowercase. It may also be a generic user such as the file OWNER, the GROUP that owns the file, or other users, as specified by EVERYONE. The permissions, as shown in Table 4-6, allow very fine-grained control. The effect varies depending on whether the object is a file or a directory.

The configuration of NFS as a client is covered in Chapter 6, with other local and network filesystems. The configuration of an NFS server is an RHCE objective covered in Chapter 16.

TABLE 4-6

Descriptions of NFSv4 ACL Permissions

Permission	Description
r	Read file or list directory
w	Write to a file or create a new file in a directory
a	Append data to a file or create a subdirectory
x	Execute a program or change a directory
d	Delete the file or directory
D	Delete the subdirectory
t	Read the attributes of the file or directory
T	Write the attributes of the file or directory
c	Read the ACLs of the file or directory
C	Write the ACLs of the file or directory
y	Allow clients to use synchronous I/O on the file or directory

CERTIFICATION OBJECTIVE 4.03

Basic Firewall Control

Traditionally, firewalls were configured only between LANs and outside networks such as the Internet. But as security threats increase, there's an increasing need for firewalls on every system. RHEL 7 includes firewalls in every default configuration.

The Linux kernel comes with a powerful framework, the Netfilter system, which enables other kernel modules to offer functionalities such as packet filtering, network address translation (NAT), and load balancing. The **iptables** command is the main tool that interacts with the Netfilter system to provide packet filtering and NAT.

Before you send a message over an IP network, the message is broken down into smaller units called *packets*. Administrative information, including the type of data, the source address, and destination address, is added to each packet. The packets are reassembled when they reach the destination computer. An **iptables** rule examines these administrative fields in each packet to determine whether to allow the packet to pass.

e x a m

w a t c h   RHEL 7 also includes a firewall command for IPv6 networks, ip6tables. The associated commands are almost identical. Unlike iptables, the ip6tables command is not listed in the Red Hat objectives.

The **iptables** tool is the basic foundation that is used by other services to manage system firewall rules. RHEL 7 comes with two such services: the new firewalld daemon and the iptables service, which was included with the previous releases of Red Hat Enterprise Linux. You can interact with firewalld using the graphical utility **firewall-config** or the command-line client **firewall-cmd**.

The iptables and firewalld services both rely on the Netfilter system within the Linux kernel to filter packets. However, whereas iptables is based on the concept of "chain of filter rules" to block or forward traffic, firewalld is "zone-based," as you will see in the next sections.

There are RHCSA and RHCE requirements related to firewall configuration and management. For the RHCSA, you need to understand how to configure a firewall to either block or allow network communication through one or more ports using **iptables, firewall-config**, or **firewall-cmd**. For the RHCE, you need a more in-depth knowledge of firewalld and its features, such as "rich rules, zones and custom rules, to implement packet filtering and configure network address translation (NAT)."

TABLE 4-7	Port	Description
	20, 21	FTP
Common TCP/IP	22	Secure Shell (SSH)
Ports	23	Telnet
	25	Simple Mail Transfer Protocol (SMTP); for example, Postfix, sendmail
	53	Domain Name Service servers
	80	Hypertext Transfer Protocol (HTTP)
	88	Kerberos
	110	Post Office Protocol, version 3 (POP3)
	139	Network Basic Input/Output System (NetBIOS) session service
	143	Internet Mail Access Protocol (IMAP)
	443	HTTP, secure (HTTPS)

Standard Ports

Linux communicates over a network, primarily using the TCP/IP protocol suite. Different services use certain ports and protocols by default, as defined in the /etc/services file. It may be useful to know some of these ports by heart, such as those described in Table 4-7. Be aware, some of these ports may communicate using the Transmission Control Protocol (TCP), the User Datagram Protocol (UDP), or even the Stream Control Transmission Protocol (SCTP). For example, as noted in the following excerpts from the /etc/services file, the FTP service has been assigned the TCP and UDP ports listed here:

```
ftp-data          20/tcp
ftp-data          20/udp
ftp               21/tcp
ftp               21/udp
```

However, you'll see shortly that the Red Hat firewall configuration tools open only TCP communications for FTP services, and the default vsFTP server configured in Chapter 1 works fine under such circumstances. This is because the default policy of the Internet Assigned Number Authority (IANA) is to register port numbers for both TCP and UDP, even if a service only supports the TCP protocol.

A Focus on iptables

The philosophy behind **iptables** is based on "chains." These are sets of rules applied to each network packet, chained together. Each rule does two things: it specifies the conditions a packet must meet to match the rule, and it specifies the action if the packet matches.

The **iptables** command uses the following basic format:

```
iptables -t tabletype <action_direction> <packet_pattern> -j <what_to_do>
```

Now let's analyze this command, step by step. First is the **-t** *tabletype* switch. There are two basic *tabletype* options for **iptables**:

- **filter**   Sets a rule for filtering packets.
- **nat**   Configures network address translation, also known as masquerading, which is discussed later in Chapter 10.

The default is **filter**; if you don't specify a **-t** *tabletype*, the **iptables** command assumes that the command is applied as a packet filter rule.

Next is the *<action_direction>*. Four basic actions are associated with **iptables** rules:

- **-A (--append)**   Appends a rule to the end of a chain.
- **-D (--delete)**   Deletes a rule from a chain. Specify the rule by the number or the packet pattern.
- **-L (--list)**   Lists the currently configured rules in the chain.
- **-F (--flush)**   Flushes all the rules in the current **iptables** chain.

If you're appending to (**-A**) or deleting from (**-D**) a chain, you'll want to apply it to network data traveling in one of three directions:

- **INPUT**   All incoming packets are checked against the rules in this chain.
- **OUTPUT**   All outgoing packets are checked against the rules in this chain.
- **FORWARD**   All packets received from a computer and being sent to another computer are checked against the rules in this chain. In other words, these are packets that are *routed* through the local server.

Typically, each of these directions is the name of a chain.

Next, you need to configure a *<packet_pattern>*. All **iptables** firewalls check every packet against this pattern. The simplest pattern is by IP address:

- **-s** *ip_address*   All packets are checked for a specific source IP address.
- **-d** *ip_address*   All packets are checked for a specific destination IP address.

Packet patterns can be more complex. In TCP/IP, packets are transported using the TCP, UDP, or ICMP protocol. You can specify the protocol with the **-p** switch, followed by the destination port (**--dport**). For example, the **-p tcp --dport 80** extension affects users outside your network who are trying to make an HTTP connection.

Once the **iptables** command finds a packet pattern match, it needs to know what to do with that packet, which leads to the last part of the command, *-j <what_to_do>*. There are three basic options:

- **DROP**   The packet is dropped. No message is sent to the requesting computer.
- **REJECT**   The packet is dropped. An error message is sent to the requesting computer.
- **ACCEPT**   The packet is allowed to proceed as specified with the **-A** action: **INPUT**, **OUTPUT**, or **FORWARD**.

Take a look at some examples of how you can use **iptables** commands to configure a firewall. The first step is always to see what is currently configured, with the following command:

```
# iptables -L
```

If an iptables firewall is configured, it should return chain rules in at least three different categories: **INPUT**, **FORWARD**, and **OUTPUT**.

Keep That Firewall in Operation

Linux firewalls such as firewalld and the iptables service are based on the **iptables** command. To review current rules, run the **iptables -L** command. Suppose all you see is the following blank list of rules:

```
Chain INPUT (policy ACCEPT)
target     prot opt source               destination

Chain FORWARD (policy ACCEPT)
target     prot opt source               destination

Chain OUTPUT (policy ACCEPT)
target     prot opt source               destination
```

This output means that the firewalld service may not be enabled. In RHEL 7, firewalld is the default firewall service. Make sure that it is running:

```
# systemctl status firewalld
```

If the service is not active, check that the iptables service is disabled, then start firewalld and ensure that it is enabled at boot:

```
# systemctl stop iptables
# systemctl disable iptables
# systemctl start firewalld
# systemctl enable firewalld
```

Before moving to the configuration of firewalld, we will briefly review the iptables service. Besides being a requirement for the RHCSA exam, a basic knowledge of the iptables service will provide a better understanding of the more advanced functionalities that come with firewalld.

The iptables Service

Whereas the iptables service was the default firewall running in RHEL 6, firewalld is the default in RHEL 7. If you wish, you can disable firewalld in RHEL 7, and switch to the old iptables service. To do so, run the following commands:

```
# systemctl stop firewalld
# systemctl disable firewalld
# systemctl start iptables
# systemctl enable iptables
```

Likewise, to switch back to firewalld, run the commands listed in the previous section. After starting the iptables service, list the existing firewall rules with **iptables -L**. The output on the default server1.example.com system is shown in Figure 4-4.

Six columns of information are shown in Figure 4-4, which correspond to various **iptables** command options. The firewall shown is based on the following rules listed in the /etc/sysconfig/iptables file. The first line in the file specifies that the rules to follow are filtering rules. Alternative rules support network address translation (NAT) or mangling.

```
*filter
```

FIGURE 4-4   Firewall rules for the iptables service

```
[root@server1 ~]# iptables -L
Chain INPUT (policy ACCEPT)
target     prot opt source               destination
ACCEPT     all  --  anywhere             anywhere             state RELATED,ESTABLISHED
ACCEPT     icmp --  anywhere             anywhere
ACCEPT     all  --  anywhere             anywhere
ACCEPT     tcp  --  anywhere             anywhere             state NEW tcp dpt:ssh
REJECT     all  --  anywhere             anywhere             reject-with icmp-host-prohibited

Chain FORWARD (policy ACCEPT)
target     prot opt source               destination
REJECT     all  --  anywhere             anywhere             reject-with icmp-host-prohibited

Chain OUTPUT (policy ACCEPT)
target     prot opt source               destination
[root@server1 ~]# █
```

Next, network traffic that is directed to the local system, intended to be forwarded and sent out, is normally accepted by default with the ACCEPT option. The [0:0] part shows the byte and packet counts.

```
:INPUT ACCEPT [0:0]
:FORWARD ACCEPT [0:0]
:OUTPUT ACCEPT [0:0]
```

The lines that follow are all applied to the **iptables** command. Every switch and option listed in this file should be available on the associated man page.

The next line keeps current network communications going. The ESTABLISHED option continues to accept incoming packets related to inbound network connections. The RELATED option accepts packets for follow-on network connections, such as for FTP data transfers.

```
-A INPUT -m state --state RELATED,ESTABLISHED -j ACCEPT
```

The next line accepts packets associated with ICMP, most commonly related with the **ping** command. When a packet is rejected, the associated message also uses the ICMP protocol.

```
-A INPUT -p icmp -j ACCEPT
```

The following line adds (**-A**) a rule to an INPUT chain, associated with the network interface (**-i**) known as the loopback adapter (**lo**). Any data processed through that device jumps (**-j**) to acceptance.

```
-A INPUT -i lo -j ACCEPT
```

The next line is the only one that directly accepts new regular network data, using the TCP protocol, over all interfaces. It looks for a match (**-m**) for a NEW connection state (**--state NEW**), for matching TCP packets, using the TCP protocol (**-p tcp**), sent to a destination port (**--dport**) of 22, which corresponds to the SSH service. Network packets that meet all of these criteria are accepted (**-j ACCEPT**). Once the connection is established, the first regular rule described in this chapter continues to accept packets on that established connection.

```
-A INPUT -p tcp -m state --state NEW -m tcp --dport 22 -j ACCEPT
```

The last two rules reject all other packets, with an **icmp-host-prohibited** message sent to the originating system:

```
-A INPUT -j REJECT --reject-with icmp-host-prohibited
-A FORWARD -j REJECT --reject-with icmp-host-prohibited
```

The COMMIT ends the list of rules:

```
COMMIT
```

As this section is associated with the RHCSA exam, a more detailed discussion can be found in Chapter 10. At this level, you need to know how to manage these firewalls with the standard configuration tools provided.

The firewalld Service

You can automate the process of configuring a firewall. For that purpose, in RHEL 7 firewalld comes with both a console and a GUI configuration tool. Although the look and feel of the two applications are different, you can use both tools to configure access to trusted services. Before starting the firewalld configuration tool, review the steps in the earlier section "Keep That Firewall in Operation" to ensure that firewalld is running and automatically starts during the boot process.

The firewalld service offers the same functionalities of the iptables tool and more. One of the new features of firewalld is *zone-based* firewalling. In a zone-based firewall, networks and interfaces are grouped into zones, with each zone configured with a different level of trust. The zones defined in firewalld are listed in Table 4-8, along with their default behavior for outgoing and incoming connections.

on the
Ⓙ o b

A zone is made up of a group of source network addresses and interfaces, plus the rules to process the packets that match those source addresses and network interfaces.

| TABLE 4-8 | Zones in firewalld |

Zone	Outgoing Connections	Incoming Connections
drop	Allowed	Dropped.
block	Allowed	Rejected with an icmp-host-prohibited message.
public	Allowed	DHCPv6 client and SSH are allowed.
external	Allowed and masqueraded to the IP address of the outgoing network interface	SSH is allowed.
dmz	Allowed	SSH is allowed.
work	Allowed	DHCPv6 client, IPP and SSH are allowed.
home	Allowed	DHCPv6 client, multicast DNS, IPP, Samba client, and SSH are allowed.
internal	Allowed	Same as the home zone.
trusted	Allowed	Allowed.

FIGURE 4-5   The graphical firewall-config tool

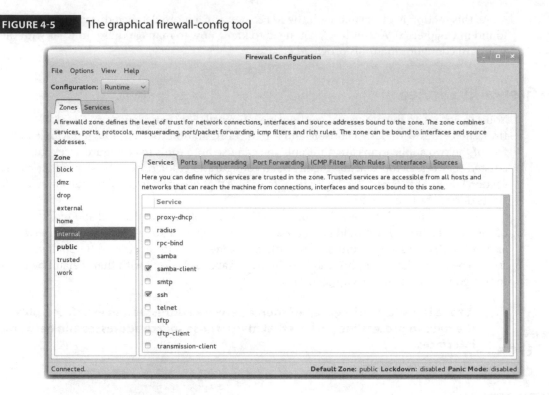

The GUI firewall-config Tool

You can start the graphical firewalld configuration tool from a GUI-based command line with the **firewall-config** command. Alternatively, in the GNOME Desktop Environment, click Applications | Sundry | Firewall. The result is shown in Figure 4-5.

As shown in the figure, the main window includes different menus and tabs. In the top-left area, there is a drop-down Configuration menu, where you can set the firewall to Runtime or Permanent mode. If it's set to Runtime, the changes applied by **firewall-config** take effect immediately, but will not survive a server reboot. Alternatively, select Permanent mode to make your changes survive a server reboot. At any time, you can click Options | Reload Firewalld to make a new firewall configuration immediately effective.

You can only modify definitions of zones and services in Permanent mode.

on the **job**

The Zone tab includes all the zones previously listed in Table 4-8. When an incoming packet hits the firewall, its source address is checked for a match with the network addresses that belong to the existing zones. If no match is found, the incoming interface of the packet is checked to verify whether it belongs to a zone. Once a correspondence is found, the packet is processed according to the rules of the zone it has been matched to.

In the main **firewall-config** window, the public zone is displayed in a bold font to indicate that this zone is the *default zone*. The default zone has a special meaning: any new network interface added to the system is automatically assigned to the default zone. In addition, the rules of the default zone are processed for all incoming packets that do not match any of the other zones. You can set a different zone to be the default by clicking Options | Change Default Zone.

To allow or deny incoming traffic through the firewall, select a zone and add or remove a checkmark in the zone's Services tab for the service you want to grant or block. As an alternative, you can also specify a protocol and port from the Ports tab.

In firewalld, a service is defined as a group of one of more protocols and ports. A service can also include a Netfilter helper module to support filtering for those applications that dynamically open multiple connections.

A variety of network services are already defined in the Services window. The most common are described in Table 4-9.

TABLE 4-9	Common TCP/IP Ports

Service	Description
amanda-client	A client of the Advanced Maryland Automatic Network Disk Archiver (AMANDA), associated with UDP and TCP port 10080.
bacula	An open-source network backup server; associated with TCP ports 9101, 9102, and 9103.
bacula-client	Client for the Bacula server; associated with TCP port 9102.
dhcp	The Dynamic Host Configuration Protocol (DHCP) is associated with UDP port 67.
dhcpv6-client	The DHCP client on IPv6 is associated with UDP port 546.
dns	Domain Name Service (DNS) server; associated with port 53, using both TCP and UDP protocols.
ftp	File Transfer Protocol (FTP) server, associated with TCP port 21; a Netfilter helper module tracks dynamic connections established for FTP data transfers.
http	The well-known web server uses TCP port 80.
https	Communications to a secure web server over the Secure Sockets Layer (SSL) uses TCP port 443.
imaps	IMAP over SSL normally uses TCP port 993.
ipsec	Associated with UDP port 500 for the Internet Security Association and Key Management Protocol (ISAKMP), along with the ESP and AH transport-level protocols.

(Continued)

| TABLE 4-9 | Common TCP/IP Ports (*Continued*) |

Service	Description
mdns	Multicast DNS (mDNS) is associated with UDP port 5353 and with the multicast IP address 224.0.0.251; mDNS is often used to support the Linux implementation of zero configuration networking (zeroconf), known as Avahi.
nfs	NFS version 4 uses TCP port 2049.
ipp	The standard network print server client uses TCP and UDP ports 631, based on the Internet Print Protocol (IPP).
ipp-client	The standard networking print client uses UDP port 631, based on the Internet Print Protocol (IPP).
openvpn	The open-source Virtual Private Network system, which uses UDP port 1194.
pop3s	POP-3 over the Secure Sockets Layer (SSL) normally uses TCP port 995.
radius	The Remote Authentication Dial-In User Service (RADIUS) protocol uses UDP ports 1812 and 1813.
samba	The Linux protocol for communication on Microsoft networks uses TCP ports 139 and 445, along with UDP ports 137 and 138.
samba-client	The Linux protocol for client communication on Microsoft networks uses UDP ports 137 and 138.
ssh	The SSH server uses TCP port 22.
smtp	The Simple Mail Transport Protocol server, such as sendmail or Postfix, uses TCP port 25.
tftp	Communications with the Trivial File Transfer Protocol (TFTP) server requires UDP port 69.
tftp-client	The TFTP client uses a dynamic port range to transfer data; a Netfilter helper module tracks those connections.

If you switch the **firewall-config** tool into Permanent mode, you can add new services or edit existing ones. To accomplish this task, scroll to the bottom of the Services window and click the corresponding icon to remove, add, or edit a service. If desired, you can also configure custom ports for an existing service by clicking the Add or Edit icon, as shown in Figure 4-6.

The Console firewall-cmd Configuration Tool

The **firewall-cmd** configuration tool has the same features and services as the corresponding GUI tool. In fact, both the graphical **firewall-config** tool and the command interface **firewall-cmd** are just client front ends that communicate to the underlying firewalld daemon.

FIGURE 4-6   Adding custom ports to a service in the firewall-config tool

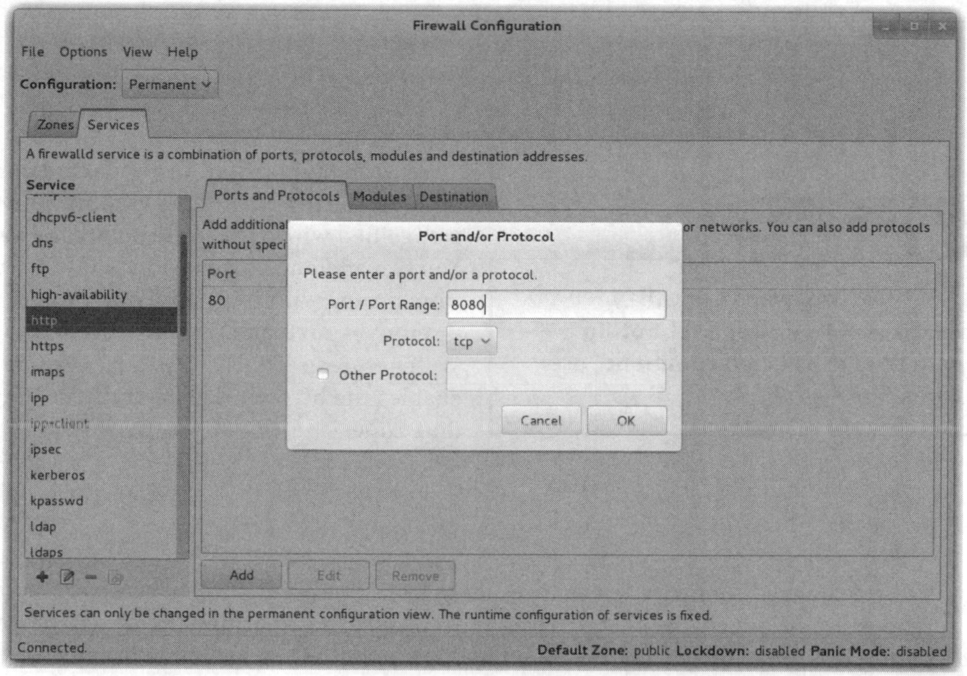

As with the GUI tool, **firewall-cmd** can display all the available zones and switch to a different default zone. In the following example, the default zone is changed from the public to the internal zone:

```
# firewall-cmd --get-default-zone
public
# firewall-cmd --set-default-zone=internal
success
# firewall-cmd --get-default-zone
internal
#
```

The option **--list-all** is particularly useful. It lists all the configured interfaces and services allowed through a zone, as illustrated next:

```
# firewall-cmd --list-all
internal (default, active)
  interfaces: eth0
  sources:
```

```
services: dhcpv6-client ipp-client mdns samba-client ssh
ports:
masquerade: no
forward-ports:
icmp-blocks:
rich rules:
#
```

e x a m

w a t c h   **You want firewall changes that survive after a reboot. To do so with the** firewall-cmd **command, use the** --permanent **switch.**

As with many of the **firewall-cmd** command options, the default zone is assumed if no zone is specified with the **--zone** command switch. You can add and remove ports and services from a zone with the **--add-port**, **--add-service**, **--remove-port**, and **--remove-service** switches, respectively. The next example enables the http service for traffic hitting the dmz zone:

```
# firewall-cmd --zone=dmz --add-service=http
success
#
```

By default, all configuration changes made by **firewall-cmd** do not survive a server reboot. To make a change that survives a reboot, add the **--permanent** switch to **firewall-cmd**. Then, run **firewall-cmd --reload** to implement the change immediately.

EXERCISE 4-2

Adjust Firewall Settings

In this exercise, you'll adjust firewalls from the command-line interface and review the results with the **nmap** and **telnet** commands. Although it does not matter how you address a problem on a Red Hat exam, in this exercise you'll see what happens when adding a new service via the **firewall-cmd** tool. Of course, it's possible to use the graphical **firewall-config** tool to perform the same tasks. This assumes a system with the default firewalld configuration described in this chapter.

1. Review current active services on the local system with the **nmap localhost** command. Note the IP address of the local system with the **ip addr** command. If the local system is server1.example.com, that IP address should be 192.168.122.50.

2. Make sure firewalld is currently operational with the **systemctl status firewalld** command.

3. Go to a different system. You can do so from a different virtual machine, or you can access it remotely with the **ssh** command. If the tester1.example.com system is running, you can log in to that system with the **ssh 192.168.122.150** command.

4. Use the **nmap** command to review what is seen through the firewall; for the noted server1.example.com system, the right command would be **nmap 192.168.122.50**. If the IP address found from Step 1 is different, substitute accordingly.

5. Return to the original system. Run the following commands to install and start the telnet service:

```
# yum install telnet-server
# systemctl start telnet.socket
```

6. Run the following command to show the current settings for the default zone:

```
# firewall-cmd --list-all
```

7. Allow telnet traffic through the default zone. Don't forget the **--permanent** switch to make the change persistent:

```
# firewall-cmd --permanent --add-service=telnet
```

8. Apply the previous change to the run-time configuration of the firewall:

```
# firewall-cmd --reload
```

9. Navigate back to the tester1.example.com system as was done in Step 3.

10. Repeat Step 4. What do you see?

CERTIFICATION OBJECTIVE 4.04

Securing SSH with Key-Based Authentication

Chapter 2 addressed SSH client programs, including **ssh**, **scp**, and **sftp**. The focus of this section is on securing SSH access with key-based authentication.

As SSH is an important tool for administering systems remotely, it's important to understand the basics of how it encrypts communication between a client and the SSH server. Then you'll see how to create a public/private key pair so connections won't even put user passwords at risk. But first, it may be helpful to review some basic information about SSH configuration commands and files.

SSH Configuration Commands

There are a few SSH-oriented utilities you need to know about:

- **sshd** The daemon service; this must be running to receive inbound Secure Shell client requests.
- **ssh-agent** A program to hold private keys used for Digital Signature Algorithm (DSA), Elliptic Curve DSA (ECDSA), and Rivest, Shamir, Adleman (RSA) authentication. The idea is that the **ssh-agent** command is started in the beginning of an X session or a login session, and other programs are started as clients to the **ssh-agent** program.
- **ssh-add** Adds private key identities to the authentication agent, **ssh-agent**.
- **ssh** The Secure Shell command, **ssh**, is a secure way to log in to a remote machine, similar to Telnet or **rlogin**. The basic use of this command was discussed in Chapter 2. To make this work with key-based authentication, you need a private key on the client and a public key on the server. Take the public key file, such as id_rsa.pub, created later in this section. Copy it to the server. Place it in the home directory of an authorized user in the ~/.ssh/authorized_keys file.
- **ssh-keygen** A utility that creates private/public key pairs for SSH authentication. The **ssh-keygen -t** *keytype* command will create a key pair based on the DSA, ECDSA, or RSA protocol.
- **ssh-copy-id** A script that copies a public key to a target remote system.

SSH Client Configuration Files

Systems configured with SSH include configuration files in two different directories. For the local system, basic SSH configuration files are stored in the /etc/ssh directory. But just as important are the configuration files in each user's home directory in the ~/.ssh/ subdirectory.

Those files configure how the given user is allowed to connect to remote systems. When DSA, ECDSA, and RSA keys are included, the user ~/.ssh/ subdirectory includes the following files:

- **authorized_keys** Includes a list of public keys from remote users. Users with public encryption keys in this file can connect to remote systems. The system users and names are listed at the end of each public key copied to this file.
- **id_dsa** Includes the local private key based on the DSA algorithm.
- **id_dsa.pub** Includes the local public key for the user based on the DSA algorithm.
- **id_ecdsa** Includes the local private key based on the ECDSA algorithm.

- **id_ecdsa.pub**   Includes the local public key for the user based on the ECDSA algorithm.
- **id_rsa**   Includes the local private key based on the RSA algorithm.
- **id_rsa.pub**   Includes the local public key for the user based on the RSA algorithm.
- **known_hosts**   Contains the public host keys from remote systems. The first time a user logs in to a system, she's prompted to accept the public key of the remote server. On RHEL 7, the ECDSA protocol is used by default to encrypt traffic. The corresponding public key on the remote server is stored on the /etc/ssh/ssh_host_ecdsa_key.pub file and is added by the client to its local ~/.ssh/known_hosts file.

Basic Encrypted Communication

Basic encryption in computer networking normally requires a private key and a public key. The principle is the same as GPG communications discussed in Chapter 10. A private key is stored by the owner, and a public key is sent to a third party. When the key pair is properly configured, a user can encrypt a message using her private key, while a third party can decrypt a message with the corresponding public key. This also works in reverse: a third party can encrypt a message using the public key of the receiver, while the receiver can decrypt the message with her private key. The SSH protocol works in a similar way: the server sends a copy of his public key to the client, and this key is used by the client to decrypt the traffic and set up a secure communication channel.

Encryption keys are based on random numbers. The numbers are so large (typically 2048 bits for RSA keys or more) that the chance someone will break into the server system, at least with a PC, is practically impossible. Private and public encryption keys are based on a matched set of these random numbers.

Private Keys

The private key must be secure. Key-based authentication relies on a private key that is accessible only to the user owner of that key in the ~/.ssh subdirectory of that user's home directory. To authenticate a user, the server sends to the client a "challenge," which is a request to perform an encryption operation that requires the knowledge of the private key. Once the server receives a response to its challenge from the client, it will be able to decrypt the message and prove that the user's identity is genuine.

Public Keys

The public key is just that, publicly available. Public keys are designed to be copied to appropriate users' ~/.ssh/ subdirectories in a file named authorized_keys.

The example shown in Figure 4-7 lists the directories and files associated with SSH usage.

FIGURE 4-7

```
[michael@server1 ~]$ ls -l .ssh/
total 20
-rw-------. 1 michael michael 1822 Jan  7 21:43 authorized_keys
-rw-------. 1 michael michael  227 Sep 12 20:29 id_ecdsa
-rw-r--r--. 1 michael michael  186 Sep 12 20:29 id_ecdsa.pub
-rw-------. 1 michael michael 1679 Nov  7 18:24 id_rsa
-rw-r--r--. 1 michael michael  406 Nov  7 18:24 id_rsa.pub
-rw-r--r--. 1 michael michael  346 Jan  7 21:44 known_hosts
[michael@server1 ~]$ █
```

Keys in a user's
.ssh/ subdirectory

e**x**a m
ⓦ a t c h   **Most of the common issues** **are set to 600 and for public keys are set**
with SSH key-based authentication are **to 644. In addition, the permissions of the**
related to file permissions. As shown in **~/.ssh directory should be 700.**
Figure 4-7, the permissions for private keys

A key is like a password used to encrypt communications data. But it's not a standard password by any means. Imagine trying to remember the 1024-bit number expressed in hexadecimal format shown here:

```
3081 8902 8181 00D4 596E 01DE A012 3CAD 51B7
7835 05A4 DEFC C70B 4382 A733 5D62 A51B B9D6
29EA 860B EC2B 7AB8 2E96 3A4C 71A2 D087 11D0
E149 4DD5 1E20 8382 FA58 C7DA D9B0 3865 FF6E
88C7 B672 51F5 5094 3B35 D8AA BC68 BBEB BFE3
9063 AE75 8B57 09F9 DCF8 FFA4 E32C A17F 82E9
7A4C 0E10 E62D 8A97 0845 007B 169A 0676 E7CF
5713
```

The private key is similar, *but you must keep it private,* or this whole system fails. Keeping it private means no one should have access to the server systems. If your PC is public, secure your private key with a passphrase (password). The procedure to set up a passphrase is described next. Don't forget the passphrase, or you'll have to create a new key pair and again copy your public key to all the target systems.

Set Up a Private/Public Pair for Key-Based Authentication

The **ssh-keygen** command is used to set up a public/private key pair. Although it creates an RSA key by default, it also can be used to create a DSA or ECDSA key. For example, some users may need DSA keys to comply with certain U.S. government standards. An example of the command sequence is shown in Figure 4-8.

FIGURE 4-8

Command to
generate an SSH
key pair

```
[michael@server1 ~]$ ssh-keygen
Generating public/private rsa key pair.
Enter file in which to save the key (/home/michael/.ssh/id_rsa):
Created directory '/home/michael/.ssh'.
Enter passphrase (empty for no passphrase):
Enter same passphrase again:
Your identification has been saved in /home/michael/.ssh/id_rsa.
Your public key has been saved in /home/michael/.ssh/id_rsa.pub.
The key fingerprint is:
3f:63:1e:4e:0e:82:f1:e9:2c:c3:2b:b8:d7:7e:57:06 michael@server1.example.net
The key's randomart image is:
+--[ RSA 2048]----+
|                 |
|                 |
|                 |
|        E        |
|      . S.       |
|       + . .o    |
|    . o. + .oB   |
|   . o =o...B +  |
|   .o oo=o.  +   |
+-----------------+
[michael@server1 ~]$
```

As shown in the figure, the command prompts for an optional passphrase to protect the
private key. When the identical passphrase is confirmed, the private key is saved in the
id_rsa file, and the corresponding public key is stored in the id_rsa.pub file. Both files for
user michael are stored in the /home/michael/.ssh directory.

If desired, you can set up RSA keys with a larger number of bits. In our testing, we were
able to set up key pairs with up to 8192 bits fairly quickly, even on a virtual machine system
with just one virtual CPU.

The command that starts the process is

```
$ ssh-keygen -b 8192
```

Alternatively, if a DSA key is needed, the following command can help. Only 1024-bit
DSA keys are allowed. The process after this command is the same as shown in Figure 4-8.

```
$ ssh-keygen -t dsa
```

The next step is to transmit the public key to a remote system. It might be one of the
servers you administer. If you're willing to transmit that public key over the network
(once per connection), the following command can work:

```
$ ssh-copy-id -i .ssh/id_rsa.pub michael@tester1.example.com
```

Strictly speaking, the **ssh-copy-id** command without the **-i** option defaults to
transmitting the most recently created public key. The preceding command automatically
appends the noted local RSA key to the end of the *remote* ~/.ssh/authorized_keys file. In
this case, that file can be found in the /home/michael directory. Of course, you may choose
to substitute the IP address for the hostname.

Sometimes, after copying a key pair to a remote system, you may get an "agent admitted failure to sign using the key" error followed by a password prompt when you try to log in. To fix this problem, log out of the console or the GUI and log back in. In most cases, the ssh command will prompt for the passphrase.

You should then be able to immediately connect to that remote system. In the preceding case, the appropriate command is either one of the following:

```
$ ssh -l michael tester1.example.com
$ ssh michael@tester1.example.com
```

When run on a console, the **ssh** command uses the following prompt for the passphrase:

```
Enter passphrase for key '/home/michael/.ssh/id_rsa'
```

When run in a GUI-based command line, it prompts with a window similar to that shown in Figure 4-9.

FIGURE 4-9

Prompt for a passphrase

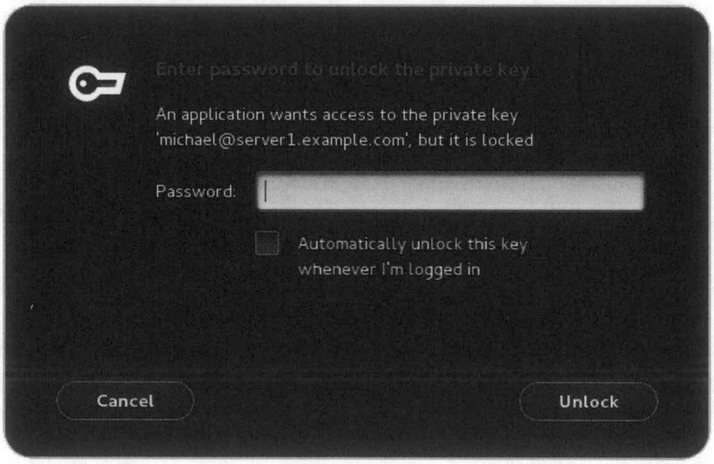

Enter password to unlock the private key

An application wants access to the private key 'michael@server1.example.com', but it is locked

Password:

☐ Automatically unlock this key whenever I'm logged in

Cancel   Unlock

CERTIFICATION OBJECTIVE 4.05

A Security-Enhanced Linux Primer

Security-Enhanced Linux (SELinux) was developed by the U.S. National Security Agency to provide a level of mandatory access control for Linux. It goes beyond the discretionary access control associated with file permissions and ACLs. In essence, SELinux enforces security rules within the kernel of the operating system. It limits the damage if there is a security breach. For example, if the system account associated with an FTP service is compromised, SELinux makes it more difficult to use that account to compromise other services.

Basic Features of SELinux

The SELinux security model is based on subjects, objects, and actions. A *subject* is a process, such as a running command or an application such as the Apache web server in operation. An *object* is a file, a device, a socket, or in general any resource that can be accessed by a subject. An *action* is what may be done by the subject to the object.

SELinux assigns different contexts to objects. A *context* is just a label, which is used by the SELinux security policy to determine whether a subject's action on an object is allowed or not.

For example, the Apache web server process can take objects such as web page files and display them for the clients of the world to see. That action is normally allowed in the RHEL 7 implementation of SELinux, as long as the object files have appropriate SELinux contexts.

The contexts associated with SELinux are fine-grained. In other words, if a "black hat" hacker breaks in and takes over your web server, SELinux contexts prevent that cracker from using that breach to break into other services.

To see the context of a particular file, run the **ls -Z** command. As an example, review what this command does in Figure 4-10, as it displays security contexts in one of this book author's /root directory.

As noted at the beginning of this chapter, five objectives relate to SELinux on the RHCSA exam. You'll explore how to meet these objectives in the following sections.

SELinux Status

As suggested in the RHCSA objectives, you need to know how to "set enforcing and permissive modes for SELinux." There are three available modes for SELinux: **enforcing**, **permissive**, and **disabled**. The **enforcing** and **disabled** modes are self-explanatory.

SELinux security contexts of different files

```
[root@server1 ~]# ls -Z
-rw-------. root root system_u:object_r:admin_home_t:s0 anaconda-ks.cfg
drwxr-xr-x. root root unconfined_u:object_r:admin_home_t:s0 backup
-rwxr--r--. root root unconfined_u:object_r:admin_home_t:s0 Ch3Lab2
-rw-r--r--. root root unconfined_u:object_r:admin_home_t:s0 Ch3Lab2testfile
-rwxr--r--. root root unconfined_u:object_r:admin_home_t:s0 Ch3Lab3
-rw-r--r--. root root unconfined_u:object_r:admin_home_t:s0 Ch3Lab3testfile
-rwxr--r--. root root unconfined_u:object_r:admin_home_t:s0 Ch3Lab4
-rw-r--r--. root root unconfined_u:object_r:admin_home_t:s0 Ch3Lab4testfile
drwxr-xr-x. root root unconfined_u:object_r:admin_home_t:s0 Desktop
drwxr-xr-x. root root unconfined_u:object_r:admin_home_t:s0 Documents
drwxr-xr-x. root root unconfined_u:object_r:admin_home_t:s0 Downloads
-rw-r--r--. root root unconfined_u:object_r:admin_home_t:s0 hosts
-rw-r--r--. root root unconfined_u:object_r:admin_home_t:s0 ifcfg-eth0
-rw-r--r--. root root unconfined_u:object_r:admin_home_t:s0 ifcfg-System_eth0
-rw-r--r--. root root system_u:object_r:admin_home_t:s0 install.log
-rw-r--r--. root root system_u:object_r:admin_home_t:s0 install.log.syslog
-rw-------. root root unconfined_u:object_r:admin_home_t:s0 ks.cfg
drwxr-xr-x. root root unconfined_u:object_r:admin_home_t:s0 Music
drwxr-xr-x. root root unconfined_u:object_r:admin_home_t:s0 Pictures
drwxr-xr-x. root root unconfined_u:object_r:admin_home_t:s0 Public
-rw-r--r--. root root system_u:object_r:net_conf_t:s0  route-System_eth0
drwxr-xr-x. root root unconfined_u:object_r:admin_home_t:s0 Templates
drwxr-xr-x. root root unconfined_u:object_r:admin_home_t:s0 Videos
[root@server1 ~]# 
```

SELinux in **permissive** mode means that any SELinux rules that are violated are logged, but the violation does not stop any action.

If you want to change the default SELinux mode, change the **SELINUX** directive in the /etc/selinux/config file, as illustrated in Table 4-10. The next time you reboot, the changes are applied to the system.

on the
job

In RHEL 6, the SELINUX configuration variable was defined in the /etc/sysconfig /selinux file. In RHEL 7, /etc/sysconfig/selinux is a symbolic link that points to /etc/selinux/config.

If SELinux is configured in **enforcing** mode, it protects systems in one of two ways: in **targeted** mode or in **mls** mode. The default is the **targeted** policy, which allows you to customize what is protected by SELinux in a fine-grained manner. In contrast, MLS goes a step further, using the Bell-La Padula model developed for the US Department of Defense. That model, as suggested in the /etc/selinux/targeted/setrans.conf file, supports layers of security between levels c0 and c3. Although the c3 level is listed as "Top Secret," the range of available levels goes all the way up to c1023. Such fine-grained levels of secrecy have yet to be fully developed. If you want to explore MLS, install the selinux-policy-mls RPM.

	Directive	Description
TABLE 4-10 Standard Directives in /etc/selinux/config	SELINUX	Basic SELinux status; may be set to **enforcing**, **permissive**, or **disabled**.
	SELINUXTYPE	Specifies the level of protection; set to **targeted** by default, where protection is limited to selected "targeted" services. The alternative is **mls**, which is associated with multi level security (MLS).

If you just want to experiment with SELinux, configure it in permissive mode. It'll log any violations without stopping anything. It's easy to set up with the SELinux Administration tool, or you can set SELINUX=permissive **in /etc/selinux/config. If the** auditd **service is running, violations are logged in the audit.log file in the /var/log/audit directory. Just remember, it's likely that Red Hat wants candidates to configure SELinux in enforcing mode during the exams.**

SELinux Configuration at the Command Line

While SELinux is still under active development, it has become much more useful with the releases of RHEL 6 and RHEL 7. Nevertheless, given the complexity associated with SELinux, it may be more efficient for system engineers who are not very familiar with it to use the SELinux Administration tool to configure SELinux settings.

The following sections show how you can configure and manage SELinux from the command-line interface. However, because it's easier to demonstrate the full capabilities of SELinux using GUI tools, a detailed discussion of such capabilities will follow later in this chapter.

Configure Basic SELinux Settings

There are some essential commands that can be used to review and configure basic SELinux settings. To see the current status of SELinux, run the **getenforce** command; it returns one of three self-explanatory options: **enforcing**, **permissive**, or **disabled**. The **sestatus** command provides more information, with output similar to the following.

```
SELinux status:                 enabled
SELinuxfs mount:                /sys/fs/selinux
SELinux root directory:         /etc/selinux
Loaded policy name:             targeted
Current mode:                   enforcing
Mode from config file:          enforcing
Policy MLS status:              enabled
Policy deny_unknown status:     allowed
Max kernel policy version:      28
```

You can change the current SELinux status with the **setenforce** command; the options are straightforward:

```
# setenforce enforcing
# setenforce permissive
```

This changes the /sys/fs/selinux/enforce boolean. For booleans, you could substitute 1 and 0, respectively, for **enforcing** and **permissive**. To make this change permanent, you'll have to modify the **SELINUX** variable in the /etc/selinux/config file. However, changes to detailed SELinux booleans require different commands.

Alternatively, if SELinux is disabled for some reason, the output would be

```
SELinux status:      disabled
```

e x a m

w a t c h **If SELinux is disabled, it may** **the process is less time-consuming than it**
take a few minutes to reboot a system after **was for the previous RHEL releases.**
setting SELinux in enforcing mode. However,

In that case, the **setenforce** command will not work. Instead, you'll have to set **SELINUX=enforcing** in the /etc/selinux/config file. And that requires a system reboot to "relabel" all files, where SELinux labels are applied to each file on the local system.

Configure Regular Users for SELinux

To review the status of current SELinux users, run the **semanage login -l** command. Based on the default installation of RHEL 7, it leads to the following output:

```
Login Name           SELinux User         MLS/MCS Range        Service
__default__          unconfined_u         s0-s0:c0.c1023       *
root                 unconfined_u         s0-s0:c0.c1023       *
system_u             system_u             s0-s0:c0.c1023       *
```

In other words, regular "default" users have the same SELinux user context of the root administrative user. To confirm, run the **id -Z** command as a regular user. Without changes, it leads to the following output, which suggests that the user is not confined by any SELinux settings:

```
unconfined_u:unconfined_r:unconfined_t:s0-s0:c0.c1023
```

The preceding string defines what is called a *label* in SELinux jargon. A label is made up of several context strings, separated by a column: a user context (which ends with a **_u**), a role context (which ends with **_r**), a type context (which ends with **_t**), a sensitivity context, and a category set. The rules of the targeted policy, which is the default SELinux policy in RHEL 7, are mostly associated with the type (**_t**) context.

Although it may not be an exam requirement, regular users should be confined by SELinux. When user accounts are compromised, and they will be compromised, you want any damage that might be caused limited by SELinux rules. The following example specifies a confinement rule that adds (**-a**) regular user michael, specifying (**-s**) the user_u context for confinement:

```
# semanage login -a -s user_u michael
```

The user_u role should not have the ability to run the **su** and **sudo** commands described in Chapter 8. If desired, you can reverse the process with the **semanage -d michael** command. Since user roles are still a work in progress, you should focus on the available user contexts listed in the latest Red Hat documentation, as shown in Table 4-11.

One other commonly seen "user" context is system_u, which typically does not apply to regular users. It is a common user seen in the output to the **ls -Z** command for system and configuration files.

When a user role is changed, it doesn't take effect until the next login. For example, if we were to change the role for user michael to user_u in a GUI-based command line, the change would not take effect until we logged out and logged back in to the GUI. If you were to try this on your system, you would no longer be able to start any administrative configuration tools, and you would not have access to the **sudo** and **su** commands.

On some networks, you may want to change the role of future users to user_u. If you don't want regular users tinkering with administrative tools, you could make that change for future default users with the following command:

```
# semanage login -m -S targeted -s "user_u" -r s0 __default__
```

TABLE 4-11	User Context	Features
	guest_u	No GUI, no networking, no access to the **su** or **sudo** command, no file execution in /home or /tmp
Options for SELinux User Roles	xguest_u	GUI, networking only via the Firefox web browser, no file execution in /home or /tmp
	user_u	GUI and networking available
	staff_u	GUI, networking, and the **sudo** command available
	sysadm_u	GUI, networking, and the **sudo** and **su** commands available
	unconfined_u	Full system access

This command modifies (**-m**) the targeted policy store (**-S**), with SELinux user (**-s**) user_u, with the MLS s0 range (**-r**) for the default user. Here, "__default__" includes two underscore characters on each side of the word. As long as user_u is in effect for the default SELinux user, regular users won't have access to use administrative tools or commands such as **su** and **sudo**. The following command reverses the process:

```
# semanage login -m -S targeted -s "unconfined_u" \
-r s0-s0:c0.c1023 __default__
```

e x a m

w a t c h   **The MLS policy adds complexity to SELinux. The targeted default policy with appropriate booleans and file**   **contexts normally provides more than adequate security.**

The full MLS range is required (s0-s0:c0.c1023) because the unconfined_u user is not normally limited by MLS restrictions.

Manage SELinux Boolean Settings

Most SELinux settings are boolean—in other words, they're activated and deactivated by setting them to 1 or 0, respectively. Once set, the booleans can be retrieved from the /sys/fs/selinux/booleans directory. One simple example is selinuxuser_ping, which is normally set to 1, which allows users to run the **ping** and **traceroute** commands. Many of these SELinux settings are associated with specific RHCE services and will be covered in the second half of this book.

These settings can be read with the **getsebool** and modified with the **setsebool** commands. For example, the following output from the **getsebool user_exec_content** command confirms that SELinux allows users to execute scripts either in their home directories or from the /tmp directory:

```
user_exec_content --> on
```

This default applies to SELinux user_u users. In other words, with this boolean, such users can create and execute scripts in the noted directories. That boolean can be disabled either temporarily or in a way that survives a reboot. One method for doing so is with the **setsebool** command. For example, the following command disables the noted boolean until the system is rebooted:

```
# setsebool user_exec_content off
```

You can choose to substitute **=0** for **off** in the command. As this is a boolean setting, the effect is the same: the flag is switched off. However, the **-P** switch is required to make the change to the boolean setting survive a system reboot. Be aware, the changes don't take effect until the next time the affected user actually logs in to the associated system.

A full list of available booleans is available in the output to the **getsebool -a** command.

For more information on each boolean, run the **semanage boolean -l** command. Although the output includes descriptions of all available booleans, it is a database that can be searched with the help of the **grep** command.

List and Identify SELinux File Contexts

If you've enabled SELinux, the **ls -Z** command lists current SELinux file contexts, as shown earlier in Figure 4-10. As an example, take the relevant output for the anaconda-ks.cfg file from the /root directory:

```
-rw-------. root root system_u:object_r:admin_home_t:s0↵
anaconda-ks.cfg
```

The output includes the regular ugo/rwx ownership and permission data. It also specifies four elements of SELinux security: the user, role, type, and MLS level for the noted file. Generally, the SELinux user associated with a file is system_u or unconfined_u, and this generally does not affect access. In most cases, files are associated with an object_r, an object role for the file. It's certainly possible that future versions of the SELinux targeted policy will include more fine-grained options for the user and role.

The key file context is the type, in this case, admin_home_t. When you configured FTP and HTTP servers in Chapter 1, you changed the type of the configured directory and the files therein to match the default type of shared files from those services with the **chcon** command.

For example, to configure a nonstandard directory for an FTP server, make sure the context matches the default FTP directory. Consider the following command:

```
# ls -Z /var/ftp/
drwxr-xr-x. root root system_u:object_r:public_content_t pub
```

The contexts are the system user (system_u) and system objects (object_r) for type sharing with the public (public_content_t). If you create another directory for FTP service, you'll need to assign the same security contexts to that directory. For example, if you create an /ftp directory as the root user and run the **ls -Zd /ftp** command, you'll see the contexts associated with the /ftp directory as shown:

```
drwxr-xr-x. root  root  unconfined_u:object_r:root_t   /ftp
```

To change the context, use the **chcon** command. If there are subdirectories, you'll want to make sure changes are made recursively with the **-R** switch. In this case, to change the user and type contexts to match /var/ftp, run the following command:

```
# chcon -R -u system_u -t public_content_t /ftp
```

If you want to support uploads to your FTP server, you'll have to assign a different type context, specifically public_content_rw_t. That corresponds to the following command:

```
# chcon -R -u system_u -t public_content_rw_t /ftp
```

In Chapter 1, you used a different variation on the **chcon** command. To use that lesson, the following command uses user, role, and context from the /var/ftp directory and applies the changes recursively:

```
# chcon -R --reference /var/ftp /ftp
```

But wait, what happens if a filesystem gets relabeled? The changes made with **chcon** won't survive a filesystem relabeling because all file contexts will be reset to the default values defined in the SELinux policy. Hence, we need a way to modify the rules that define the default file context for each file. This subject will be covered in the next section.

on the job

Using restorecon **is the preferred way to change file contexts because it sets the contexts to the values configured in the SELinux policy. The** chcon **command can modify file contexts to any value passed as an argument, but the change may not survive a filesystem relabeling if a context differs from the default value defined in the SELinux policy. Hence, to avoid mistakes, you should modify contexts in the SELinux policy with** semanage fcontext **and use** restorecon **to change file contexts.**

Restore SELinux File Contexts

Default contexts are configured in /etc/selinux/targeted/contexts/files/file_contexts. If you make a mistake and want to restore the original SELinux settings for a file, the **restorecon** command restores those settings based on the file_contexts configuration file. However, the defaults in a directory may vary. For example, the following command (with the **-F** switch forcing a change to all contexts rather than just the type context) leads to a different set of contexts for the /ftp directory:

```
# restorecon -F /ftp
# ls -Zd /ftp
drwxr-xr-x.  root  root  system_u:object_r:default_t  ftp
```

FIGURE 4-11   SELinux context definitions

```
/var/ftp(/.*)?                         all files      system_u:object_r:public_content_t:s0
/var/ftp/bin(/.*)?                     all files      system_u:object_r:bin_t:s0
/var/ftp/etc(/.*)?                     all files      system_u:object_r:etc_t:s0
/var/ftp/lib(/.*)?                     all files      system_u:object_r:lib_t:s0
/var/ftp/lib/ld[^/]*\.so(\.[^/]*)*     regular file   system_u:object_r:ld_so_t:s0
/var/games(/.*)?                       all files      system_u:object_r:games_data_t:s0
/var/imap(/.*)?                        all files      system_u:object_r:cyrus_var_lib_t:s0
/var/kerberos/krb5kdc(/.*)?            all files      system_u:object_r:krb5kdc_conf_t:s0
/var/kerberos/krb5kdc/from_master.*    all files      system_u:object_r:krb5kdc_lock_t:s0
/var/kerberos/krb5kdc/kadm5\.keytab    regular file   system_u:object_r:krb5_keytab_t:s0
/var/kerberos/krb5kdc/principal.*      all files      system_u:object_r:krb5kdc_principal_t:s0
/var/kerberos/krb5kdc/principal.*\.ok  all files      system_u:object_r:krb5kdc_lock_t:s0
```

You may notice that the user context is different from when the /ftp directory was created. That's due to the first line in the aforementioned file_contexts file, which applies the noted contexts:

```
/.*        system_u:object_r:default_t:s0
```

You may also list all default file contexts rules in file_contexts with the **semanage fcontext -l** command. See Figure 4-11 for an excerpt of the output.

As you can see, SELinux context definitions use regular expressions, such as the following:

```
(/.*)?
```

The preceding regular expression matches the / character, followed by an arbitrary number of characters (the **.***). The **?** character means that the entire regular expression within parentheses can be matched zero or one time. Hence, the overall result is to match a / followed by an arbitrary amount of characters, or nothing. This regular expression is widely used to match a directory and all the files in it.

As an example, a regular expression that matches the /ftp directory and all files in it is given by the following:

```
/ftp(/.*)?
```

Using this regular expression, we can define a SELinux policy rule that assigns to the /ftp directory and all files in it a default type context. This can be done with the **semanage fcontext -a** command. For example, the following command assigns a default type context of public_content_t to the /ftp directory and all the files in it:

```
# semanage fcontext -a -t public_content_t '/ftp(/.*)?'
```

Once you have defined a new default policy context for a filesystem path, you can run the **restorecon** command to set the contexts to the corresponding default policy values.

The following command restores the context recursively (**-R**) to the public_content_t value defined previously:

```
# restorecon -RF /ftp
# ls -Zd /ftp
drwxr-xr-x.  root  root  system_u:object_r:public_content_t  ftp
```

Identify SELinux Process Contexts

As discussed in Chapter 9, the **ps** command lists currently running processes. In a SELinux system, there are contexts for each running process. To see those contexts for all processes currently in operation, run the **ps -eZ** command, which lists every (**-e**) process SELinux context (**-Z**). Figure 4-12 includes a varied excerpt from the output of that command on our system.

Although the user and role don't change often, the process type varies widely, frequently matching the purpose of the running process. For example, from the bottom of the figure, you can see how the Avahi daemon (avahi-daemon) is matched by the avahi_t SELinux type. You should be able to identify how at least some of the other SELinux types match the associated service.

In other words, although there is a large variety of SELinux types, they're consistent with the running process.

FIGURE 4-12

SELinux security contexts of different processes

```
system_u:system_r:kernel_t:s0          486 ?   00:00:00 rpciod
system_u:system_r:syslogd_t:s0         499 ?   00:00:00 systemd-journal
system_u:system_r:lvm_t:s0             502 ?   00:00:00 lvmetad
system_u:system_r:udev_t:s0-s0:c0.c1023 517 ?  00:00:00 systemd-udevd
system_u:system_r:kernel_t:s0          537 ?   00:00:00 vballoon
system_u:system_r:kernel_t:s0          562 ?   00:00:00 kvm-irqfd-clean
system_u:system_r:kernel_t:s0          569 ?   00:00:00 hd-audio0
system_u:system_r:kernel_t:s0          588 ?   00:00:00 xfs-data/vda1
system_u:system_r:kernel_t:s0          591 ?   00:00:00 xfs-conv/vda1
system_u:system_r:kernel_t:s0          592 ?   00:00:00 xfs-cil/vda1
system_u:system_r:kernel_t:s0          594 ?   00:00:00 xfsaild/vda1
system_u:system_r:auditd_t:s0          600 ?   00:00:00 auditd
system_u:system_r:audisp_t:s0          608 ?   00:00:00 audispd
system_u:system_r:audisp_t:s0          613 ?   00:00:00 sedispatch
system_u:system_r:alsa_t:s0            627 ?   00:00:00 alsactl
system_u:system_r:firewalld_t:s0       629 ?   00:00:00 firewalld
system_u:system_r:avahi_t:s0           632 ?   00:00:00 avahi-daemon
system_u:system_r:syslogd_t:s0         633 ?   00:00:00 rsyslogd
system_u:system_r:tuned_t:s0           634 ?   00:00:00 tuned
system_u:system_r:abrt_t:s0-s0:c0.c1023 636 ?  00:00:00 abrtd
system_u:system_r:abrt_watch_log_t:s0 637 ?    00:00:00 abrt-watch-log
system_u:system_r:abrt_watch_log_t:s0 640 ?    00:00:00 abrt-watch-log
system_u:system_r:avahi_t:s0           650 ?   00:00:00 avahi-daemon
:
```

Diagnose and Address SELinux Policy Violations

If there's a problem, SELinux is running in enforcing mode, and you're sure there are no problems with the target service or application, don't disable SELinux! Red Hat has made it easier to manage and troubleshoot. According to Red Hat, the top two causes of SELinux-related problems are contexts and boolean settings.

SELinux Audits

Problems with SELinux should be documented in the associated log file, audit.log, in the /var/log/audit directory. The file may be confusing, especially the first time you read it. A number of tools are available to help decipher this log.

First, the audit search (**ausearch**) command can help filter for specific types of problems. For example, the following command lists all SELinux events associated with the use of the **sudo** command:

```
# ausearch -m avc -c sudo
```

Such events are known as Access Vector Cache (**-m avc**) messages; the **-c** allows you to specify the name commonly used in the log, such as httpd or su. If you've experimented with the user_u SELinux user described earlier in this chapter, there should be several related messages available from the audit.log file.

Even for most administrators, the output is still a lot of gobbledygook. However, it should include identifying information such as the audited user ID (shown as auid), which can help you identify the offending user. Perhaps the user needs such access, or perhaps that user's account has been compromised. In any case, the alert may cause you to pay more attention to that account.

In contrast, the **sealert -a /var/log/audit/audit.log** command may provide more clarity. An excerpt is shown in Figure 4-13.

SELinux Label and Context Issues

Considering Figure 4-13 and the SELinux concepts described so far, you might wonder if the user in question is allowed to run the **su** command. If the problem were in the /etc/sudoers file covered in Chapter 8, the SELinux alert message might not even appear. So you should pay attention to the source and target contexts. As they match, the file context is not the issue.

By process of elimination, that points to the user context described earlier as the problem. The UID of the user in question should be listed later in the file, under "Raw Audit Messages." If the user in question requires access to the **su** and **sudo** commands, you should change the role of that user with the **semanage login** command described earlier. Otherwise, the user might just be experimenting with Linux. Any access to the **sudo** command will be documented in the /var/log/secure log file.

A SELinux alert

```
SELinux is preventing /usr/bin/su from using the setuid capability.

*****  Plugin catchall_boolean (89.3 confidence) suggests   ******************

If you want to allow user  to use ssh chroot environment.
Then you must tell SELinux about this by enabling the 'selinuxuser_use_ssh_chroot'
 boolean.
You can read 'user_selinux' man page for more details.
Do
setsebool -P selinuxuser_use_ssh_chroot 1

*****  Plugin catchall (11.6 confidence) suggests   **************************

If you believe that su should have the setuid capability by default.
Then you should report this as a bug.
You can generate a local policy module to allow this access.
Do
allow this access for now by executing:
# grep su /var/log/audit/audit.log | audit2allow -M mypol
# semodule -i mypol.pp


Additional Information:
Source Context             user_u:user_r:user_t:s0
Target Context             user_u:user_r:user_t:s0
Target Objects             [ capability ]
Source                     su
Source Path                /usr/bin/su
Port                       <Unknown>
Host                       <Unknown>
Source RPM Packages        sudo-1.8.6p7-11.el7.x86_64
Target RPM Packages
Policy RPM                 selinux-policy-3.12.1-153.el7_0.13.noarch
Selinux Enabled            True
Policy Type                targeted
Enforcing Mode             Enforcing
:█
```

SELinux Boolean Issues

After deactivating the user_exec_content boolean described earlier, we created a simple script named script1 for a user governed by the user_u label. After making that script executable, we tried running it with the **/home/examprep/script1** command. Even though that user had ownership of the file, with executable permissions set, that attempt led to the following message:

```
-bash: /home/examprep/script1: Permission denied
```

That led to the log excerpt shown in Figure 4-14. Note the section on the top; it explicitly cites the command required to address the problem. As an administrator, you need to decide whether such users should be given the ability to execute their own scripts. If so, then the noted command would address the problem.

A SELinux alert
and a solution

```
-------------------------------------------------------------------------------
SELinux is preventing /usr/bin/bash from execute access on the file .

*****  Plugin catchall_boolean (89.3 confidence) suggests   ******************

If you want to allow user to exec content
Then you must tell SELinux about this by enabling the 'user_exec_content' boolean.
You can read 'user_selinux' man page for more details.
Do
setsebool -P user_exec_content 1

*****  Plugin catchall (11.6 confidence) suggests   **************************

If you believe that bash should be allowed execute access on the  file by default.
Then you should report this as a bug.
You can generate a local policy module to allow this access.
Do
allow this access for now by executing:
# grep bash /var/log/audit/audit.log | audit2allow -M mypol
# semodule -i mypol.pp


Additional Information:
Source Context                   user_u:user_r:user_t:s0
Target Context                   unconfined_u:object_r:user_home_t:s0
Target Objects                    [ file ]
Source                           bash
:█
```

The GUI SELinux Administration Tool

If you've taken the time to learn SELinux from the command line, this section should be just a review. For many users, the easiest way to change SELinux settings is with the SELinux Administration tool, which you can start with the **system-config-selinux** command. As shown in Figure 4-15, it starts with a basic view of the status of SELinux on the local system, reflecting some of the information shown in the output to the **sestatus** command.

As you can see, there are options labeled Default Enforcing Mode and Current Enforcing Mode, which you can set to Enforcing, Permissive, or Disabled. Although the focus of SELinux is on a Targeted policy, MLS is also available if you install the selinux-policy-mls package. Generally, you don't need to activate the Relabel On Next Reboot option unless you've changed the default policy type.

There are a number of categories shown in the left pane of the SELinux Management Tool window described in the following sections. In the RHCE half of this book, you'll revisit this tool with more of a focus on boolean settings.

SELinux Boolean Settings

In the SELinux Administration tool, click Boolean in the left panel. Scroll through available modules. As you can see, a SELinux policy can be modified in a number of different

FIGURE 4-15   SELinux status in the Administration tool

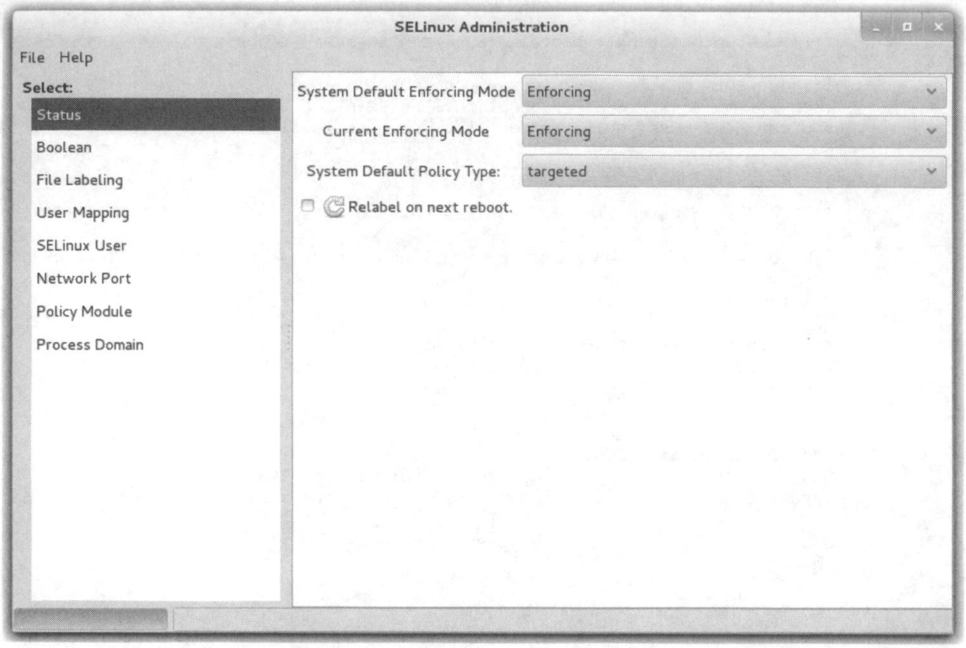

categories, some related to administrative functions, others to specific services. A select number of these options are shown in Figure 4-16. Any changes you make are reflected in boolean variables in the /sys/fs/selinux/booleans directory. Module categories of interest for the RHCSA exam include cron, mount, virt, and that catch-all category: unknown. A list of selected booleans is included in Table 4-12. The booleans appear in the order shown in the SELinux Management tool.

File Labeling

You can change the default labels associated with files, some of which are described earlier in this chapter (and in other chapters discussing SELinux contexts). Some of the options are shown in Figure 4-17. Any changes to this screen are written to the file_contexts.local file in the /etc/selinux/targeted/contexts/files directory.

User Mapping

The User Mapping section allows you to go beyond the defaults for regular and administrative users. The display here illustrates the current output to the **semanage login -l**

FIGURE 4-16   Booleans in the SELinux Administration tool

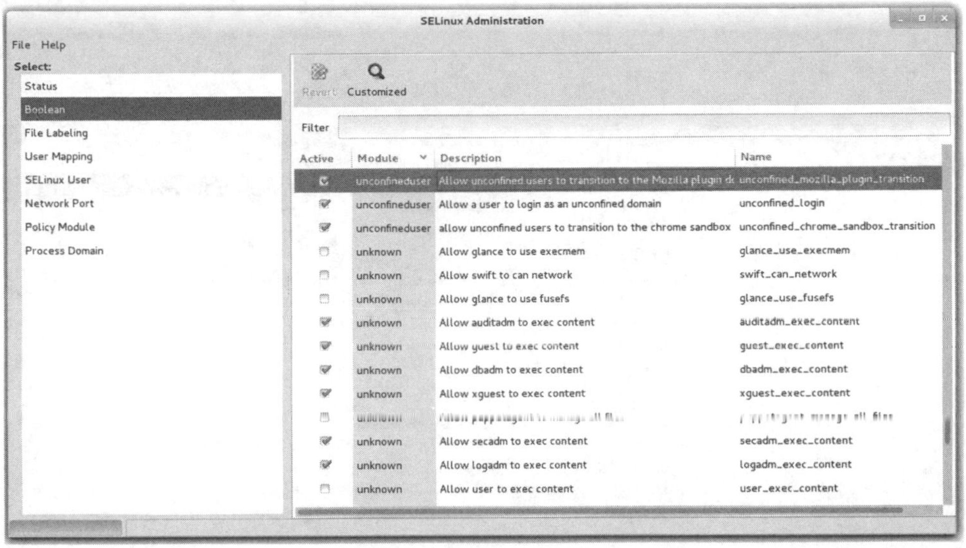

TABLE 4-12   Selected SELinux Boolean Options

Boolean	Description
fcron_crond	Supports fcron rules for job scheduling
cron_can_relabel	Allows cron jobs to change the SELinux file context label
mount_anyfile	Permits the use of the **mount** command on any file
daemons_use_tty	Lets service daemons use terminals as needed
daemons_dump_core	Supports writing of core files to the top-level root directory
virt_use_nfs	Supports the use of NFS filesystems for virtual machines
virt_use_comm	Supports a connection for virtual machines to serial and parallel ports
virt_use_usb	Supports the use of USB devices for virtual machines
virt_use_samba	Supports the use of CIFS (Common Internet File System) filesystems for virtual machines
guest_exec_content	Allows guest_u users the right to execute scripts
xguest_exec_content	Allows xguest_u users the right to execute scripts
user_exec_content	Allows user_u users the right to execute scripts
staff_exec_content	Allows staff_u users the right to execute scripts
sysadm_exec_content	Allows sysadm_u users the right to execute scripts

FIGURE 4-17   File types in the SELinux Administration tool

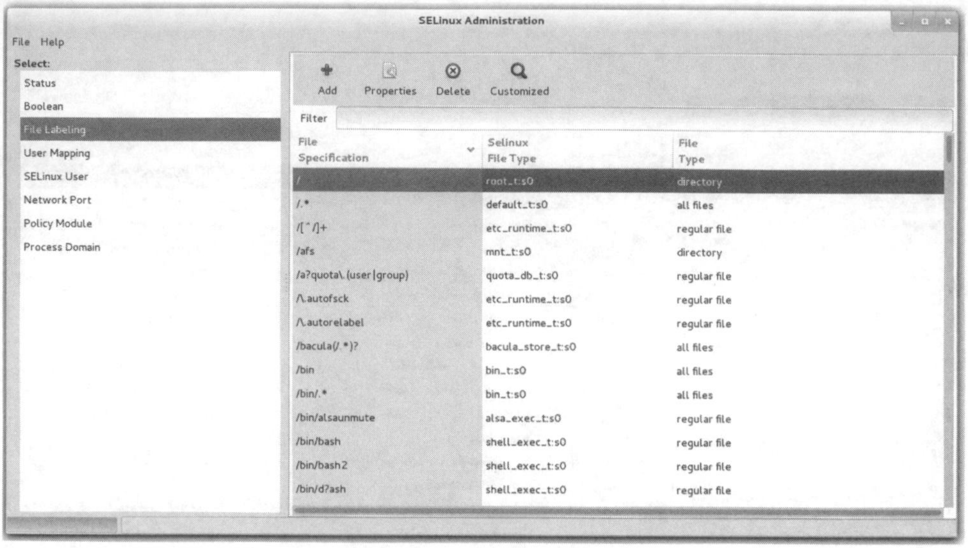

command. If you don't remember the intricacies of the **semanage** command, it may be easier to use this screen to map existing users to different contexts. Click Add to open the Add User Mapping window shown in Figure 4-18. This figure also illustrates how you might reclassify a user named michael as a SELinux user_u user type.

SELinux User

The SELinux User section allows you to specify and modify default roles for standard users, such as regular users (user_u), system users (system_u), and unconfined users (unconfined_u).

Network Port

The Network Port section associates standard ports with services.

Policy Module

The Policy Module section specifies the SELinux policy version number applied to each module.

| FIGURE 4-18 | Map a user in the SELinux Management tool. |

Process Domain

The Process Domain allows you to change the status of SELinux to Permissive or Enforcing mode for a single process domain, rather than for the whole system.

The SELinux Troubleshoot Browser

RHEL 7 includes the SELinux Troubleshoot Browser shown in Figure 4-19. It provides tips and advice on any problems you may encounter in a language that Linux administrators can understand, often including commands that you can run and that will address the subject problem.

To start the browser from the GNOME desktop, click Applications | Sundry | SELinux Troubleshooter or run **sealert -b** from a GUI-based command line. The command is available from the setroubleshoot-server package.

FIGURE 4-19   Security alerts with the SELinux Troubleshoot Browser

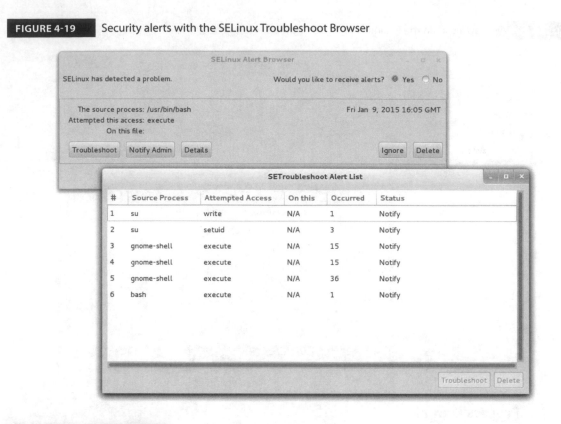

EXERCISE 4-3

Test a SELinux User Type

In this exercise, you'll configure a user with the staff_u SELinux user type and test the results. You'll need a GUI and at least one regular user other than the root administrative user.

1. If necessary, create a regular user. Even if you already have a regular user, a second regular user for the purpose of this exercise may reduce risks. Users can always be deleted, as discussed in Chapter 8. To that end, the **useradd user1** and **passwd user1** commands create a user named user1 with a password.

2. Review the SELinux types of current users with the **semanage login -l** command.

3. Configure the desired user as a staff_u user with the **semanage login -a -s staff_u user1** command. Substitute as desired for user1.

4. If you're completely logged in to the GUI, log out. Click System | Log Out, and click Log Out in the window that appears.

5. Log in to the GUI with the newly revised staff_u account, user1 (or whatever else you may have configured in Step 3). If you don't already see a GUI login screen, press ALT-F1 or ALT-F7.

6. Try various administrative commands. Do you have access to the **su** command? What of **sudo**? You may want to review this exercise after reading Chapter 8 if you don't know how to use **sudo**. What administrative tools discussed so far in this book are accessible? Is there a difference whether that tool is started from the GUI command line or from the GUI menu?

7. Log out of the new user1 account, and log back in to the regular account.

8. Delete the new user from the staff_u list; if that's user1, you can do so with the **semanage login -d user1** command.

9. Confirm the restored configuration with the **semanage login -l** command.

SCENARIO & SOLUTION

A file can't be read, written to, or executed.	Review current ownership and permissions with the **ls -l** command. Apply ownership changes with the **chown** and **chgrp** commands. Apply permission changes with the **chmod** command.
Access to a secure file is required for a single user.	Configure an ACL using the **setfacl** command to provide access.
The SSH service is not accessible on a server.	Assuming the SSH service is running (a RHCE requirement), make sure the firewall supports SSH access with the **firewall-cmd --list-all** command; revise as needed with the **firewall-config** tool.
Enforcing mode is not set for SELinux.	Set enforcing mode with the **setenforce enforcing** command. Check the default boot settings in /etc/selinux/config.
Need to restore SELinux default file contexts on a directory.	Apply the **restorecon -F** command to the target directory. Use the **-R** switch to change the contexts recursively for all files and subdirectories.
Unexpected failure when SELinux is set in enforcing mode.	Use the **sealert -a /var/log/audit/audit.log** command or the SELinux Troubleshooter to find more information about the failure; sometimes a suggested solution is included.
Need to change SELinux options for a user.	Apply the **setsebool -P** command to the appropriate boolean setting.

CERTIFICATION SUMMARY

This chapter focused on the basics of RHCSA-level security. On any Linux system, security starts with the ownership and permissions associated with a file. Ownership may be divided into users, groups, and others. Permissions may be divided into read, write, and execute in a scheme known as discretionary access controls. Default file permissions are based on the value of **umask** for a user. Permissions may be extended with the SUID, SGID, and sticky bits.

ACLs can add another dimension to discretionary access controls. When configured on a mounted volume, ACLs can be configured to supersede basic ugo/rwx permissions. ACLs can be included in NFSv4 shared directories.

Firewalls can prevent communication on all but the desired ports. Standard ports for most services are defined in the /etc/services file. However, some services may not use all of the protocols defined in that file. The default RHEL 7 firewall supports access only to a local SSH server.

The **ssh-keygen** command creates passphrase-protected key pairs, which can be used to authenticate to an SSH server without transmitting a user's password over the network.

SELinux provides another layer of protection using mandatory access control. With a variety of available SELinux users, objects, file types, and MLS ranges, SELinux controls can help ensure that a breach in one service doesn't lead to trouble with other services.

✔ TWO-MINUTE DRILL

Here are some of the key points from the certification objectives in Chapter 4.

Basic File Permissions

❑ Standard Linux file permissions are read, write, and execute, which may vary for the user owner, the group owner, and other users.

❑ Special permissions include the SUID, SGID, and sticky bits.

❑ Default user permissions are based on the value of the **umask**.

❑ Ownership and permissions can be changed with the **chown**, **chgrp**, and **chmod** commands.

❑ Special file attributes can be listed with the **lsattr** command and modified by the **chattr** command.

Access Control Lists and More

❑ ACLs can be listed and modified on filesystems mounted with the **acl** option. The XFS and ext4 filesystems created on RHEL 7 have such an option enabled by default.

❑ Every file already has ACLs based on standard ownership and permissions.

❑ You can configure ACLs on a file to supersede standard ownership and permissions for specified users and groups on selected files. Actual ACLs may depend on the mask.

❑ Custom ACLs on a file are not enough; selected users and groups also need access to the directories that contain such files.

❑ Just as custom ACLs can support special access for selected users, they can also deny access to other selected users.

❑ ACLs can be configured on shared NFS directories.

Basic Firewall Control

❑ Standard Linux firewalls are based on the Netfilter kernel system and on the **iptables** tool.

❑ Standard Linux firewalls assume the use of some of the ports and protocols listed in /etc/services.

❑ The default RHEL 7 firewall supports remote access to the local SSH server.

❑ The RHEL 7 firewall can be configured with the GUI **firewall-config** tool or the console-based tool **firewall-cmd** command.

Securing SSH with Key-Based Authentication

❑ SSH configuration commands include **ssh-keygen** and **ssh-copy-id**.

❑ User home directories include their own .ssh subdirectory of configuration files, with private and public SSH keys, suitable for passphrases.

❑ Private/public key pairs can be configured with passphrases using the **ssh-keygen** command.

❑ Public keys can be transmitted to users' home directories on remote systems with the **ssh-copy-id** command.

A Security-Enhanced Linux Primer

❑ SELinux may be configured in enforcing, permissive, or disabled mode, with targeted or MLS policies, with the help of the **setenforce** command. Default boot settings are stored in the /etc/selinux/config file.

❑ User options for SELinux can be set with the **semanage login** command.

❑ SELinux labels contain different contexts, such as user, roles, types, and MLS levels.

❑ SELinux booleans can be managed with the **setsebool** command; permanent changes require the **-P** switch.

❑ SELinux contexts can be changed with the **chcon** command and restored to defaults with the **restorecon** command.

❑ The **sealert** command and the SELinux Troubleshoot Browser can be used to interpret problems documented in the audit.log file in the /var/log/audit directory.

SELF TEST

The following questions will help you measure your understanding of the material presented in this chapter. As no multiple choice questions appear on the Red Hat exams, no multiple choice questions appear in this book. These questions exclusively test your understanding of the chapter. Getting results, not memorizing trivia, is what counts on the Red Hat exams. There may be more than one right answer to many of these questions.

Basic File Permissions

1. What command configures read and write permissions on the file named question1 in the local directory, for the file owner, with no permissions for any other user?

   _____

2. What single command changes the user owner to professor and group owner to assistants for the local file named question2?

   _____

3. What command would change the attributes of a file named question3 to allow you to only append to that file?

   _____

Access Control Lists and More

4. What command reads current ACLs for the local file named question4? Assume that file is on a filesystem with ACL support enabled.

_____

5. What single command gives members of the group named managers read access to the project5 file in the /home/project directory? Assume the managers group already has read and execute access to the directory.

_____

6. What command prevents members of the group named temps from having any access to the secret6 file in the /home/project directory?

_____

Basic Firewall Control

7. What TCP/IP port number is associated with the HTTP service?

_____

8. List the full **firewall-cmd** command to permanently allow incoming HTTP traffic for the default firewalld zone.

_____

Securing SSH with Key-Based Authentication

9. What command configures a private/public key pair using DSA?

_____

10. What subdirectory of a user home directory contains the authorized_keys file?

_____

A Security-Enhanced Linux Primer

11. What command configures SELinux in enforcing mode?

_____

12. What command lists the SELinux status of current users?

_____

13. What command lists all boolean settings for SELinux?

_____

LAB QUESTIONS

Several of these labs involve configuration exercises. You should do these exercises on test machines only. It's assumed that you're running these exercises on virtual machines such as KVM and they're not used for production.

Red Hat presents its exams electronically. For that reason, most of the labs in this and future chapters are available from the media that accompanies the book. For this chapter's lab, look in the Chapter4/ subdirectory. In case you haven't yet set up RHEL 7 on a system, refer to Chapter 1 for installation instructions.

The answers for each lab follow the Self Test answers for the fill-in-the-blank questions.

SELF TEST ANSWERS

Basic File Permissions

1. The command that configures read and write permissions on the file named question1 in the local directory, with no permissions for any other user, is

   ```
   # chmod 600 question1
   ```

2. The single command that changes the user owner to professor and group owner to assistants for the noted file is

   ```
   # chown professor.assistants question2
   ```

   It's acceptable to substitute a colon (:) for the dot (.).

3. The command that changes the attributes of a file named question3 to allow you to only append to that file is

   ```
   # chattr +a question3
   ```

Access Control Lists and More

4. The command that reads current ACLs for the local file named question4 is

```
# getfacl question4
```

5. The single command that gives members of the group named managers read access to the project5 file in the /home/project directory is

```
# setfacl -m g:managers:r /home/project/project5
```

6. The command that prevents members of the group named temps from having any access to the secret6 file in the /home/project directory is

```
# setfacl -m g:temps:- /home/project/secret6
```

Basic Firewall Control

7. The TCP/IP port number associated with the HTTP service is 80.

8. The **firewall-cmd** command that permanently allows incoming HTTP traffic for the default firewalld zone is

```
# firewall-cmd --permanent --add-service=http
```

Securing SSH with Key-Based Authentication

9. The command is **ssh-keygen -t dsa**.

10. Every user with public keys stored in the authorized_keys file can find that file in the .ssh/ subdirectory of her home directory.

A Security-Enhanced Linux Primer

11. The command that configures SELinux in enforcing mode is

```
# setenforce enforcing
```

12. The command that lists the SELinux status of current users is

```
# semanage login -l
```

13. The command that lists all boolean settings for SELinux is

```
# semanage boolean -l
```

LAB ANSWERS

Lab 1

Lab 1 is designed to let you practice configuring permissions associated with the SUID bit of /usr/bin/passwd.

Lab 2

Lab 2 shows an approach to making a script owned by a user executable by another user. If the script is properly executed by the ACL-configured regular user, you'll find a file named filelist in the local directory.

Lab 3

The configuration of ACLs on the /root administrative directory is a bad security practice. However, it is an excellent way to illustrate the capabilities of ACLs on a system and how it can allow access by selected regular users to the inner sanctums of the root administrative account. Because of the risks, disable the ACLs when the lab is complete. If the selected user is michael, one method is with the following command:

```
# setfacl -b u:michael /root
```

Lab 4

This lab is designed to raise awareness of the time and effort required to disable and re-enable SELinux in enforcing mode. If you switch between disabled and permissive mode, the time and effort required should be about the same. If you have to reconfigure SELinux in enforcing mode, you may lose precious time during a Red Hat exam because nothing else can be done while the system is being rebooted and relabeled.

Lab 5

Standard users in RHEL 7 run as unconfined_u SELinux user types. As such, there are few limits on their user accounts. If instructions on an exam or from a corporate policy require certain limits on regular users, you may want to set up the __default__ user with the SELinux user_u user type. Alternatively, if you're told to set up specific users to a limited type, such as xguest_u or staff_u, multiple **semanage login** commands may be appropriate. If you need to review the syntax of the **semanage login** command, run **man semanage-login**.

Lab 6

After testing a user as a guest_u user, most administrators will want regular users to have more privileges. However, the guest_u user is suitable for systems such as an edge server, where you want user accounts to be locked down.

Lab 7

Users configured with the guest_u SELinux user type are normally allowed to execute scripts even in their own home directories. That can change with the guest_exec_content boolean described in the lab. Success in this lab is based on a simple comparison: whether a binary can be executed with and without the active boolean.

Although the easiest way to restore the original configuration is with the GUI SELinux management tool, you should also know how to use commands such as the following, which disables a custom SELinux user type for user michael:

```
# semanage login -d michael
```

Lab 8

Success in this lab can be measured first with the **ls -Zd** command. When applied to both the /ftp and the /var/ftp/pub directories, it should lead to the same list of SELinux roles, objects, types, and MLS options for each directory.

Then, run the **restorecon -R /ftp** command and check again the SELinux type of the /ftp directory. If it has changed, it means you have missed the **semanage fcontext** command to modify the default file contexts described in the chapter.

Lab 9

Everyone will experiment with SELinux in different ways. So the results of this lab are up to you. The objective is to analyze a current relevant log file and process it at the command line. Try to identify the problems associated with each alert. Although you may not be able to address many SELinux issues, at least until the second half of this book, you should be able to identify the problems or at least the users and/or commands associated with each alert.

Chapter 5

The Boot Process

This chapter is focused on what happens from the moment a system is powered up to the time a login prompt is available. This is called the boot process. When RHEL 7 is properly installed, the BIOS/UEFI points to a specific media device. Assuming it's a local hard drive, the GUID Partition Table (GPT) or Master Boot Record (MBR) of that device points to the GRUB 2 bootloader. Once an option to boot RHEL 7 is selected in GRUB 2, the associated commands point to and initialize the Linux kernel, which then starts **systemd**, the first Linux process. The **systemd** process then initializes the system and activates appropriate system units. When Linux boots into a specific target, it starts a series of units, including the client associated with the Network Time Protocol (NTP). You can customize this process.

INSIDE THE EXAM

Understanding the Boot Process

Objectives related to the boot process have been consolidated into the RHCSA exam. Perhaps the most basic skill related to the boot process is an understanding of the commands that start and stop the boot process, such as **systemctl poweroff** and **systemctl reboot**:

- Boot, reboot, and shut down a system normally

Of course, that starts with the way a system is powered up. In this chapter, you'll be introduced to systemd targets, which replace the traditional runlevels in RHEL 6 and other older Linux distributions. From the standard RHEL 7 boot menu, you need to know how to

- Boot systems into different targets manually

Closely related to this objective is this one:

- Interrupt the boot process in order to gain access to a system

If you are already familiar with single-user mode in RHEL 6, you should understand that "access" in single-user mode is password-free access to the root administrative account in a limited environment. You should be able to achieve the same objective in RHEL 7 and gain access to a system to recover a lost root password or to troubleshoot issues during the boot process.

Also closely related is this objective, focused on the configuration of different targets:

- Configure systems to boot into a specific target automatically

As Linux is a network operating system, and as most users can't do much without networking, it's important to know how to

- Configure network services to start automatically at boot

The following RHCSA objective is strictly related to the previous one:

- Start and stop services and configure services to start automatically at boot

With the focus on the boot process, you'll also learn how to

- Modify the system bootloader

Closely related to these objectives, and part of the boot process, are objectives related to how filesystems are mounted, as covered in Chapter 6.

The Network Time Service

This chapter covers the configuration of NTP, based on the following objective:

- Configure a system to use time services

CERTIFICATION OBJECTIVE 5.01

The BIOS and the UEFI

Although not officially a Red Hat exam prerequisite or requirement, a basic understanding of the BIOS and the UEFI is a fundamental skill for all serious computer users. The UEFI has replaced the BIOS on many modern systems and can do so much more. But as the UEFI supports changes to boot media in similar ways, the functionality for our purposes is the same.

Because of the variety of BIOS/UEFI software available, this discussion is general. It's not possible to provide any sort of step-by-step instructions for modifying the wide array of available BIOS/UEFI menus. In any case, such instructions are not directly relevant either to the administration of Linux or to any of the Red Hat exams. However, these skills can help you boot from different Linux installation media, access default virtualization settings, and more.

Basic System Configuration

When a computer is powered up, the first thing that starts is the BIOS/UEFI. Based on settings stored in stable, read-only memory, the BIOS/UEFI system performs a series of diagnostics to detect and connect the CPU and key controllers. This is known as the Power On Self Test (POST). If you hear beeps during this process, there may be a hardware problem such as an improperly connected hard drive controller. The BIOS/UEFI system then looks for attached devices such as the graphics card. After the graphics hardware is detected, you may see a screen similar to Figure 5-1, which displays other hardware as detected, tested, and verified.

If your system has an UEFI menu, it may include a Trusted Platform Module (TPM). Although it's built to enhance security on a system, it has caused controversy within the open-source community due to privacy and vendor lock-in issues. Many open-source

FIGURE 5-1	`F2  = System Setup`
	`F10 = Lifecycle Controller`
	`F11 = Boot Manager`
	`Force PXE Boot Requested via Attribute`

The BIOS
Initialization menu
	`Initializing Serial ATA devices...`
	` Port J: PLDS DVD+/-RW DS-8ABSH`
	
	`Initializing Intel(R) Boot Agent XE v2.3.27`
	`PXE 2.1 Build 092 (WfM 2.0)`
	
	.
	
	`PowerEdge Expandable RAID Controller BIOS`
	`Copyright(c) 2014 LSI Corporation`
	`Press <Ctrl><R> to Run Configuration Utility`
	`F/W Initializing Devices 26%`

professionals are working to minimize any such problems through the Open Trusted Computing (OpenTC) group of the European Union. RHEL 7 takes advantage of TPM hardware features to enhance system security.

Once complete, the BIOS/UEFI passes control to the boot device, typically the first hard drive. The first stage of the GRUB 2 bootloader is normally copied to the MBR or GUID Partition Table (GPT). It serves as a pointer to the other information from the GRUB 2 menu. At that point, you should see a bootloader screen.

Startup Menus

Generally, the only reason to access the BIOS/UEFI menu during the Red Hat exams is to boot from different media, such as a CD, floppy, or USB key. In many cases, you can bypass this process.

Sometimes, all you see after POST is a blank screen. The BIOS/UEFI is often configured in this way. In that case, you'll need to do some guessing based on your experience on how to access the boot or BIOS menu.

In many cases, boot menus are directly accessible by pressing a key such as ESC, DEL, F1, F2, or F12. Such boot menus may have entries similar to the following:

```
     Boot Menu
1. Removable Devices
2. Hard Drive
3. CD-ROM Drive
4. USB Drive
5. Built-In LAN
```

From that or similar menus, you should be able to select the desired boot device using the ARROW and ENTER keys. If that doesn't work, you'll have to use the BIOS/UEFI menu to boot from the desired drive.

Access to Linux Bootloaders

As noted in Chapter 2, the default bootloader is GRUB 2, and the first part of it (known as stage 1) is installed in the MBR or GUID table of the default drive. Normally, the BIOS should automatically start the bootloader, with a message similar to

```
Red Hat Enterprise Linux Server, with Linux 3.10.0-123.el7.x86_64
Red Hat Enterprise Linux Server, with Linux 0-rescue-662ce234911596f1a75
...
The selected entry will be started automatically in 5s.
```

FIGURE 5-2   The GRUB menu

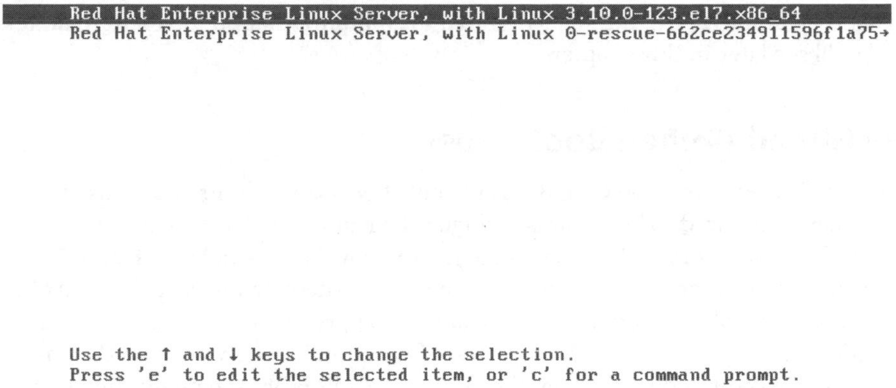

```
Red Hat Enterprise Linux Server, with Linux 3.10.0-123.el7.x86_64
Red Hat Enterprise Linux Server, with Linux 0-rescue-662ce234911596f1a75→
```

```
Use the ↑ and ↓ keys to change the selection.
Press 'e' to edit the selected item, or 'c' for a command prompt.
```

Alternatively, if you press a key before those five seconds are complete, GRUB will present a menu similar to that shown in Figure 5-2.

If the system includes more than one Linux kernel, or more than one operating system, there may be multiple choices available, which you can highlight with the UP ARROW and DOWN ARROW keys. To boot Linux from the highlighted option, press ENTER.

On old PCs (pre-21st century), some BIOSes could not find your bootloader unless it was located within the first 1024 cylinders of the hard disk. For that reason, the partition where the /boot directory is configured is normally the first available primary partition.

RHEL 7 supports the traditional MBR partitioning layout and the newer GUID Partition Table (GPT) format. Whereas the MBR partitioning scheme supports a maximum size of 2TB per disk, GPT does not have such limitation. However, to boot RHEL from a disk with a GPT partition layout, you need a system with the UEFI firmware interface, rather than a traditional BIOS firmware. You should check with your hardware vendor if UEFI is supported by your system.

CERTIFICATION OBJECTIVE 5.02

Bootloaders and GRUB 2

The standard bootloader associated with Red Hat Enterprise Linux (RHEL) is GRUB 2, the GRand Unified Bootloader version 2. As suggested by the Red Hat exam requirements, for the RHCSA exam you need to know how to use the GRUB 2 menu to boot into different targets and diagnose and correct boot failures arising from bootloader errors. In GRUB version 1, which was the default in RHEL 6, the associated configuration file was relatively easy to understand and customize. However, although the GRUB 2.0 menu is similar to what's seen on RHEL 6, the steps required to configure that bootloader are quite different, as you'll see later in this chapter.

GRUB, the GRand Unified Bootloader

Red Hat has implemented GRUB 2 as the only bootloader for its Linux distributions. It's normally configured to boot into a configured default kernel. GRUB 2 finds the configuration in the /boot directory and displays a menu, which will look similar to Figure 5-2. You can use the GRUB 2 menu to boot any operating system detected during the Linux installation process, or any other operating system added to appropriate configuration files.

GRUB 2 is flexible. Not only can the configuration be easily generated from the CLI, but also it can be edited directly from the GRUB 2 menu. From the menu shown in Figure 5-2, you can press E to temporarily edit the file, or press C to open a GRUB 2 command prompt. This section is focused on booting into different systemd targets.

Boot into Different Targets

To pass a parameter to the kernel through GRUB 2, press E at the first GRUB menu. This allows you to edit the boot parameters sent to the kernel. Locate the line that starts with the directive **linux16**. Scroll down with the DOWN ARROW key if necessary. You might then see a line of commands similar to the following:

```
linux16 /vmlinuz-3.10.0-123.el7.x86_64 root=/dev/mapper/rhel-root
ro rd.lvm.lv=rhel/root vconsole.font=latarcyrheb-sun16
rd.lvm.lv=rhel/swap crashkernel=auto  vconsole.keymap=uk rhgb
quiet LANG=en_GB.UTF-8
```

Yeah, that's a lot of stuff that will be explained shortly. What matters for the RHCSA is that you can add more kernel parameters to the end of this line. For example, if you add the string **systemd.unit=emergency.target** to the end of this line and press CTRL-X, Linux starts in a mode of operation called *emergency target*, which runs a rescue shell.

From the emergency target, type **exit**. The system will go into the default target, which normally is either the multiuser or graphical target. If you have made changes or repairs to any partitions, the next step is to reboot the computer with the **systemctl reboot** command. At some point, changes made during a Red Hat exam should be tested with a reboot.

on the job

On RHEL 7, the shutdown, reboot**, and** halt **commands are symbolic links to** systemctl**. They have the same effect as the** systemctl poweroff**,** systemctl reboot**, and** systemctl halt **commands, respectively.**

To a certain extent, the concept of the systemd targets is similar to that of runlevels in
RHEL 6, and is detailed later in this chapter. For now, all you need to know is that when
RHEL 7 is configured to boot into a GUI, it's configured to boot into the graphical target by
default. That target can be changed by appending a **systemd.unit=***name***.target** string to the
end of the kernel command line.

If you encounter a problem with a system booting into the GUI, the first thing to try is to
add a **systemd.unit=multi-user.target** at the end of the kernel command line. If successful,
it will boot RHEL 7 into text mode with a command-line console-based login.

If you need direct access into a recovery shell, add the string **systemd.unit=rescue.target**
to the end of the kernel command line. In rare cases, some systems are so troubled, they
don't boot into the rescue target. In that case, two other options are available:

- **systemd.unit=emergency.target**   No filesystem is mounted, apart from the root
  filesystem in read-only mode.
- **init=/sysroot/bin/sh**   Starts a shell and mounts the root filesystem in read-only
  mode; does not require a password.

The emergency and rescue targets require the root password to log in and get full root
administrative privileges. If you have lost the root password, you will need to add the
string **init=/sysroot/bin/sh** or **rd.break** to the end of the kernel command line and follow
the procedure illustrated in Exercise 5-2. As that supports full administrative privileges,
including changes to the root administrative password, it's important to password-protect
the GRUB 2 menu. Somebody who can change the boot order can achieve the same thing
with a bootable USB drive, so it is also important to protect your BIOS or UEFI to ensure
the system only boots the local disk without a password.

Now you should understand how to boot into different targets during the boot process.
As defined in the Red Hat Exam Prep guide, this is explicitly described as a RHCSA
requirement:

- Boot systems into different targets manually

e x a m

w a t c h

Red Hat exams are "closed book." Although you are allowed to use all documentation that can be found on your RHEL installation, during recovery or emergency procedures you may not have access to man pages or other documentation resources. Therefore, it is extremely important that you practice the exercises in this chapter without the help of any documentation. You should memorize the steps to boot into an emergency shell or to recover a root password; otherwise, you may be in trouble, not just during the RHCSA exam, but also in real life when performing your job duties as a Linux sysadmin.

EXERCISE 5-1

Boot into a Different Target

One key skill is knowing how to boot into a different systemd target. This exercise assumes you've configured RHEL 7 per Chapter 2, which sets the graphical target as the default. Run the **ls -l /etc/systemd/system/default.target** command to verify. If the current system reflects the defaults, this file should be a symbolic link to the graphical.target file within the directory /usr/lib/systemd/system. As an alternative, run the following command:

```
# systemctl get-default
```

It should return the string "graphical.target." Now you can start the exercise.

1. Reboot your system using the **reboot** command.

2. When you see the following message, make sure to press any key to access the GRUB menu:

```
The selected entry will be started automatically in 5s.
```

3. Press E to edit the current menu entry.

4. Scroll down with the DOWN ARROW key to locate the line starting with **linux16**. First, delete the kernel options **rhgb quiet**. Then, at the end of the line, type **systemd.unit=multi-user.target** and press CTRL-X to boot this kernel.

5. Watch the boot messages. What kind of login screen do you see?

6. Log in to this system. You can use any existing user account.

7. Run the **reboot** command to restart this system.

8. Repeat Steps 2 through 4, but boot this system into the rescue target by passing the option **systemd.unit=rescue.target** to the kernel.

9. Watch the boot messages. What kind of login screen do you see? Which filesystems are mounted?

10. Repeat Steps 2 through 4, but boot this system into the emergency target by passing the option **systemd.unit=emergency.target** to the kernel.

11. Watch the boot messages. What kind of login screen do you see? Do you have to log in at all? Which filesystems are mounted?

12. Repeat Steps 2 through 4, but this time append **rd.break** to the kernel line.

13. Watch the boot messages. What kind of login screen do you see? Do you have to log in at all? Is the root filesystem mounted from the hard drive?

14. Run **exit** to continue the boot sequence.

15. Repeat Steps 2 through 4, but boot this system into an emergency shell by passing the string **init=/sysroot/bin/sh**.

16. Watch the boot messages. What kind of login screen do you see?

17. Type **reboot** to log out and restart the system.

EXERCISE 5-2

Recover the Root Password

If you boot a RHEL 7 system into the rescue or emergency target, you are prompted for the root password. But what if you have forgotten the password? This exercise shows the steps required to reset a lost password for the root user. During the password-recovery process, you probably won't have access to documentation. Hence, you should practice the following procedure until you can use it in a crisis:

1. Use the following command to change the root password to a random string. This command hides the random password from you:

   ```
   # pwmake 128 | passwd --stdin root
   ```

2. Log out from your session. Try to log in again as the root user. You shouldn't be able to log in to the system with the old known root password.

3. Reboot the server.

4. When you see the following message, press a key to access the GRUB menu:

   ```
   The selected entry will be started automatically in 5s.
   ```

5. Press E to edit the current menu entry.

6. Scroll down with the DOWN ARROW key to locate the line starting with **linux16**. Press CTRL-E or END to move to the end of the line, and then type the string **rd.break**.

7. Press CTRL-X to boot the system.

8. The **rd.break** directive interrupts the boot sequence before the root filesystem is properly mounted. Confirm this by running **ls /sysroot**. If you know the contents of the root filesystem, the output should look familiar.

9. Remount the root /sysroot filesystem as read-write and change the root directory to /sysroot:

```
# mount -o remount,rw /sysroot
# chroot /sysroot
```

10. Change the root password:

```
# passwd
```

11. Because SELinux is not running, the **passwd** command does not preserve the context of the /etc/passwd file. To ensure that the /etc/passwd file is labeled with the correct SELinux context, instruct Linux to relabel all files at the next boot with the following command:

```
# touch /.autorelabel
```

12. Type **exit** to close the chroot jail, and then type **exit** again to reboot the system.

13. It may take a few minutes for SELinux to relabel all files. Once you get a login prompt, confirm that you are able to log in as the root user.

Modify the System Bootloader

The RHCSA specifically requires that you need to know how to "modify the system bootloader." That means you need to know how to configure GRUB 2 in detail. The configuration is available in the file /etc/grub2.cfg, which is a symbolic link that points to /boot/grub2/grub.cfg on systems configured in BIOS mode, or /boot/efi/EFI/redhat/grub.cfg for servers that use an UEFI boot manager. In the rest of this chapter, we will assume that you run a traditional BIOS-based system or a UEFI-capable system in BIOS mode. We'll refer to /boot/grub2/grub.cfg as the standard path of the configuration file.

The grub.cfg file is organized into a header section and different **menuentry** stanzas, one for each kernel installed on the system. An excerpt of the file is shown in Figure 5-3. Each **menuentry** block contains two lines starting with the **linux16** and **initrd16** directives. These specify the path of the kernel and of the RAM disk filesystem to be loaded during the

An excerpt of the grub.cfg file

```
menuentry 'Red Hat Enterprise Linux Server (3.10.0-123.13.2.el7.x86_64) 7.0 (Maipo)' --class
 red --class gnu-linux --class gnu --class os --unrestricted $menuentry_id_option 'gnulinux-
3.10.0-123.el7.x86_64-advanced-d055418f-1ff6-46bf-8476-b391e82a6f51' {
        load_video
        set gfxpayload=keep
        insmod gzio
        insmod part_msdos
        insmod xfs
        set root='hd0,msdos1'
        if [ x$feature_platform_search_hint = xy ]; then
          search --no-floppy --fs-uuid --set=root --hint='hd0,msdos1'  26740bbd-3aea-44b9-94
9d-c2ed4017f193
        else
          search --no-floppy --fs-uuid --set=root 26740bbd-3aea-44b9-949d-c2ed4017f193
        fi
        linux16 /vmlinuz-3.10.0-123.13.2.el7.x86_64 root=/dev/mapper/rhel-root ro rd.lvm.lv=
rhel/root vconsole.font=latarcyrheb-sun16 rd.lvm.lv=rhel/swap crashkernel=auto  vconsole.key
map=uk rhgb quiet LANG=en_GB.UTF-8
        initrd16 /initramfs-3.10.0-123.13.2.el7.x86_64.img
}
menuentry 'Red Hat Enterprise Linux Server (3.10.0-123.el7.x86_64) 7.0 (Maipo)' --class red
--class gnu-linux --class gnu --class os --unrestricted $menuentry_id_option 'gnulinux-3.10.
0-123.el7.x86_64-advanced-d055418f-1ff6-46bf-8476-b391e82a6f51' {
        load_video
        set gfxpayload=keep
        insmod gzio
        insmod part_msdos
        insmod xfs
        set root='hd0,msdos1'
```

boot process. As you saw in the previous section, the **linux16** line is especially important. This is the entry that you can edit interactively during the boot process to pass additional kernel parameters or to boot into a non default systemd target.

Although the number of options and directives in the grub.cfg file may seem overwhelming, don't panic. You never need to touch this file directly. The right approach is to generate a new version of this file with the **grub2-mkconfig** tool, based on the /etc/default/grub configuration file and on the scripts in the /etc/grub.d/ directory. The /etc/default/grub file is much simpler to understand, safer, and more convenient to edit than grub.cfg. Once you have made a modification to /etc/default/grub, generate the new GRUB configuration file by running

```
# grub2-mkconfig -o /boot/grub2/grub.cfg
```

Do not manually edit the /etc/grub2/grub.cfg file. This file is automatically generated when a kernel is installed or updated, and as a result any direct customizations to this file would be lost. Use grub2-mkconfig **and the /etc/default/grub file to make modifications to grub.cfg.**

The following is a detailed analysis of a typical version of the /etc/default/grub file:

```
GRUB_TIMEOUT=5
GRUB_DISTRIBUTOR="$(sed 's, release .*$,,g' /etc/system-release)"
GRUB_DEFAULT=saved
GRUB_DISABLE_SUBMENU=true
GRUB_TERMINAL_OUTPUT="console"
GRUB_CMDLINE_LINUX="rd.lvm.lv=rhel/root vconsole.font=latarcyrheb-sun16 ↵
rd.lvm.lv=rhel/swap crashkernel=auto  vconsole.keymap=uk rhgb quiet"
GRUB_DISABLE_RECOVERY="true"
```

In the first line, the GRUB_TIMEOUT variable specifies the time in seconds before GRUB 2 automatically boots the default operating system. You can interrupt the countdown by pressing any key on the keyboard. If this variable is set to 0, GRUB 2 will not display a list of bootable kernels, unless you press and hold an alphanumeric key during the BIOS initial screen.

The value of the GRUB_DISTRIBUTOR variable returns "Red Hat Enterprise Linux Server" on a standard RHEL installation, and is displayed before each kernel-bootable entry. You can modify this entry to any string of your choice if you wish.

The next directive is GRUB_DEFAULT and is related to the default kernel that GRUB 2 loads at boot. The value "saved" instructs GRUB 2 to look at the saved_entry variable in the file /boot/grub2/grubenv. This variable is updated with the name of the latest kernel every time that a new kernel is installed.

You can update the saved_entry variable and instruct GRUB 2 to boot a different default kernel via the **grub2-set-default** command. As an example,

```
# grub2-set-default 1
```

sets the second menu entry in /etc/grub2.cfg as the default kernel. This may be slightly confusing because GRUB 2 starts counting from 0. Hence, **grub2-set-default 0** points to the first available menu entry in /etc/grub2.cfg. Similarly, the command **grub2-set-default 1** points to the second kernel entry, and so on, if included in the configuration file.

The next configuration line in /etc/default/grub defines the variable GRUB_DISABLE_ SUBMENU. This is set to "true" by default to disable any submenu entries at boot. Then follows the directive GRUB_TERMINAL_OUTPUT, which tells GRUB 2 to use a text console as the default output terminal. The last variable defined in the file is GRUB_ DISABLE_RECOVERY, which disables the generation of recovery menu entries.

The directive GRUB_CMDLINE_LINUX is more interesting. It specifies the options to pass to the Linux kernel. For example, **rd.lvm.lv** tells the name of the logical volumes where the root filesystem and swap partition are located. The next options, **vconsole.font** and **vconsole.keymap**, list the default font and keyboard map, respectively. The **crashkernel** option is used to reserve some memory for kdump, which is invoked to capture a kernel core dump if the system crashes. Finally, at the end of the line, the **rhgb quiet** directives enable the Red Hat graphical boot and hide the boot messages by default. If you want to enable verbose boot messages, remove the **quiet** option from this line.

How to Update GRUB

If you've previously installed a different bootloader to the MBR, such as Microsoft's NTLDR or BOOTMGR, just run the **grub2-install** command. If it doesn't automatically write the GRUB 2 pointer to the MBR, or if multiple hard drives are available, you may need to include the hard drive device, such as /dev/sdb. It's also possible to set up GRUB 2 on a portable drive; just specify the device with the command.

When the GRUB 2 configuration file is generated using **grub2-mkconfig**, no additional commands are required. The pointer from the MBR automatically reads the current version of the /boot/grub2/grub.cfg file.

The GRUB 2 Command Line

An error in grub.cfg can result in an unbootable system. For example, if GRUB 2 identifies the wrong volume as the root partition (/), Linux will hang during the boot process. Other configuration errors in /boot/grub2/grub.cfg can lead to a kernel panic during the boot process.

Now that you've analyzed the GRUB 2 configuration file, you can probably visualize some of the effects of errors in this file. If some of the filenames or partitions are wrong, GRUB 2 won't be able to find critical files such as the Linux kernel. If the GRUB 2 configuration file is completely missing, you'll see a prompt similar to this:

```
grub>
```

You can access a GRUB 2 command line by pressing the c key when the menu is displayed. To see a list of available commands, press the TAB key at the **grub>** prompt, or type the **help** command.

Command completion is also available. For example, if you don't remember the name of the kernel file, type **linux /** and then press the TAB key to review the available files in the /boot directory.

You should be able to find all detected hard drives on a standard PC from the BIOS/UEFI menus with the **ls** command. As an example, let's find the /boot partition and grub.cfg file on this particular system. By default, the /boot directory is mounted on a separate partition. First, run **ls** at the **grub>** command line:

```
grub> ls
(proc) (hd0) (hd0,msdos1) (hd0,msdos2)
```

The string **hd0** denotes the first hard drive, whereas **msdos1** is the first partition, created with the MBR format (msdos). If a server was partitioned using the newer GPT partition format, GRUB 2 would identify the first partition as **gpt1** rather than **msdos1**. Similarly, **hd0,msdos2** denotes the second partition on the first hard drive.

Next, use that information to find the grub.cfg file:

```
grub> ls (hd0,msdos1)/grub2/grub.cfg
grub.cfg
```

If the file is not on the noted partition, you'll see an "error: file '/grub2/grub.cfg' not found" error message. You may also see "error: unknown filesystem" if the noted partition does not contain a valid filesystem.

We know that the /boot directory is on **(hd0,msdos1)**. To confirm the location of grub.cfg, run the following command:

```
grub> cat (hd0,msdos1)/grub2/grub.cfg
```

You should see the contents of the grub.cfg file in the output. Press a key to scroll through the content of the file until you are back to the GRUB 2 command line.

There's one more way to identify the partition with the /boot directory. Run the **search.file** command to find grub.cfg:

```
grub> search.file /grub2/grub.cfg
```

GRUB 2 should return the partition with the /boot directory. In this case, it's the first partition on the first hard drive:

```
hd0,msdos1
```

Now you can use these commands from the GRUB 2 configuration file to boot Linux from the **grub>** prompt. If the top-level root directory is normally mounted on a partition, you may even confirm the contents of the /etc/fstab file with a command like the following:

```
grub> cat (hd0,msdos2)/etc/fstab
```

If the root file system resides on an LVM volume, the preceding command would return an "error: unknown filesystem" message. To solve this problem, load the LVM module using the following command:

```
grub> insmod lvm
```

Now, the **ls** command should also include logical volumes in its output:

```
grub> ls
(proc) (hd0) (hd0,msdos2) (hd0,msdos1) (lvm/rhel-root) (lvm/rhel-swap)
```

Finally, to print the content of /etc/fstab, run the following command:

```
grub> cat (lvm/rhel-root)/etc/fstab
```

EXERCISE 5-3

Using the GRUB 2 Command Line

In this exercise, you'll boot RHEL 7 manually. Look at the contents of /etc/grub2.cfg and identify the desired commands in the stanza. Now follow these steps:

1. Boot the system. When you see the following line at the top of the screen, press any key to access the GRUB 2 menu:

   ```
   The selected entry will be started automatically in 5s.
   ```

2. Press C for a GRUB-based command-line interface. You should see the **grub>** prompt.

3. Load the LVM module by typing the following command:

   ```
   grub> insmod lvm
   ```

4. List all partitions and logical volumes:

   ```
   grub> ls
   ```

5. Identify the root partition. This may be named something like (lvm/rhel-root). You may need to use some trial and error to find out (for example, by trying to display the /etc/fstab file from all the devices names previously listed by GRUB 2).

   ```
   grub> cat (lvm/rhel-root)/etc/fstab
   ```

6. Set the root variable to the device that you have identified as that containing the root file system:

   ```
   grub> set root=(lvm/rhel-root)
   ```

7. Enter the **linux** command, which specifies the kernel and root directory partition. Yes, this is a long line; however, you can use command completion (press the TAB key) to make it faster. In addition, the only important parts of the line are the kernel file and the location of the top-level root directory.

   ```
   linux (hd0,msdos1)/vmlinuz-3.10.0-123.el7.x86_64↵
   root=/dev/mapper/rhel-root
   ```

8. Enter the **initrd** command, which specifies the initial RAM disk command and file location. Again, you can use the TAB key for filename completion.

   ```
   initrd (hd0,msdos1)/initramfs-3.10.0-123.el7.x86_64.img
   ```

9. Now enter the **boot** command. If this command is successful, Linux should now boot the selected kernel and initial RAM disk just as if you selected that option from the GRUB 2 configuration menu.

Reinstall GRUB 2

In some situations, you may need to reinstall GRUB 2 from scratch. This may occur if **grub2-mkconfig** does not work, or if the configuration file that it generates contains errors due to a corrupt or incorrect script file. In this case, you need to reinstall the grub2-tools RPM package. Before proceeding with this operation, list and remove all GRUB 2 configuration and script files. This can be done using the following commands:

```
# rpm -qc grub2-tools
/etc/default/grub
/etc/grub.d/00_header
/etc/grub.d/10_linux
/etc/grub.d/20_linux_xen
/etc/grub.d/20_ppc_terminfo
/etc/grub.d/30_os-prober
/etc/grub.d/40_custom
/etc/grub.d/41_custom
# rm -f /etc/default/grub
# rm -f /etc/grub.d/*
```

Then, reinstall GRUB 2 by running the following command:

```
# yum reinstall grub2-tools
```

(You will find a full introduction to the **rpm** and **yum** commands in Chapter 7.)

Finally, regenerate the grub.cfg configuration file. On machines that run traditional BIOS firmware, the **grub2-mkconfig** command would look like this:

```
# grub2-mkconfig -o /boot/grub2/grub.cfg
```

Of course, if the GRUB 2 configuration file is missing and you weren't able to boot the system to even display the GRUB 2 menu, you might need to resort to an option known as rescue mode.

An Option for Booting from GRUB 2: Rescue Mode

The troubleshooting objectives associated with a previous version of the RHCE exam prep guide suggested that you needed to be able to recover from a complete boot failure, such as if the GRUB 2 configuration file were corrupt or missing. In other words, if you've tried to boot directly from the **grub>** prompt described earlier and failed, you might need to resort to the option known as rescue mode. That requires access to the installation DVD or the network boot disk.

e x a m

w a t c h   The RHCSA and RHCE objectives no longer include a requirement associated with rescue mode. However, because the rescue of unbootable systems is an important skill, it may be included in future versions of one of these exams.

To that end, boot from one of those media options. You should see the installation screen with the following options:

```
Install Red Hat Enterprise Linux 7.0
Test this media & install Red Hat Enterprise Linux 7.0
Troubleshooting
```

Select the Troubleshooting option and press ENTER. You will see a second screen with the following options:

```
Install Red Hat Enterprise Linux 7.0 in basic graphics mode
Rescue a Red Hat Enterprise Linux system
Run a memory test
Boot from local drive
Return to main menu
```

Select the Rescue a Red Hat Enterprise Linux system option and press ENTER. Rescue mode runs a stable minimal version of the RHEL 7 operating system on the local machine. It's in essence a text-only version of the "Live DVD" media available on other Linux distributions such as Knoppix, Ubuntu, and, yes, even the Scientific Linux rebuild distribution.

o n t h e

j o b   For RHEL 7, it's best to use RHEL 7 rescue media. Such media uses a kernel compiled by Red Hat, customized for supported software. Nevertheless, options such as Knoppix are excellent.

You can use the rescue environment to recover unbootable systems. If you've used rescue mode in RHEL 6, you should feel comfortable here. In most cases, the next step you see is shown in Figure 5-4.

The Continue option, as suggested in Figure 5-5, mounts all detected volumes as subdirectories of the /mnt/sysimage directory. The Read-Only option mounts detected volumes in read-only mode. The Skip option moves straight to a command-line interface. Select Continue. After confirmation, you'll be presented with a shell prompt, as shown in Figure 5-6.

FIGURE 5-4   Options for the rescue environment

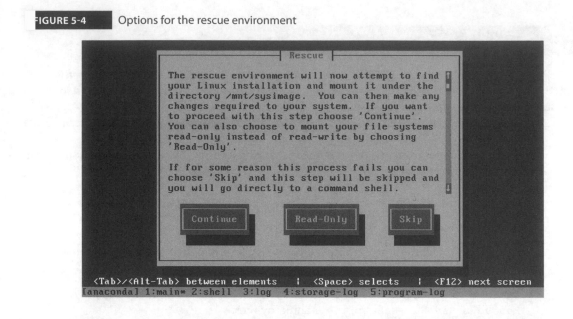

FIGURE 5-5   Mounting the root filesystem in the rescue environment

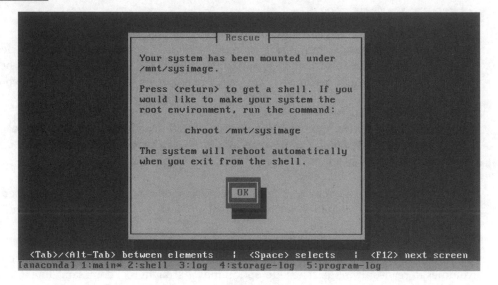

FIGURE 5-6	Rescue environment shell

```
Starting installer, one moment...
anaconda 19.31.79-1 for Red Hat Enterprise Linux 7.0 started.

Your system is mounted under the /mnt/sysimage directory.
When finished please exit from the shell and your system will reboot.

sh-4.2#
```

```
[anaconda] 1:main* 2:shell  3:log  4:storage-log  5:program-log
```

From the shell prompt, enter the **chroot /mnt/sysimage** command. As the regular top-level root directory for the system is mounted on the /mnt/sysimage directory, the **chroot** command changes the root directory, as if the /mnt/sysimage filesystem was mounted under /.

Do practice what you've learned about GRUB 2 in this section. It could help you recover from a real-world problem—and Red Hat does say that their exams are filled with "real-world tasks." However, don't assume that you have access to a CD or a DVD during a Red Hat exam. If a rescue media is not available, that should mean that there's at least one alternative method you can use to address the problem.

CERTIFICATION OBJECTIVE 5.03

Between GRUB 2 and Login

This section provides a basic overview of the boot process after the GRUB 2 bootloader finds the kernel. If you understand this process, you can diagnose a wide variety of boot problems. The messages associated with the kernel provide a step-by-step view of the process.

The loading of Linux depends on a temporary filesystem, known as the initial RAM disk. Once the boot process is complete, control is given to systemd, known as the first process. This section will describe the contents of systemd in detail, through the configuration of units and targets.

> **Most Linux distributions, including RHEL 7, have replaced Upstart and SysVinit with the new systemd service manager.**

In this section, you'll also review the commands that allow you to reboot and shut down a system normally.

> **In systemd, the Unix philosophy that "everything is a file" can be paraphrased as "everything is a unit." Units are the basic building blocks of systemd.**

Kernels and the Initial RAM Disk

After you select a kernel from the GRUB 2 configuration menu, Linux hands over boot responsibilities to the kernel with the help of the initial RAM disk, also known by its filename in the /boot directory, initramfs. As suggested by its name, it is actually a filesystem.

During the boot process, Linux loads that temporary filesystem into your RAM. Linux then loads hardware drivers and starts the first process, systemd.

Next, systemd activates all the system units for the initrd.target and mounts the root filesystem under /sysroot. Finally, systemd restarts itself in the new root directory and activates all units for the default target (we will look in more detail at units and targets in the next section).

To learn more, disable the **quiet** directive for the desired kernel in the GRUB configuration file. Boot your system. Watch as the messages pass quickly through the screen. After logging in, you can review these messages in the /var/log/dmesg file or by running the **dmesg** command.

You can find more log information in the systemd journal. Display its contents with the **journalctl** command. What you see depends on the hardware and configuration of the local system. Key messages include the following:

- The version of the kernel.
- SELinux status, if active. By default, SELinux first starts in permissive mode, until the configured policy (enforcing) is loaded near the end of the boot process.
- The amount of recognized RAM (which does not necessarily match the actual amount of installed RAM).
- CPUs.
- Kernel command line, specifying the logical volume or root filesystem.

- Freeing of memory associated with the initial RAM disk (initramfs).
- Hard drives and partitions (as defined by their device filenames, such as /dev/sda or /dev/vda1).
- Active filesystems.
- Swap partitions.

The log file is filled with excellent information. If the system is loading the wrong kernel, you'll see evidence of that here. If Linux isn't using a partition that you've configured, you'll also see it here (indirectly). If SELinux isn't loading properly, you'll see it in messages toward the end of the file.

The First Process, Targets, and Units

The Linux kernel continues the boot process by calling the first process, **systemd**. In RHEL 7, the legacy **init** process is configured with a symbolic link to **systemd**.

Units are the basic building blocks of systemd. The most common are *service units,* which have a .service extension and activate a system service. To show a list of all service units, type the following command:

```
# systemctl list-units --type=service --all
```

The **--all** flag includes all units, not just the active ones. There are other types of units, such as mount and automount units, which manage mount points; path units, which activate a service when there is a change on a filesystem path (such as a spool directory); socket units, which start a service only when a client connection is made (if you have used the **xinetd** daemon, this is similar to how **xinetd** starts services on demand); and many, many more.

A special type of unit is a *target unit,* which is used to group together other system units and to transition the system into a different state. To list all target units, type the following command:

```
# systemctl list-units --type=target --all
```

The most important target units are described in Table 5-1.

TABLE 5-1

The systemd
Target Units

Target Unit	Description
emergency.target	Emergency shell; only the / filesystem is mounted in read-only mode.
graphical.target	The default target for multiuser graphical systems.
multi-user.target	Nongraphical multiuser system.
rescue.target	Emergency shell; all filesystems are mounted.

In systemd, targets serve the same function as runlevels in previous RHEL distributions. In RHEL 6, seven runlevels, 0 through 6, were available. Linux services were organized by runlevel. Each runlevel was associated with a level of functionality.

For example, in runlevel 1, only one user was allowed to log in to that Linux system. X11 mode, also known as runlevel 5, was used to start Linux with a GUI login screen, if appropriate packages were installed. Table 5-2 compares systemd targets and the runlevels defined in RHEL 6.

Run the following command:

```
# ls -l /usr/lib/systemd/system/runlevel?.target
```

Note the symbolic links in the output. See how files such as runlevel0.target, runlevel1 .target, and so on are linked to systemd targets such as poweroff.target and rescue.target. These links provide backward compatibility with the old SysV runlevels. You can even refer to graphical.target as runlevel5.target and multi-user.target as runlevel3.target.

Targets are controlled by units, organized in unit files. Although the default target is defined in /etc/systemd/system, you can override the default during the boot process from the GRUB 2 menu.

TABLE 5-2   RHEL 6 Runlevels and RHEL 7 systemd Targets

Runlevel	systemd Target	Description
0	poweroff.target	Halt the system
1	rescue.target	Single-user mode for maintenance and repair
2	multi-user.target	Multiuser, without NFS
3	multi-user.target	Full multiuser mode
4	multi-user.target	Not used in RHEL 6
5	graphical.target	X11 GUI with networking
6	reboot.taget	Reboot the system

Each target may be associated with several systemd units. Each unit can start or stop Linux services such as printing (**cupsd**), scheduling (**crond**), the Apache web server (**httpd**), the Samba file server (**smbd**), and more. When configured, the boot process starts and stops the systemd units of your choice. These units are known as dependencies. To list all dependencies of the default graphical.target unit, run the following command:

```
# systemctl list-dependencies graphical.target
```

The default target is specified as a symbolic link from the /etc/systemd/system/default.target file to either multi-user.target or graphical.target. You can also use the **systemctl** command to retrieve the current default target or to change the current settings, as shown here:

```
# systemctl get-default
graphical.target
# systemctl set-default multi-user.target
rm '/etc/systemd/system/default.target'
ln -s '/usr/lib/systemd/system/multi-user.target'↵
'/etc/systemd/system/default.target'
```

As you can see from this output, the **systemctl set-default multi-user.target** command creates a symbolic link from /etc/systemd/system/default.target.

Switch Between Targets

Now that you've examined the different targets available on RHEL 7, it's time to explore how to switch between targets. On earlier versions of RHEL, this is functionally equivalent to switching runlevels. First, establish the default target with the following command:

```
# systemctl get-default
graphical.target
```

RHEL 7 normally boots to either graphical.target or multi-user.target. After logging in as the administrative user, you can move to a different target with the **systemctl isolate** command. For example, the following command moves the system to the multi-user target:

```
# systemctl isolate multi-user.target
```

After that command is complete, rerun the **systemctl get-default** command. The output confirms that the default target has not changed:

```
graphical.target
```

Now try something else. What do you think happens when the following command is executed?

```
# systemctl isolate poweroff.target
```

Reboot and Shut Down a System Normally

The commands required to reboot and shut down a system are straightforward. As just suggested in the previous section, the following commands provide one way to shut down and reboot a system, respectively:

```
# systemctl poweroff
# systemctl reboot
```

For legacy purposes, Red Hat has created symbolic links from the following commands to **systemctl**. These commands work just as they did in earlier versions of RHEL.

```
# shutdown
# reboot
```

systemd Replaces Upstart and SysVinit

The systemd process is the first process started at boot. It takes charge of activating all services. It replaces the traditional init daemon and the Upstart system, which is also a substitute for init and was the default init daemon on RHEL 6. The design and philosophy of Upstart are very similar to the old SysVinit system, which relies on init scripts to activate services, and on the concept of runlevels, which was introduced in the previous sections.

In contrast, systemd introduces a lot of new tools and can do much more, while maintaining compatibility with SysVinit. The design of systemd is based on optimal efficiency. First, at boot, systemd activates only the services that are strictly required, whereas others are started on demand. As an example, systemd starts the CUPS printing service only when a print job is sent to the /var/spool/cups queue. In addition, systemd parallelizes the initialization of services.

As a result, the boot process under systemd is faster. To display the time required to boot your system, run the following command:

```
# systemd-analyze time
Startup finished in 506ms (kernel) + 1.144s↵
(initrd) + 6.441s (userspace) = 8.092s.
```

This output shows the time required to initialize the kernel, plus the time to load the initial RAM disk (initrd) and the time to activate systemd units (userspace). The total time is 8.092 seconds. But there's more. You can display a detailed account of the time required to activate each systemd unit by running **systemd-analyze blame**. An example is shown in Figure 5-7.

The numbers in Figure 5-7 don't equal the total userspace time reported by **systemd-analyze time**. That happens because systemd starts multiple services simultaneously.

Initialization time
of systemd units

```
[root@server1 ~]# systemd-analyze blame
       4.604s kdump.service
       2.610s postfix.service
       2.333s firewalld.service
       1.629s tuned.service
       1.370s network.service
       1.365s plymouth-quit-wait.service
        953ms iprupdate.service
        845ms accounts-daemon.service
        729ms avahi-daemon.service
        699ms iprinit.service
        666ms ModemManager.service
        638ms systemd-logind.service
        596ms lvm2-monitor.service
        568ms rsyslog.service
        560ms rtkit-daemon.service
        536ms nfs-lock.service
        520ms iprdump.service
        482ms NetworkManager.service
        477ms libvirtd.service
        442ms gdm.service
        412ms chronyd.service
        338ms ksmtuned.service
        324ms netcf-transaction.service
```

But there's even more. Although an in-depth knowledge of all the features of systemd is outside of the scope of the RHCSA exam, systems administrators can take advantage of some of its capabilities.

Some Linux developers have argued that systemd does too much and breaks the Unix philosophy of writing programs that "do one thing and do it well." However, as of today, systemd has been adopted by most of the major Linux distributions.

Logging

The systemd process includes a powerful logging system. You can display all collected logs with the **journalctl** command. By default, the journal log files are temporarily stored in RAM in a ring buffer in the /run/log/journal directory. To get Linux to write journal log files persistently on disk, run the following commands:

```
# mkdir /var/log/journal
# chgrp systemd-journal /var/log/journal
# chmod 2775 /var/log/journal
# systemctl restart systemd-journald.service
```

Once persistent logging is enabled, you can show log messages from a specific boot with the **-b** switch: **journalctl -b 0** displays the log messages since the last boot, **journalctl -b 1** from the boot before the last one, and so on. You don't have to switch through different log files because **journactl** automatically aggregates available data from the current and all rotated log files.

You can also filter log messages based on their priority using the **-p** command option. As an example, **journalctl -p warning** displays all messages with a priority level of "warning" or higher. Log messages of a "warning" priority level are displayed in a bold font character, whereas messages with priority levels of "err" and higher are shown in red.

cgroups

Control groups (or cgroups) are a feature of the Linux kernel to group processes together and control or limit their resource usage (such as CPU, memory, and so on). In systemd, cgroups are primarily used to track processes and to ensure that all processes that belong to a service are terminated when a service is stopped.

Under the traditional SysVinit system, it is difficult to identify the service associated with a process. In fact, services often start multiple processes. When you stop a SysVinit service, that service may not be able to terminate all dependent (child) processes. You're stuck with either stopping all dependent processes manually (with the **ps** and **kill** commands) or accepting a system with orphaned processes in an unknown state until the next reboot.

To address this limitation, systemd labels processes associated with a service using cgroups. In this way, systemd uses cgroups to kill all processes in a group, if required.

The command **systemd-cgls** displays the cgroup hierarchy in a tree format, as shown in Figure 5-8. From the excerpt in Figure 5-8, you can identify cgroups such as rsyslog.service and avahi-daemon.service, along with the processes they have spawned. Note the one-to-one correspondence between cgroups and systemd service units.

FIGURE 5-8

The cgroup
hierarchy

```
      ├─1673 pickup -l -t unix -u
      └─1674 qmgr -l -t unix -u
    ─rsyslog.service
      └─633 /usr/sbin/rsyslogd -n
    ─rhsmcertd.service
      └─1283 /usr/bin/rhsmcertd
    ─NetworkManager.service
      └─828 /usr/sbin/NetworkManager --no-daemon
    ─avahi-daemon.service
      ├─632 avahi-daemon: running [server1.local]
      └─643 avahi-daemon: chroot helpe
    ─crond.service
      └─698 /usr/sbin/crond -n
    ─pcscd.service
      └─1324 /usr/sbin/pcscd --foreground --auto-exit
    ─dbus.service
      └─683 /bin/dbus-daemon --system --address=systemd: --nofork --nopidfile --sy
    ─firewalld.service
      └─629 /usr/bin/python -Es /usr/sbin/firewalld --nofork --nopid
    ─iprdump.service
      └─746 /sbin/iprdump --daemon
    └─iprupdate.service
      └─714 /sbin/iprupdate --daemon
lines 120-142/142 (END)
```

FIGURE 5-9

Dependencies between systemd units

```
default.target
  ┬accounts-daemon.service
  ├gdm.service
  ├iprdump.service
  ├iprinit.service
  ├iprupdate.service
  ├network.service
  ├rhnsd.service
  ├rtkit-daemon.service
  ├systemd-readahead-collect.service
  ├systemd-readahead-replay.service
  ├systemd-update-utmp-runlevel.service
  └multi-user.target
     ┬abrt-ccpp.service
     ├abrt-oops.service
     ├abrt-vmcore.service
     ├abrt-xorg.service
     ├abrtd.service
     ├atd.service
     ├auditd.service
     ├avahi-daemon.service
     ├brandbot.path
     ├chronyd.service
lines 1-23
```

Dependencies

The traditional SysVinit system starts services sequentially. In contrast, systemd can activate services in parallel by keeping track of all dependencies between units. The **systemctl list-dependencies** command displays a tree with all dependencies between units. An excerpt of the output is shown in Figure 5-9.

You can show the dependencies for any available unit. Dependent units must be started first. For example, the following command shows the units that must be started before the rsyslog service:

```
# systemctl list-dependencies rsyslog.service
```

systemd Units

The first process is systemd. The systemd process uses various configuration files to start other processes. You can find these configuration files in the following directories: /etc/systemd/system and /usr/lib/systemd/system.

The default configuration files are stored in /usr/lib/systemd/system. Custom files, stored in /etc/systemd/system, supersede these files. Don't change files in the /usr/lib/systemd /system directory. Any software updates may overwrite those files.

We have already discussed *service* and *target* units, but there are more. Table 5-3 gives a brief description of all available unit types.

Examine the contents of the /usr/lib/systemd/system directory. Each file contains the configuration of a systemd unit whose type matches the filename extension. As an example, the file graphical.target defines the configuration for the graphical login target unit, whereas the file rsyslog.service includes the configuration for the rsyslog service unit.

Unit Type	Description
Target	A group of units. It is used as a synchronization point at startup to define a set of units to be activated.
Service	A service, such as a daemon like the Apache web server.
Socket	An IPC or network socket, used to activate a service when traffic is received on a listening socket (similar to the activation of services on demand performed by the **xinetd** daemon).
Device	A device unit, such as a drive or partition.
Mount	A filesystem mount point controlled by systemd.
Automount	A filesystem automount point controlled by systemd.
Swap	A swap partition to be activated by systemd.
Path	A path monitored by systemd, used to activate a service when the path changes.
Timer	A timer controlled by systemd, used to activate a service when the timer elapses.
Snapshot	Used to create a snapshot of the systemd run-time state.
Slice	A group of system resources (such as CPU, memory, and so on) that can be assigned to a unit via the cgroup interface.
Scope	A unit for organizing and managing resource utilization of a set of system processes.

You can list all active systemd units using the following command:

```
# systemctl list-units
```

The **list-units** keyword is optional because it is the default. If you want to include inactive, maintenance, and failed units, add the **--all** command switch. An excerpt of the output of the command is shown in Figure 5-10.

In the output, the first column lists the unit name, and the second column tells whether or not the unit was properly loaded. The third column displays the state of the unit: active, inactive, failed, or maintenance. The next column includes more detail. Finally, the last column shows a brief description of the unit.

Whereas the **systemctl list-units** command gives a run-time snapshot of the state of each unit, the following command shows whether a unit is enabled or disabled at startup:

```
# systemctl list-unit-files
```

An example of the output is shown in Figure 5-11. As you can see, units can be "enabled" or "disabled." There is also another state, named "static," which means that a unit is enabled and it cannot be manually disabled.

FIGURE 5-10   systemd units

```
systemd-as...sword-plymouth.path loaded active   waiting  Forward Password Requests to Plym
systemd-ask-password-wall.path    loaded active   waiting  Forward Password Requests to Wall
session-4.scope                   loaded active   running  Session 4 of user alex
abrt-ccpp.service                 loaded active   exited   Install ABRT coredump hook
abrt-oops.service                 loaded active   running  ABRT kernel log watcher
abrt-vmcore.service               loaded inactive dead     Harvest vmcores for ABRT
abrt-xorg.service                 loaded active   running  ABRT Xorg log watcher
abrtd.service                     loaded active   running  ABRT Automated Bug Reporting Tool
accounts-daemon.service           loaded active   running  Accounts Service
alsa-restore.service              loaded inactive dead     Restore Sound Card State
alsa-state.service                loaded active   running  Manage Sound Card State (restore
alsa-store.service                loaded inactive dead     Store Sound Card State
atd.service                       loaded active   running  Job spooling tools
auditd.service                    loaded active   running  Security Auditing Service
avahi-daemon.service              loaded active   running  Avahi mDNS/DNS-SD Stack
bluetooth.service                 loaded active   running  Bluetooth service
brandbot.service                  loaded inactive dead     Flexible Branding Service
chronyd.service                   loaded active   running  NTP client/server
colord.service                    loaded active   running  Manage, Install and Generate Colo
cpupower.service                  loaded inactive dead     Configure CPU power related setti
crond.service                     loaded active   running  Command Scheduler
cups.service                      loaded active   running  CUPS Printing Service
dbus.service                      loaded active   running  D-Bus System Message Bus
dm-event.service                  loaded inactive dead     Device-mapper event daemon
lines 53-76/250 30%
```

FIGURE 5-11

Installed unit files

```
dbus-org.freedesktop.timedate1.service    static
dbus.service                              static
debug-shell.service                       disabled
display-manager.service                   enabled
dm-event.service                          disabled
dmraid-activation.service                 enabled
dnsmasq.service                           disabled
dracut-cmdline.service                    static
dracut-initqueue.service                  static
dracut-mount.service                      static
dracut-pre-mount.service                  static
dracut-pre-pivot.service                  static
dracut-pre-trigger.service                static
dracut-pre-udev.service                   static
dracut-shutdown.service                   static
ebtables.service                          disabled
emergency.service                         static
fcoe.service                              disabled
firewalld.service                         enabled
firstboot-graphical.service               disabled
fprintd.service                           static
gdm.service                               enabled
getty@.service                            enabled
halt-local.service                        static
lines 66-89
```

Virtual Terminals and Login Screens

The login terminals in Linux are virtual terminals. Most Linux systems, including RHEL 7, are configured with six standard command-line virtual terminals. These consoles are numbered from 1 to 6. When configured with a GUI and a login manager, RHEL 7 substitutes the graphical login screen for the first virtual terminal.

What does that all mean? In Linux, you can switch between virtual terminals with an ALT-function key combination. For example, ALT-F2 brings you to the second virtual terminal. You can switch between adjacent virtual terminals by pressing ALT-RIGHT ARROW or ALT-LEFT ARROW. For example, to move from virtual terminal 2 to virtual terminal 3, press ALT-RIGHT ARROW. If you're in a GUI virtual terminal, add the CTRL key. So in RHEL 7, if the GUI is installed and you're in the first virtual terminal, you'd press CTRL-ALT-F2 to get to the second virtual terminal.

When you log in to a regular virtual terminal, Linux returns a command-line shell. The default shell for a user is defined in the /etc/passwd file described in Chapter 6. When you log in to a GUI virtual terminal, Linux returns the configured GUI desktop. For more information on the Linux GUI, see Chapter 8.

Through RHEL 6, virtual terminals were configured in files in /etc/sysconfig/init and the /etc/init directory. Now that systemd has replaced Upstart, they are defined by the logind.conf file in the /etc/systemd directory.

Virtual terminals bring the multiuser capabilities of Linux to life. At work (or during a Red Hat exam), you might review a man page on one terminal, compile a program in another, and edit a configuration file in a third virtual terminal. Other users who are connected can do the same thing at the same time.

CERTIFICATION OBJECTIVE 5.04

Control by Target

With systemd, Red Hat Enterprise Linux service management is customized by target. Since systemd includes links to runlevels for backward compatibility with SysVinit, you can still refer to the runlevels listed in Table 5-2 with commands such as **init** and **telinit**. However, you should get familiar with targets because this is the standard method of activating services at boot.

Linux is highly customizable. Therefore, it makes sense that the systemd units that start in each target can be customized. Although GUI tools are available to customize systemd units, configuring them from the command-line interface is generally a lot faster.

Functionality by Target

As described earlier, the basic functionality of each target is listed in the configuration files in the directories /etc/systemd/systemd and /usr/lib/systemd/system. For example, let's start with the default target, which in a RHEL 7 system with graphical login is

```
# systemctl get-default
graphical.target
```

The system knows that graphical.target is the default thanks to a symbolic link from the /etc/systemd/system/default.target file to the graphical.target file in /usr/lib/system/system. Take a look at one of those files. An excerpt is shown here:

```
[Unit]
Description=Graphical Interface
Documentation=man:systemd.special(7)
Requires=multi-user.target
After=multi-user.target
Conflicts=rescue.target
Wants=display-manager.service
AllowIsolate=yes
```

This means that a target can include another target. In this case, graphical.target is a superset of multi-user.target. After all systemd units in multi-user.target have started, graphical.target activates display-manager.service, as indicated by the Wants directive in the graphical.target configuration file.

Other services started by graphical.target may be listed in the graphical.target.wants subdirectory in /etc/systemd/system or /usr/lib/systemd/system. In a default RHEL 7 installation, we see the following files:

```
# ls /etc/systemd/system/graphical.target.wants
accounts-daemon.service rtkit-daemon.service
```

These are symbolic links to the unit configuration files of the Accounts and RealtimeKit services.

The Innards of systemd Units

The systemd units are activated whenever a system moves to a different target. Therefore, the units associated with the default target are executed during the boot process. Appropriate units are also started when you change targets; for example, when you run the **systemctl isolate multi-user.target** command from the graphical.target, Linux stops all service units that were started by the graphical target.

But you can control systemd units directly. For example, examine the content of the file rsyslog.service from the /usr/lib/systemd/system directory, as shown in Figure 5-12.

FIGURE 5-12

The configuration
file of the rsyslog
service unit

```
[root@server1 ~]# cat /usr/lib/systemd/system/rsyslog.service
[Unit]
Description=System Logging Service
;Requires=syslog.socket

[Service]
Type=notify
EnvironmentFile=-/etc/sysconfig/rsyslog
ExecStart=/usr/sbin/rsyslogd -n $SYSLOGD_OPTIONS
StandardOutput=null

[Install]
WantedBy=multi-user.target
;Alias=syslog.service
[root@server1 ~]# █
```

The configuration starts with the Unit section, which contains a description of the service. Then comes the service configuration, which includes the type of the service, a pointer to a file with some environment variables that configure the service behavior, the main executable to run to activate the service, and a directive that sends all standard output from the service to /dev/null.

Finally, the WantedBy directive tells us that this service will be activated at boot when the system enters into the multi-user target.

Now, run the following command:

```
# systemctl status rsyslog.service
```

If you specify a unit name without an extension, by default systemd assumes that it is a service unit. Hence, a short version of the previous command is

```
# systemctl status rsyslog
```

This command should return an output similar to that shown in Figure 5-13, including the status of the service unit, its main process ID, and up to the 10 most recent log lines. If some of the log lines are truncated, use the **-l** switch to display them in full.

You can stop a service by running a command such as this:

```
# systemctl stop rsyslog.service
```

FIGURE 5-13

Displaying the
status of a service

```
[root@server1 ~]# systemctl status rsyslog.service
rsyslog.service - System Logging Service
   Loaded: loaded (/usr/lib/systemd/system/rsyslog.service; enabled)
   Active: active (running) since Thu 2015-01-22 08:47:34 GMT; 8h ago
 Main PID: 634 (rsyslogd)
   CGroup: /system.slice/rsyslog.service
           └─634 /usr/sbin/rsyslogd -n

Jan 22 08:47:33 server1.example.net systemd[1]: Starting System Logging Service.
Jan 22 08:47:34 server1.example.net systemd[1]: Started System Logging Service.
```

	Command	Description
TABLE 5-4	start	Starts the service if it's currently not running.
	stop	Stops the service if it's currently running.
systemctl Service Control Commands	restart	Stops and then starts the service.
	reload	If supported, it loads the current version of the configuration file(s). The service is not stopped, and clients that have previously connected are not kicked off.
	try-restart	Stops and then restarts the service only if it is already running.
	condrestart	Same as try-restart.
	status	Lists the current operational status of the service.

Alternatively, the **systemctl** command can be used with the options shown in Table 5-4; for example, the following command reloads the SSH configuration file without stopping or starting the service:

```
# systemctl reload sshd.service
```

Service Configuration

The **systemctl** command gives you a simple way to enable a service for the default target. First, try the following command:

```
# systemctl list-unit-files --type=service
```

This gives an output similar to Figure 5-11, but limited to service units. You'll see the whole list of installed services in the system, along with their activation status at boot.

The **systemctl** command can do more. With that command, you can change the boot state of a particular service. For example, the following command checks if the Postfix service is configured to start at boot:

```
# systemctl list-unit-files | grep postfix.service
postfix.service                                     enabled
```

An equivalent command is

```
# systemctl is-enabled postfix.service
enabled
```

This indicates that the Postfix e-mail server is configured to start in the default target. If you want to make sure the Postfix service does not start in the default target, execute the following command:

```
# systemctl disable postfix.service
```

Run the **systemctl list-unit-files** command again to confirm the change. To turn it back on for the default target, run the same command, substituting **enable** for **disable**, as shown here:

```
# systemctl enable postfix.service
```

When you enable a service, the **systemctl enable** command creates a symbolic link in the directory /etc/systemd/system/multi-user.target.wants that points to the corresponding unit configuration file in /usr/lib/systemd/system. If you wish, you can enable or disable services manually by creating symbolic links in the appropriate systemd directories. However, using **systemctl** is the preferred way because it is less error-prone.

When a service is disabled, you can still start and stop it manually via the **systemctl start** and **stop** commands. This means that the **systemctl disable** command does not prevent a user from accidentally starting a service by mistake. If you want to disable a service unit at boot and ensure that it cannot be started anymore, you should use the **mask** command, as illustrated here:

```
# systemctl mask postfix.service
ln -s '/dev/null' '/etc/systemd/system/postfix.service'
```

As shown, this command creates a symbolic link in /etc/systemd/system named postfix .service, which points to /dev/null. A configuration file in /etc/systemd/system always takes precedence over a corresponding file in /usr/lib/systemd/system. Hence, the result is that the default postfix.service file in /usr/lib/systemd/system is "masked" by the symbolic link in /etc/systemd/system to /dev/null.

CERTIFICATION OBJECTIVE 5.05

Time Synchronization

The configuration of a Network Time Protocol (NTP) client is straightforward. Therefore, this section provides an overview of the configuration files and the associated command tools.

There are good reasons to keep different systems running on the same clock. For example, a web server and a client logging in different times would make troubleshooting extremely difficult. Several services rely on accurate timestamps. As an example, a time drift of more than five minutes would cause a Kerberos client to fail authentication.

RHEL 7 includes RPMs for two NTP daemons: ntpd and chronyd. Don't install both. Typically, ntpd is recommended for systems that are always connected to the network, such as servers, whereas chronyd is the preferred choice for virtual and mobile systems. We will describe the configuration of the default time synchronization service, chronyd. But first, we will explain how to configure the time zone.

Time Zone Configuration

Every system, real or virtual, starts with a hardware clock. The time on that clock may depend on the power in a battery; over time, batteries lose power, and many hardware clocks end up losing time. The installation process on RHEL 7 normally sets the hardware clock to local time, rather than UTC. However, UTC (which is essentially identical to Greenwich Mean Time, or GMT) is usually the best setting for servers to avoid issues when switching to daylight saving time.

Every RHEL 7 system includes a time zone configured in the /etc/localtime file. This is a symbolic link that points to one of the time zones files in /usr/share/zoneinfo. As an example, /etc/localtime should point to /usr/share/zoneinfo/America/Los_Angeles if you are based in California.

Rather than manually setting a symbolic link to a time zone file, you can use the **timedatectl** utility. If you run the command alone with no arguments, it will show a summary of the current time settings, including the current time, time zone, and NTP status. Some sample output is shown in Figure 5-14.

You can display a list of the available time zones by running the following command:

```
# timedatectl list-timezones
```

Then, to switch to a different time zone, run **timedatectl** with the **set-timezone** command. Here's an example:

```
# timedatectl set-timezone America/Los_Angeles
```

FIGURE 5-14	
Date and time settings	

```
[root@server1 ~]# timedatectl
      Local time: Thu 2015-01-22 19:38:06 GMT
  Universal time: Thu 2015-01-22 19:38:06 UTC
        RTC time: Thu 2015-01-22 19:38:06
        Timezone: Europe/London (GMT, +0000)
     NTP enabled: yes
 NTP synchronized: yes
 RTC in local TZ: no
      DST active: no
 Last DST change: DST ended at
                  Sun 2014-10-26 01:59:59 BST
                  Sun 2014-10-26 01:00:00 GMT
 Next DST change: DST begins (the clock jumps one hour forward) at
                  Sun 2015-03-29 00:59:59 GMT
                  Sun 2015-03-29 02:00:00 BST
[root@server1 ~]#
```

Sync the Time with chronyd

The default chronyd configuration file, /etc/chrony.conf, is set up to connect to multiple public servers from the NTP pool project. When used collectively, the chronyd daemon minimizes time errors.

```
server 0.rhel.pool.ntp.org iburst
server 1.rhel.pool.ntp.org iburst
server 2.rhel.pool.ntp.org iburst
server 3.rhel.pool.ntp.org iburst
```

Users of rebuild distributions such as CentOS will see different hostnames, such as 0.centos .pool.ntp.org. The **iburst** configuration option shown here speeds the initial synchronization when the chronyd service is started.

To configure chronyd to synchronize with a different NTP server, just modify the **server** directives in /etc/chrony.conf and restart chronyd:

```
# systemctl restart chrnoyd
```

You can display information about the current time sources using the **chronyc sources -v** command. An example is shown in Figure 5-15.

Sync the Time with ntpd

A basic configuration of the ntpd daemon is straightforward. First, you should ensure that chronyd is stopped and disabled at boot because you cannot have both chronyd and ntpd running on the same machine:

```
# systemctl stop chronyd.service
# systemctl disable chronyd.service
```

FIGURE 5-15

NTP server statistics

```
[root@server1 ~]# chronyc sources -v
210 Number of sources = 4

  .-- Source mode  '^' = server, '=' = peer, '#' = local clock.
 / .- Source state '*' = current synced, '+' = combined , '-' = not combined,
| /   '?' = unreachable, 'x' = time may be in error, '~' = time too variable.
||                                                 .- xxxx [ yyyy ] +/- zzzz
||                                                /   xxxx = adjusted offset,
||            Log2(Polling interval) -.          |   yyyy = measured offset,
||                                     \         |   zzzz = estimated error.
||                                      |        |
MS Name/IP address         Stratum Poll Reach LastRx Last sample
===============================================================================
^* kvm1.websters-computers.c   2   6    77    33  +717us[ -992us] +/-   26ms
^+ static.132.14.76.144.clie   2   6    37    97 +3483us[+1774us] +/-   67ms
^+ ntp-ext.cosng.net           2   6    77    31 -2928us[-2928us] +/-   42ms
^+ ghost-networks.de           2   6    77    32 -1419us[-1419us] +/-   51ms
[root@server1 ~]#
```

Then, install the ntp RPM package:

```
# yum install ntp
```

The default ntpd configuration file is /etc/ntp.conf. It is similar to the /etc/chronyd.conf file and contains four server directives, pointing to public servers that are part of the NTP pool project. You can customize the configuration or run ntpd with the default settings. Once you have made your changes to the file, start and enable ntpd:

```
# systemctl start ntpd.service
# systemctl enable ntpd.service
```

To display information about the NTP sources, run the **ntpq -p** command.

CERTIFICATION SUMMARY

This chapter covered the basic boot process of a RHEL system. It starts with the hardware POST and continues with the BIOS or UEFI system. Once boot media is found, the process moves to the first stage of the GRUB 2 bootloader. The GRUB 2 menu allows you to select and customize the kernel to be booted.

Once you've selected an option, GRUB 2 hands control to the kernel. The kernel loads a temporary filesystem known as the initial RAM disk. Once essential drivers and filesystems are loaded, you can review the systemd journal with the **journalctl** command. Then the kernel executes the first process, also known as **systemd**.

Linux services are controlled by systemd targets, which group together other systemd units. The default target is configured as a symbolic link in the directory /etc/systemd /system, and the unit configuration files are stored in this directory and in /usr/lib/systemd /system. The status of those systemd units can be configured and queried using the **systemctl** command. The systemd targets are linked to other targets and to unit configuration files. **systemctl** can also be used to start, stop, restart, reload systemd units, and more.

You may need to set up local systems as NTP clients. The default NTP service in RHEL 7 is chronyd.

TWO-MINUTE DRILL

Here are some of the key points from the certification objectives in Chapter 5.

The BIOS and the UEFI

❑ Although not strictly a part of the exam, it's important to know the basics of the BIOS and the UEFI.

❑ You can change the boot sequence from the BIOS/UEFI menu.

❑ Once the BIOS/UEFI detects the designated boot drive(s), it hands control to GRUB 2 via the Master Boot Record (MBR) or GUID Partition Table (GPT) of the appropriate drive.

Bootloaders and GRUB 2

❑ RHEL 7 uses GRUB 2.

❑ The GRUB 2 configuration file is organized into sections.

❑ From the GRUB 2 menu, you can boot into a systemd target other than the default.

❑ You can even boot from a GRUB 2 menu into a rescue shell that provides root administrative access without an account password.

❑ The GRUB 2 configuration file specifies a kernel, a root directory volume, and an initial RAM disk for each operating system.

❑ If the GRUB 2 configuration file is missing, you may be able to boot from the grub> prompt with information on the /boot directory partition, the Linux kernel file, the top-level root directory, and the initial RAM disk file.

Between GRUB 2 and Login

❑ You can analyze boot messages through the **journalctl** command.

❑ Default system targets are configured as a symbolic link from the /etc/systemd /system directory.

❑ The systemd process has replaced Upstart and SysVinit as the first process. It has configuration files in the /etc/systemd/system and /usr/lib/systemd/system directories.

❑ Once the kernel boots, it hands control to systemd, also known as the first process.

Control by Target

❑ The default target configured in /etc/systemd/system activates systemd units in the /usr/lib/systemd/system directory.

❑ Target units can include other targets and units to be activated.

❑ You can use **systemctl** to control a service with the start, stop, restart, reload, and other commands.

❑ The services that start in each target can also be controlled with **systemctl** and the enable/disable commands.

Time Synchronization

❑ The **timedatectl** tool can be used to check the current time, date, time zone, and NTP service status.

❑ The default NTP service in RHEL 7 is chronyd. It keeps time in sync with servers configured in the /etc/chrony.conf file.

❑ An alternative to chronyd is ntpd, which keeps its configuration settings in the /etc/ntp.conf file.

❑ Do not run both chronyd and ntpd at the same time.

Q SELF TEST

The following questions will help measure your understanding of the material presented in this chapter. As no multiple choice questions appear on the Red Hat exams, no multiple choice questions appear in this book. These questions exclusively test your understanding of the chapter. It is okay if you have another way of performing a task. Getting results, not memorizing trivia, is what counts on the Red Hat exams. There may be more than one answer for many of these questions.

The BIOS and the UEFI

1. On what part of the boot hard drive is the first stage of the GRUB 2 bootloader typically located?

_____

Bootloaders and GRUB 2

2. When you see the GRUB 2 configuration menu, what command would you use to modify the configuration?

_____

3. What string would you add to the **linux16** command line to boot into the emergency target?

   _____

4. If you see the **set root='hd0,msdos1'** directive in the GRUB 2 configuration file, on what partition is the /boot directory? Assume the GRUB 2 configuration file is properly configured.

   _____

Between GRUB 2 and Login

5. What temporary file system is loaded directly from the GRUB 2 menu?

   _____

6. What one-word command can you use to read systemd log messages?

   _____

7. In what directories can you find the configuration files associated with the first process?

   _____

8. How do you switch from the graphical target to the multi-user target?

   _____

Control by Target

9. What command lists the default target?

   _____

10. Name three commands that can be typically run from **systemctl** to control the status of systemd units.

    _____

    _____

    _____

11. What command lists the state of all systemd units currently available on the local system, including those that are not active?

    _____

Time Synchronization

12. What command lists the current time, time zone, and status of the NTP service?

_____

13. Which configuration file is used by chronyd?

_____

LAB QUESTIONS

Several of these labs involve installation exercises. You should do these exercises on test machines only. The second lab of Chapter 1 sets up KVM for this purpose.

Red Hat presents its exams electronically. For that reason, the labs in this and future chapters are available from the media that accompanies the book. Look in the Chapter5/ subdirectory for this chapter's labs. They're available in .doc, .html, and .txt formats. In case you haven't yet set up RHEL 7 on a system, refer to the first lab of Chapter 2 for installation instructions. The answers for each lab follow the Self Test answers for the fill-in-the-blank questions.

A SELF TEST ANSWERS

The BIOS and the UEFI

1. For the BIOS/UEFI to hand control over to Linux, it needs to identify the Master Boot Record (MBR) or the GUID Partition Table (GPT) of the boot hard drive.

Bootloaders and GRUB 2

2. From the GRUB 2 menu, the command that modifies the configuration is **e**.

3. To boot into the emergency target from the GRUB 2 **linux16** command line, you'd append the string **systemd.unit=emergency.target**.

4. The **set root='hd0,msdos1'** directive documents the /boot directory on the first partition on the first hard drive.

Between GRUB 2 and Login

5. The temporary filesystem loaded from the GRUB 2 menu is the initial RAM disk filesystem, also known by its filename, initramfs.

6. The one-word command that you can use to read systemd log messages is **journalctl**.

7. The configuration files associated with the first process are located in the /etc/systemd/system and /usr/lib/systemd/system directories.

8. The command to switch from the graphical target to the multi-user target is **systemctl isolate multi-user.target**.

Control by Target

9. The command that lists the default target is **systemctl get-default**.

10. Typical commands that can be run from **systemctl** include **start**, **stop**, **restart**, **reload**, **enable**, **disable**, and more.

11. The **systemctl list-units --all** command (or just **systemctl --all**) lists the state of all units, including inactive ones.

Time Synchronization

12. The **timedatectl** command lists the current time, time zone, and the status of the NTP service.

13. The chronyd configuration file is /etc/chrony.conf.

LAB ANSWERS

Yes, there are many Linux systems that run for years at a time without a reboot. But reboots are sometimes required, such as when newer kernels are installed. So when configuring a Linux system, make sure any changes survive a reboot. On a Red Hat exam, you won't get credit unless your changes survive a reboot.

Lab 1

If successful, this lab will show you how to change the default target, along with the relative importance of the options in the GRUB bootloader. Remember, you can modify the default target via the **systemctl** command

```
# systemctl set-default multi-user.target
```

or manually by modifying the /etc/systemd/system/default.target symbolic link:

```
# rm -f /etc/systemd/system/default.target
# ln -s /usr/lib/systemd/system/multi-user.target ↵
/etc/systemd/system/default.target
```

Lab 2

This lab is the same as Exercise 5-2. Practice with the root password recovery procedure until you are familiar with all the steps and you don't need to rely on the documentation. Remember, Red Hat exams are "closed book."

Lab 3

After completing this lab, you should have modified the variables GRUB_TIMEOUT and GRUB_CMDLINE_LINUX in /etc/default/grub, as shown here:

```
GRUB_TIMEOUT=10
GRUB_CMDLINE_LINUX="rd.lvm.lv=rhel/root vconsole.font↵
=latarcyrheb-sun16 rd.lvm.lv=rhel/swap crashkernel↵
=auto  vconsole.keymap=uk rhgb"
```

Note that the "quiet" keyword has been removed from GRUB_CMDLINE_LINUX, to enable verbose messages at boot.

Then, run the **grub2-mkconfig** command to generate a new GRUB configuration file:

```
# grub2-mkconfig -o /boot/grub2/grub.cfg
```

To really test the result, reboot the system. What happens? Finally, revert back your changes.

Lab 4

The script executed in this lab moved the grub.cfg configuration file to the /root/backup directory. If you understand GRUB 2 well, you should have been able to boot the system from the grub> prompt.

Otherwise, you can recover the grub.cfg file by booting into the rescue target described in this chapter. From the rescue mode command-line prompt, you should be able to restore the original configuration with the following commands:

```
# chroot /mnt/sysimage
# cp /root/backup/grub.cfg /boot/grub2/
```

Alternatively, generate a new grub.cfg configuration file with the **grub2-mkconfig** command.

Lab 5

It's possible to configure up to 12 virtual terminals, which match the number of function keys available on most keyboards. If you want to set up 12 virtual terminals (and that would be an interesting problem for the RHCSA exam), look at the /etc/securetty file and related man pages with the **man -k securetty** command. One way to accomplish the tasks in this lab is with the following steps:

1. Open the /etc/systemd/logind.conf file. Change the following directive to limit the active consoles to terminals 1 and 2:

   ```
   NAutoVTs=2
   ```

2. To test the result, reboot the system.
3. What happens? Can you still log in to terminals 3, 4, 5, and 6?
4. When complete, just remember to restore the original version of the /etc/systemd/logind.conf file.

Chapter 6

Linux Filesystem Administration

L inux installation is easy, at least for anyone serious about Red Hat certification.

However, most administrators have to maintain existing systems. Critical skills related to filesystems include adding new partitions, creating logical volumes, mounting filesystems, and more. In many cases, you'll want to make sure these filesystems are mounted automatically during the boot process, and that requires a detailed knowledge of the /etc/fstab configuration file.

Some filesystems, such as those that are not accessed frequently, should be mounted only on a temporary basis; that is the job of the automounter.

INSIDE THE EXAM

Inside the Exam

Some of the RHCSA objectives listed in this chapter overlap and may be covered in multiple sections. The objectives all relate in some way to filesystem management and should be considered as a whole in this chapter.

Partition Management

As in the real world, it is the results that matter. It doesn't matter whether you use **fdisk** or **parted** to create an MBR-style partition. However, you should know that the Red Hat implementation of **fdisk** does not support GPT partitions, whereas **gdisk** and **parted** do. Make sure that appropriate partitions meet the requirements of the exam.

The current RHCSA objectives include the following related requirements:

- Add new partitions, logical volumes and swap to a system non-destructively
- List, create, delete partitions on MBR and GPT disks

Logical Volumes

Partitions and disks are components of logical volumes. Related RHCSA objectives describe some of the skills required. For example, the following objective suggests that you need to know the process starting with physical volumes:

- Create and remove physical volumes, assign physical volumes to volume groups, and create and delete logical volumes

Of course, a logical volume isn't fulfilling its full potential unless you can increase its size, as suggested by the following objective:

- Extend existing logical volumes

Filesystem Management

Partitions and logical volumes must be formatted before they're ready to store files. To that end, you need to know how to meet the following RHCSA objectives:

- Create, mount, unmount, and use vfat, ext4, and xfs file systems
- Mount and unmount CIFS and NFS network file systems
- Configure systems to mount file systems at boot by Universally Unique ID (UUID) or label

Storage Management and Partitions

While it's easier to create partitions, logical volumes, and RAID arrays during the installation process, not every administrator has that privilege. Although this section is focused on the management of regular partitions, the techniques described in this section are also used to create the partition-based components of both logical volumes and RAID arrays. Once configured, a partition, a logical volume, and a RAID array can each be referred to generically as a volume. In Linux, three tools still predominate for administrators who need to create and manage partitions: **fdisk**, **gdisk**, and **parted**. While these tools are primarily applied to local hard disks, they can also be used for other media such as drives attached over a network.

Current System State

Before using the **fdisk**, **gdisk**, or **parted** utilities to create or modify a partition, do check currently available free space along with currently mounted filesystems. The following commands make it easy: **df** and **fdisk -l**. The following example in Figure 6-1 illustrates how the **df** command displays the total, used, and available free space on all currently mounted filesystems.

on the job **The terms *filesystem* and *file system* are interchangeable. Both are used in official Linux documentation.**

Note the numbers under the "1K-blocks" column. In this case (except for the temporary filesystems, tmpfs, and devtmpfs), they add up to about 11.5GB of allocated space. If the hard drive is larger, unallocated space may be used for another partition. Partitions can be

FIGURE 6-1

Disk space usage shown by the df command

```
[root@server1 ~]# df
Filesystem                     1K-blocks     Used  Available Use% Mounted on
/dev/mapper/rhel_server1-root  10229760  3387916    6841844  34% /
devtmpfs                         499652        0     499652   0% /dev
tmpfs                            508936       92     508844   1% /dev/shm
tmpfs                            508936     7120     501816   2% /run
tmpfs                            508936        0     508936   0% /sys/fs/cgroup
/dev/mapper/rhel_server1-home   1020588    70580     950008   7% /home
/dev/vda1                        508588   121244     387344  24% /boot
```

```
[root@server1 ~]# df -h
Filesystem                     Size  Used Avail Use% Mounted on
/dev/mapper/rhel_server1-root  9.8G  3.3G  6.6G  34% /
devtmpfs                       488M     0  488M   0% /dev
tmpfs                          498M  148K  497M   1% /dev/shm
tmpfs                          498M  7.0M  491M   2% /run
tmpfs                          498M     0  498M   0% /sys/fs/cgroup
/dev/mapper/rhel_server1-home  997M   74M  924M   8% /home
/dev/vda1                      497M  119M  379M  24% /boot
[root@server1 ~]#
```

Output of the
df command in
human-readable
format

combined with others to configure additional space in logical volumes and RAID arrays, and that can be useful when you need to expand the space available to appropriate filesystems, such as /home, /tmp, and /var.

To print the partition sizes in a more readable format, you can use the **-h** command option shown in Figure 6-2.

The second command, **mount**, lists the format and mount options for each filesystem. From the figure, examine the partition represented by device /dev/mapper/rhel_server1-home. Note how it is mounted on the /home directory with the xfs file type. It separates the home directories of regular users in a dedicated partition:

```
[root@server1 ~]# mount | grep home
/dev/mapper/rhel_server1-home on /home type xfs ↵
(rw,relatime,seclabel,attr2,inode64,noquota)
```

If the output of the **mount** command confuses you, consider the **findmnt** command, which prints all mounted filesystems in a tree-like format, as shown in Figure 6-3.

In the output, note the presence of "special filesystems" such as proc and sysfs, which we cover later in this chapter.

The fdisk Utility

The **fdisk** utility is common to many operating systems. The Mac OS has a fully featured version of **fdisk**. Older versions of Microsoft Windows have a simplified version of **fdisk**.

Although the Linux implementation of **fdisk** includes a wide variety of commands, you need to know only the few discussed here.

fdisk works with partitions created using the traditional Master Boot Record (MBR) partitioning scheme. On newer systems that run UEFI firmware rather than a traditional BIOS, you may see a different partitioning standard: the GUID Partition Table (GPT). The **fdisk** support of GPT is considered experimental. The preferred tools to manage GPT partitions are **gdisk** and **parted**.

Output of the findmnt command

```
[root@server1 ~]# findmnt
TARGET                          SOURCE     FSTYPE    OPTIONS
/                               /dev/mapper/rhel_server1-root
                                           xfs       rw,relatime,seclabel,attr2,inode64,n
├─/proc                         proc       proc      rw,nosuid,nodev,noexec,relatime
│ ├─/proc/sys/fs/binfmt_misc    systemd-1  autofs    rw,relatime,fd=33,pgrp=1,timeout=300
│ └─/proc/fs/nfsd               sunrpc     nfsd      rw,relatime
├─/sys                          sysfs      sysfs     rw,nosuid,nodev,noexec,relatime,secl
│ ├─/sys/kernel/security        securityfs securityf rw,nosuid,nodev,noexec,relatime
│ ├─/sys/fs/cgroup              tmpfs      tmpfs     rw,nosuid,nodev,noexec,seclabel,mode
│ │ ├─/sys/fs/cgroup/systemd    cgroup     cgroup    rw,nosuid,nodev,noexec,relatime,xatt
│ │ ├─/sys/fs/cgroup/cpuset     cgroup     cgroup    rw,nosuid,nodev,noexec,relatime,cpus
│ │ ├─/sys/fs/cgroup/cpu,cpuacct cgroup    cgroup    rw,nosuid,nodev,noexec,relatime,cpua
│ │ ├─/sys/fs/cgroup/memory     cgroup     cgroup    rw,nosuid,nodev,noexec,relatime,memo
│ │ ├─/sys/fs/cgroup/devices    cgroup     cgroup    rw,nosuid,nodev,noexec,relatime,devi
│ │ ├─/sys/fs/cgroup/freezer    cgroup     cgroup    rw,nosuid,nodev,noexec,relatime,free
│ │ ├─/sys/fs/cgroup/net_cls    cgroup     cgroup    rw,nosuid,nodev,noexec,relatime,net_
│ │ ├─/sys/fs/cgroup/blkio      cgroup     cgroup    rw,nosuid,nodev,noexec,relatime,blki
│ │ ├─/sys/fs/cgroup/perf_event cgroup     cgroup    rw,nosuid,nodev,noexec,relatime,perf
│ │ └─/sys/fs/cgroup/hugetlb    cgroup     cgroup    rw,nosuid,nodev,noexec,relatime,huge
│ ├─/sys/fs/pstore              pstore     pstore    rw,nosuid,nodev,noexec,relatime
│ ├─/sys/kernel/config          configfs   configfs  rw,relatime
│ ├─/sys/fs/selinux             selinuxfs  selinuxfs rw,relatime
│ ├─/sys/kernel/debug           debugfs    debugfs   rw,relatime
│ └─/sys/fs/fuse/connections    fusectl    fusectl   rw,relatime
├─/dev                          devtmpfs   devtmpfs  rw,nosuid,seclabel,size=499652k,nr_i
│ ├─/dev/shm                    tmpfs      tmpfs     rw,nosuid,nodev,seclabel
│ ├─/dev/pts                    devpts     devpts    rw,nosuid,noexec,relatime,seclabel,g
│ ├─/dev/hugepages              hugetlbfs  hugetlbfs rw,relatime,seclabel
│ └─/dev/mqueue                 mqueue     mqueue    rw,relatime,seclabel
├─/run                          tmpfs      tmpfs     rw,nosuid,nodev,seclabel,mode=755
│ └─/run/user/1000/gvfs         gvfsd-fuse fuse.gvfs rw,nosuid,nodev,relatime,user_id=100
├─/var/lib/nfs/rpc_pipefs       sunrpc     rpc_pipef rw,relatime
```

Start fdisk: Help and More

The following screen output lists commands that show how to start **fdisk**, how to get help, and how to quit the program. The /dev/vda drive is associated with the first virtual drive on a KVM-based virtual machine. As other systems may be configured with different hard drive device files, you may need to check the output from the **df** and **fdisk -l** commands for clues.

When you start **fdisk**, type **m** to list basic **fdisk** commands:

```
# fdisk /dev/vda
Welcome to fdisk (util-linux 2.23.2).

Changes will remain in memory only, until you decide to write them.
Be careful before using the write command.
```

```
Command (m for help): m
Command action
   a   toggle a bootable flag
   b   edit bsd disklabel
   c   toggle the dos compatibility flag
   d   delete a partition
   g   create a new empty GPT partition table
   G   create an IRIX (SGI) partition table
   l   list known partition types
   m   print this menu
   n   add a new partition
   o   create a new empty DOS partition table
   p   print the partition table
   q   quit without saving changes
   s   create a new empty Sun disklabel
   t   change a partition's system id
   u   change display/entry units
   v   verify the partition table
   w   write table to disk and exit
   x   extra functionality (experts only)

Command (m for help): q
#
```

A wide variety of commands are associated with **fdisk**—and more if you run the **x** command to access **fdisk**'s extra functionality.

Using fdisk: A New Drive with No Partitions

After a new drive is installed on Linux, that drive normally isn't configured with partitions. The **fdisk** utility can be used to configure partitions on physical or virtual disks attached to the system. For example, the baseline virtual system for this book includes three drives: /dev/vda, /dev/vdb, and /dev/vdc.

on the
job

SATA, PATA, and SAS SCSI drives are all represented by device files such as /dev/sda, /dev/sdb, and so on.

If a newly added drive hasn't been used by the RHEL installation program (or some other disk management program), it'll return the following message the first time it's opened by **fdisk**:

```
Device does not contain a recognized partition table
Building a new DOS disklabel with disk identifier 0xcb0a51f1.
```

In other words, even if you don't create a partition after opening it in **fdisk**, it will automatically write a DOS disk label to the drive if you save your changes.

If you need more than four partitions on the new physical disk, configure the first three partitions as primary partitions, and then configure the fourth partition as an extended partition. That extended partition should typically be large enough to fill the rest of the disk; all logical partitions must fit in that space.

Using fdisk: In a Nutshell

At the **fdisk** command-line prompt, start with the print command (**p**) to examine the partition table. This allows you to review the current entries in the partition table. Assuming free space is available, you can then create a new (**n**) partition.

Generally, partitions are either primary (**p**) or logical (**l**). If it doesn't already exist, you can also create an extended partition (**e**) to contain logical partitions. Remember that in a drive formatted with the MBR scheme, you can have up to four primary partitions, which would correspond to numbers 1 through 4. One of the primary partitions can be configured as an extended partition. The remaining partitions are logical partitions, numbered 5 and above. With an extended partition, you can create a maximum of 12 logical partitions on a drive.

If free space is available, **fdisk** normally starts the new partition at the first available sector or cylinder. The actual size of the partition depends on disk geometry.

Using fdisk: Create a Partition

The following screen output sample shows the steps used to create (**n**) the first partition, make it bootable (**a**), and then finally write (**w**) the partition information to the disk. (Note that although you may specify a 500MB partition, the geometry of the disk may not allow that precise size.)

```
# fdisk /dev/vdb

Command (m for help): n
Command action
   p   primary partition (0 primary, 0 extended, 4 free)
   e   extended
Select (default p): p
Partition number (1-4, default 1): 1
First sector (2048-2097151, default 2048):
Using default value 2048
Last sector, +sectors or +size{K,M,G} (2048-2097151, default
2097151): +500M
Partition 1 of type Linux and of size 500 MiB is set
```

```
Command (m for help): a
Selected partition 1

Command (m for help): p
Disk /dev/vdb: 1073 MB, 1073741824 bytes, 2097152 sectors
...
   Device Boot      Start         End      Blocks   Id  System
/dev/vdb1    *        2048     1026047      512000   83  Linux

Command (m for help):
```

Note how the number of blocks matches the binary representation of 500MB. Repeat the commands to create any other partitions you might need.

When partitions are added or changed, you generally don't have to reboot to get Linux to read the new partition table, unless another partition on that drive has been formatted and mounted. If so, an attempt to write the partition table with the **w** command fails temporarily with the following message:

```
WARNING: Re-reading the partition table failed with error 16:
 Device or resource busy.
 The kernel still uses the old table. The new table will be used at
 the next reboot or after you run partprobe(8) or kpartx(8)
```

If you run **partprobe /dev/vdb**, the kernel will read the new partition table and you'd be able to use the newly created partition.

Using fdisk: Many Partition Types

One feature of special interest is based on the **t** command to change the partition system identifier. If you need space for logical volumes, RAID arrays, or even swap space, that command is important. After pressing **t**, you're prompted to enter the partition number (if there's more than one configured). You can then list available partition types with the **L** command, as shown here. (If there's only one partition on the drive, it is selected automatically.)

```
Command (m for help): t
Selected partition 1
Hex code (type L to list all codes): L
```

The list of available partition identifiers, as shown in Figure 6-4, is impressive. Note how it's not limited to Linux partitions. However, as this book covers Linux, Table 6-1 lists associated partition types.

Unless you're making a change, type in identifier **83**. You'll be returned to the **fdisk** command prompt.

FIGURE 6-4   Linux partition types in fdisk

```
 0   Empty             24  NEC DOS           81  Minix / old Lin bf  Solaris
 1   FAT12             27  Hidden NTFS Win   82  Linux swap / So c1  DRDOS/sec (FAT-
 2   XENIX root        39  Plan 9            83  Linux           c4  DRDOS/sec (FAT-
 3   XENIX usr         3c  PartitionMagic    84  OS/2 hidden C:  c6  DRDOS/sec (FAT-
 4   FAT16 <32M        40  Venix 80286       85  Linux extended  c7  Syrinx
 5   Extended          41  PPC PReP Boot     86  NTFS volume set da  Non-FS data
 6   FAT16             42  SFS               87  NTFS volume set db  CP/M / CTOS / .
 7   HPFS/NTFS/exFAT   4d  QNX4.x            88  Linux plaintext de  Dell Utility
 8   AIX               4e  QNX4.x 2nd part   8e  Linux LVM       df  BootIt
 9   AIX bootable      4f  QNX4.x 3rd part   93  Amoeba          e1  DOS access
 a   OS/2 Boot Manag   50  OnTrack DM        94  Amoeba BBT      e3  DOS R/O
 b   W95 FAT32         51  OnTrack DM6 Aux   9f  BSD/OS          e4  SpeedStor
 c   W95 FAT32 (LBA)   52  CP/M              a0  IBM Thinkpad hi eb  BeOS fs
 e   W95 FAT16 (LBA)   53  OnTrack DM6 Aux   a5  FreeBSD         ee  GPT
 f   W95 Ext'd (LBA)   54  OnTrackDM6        a6  OpenBSD         ef  EFI (FAT-12/16/
10   OPUS              55  EZ-Drive          a7  NeXTSTEP        f0  Linux/PA-RISC b
11   Hidden FAT12      56  Golden Bow        a8  Darwin UFS      f1  SpeedStor
12   Compaq diagnost   5c  Priam Edisk       a9  NetBSD          f4  SpeedStor
14   Hidden FAT16      61  SpeedStor         ab  Darwin boot     f2  DOS secondary
16   Hidden FAT16      63  GNU HURD or Sys   af  HFS / HFS+      fb  VMware VMFS
17   Hidden HPFS/NTF   64  Novell Netware    b7  BSDI fs         fc  VMware VMKCORE
18   AST SmartSleep    65  Novell Netware    b8  BSDI swap       fd  Linux raid auto
1b   Hidden W95 FAT3   70  DiskSecure Mult   bb  Boot Wizard hid fe  LANstep
1c   Hidden W95 FAT3   75  PC/IX             be  Solaris boot    ff  BBT
1e   Hidden W95 FAT1   80  Old Minix
Hex code (type L to list all codes): ▮
```

TABLE 6-1   Linux Partition Types in fdisk

Partition Identifier	Description
5	Extended partition; while not a Linux partition type, such partitions are a prerequisite for logical partitions. Also see 85.
82	Linux swap.
83	Linux; applicable for all standard Linux partition formats.
85	Linux extended partition; not recognized by other operating systems.
88	Linux plaintext partition table; rarely used.
8e	Linux LVM for partitions used as physical volumes.
fd	Linux RAID; for partitions used as components of a RAID array.

Using fdisk: Delete a Partition

The following example removes the only configured partition. The sample output screen first starts **fdisk**. Then you can print (**p**) the current partition table, delete (**d**) the partition by number (**1** in this case), write (**w**) the changes to the disk, and quit (**q**) from the program. Needless to say, *do not perform this action on any partition where you need the data*.

Assuming only one partition on this drive, it is selected automatically after you run the **d** command.

```
# fdisk /dev/vdb
Command (m for help): p

Disk /dev/vdb: 1073 MB, 1073741824 bytes, 2097152 sectors
Units = sectors of 1 * 512 = 512 bytes
Sector size (logical/physical): 512 bytes / 512 bytes
I/O size (minimum/optimal): 512 bytes / 512 bytes
Disk label type: dos
Disk identifier: 0x2e3c116d

Device     Boot     Start        End      Blocks    Id  System
/dev/vdb1           2048     1026047      512000    83  Linux
Command (m for help): d
Selected partition 1
Partition 1 is deleted
```

This is the last chance to change your mind before deleting the current partition. To avoid writing the change, exit from **fdisk** with the **q** command. If you're pleased with the changes that you've made and want to make them permanent, proceed with the **w** command:

```
Command (m for help): w
```

Unless the aforementioned error 16 message appears, that's it. You should now have an empty hard drive.

on the **Job**
If you remove a partition, the partition table on disk is modified to reflect the change, but the actual data on the partition isn't removed. This means that if you re-create the partition using the same layout (same start/end sectors), your data will still be there. It's worth trying this procedure in case you accidentally delete a partition by mistake.

Using fdisk: Create a Swap Partition

Now that you know how to create partitions with **fdisk**, just one additional step is required to set up that partition for swap space. Once you have a swap partition of the desired size, run the **t** command to select a partition, and then run the **l** command to show the partition ID types listed in Figure 6-4.

In this case, at the following prompt, type in **82** for a Linux swap partition:

```
Hex code (type L to list codes): 82
```

For example, you could run the following sequence of commands to set up a new swap partition on the second hard drive. The details of what you see depend on the partitions you may have created. It'll be a 900MB swap space on the first primary partition (/dev/vdb1).

```
Command (m for help): n
Command action
   e   extended
   p   primary partition (1-4)
Select (default p): p
Partition number (1-4, default 1): 1
First sector (2048-2097151, default 2048): 2048
Last sector, +sectors or +size{K,M,G} (2048-2097151, default
2097151): +900M
Partition 1 of type Linux and of size 900 MiB is set

Command (m for help): p

Disk /dev/vdb: 1073 MB, 1073741824 bytes, 2097152 sectors
...

   Device Boot      Start         End      Blocks   Id  System
/dev/vdb1             2048     1845247      921600   83  Linux

Command (m for help): t
Selected partition 1
Hex code (type L to list all codes): 82
Changed system type of partition 'Linux' to 'Linux swap / Solaris'

Command (m for help): w
The partition table has been altered!

Calling ioctl() to re-read partition table.
Syncing disks.
```

The **fdisk** utility doesn't actually write the changes to disk until you run the write (**w**) command. Alternatively, you can cancel these changes with the quit (**q**) command. If you don't have the error 16 message described earlier, the changes are written to disk. As described later in this chapter, additional work is required to configure RHEL to use that newly created swap partition.

The gdisk Utility

As we have illustrated in the previous section, the MBR partitioning scheme supports a maximum of 15 partitions for data (3 primary and 12 logical), plus an extended partition, which is simply a "container" for logical partitions. In contrast, the GPT partitioning scheme can hold up to 128 partitions.

Another limitation of MBR is the disk size. The MBR scheme uses 32-bit logical addresses, which support disk drives up to 2TB. On the other hand, the GPT format relies on 64-bit addresses, which support drives of up to 8 million terabytes!

Although you could use **fdisk** and select the **g** command to switch to a GPT partition table format, the **gdisk** utility is preferred for GPT partitions. If you're familiar with **fdisk**, **gdisk** should seem familiar too. When you start **gdisk** on a disk with an MBR partition table, you will see the following warning:

```
[root@server1 ~]# gdisk /dev/vdb
...
*****************************************************************
Found invalid GPT and valid MBR; converting MBR to GPT format.
THIS OPERATION IS POTENTIALLY DESTRUCTIVE! Exit by typing 'q' if
you don't want to convert your MBR partitions to GPT format!
*****************************************************************
```

As suggested by the message, type **q** to exit; otherwise, you may lose any data on your drive. Once started, **gdisk** works in a similar way to **fdisk**. Type the question mark (**?**) to get a list of commands:

```
Command (? for help): ?
b       back up GPT data to a file
c       change a partition's name
d       delete a partition
i       show detailed information on a partition
l       list known partition types
n       add a new partition
o       create a new empty GUID partition table (GPT)
q       quit without saving changes
r       recovery and transformation options (experts only)
s       sort partitions
t       change a partition's type code
v       verify disk
w       write table to disk and exit
x       extra functionality (experts only)
?       print this menu

Command (? for help):
```

The next screen output shows the steps used to create a new 500MB partition (**n**) on the disk device /dev/vdc:

```
[root@server1 ~]# gdisk /dev/vdc
GPT fdisk (gdisk) version 0.8.6

Partition table scan:
  MBR: not present
  BSD: not present
  APM: not present
  GPT: not present

Creating new GPT entries

Command (? for help): n
Partition number (1-128, default 1): 1
First sector (34-2097118, default = 2048) or {+-}size{KMGTP}: 2048
Last sector (2048-2097118, default = 2097118) or {+-}size{KMGTP}:
+500M
Current type is 'Linux filesystem'
Hex code or GUID (L to show codes, Enter = 8300):
Changed type of partition to 'Linux filesystem'

Command (? for help): w
```

As with **fdisk**, the **gdisk** tool doesn't write the changes to disk until you type the write (**w**) command. At any time you can quit the utility without saving any changes with the quit (**q**) command.

The parted Utility

In its different forms, the **parted** utility is becoming increasingly popular. It's an excellent tool developed by the Free Software Foundation. As with **fdisk**, you can use it to create, check, and destroy partitions, but it can do more. You can also use it to resize and copy partitions, as well as the filesystems contained therein. It's the foundation for multiple GUI-based partition management tools, including GParted and QtParted. For more information, see www.gnu.org/software/parted.

on the **Job**

In some ways, the parted **utility may be more risky. For example, one of the authors of this book accidentally ran the** mklabel **command from the** (parted) **prompt on an existing RHEL system. It deleted all existing partitions. Changes were written immediately while** parted **was still running. Fortunately, there was a backup of this virtual system and it could be restored with little trouble.**

During our discussion of **parted**, we'll proceed from section to section, assuming that **parted** is still open with the following prompt:

```
(parted)
```

Using parted: Starting, Getting Help, and Quitting

The next screen output lists commands that show how to start the **parted** utility, how to get help, and how to quit the program. In this case, the /dev/vdb drive is associated with the second virtual drive on a virtual machine. Your computer may have a different hard drive; you can check the output from the **df** and **fdisk -l** commands for clues.

As you can see in Figure 6-5, when **parted** is run, it opens its own command-line prompt. Enter **help** for a list of available commands.

A wide variety of commands are available at the **parted** interface. When compared to **fdisk** and **gdisk**, **parted** can do more in some ways, as you will see in the next sections.

Using parted: In a Nutshell

At the **parted** command-line prompt, start with the **print** command to list the current partition table. Assuming sufficient unallocated space is available, you can then make a

FIGURE 6-5   The parted command options

```
(parted) help
  align-check TYPE N                      check partition N for TYPE(min|opt)
        alignment
  help [COMMAND]                          print general help, or help on
        COMMAND                           COMMAND
  mklabel,mktable LABEL-TYPE              create a new disklabel (partition
        table)
  mkpart PART-TYPE [FS-TYPE] START END    make a partition
  name NUMBER NAME                        name partition NUMBER as NAME
  print [devices|free|list,all|NUMBER]   display the partition table,
        available devices, free space, all found partitions, or a particular
        partition
  quit                                    exit program
  rescue START END                        rescue a lost partition near START
        and END
  rm NUMBER                               delete partition NUMBER
  select DEVICE                           choose the device to edit
  disk_set FLAG STATE                     change the FLAG on selected device
  disk_toggle [FLAG]                      toggle the state of FLAG on selected
        device
  set NUMBER FLAG STATE                   change the FLAG on partition NUMBER
  toggle [NUMBER [FLAG]]                  toggle the state of FLAG on partition
        NUMBER
  unit UNIT                               set the default unit to UNIT
  version                                 display the version number and
        copyright information of GNU Parted
(parted)
```

new (**mkpart**) partition or even make and format the filesystem (**mkpartfs**). For more information about **parted** command options, use the **help** command; for example, the following command provides more information about **mkpart**:

```
(parted) help mkpart
  mkpart PART-TYPE [FS-TYPE] START END     make a partition

        PART-TYPE is one of: primary, logical, extended
        FS-TYPE is one of: btrfs, nilfs2, ext4, ext3, ext2, fat32, fat16, hfsx,
        hfs+, hfs, jfs, swsusp, linux-swap(v1), linux-swap(v0), ntfs, reiserfs,
        hp-ufs, sun-ufs, xfs, apfs2, apfs1, asfs, amufs5, amufs4, amufs3,
        amufs2, amufs1, amufs0, amufs, affs7, affs6, affs5, affs4, affs3, affs2,
        affs1, affs0, linux-swap, linux-swap(new), linux-swap(old)
        START and END are disk locations, such as 4GB or 10%.  Negative values
        count from the end of the disk.  For example, -1s specifies exactly the
        last sector.

        'mkpart' makes a partition without creating a new file system on the
        partition.  FS-TYPE may be specified to set an appropriate partition
        ID.
```

If that's too much information, just run the command. You'll be prompted for the necessary information.

Using parted: A New PC (or Hard Drive) with No Partitions

The first step with any truly new hard drive is to create a partition table. For example, after you add a new hard drive to your virtual RHEL system, just about any command you run in **parted** leads to the following message:

```
Error: /dev/vdb: unrecognised disk label
```

Before you can do anything else with this drive, you need to create a label. As shown from the list of available commands, you can do so with the **mklabel** command. If you type **msdos**, the MBR-style partition scheme will be used. To use the GTP format, type **gpt** at the command prompt:

```
(parted) mklabel
New disk label type? msdos
```

Using parted: Create a New Partition

Now you can create a new partition in **parted** with the **mkpart** command. Naturally, if you have selected the MBR partition scheme, you need to specify the partition type:

```
(parted) mkpart
Partition type?  primary/extended? primary
File system type?  [ext2]? xfs
Start? 1MB
End? 500MB
```

For **parted**, we used 1MB to start the partition at sector 2,048. Although we could have used "0MB" as the starting point, that would have generated a warning because the partition would have not been properly aligned at the 1MB boundary for best performance. Now review the results with the **print** command:

```
(parted) print
Model: Virtio Block Device (virtblk)
Disk /dev/vdb: 1074MB
Sector size (logical/physical): 512B/512B
Partition Table: msdos
Disk Flags:

Number  Start   End    Size   Type     File system  Flags
 1      1049kB  500MB  499MB  primary
```

If this is the first partition you've created, the file system type column will be empty. However, for the purposes of this chapter, don't exit from **parted** just yet.

on the Job

The GUI parted tools (GParted and QtParted) do support formatting to a wider variety of filesystem formats, even though they're just "front ends" to parted. They might be available from third-party repositories such as those described in Chapter 7.

Using parted: Delete a Partition

It's easy to delete a partition in **parted**. All you need to do from the **(parted)** prompt is use the **rm** command to delete the target partition by number.

Of course, before deleting any partition, you should do the following:

■ Save any data you need from that partition.

■ Unmount the partition.

■ Make sure it isn't configured in /etc/fstab so Linux doesn't try to mount it the next time you boot.

■ After starting **parted**, run the **print** command to identify the partition you want to delete, as well as its ID number.

For example, to delete partition /dev/vdb10 from the **(parted)** prompt, run the following command:

```
(parted) rm 10
```

Using parted: Create a Swap Partition

Now let's repeat the process to create a swap partition. If necessary, delete the previously created partition to make room. Make the start of the new partition 1MB after the end of the previous partition. You can still use the same commands, just substitute the **linux-swap** filesystem type as appropriate:

```
(parted) mkpart
Partition type?  primary/extended? primary
File system type?  [ext2]? linux-swap
Start? 501MB
End? 1000MB
```

Now review the result with the **print** command:

```
(parted) print
Model: Virtio Block Device (virtblk)
Disk /dev/vdb: 1074MB
Sector size (logical/physical): 512B/512B
Partition Table: msdos
Disk Flags:

Number  Start   End     Size    Type     File system  Flags
 1      1049kB  500MB   499MB   primary
 2      501MB   1000MB  499MB   primary
```

Now exit from **parted**. To use these partitions, you need to run commands such as **mkswap**, **swapon**, and **mkfs.xfs**. We cover these commands later in this chapter.

```
(parted) quit

# mkswap /dev/vdb2
# swapon /dev/vdb2
```

Now you can format the new regular Linux partition with the following command:

```
# mkfs.xfs /dev/vdb1
```

Using parted: Set Up a Different Partition Type

When a partition is created in **parted**, you can change its type with the **set** command. If you have a hard drive with unused partitions, open it with the **parted** command. For example, the following command opens the second virtual hard drive:

```
# parted /dev/vdb
```

Run the **print** command. The Flags column for existing partitions should be empty. Now you'll set that flag with the **set** command. From the commands shown here, the flags are set to use that first partition of the second drive as an LVM partition:

```
(parted) set
Partition number? 1
Flag to Invert? lvm
New state? [on]/off on
```

Now review the result with the **print** command:

```
(parted) print
Model: Virtio Block Device (virtblk)
Disk /dev/vdb: 1074MB
Sector size (logical/physical): 512B/512B
Partition Table: msdos
Disk Flags:

Number  Start   End      Size   Type     File system  Flags
 1      1049kB  500MB    499MB  primary  xfs          lvm
 2      501MB   1000MB   499MB  primary  linux-swap(v1)
```

You can use similar steps to configure a partition or a component of a RAID array. It's also a flag; just substitute **raid** for **lvm** in response to the Flag to Invert prompt just shown. If you're following along with a RHEL 7 system, first confirm the result. Exit from **parted** and then run the following commands:

```
# parted /dev/vdb print
# fdisk -l /dev/sdb
```

You'll see the **lvm** flag as shown previously from the **parted** command; you'll see the following confirmation in the output to the **fdisk** command:

```
  Device   Boot  Start     End   Blocks   Id  System
/dev/vdb1         2048   976895  487424   8e  Linux LVM
```

If you've set up the baseline virtual system described in Chapter 2, this is an excellent opportunity to set up partitions as components of LVM volumes. Now that you have the tools, it does not matter whether you use **fdisk**, **gdisk**, or **parted** for this purpose. You can choose to use all the free space. Just be sure to create a partition on more than one hard disk for this purpose to help illustrate the power of logical volumes.

Graphical Options

As suggested earlier, excellent graphical front ends are available for disk partitions. The GParted and QtParted options are based on **parted** and are designed for the GNOME and KDE desktop environments, respectively. As they are not available from the Red Hat

FIGURE 6-6   The Disk Utility

Network, they are not supported by Red Hat and therefore won't be available for any Red Hat exams.

One graphical option available for RHEL 7 is known simply as Disk Utility, available from the gnome-disk-utility package. Once appropriate packages are installed, you can open Disk Utility from the command-line interface with the **gnome-disks** command.

The Disk Utility screen shown in Figure 6-6 depicts the baseline virtual machine created in Chapter 2; it lists the virtual hard drive, device /dev/vda, as well as its root and home partitions, the two additional drives, and the DVD drive.

The functionality includes the following clickable options from the settings menu ("gear" icon):

- ■ **Format**   On a drive, sets the MBR or GPT-style partition formats. On a partition, formats a partition for a number of filesystem formats.
- ■ **Edit Partition**   Sets the partition type, such as Linux swap or Linux LVM.
- ■ **Edit Filesystem**   Sets the filesystem label; labels were commonly used on RHEL 5.
- ■ **Edit Mount Option**   Configures the filesystem mount options, such as mount points and filesystem type.

- **Create Disk Image** Creates an image file with the content of a drive or partition.
- **Restore Disk Image** Restores the content of a drive from a disk image.
- **Benchmark** Allows measurements of read and write performance.
- **Unmount the Filesystem** Unmounts a filesystem. (This option appears as the "stop" icon.)
- **Delete Partition** Deletes a partition. (This option appears as the "minus" icon.)
- **Create Partition** Creates a new partition. (This option appears as the "plus" icon.)

Not all of these options appear in Figure 6-6; for example, the Create Partition option does not appear unless you've selected a "free" area of the target hard drive. In addition, you may note that the functionality of the Disk Utility goes beyond mere partitioning.

EXERCISE 6-1

Work with fdisk and parted

In this exercise, you'll work with both the **fdisk** and **parted** utilities. It assumes you have a new empty drive, such as a drive on a virtual machine. For the purpose of this exercise, **fdisk** and **parted** will be used on drives /dev/vdb and /dev/vdc, respectively. Feel free to substitute accordingly. Do save the results of this work. You'll use it for exercises that follow later in this chapter.

1. Run the **fdisk -l /dev/vdb** command to review the current status of the /dev/vdb drive (if your first disk drive has a different device name, substitute with the correct name, such as /dev/sdb.)
2. Open disk /dev/vdb with the **fdisk /dev/vdb** command.
3. Run the **p** command to display any previously configured partitions.
4. Create a new partition with the **n** command. If primary partitions are available, create one with the **p** command. If options for primary partition numbers are presented, select the first available.
5. When presented with a request similar to the following to specify the first sector of the new partition, specify something else. First try to specify sector 1 to see the response. Then try a sector somewhere after the default. For the purpose of this example, specify 10,000 here:

```
First sector (1845248-2097151, default 1845248): 10000
```

6. When presented with a request similar to the following to specify the last sector of the new partition, enter a number somewhere in the middle of the listed range. For the purpose of this example, specify 1,950,000 here:

```
Last sector, +sectors or +size{K,M,G} (1845248-2097151, default 2097151):
1950000
```

7. Run the **p** command again to review the result. Run the **w** command to write the result to disk.

8. Review the result on the /dev/vdb disk with the **parted /dev/vdb print** command.

9. Open the other available free disk (/dev/vdc) with the **parted /dev/vdc** command.

10. From the **(parted)** prompt, run the **print** command to review the current status of partitions. If you see an "unrecognized disk label" error message, run the **mklabel msdos** command and run the **print** command again.

11. Create a new partition with the **mkpart** command. Follow the prompts. It does not matter whether the partition is primary or logical (avoid an extended partition for now). Enter **xfs** as a filesystem type; start the partition at **100M** (100MB) and end it at **600M** (600MB). Run the **print** command to confirm the new partition, and identify the partition number.

12. Run the **quit** command to exit from **parted**.

13. Run the **fdisk -l /dev/vdc** command to review the result.

14. Exit from **fdisk** with the **q** command.

CERTIFICATION OBJECTIVE 6.02

Filesystem Formats

The number of filesystem types may exceed the number of operating systems. While RHEL can work with many of these formats, the default is XFS. Although many users enable other filesystems such as Btrfs, Red Hat may not support them.

Linux supports a rich variety of filesystems. Except for some old filesystems such as ext2, most filesystems incorporate features such as journal-based transactions, large storage support, delayed allocation, and complex algorithms to optimize read and write performance. In the following sections we split filesystems into two broad categories: "standard formatting" and journaling. While this is an oversimplification, it is sufficient to categorize the filesystem important to Linux.

The filesystems described in this book are just a subset of those that can be configured on a RHEL system. The Linux kernel makes it possible to set up more.

Standard Formatting Filesystems

Linux is a clone of Unix. The Linux filesystems were developed to mimic the functionality of Unix filesystems available at the time. The first versions of the Linux operating systems used the Extended Filesystem (ext). In the twentieth century, Red Hat formatted its partitions to the Second Extended Filesystem (ext2). Starting with RHEL 5, Red Hat moved to the Third Extended Filesystem (ext3). For RHEL 6, Red Hat progressed to the Fourth Extended Filesystem (ext4). Both ext3 and ext4 are journaling filesystems.

The size of current filesystems has increased the importance of journaling because such filesystems are more resilient to failure. So in general, the nonjournaling filesystems described in Table 6-2 are legacy filesystems. Of course, filesystems such as ISO 9660 and swap are still in common use.

TABLE 6-2   Some Standard Filesystems

Filesystem Type	Description
ext	The first Linux filesystem, used only on early versions of the operating system.
ext2 (Second Extended)	The foundation for ext3, the default filesystem for RHEL 5. The ext3 filesystem is essentially ext2 with journaling.
swap	The Linux swap filesystem is associated with dedicated swap partitions. You probably created at least one swap partition when you installed RHEL.
MS-DOS and VFAT	These filesystems allow you to read MS-DOS-formatted filesystems. MS-DOS lets you read pre–Windows 95 partitions or regular Windows partitions within the limits of short filenames. VFAT lets you read Windows 9x/NT/2000/XP/Vista/7 partitions formatted to the FAT16 or FAT32 filesystem.
ISO 9660	The standard filesystem for CD-ROMs. It is also known as the High Sierra File System, or HSFS, on other Unix systems.
proc and sys	Two Linux virtual filesystems. *Virtual* means that the filesystem doesn't occupy real disk space. Instead, files are created as needed. Used to provide information on kernel configuration and device status.
devpts	The Linux implementation of the Open Group's Unix98 PTY support.
tmpfs	A filesystem stored in memory. Used on RHEL 7 for the /run partition.

Journaling Filesystems

Journaling filesystems have two main advantages. First, they're faster for Linux to check during the boot process. Second, if a crash occurs, a journaling filesystem has a log (also known as a journal) that can be used to restore the metadata for the files on the relevant partition.

For RHEL 7, the default filesystem is XFS, a highly scalable, journal-based filesystem.

This isn't the only journaling filesystem options available, however. We list a few of the options commonly used for RHEL in Table 6-3. From this list, Red Hat officially supports only ext3, ext4, and XFS. At the time of writing, Btrfs is considered to be a "technology preview" and is not fully supported by Red Hat.

The Red Hat move to XFS is a testament to its use as a server operating system. For example, volumes formatted to XFS can theoretically be as large as 8 exabytes (EB). That's a serious increase over the maximum size of an ext4 volume: 16 terabytes (TB).

XFS supports a large number of concurrent operations, guarantees space for files, guarantees faster checks, and more. As XFS has been a part of the Linux kernel since 2004, it is proven technology.

Filesystem Format Commands

Several commands can help you create a Linux filesystem. They're all based on the **mkfs** command, which works as a front end to filesystem-specific commands such as **mkfs.ext3**, **mkfs.ext4**, and **mkfs.xfs**.

TABLE 6-3   Some Journaling Filesystems

Filesystem Type	Description
ext3	The default filesystem for RHEL 5.
ext4	The default filesystem for RHEL 6.
XFS	Developed by Silicon Graphics as a journaling filesystem, it supports very large files and features such as B-tree indexing and dynamic allocation inodes.
JFS	IBM's journaled filesystem, commonly used on IBM enterprise servers.
Btrfs	The B-tree filesystem was developed to offer a set of features comparable with Oracle ZFS. It offers some advanced features such as snapshots, storage pools, and compression.
NTFS	The current Microsoft Windows filesystem.

If you want to reformat an existing partition, logical volume, or RAID array, take the following precautions:

- Back up any existing data on the partition.
- Unmount the partition.

There are two ways to format a volume. (As noted earlier in this chapter, a volume is a generic name that can describe a partition, a RAID array, or a logical volume.) For example, if you've just created a partition on /dev/sdb5, you can format it to the XFS filesystem using one of the following commands:

```
# mkfs -t xfs /dev/sdb5
# mkfs.xfs /dev/sdb5
```

You can format partitions, logical volumes, and RAID arrays to other filesystems. The options available in RHEL 7 include the following:

- **mkfs.cramfs** creates a compressed ROM filesystem.
- **mkfs.ext2** formats a volume to the ext2 filesystem.
- **mkfs.ext3** formats a volume to the RHEL 5 default ext3 filesystem.
- **mkfs.ext4** formats a volume to the RHEL 6 default ext4 filesystem.
- **mkfs.fat** (or **mkfs.vfat**, **mkfs.msdos**, **mkdosfs**) formats a partition to the Microsoft-compatible FAT filesystem; it does not create bootable filesystems. (All these commands are the same because they are symbolic links to mkfs.fat.)
- **mkfs.xfs** formats a volume to the RHEL 7 default XFS filesystem.
- **mkswap** sets up a Linux swap area.

These commands assume you've configured an appropriate partition in the first place; for example, before the **mkswap** command can be properly applied to a partition, the Linux swap partition ID type must be configured for that partition. If you've created a RAID array or logical volume, as described later in this chapter, similar rules apply.

Swap Volumes

Although Linux can use swap files, the swap space is generally configured in properly formatted partitions or logical volumes. To see the swap space currently configured, run the **cat /proc/swaps** command.

As suggested in the previous section, swap volumes are formatted with the **mkswap** command. But that's not enough. First, swap volumes must be activated with the **swapon** command. If the new swap volume is recognized, you'll see it in both the /proc/swaps file and the output to the **top** command. Second, you'll need to make sure to configure the new swap volume in the /etc/fstab file, as described later in this chapter.

Filesystem Check Commands

The **fsck** command analyzes the specified filesystem and performs repairs as required. Assume, for example, you're having problems with files in the /var directory, which happens to be mounted on /dev/sda7. If you want to run **fsck**, unmount that filesystem first. In some cases, you may need to go into rescue mode before you can unmount a filesystem. To unmount, analyze, and then remount the filesystem noted in this section, run the following commands:

```
# umount /var
# fsck -t xfs /dev/sda7
# mount /dev/sda7 /var
```

The **fsck** command also serves as a "front end," depending on the filesystem format. For example, if you're formatting an ext2, ext3, or ext4 filesystem, **fsck** by itself automatically calls the **e2fsck** command. In fact, the **fsck.ext2**, **fsck.ext3**, **fsck.ext4**, and **e2fsck** files are all different names for the same command! They have the same inode number. You can confirm this by applying the **ls -i** command to all four files, which are part of the /sbin directory.

EXERCISE 6-2

Format, Check, and Mount Different Filesystems

In this exercise, you'll work with the file format and checking commands **mkfs** and **fsck** and then review the results with the **mount** command. This exercise assumes you've completed Exercise 6-1, or at least have unmounted Linux partitions with no data.

1. Review the current status of partitions on the drives discussed in Exercise 6-1 with the **parted /dev/vdb print** and **fdisk -l /dev/vdc** commands.

2. Format the partition created by the first drive with the **mkfs.ext2 /dev/vdb1** command. Review the current status of the volume with the **dumpe2fs -h /dev/vdb1 | grep features** command. What features do you see in the output? Save the output temporarily. One way to do so is to open a new command-line console. Check the system with the **fsck.ext2 /dev/vdb1** command.

3. Mount the newly formatted partition with the **mount /dev/vdb1 /mnt** command. Review the output with the **mount** command by itself. If the mount and format worked, you'll see the following output:

```
/dev/vdb1 on /mnt type ext2 (rw,relatime,seclabel)
```

4. Unmount the formatted partition with the **umount /mnt** command.

5. Run the **mkfs.ext4 /dev/vdb1** command and rerun the **dumpe2fs** command from the previous step. What's the difference between the output now and the output when the partition was formatted to the ext2 filesystem?

6. Repeat Steps 3 and 4. What's the difference in the output to the **mount** command?

7. Now on the other partition created in Exercise 6-1, apply the **mkfs.xfs /dev/vdc1** command.

8. Mount the newly formatted partition on the **/mnt** directory and then run the **mount** command by itself. Can you confirm the filesystem of the /dev/vdc1 partition?

CERTIFICATION OBJECTIVE 6.03

Basic Linux Filesystems and Directories

Everything in Linux can be reduced to a file. Partitions are associated with *filesystem device nodes* such as /dev/sda1. Hardware components are associated with node files such as /dev/cdrom. Detected devices are documented as files in the /sys directory. The Filesystem Hierarchy Standard (FHS) is the official way to organize files in Unix and Linux directories. As with the other sections, this introduction provides only the most basic overview of the FHS. More information is available from the official FHS home page at http://refspecs .linuxfoundation.org/fhs.shtml.

Separate Linux Filesystems

Several major directories are associated with all modern Unix/Linux operating systems. Files, drivers, kernels, logs, programs, utilities, and more are organized in these directories. The way these components are organized on storage media is known as a filesystem. The FHS makes it easier for Linux distributions to adhere to a common directory structure.

Every FHS starts with the top-level root directory, also known by its symbol, the single forward slash (/). All the other directories shown in Table 6-4 are subdirectories of the root directory. Unless they are mounted separately, you can also find their files on the same partition as the root directory. You may not see some of the directories shown in the table if associated packages have not been installed. Not all directories shown are officially part of the FHS. More importantly, not all listed directories can or should be mounted separately.

Mounted directories are often known as *volumes,* which can span multiple partitions if used with the Logical Volume Manager (LVM). While the root directory (/) is the top-level directory in the FHS, the root user's home directory (/root) is just a subdirectory.

| TABLE 6-4 | Basic Filesystem Hierarchy Standard Directories |

Directory	Description
/	The root directory, the top-level directory in the FHS. All other directories are subdirectories of root, which is always mounted on some volume.
/bin	Essential command-line utilities. Should not be mounted separately; otherwise, it could be difficult to get to these utilities when using a rescue disk. On RHEL 7, it is a symbolic link to /usr/bin.
/boot	Includes Linux startup files, including the Linux kernel. The default, 500MB, is usually sufficient for a typical modular kernel and additional kernels that you might install during the RHCE or RHCSA exam.
/dev	Hardware and software device drivers for everything from floppy drives to terminals. Do not mount this directory on a separate volume.
/etc	Most basic configuration files. Do not mount this directory on a separate volume.
/home	Home directories for almost every user.
/lib	Program libraries for the kernel and various command-line utilities. Do not mount this directory on a separate volume. On RHEL 7, this is a symbolic link to /usr/lib.
/lib64	Same as /lib, but includes 64-bit libraries. On RHEL 7, this is a symbolic link to /usr/lib64.
/media	The mount point for removable media, including DVDs and USB disk drives.
/misc	The standard mount point for local directories mounted via the automounter.
/mnt	A mount point for temporarily mounted filesystems.
/net	The standard mount point for network directories mounted via the automounter.
/opt	Common location for third-party application files.
/proc	A virtual filesystem listing information for currently running kernel-related processes, including device assignments such as IRQ ports, I/O addresses, and DMA channels, as well as kernel-configuration settings such as IP forwarding. As a virtual filesystem, Linux automatically configures it as a separate filesystem in RAM.
/root	The home directory of the root user. Do not mount this directory on a separate volume.
/run	A tmpfs filesystem for files that should not persist after a reboot. On RHEL 7, this filesystem replaces /var/run, which is a symbolic link to /run.
/sbin	System administration commands. Don't mount this directory separately. On RHEL 7, this is a symbolic link to /usr/bin.
/smb	The standard mount point for remote shared Microsoft network directories mounted via the automounter.
/srv	Commonly used by various network servers on non–Red Hat distributions.

(Continued)

TABLE 6-4	Basic Filesystem Hierarchy Standard Directories (*continued*)	

Directory	Description
/sys	Similar to the /proc filesystem. Used to expose information about devices, drivers, and some kernel features.
/tmp	Temporary files. By default, Red Hat Enterprise Linux deletes all files in this directory periodically.
/usr	Programs and read-only data. Includes many system administration commands, utilities, and libraries.
/var	Variable data, including log files and printer spools.

In Linux, the word *filesystem* has different meanings. It can refer to the FHS or to a format such as ext3. A filesystem mount point such as /var represents the directory on which a filesystem can be mounted.

Directories That Can Be Mounted Separately

If space is available, several directories listed in Table 6-4 are excellent candidates to be mounted separately. As discussed in Chapter 1, it's typical to mount directories such as /, /boot, /home, /opt, /tmp, and /var on separate volumes. Sometimes, it makes sense to mount lower-level subdirectories on separate volumes, such as /var/ftp for an FTP server or /var/www for a web server.

But first, several directories should always be maintained as part of the top-level root directory filesystem. These directories include /dev, /etc, and /root. Files within these directories are essential to the smooth operation of Linux as an operating system. Although the same argument can be made for the /boot directory, it is a special case. The storage of the Linux kernel, initial RAM disk, and bootloader files in this directory can help protect the core of the operating system when there are other problems.

Files in the /proc and /sys directories are filled only during the boot process and disappear when a system is shut down, and as such they are stored in a special in-memory virtual filesystem.

Some directories listed in Table 6-4 are designed for use only as mount points. In other words, they should normally be empty. If you store files on those directories, they won't be accessible if, say, a network share is mounted on them. Typical network mount points include the /media, /mnt, /net, and /smb directories.

CERTIFICATION OBJECTIVE 6.04

Logical Volume Management (LVM)

Logical Volume Management (LVM, also known as the Logical Volume Manager) creates an abstraction layer between physical devices, such as disks and partitions, and volumes that are formatted with a filesystem.

LVM can simplify disk management. As an example, assume that the /home filesystem is configured on its own logical volume. If extra space is available on the volume group associated with /home, you can easily resize the filesystem. If no space is available, you can make more room by adding a new physical disk and allocate its storage capacity to the volume group. On LVM, volume groups are like storage pools and they aggregate together the capacity of multiple storage devices. Logical volumes reside on volume groups and can span multiple physical disks.

LVM is an important tool to manage the space available to different volumes.

Definitions in LVM

To work with LVM, you need to understand how partitions configured for that purpose are used. First, with the **fdisk**, **gdisk** or **parted** utilities, you need to create partitions configured to the LVM partition type. You can also use an entire disk device.

Once those partitions or disk devices are available, they need to be set up as physical volumes (PVs). That process initializes a disk or partition for use by LVM. Then, you create volume groups (VGs) from one or more physical volumes. Volume groups organize the physical storage in a collection of manageable disk chunks known as physical extents (PEs). With the right commands, you can then organize those PEs into logical volumes (LVs). Logical volumes are made of logical extents (LEs), which map to the underlining PEs. You can then format and mount the LVs. For those who are new to LVM, it may be important to break out each definition:

- **Physical volume (PV)**   A PV is a partition or a disk drive initialized to be used by LVM.
- **Physical extent (PE)**   A PE is a small uniform segment of disk space. PVs are split into PEs.
- **Volume group (VG)**   A VG is a storage pool, made of one or more PVs.

■ **Logical extent (LE)**   Every PE is associated with an LE, and these PEs can be combined into a logical volume.

■ **Logical volume (LV)**   An LV is a part of a VG and is made of LEs. An LV can be formatted with a filesystem and then mounted on the directory of your choice.

You'll see this broken down in the following sections. In essence, to create an LV system, you need to create a new PV using a command such as **pvcreate**, assign the space from one or more PVs to a VG with a command such as **vgcreate**, and allocate the space from some part of available VGs to an LV with a command such as **lvcreate**.

To add space to an existing logical volume, you need to add free space from an existing VG with a command such as **lvextend**. If you don't have any existing VG space, you'll need to add to it with unassigned PV space with a command such as **vgextend**. If all of your PVs are taken, you may need to create a new PV from an unassigned partition or hard drive with the **pvcreate** command.

Create a Physical Volume

The first step is to start with a physical partition or a hard disk drive. Based on the discussion earlier in this chapter, you should be able to set up partitions to match the Linux LVM identifier. Then, to set up a new PV on a properly configured partition, such as /dev/sda1, apply the **pvcreate** command to that partition:

```
# pvcreate /dev/sda1
```

If there is more than one partition to be configured as a PV, the associated device files can all be listed in the same command:

```
# pvcreate /dev/sda1 /dev/sda2 /dev/sdb1 /dev/sdb2
```

Create a Volume Group

From one or more PVs, you can create a volume group (VG). In the following command, substitute the name of your choice for *volumegroup*:

```
# vgcreate volumegroup /dev/sda1 /dev/sda2
```

You can include additional PVs in any VG. Assume there are existing PVs based on /dev/sdb1 and /dev/sdb2 partitions, you can add to the *volumegroup* VG with the following command:

```
# vgextend volumegroup /dev/sdb1 /dev/sdb2
```

Create a Logical Volume

However, a new VG isn't enough since you can't format or mount a filesystem on it. So you need to create a logical volume (LV) for this purpose. The following command creates an LV. You can add as many chunks of disk space, in PEs, as you need.

```
# lvcreate -l number_of_PEs volumegroup -n logvol
```

This creates a device named /dev/*volumegroup/logvol*. You can format this device as if it were a regular disk partition and then mount that new logical volume on a directory.

But this isn't useful if you don't know how much space is associated with each PE. You can use the **vgdisplay** command to display the size of the PEs, or specify the size with the **-s** option of the **vgcreate** command when you initialize the volume group. Alternatively, you can use the -**L** switch to set a size in MB, GB, or another unit of measure. For example, the following command creates an LV named flex of 200MB:

```
# lvcreate -L 200M volumegroup -n flex
```

Make Use of a Logical Volume

But that's not the last step. You may not get full credit unless the logical volume gets formatted and mounted when the system is rebooted. This process is described later in this chapter in the discussion of the /etc/fstab configuration file.

More LVM Commands

A wide variety of LVM commands related to PVs, LVs, and VGs are available. Generally, they are **pv***, **lv***, and **vg*** in the /usr/sbin directory. Physical volume commands include those listed in Table 6-5.

As you assign PVs to VGs to LVs, you may need commands to control and configure them. Table 6-6 includes an overview of most related volume group commands.

As you assign PVs to VGs and then subdivide VGs into LVs, you may need commands to control and configure them. Table 6-7 includes an overview of related LVM commands.

TABLE 6-5   Physical Volume Management Commands

Physical Volume Command	Description
pvchange	Changes attributes of a PV: the **pvchange -x n /dev/sda10** command disables the allocation of PEs from the /dev/sda10 partition.
pvck	Checks the consistency of a physical volume's metadata.
pvcreate	Initializes a disk or partition as a PV; the partition should be flagged with the LVM file type.

(Continued)

TABLE 6-5 Physical Volume Management Commands (*continued*)

Physical Volume Command	Description
pvdisplay	Displays currently configured PVs.
pvmove	Moves PEs in a VG from the specified PV to free locations on other PVs; prerequisite to disabling a PV. One example: **pvmove /dev/sda10**.
pvremove	Removes a given PV from a list of recognized volumes: for example, **pvremove /dev/sda10**.
pvresize	Changes the amount of a partition allocated to a PV. If you've expanded partition /dev/sda10, **pvresize /dev/sda10** takes advantage of the additional space. Alternatively, **pvresize --setphysicalvolumesize 100M /dev/sda10** reduces the amount of PVs taken from that partition to the noted space.
pvs	Lists configured PVs and the associated VGs, if so assigned.
pvscan	Scans disks for physical volumes.

TABLE 6-6 Volume Group Commands

Volume Group Command	Description
vgcfgbackup vgcfgrestore	Used to back up and restore the metadata associated with LVM; by default, the backup files are in the /etc/lvm directory.
vgchange	Similar to **pvchange**, this command allows you to change the configuration settings of a VG. For example, **vgchange -a y** enables all local VGs.
vgck	Checks the consistency of a volume group metadata.
vgconvert	Supports conversions from LVM1 systems to LVM2: **vgconvert -M2 VolGroup00** converts VolGroup00 to the LVM2 metadata format.
vgcreate	Creates a VG, from one or more configured PVs: for example, **vgcreate vgroup00 /dev/sda10 /dev/sda11** creates vgroup00 from PVs as defined on /dev/sda10 and /dev/sda11.
vgdisplay	Displays characteristics of currently configured VGs.
vgexport vgimport	Used to export and import unused VGs from those available; the **vgexport -a** command exports all inactive VGs.
vgextend	If you've created a new PV, **vgextend vgroup00 /dev/sda11** adds the space from /dev/sda11 to vgroup00.
vgmerge	If you have an unused VG vgroup01, you can merge it into vgroup00 with the following command: **vgmerge vgroup00 vgroup01**.
vgmknodes	Run this command if you have a problem with VG device files.

TABLE 6-6 Volume Group Commands (*continued*)

Volume Group Command	Description
vgreduce	The **vgreduce vgroup00 /dev/sda11** command removes the /dev/sda11 PV from vgroup00, assuming /dev/sda11 is unused.
vgremove	The **vgremove vgroup00** command removes vgroup00, assuming it has no LVs assigned to it.
vgrename	Allows the renaming of LVs.
vgs	Displays basic information on configured VGs.
vgscan	Scans all devices for VGs.
vgsplit	Splits a volume group.

TABLE 6-7 Logical Volume Commands

Logical Volume Command	Description
lvchange	Similar to **pvchange**, this command changes the attributes of an LV: for example, the **lvchange -a n vgroup00/lvol00** command disables the use of the LV labeled lvol00.
lvconvert	Converts a logical volume between different types, such as linear, mirror, or snapshot.
lvcreate	Creates a new LV in an existing VG. For example, **lvcreate -l 200 volume01 -n lvol01** creates lvol01 using 200 extents in the VG named volume01.
lvdisplay	Displays currently configured LVs.
lvextend	Adds space to an LV: the **lvextend -L 4G /dev/volume01/lvol01** command extends lvol01 to 4GB, assuming space is available.
lvreduce	Reduces the size of an LV; if there's data in the reduced area, it is lost.
lvremove	Removes an active LV: the **lvremove volume01/lvol01** command removes the LV lvol01 from VG volume01.
lvrename	Renames an LV.
lvresize	Resizes an LV; can be done by **-L** for size. For example, **lvresize -L +4GB volume01 /lvol01** adds 4GB to the size of lvol01.
lvs	Lists all configured LVs.
lvscan	Scans for all LVs.

FIGURE 6-7

Configuration of a
volume group (VG)

```
[root@server1 ~]# vgdisplay
  --- Volume group ---
  VG Name               rhel_server1
  System ID
  Format                lvm2
  Metadata Areas        1
  Metadata Sequence No  3
  VG Access             read/write
  VG Status             resizable
  MAX LV                0
  Cur LV                2
  Open LV               2
  Max PV                0
  Cur PV                1
  Act PV                1
  VG Size               14.53 GiB
  PE Size               4.00 MiB
  Total PE              3720
  Alloc PE / Size       2750 / 10.74 GiB
  Free  PE / Size       970 / 3.79 GiB
  VG UUID               oYuR2x-uaUH-AZsZ-McNz-92Jh-qfYk-Ma0FDT

[root@server1 ~]# █
```

Here's an example how this works. Try the **vgscan** command. You can verify configured volume groups (VGs) with the **vgdisplay** command. For example, Figure 6-7 illustrates the configuration of VG rhel_server1.

Although a number of **lvm*** commands are installed, just four of them are active: **lvm**, **lvmconf**, **lvmdiskscan**, and **lvmdump**. Other **lvm*** commands are obsolete or not implemented yet. The **lvm** command moves to an **lvm>** prompt. It's rather interesting, as the **help** command at that prompt provides a nearly full list of available LVM commands.

The **lvmconf** command can modify the default settings in the related configuration file, /etc/lvm/lvm.conf. The **lvmdiskscan** command scans all available drives for LVM-configured physical volumes. Finally, the **lvmdump** command sets up a configuration report in the root administrative user's home directory (/root).

Remove a Logical Volume

The removal of an existing LV is straightforward, with the **lvremove** command. This assumes that any directories previously mounted on LVs have been unmounted. At that point, the basic steps are simple:

1. Save any data in directories that are mounted on the LV.
2. Unmount the filesystem associated with the LV. As an example, you can use a command similar to the following:

   ```
   # umount /dev/vg_01/lv_01
   ```

3. Apply the **lvremove** command to the LV with a command such as this:

```
# lvremove /dev/vg_01/lv_01
```

4. You should now have the LEs from this LV free for use in other LVs.

Resize Logical Volumes

If you need to increase the size of an existing LV, you can add the space from a newly created PV to it. All it takes is appropriate use of the **vgextend** and **lvextend** commands. For example, to add the PEs to the VG associated with a /home directory mounted on an LV, take the following basic steps:

1. Back up any data existing on the /home directory. (This is a standard precaution that isn't necessary if everything goes right. You might even skip this step on the Red Hat exams. But do you really want to risk user data in practice?)

2. Extend the VG to include new partitions configured to the appropriate type. For example, to add /dev/sdd1 to the vg_00 VG, run the following command:

```
# vgextend vg_00 /dev/sdd1
```

3. Make sure the new partitions are included in the VG with the following command:

```
# vgdisplay vg_00
```

4. Now you can extend the space given to the current LV. For example, to extend the LV to 2000MB, run the following command:

```
# lvextend -L 2000M /dev/vg_00/lv_00
```

5. The **lvextend** command can increase the space allocated to an LV in KB, MB, GB, or even TB. For example, you could specify a 2GB LV with the following command:

```
# lvextend -L 2G /dev/vg_00/lv_00
```

If you prefer to specify the extra space to be added rather than the total space, you can use the syntax in the following example, which adds 1GB to the logical volume:

```
# lvextend -L +1G /dev/vg_00/lv_00
```

6. Resize the formatted volume with the **xfs_growfs** command (or with **resize2fs**, if it is an ext2/ext3/ext4 filesystem). If you're using the entire extended LV, the command is simple:

```
# xfs_growfs /dev/vg_00/lv_00
```

7. Alternatively, you can reformat the LV, using commands described earlier, so the filesystem can take full advantage of the new space—and then restore data from the backup. (If you've already successfully resized an LV, *don't* reformat it. It isn't necessary and would destroy existing data!)

```
# mkfs.xfs -f /dev/vg_00/lv_00
```

8. In either case, you'd finish the process by checking the new filesystem size with the **df** command:

```
# df -h
```

CERTIFICATION OBJECTIVE 6.05

Filesystem Management

Before you can access the files in a directory, that directory must be mounted on a partition formatted to some readable filesystem. Linux normally automates this process using the /etc/fstab configuration file. When Linux goes through the boot process, directories specified in /etc/fstab are mounted on configured volumes, with the help of the **mount** command. Of course, you can run that command with any or all appropriate options, so that's an excellent place to start this section.

The remainder of this section focuses on options for /etc/fstab. While it starts with the default using the baseline configuration for the standard virtual machine, it includes options to customize that file for local, remote, and removable filesystems.

The /etc/fstab File

To look at the contents of the /etc/fstab file, run the **cat /etc/fstab** command. From the example shown in Figure 6-8, different filesystems are configured on each line.

In RHEL 7 the default is to use UUIDs to mount non-LVM filesystems. As you'll see in the next section, UUIDs can represent a partition, a logical volume, or a RAID array. In all cases, volumes should be formatted to the filesystem noted on each line and are mounted on the directory listed in the second column. The advantage of UUIDs and logical volume devices is that they are unique, whereas device names such as /dev/sdb2 may change after a reboot, depending on the order in which the disks are initialized.

But to some extent, UUIDs are beside the point. As shown in Figure 6-8, six fields are associated with each filesystem, described from left to right in Table 6-8. You can verify how partitions are actually mounted in the /etc/mtab file, as shown in Figure 6-9.

FIGURE 6-8   Sample /etc/fstab

```
[root@server1 ~]# cat /etc/fstab

#
# /etc/fstab
# Created by anaconda on Mon Feb  2 17:41:03 2015
#
# Accessible filesystems, by reference, are maintained under '/dev/disk'
# See man pages fstab(5), findfs(8), mount(8) and/or blkid(8) for more info
#
/dev/mapper/rhel_server1-root /                        xfs      defaults         1 1
UUID=c89968bc-acc5-4d60-8deb-97542cb766c6 /boot                 xfs      defaults         1 2
/dev/mapper/rhel_server1-home /home                    xfs      defaults         1 2
UUID=9d37eaf0-2c0b-4e57-b05f-87c2e21d3a95 swap                  swap     defaults         0 0
[root@server1 ~]#
```

FIGURE 6-9   Sample /etc/mtab

```
[root@server1 ~]# cat /etc/mtab
rootfs / rootfs rw 0 0
proc /proc proc rw,nosuid,nodev,noexec,relatime 0 0
sysfs /sys sysfs rw,seclabel,nosuid,nodev,noexec,relatime 0 0
devtmpfs /dev devtmpfs rw,seclabel,nosuid,size=499652k,nr_inodes=124913,mode=755 0 0
securityfs /sys/kernel/security securityfs rw,nosuid,nodev,noexec,relatime 0 0
tmpfs /dev/shm tmpfs rw,seclabel,nosuid,nodev 0 0
devpts /dev/pts devpts rw,seclabel,nosuid,noexec,relatime,gid=5,mode=620,ptmxmode=000 0 0
tmpfs /run tmpfs rw,seclabel,nosuid,nodev,mode=755 0 0
tmpfs /sys/fs/cgroup tmpfs rw,seclabel,nosuid,nodev,noexec,mode=755 0 0
cgroup /sys/fs/cgroup/systemd cgroup rw,nosuid,nodev,noexec,relatime,xattr,release_agent=/usr/
lib/systemd/systemd-cgroups-agent,name=systemd 0 0
pstore /sys/fs/pstore pstore rw,nosuid,nodev,noexec,relatime 0 0
cgroup /sys/fs/cgroup/cpuset cgroup rw,nosuid,nodev,noexec,relatime,cpuset 0 0
cgroup /sys/fs/cgroup/cpu,cpuacct cgroup rw,nosuid,nodev,noexec,relatime,cpuacct,cpu 0 0
cgroup /sys/fs/cgroup/memory cgroup rw,nosuid,nodev,noexec,relatime,memory 0 0
cgroup /sys/fs/cgroup/devices cgroup rw,nosuid,nodev,noexec,relatime,devices 0 0
cgroup /sys/fs/cgroup/freezer cgroup rw,nosuid,nodev,noexec,relatime,freezer 0 0
cgroup /sys/fs/cgroup/net_cls cgroup rw,nosuid,nodev,noexec,relatime,net_cls 0 0
cgroup /sys/fs/cgroup/blkio cgroup rw,nosuid,nodev,noexec,relatime,blkio 0 0
cgroup /sys/fs/cgroup/perf_event cgroup rw,nosuid,nodev,noexec,relatime,perf_event 0 0
cgroup /sys/fs/cgroup/hugetlb cgroup rw,nosuid,nodev,noexec,relatime,hugetlb 0 0
configfs /sys/kernel/config configfs rw,relatime 0 0
/dev/mapper/rhel_server1-root / xfs rw,seclabel,relatime,attr2,inode64,noquota 0 0
selinuxfs /sys/fs/selinux selinuxfs rw,relatime 0 0
systemd-1 /proc/sys/fs/binfmt_misc autofs rw,relatime,fd=33,pgrp=1,timeout=300,minproto=5,maxp
roto=5,direct 0 0
hugetlbfs /dev/hugepages hugetlbfs rw,seclabel,relatime 0 0
debugfs /sys/kernel/debug debugfs rw,relatime 0 0
mqueue /dev/mqueue mqueue rw,seclabel,relatime 0 0
sunrpc /var/lib/nfs/rpc_pipefs rpc_pipefs rw,relatime 0 0
sunrpc /proc/fs/nfsd nfsd rw,relatime 0 0
/dev/mapper/rhel_server1-home /home xfs rw,seclabel,relatime,attr2,inode64,noquota 0 0
/dev/vda1 /boot xfs rw,seclabel,relatime,attr2,inode64,noquota 0 0
fusectl /sys/fs/fuse/connections fusectl rw,relatime 0 0
gvfsd-fuse /run/user/1000/gvfs fuse.gvfsd-fuse rw,nosuid,nodev,relatime,user_id=1000,group_id=
1000 0 0
/dev/sr0 /run/media/alex/RHEL-7.0\040Server.x86_64 iso9660 ro,nosuid,nodev,relatime,uid=1000,g
id=1000,iocharset=utf8,mode=0400,dmode=0500 0 0
[root@server1 ~]#
```

| TABLE 6-8 | Description of /etc/fstab by Column, Left to Right |

Field Name	Description
Device	Lists the device to be mounted; you may substitute the UUID or the device path.
Mount Point	Notes the directory where the filesystem will be mounted.
Filesystem Format	Describes the filesystem type. Valid filesystem types are xfs, ext2, ext3, ext4, msdos, vfat, iso9660, nfs, smb, swap, and many others.
Mount Options	Covered in the following section.
Dump Value	Either 0 or 1. If you use the **dump** command to back up filesystems, this field controls which filesystems need to be dumped.
Filesystem Check Order	Determines the order that filesystems are checked by the **fsck** command during the boot process. The root directory (/) filesystem should be set to 1, and other local filesystems should be set to 2. Removable filesystems such as those associated with CD/DVD drives should be set to 0, which means that they are not checked during the Linux boot process.

Note the differences, especially the use of the device file in place of UUIDs, and the presence of virtual filesystems such as tmpfs and sysfs, which are discussed later in this chapter.

When adding a new partition, you could just add the device file associated with the partition or logical volume to the first column.

Universally Unique Identifiers in /etc/fstab

In /etc/fstab, note the focus on UUIDs, short for Universally Unique Identifiers. Every formatted volume has a UUID, a unique 128-bit number. Each UUID represents either a partition, a logical volume, or a RAID array.

To identify the UUID for available volumes, run the **blkid** command with the name of the device as an argument. The output will give the UUID of the device. As an example, to retrieve the UUID of the "root" logical volume in the "rhel_server1" volume group, run the following command:

```
# blkid /dev/rhel_server1/root
/dev/rhel_server1/root: UUID="2142e97a-dbec-495c-b7d9-1369270089ff" ↵
TYPE="xfs"
```

Alternatively, you could use the **xfs_admin** and **dumpe2fs** commands for the XFS and ext2/ext3/ext4 filesystems, respectively; for example, the following command identifies the UUID associated with the noted LV:

```
# xfs_admin -u /dev/rhel_server1/root
```

As UUIDs are not limited to LVs, you should be able to get equivalent information for a partition from a command such as the following:

```
# xfs_admin -u /dev/vda1
```

Of course, the same is true if you have a configured and formatted ext volume, with a command such as the following:

```
# dumpe2fs /dev/mapper/rhel_server1-test | grep UUID
```

The mount Command

The **mount** command can be used to attach local and network partitions to specified directories. Mount points are not fixed; you can mount a CD drive or even a shared network directory to any empty directory if appropriate ownership and permissions are set. Closely related is the **umount** (not unmount) command, which unmounts selected volumes from associated directories.

First, try the **mount** command by itself. It'll display all currently mounted filesystems, along with important mount options. For example, the following output suggests that the /dev/mapper/rhel_server1-root volume is mounted on the top-level root directory in read-write mode and formatted to the xfs filesystem:

```
/dev/mapper/rhel_server1-root on / type xfs ↵
(rw,relatime,seclabel,attr2,inode64,noquota)
```

As suggested earlier, the **mount** command is closely related to the /etc/fstab file. If you've unmounted a directory and have made changes to the /etc/fstab file, the easiest way to mount all filesystems currently configured in the /etc/fstab file is with the following command:

```
# mount -a
```

However, if a filesystem is already mounted, this command doesn't change its status, no matter what has been done to the /etc/fstab file. But if the system is subsequently rebooted, the options configured in /etc/fstab are used automatically.

If you're not sure about a possible change to the /etc/fstab file, it's possible to test it out with the **mount** command. For example, the following command remounts the volume associated with the /boot directory in read-only mode:

```
# mount -o remount,ro /boot
```

You can confirm the result by rerunning the **mount** command. The following output should reflect the result on the /boot directory:

```
/dev/vda1 on /boot type xfs (ro,relatime,seclabel,attr2,inode64,noquota)
```

If you've read this book from the beginning, you've already seen the **mount** command at work with access control lists (ACLs), and even the ISO files associated with downloaded CD/DVDs. To review, the following command remounts the noted /home directory with ACLs:

```
# mount -o remount,acl /dev/vda5 /home
```

And for ISO files, the following command mounts the noted RHEL 7 ISO file on the /mnt directory:

```
# mount -o loop rhel-server-7.0-x86_64-dvd.iso /mnt
```

More Filesystem Mount Options

Many **mount** command options are appropriate for the /etc/fstab file. One option most commonly seen in that file is **defaults**. Although that is the appropriate mount option for most /etc/fstab filesystems, there are other options, such as those listed in Table 6-9. If you want to use multiple options, separate them by commas. Don't use spaces between options. The list in Table 6-9 is not comprehensive. You can find out more from the mount man page, available with the **man mount** command.

TABLE 6-9   Options for the mount Command and /etc/fstab

Mount Option	Description
async	All I/O is done asynchronously on this filesystem.
atime	Updates the inode access time every time the file is accessed.
auto	Can be mounted with the **mount -a** command.
defaults	Uses default mount options **rw**, **suid**, **dev**, **exec**, **auto**, **nouser**, and **async**.
dev	Permits access to character devices such as terminals or consoles and block devices such as drives.
exec	Allows binaries (compiled programs) to be run on this filesystem.
noatime	Does not update the inode access time every time the file is accessed.
noauto	Requires explicit mounting. This is a common option for CD drives and removable media.
nodev	Device files on this filesystem are not read or interpreted.
noexec	Binaries (compiled programs) cannot be run on this filesystem.
nosuid	Disallows **setuid** and **setgid** permissions on this filesystem.
nouser	Only root users are allowed to mount the specified filesystem.

TABLE 6-9	Options for the mount Command and /etc/fstab (*continued*)

Mount Option	Description
remount	Remounts a currently mounted filesystem.
ro	Mounts the filesystem as read-only.
rw	Mounts the filesystem as read/write.
suid	Allows **setuid** and **setgid** permissions on programs on this filesystem.
sync	All I/O is done synchronously on this filesystem.
user	Allows non-root users to mount this filesystem. By default, this also sets the **noexec**, **nosuid**, and **nodev** options.

Virtual Filesystems

This section describes some of the virtual filesystems used by RHEL 7 and listed in /etc/mtab. Here are the most common:

- **tmpfs**   This virtual memory filesystem uses both RAM and swap space.
- **devpts**   This filesystem relates to pseudo-terminal devices.
- **sysfs**   This filesystem provides dynamic information about system devices. Explore the associated /sys directory. You'll find a wide variety of information related to the devices and drivers attached to the local system.
- **proc**   This filesystem is especially useful because it provides dynamically configurable options for changing the behavior of the kernel. As an RHCE skill, you may learn more about options in the proc filesystem in Chapter 12.
- **cgroups**   This filesystem is associated with the control group feature of the Linux kernel, which allows you to set limits on system resource usage for a process or a group of processes.

Add Your Own Filesystems to /etc/fstab

If you need to set up a special directory, it sometimes makes sense to set it up on a separate volume. Different volumes for different directories means that files in that volume can't overload critical directories such as /boot. While it's nice to follow the standard format of the /etc/fstab file, it is an extra effort. If required on a Red Hat exam, it'll be in the instructions that you see.

So in most cases, it's sufficient to set up a new volume in /etc/fstab with the associated device file, such as a /dev/vda6 partition, a UUID, or a LVM device such as

/dev/mapper/NewVol-NewLV or /dev/NewVol/NewLV. Make sure the device file reflects the new volume you've created, the intended mount directory (such as /special), and the filesystem format you've applied (such as xfs).

Removable Media and /etc/fstab

In general, removable media should not be mounted automatically during the boot process. That's possible in the /etc/fstab configuration file with an option such as **noauto**, but in general it's not standard in RHEL to set up removable media in /etc/fstab.

To read removable media such as smartcards and CD/DVDs, RHEL partially automates the mounting of such media in the GNOME Desktop Environment. Although the details of this process are not part of the Red Hat Exam Prep guide, the process is based on configuration files in the /usr/lib/udev/rules.d directory. If RHEL detects your hardware, click Places; in the menu that appears, select the entry for the removable media. If multiple removable media options are loaded, you can select the media to mount in the Removable Media submenu.

If that doesn't work for some reason, you can use the **mount** command directly. For example, the following command mounts a CD/DVD in a drive:

```
# mount -t iso9660 /dev/sr0 /mnt
```

The **-t** switch specifies the type of filesystem (iso9660). The device file /dev/sr0 represents the first CD/DVD drive; /mnt is the directory through which you can access the files from the CD/DVD after mounting. But /dev/sr0? How is anyone supposed to remember that?

Fortunately, Linux addresses this in a couple of ways. First, it sets up links from more sensibly named files such as /dev/cdrom, which you can confirm with the **ls -l /dev/cdrom** command. Second, it provides the **blkid** command. Try it. If removable media (other than a CD/DVD) are connected, you'll see it in the output to the command, including the associated device file.

Just remember that it is important to unmount removable media such as USB keys before removing them. Otherwise, the data you thought was written to the disk might still be in the unwritten RAM cache. In that case, you would lose that data.

Given these examples of how removable media can be mounted, you should have a better idea on how such media can be configured in the /etc/fstab configuration file. The standard **defaults** option is inappropriate in most cases because it mounts a system in read-write mode (even for read-only DVDs), attempts to mount automatically during the boot process, and limits access to the root administrative user. But that can be changed with the right options. For example, to configure a CD drive that can be mounted by regular users, you could add the following line to /etc/fstab:

```
/dev/sr0 /cdrom auto ro,noauto,users 0 0
```

This line sets up a mount in read-only mode, does not try to mount it automatically during the boot process, and supports access by regular users.

As desired, similar options are possible for removable media such as USB keys, but that can be more problematic with multiple USB keys; for example, one may be detected as /dev/sdc once, and then later detected as /dev/sdd, if there's a second USB key installed. However, if properly configured, each USB key should have a unique UUID. There's another option: rather than using static mounts for removable devices, you can rely on the automounter, as we will illustrate later in this chapter.

Networked Filesystems

The /etc/fstab file can be used to automate mounts from shared directories. The two major sharing services of interest are NFS and Samba. This section provides only a brief overview to how such shared directories can be configured in the /etc/fstab file; for more information, see Chapters 15 and 16.

In general, shares from networked directories should be assumed to be unreliable. People step on power lines, on Ethernet cables, and so on. If your system uses a wireless network, that adds another level of unreliability. In other words, the settings in the /etc/fstab file should account for that. So if there's a problem either in the network connection or perhaps a problem such as a power failure on the remote NFS server, you should specify in the mount options how you want the client to behave.

A connection to a shared NFS directory is based on its hostname or IP address, along with the full path to the directory on the server. So to connect to a remote NFS server on system *server1* that shares the /pub directory, you could mount that share with the following command (assuming the /share directory exists):

```
# mount -t nfs server1.example.com:/pub /share
```

But that mount does not specify any options. You can try the following entry in /etc/fstab:

```
server1:/pub  /share  nfs rsize=65536,wsize=65536,hard,udp 0 0
```

The **rsize** and **wsize** variables determine the maximum size (in bytes) of the data to be read and written in each request. The **hard** directive specifies that the client will retry failed NFS requests indefinitely, blocking client requests potentially until the NFS server becomes available. Conversely, the **soft** option will cause the client to fail after a predefined amount of retransmissions, but at the cost of risking the integrity of the data. The **udp** specifies a connection using the User Datagram Protocol (UDP). If the connection is to a NFS version 4 server, substitute **nfs4** for **nfs** in the third column. Note that NFS version 4 requires TCP. In contrast, shared Samba directories use a different set of options. The following line is generally all that's needed for a share of the same directory and server:

```
//server1/pub  /share  cifs rw,username=user,password=pass, 0 0
```

If you're disturbed by the open display of a username and password in the /etc/fstab file, which is world-readable, try the following option:

```
//server1/pub  /share  cifs rw,credentials=/etc/secret 0 0
```

You can then set up the /etc/secret file as accessible only to the root administrative user, with the username and password in the following format:

```
username=user
password=password
```

CERTIFICATION OBJECTIVE 6.06

The Automounter

With network mounts and portable media, problems may come up if connections are lost or media are removed. During the server configuration process, you could be mounting directories from a number of remote systems. You may also want temporary access to removable media such as USB keys. The automount daemon, also known as the automounter or **autofs**, can help. It can automatically mount a specific filesystem as needed. It can unmount a filesystem automatically after a fixed period of time.

Mounting via the Automounter

Once a partition is mounted manually with the **mount** command or via /etc/fstab, it stays mounted until you unmount it or shut down the system. The permanence of the mount can cause problems. For example, if you've mounted a USB key and then physically remove the key, Linux may not have had a chance to write the file to the disk. Data would be lost. The same issue applies to secure digital cards or other hot-swappable removable drives.

Another issue: mounted NFS filesystems may cause problems if the remote computer fails or the connection is lost. Systems may slow down or even hang as the local system looks for the mounted directory.

This is where the automounter can help. It relies on the **autofs** daemon to mount configured directories as needed on a temporary basis. In RHEL, the relevant configuration files are auto.master, auto.misc, auto.net, and auto.smb, all in the /etc directory. If you use the automounter, keep the /misc and /net directories free. Red Hat configures automounts on these directories by default, and they won't work if local files or directories are stored there. Subsections will cover each of these files.

on the **job**

You won't even see the /misc and/or /net directories unless you properly configure /etc/auto.master and the autofs daemon is running.

Default automounter settings are configured in /etc/sysconfig/autofs. The default settings include a timeout of 300 seconds; in other words, if nothing happens on an automount within that time, the share is automatically unmounted:

```
TIMEOUT=300
```

BROWSE_MODE can allow you to search from available mounts. The following directive disables it by default:

```
BROWSE_MODE="no"
```

A wide variety of additional settings are available, as commented in /etc/sysconfig/autofs.

/etc/auto.master

The standard /etc/auto.master file includes a series of directives, with four uncommented lines by default. The first refers to the /etc/auto.misc file as the configuration file for the /misc directory. The **/net -hosts** directive allows you to specify the host to automount a network directory, as specified in /etc/auto.net.

```
/misc /etc/auto.misc
/net  -hosts
+dir:/etc/auto.master.d
+auto.master
```

In any case, these directives point to configuration files for each service. Shared directories from each service are automatically mounted on demand on the given directory (/misc and /net).

You can set up the automounter on other directories. One popular option is to set up the automounter on the /home directory. In this way, you can configure user home directories on remote servers mounted on demand. Users are given access to their home directories upon login, and based on the **TIMEOUT** directive in the /etc/sysconfig/autofs file, all mounted directories are automatically unmounted 300 seconds after users are logged off from the system.

```
# /home /etc/auto.home
```

This works only if a /home directory doesn't already exist on the local system. As the Red Hat exam requires the configuration of a number of regular users, your systems should include a /home directory for regular users. In that case, you could substitute a different directory, leading to a line such as the following:

```
/shared /etc/auto.home
```

Just remember, for any system accessed over a network, you'll need to be sure that the firewall allows traffic associated with the given service.

/etc/auto.misc

Red Hat conveniently provides standard automount directives in comments in the /etc/auto .misc file. It's helpful to analyze this file in detail. We use the default RHEL version of this file. The first four lines are comments, which we skip. The first directive is

```
cd      -fstype=iso9660,ro,nosuid,nodev    :/dev/cdrom
```

In RHEL, this directive is active by default, assuming you've activated the **autofs** service. In other words, if you have a CD in the /dev/cdrom drive, you can access its files through the automounter with the **ls /misc/cd** command, even as a regular user. The automounter accesses it using the ISO9660 filesystem. It's mounted read-only (**ro**), set owner user ID permissions are not allowed (**nosuid**), and device files on this filesystem are not used (**nodev**).

A number of other directives are commented out, ready for use. Of course, you would have to delete the comment character (#) before using any of these configuration lines, and you'd have to adjust names and device files accordingly; for example, /dev/hda1 is no longer used as a device file on the latest Linux systems, even for PATA hard drives.

As suggested by one of the comments, "The following entries are samples to pique your imagination." The first of these commented lines allows you to set up a /misc/linux mount point from a shared NFS directory, /pub/linux, from the ftp.example.org host:

```
#linux   -ro,soft,intr     ftp.example.org:/pub/linux
```

The next line assumes that a filesystem is stored on the /dev/hda1 partition. With this directive, you can automount the filesystem in /misc/boot.

```
#boot    -fstype=ext2      :/dev/hda1
```

The following three lines apply to a floppy disk drive. Don't laugh; virtual floppies are fairly easy to create and configure on most virtual machine systems. The first directive, set to an "auto" filesystem type, searches through /etc/filesystems to try to match what's on your floppy. The next two directives assume that the floppy is formatted to the ext2 filesystem.

```
#floppy        -fstype=auto      :/dev/fd0
#floppy        -fstype=ext2      :/dev/fd0
#e2floppy      -fstype=ext2      :/dev/fd0
```

The next line points to the first partition on the third SCSI drive. The **jaz** at the beginning suggests this is suitable for an old Iomega-type Jaz drive.

```
#jaz       -fstype=ext2      :/dev/sdc1
```

Finally, the last command is based on an older system where the automounter is applied to a legacy PATA drive. Of course, the /dev/hdd device file is no longer used, so substitute accordingly. But the **removable** at the beginning suggests this is also suitable for removable hard drives. Of course, you'd likely have to change the filesystem format to something like XFS. As suggested earlier in this chapter, the **blkid** command can help identify available device files from removable systems such as USB keys and portable drives.

```
#removable    -fstype=ext2        :/dev/hdd
```

In general, you'll need to modify these lines for available hardware.

/etc/auto.net

With the /etc/auto.net configuration script, you can review and read shared NFS directories. It works with the hostnames or IP addresses of NFS servers. By default, executable permissions are enabled on this file.

Assuming the automounter is active and can connect to an NFS server with an IP address of 192.168.122.1, you can review shared NFS directories on that system with the following command:

```
# /etc/auto.net 192.168.122.1 -fstype=nfs,hard,intr,nodev,nosuid \
        /srv/ftp 192.168.122.1:/srv/ftp
```

This output tells that the /srv/ftp directory on the 192.168.122.1 system is shared via NFS. Based on the directives in /etc/auto.master, you could access this share (assuming appropriate firewall and SELinux settings) with the following command:

```
# ls /net/192.168.122.1/srv/ftp
```

/etc/auto.smb

One of the problems associated with the configuration of a shared Samba or CIFS directory is that it works, at least in its standard configuration, only with public directories. In other words, if you activate the /etc/auto.smb file, it'll only work with directories shared without a username or a password.

If you accept these unsecure conditions, it's possible to set up the /etc/auto.smb file in the same way as the /etc/auto.net file. First, you'd have to add it to the /etc/auto.master file in a similar fashion, with the following directive:

```
/smb  /etc/auto.smb
```

You'd then need to specifically restart the automounter service with the following command:

```
# systemctl restart autofs
```

You'll then be able to review shared directories with the following command; substitute a hostname or IP address if desired. Of course, this won't work unless the Samba server is activated on the noted server1.example.com system and the firewall is configured to allow access through associated TCP/IP ports.

```
# /etc/auto.smb server1.example.com
```

Activate the Automounter

Once appropriate files have been configured, you can start, restart, or reload the automounter. As it is governed by the **autofs** daemon, you can stop, start, restart, or reload that service with one of the following commands:

```
# systemctl stop autofs
# systemctl start autofs
# systemctl restart autofs
# systemctl reload autofs
```

With the default command in the /etc/auto.misc file, you should now be able to mount a CD on the /misc/cd directory automatically, just by accessing the configured directory. Once you have a CD in the drive, the following command should work:

```
# ls /misc/cd
```

If you navigate to the /misc/cd directory, the automounter would ignore any timeouts. Otherwise, /misc/cd is automatically unmounted according to the timeout, which according to the **TIMEOUT** directive in /etc/sysconfig/autofs is 300 seconds.

EXERCISE 6-3

Configure the Automounter

In this exercise, you'll test the automounter. You'll need at least a CD. Ideally, you should also have a USB key or a secure digital (SD) card. First, however, you need to make sure that the **autofs** daemon is in operation, modify the appropriate configuration files, and then restart **autofs**. You can then test the automounter in this lab.

1. From the command-line interface, run the following command to make sure the **autofs** daemon is running:

   ```
   # systemctl start autofs
   ```

2. Review the /etc/auto.master configuration file in a text editor. The defaults are sufficient to activate the configuration options in /etc/auto.misc and /etc/auto.net.

3. Check the /etc/auto.misc configuration file in a text editor. Make sure it includes the following line (which should already be there by default). Save and exit from /etc/auto.misc.

   ```
   cd     -fstype=iso9660,ro,nosuid,nodev    :/dev/cdrom
   ```

4. Now reload the **autofs** daemon. Since it's already running, all you need to do is make sure it rereads associated configuration files.

```
# systemctl reload autofs
```

5. The automounter service is now active. Insert a CD or DVD into an appropriate drive and run the following command. If successful, it should display the contents of the CD or DVD:

```
# ls /misc/cd
```

6. Run the **ls /misc** command immediately. You should see the CD directory in the output.

7. Wait at least five minutes and then repeat the previous command. What do you see?

SCENARIO & SOLUTION

You need to configure several new partitions for a standard Linux partition, for swap space, and for a logical volume.	Use the **fdisk**, **gdisk** or **parted** utility to create partitions, and then modify their partition types with the **t** or **set** command.
You want to set up a mount during the boot process based on the UUID.	Identify the UUID of the volume with the **blkid** command, and use that UUID in the /etc/fstab file.
You need to format a volume to the XFS filesystem type.	Format the target volume with the command **mkfs.xfs**.
You need to format a volume to the ext2, ext3, or ext4 filesystem type.	Format the target volume with a command such as **mkfs.ext2**, **mkfs.ext3**, or **mkfs.ext4**.
You want to set up a logical volume.	Use the **pvcreate** command to create PVs; use the **vgcreate** command to combine PVs in VGs; use the **lvcreate** command to create an LV; format that LV for use.
You want to add new filesystems without destroying others.	Use the free space available on existing or newly installed hard drives.
You want to expand the space available to an LV formatted with the XFS filesystem.	Use the **lvextend** command to increase the space available to an LV, and then use the **xfs_growfs** command to expand the formatted filesystem accordingly.
You need to configure automated mounts to a shared network filesystem.	Configure the filesystem either in /etc/fstab or through the automounter.

CERTIFICATION SUMMARY

As a Linux administrator, you should know how to create and manage new filesystem volumes. To create a new filesystem, you need to know how to create, manage, and format partitions as well as how to set up those partitions for logical volumes.

RHEL 7 also supports the configuration of logical volumes. The process is a bit intricate, as it requires the configuration of a partition as a PV. One or more PVs can then be configured as a VG. Logical volumes can then be configured from desired portions of a VG. Associated commands are **pv***, **vg***, and **lv***; those and others can be accessed from the **lvm>** prompt.

Linux supports the format of partitions, RAID arrays, and logical volumes to a wide variety of filesystems. Although the default is XFS, Linux supports formats and checks associated with regular and journaling filesystems associated with Linux, Microsoft, and other operating systems.

Once configured, partitions and logical volumes, whether encrypted or not, can be configured in the /etc/fstab file. That configuration is read during the boot process and can also be used by the **mount** command. If desired, removable filesystems and shared network directories can also be configured in /etc/fstab.

The /etc/fstab file is not the only option to set up mounts. You can automate this process for regular users with the automounter. Properly configured, it allows users to access shared network directories, removable media, and more through paths defined in /etc/auto.master.

✓ TWO-MINUTE DRILL

Here are some of the key points from the certification objectives in Chapter 6.

Storage Management and Partitions

❑ The **fdisk**, **gdisk** and **parted** utilities can help you create and delete partitions.

❑ **fdisk**, **gdisk**, and **parted** can be used to configure partitions for logical volumes and RAID arrays.

❑ Disks can use the traditional MBR-style partitioning scheme, which supports primary, extended, and logical partitions, or the GPT scheme, which supports up to 128 partitions.

Filesystem Formats

❑ Linux tools can be used to configure and format volumes to a number of different filesystems.

❑ Examples of standard filesystems include MS-DOS and ext2.

❑ Journaling filesystems, which include logs that can restore metadata, are more resilient; the default RHEL 7 filesystem is XFS.

❑ RHEL 7 supports a variety of **mkfs.*** filesystem format-check and **fsck.*** filesystem-check commands.

Basic Linux Filesystems and Directories

❑ Linux files and filesystems are organized into directories based on the FHS.

❑ Some Linux directories are well suited to configuration on separate filesystems.

Logical Volume Management (LVM)

❑ LVM is based on physical volumes, logical volumes, and volume groups.

❑ You can create and add LVM systems with a wide variety of commands, starting with **pv***, **lv***, and **vg***.

❑ The space from new partitions configured as PVs can be allocated to existing volume groups with the **vgextend** command; they can be added to LVs with the **lvcreate** and **lvextend** commands.

❑ The extra space can be used to extend an existing XFS filesystem with the **xfs_growfs** command.

Filesystem Management

❑ Standard filesystems are mounted as defined in /etc/fstab.

❑ Filesystem volumes are usually identified by their UUIDs; for a list, run the **blkid** command.

❑ The **mount** command can either use the settings in /etc/fstab or mount filesystem volumes directly.

❑ It's also possible to configure mounts of shared network directories from NFS and Samba servers in /etc/fstab.

The Automounter

❑ With the automounter, you can configure automatic mounts of removable media and shared network drives.

❑ Key automounter configuration files are auto.master, auto.misc, and auto.net, in the /etc directory.

SELF TEST

The following questions will help measure your understanding of the material presented in this chapter. As no multiple choice questions appear on the Red Hat exams, no multiple choice questions appear in this book. These questions exclusively test your understanding of the chapter. Getting results, not memorizing trivia, is what counts on the Red Hat exams. There may be more than one correct answer to many of these questions.

Storage Management and Partitions

1. What **fdisk** command option lists configured partitions from all attached hard drives?

   _____

2. After a swap partition has been created, what command activates it?

   _____

Filesystem Formats

3. What is the primary advantage of a journaling filesystem such as XFS?

   _____

4. What command formats /dev/sdb3 to the default Red Hat filesystem format?

   _____

Basic Linux Filesystems and Directories

5. What filesystem is mounted on a directory separate from the top-level root directory in the default RHEL 7 installation?

   _____

6. Name three directories just below / that are not suitable for mounting separately from the volume with the top-level root directory.

   _____

Logical Volume Management (LVM)

7. Once you've created a new partition and set it to the Logical Volume Management type, what command adds it as a PV?

_____

8. Once you've added more space to an LV, what command would expand the underlining XFS filesystem to fill the new space?

_____

Filesystem Management

9. To change the mount options for a local filesystem, what file would you edit?

_____

10. What would you add to the /etc/fstab file to set up access to the partition /dev/vda6, mounted on the /usr directory as read-only with other default options? Assume you can't find the UUID of /dev/vda6. Also assume a dump value of 1 and a filesystem check order of 2.

_____

The Automounter

11. If you've started the **autofs** daemon and want to read the list of shared NFS directories from the server1.example.com computer, what automounter-related command would you use?

_____

12. Name three configuration files associated with the default installation of the automounter on RHEL 7.

_____

LAB QUESTIONS

Several of these labs involve format exercises. You should do these exercises on test machines only. The instructions in these labs delete all of the data on a system. The second lab sets up KVM for this purpose.

Red Hat presents its exams electronically. For that reason, the labs in this and future chapters are available from the DVD that accompanies the book; look for this chapter's labs in the Chapter6/ subdirectory. The labs are available in .doc, .html, and .txt formats. In case you haven't yet set up RHEL 7 on a system, refer to the first lab of Chapter 2 for installation instructions. However, the answers for each lab follow the Self Test answers for the fill-in-the-blank questions.

SELF TEST ANSWERS

Storage Management and Partitions

1. The **fdisk** command option that lists configured partitions from all attached hard drives is **fdisk -l**.

2. After creating a swap partition, you can use the **mkswap** *devicename* and **swapon** *devicename* commands to initialize and activate the volume; just substitute the device file associated with the volume (such as /dev/sda1 or /dev/VolGroup00/LogVol03) for *devicename.*

Filesystem Formats

3. The primary advantage of a journaling filesystem such as XFS is faster data recovery.

4. The command that formats /dev/sdb3 to the default Red Hat filesystem format is **mkfs.xfs /dev/sdb3**. The **mkfs -t xfs /dev/sdb3** command is also an acceptable answer.

Basic Linux Filesystems and Directories

5. The /boot filesystem is mounted separately from /.

6. There are many correct answers to this question; some of the directories not suitable for mounting separately from / include /dev, /etc, and /root. (In contrast, several directories are essentially shown as placeholders for mounting, including /media and /mnt.)

Logical Volume Management (LVM)

7. Once you've created a new partition and set it to the Logical Volume Management file type, the command that adds it as a PV is **pvcreate**. For example, if the new partition is /dev/sdb2, the command is **pvcreate /dev/sdb2**.

8. Once you've added more space to an LV, the command that would expand the underlining XFS filesystem to fill the new space is **xfs_growfs**.

Filesystem Management

9. To change the mount options for a local filesystem, edit /etc/fstab.

10. Since the UUID is unknown, you'll need to use the device file for the volume (in this case, /dev/vda6). Thus, the line to be added to /etc/fstab is

```
/dev/vda6 /usr    xfs    defaults,ro      1 2
```

The Automounter

11. If you've started the **autofs** daemon and want to read the list of shared NFS directories from the first.example.com computer, the automounter-related command you'd use to list those directories is **/etc/auto.net server1.example.com**.

12. The configuration files associated with the default installation of the automounter include auto .master, auto.misc, auto.net, and auto.smb, all in the /etc directory, as well as /etc/sysconfig/autofs.

LAB ANSWERS

One of the assumptions with these labs is that where a directory such as /test1 is specified, you create it before mounting a volume device file on it or including it in a key configuration file such as /etc/fstab. Otherwise, you'll possibly encounter unexpected errors.

Lab 1

1. It shouldn't matter whether partitions are created in the **fdisk** or **parted** utility. If the partition types were correctly configured, you should see one Linux partition and one Linux swap partition in the configured hard drives in the output to the **fdisk -l** command.

2. If you're confused about what UUID to use in /etc/fstab, run the **blkid** command. If the given partitions have been properly formatted (with the **mkfs.xfs** and **mkswap** commands), you'll see the UUID for the new partitions in the output to **blkid**. You should be able to test the configuration of a new partition and directory in /etc/fstab with the **mount -a** command. Then a **mount** command by itself should be able to confirm appropriate configuration in /etc/fstab.

3. You should be able to confirm the configuration of a new swap partition in the output to the **cat /proc/swaps** command. You should also be able to verify the result in the **Swap** line associated with the **top** command, as well as in the output of the **free -h** command.

4. Remember, all changes should survive a reboot. For the purpose of this lab, you may want to reboot this system to confirm this. However, reboots take time; if you have multiple tasks during an exam, you may want to wait until completing as much as possible before rebooting a system.

Lab 2

This discussion is focused on how you can verify the results of this lab. Even if you've configured the exact spare partitions described in this lab and followed exact instructions, it's quite possible that your LV won't be exactly 900MB. Some of that variance comes from the differences between units of measure that rely on base 2 or base 10 numbers. Don't panic; that variance is normal. The same proviso applies to Lab 3 as well.

Keep in mind that logical volumes are based on appropriately configured partitions, set up as PVs, collected into a VG, and then subdivided into an LV. That LV is then formatted and mounted on an appropriate directory; for the purpose of this lab, that directory is /test2. The UUID of that formatted volume can then be used to set up that LV as a mount in the /etc/fstab file.

1. To verify the partitions prepared for logical volumes, run the **fdisk -l** command. Appropriate partitions should appear with the "Linux LVM" label. To verify the configuration of PVs, run the **pvs** command. The output should report the devices and space allocated to PVs.

2. To verify the configuration of a VG, run the **vgs** command. The output should list the VG created during the lab from the PVs, including the space available.

3. To verify the configuration of an LV, run the **lvs** command. The output should list the LV, the VG from where it was created, and the amount of space allocated to that LV.

4. To verify the UUID of the newly formatted volume, run the following command:

```
# blkid <device_path>
```

5. If the /etc/fstab file is properly configured, you should be able to run the **mount -a** command. Then you should see the logical volume mounted on the /test2 directory.

6. As with Lab 1, all changes should survive a reboot. At some point, you'll want to reboot the local system to check for success or failure of this and other labs.

Lab 3

Based on the information from Lab 2, you should already know what the size of the current LV is. The associated **df** command should confirm the result; the **df -m** command, with its output in MB, could help.

The key commands in this lab are **lvextend** and **xfs_growfs**. While there are a number of excellent command options available, all you really need with that command is the device file for the LV. As with Lab 2, the result can be confirmed after an appropriate **mount** and **df** command. However, to ensure that no data have been lost during the process, you could create some test files before resizing the LV and the filesystem.

Lab 4

There are several steps associated with this lab:

1. Ensure that all the partitions and volumes created in the previous labs have been unmounted, eliminated from /etc/fstab, and removed (with **{lv,vg,pv}remove**).

2. You don't need to partition the /dev/vdb and /dev/vdc drives. It is sufficient to initialize the entire drives as PVs, using the **pvcreate /dev/vdb** and **pvcreate /dev/vdc** commands.

3. Run the **vgcreate -s 2M vg01 /dev/vdb /dev/vdc** command to create the VG.

4. Create the LV with the **lvcreate -l 800 -n lv01 vg01** command.

5. Format the filesystem with the **mkfs.ext4 /dev/vg01/lv01** command.

6. Add the correct entry to /etc/fstab.

7. Create the mount point (**mkdir /test4**).

If the /etc/fstab file is properly configured, you should be able to run the **mount -a** command. Then you should see /dev/mapper/vg01-lv01 mounted on the /test4 directory.

Lab 5

The configuration of the automounter on a shared NFS directory is easier than it looks. Before you begin, make sure the shared NFS directory is available from the remote computer with the **showmount -e** *remote_ipaddr* command, where *remote_ipaddr* is the IP address of the remote NFS server. If that doesn't work, you may have skipped a step described in the lab. For more information on NFS servers, refer to Chapter 16.

Of course, there's the CD/DVD. If the automounter is running and a CD/DVD drive is in the appropriate location, you should be able to read the contents of that drive with the **ls /misc/cd** command. That matches the default configuration of the /etc/auto.master and /etc/auto.misc files.

As for the shared NFS directory, there are two approaches. You could modify the following commented sample NFS configuration directive. Of course, you'd have to at least change ftp.example.org to the name or IP address of the NFS server and /pub/linux to /tmp (or whatever is the name of the directory being shared).

```
linux   -ro,soft,intr  ftp.example.org:/pub/linux
```

Alternatively, you could just directly take advantage of the **/etc/auto.net** script. For example, if the remote NFS server is on IP address 192.168.122.50, run the following command:

```
# /etc/auto.net 192.168.122.50
```

You should see the /tmp directory shared in the output. If so, you'll be able to access it more directly with the following command:

```
# ls /net/192.168.122.50/tmp
```

If you really want to learn the automounter, try modifying the aforementioned directive in the /etc/auto.misc configuration file. Assuming the automounter is already running, you can make sure the automounter rereads the applicable configuration files with the **systemctl reload autofs** command.

If you use the same first directive in the aforementioned line, you'll be able to use the automounter to access the same directory with the **ls /misc/linux** command.

Chapter 7

Package Management

A fter installation is complete, systems are secured, filesystems are configured, and other initial setup tasks are completed, you still have work to do. Almost certainly before your system is in the state you desire, you will be required to install or remove packages. To make sure the right updates are installed, you need to know how to get a system working with Red Hat Subscription Management (RHSM) or the repository associated with a rebuild distribution.

To accomplish these tasks, you need to understand how to use the **rpm** and **yum** commands in detail. Although these are "just" two commands, they are rich in detail. Entire books have been dedicated to the **rpm** command, such as the *Red Hat RPM Guide* by Eric

Foster-Johnson. For many, that degree of in-depth knowledge of the **rpm** command is no longer necessary, given the capabilities of the **yum** command and the additional package management tools provided in RHEL 7.

The Red Hat Package Manager

One of the major duties of a system administrator is software management. New applications are installed. Services are updated. Kernels are patched. Without the right tools, it can be difficult to figure out what software is on a system, what is the latest update, and what applications depend on other software. Worse, you may install a new software package only to find it has overwritten a crucial file from a currently installed package.

INSIDE THE EXAM

Administrative Skills

As the management of RPM packages is a fundamental skill for Red Hat administrators, it's reasonable to expect to use the **rpm**, **yum**, and related commands on the RHCSA exam. In fact, the RHCE exam effectively assumes knowledge of such commands and more as prerequisite skills. The RHCSA objectives include two specific requirements addressed in this chapter:

- Install and update software packages from Red Hat Network, a remote repository, or from the local filesystem
- Update the kernel package appropriately to ensure a bootable system

Another closely related objective is the **tar** archiving utility, which is covered in Chapter 9. Before Red Hat introduced RPM packages, tar archives were the standard method for distributing software.

Now let's break down these skills a bit. If you don't have access to the RHN, don't be intimidated. For RHEL 7, the RHN-hosted service has been phased out in favor of Red Hat Subscription Management (RHSM, which can be accessed via a web interface from the Red Hat Customer Portal). You can use **yum** to install and update packages from RHSM; you can use the same **yum** commands to install and update packages from a remote third-party repository.

The Red Hat Package Manager (RPM) was designed to alleviate these problems. With RPM, software is managed in discrete *packages.* An RPM package includes the software with instructions for adding, removing, and upgrading those files. When properly used, the RPM system can back up key configuration files before proceeding with upgrades and removals. It can also help you identify the currently installed version of any RPM-based application.

RPMs and the **rpm** command are very focused on individual packages, which in many cases is far from ideal and is why **rpm** has been supplemented with the **yum** command. With a connection to a repository such as that available from RHSM or third-party "rebuilds" such as Scientific Linux, you'll be able to use **yum** to satisfy dependencies automatically.

What Is a Package?

In the generic sense, an RPM package is a container of files. It includes the group of files associated with a specific program or application, which normally contains binary files, installation scripts, as well as configuration and documentation files. It also includes instructions on how and where these files should be installed and uninstalled.

An RPM package name usually consists of the version, the release, and the architecture for which it was built. For example, the fictional penguin-3.4.5-26.el7.x86_64.rpm package is version 3.4.5, release 26.el7. The x86_64 indicates that it is suitable for computers built to the AMD/Intel 64-bit architecture.

on the **Job**
Many RPM packages include software compiled for a specific CPU type (for example, x86_64). You can identify the CPU type for the system with the uname -i or uname -p command. More information about your processor can be found in /proc/cpuinfo.

What Is the RPM Database?

At the heart of this system is the RPM database, which is stored locally on each machine in the /var/lib/rpm directory. Among other things, this database tracks the version and location of every file in each RPM. The RPM database also maintains an MD5 checksum of each file. With the checksum, you can use the **rpm -V** *package* command to determine whether any file from that RPM package has changed. The RPM database makes it easy to add, remove, and upgrade individual packages because it's configured to know which files to handle and where to put them.

RPM also manages conflicts between packages. For example, assume you have a package that installs a configuration file, and you want to update from an older to a newer version of the software. Call the original configuration file /etc/*someconfig*.conf. You've already installed package X. If you then try to install a more recent version of package X, the RPM can be configured to preserve the original configuration file and install the new one as /etc/*someconfig*.conf.rpmnew.

Alternatively, the RPM creator can build the RPM in such a way that it will back up the original /etc/*someconfig*.conf file (with a filename such as /etc/*someconfig*.conf.rpmsave) before upgrading package X and then replace the configuration file with a new version. This may occur if the format of the old configuration file is incompatible with the new release of the software.

on the **Job**

Although RPM upgrades are supposed to preserve or save existing configuration files, there are no guarantees, especially if the RPM is created by someone other than Red Hat. It's best to back up all applicable configuration files before upgrading any associated RPM package.

What Is a Repository?

RPM packages are frequently organized into repositories. Generally, such repositories include groups of packages with different functions. For example, the Red Hat Portal gives access to the following RHEL 7 Server repositories (additional repositories are available):

- **Red Hat Enterprise Linux Server**   The main repository, which includes both the packages associated with the original installation of RHEL 7, along with updates.
- **RHEL Server Optional**   A large group of open-source packages, provided with no support from Red Hat.
- **RHEL Server Supplementary**   A collection of packages released under licenses other than open source, such as the IBM Java Runtime and Development Kit.
- **RHEL Extras**   Includes Docker, a platform for packaging and managing applications using a lightweight form of virtualization known as Linux Containers.
- **RHN Tools**   Client tools to subscribe to the Red Hat Network via a Satellite server, along with utilities for automating Kickstart installations.

In contrast, the repository categories for third-party Red Hat clones vary. Generally, they include categories such as main and extras. In most cases, whereas the main repository includes just the packages available from the released DVD, updated packages are configured in their own repository.

Each repository includes a database of packages in a repodata/ subdirectory. That database includes information on each package and allows installation requests to include all dependencies. If you have a subscription to RHSM, access to the Red Hat repositories is enabled in the product-id.conf and subscription-manager.conf files, in the /etc/yum/pluginconf.d directory. Those files are discussed later in this chapter.

Later in this chapter, you'll examine how to configure connections to repositories with the configuration files associated with the **yum** command.

on the
job

A dependency is a package that needs to be installed to make sure all the features of a target package work as designed.

Install an RPM Package

There are three basic commands that *may* install an RPM. They won't work if there are dependencies. For example, if you haven't installed the SELinux policy development tool package (policycoreutilis-devel) and try to install the SELinux configuration GUI (policycoreutilis-gui), you'll get the following message (version numbers may vary):

```
# rpm -i policycoreutils-gui-2.2.5-11.el7.x86_64.rpm
error: Failed dependencies:
        policycoreutils-devel = 2.2.5-11.el7 is needed by↵
policycoreutils-gui-2.2.5-11.el7.x86_64
```

One way to test this is to mount the RHEL 7 DVD with the **mount /dev/cdrom /media** command. Next, find the noted policycoreutils-gui package in the Packages/ subdirectory. Alternatively, you could download that package directly from the Red Hat Portal or a configured repository with the **yumdownloader policycoreutils-gui** command. This and other **yum** commands are discussed later in this chapter. Be aware that some Linux GUI desktop environments automatically mount a CD/DVD media that is inserted into an associated drive. If so, you'll see the mount directory in the output to the **mount** command.

When dependency messages are shown, **rpm** does not install the given package. Note the dependency messages: policycoreutils-gui requires a policycoreutils-devel package of the same version number.

on the
job

Sure, you can use the --nodeps option to make rpm ignore dependencies, but that can lead to other problems, unless you install those dependencies as soon as possible. The best option is to use an appropriate yum command, described later in this chapter. In this case, a yum install policycoreutils-gui command would automatically install the other dependent RPM as well.

If you're not stopped by dependencies, the following three basic commands can install RPM packages:

```
# rpm -i packagename
# rpm -U packagename
# rpm -F packagename
```

The **rpm -i** option installs the package, if it isn't already installed. The **rpm -U** option upgrades any existing package or installs it if an earlier version isn't already installed.

The **rpm -F** option upgrades only existing packages. It does not install a package if it wasn't previously installed.

We like to add the **-vh** options with the **rpm** command. These options add verbose mode and use hash marks that can help monitor the progress of the installation. So when we use **rpm** to install a package, we run the following command:

```
# rpm -ivh packagename-version.arch.rpm
```

There's one more thing associated with a properly designed RPM package. When unpacking a package, the **rpm** command checks to see whether it would overwrite any configuration files. The **rpm** command tries to make intelligent decisions about what to do in this situation. As suggested earlier, if the **rpm** command chooses to replace an existing configuration file, it provides a warning (in most cases) similar to this:

```
# rpm -U penguin-3.26.x86_64.rpm
warning: /etc/someconfig.conf saved as /etc/someconfig.conf.rpmsave
```

The **rpm** command normally works in the same fashion when a package is erased with the **-e** switch. If a configuration file has been changed, it's also saved with an .rpmsave extension in the same directory.

It's up to you to look at both files and determine what modifications, if any, need to be made. Of course, as not every RPM package is perfect, there's always a risk that such an update would overwrite that critical customized configuration file. In that case, backups are important.

In general, the **rpm** commands to upgrade a package work only if the package being installed is of a newer version. Sometimes, an older version of a package is desirable. As long as there are no security issues with the older package, administrators may be more comfortable with slightly older releases. Bugs that may be a problem on a newer package may not exist in an older version of that package. So if you want to "downgrade" a package with the **rpm -i**, **-U**, or **-F** command, the **--force** switch can help.

on the
job

If you've already customized a package and then upgraded it with rpm, check if there is a saved configuration file ending with an .rpmnew extension. Use it as a guide to change the settings in the new configuration file. But remember, with upgrades, there may be additional required changes. Therefore, you should test the result for every conceivable production environment.

Uninstall an RPM Package

The **rpm -e** command uninstalls a package. But first, RPM checks a few things. It performs a dependency check to make sure no other packages need what you're trying to uninstall. If dependent packages are found, **rpm -e** fails with an error message identifying these packages. With properly configured RPMs, if you have modified related configuration files,

RPM makes a copy of the file, adds an .rpmsave extension to the end of the filename, and then erases the original. It can then proceed with the uninstallation. When the process is complete, it removes the package from the database.

on the job

Be very careful about which packages you remove from a system. Like many other Linux utilities, RPM may silently let you shoot yourself in the foot. For example, if you were to remove the packages that include the running kernel, it could render that system unusable at the next boot.

Install RPMs from Remote Systems

With the RPM system, you can even specify package locations similar to an Internet address, in URL format. For example, if you want to apply the **rpm** command to the foo.rpm package on the /pub directory of the ftp.rpmdownloads.com FTP server, you can install this package with a command such as the following:

```
# rpm -ivh ftp://ftp.rpmdownloads.com/pub/foo.rpm
```

Assuming you have a network connection to that remote server, this particular **rpm** command logs on to the FTP server anonymously and downloads the file. Unfortunately, an attempt to use wildcards in the package name with this command leads to an error message associated with "file not found." The complete package name is required, which can be an annoyance.

If you installed RHEL 7 from an FTP server as instructed in Chapters 1 and 2, you could substitute the associated URL, along with the exact name of the package. For example, based on the FTP server configured in Chapter 1 and the aforementioned policycoreutils-gui package, the appropriate command would be

```
# rpm -ivh ftp://192.168.122.1/pub/inst/policycoreutils-gui ↵
-2.2.5-11.el7.x86_64.rpm
```

If the FTP server requires a username and password, you can include them in the following format

```
ftp://username:password@hostname:port/path/to/remote/package.rpm
```

where *username* and *password* are the username and password you need to log on to this system, and *port*, if required, specifies a nonstandard port used on the remote FTP server.

Based on the preceding example, if the username is **mjang** and the password is **Ila451MS**, you could install an RPM directly from a server with the following command:

```
# rpm -ivh ftp://mjang:Ila451MS@192.168.122.1/pub/inst/policycoreutils-gui ↵
-2.2.5-11.el7.x86_64.rpm
```

RPM Installation Security

Security can be a concern, especially with RPM packages downloaded over the Internet. If a "black hat" hacker were to somehow penetrate a third-party repository, how would you know that packages from those sources were genuine? The key is GNU Privacy Guard (GPG), which is the open-source implementation of Pretty Good Privacy (PGP). If an RPM file is signed using a private GPG key, the integrity of the package can be verified with the corresponding public GPG key. A valid signature also ensures that the package has been signed by an authorized party and does not come from a malicious hacker.

If you haven't imported or installed the Red Hat public GPG keys, you might have noticed something similar to the following message when packages are installed:

```
warning: vsftpd-3.0.2-9.el7.x86_64.rpm: Header V3 RSA/SHA256
Signature, key ID fd431d51: NOKEY
```

If you're concerned about security, this warning should raise alarm bells. During the RHEL 7 installation process, GPG keys are stored in the /etc/pki/rpm-gpg directory. Take a look at the contents of this directory. You'll find files such as RPM-GPG-KEY-redhat-release. To actually use the key to verify packages, it has to be imported—and the command to import the GPG key is fairly simple:

```
# rpm --import /etc/pki/rpm-gpg/RPM-GPG-KEY-redhat-release
```

If there's no output, the **rpm** command probably successfully imported the GPG key. Even if this command succeeds, if you repeat it, an "import failed" message will appear. In addition, the GPG key is now included in the RPM database, which can be verified with the **rpm -qa gpg-pubkey** command.

In the /etc/pki/rpm-gpg directory, there are normally five GPG keys available, as described in Table 7-1.

Later in this chapter, you'll see how GPG keys are imported automatically from remote repositories when new packages are installed.

Special RPM Procedures with the Kernel

Updated kernels incorporate new features, address security issues, and generally help Linux systems work better. However, kernel updates can go wrong and prevent systems booting or cause applications to break; this is particularly common if specialized packages that depend on an existing version of a kernel have been installed.

If you are aware of any software that relies on a custom kernel module, don't upgrade a kernel if you're not ready to repeat every step taken to customize software with the existing kernel, whether that be obtaining new closed-source kernel modules from the vendor for the new version, rebuilding specialized modules for the new kernel, or other manual work. For example, the drivers for a few wireless network cards and printers

TABLE 7-1   GPG Keys to Verify Software Updates

GPG Key	Description
RPM-GPG-KEY-redhat-beta	Packages built for the RHEL 7 beta
RPM-GPG-KEY-redhat-legacy-former	Packages for pre–January 2007 releases (and updates)
RPM-GPG-KEY-redhat-legacy-release	Packages for post–January 2007 releases
RPM-GPG-KEY-redhat-legacy-rhx	Packages associated with Red Hat Exchange
RPM-GPG-KEY-redhat-release	Released packages for RHEL 7

without in-tree open-source drivers may be tied to a specific version of a kernel. Some virtual machine software components (not including KVM) may be installed against a specific version of a kernel.

If you see an available update for a kernel RPM, the temptation is to run the **rpm -U** *newkernel* command. Don't do it! It overwrites your existing kernel, and if the updated kernel doesn't work with the system, you're out of luck. (Well, not completely out of luck, but if you reboot and have problems, you'll have to use rescue mode, discussed in Chapter 5, to boot the system and reinstall the existing kernel. In the days where there were separate Troubleshooting and System Maintenance sections on the Red Hat exams, that might have made for an interesting test scenario.) The best option for upgrading to a new kernel is to install it, specifically with a command such as this:

```
# rpm -ivh newkernel
```

If you're connected to an appropriate repository, the following command works equally well:

```
# yum install kernel
```

This installs the new kernel, along with related files, side by side with the current working kernel. One example of the result is shown in Figure 7-1, in the output to the **ls /boot** command.

on the
ṏ o b   **It is also safe to install a new kernel by running** yum update kernel. **In fact, by default, yum is configured to always install a kernel package and leave any old kernel in place. This applies to a maximum of three kernels installed at the same time.**

Table 7-2 briefly describes the different files for the various parts of the boot process in the /boot directory.

New and existing
kernel files in the
/boot directory

```
[root@server1 ~]# ls /boot
config-3.10.0-123.13.2.el7.x86_64
config-3.10.0-123.el7.x86_64
grub2
initramfs-0-rescue-b37be8dd26f97ac4ba4a6152f5e92b44.img
initramfs-3.10.0-123.13.2.el7.x86_64.img
initramfs-3.10.0-123.el7.x86_64.img
initrd-plymouth.img
symvers-3.10.0-123.13.2.el7.x86_64.gz
symvers-3.10.0-123.el7.x86_64.gz
System.map-3.10.0-123.13.2.el7.x86_64
System.map-3.10.0-123.el7.x86_64
vmlinuz-0-rescue-b37be8dd26f97ac4ba4a6152f5e92b44
vmlinuz-3.10.0-123.13.2.el7.x86_64
vmlinuz-3.10.0-123.el7.x86_64
[root@server1 ~]#
```

The installation of a new kernel adds options to boot the new kernel in the GRUB configuration file (/boot/grub2/grub.cfg), without erasing existing options. A condensed version of the revised GRUB configuration file is shown in Figure 7-2.

A careful reading of the two "menuentry" stanzas reveals that the only difference is in the version numbers listed in the title for the Linux kernel and for the initial RAM disk filesystem. By default, the system will boot with the newly installed kernel. Therefore, if that kernel does not work, you can restart the system, access the GRUB menu, and then boot from the older, previously working kernel.

TABLE 7-2

Files in the /boot
Directory

File	Description
config-*	Kernel configuration settings; a text file
grub2/	Directory with GRUB configuration files
initramfs-*	The initial RAM disk filesystem, a root filesystem called during the boot process to help load other kernel components, such as block device modules
initrd-plymouth.img	RAM disk filesystem containing files for the graphical animation displayed at boot by Plymouth
symvers-*	List of modules
System.map-*	Map of system names for variables and functions, with their locations in memory
vmlinuz-*	The actual Linux kernel

FIGURE 7-2   GRUB with a second kernel

```
menuentry 'Red Hat Enterprise Linux Server (3.10.0-123.13.2.el7.x86_64) 7.0 (Maipo)' --class
red --class gnu-linux --class gnu --class os --unrestricted $menuentry_id_option 'gnulinux-3.
10.0-123.el7.x86_64-advanced-d055418f-1ff6-46bf-8476-b391e82a6f51' {
        # output removed for brevity
        set root='hd0,msdos1'
        linux16 /vmlinuz-3.10.0-123.13.2.el7.x86_64 root=/dev/mapper/rhel-root ro rd.lvm.lv=r
hel/root vconsole.font=latarcyrheb-sun16 rd.lvm.lv=rhel/swap crashkernel=auto  vconsole.keyma
p=uk rhgb quiet LANG=en_GB.UTF-8
        initrd16 /initramfs-3.10.0-123.13.2.el7.x86_64.img
}
menuentry 'Red Hat Enterprise Linux Server (3.10.0-123.el7.x86_64) 7.0 (Maipo)' --class red -
-class gnu-linux --class gnu --class os --unrestricted $menuentry_id_option 'gnulinux-3.10.0-
123.el7.x86_64-advanced-d055418f-1ff6-46bf-8476-b391e82a6f51' {
        # output removed for brevity
        set root='hd0,msdos1'
        linux16 /vmlinuz-3.10.0-123.el7.x86_64 root=/dev/mapper/rhel-root ro rd.lvm.lv=rhel/r
oot vconsole.font=latarcyrheb-sun16 rd.lvm.lv=rhel/swap crashkernel=auto  vconsole.keymap-uk
rhgb quiet LANG=en_GB.UTF-8
        initrd16 /initramfs-3.10.0-123.el7.x86_64.img
}
```

CERTIFICATION OBJECTIVE 7.02

More RPM Commands

The **rpm** command is rich with details. All this book can do is cover some of the basic ways **rpm** can help you manage RHEL. You've already read about how **rpm** can install and upgrade packages in various ways. Queries can help you identify what's installed in detail. Verification tools can help you check the integrity of packages and individual files. You can use related tools to help identify the purpose of different RPMs, as well as a full list of those RPMs already installed.

Package Queries

The simplest RPM query verifies whether a specific package is installed. The following command verifies the installation of the systemd package (the version number may vary):

```
# rpm -q systemd
systemd-208-11.el7.x86_64
```

You can do more with RPM queries, as described in Table 7-3. Note how queries are associated with -**q** or --**query**; full-word switches such as --**query** are usually associated with a double-dash.

rpm Query Command	Meaning
rpm -qa	Lists all installed packages.
rpm -qf /path/to/file	Identifies the package associated with /path/to/file.
rpm -qc *packagename*	Lists only configuration files from *packagename*.
rpm -qd *packagename*	Lists only documentation files from *packagename*.
rpm -qi *packagename*	Displays basic information for *packagename*.
rpm -ql *packagename*	Lists all files from *packagename*.
rpm -qR *packagename*	Notes all dependencies; you can't install *packagename* without them.
rpm -q --changelog *packagename*	Displays change information for *packagename*.

If you want to query an RPM package file rather than the local RPM database, all you have to do is add the **-p** switch and specify the path or URL of the package file. As an example, the following command lists all the files of the RPM package epel-release-7-5.noarch.rpm:

```
# rpm -qlp epel-release-7-5.noarch.rpm
```

Package Signatures

RPM uses several methods for checking the integrity of a package. You've seen how to import the GPG key. Some of the available methods are shown when you verify a package with the **rpm --checksig** *pkg.rpm* command. (The **-K** switch is equivalent to **--checksig**.) For example, if you've downloaded a package from a third party such as the hypothetical pkg-1.2.3-4.noarch.rpm package and want to check it against the imported GPG keys, run the following command:

```
# rpm --checksig pkg-1.2.3-4.noarch.rpm
```

If successful, you'll see output similar to the following:

```
pkg-1.2.3-4.noarch.rpm: rsa sha1 (md5) pgp md5 OK
```

This guarantees that the package is authentic and the RPM file was not modified by a third party. You may already recognize the algorithms used to verify package integrity:

- **rsa**   Named for its creators, Rivest, Shamir, and Adleman, it's a public key encryption algorithm.
- **sha1**   A 160-bit message digest Secure Hash Algorithm; a cryptographic hash function.
- **md5**   Message Digest 5, a cryptographic hash function.
- **pgp**   PGP, as implemented in Linux by GPG.

File Verification

The verification of an installed package compares information about that package with information from the RPM database on a system. The **--verify** (or **-v**) switch checks the size, MD5 checksum, permissions, type, owner, and group of each file in the package. Verification can be done in a number of ways. Here are a few examples:

- Verify all files. Naturally, this may take a long time on your system. (Of course, the **rpm -Va** command performs the same function.)

  ```
  # rpm --verify -a
  ```

- Verify all files within a package against a downloaded RPM.

  ```
  # rpm --verify -p vsftpd-3.0.2-9.el7.x86_64.rpm
  ```

- Verify a file associated with a particular package.

  ```
  # rpm --verify --file /bin/ls
  ```

If the integrity of the files or packages is verified, you will see no output. Any output means that a file or package is different from the original. There's no need to panic if certain changes appear; after all, administrators do edit configuration files. There are eight tests. If there has been a change, the output is a string of up to eight failure code characters, each of which tells you what happened during each test.

If you see a dot (.), that test passed. The following example shows /bin/vi with an incorrect group ID assignment:

```
# rpm --verify --file /bin/vi
......G.   /bin/vi
```

Table 7-4 lists the failure codes and their meanings.

Now here's an interesting experiment: When you have one version of a package installed, use the **rpm --verify -p** command with a second version of the same package. Finding such

Failure Code	Meaning
5	MD5 checksum
S	File size
L	Symbolic link
T	File modification time
D	Device
U	User
G	Group
M	Mode

a package should not be too difficult because Red Hat updates packages for feature updates, security patches, and, yes, bug fixes frequently. For example, when we wrote this book for RHEL 7, we had access to both sssd-client-1.11.2-65.el7.x86_64.rpm and sssd-client-1.11.2-28 .el7.x86_64.rpm. When the latter version was installed, we ran the command

```
# rpm --verify -p sssd-client-1.11.2-65.el7.x86_64.rpm
```

and got a whole list of changed files, as shown in Figure 7-3. This command provides information on what was changed between different versions of the sssd-client package.

FIGURE 7-3

Verifying changes
between packages

```
[root@server1 Packages]# rpm --verify -p sssd-client-1.11.2-65.el7.x86_64.rpm
S.5....T.    /usr/lib64/krb5/plugins/authdata/sssd_pac_plugin.so
S.5....T.    /usr/lib64/krb5/plugins/libkrb5/sssd_krb5_locator_plugin.so
S.5....T.    /usr/lib64/libnss_sss.so.2
S.5....T.    /usr/lib64/security/pam_sss.so
missing     /usr/share/doc/sssd-client-1.11.2
missing   d /usr/share/doc/sssd-client-1.11.2/COPYING
missing   d /usr/share/doc/sssd-client-1.11.2/COPYING.LESSER
missing   d /usr/share/man/ca/man8/pam_sss.8.gz
missing   d /usr/share/man/es/man8/pam_sss.8.gz
S.5....T. d /usr/share/man/es/man8/sssd_krb5_locator_plugin.8.gz
S.5....T. d /usr/share/man/fr/man8/pam_sss.8.gz
S.5....T. d /usr/share/man/fr/man8/sssd_krb5_locator_plugin.8.gz
missing   d /usr/share/man/ja/man8/pam_sss.8.gz
S.5....T. d /usr/share/man/ja/man8/sssd_krb5_locator_plugin.8.gz
S.5....T. d /usr/share/man/man8/pam_sss.8.gz
S.5....T. d /usr/share/man/man8/sssd_krb5_locator_plugin.8.gz
S.5....T. d /usr/share/man/uk/man8/pam_sss.8.gz
S.5....T. d /usr/share/man/uk/man8/sssd_krb5_locator_plugin.8.gz
[root@server1 Packages]#
```

CERTIFICATION OBJECTIVE 7.03

Dependencies and the yum Command

The **yum** command makes it easy to add and remove software packages to and from a system. It maintains a database regarding the proper way to add, upgrade, and remove packages. This makes it relatively simple to add and remove software with a single command. That single command overcame what was known as "dependency hell."

The **yum** command was originally developed for Yellow Dog Linux. The name is based on the Yellow Dog updater, modified. Given the trouble associated with dependency hell, Linux users were motivated to find a solution. It was adapted for Red Hat distributions with the help of developers from Duke University.

The configuration of **yum** depends on package libraries known as repositories. Red Hat repositories are available through the Red Hat Portal, while repositories of third-party rebuild distributions use their own publicly available servers. In either case, it's important to know the workings of the **yum** command as well as how it installs and updates individual packages and package groups.

An Example of Dependency Hell

To understand more about the need for the **yum** command, examine Figure 7-4. You do not need the kernel.spec file. The packages listed in that figure are what's required to build an RPM. Although the building of an RPM package is not an exam requirement, the associated packages illustrate the need for **yum**.

You could try to use the **rpm** command to install each of these packages. To do so, take the following steps:

1. Include the RHEL 7 DVD. Insert it into its drive, or make sure it's included in the configuration for the target virtual machine.

FIGURE 7-4	

Packages required to build RPMs

```
[root@server1 SPECS]# rpmbuild -ba kernel.spec
error: Failed build dependencies:
        gcc >= 3.4.2 is needed by kernel-3.10.0-123.13.2.el7.x86_64
        xmlto is needed by kernel-3.10.0-123.13.2.el7.x86_64
        hmaccalc is needed by kernel-3.10.0-123.13.2.el7.x86_64
        elfutils-devel is needed by kernel-3.10.0-123.13.2.el7.x86_64
        binutils-devel is needed by kernel-3.10.0-123.13.2.el7.x86_64
        python-devel is needed by kernel-3.10.0-123.13.2.el7.x86_64
        perl(ExtUtils::Embed) is needed by kernel-3.10.0-123.13.2.el7.x86_64
        bison is needed by kernel-3.10.0-123.13.2.el7.x86_64
        audit-libs-devel is needed by kernel-3.10.0-123.13.2.el7.x86_64
        numactl-devel is needed by kernel-3.10.0-123.13.2.el7.x86_64
[root@server1 SPECS]#
```

2. Unless it's already mounted, mount that DVD with the following command. Of course, a different empty directory can be substituted for /media.

```
# mount /dev/cdrom /media
```

3. Navigate to the directory where the DVD is mounted (that is, /media or some subdirectory of /media).

4. The RPM packages on the RHEL 7 DVD can be found in the Packages/ subdirectory of the DVD. Navigate to that subdirectory.

5. Enter the **rpm -ivh** command, and then type in the names of the packages listed in Figure 7-4. It may be easiest to use command completion for this purpose; for example, if you were to type in

```
# rpm -ivh gcc-
```

you could then press the TAB key twice and review available packages that start with **gcc-**. You could then enter additional keys and press the TAB key again to complete the name of the package. After a bit of work, you'd end up with something similar to the command and results shown in Figure 7-5. What actually appears depends on the current revision level of each package, as well as what's already installed on the local system.

6. The next step is to try to include the missing dependencies in the list of packages to be installed. When we try this step, it leads to more dependencies, as shown in Figure 7-6.

At this point, the addition of more packages to the installation becomes somewhat more difficult. How would you know, except from experience, that the mpfr-* package would

FIGURE 7-5   These packages have dependencies.

```
[root@server1 Packages]# rpm -ivh gcc-4.8.2-16.el7.x86_64.rpm xmlto-0.0.25-7.el7.x86_64.rpm
hmaccalc-0.9.13-4.el7.x86_64.rpm elfutils-devel-0.158-3.el7.x86_64.rpm binutils-devel-2.23.5
2.0.1-16.el7.x86_64.rpm python-devel-2.7.5-16.el7.x86_64.rpm perl-ExtUtils-Embed-1.30-283.el
7.noarch.rpm bison-2.7-4.el7.x86_64.rpm audit-libs-devel-2.3.3-4.el7.x86_64.rpm numactl-deve
l-2.0.9-2.el7.x86_64.rpm
error: Failed dependencies:
        cpp = 4.8.2-16.el7 is needed by gcc-4.8.2-16.el7.x86_64
        glibc-devel >= 2.2.90-12 is needed by gcc-4.8.2-16.el7.x86_64
        libmpc.so.3()(64bit) is needed by gcc-4.8.2-16.el7.x86_64
        libmpfr.so.4()(64bit) is needed by gcc-4.8.2-16.el7.x86_64
        flex is needed by xmlto-0.0.25-7.el7.x86_64
        elfutils-libelf-devel(x86-64) = 0.158-3.el7 is needed by elfutils-devel-0.158-3.el7.
x86_64
        perl-devel is needed by perl-ExtUtils-Embed-0:1.30-283.el7.noarch
        kernel-headers >= 2.6.29 is needed by audit-libs-devel-2.3.3-4.el7.x86_64
[root@server1 Packages]#
```

| FIGURE 7-6 | There are even more dependencies. |

```
[root@server1 Packages]# rpm -ivh gcc-4.8.2-16.el7.x86_64.rpm xmlto-0.0.25-7.el7.x86_64.rpm
hmaccalc-0.9.13-4.el7.x86_64.rpm elfutils-devel-0.158-3.el7.x86_64.rpm binutils-devel-2.23.5
2.0.1-16.el7.x86_64.rpm python-devel-2.7.5-16.el7.x86_64.rpm perl-ExtUtils-Embed-1.30-283.el
7.noarch.rpm bison-2.7-4.el7.x86_64.rpm audit-libs-devel-2.3.3-4.el7.x86_64.rpm numactl-deve
l-2.0.9-2.el7.x86_64.rpm cpp-4.8.2-16.el7.x86_64.rpm glibc-devel-2.17-55.el7.x86_64.rpm libm
pc-1.0.1-3.el7.x86_64.rpm mpfr-3.1.1-4.el7.x86_64.rpm flex-2.5.37-3.el7.x86_64.rpm elfutils-
libelf-devel-0.158-3.el7.x86_64.rpm perl-devel-5.16.3-283.el7.x86_64.rpm kernel-headers-3.10
.0-123.el7.x86_64.rpm
error: Failed dependencies:
        glibc-headers is needed by glibc-devel-2.17-55.el7.x86_64
        glibc-headers = 2.17-55.el7 is needed by glibc-devel-2.17-55.el7.x86_64
        gdbm-devel is needed by perl-devel-4:5.16.3-283.el7.x86_64
        libdb-devel is needed by perl-devel-4:5.16.3-283.el7.x86_64
        perl(ExtUtils::Installed) is needed by perl-devel-4:5.16.3-283.el7.x86_64
        perl(ExtUtils::MakeMaker) is needed by perl-devel-4:5.16.3-283.el7.x86_64
        perl(ExtUtils::ParseXS) is needed by perl-devel-4:5.16.3-283.el7.x86_64
        systemtap-sdt-devel is needed by perl-devel-4:5.16.3-283.el7.x86_64
[root@server1 Packages]# █
```

satisfy the "Failed Dependencies" message for libmpfr.so.4()(64bit)? Even if you do already understand, the inclusion of such packages is not enough. There's even one more level of dependent packages. This pain is known as dependency hell.

Relief from Dependency Hell

Before **yum**, some attempts to use the **rpm** command were stopped by the dependencies described earlier. Sure, you could install those dependent packages with the same command, but what if those dependencies themselves have dependencies? That perhaps is the biggest advantage of the **yum** command.

Before **yum**, RHEL incorporated dependency resolution into the update process. Through RHEL 4, this was done with **up2date**. Red Hat incorporated **yum** starting with RHEL 5. The **yum** command uses subscribed Red Hat Portal channels and any other repositories configured in the /etc/yum.repos.d directory.

All you need to do to install the packages listed in Figure 7-4 is run the following command:

```
# yum install gcc xmlto hmaccalc elfutils-devel binutils-devel \
> python-devel perl-ExtUtils-Embed bison audit-libs-devel numactl-devel
```

If so prompted, accept the request to install additional dependent packages, and then all of the noted dependencies are installed automatically. (Yes, the **-y** switch would perform the same function.) If updates are available from connected repositories, the latest available version of each package is installed. The **yum** command is described in more detail later in this chapter.

But if you're running RHEL 7 without a connection to Red Hat Portal, nothing happens. Shortly, you'll see how to create a connection between **yum** and the installation server created in Chapter 1.

A number of third-party repositories are available for RHEL. They include several popular applications that are not supported by Red Hat. For example, one of the authors of this book uses an external repository to install packages associated with his laptop wireless network card.

Although the owners of these repositories work closely with some Red Hat developers, there are some reports where dependencies required from one repository are unavailable from other repositories, leading to a different form of "dependency hell." However, the more popular third-party repositories are excellent; we have never encountered "dependency hell" when using these repositories.

on the **Job**

There are two main reasons why Red Hat does not include most proven and popular packages available from third-party repositories. Some are not released under open-source licenses, and others are packages that Red Hat simply chooses not to support.

Basic yum Configuration

Relief from dependency hell depends on the proper configuration of **yum**. Not only do you need to know how to configure **yum** to connect to repositories over the Internet, but also you need to know how to configure **yum** to connect to repositories on a local network. With this knowledge, you can connect **yum** to repositories on Red Hat Portal, to repositories configured by third parties, and to custom repositories configured for specialized networks. And remember, during the Red Hat exams, you won't have access to the Internet.

To that end, you have to understand how yum is configured in some detail. It starts with the /etc/yum.conf configuration file and continues with files in the /etc/yum and /etc/yum .repos.d directories. To get the full list of yum configuration directives and their current values, run the following command:

```
# yum-config-manager
```

This command requires the installation of the yum-utils package.

The Basic yum Configuration File: yum.conf

This section analyzes the default version of the /etc/yum.conf file, line by line. Although you won't make changes to this file in most cases, you need to understand at least the standard directives in this file if something goes wrong. The following lines are straight excerpts from the default version of this file. The first directive is a header; the **[main]** header suggests that all directives that follow apply globally to **yum**:

```
[main]
```

The **cachedir** directive specifies where caches of packages, package lists, and related databases are to be downloaded. Based on the standard 64-bit architecture for RHEL 7, this translates to the /var/cache/yum/x86_64/7Server directory.

```
cachedir=/var/cache/yum/$basearch/$releasever
```

The **keepcache** boolean directive specifies whether **yum** actually stores downloaded headers and packages in the directory specified by **cachedir**. The standard shown here suggests that caches are not kept, which helps make sure that a system is kept up to date with the latest available packages (at the expense of slightly slower executions of **yum** as metadata is pulled down on each execution).

```
keepcache=0
```

The **debuglevel** directive is closely related to the **errorlevel** and **logfile** directives, as they specify the detail associated with debug and error messages. Even though the **errorlevel** directive is not shown, both it and **debuglevel** are set to 2 by default. The available range is 0–10, where 0 provides almost no information, and 10 provides perhaps too much information, even for developers.

```
debuglevel=2
logfile=/var/log/yum.log
```

The **exactarch** boolean directive makes sure the architecture matches the actual processor type, as defined by the **arch** command.

```
exactarch=1
```

The **obsoletes** boolean directive can support the uninstallation of obsolete packages in conjunction with a **yum update** command.

```
obsoletes=1
```

The **gpgcheck** boolean directive makes sure the **yum** command actually checks the GPG signature of downloaded packages.

```
gpgcheck=1
```

The **plugins** boolean directive provides a necessary link to Python-based RHN plugins in the /usr/share/yum-plugins directory. It also refers indirectly to plugin configuration files in the /etc/yum/pluginconf.d directory.

```
plugins=1
```

The **installonly_limit** directive specifies how many of the packages listed in the **installonlypkgs** option (usually the kernel) can be installed at the same time:

```
installonly_limit=3
```

To make sure the header data downloaded from the RHN (and any other repositories) is up to date, the **metadata_expire** directive specifies a lifetime for headers. Although the comments in yum.conf state that the default value is 90 minutes, the actual default on RHEL 7 is six hours. In other words, if you haven't used the **yum** command in the last six hours, the next use of the **yum** command downloads the latest header information.

```
#metadata_expire=90m
```

The final directive of interest, in comments, happens to be the default; it's a reference to the noted directory for actual configuration information for repositories:

```
# PUT YOUR REPOS HERE OR IN separate files named file.repo
# in /etc/yum.repos.d
```

Configuration Files in the /etc/yum/pluginconf.d Directory

The default files in the /etc/yum/pluginconf.d directory configure a connection between **yum** and the Red Hat Portal or a local Satellite server. If you're studying from a RHEL rebuild distribution such as CentOS, you'll see a different set of files in this directory. In CentOS, the files in this directory are focused on connecting the local system to better repositories over the Internet. This is a Red Hat book, however, so the focus will be on the two basic files in the RHEL 7 installation.

Red Hat Network Plugins

If you have a subscription to the RHN via an old version of Red Hat Satellite Server, the rhnplugin.conf file in this directory is especially important. Although the directives, shown next, may seem simple, they enable access and check GPG signatures:

```
[main]
enabled = 1
gpgcheck = 1
timeout = 120
```

In comments, this file suggests that different settings can be configured for different repositories. The repositories enclosed in brackets should match those associated with the actual RHN repositories.

Red Hat Subscription Management Plugins

The subscription-manager.conf and product-id.conf files are designed to connect the **yum** system to Red Hat Portal using Subscription Manager. As discussed later in this chapter, Subscription Manager is a system designed to replace RHN for system updates. The file subscription-manager.conf is very simple, with two directives that enable a connection between **yum** and the Subscription Manager plugin:

```
[main]
enabled=1
```

Configuration Files in the /etc/yum.repos.d Directory

The configuration files in the /etc/yum.repos.d directory are designed to connect systems to actual repositories. If you're running a rebuild distribution such as CentOS, you'll see files that connect to public repositories on the Internet. If you're running RHEL 7, this directory may be empty, unless the system was registered with Red Hat Subscription Management. In that case, you'll see a redhat.repo file in that directory, which is designed to get further updates from the Red Hat Portal.

A couple of elements in common for configuration files in the /etc/yum.repos.d directory are the file extension (.repo) and the documentation, available with the **man yum.conf** command.

A properly configured .repo file in the /etc/yum.repos.d directory can be a terrific convenience to enable the installation of groups of packages with the **yum** command. As the /etc/yum.repos.d directory may be empty on a RHEL 7 system, you should know how to create that file from scratch, using data for the installation server and information available in the yum.conf man page.

Understand /etc/yum.repos.d Configuration Files for Rebuild Distributions

If you're running a rebuild distribution, the files in the /etc/yum.repos.d directory may connect the local system to one or more remote repositories. One example comes from CentOS 7, as shown in Figure 7-7. Although it includes a number of different repositories, you can learn from the pattern of directives configured for each repository.

FIGURE 7-7   Several repositories configured in one file

```
[base]
name=CentOS-$releasever - Base
mirrorlist=http://mirrorlist.centos.org/?release=$releasever&arch=$basearch&repo=os
#baseurl=http://mirror.centos.org/centos/$releasever/os/$basearch/
gpgcheck=1
gpgkey=file:///etc/pki/rpm-gpg/RPM-GPG-KEY-CentOS-7

#released updates
[updates]
name=CentOS-$releasever - Updates
mirrorlist=http://mirrorlist.centos.org/?release=$releasever&arch=$basearch&repo=updates
#baseurl=http://mirror.centos.org/centos/$releasever/updates/$basearch/
gpgcheck=1
gpgkey=file:///etc/pki/rpm-gpg/RPM-GPG-KEY-CentOS-7

#additional packages that may be useful
[extras]
name=CentOS-$releasever - Extras
mirrorlist=http://mirrorlist.centos.org/?release=$releasever&arch=$basearch&repo=extras
#baseurl=http://mirror.centos.org/centos/$releasever/extras/$basearch/
gpgcheck=1
gpgkey=file:///etc/pki/rpm-gpg/RPM-GPG-KEY-CentOS-7

#additional packages that extend functionality of existing packages
[centosplus]
name=CentOS-$releasever - Plus
mirrorlist=http://mirrorlist.centos.org/?release=$releasever&arch=$basearch&repo=centosplus
#baseurl=http://mirror.centos.org/centos/$releasever/centosplus/$basearch/
gpgcheck=1
enabled=0
gpgkey=file:///etc/pki/rpm-gpg/RPM-GPG-KEY-CentOS-7
```

There are four stanzas in Figure 7-7. Each stanza represents a connection to a CentOS repository. For example, the first stanza includes the basic elements of a repository and more. The first line, in brackets, provides a name for the repository. In this case, **[base]** just stands for the base repository used by the CentOS 7 distribution. It doesn't represent the directory where the associated packages are installed.

```
[base]
```

However, when you run the **yum update** command to update the local database of those remote packages, it includes **base** as the name of the repository in output similar to the following, which suggests that it took one second to download the 3.6KB database of existing repository data:

```
base          | 3.6 kB  00:00:01
```

Although the name of the repository follows, it's just for documentation purposes and does not affect how packages or package databases are read or downloaded. However, the inclusion of the **name** directive does avoid a nonfatal error message.

```
name=CentOS-$releasever - Base
```

Note the **mirrorlist** directive that follows. It specifies a URL to a file that contains a list of multiple URLs to the closest remote servers with a copy of the actual repository of packages. It commonly works with either the HTTP or FTP protocol. (It can even work with local directories or mounted Network File System shares, as described in Exercise 7-1.)

```
mirrorlist=http://mirrorlist.centos.org/?release=$releasever ↵
&arch=$basearch&repo=os
```

Alternatively, these repositories can be set up in a file downloaded with the **baseurl** directive:

```
#baseurl=http://mirror.centos.org/centos/$releasever/os/$basearch/
```

Repositories configured in .repo files in the /etc/yum.repos.d directory are **enabled** by default. The following directive provides an easy way to deactivate a connection to such (**enabled=1** would activate the connection):

```
enabled=0
```

If you want to disable the GPG signatures of each package to be downloaded, the following command puts that wish into effect:

```
gpgcheck=0
```

Of course, if you enable **gpgcheck**, any GPG check requires a GPG key; the following directive specifies one key from the local /etc/pki/rpm-gpg directory for that purpose:

```
gpgkey-file:///etc/pki/rpm-gpg/RPM-GPG-KEY-CentOS-7
```

Create Your Own /etc/yum.repos.d Configuration File

You'll want to know how to create a local configuration file in the /etc/yum.repos.d directory. It enables the use of the **yum** command, which is the easiest way to install groups of packages such as the Apache web server or any of the groups of packages discussed in the book.

To do so, you'll need to set up a text file with a .repo extension in the /etc/yum.repos.d directory. All that file needs is three lines. In fact, if you're willing to accept some nonfatal errors, two lines are sufficient.

On RHEL 7, especially during an exam, the /etc/yum.repos.d directory may be empty. So you may not have access to examples such as those available for CentOS, as shown in Figure 7-7. The first guidance comes from the following comments at the bottom of the /etc/yum.conf file, which confirm that the file must have a .repo extension in the /etc/yum.repos.d directory:

```
# PUT YOUR REPOS HERE OR IN separate files named file.repo
# in /etc/yum.repos.d
```

```
[repository] OPTIONS
     The repository section(s) take the following form:

       Example: [repositoryid]
       name=Some name for this repository
       baseurl=url://path/to/repository/

       repositoryid  Must be a unique name for each repository, one
       word.

       name A human readable string describing the repository.

       baseurl Must be a URL to the directory  where  the  yum  reposi-
       tory's `repodata' directory lives. Can be an http://, ftp:// or
       file:// URL. You can specify multiple URLs in one baseurl state-
       ment. The best way to do this is like this:
       [repositoryid]
       name=Some name for this repository
       baseurl=url://server1/path/to/repository/
               url://server2/path/to/repository/
               url://server3/path/to/repository/

       If you list more than one baseurl= statement in a repository you
       will find yum will ignore the  earlier  ones  and  probably  act
       bizarrely. Don't do this, you've been warned.
```

In addition, you could configure the three lines in the /etc/yum.conf file. If you forget what three lines to add, there is an example in the man page for the yum.conf file, as shown in Figure 7-8.

If you forget what to do, run the **man yum.conf** command and scroll down to this part of the man page. The identifier for the repository is shown in brackets. Unless specified by the RHCSA exam, it doesn't matter what single word you put between the brackets as the identifier.

For the purpose of this chapter, we open a new file named whatever.repo in the /etc/yum .repos.d directory. (To some extent, the filename of the .repo file does not matter, as long as it has a .repo extension in the /etc/yum.repos.d directory.) In that file, we add the following identifier:

```
[test]
```

Next comes the **name** directive for the repository. As suggested by the listing in the man page, that name should be "human readable." In Linux parlance, that also means the name does not affect the functionality of the repository. To demonstrate, we add the following directive:

```
name=somebody likes Linux
```

exam

watch You should learn how to create a working .repo file in the /etc/yum .repos.d directory during Red Hat exams. It can be a big time saver when you need to install additional packages.

Finally, there's the **baseurl** directive, which can be configured to point to an installation server. The RHCSA requirements imply that you need to know how to install Linux from a remote server. They also suggest that you need to know how to install and update packages from a remote repository. To meet either objective, you need to know the URL of that remote server or repository. It's reasonable to expect that URL to be provided during the exam. In Chapter 1, you created FTP and HTTP installation servers on the host system for virtual machines, which are "remote" from those systems.

The FTP and HTTP installation servers that you created in Chapter 1 can also be used as remote repositories. To set up access to those repositories, all you need to include is one of the following **baseurl** directives:

```
baseurl=ftp://192.168.122.1/pub/inst
baseurl=http://192.168.122.1/inst
```

As suggested in the yum.conf man page, you should not include both URLs in separate **baseurl** directives. Make a choice and save the resulting file. That's all you need. There's no reason (except for better security) to include the **enabled**, **gpgcheck**, or **gpgkey** directive described earlier. Of course, security is important in real life, but if your focus is on the exam, the best advice is often to keep things as simple as possible.

Once the file is saved, run the following commands to first clear out databases from previously accessed repositories and then to update the local database cache from the repository newly configured in the /etc/yum.repos.d/*whatever*.repo file:

```
# yum clean all
# yum makecache
```

For a system not registered with Red Hat Subscription Management, it'll lead to the following output:

```
Loaded plugins: langpacks, product-id, subscription-manager
test                                         | 3.7 kB     00:00
test/primary_db                              | 2.9 MB     00:00
Metadata Cache Created
```

The system is now ready for the installation of new packages. Try running the following command:

```
# yum install system-config-date
```

Given the virtual machines configured earlier in this book, you might see the result shown in Figure 7-9. If confirmed, the **yum** command would download and then install not only the system-config-date RPM, but also the dependent package shown in the figure to make sure the system-config-date package is fully supported.

FIGURE 7-9 Installation of one package can include dependencies.

```
Dependencies Resolved

================================================================================
 Package                    Arch        Version            Repository    Size
================================================================================
Installing:
 system-config-date         noarch      1.10.6-2.el7       test         619 k
Installing for dependencies:
 system-config-date-docs    noarch      1.0.11-4.el7       test         527 k

Transaction Summary
================================================================================
Install  1 Package (+1 Dependent package)

Total download size: 1.1 M
Installed size: 3.5 M
Is this ok [y/d/N]: ▇
```

EXERCISE 7-1

Create a yum Repository from the RHEL 7 DVD

This exercise requires access to the RHEL 7 DVD. If you don't have a lot of space for this exercise, it's acceptable to set up the repository directly on the mounted DVD. Alternatively, you can copy the contents to a specified directory. It also assumes an available installation repository, such as one of those created in Chapter 1.

This exercise assumes you'll be starting with no files in the /etc/yum.repos.d directory described in this chapter.

1. If there are existing files in the /etc/yum.repos.d directory, copy them to a backup location such as the root user's home directory, /root. Delete any existing .repo files in the /etc/yum.repos.d directory.

```
# cp  -a /etc/yum.repos.d /root/
# rm -f /etc/yum.repos.d/*.repo
```

2. Mount the RHEL 7 DVD on the /mnt directory with the following command (you may need to substitute /dev/sr0 or /dev/dvd for /dev/cdrom):

```
# mount /dev/cdrom /mnt
```

Alternatively, if you have only the RHEL 7 DVD as an ISO file, mount it with the following command:

```
# mount -o loop rhel-server-7.0-x86_64-dvd.iso /mnt
```

Of course, if desired, you can copy the files from a different mount point, such as from /mnt to the /opt/repos/rhel7 directory, with a command like this:

```
# mkdir -p /opt/repos/rhel7
# cp -a /mnt/. /opt/repos/rhel7
```

The dot (.) in front of the /mnt directory ensures the copying of the contents of the directory, rather than of the directory itself.

3. Navigate to the /etc/yum.repos.d directory.

4. Open a new file in a text editor. Use a name such as rhel7.repo.

5. Edit the rhel7.repo file. Create a new stanza of directives. Use an appropriate stanza title such as [**rhel**].

6. Specify an appropriate **name** directive for the repository.

7. Include a **baseurl** directive set to **file:///opt/repos/rhel7/**. Include an **enabled=1** directive.

8. Save and close the file.

9. Assuming you're running RHEL 7 (and not a rebuild distribution), open the subscription-manager.conf file in the /etc/yum/pluginconf.d directory and set **enabled=0**.

10. Run the **yum clean all** and **yum update** commands.

11. If successful, you should see the following output:

```
Loaded plugins: langpacks, product-id
rhel                                            |  3.8 kB  00:00:00
(1/2): rhel/group_gz                            |  133 kB  00:00:00
(2/2): rhel/primary_db                          |  3.4 MB  00:00:00
No packages marked for update
```

You've now set up a repository on the local /opt/repos/rhel7 directory.

12. Restore the original files. Open the subscription-manager.conf file in the /etc/yum/pluginconf.d directory and then set **enabled=1**. Move the backed-up files from the /root directory to /etc/yum.repos.d. If you want to restore the original configuration, delete or move the rhel7.repo file from that directory. Run the **yum clean all** command again.

Third-party Repositories

Other groups of third-party developers create packages for RHEL 7. They include packages for some popular software not supported by Red Hat. The websites for two of these third parties can be found at https://fedoraproject.org/wiki/EPEL and http://repoforge.org.

To add third-party repositories to a system, you'd create a custom .repo file in the /etc/yum.repos.d directory.

Some repositories, such as EPEL (Extra Packages for Enterprise Linux), simplify the configuration by providing an RPM package that includes a .repo configuration file and a GPG key to verify the packages. To configure the repository, all you have to do is install that RPM file:

```
# rpm -ivh https://dl.fedoraproject.org/pub/epel/7/x86_64/e/ ↵
epel-release-7-5.noarch.rpm
```

If you want to disable any repository in the /etc/yum.repos.d directory, add the following directive to the applicable repository file:

```
enabled=0
```

Basic yum Commands

If you want to learn more about the intricacies of the **yum** command, run the command by itself. You'll see the following output scroll by, probably far too fast. Of course, you can pipe the output to the **less** command pager with the **yum | less** command.

```
# yum
Loaded plugins: langpacks, product-id, subscription-manager
You need to give some command
usage: yum [options] COMMAND

List of Commands
...
```

You'll examine how a few of these commands and options work in the following sections. Although you won't have Internet access during a Red Hat exam, you might have a network connection to a locally configured repository, which you should be ready to configure via the appropriate file in the /etc/yum.repos.d directory, as described earlier. As well as during the exam, yum is an excellent tool for administering Red Hat systems.

Start with a simple command: **yum list**. It'll return a list of all packages, whether they're installed or available, along with their version numbers and repositories. **yum list | grep** *packagename* tells you what version of a package you will get with a yum install. If you want to show all the configured repositories, you can do this with **yum repolist all**. More information about a specific package can be obtained via the **yum info** command. For example, the following command is functionally equivalent to **rpm -qi samba**:

```
# yum info samba
```

The **rpm -qi** command works if the queried package is already installed. The **yum info** command is not subject to that limitation.

Installation Mode

There are two basic installation commands. If you haven't installed a package before, or you want to update it to the latest stable version, run the **yum install** *packagename* command. You don't need to specify the version or release number. Only the package name is required. For example, if you're checking for the latest version of the Samba RPM, the following command will update it or add it if it isn't already installed on the target system:

```
# yum install samba
```

If you just want to keep the packages on a system up to date, run the **yum update** *packagename* command. For example, if you already have the Samba RPM installed, the following command makes sure it's updated to the latest version:

```
# yum update samba
```

If you haven't installed Samba, this command doesn't add it to your installed packages. In that way, the **yum update** command is analogous to the **rpm -F** command.

Of course, the **yum** command is not complete without options that can remove a package. The first one is straightforward because it uninstalls the Samba package along with any dependencies:

```
# yum remove samba
```

The **yum update** command by itself is powerful; if you want to make sure that all installed packages are updated to the latest stable versions, run the following command:

```
# yum update
```

The **yum update** command may take some time as it communicates with the Red Hat Portal or other repositories. It may need to download the current database of packages with all dependencies. It then finds all packages with available updates and adds them to the list of packages to be updated. It finds all dependent packages if they're not already included in the list of updates.

What if you just want a list of available updates? The **yum list updates** command can help there. It's functionally equivalent to the **yum check-update** command.

But what if you aren't quite sure what to install? For example, if you want to install the Evince document reader and think the operational command includes the term "evince," then the **yum whatprovides** "*evince*" command can help.

Alternatively, to search for all instances of files with the .repo extension, run the following command:

```
# yum whatprovides "*.repo"
```

It lists all instances of the packages with files that end with the .repo extension, with the associated RPM package. The wildcard is required because the **whatprovides** option requires the full path to the file. It accepts partial filenames; for example, the **yum whatprovides** "/etc/systemd/*" command returns the RPM associated with files in the /etc/systemd directory. Once the needed package is known, you can proceed with the **yum install** *packagename* command.

In many cases, problems with yum can be solved with the yum clean all **command. If there are recent updates to Red Hat packages (or third-party repositories), this command flushes the current cache of headers, allowing you to synchronize headers with configured repositories, without having to wait the default six hours before the cache is automatically flushed.**

Security and yum

GPG digital signatures can verify the integrity and authenticity of yum updates. It's the same system described earlier in this chapter for RPM packages. As an example, look at the output the first time a new package is installed over a network on RHEL 7:

```
# yum install samba
```

After packages are downloaded, you'll see something similar to the following messages:

```
Importing GPG key 0xFD431D51:
 Userid     : "Red Hat, Inc. (release key 2) <security@redhat.com>"
 Fingerprint: 567e 347a d004 4ade 55ba 8a5f 199e 2f91 fd43 1d51
 Package    : redhat-release-server-7.0-1.el7.x86_64 (@anaconda/7.0)
 From       : /etc/pki/rpm-gpg/RPM-GPG-KEY-redhat-release
Is this ok [y/N]: y
Importing GPG key 0x2FA658E0:
 Userid     : "Red Hat, Inc. (auxiliary key) <security@redhat.com>"
 Fingerprint: 43a6 e49c 4a38 f4be 9abf 2a53 4568 9c88 2fa6 58e0
 Package    : redhat-release-server-7.0-1.el7.x86_64 (@anaconda/7.0)
```

```
From        : /etc/pki/rpm-gpg/RPM-GPG-KEY-redhat-release
Is this ok [y/N]: y
```

If you're simultaneously downloading packages from other repositories, additional GPG keys may be presented for approval. As suggested by the last line, **N** is the default response; you actually have to type in **y** to proceed with the download and installation—not only of the GPG key, but also of the package in question.

You may notice that the GPG key used is from the same directory of keys associated with the **rpm** command earlier in this chapter.

Updates and Security Fixes

Red Hat maintains a public list of errata, classified by RHEL release, at https://rhn.redhat .com/errata. If you have a RHEL subscription, affected packages are normally made available through the Red Hat Portal; for RHSM-connected machines, all you need to do is run the **yum update** command periodically. This list is useful for those third parties who use RHEL source code, such as CentOS, Scientific Linux, and even Oracle Linux; typically RHEL rebuilds provide similar errata shortly after Red Hat.

Package Groups and yum

The **yum** command can do more. It can install and remove packages in groups. These are the groups defined in the *-comps-Server.x86_64.xml file described in Chapter 2. One location for that file is on the RHEL 7 DVD in the /repodata subdirectory. At the start of most of those stanzas, you'll see the **<id>** and **<name>** XML directives, which list two identifiers for each of those groups.

But that's a lot of work to find a package group. The **yum** command makes it simpler. With the following command, you can identify available package groups from configured repositories:

```
# yum group list
```

Note how the groups are divided into installed and available groups. Some of the groups listed may be of particular interest, such as "Basic Web Server," which you'll use in Chapter 14. To find out more about this group, run the following command. The output is shown in Figure 7-10.

```
# yum group info "Basic Web Server"
```

There are two types of groups in yum: regular groups, which include standard RPM packages, and environment groups, which are made of other groups. "Basic Web Server" in Figure 7-10 is identified as an "environment group" and is in fact a collection of regular groups. Environment groups and regular groups are associated with an environment ID and group ID, respectively, which is shown by the **yum group info** command. These IDs are

FIGURE 7-10

Packages in the
Basic Web Server
group

```
[root@server1 ~]# yum group info "Basic Web Server"
Loaded plugins: langpacks, product-id

Environment Group: Basic Web Server
 Environment-Id: web-server-environment
 Description: Server for serving static and dynamic internet content.
 Mandatory Groups:
    base
    core
    web-server
 Optional Groups:
   +backup-client
   +directory-client
    guest-agents
   +hardware-monitoring
   +java-platform
   +large-systems
   +load-balancer
   +mariadb-client
   +network-file-system-client
   +performance
   +perl-web
   +php
   +postgresql-client
   +python-web
   +remote-system-management
   +web-servlet
[root@server1 ~]# █
```

alternative names for the groups, without spaces or uppercase characters, and they are often used in Kickstart configuration files.

To list all groups, you can type

```
# yum group list hidden
```

Let's get some information about one of the regular groups:

```
# yum group info "Remote Desktop Clients"
```

Note how the packages are all listed as "Optional Packages." In other words, they're not normally installed with the package group. Thus, suppose you were to run the following command:

```
# yum group install "Remote Desktop Clients"
```

Nothing would be installed. Desired packages from this package group have to be specifically named to be installed with commands like the following:

```
# yum install tigervnc
```

FIGURE 7-11

Packages in the
Print Server group

```
[root@server1 ~]# yum group info "Print Server"
Loaded plugins: langpacks, product-id

Group: Print Server
 Group-Id: print-server
 Description: Allows the system to act as a print server.
 Mandatory Packages:
   +cups
   +ghostscript-cups
 Default Packages:
   +foomatic
   +foomatic-filters
   +gutenprint
   +gutenprint-cups
   +hpijs
   +paps
[root@server1 ~]# 
```

But optional packages are not the only category. The following command lists all packages in the "Print Server" package group. The output is shown in Figure 7-11.

```
# yum group info "Print Server"
```

Packages in the Print Server group are classified in two other categories. Mandatory packages are always installed with the package group. Default packages are normally installed with the package group; however, specific packages from this group can be excluded with the **-x** switch. For example, the following command installs the two mandatory and six default packages:

```
# yum group install "Print Server"
```

In contrast, the following command excludes the paps and the gutenprint-cups packages from the list of those to be installed:

```
# yum group install "Print Server" -x paps -x gutenprint-cups
```

After running this command, show again a list of the packages in the Print Server package group:

```
# yum group info "Print Server"
```

The output is shown in Figure 7-12. Compare this with Figure 7-11. You will notice that some of the packages have an equal sign (=) marker in front. This means that the corresponding package was installed using the **yum group install** command. Conversely, the minus marker (-) indicates that a package was excluded from installation and will not be installed if we upgrade or install the group. Similarly, the plus marker (+) indicates that a package is not installed, but it

Packages after the
Print Server group
is installed

```
[root@server1 ~]# yum group info "Print Server"
Loaded plugins: langpacks, product-id

Group: Print Server
 Group-Id: print-server
 Description: Allows the system to act as a print server.
 Mandatory Packages:
   =cups
   =ghostscript-cups
 Default Packages:
   =foomatic
   =foomatic-filters
   =gutenprint
   -gutenprint-cups
   =hpijs
   -paps
[root@server1 ~]#
```

will be added to the system if we install or upgrade the group. If no marker is present, then the
package was installed, but not as part of a **yum group install** command.

The options to the **yum** command are not complete unless there's a command that can
reverse the process. As suggested by the name, the **group remove** command uninstalls all
packages from the noted package group:

```
# yum group remove "Print Server"
```

Exclusions are not possible with the **yum group remove** command. If you don't want to
remove all packages listed in the output to the command, it may be best to remove target
packages individually.

More yum Commands

A number of additional **yum**-related commands are available. Two of them may be of
particular interest to those studying for the Red Hat exams: **yum-config-manager** and
yumdownloader, which can display all current settings for each repository as well as
download individual RPM packages. One more related command is **createrepo**, which can
help you set up a local repository.

View All Directives with yum-config-manager

To some extent, the directives listed in the yum.conf and related configuration files provide
only a small snapshot of available directives. To review the full list of directives, run the
yum-config-manager command. Pipe it to the **less** command as a pager. It includes more
than 300 lines. The excerpt from the [**main**] section shown in Figure 7-13 includes settings
that apply to all the configured repositories.

FIGURE 7-13	

A partial list of
yum directives

```
fssnap_automatic_keep = 1
fssnap_automatic_post = False
fssnap_automatic_pre = False
fssnap_devices = !*/swap,
   !*/lv_swap
fssnap_percentage = 100
gaftonmode = False
gpgcheck = True
group_command = objects
group_package_types = mandatory,
   default
groupremove_leaf_only = False
history_list_view = single-user-commands
history_record = True
history_record_packages = yum,
   rpm
http_caching = all
installonly_limit = 3
installonlypkgs = kernel,
   kernel-bigmem,
   installonlypkg(kernel-module),
   installonlypkg(vm),
   kernel-enterprise,
   kernel-smp,
   kernel-debug,
   kernel-unsupported,
   kernel-source,
   kernel-devel,
   kernel-PAE,
   kernel-PAE-debug
```

Some of the directives associated with **yum** are not filled in, such as **exactarchilist**; some don't really matter, such as the color directives. Some of the other significant directives are shown in Table 7-5. It is not a comprehensive list. If you're interested in a directive not shown, it's defined in the man page for the yum.conf file.

yum-config-manager can also manage repositories. For example, if you know the URL of a repository, you can automatically generate a configuration file using a command similar to the following:

```
# yum-config-manager --add-repo="http://192.168.122.1/inst"
```

Package Downloads with yumdownloader

As suggested by the name, the **yumdownloader** command can be used to download packages from yum-based repositories. It's a fairly simple command. For example, the following command reviews the contents of configured repositories for a package named cups:

```
# yumdownloader cups
```

| TABLE 7-5 | Configuration Parameters from yum-config-manager |

Configuration Directive in yum	Description
alwaysprompt	Prompts for confirmation on package installation or removal.
assumeyes	Set to no by default; if set to 1, yum proceeds automatically with package installation and removal.
cachedir	Set to the directory for database and downloaded package files.
distroverpkg	Lists the RPM packages that yum checks to find the version of the Linux distribution installed on the current machine.
enablegroups	Supports **yum group*** commands.
installonlypkgs	Lists packages that should never be updated; normally includes Linux kernel packages.
logfile	Specifies the name of file with log information, normally /var/log/yum.log.
pluginconfpath	Notes the directory with plugins, normally /etc/yum/pluginconf.d.
reposdir	Specifies the directory with repository configuration files.
ssl*	Supports the use of the Secure Sockets Layer (SSL) for secure updates.
tolerant	Determines whether yum stops if an error is encountered with one of the packages.

Either the RPM package is downloaded to the local directory or the command returns the following error messages:

```
No Match for argument cups
Nothing to download
```

Sometimes, more specifics are required. If there are multiple versions of a package stored on a repository, the default is to download the latest version of that package. That may not always be what you want. For example, if you want to use the originally released RHEL 7 kernel, use the following command:

```
# yumdownloader kernel-3.10.0-123.el7
```

Create Your Own Repository with createrepo

An earlier version of the RHCE objectives for RHEL 6 suggested that you should know how to "create a private yum repository." Although that objective has since been removed, it's a necessary job skill for a Red Hat system engineer.

Custom repositories can provide additional control. Enterprises that want to control the packages installed on their Linux systems can create their own customized repository. Although this can be based on the standard repositories developed for a distribution, it can include additional packages such as custom software unique to an organization. Just as easily, it can omit packages that may violate organizational policies such as games. Limits on the choices for certain functions such as browsers can minimize related support requirements.

To create a customized repository, you need to collect desired packages in a specific directory. The **createrepo** command can process all packages in that directory. The database is created in XML files in a repodata/ subdirectory. An example of this package database already exists in the repodata/ subdirectory of the RHEL 7 DVD.

The Red Hat Portal enables support of customized repositories with related products, such as Red Hat Satellite Server. For more information on repository management, see *Linux Patch Management* written by Michael Jang and published by Prentice Hall.

CERTIFICATION OBJECTIVE 7.04

More Package Management Tools

Whether a Red Hat system is connected to Red Hat Customer Portal or repositories provided by a distribution such as CentOS or Scientific Linux, it will use the same basic package management tools. Regardless of source, the **rpm** command is used to process RPM packages. Higher-level tools such as the **yum** command are used to satisfy dependencies and install groups of packages. This makes sense because the rebuild distributions are based on the same source code as RHEL 7 and all are distributed via RPM.

These similarities extend to GUI-based package management tools. While the identity of these tools has changed between RHEL 6 and RHEL 7, they are still front ends to the **rpm** and **yum** commands. They take advantage of the package groups configured in the .xml file described in Chapter 2. Since Red Hat uses GNOME as the default GUI desktop environment, the associated software management tools are based on that interface.

In RHEL 7, GUI-based package management tools rely on PackageKit, a common abstraction layer that provides a unified interface to all Linux software management applications. However, it's quite possible that PackageKit won't be available on a server, or perhaps even a system configured for a Red Hat exam. If you absolutely need PackageKit, install the required RPMs with the **yum install gnome-packagekit** command. Of course, if you're already comfortable with the **yum** command, you may not need PackageKit.

Although the RHN is listed as part of the RHCSA objectives, it's listed in context as a choice. Whether you're installing or updating software packages from RHN, "a remote repository, or a local filesystem," you can use the rpm and yum commands. Of course, it's simplest if you have an official Red Hat subscription.

The GNOME Software Update Tool

The Software Update tool can be started from a GUI terminal with the **gpk-update-viewer** command. Alternatively, from the GNOME Desktop Environment, click Applications | System Tools | Software Update. The tool, as shown in Figure 7-14, lists packages that are available for update.

FIGURE 7-14   The GNOME Software Update tool

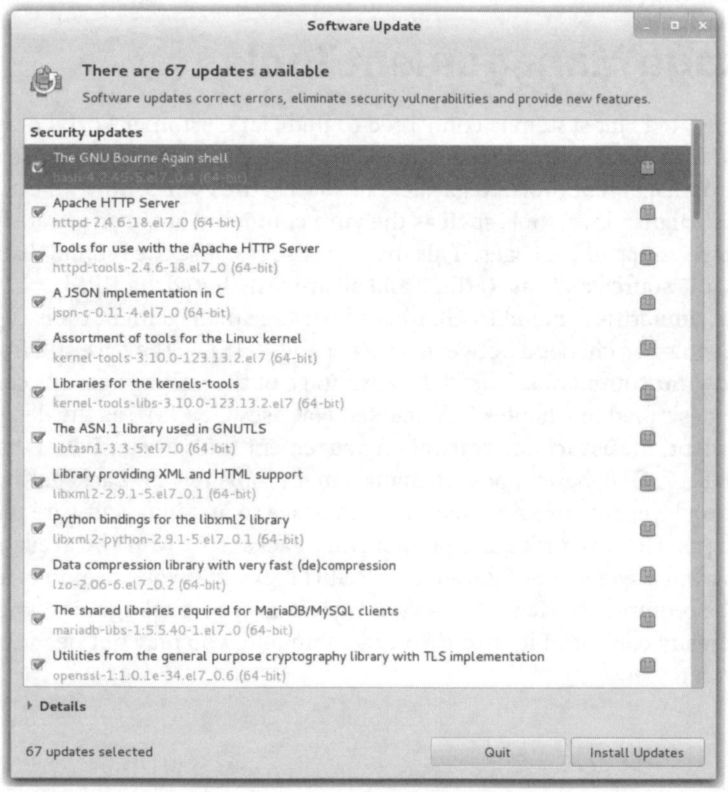

The GNOME Software Update Preferences tool

It's a pretty straightforward interface. It's effectively a front end to the **yum update** command. Note the additional information, with a description of changes.

Automated Updates

It is important to install the latest security updates as quickly as possible. To do that, open the Software Update Preferences tool shown in Figure 7-15. You can open it from a GUI command line with the **gpk-prefs** command. You can configure the system to check for updates on an hourly, daily, or a weekly basis, or not at all. When updates are found, you can configure automatic installation of all available updates, of only security updates, or of nothing at all.

GNOME Software Tool

You can add, update, and remove packages with a graphical tool. To start the GNOME Software tool from a GUI command line, run the **gpk-application** command, or click Applications | System Tools | Software. This opens the tool shown in Figure 7-16. Here, you can install more than one package or package group at a time. Once packages are selected

FIGURE 7-16   The GNOME Software tool

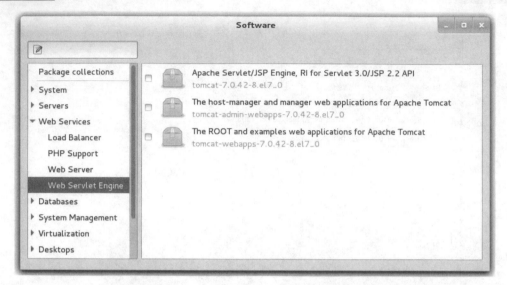

(or deselected), the tool automatically calculates dependencies and installs (or removes) them, along with the selected packages.

You can use the GNOME Software tool to add the packages or package groups of your choice. In the upper-left part of the screen is the **Package Collections** option, which lists the same groups shown in the output to the **yum group list** command described earlier.

Software packages are further subdivided in the lower-left part of the screen. When a package or package group is selected or deselected for installation or removal, the Apply Changes button becomes clickable. Once clicked, the tool uses the **yum** command to calculate dependencies. If there are no dependencies, the installation proceeds immediately. If there are dependencies, the entire list of packages to be installed or removed is presented for your approval.

EXERCISE 7-2

Installing More with yum and the GNOME Software Tool

This exercise requires a network connection to a remote repository, or at least a RHEL 7 DVD copied or mounted as a repository, as configured earlier in this chapter. If you're using a rebuild of RHEL 7, you'll need to make sure the connection to the core repository is active, perhaps with a **ping** command to the host of that repository, as defined in the appropriate file in the /etc/yum.repos.d directory. Given the possible variations, exact steps are not possible.

1. Run the **yum list** command. Assuming an active network connection and a responsive repository, you'll see a full list of available packages, including those already installed. Note the label in the right column; it will either show the repository where a package is available or note that the package is already installed.

2. Enter the **gpk-application** command in a GUI command line. This should open the GNOME Software tool.

3. In a second command-line console, type in the **yum group list** command. In the GNOME Software tool, select Package Collections. Compare the list of package groups in each output.

4. Review available package groups in the GNOME Software tool. For example, click the arrow next to Servers. Under the options that appear, click FTP Server. There are only two official packages in the RHEL 7 configuration of this group. Select the packages, which will be installed when you click Apply Changes.

5. Locate the text box in the upper-left corner of the GNOME Software tool. Type in a common search term such as *gnome* and watch as a long list of packages are shown. Compare the result to the output of the **yum search gnome** command.

6. Use a less common search term such as *iptables.* Highlight the iptables package and review it in the lower-right part of the screen. Compare the result to the output of the **yum info iptables** command.

7. Select again the iptables packages and click the Files and Dependent Packages buttons in the lower-right part of the screen. Compare the results to the output of the commands **repoquery -l iptables** and **yum deplist iptables**.

8. Once you've selected some packages, click Apply Changes. If there are dependencies, they will be automatically installed.

9. Wait as packages are installed. When finished, close the GNOME Software tool.

Red Hat Subscription Manager

The RHCSA exam objectives require candidates to be able to "install and update software packages from Red Hat Network." However, at the time of writing, RHEL 7 systems no longer support the use of the Red Hat Network (RHN). Subscriptions to RHN repositories are available only through a local installation of older version of Red Hat Satellite. Newer versions of Red Hat Satellite Server and stand-alone RHEL 7 systems use the Red

Hat Customer Portal Subscription Management (RHSM) to access Red Hat software repositories.

Remember, the related objective suggests that all you need to know is how to install and update packages from the RHN. And that skill was already covered with the **rpm** and **yum** commands, along with the related GUI tools discussed in most of this chapter.

Perhaps the key benefit of Red Hat Satellite (or an alternative such as Spacewalk or Katello) is the ability to manage all RHEL and rebuild distribution systems remotely over a web-based interface. Once an appropriate connection is configured from the client systems, Satellite Server can even run remote commands on any schedule. If you're administering a whole bunch of systems, Red Hat Satellite supports configuration of systems in groups. For example, if there are 10 systems configured as RHEL 7–based web servers, you can configure those systems as a single group. You can then schedule a single command that's applied to all of those systems remotely. For more information on Red Hat Satellite, see the latest version of the documentation, available from https://access.redhat.com/documentation/.

If you have access to the Red Hat Customer Portal Subscription Management (RHSM), take the following steps to register and subscribe to a RHEL 7 system:

1. Run the following command to register a system with RHSM. Include a username and password of a valid Red Hat account. If the system is already registered, use the **--force** command option to re-register the machine.

   ```
   # subscription-manager --username=USERNAME --password=PASSWORD
   ```

2. Subscribe the system to a Red Hat product. In the following command, the **--auto** option finds the most appropriate subscription:

   ```
   # subscription-manager attach --auto
   ```

3. Alternatively, list all available subscriptions. Take note of the pool IDs.

   ```
   # subscription-manager list --available
   ```

   Then, use the pool ID that you have retrieved from the last command to attach a system to a subscription:

   ```
   # subscription-manager attach --pool=8a85f98146f719180146fd9593b7734c
   ```

4. Review current settings. Run the following command to list the subscriptions attached to the system:

   ```
   # subscription-manager list
   ```

5. Show all available repositories for the system:

   ```
   # subscription-manager repos
   ```

6. You can enable additional repositories with the following command:

   ```
   # subscription-manager repos --enable=REPOID
   ```

7. If you prefer, you can use the GUI version of Subscription Manager, which can be started with the **subscription-manager-gui** command. Alternatively, from the GNOME Desktop Environment, click Applications | System Tools | Red Hat Subscription Manager.

CERTIFICATION SUMMARY

This chapter focuses on the management of RPM packages. With different command options, you also saw how the **rpm** tool installs, removes, and upgrade packages, as well as how it works locally and remotely. When presented with a new version of a kernel, it's important to never replace the existing kernel with **rpm.** A properly configured installation of a later kernel version does not overwrite, but brings the kernels together, side by side. You'll then be able to boot into either kernel.

With the **rpm** command, you also learned how to query packages, to examine to which package a file belongs, to validate a package signature, and to find the current list of installed RPMs. You also saw the difficulties associated with dependencies that drove users to the **yum** command.

The **yum** command is, in part, a front end to the **rpm** command. When there are dependencies, it installs those packages simultaneously. You learned how to configure Red Hat and other repositories to work with the **yum** command. You should now be able to configure even the RHEL 7 DVD as its own repository. As you saw, the **yum** command also can install or remove package groups, as defined by the XML database file of packages on the RHEL 7 DVD and other repositories. The **yum** command is fully compatible with the RHSM.

Although additional package management tools are available from the GUI, they are front ends to the **yum** and **rpm** commands. With the **gpk-update-viewer** command, you started the Software Update tool to identify and install available updates. With the **gpk-prefs** command, you started the Software Update Preferences tool, which can check for and install security or all available updates on a regular schedule. With the **gpk-application** command, you opened the GNOME Software tool, which also can be used to add or remove packages and package groups. If you have a RHEL subscription, systems can also be kept up to date and registered to RHSM through the **subscription-manager** command.

TWO-MINUTE DRILL

Here are some of the key points from the certification objectives in Chapter 7.

The Red Hat Package Manager

❑ The RPM database tracks where each file in a package is located, its version number, and much more.

❑ The **rpm -i** command installs RPM packages.

❑ The **rpm -e** command uninstalls RPM packages.

❑ The **rpm** command can even install RPMs directly from remote servers.

❑ RPM package verification is supported by the GPG keys in the /etc/pki/rpm-gpg directory.

❑ Kernel RPMs should always be installed, never upgraded.

❑ The Upgrade mode of RPM replaces the old version of the package with the new one.

More RPM Commands

❑ The **rpm -q** command determines whether packages are installed on a system; with additional switches, it can list more about a package and identify the package for a specific file.

❑ Package signatures can be checked with the **rpm --checksig** (or -K) command.

❑ The **rpm -V** command can identify files that have changed from the original installation of the package before the RPM is installed.

❑ The **rpm -qa** command lists all currently installed packages.

Dependencies and the yum Command

❑ By including additional required packages, the **yum** command can help avoid "dependency hell."

❑ The behavior of the **yum** command is configured in the /etc/yum.conf file, plugins in the /etc/yum/pluginconf.d directory, and repositories configured in the /etc/yum.repos.d directory.

❑ Red Hat organizes packages in several different repositories for RHEL 7.

❑ Repositories for rebuild distributions and from third parties are accessible online.

❑ The **yum** command can install, erase, and update packages. It also can be used to search in different ways.

❑ The **yum** command uses the GPG keys developed for RPM packages.

❑ The **yum** command can install, remove, and list package groups.

More Package Management Tools

❑ RHEL 7 package management tools are based on the PackageKit built for GNOME.

❑ With the GNOME Software tool, you can install and remove packages and package groups.

❑ The PackageKit also includes tools focused on current updates. It can also set up updates of security packages or all packages on a schedule.

❑ The RHSM and Red Hat Satellite can help you manage subscribed systems remotely using a web-based interface.

SELF TEST

The following questions will help measure your understanding of the material presented in this chapter. As no multiple choice questions appear on the Red Hat exams, no multiple choice questions appear in this book. These questions exclusively test your understanding of the chapter. It is okay if you have another way of performing a task. Getting results, not memorizing trivia, is what counts on the Red Hat exams. There may be more than one answer to many of these questions.

The Red Hat Package Manager

1. What command would you use to install the penguin-3.26.x86_64.rpm package, with extra messages in case of errors? The package is on the local directory.

   _____

2. What command would you use to upgrade the penguin RPM with the penguin-3.27.x86_64.rpm package? The package is on the ftp.remotemj02.abc server.

   _____

3. If you've downloaded a later version of the Linux kernel to the local directory and the package filename is kernel-3.10.0-123.13.2.el7.x86_64.rpm, what's the best command to make it a part of your system?

   _____

4. What directory contains RPM GPG keys on an installed system?

   _____

More RPM Commands

5. What command lists all currently installed RPMs?

   _____

6. What command lists all the files in the package penguin-3.26.x86_64.rpm?

   _____

7. If you've downloaded an RPM from a third party called third.i686.rpm, how can you validate the associated package signature?

   _____

Dependencies and the yum Command

8. What is the full path to the directory where the location of **yum** repositories are normally configured?

   _____

9. What command searches **yum** repositories for the package associated with the /etc/passwd file?

   _____

More Package Management Tools

10. What command-line command lists the package groups shown in the GNOME Software tool?

    _____

11. Name two allowable time periods for automatic updates, as defined by the Software Update Preferences tool.

    _____

    _____

12. What command from the console starts the process of registration on RHSM?

    _____

LAB QUESTIONS

Red Hat presents its exams electronically. For that reason, the labs in this chapter are available from the DVD that accompanies the book in the Chapter7/ subdirectory. They're available in .doc, .html, and .txt format to reflect standard options associated with electronic delivery on a live RHEL 7 system. In case you haven't yet set up RHEL 7 on a system, refer to the first lab of Chapter 2 for installation instructions. The answers for each lab follow the Self Test answers for the fill-in-the-blank questions.

SELF TEST ANSWERS

The Red Hat Package Manager

1. The command that installs the penguin-3.26.x86_64.rpm package, with extra messages in case of errors, from the local directory is

    ```
    # rpm -iv penguin-3.26.x86_64.rpm
    ```

    Additional switches that don't change the functionality of the command, such as **-h** for hash marks, are acceptable. This applies to subsequent questions as well.

2. The command that upgrades the aforementioned penguin RPM with the penguin-3.27.x86_64 .rpm package from the ftp.remotemj02.abc server is

    ```
    # rpm -Uv ftp://ftp.remotemj02.abc/penguin-3.26.x86_64.rpm
    ```

    If you use the default vsFTP server, the package may be in the pub/Packages/ subdirectory. In other words, the command would be

    ```
    # rpm -Uv ftp://ftp.remotemj02.abc/pub/Packages/penguin-3.26.i386.rpm
    ```

    Yes, the question is not precise—but that's what you see in real life.

3. If you've downloaded a later version of the Linux kernel to the local directory and the package filename is kernel-3.10.0-123.13.2.el7.x86_64.rpm, the best way to make it a part of your system is to install it—and not upgrade the current kernel. Kernel upgrades overwrite existing kernels. Kernel installations allow kernels to exist side by side; if the new kernel doesn't work, you can still boot into the working kernel. As the desired package is already downloaded, you'd use a command similar to the following:

    ```
    # rpm -iv kernel-3.10.0-123.13.2.el7.x86_64.rpm
    ```

    Variations of the **rpm** command, such as **rpm -i** and **rpm -ivh**, are acceptable. However, variations that upgrade, with the **-U** or **-F** switches, are incorrect.

4. The directory with RPM GPG keys on an installed system is /etc/pki/rpm-gpg. The GPG keys on the RHEL 7 CD/DVD are not "installed" on a system.

More RPM Commands

5. The command that lists all installed RPMs is

    ```
    # rpm -qa
    ```

6. The command that lists all the files in the package penguin-3.26.x86_64.rpm is

    ```
    # rpm -ql penguin-3.26.x86_64.rpm
    ```

7. If you've downloaded an RPM from a third party, call it third.i686.rpm, you'll first need to download and install the RPM-GPG-KEY file associated with that repository. You can then validate the associated package signature with a command like the following (note the uppercase **-K**; **--checksig** is equivalent to **-K**):

    ```
    # rpm -K third.i386.rpm
    ```

Dependencies and the yum Command

8. The **yum** command repositories are normally configured in files in the /etc/yum.repos.d directory. Technically, **yum** command repositories can also be configured directly in the /etc/yum.conf file.

9. The **yum whatprovides /etc/passwd** command identifies packages associated with that file.

More Package Management Tools

10. This is a slightly tricky question because the **yum group list** command lists the package groups also shown in the GNOME Software tool.

11. Allowable time periods for updates, as defined by the Software Update Preferences tool, are hourly, daily, and weekly.

12. The **subscription-manager** command starts the process of registering a system on RHSM.

LAB ANSWERS

Lab 1

When the lab is complete, run the following commands to verify the connection:

```
# yum clean all
# yum update
```

The output should look similar to the following:

```
Loaded plugins: langpacks, product-id, subscription-manager
inst                                    | 3.7 kB      00:00
inst/primary_db                         | 2.9 MB      00:00
Setting up Update Process
```

This output verifies a successful connection to the FTP server. If you see something significantly different, check the following in the /etc/yum.repos.d/file.repo file:

- Make sure the stanza in this file starts with [**inst**].
- Check the URL associated with the **baseurl** directive. It should match the URL of the FTP server defined in Chapter 1, Lab 2. You should be able to run the **lftp** and **ftp** commands with that URL from a command-line interface. If that doesn't work, either the FTP server is not running or messages to that server are blocked by a firewall.
- If there were problems, fix them. Then try the previous commands again.

Lab 2

One way to check all of the files in the /usr/sbin directory is to use the **rpm -Va | grep /usr/sbin** command.

If successful, you'll identify the /usr/sbin/vsftpd and /etc/vsftpd/vsftpd.conf files as different from their original versions, as installed from the RPM. Changes to a configuration file are not a big deal, especially if it has been customized in any way. However, changes to the binary file are a reason for suspicion.

Assuming standard Red Hat RPM packages, removal and reinstallation should preserve changes to the vsftpd.conf file in a vsftpd.conf.rpmsave file.

If you really do have a security concern, additional measures are appropriate. For example, some security professionals might compare all files on a suspect system to the files on a verified baseline system.

In that case, it may be simplest to take a copy or clone of the baseline system, reinstall the vsftpd RPM, and reconfigure it as needed. Assuming the baseline system is secure, you'd then be reasonably sure the new server would also be secure.

The changes made by the script to this lab set a new modification time for the /usr/sbin/vsftpd binary and appended a comment to the end of the vsftpd.conf configuration file. If you want to restart with fresh copies of these packages, back up your current vsftpd.conf file and run the **rpm -e vsftpd** command to uninstall the package. If the RPM package was reconfigured, you should see at least the following warning message:

```
warning: /etc/vsftpd/vsftpd.conf saved as /etc/vsftpd/vsftpd.conf.rpmsave
```

You can then reinstall the original package from either the installation DVD or a remote repository. Alternatively, you could delete (or move) the changed files and then run the following command to force the **rpm** command to provide the original copies of these files from the associated package. The version number is based on the RHEL 7.0 DVD.

```
# rpm -ivh --force vsftpd-3.0.2-9.el7.x86_64.rpm
```

Lab 3

This lab is intended to help you examine what the **yum update** command can do. It's the essential front end to GUI update tools. As you can see from the update.txt file created in this lab, the messages display how **yum** appears for all newer packages from configured repositories or the RHN, downloads their headers, and uses them to check for dependencies that also need to be downloaded and installed.

Lab 4

This lab should be straightforward because it involves the use of the Software Update Preferences tool, which you can start from a GUI command line with the **gpk-prefs** command.

Lab 5

This lab is somewhat self-explanatory and is intended to help you explore what happens when you properly install a new kernel RPM. As with other Linux distributions, when you install (and do not use upgrade mode for) a new kernel, two areas are affected.

The new kernel is added as a new option in the GRUB2 configuration menu. The existing kernel should be retained as an option in that menu. When you reboot the system, try the new kernel. Don't hesitate to reboot the system again and then try the other option, probably the older kernel.

When you review the /boot directory, all of the previously installed boot files should be there. The new kernel RPM should add matching versions of all of the same files—with different revision numbers.

To keep this all straight, it helps if you made copies of the original versions of the GRUB 2 configuration file and the file list in the /boot directory. If you choose to retain the newly installed kernel, great. Otherwise, uninstall the newly installed kernel. This is one case where revision numbers are required with the **rpm -e** command; the following is based on the removal of the kernel and kernel-firmware packages, based on version number 3.10.0-229.el7:

```
# rpm -e kernel-3.10.0-229.el7.x86_64
# rpm -e linux-firmware-20140911-0.1.git365e80c.el7
```

If the revision number of the kernel or kernel-firmware package that you installed during this lab is different, adjust the commands accordingly.

Lab 6

This lab is designed to give you practice with both the **yum** command and the Add/Remove Software tool. It should help you prepare for Chapter 9 and provide the skills required to install services for other chapters. You should realize by now that because all packages in the Remote Desktop Clients package group are optional, the **yum group install "Remote Desktop Clients"** command doesn't install anything. You'll need to install each of the optional packages by name.

To identify the names of the packages to be installed, run the **yum group info "Remote Desktop Clients"** command. Be sure to install every package from that group on both systems. The best method is with the **yum install** package1 package2 ... command, where *package1*, *package2*, and so on, are names of packages in the "Remote Desktop Clients" package group.

Chapter 8

User Administration

Fundamental to Linux administration is the management of users and groups. In this chapter, you'll examine different ways to manage the variety of users and groups available to Linux. Important skills in this area range from the simple login to user account management, group membership, group collaboration, and network authentication. The configuration of administrative privileges for Linux users can help the master administrator distribute responsibilities to others.

You'll see how to manage these tasks from the command line, with the help of the files of the shadow password suite. You'll also use tools such as the User Manager and the Authentication Configuration tool to set up some of these tasks. As you should expect, Red Hat GUI tools can't do it all, which emphasizes the importance of understanding user management from the command line.

INSIDE THE EXAM

Inside the Exam

This chapter addresses several RHCSA objectives. Briefly explained, these objectives include the following:

- Log in and switch users in multiuser targets

Briefly, that means you need to know how to log in with regular accounts when RHEL 7 is running in the multiuser or graphical targets. To switch users, you need to know how to log out and log back in with a second account. Simple enough.

- Create, delete, and modify local user accounts
- Change passwords and adjust password aging for local user accounts
- Create, delete, and modify local groups and group memberships

You could use commands such as **useradd**, **usermod**, **groupadd**, **groupmod**, and **chage** as well as the User Manager to accomplish these tasks. While this chapter explains how you can use both types of tools, there is no guarantee that the User Manager will be available during an exam.

- Create and configure set-GID directories for collaboration

When the RHCT exam was available, the related objective was "Configure filesystem permissions for collaboration." In other words, the objective is now more specific—you're told how to set one or more directories for collaboration between a group of users.

- Configure a system to use an existing authentication service for user and group information

In the previous version of the RHCSA exam for RHEL 6, this objective was limited to "Attach a system to a centralized Lightweight Directory Access Protocol (LDAP) server." Now the scope of the objective is broader, and may include any service such as Kerberos, Microsoft Active Directory, or an Identity, Policy, and Audit (IPA) server.

CERTIFICATION OBJECTIVE 8.01

User Account Management

You need to know how to create and configure users. This means knowing how to configure and modify accounts, work with passwords, and organize users in groups. You also need to know how to configure the environment associated with each user account: in configuration files and in user settings.

If you've installed RHEL 7 via Kickstart or in text mode, or otherwise avoided the Firstboot process described in Chapter 1, the default Red Hat installation includes just a single login account: root. Although no other accounts are required, it's important to set up some regular user accounts. Even if you're going to be the only user on the system, do create at least one non-administrative account for day-to-day work. Then you can use the root account only when it's necessary to administer the system. You can add accounts to Red Hat Enterprise Linux systems using various utilities, including direct editing of password configuration files (the manual method), the **useradd** command (the command-line method), and the User Manager utility (the graphical method).

Different Kinds of Users

There are three basic types of Linux user accounts: administrative (root), regular, and service. The administrative root account is automatically created when Linux is installed, and it has administrative privileges for all services on a Linux system. A "black hat" hacker who has a chance to take control of this account can take full control of that system.

For the times when you do log in as an administrator, RHEL builds in safeguards for root users. Log in as the root user, and then run the **alias** command. You'll see entries such as the following:

```
alias rm='rm -i'
```

Due to this particular alias, when the root user runs the **rm** command, the shell actually executes the **rm -i** command, which prompts for confirmation before the **rm** command deletes a file. Unfortunately, a command such as **rm -rf** *directoryname* supersedes this safety setting.

Regular users have the necessary privileges to perform standard tasks on a Linux computer. They can access programs such as word processors, databases, and web browsers. They can store files in their own home directories. Since regular users do not normally have administrative privileges, they cannot accidentally delete critical operating system configuration files. You can assign a regular account to most users, safe in the knowledge that they can't disrupt a system with the privileges they have on that account.

Services such as Apache, Squid, mail, and printing have their own individual service accounts. These accounts exist to allow each of these services to interact with Linux systems. Normally, you won't need to change any service account, but if you see that someone is running a Bash shell through one of these accounts, be wary. Someone may have broken into your system.

on the !job **To review recent logins, run the** last | less **command. If the login is from a remote location, it will be associated with a specific IP address outside your network.**

The Shadow Password Suite

When Unix was first developed back in the 1970s, security was not a serious concern. Everything required for user and group management was contained in the /etc/passwd and /etc/group files. As suggested by the name, passwords were originally in the /etc/passwd file. The problem is that file is "world readable." Anyone with a copy of that file, before the shadow password suite, would have a copy of the password for every user. Even passwords that are encrypted in that file may eventually be decrypted. That is the motivation behind the development of the shadow password suite, where more sensitive information was moved to other files, readable only by the root administrative user.

The four files of the shadow password suite are /etc/passwd, /etc/group, /etc/shadow, and /etc/gshadow. Defaults in these files are driven by the /etc/login.defs file.

The /etc/passwd File

The /etc/passwd file contains basic information about every user. Open that file in a text editor and browse around a bit. At the top of the file is basic information for the root administrative user. Other users in this file may relate to services such as mail, ftp, and sshd. They may be specific users designed for logins.

There are seven columns of information in the /etc/passwd file, delineated by colons. Each column in /etc/passwd includes specific information described in Table 8-1.

The RHEL 7 version of /etc/passwd includes more secure features for user accounts when compared to some other Linux distributions. The only accounts with a real login shell are user accounts. If a "black hat" hacker somehow breaks into a service account, such as mail or nobody, with the false /sbin/nologin shell, that user doesn't automatically get access to the command line.

The /etc/group File

Every Linux user is assigned to a group. By default, in RHEL 7 every user gets his own private group. The user is the only member of that group, as defined in the /etc/group configuration file. Open that file in a text editor. Browse around a bit. The first line in this

TABLE 8-1   The Anatomy of /etc/passwd

Field	Example	Purpose
Username	mj	The user logs in with this name. Usernames can include digits, hyphens (-), dots (.), and underscores (_). However, they should not start with a hyphen or be longer than 32 characters.
Password	x	The password. You should see either an x, an asterisk (*), or a seemingly random group of letters and numbers. An x points to /etc/shadow for the actual password. An asterisk means the account is disabled. A random group of letters and numbers represents the encrypted password.
User ID	1000	The unique numeric user ID (UID) for that user. By default, Red Hat starts user IDs at 1000.
Group ID	1000	The primary group ID (GID) associated with that user. By default, RHEL creates a new group for every new user, and the number matches the UID, if the corresponding GID is available. Some other Linux and Unix systems assign all users to a default Users group.
User info	Michael Jang	You can enter any information of your choice in this field. Standard options include the user's full name, telephone number, e-mail address, and physical location. You can leave this blank.
Home Directory	/home/mj	By default, RHEL places new home directories in /home/*username*.
Login Shell	/bin/bash	By default, RHEL assigns users to the bash shell. You can change this to any legal shell you have installed.

file specifies information for the root administrative user's group. Some service users include other users as members of that group. For example, user qemu is a member of the kvm group, which gives services associated with the QEMU emulator privileges with the Kernel-based Virtual Machine (KVM).

There are four columns of information in the /etc/group file, delineated by colons. Each column in the /etc/group specifies information described in Table 8-2.

The /etc/shadow File

The /etc/shadow file is a supplement to /etc/passwd. It contains eight columns of information, and the first column contains the same list of usernames as documented in /etc/passwd. As long as there's an x in the second column of each /etc/passwd entry, Linux knows to look at /etc/shadow for more information. Open that file in a text editor and browse around a bit. You'll see the same pattern of information, starting with the root administrative user.

| TABLE 8-2 | The Anatomy of /etc/group |

Field	Example	Purpose
Groupname	mj	Each user gets his own group, with the same name as his username. You can also create unique group names.
Password	x	The password. You should see either an *x* or a seemingly random group of letters and numbers. An *x* points to /etc/gshadow for the actual password. A random group of letters and numbers represents the encrypted password.
Group ID	1000	The numeric group ID (GID) associated with the group. By default, RHEL creates a new group for every new user. If you want to create a special group such as managers, you should assign a GID number outside the standard range; otherwise, Red Hat GIDs and UIDs would probably get out of sequence.
Group members	mj,vp,ao	Lists the usernames that are members of the group. If there is a username that lists the GID of the group as its primary group in /etc/passwd, that username is also a member of the group.

As shown in Table 8-3, /etc/shadow includes the encrypted password in the second column, and the remaining information relates to the way passwords are managed. In fact, the first two characters of the second column are based on the encryption hash for the password. If you see a $1, the password is hashed to the Message Digest 5 (MD5) algorithm, the standard through RHEL 5. If you see a $6, the password is protected with the 512-bit Secure Hash Algorithm (SHA-512), the standard for RHEL 6 and 7.

| TABLE 8-3 | The Anatomy of /etc/shadow |

Column	Field	Description
1	Username	Username
2	Password	Encrypted password; requires an *x* in the second column of /etc/passwd
3	Password history	Date of the last password change, in number of days after January 1, 1970
4	mindays	Minimum number of days that a user must keep a password
5	maxdays	Maximum number of days after which a password must be changed
6	warndays	Number of days before password expiration when a warning is given
7	inactive	Number of days after password expiration during which the password is still accepted, but the user is prompted to change her password
8	disabled	Number of days since January 1, 1970, after which an account is disabled

TABLE 8-4		The Anatomy of /etc/gshadow
Field	**Example**	**Purpose**
Groupname	mj	The group name.
Password	!	Most groups have a !, which indicates no password; some groups may have a hashed password similar to that shown in the /etc/shadow file.
Administrators	mj	A comma-separated list of users who are part of the group and can change the members or the password of the group using the **gpasswd** command.
Group members	vp,ao	A comma-delineated list of usernames that are members of the group.

The /etc/gshadow File

The /etc/gshadow file is the group configuration file in the shadow password suite. It includes the group administrators, which can add other group members using the **gpasswd** command. If desired, you can even configure a hashed password. Once a password is set, other users can become members of the group by using the **newgrp** command and typing the required password. Table 8-4 describes the columns in /etc/gshadow, from left to right.

The /etc/login.defs File

The /etc/login.defs file provides the baseline for a number of parameters in the shadow password suite. This section provides a brief analysis of each active directive in the default version of this file. As you'll see, the directives go somewhat beyond authentication. The first configuration parameter specifies the directory with locally delivered e-mail, listed by username:

```
MAIL_DIR /var/spool/mail
```

The next four directives relate to default password aging information. The directives are explained in the file comment and in Table 8-5.

TABLE 8-5	/etc/login.defs Password-Aging Configuration Parameters
Configuration Parameter	**Purpose**
PASS_MAX_DAYS	After this number of days, the password must be changed.
PASS_MIN_DAYS	Passwords must be kept for at least this number of days.
PASS_MIN_LEN	The length of a password must be at least this number of characters.
PASS_WARN_AGE	Users are warned this number of days before PASS_MAX_DAYS.

As suggested earlier, User ID (UID) and Group ID (GID) numbers for regular users and groups start at 1000. Since Linux supports UID and GID numbers above 4 billion (actually, up to $2^{32}-1$), the maximum UID and GID numbers of 60000, as defined in the /etc/login.defs file, may seem strange. However, it leaves higher numbers available for other authentication databases, such as those associated with LDAP and Microsoft Windows (via Winbind). As suggested by the directives, **UID_MIN** specifies the minimum UID, **UID_MAX** specifies the maximum UID, and so on:

```
UID_MIN   1000
UID_MAX   60000
GID_MIN   1000
GID_MAX   60000
```

Similarly, the **useradd** and **groupadd** commands with the **-r** switch create a system user or system group, respectively, whose ID is chosen within the following range:

```
SYS_UID_MIN 201
SYS_UID_MAX 999
SYS_GID_MIN 201
SYS_GID_MAX 999
```

Normally, when the **useradd** command is run to create a new user, it automatically creates home directories as well, which is confirmed by the following directive:

```
CREATE_HOME yes
```

As described later in this chapter, other files set the value of the umask. But if those other files did not exist, this directive would govern the default umask for regular users:

```
UMASK     077
```

The following directive is critical in the implementation of the User Private Group scheme, where new users are also made members of their own private group, normally with the same UID and GID numbers. It means when new users are created (or deleted), the associated group is also added (or deleted):

```
USERGROUPS_ENAB yes
```

Finally, the following directive determines the algorithm used to encrypt passwords, normally SHA 512 for RHEL 7:

```
ENCRYPT_METHOD SHA512
```

Different encryption methods may be set up with the Authentication Configuration tool described later in this chapter.

Command-Line Tools

There are two basic ways to add users through the command-line interface. You can add users directly by editing the /etc/passwd file in a text editor such as vi. To this end, both **vipw** and **vigr** were described in Chapter 3. Alternatively, you can use text commands customized for the purpose.

Add Users Directly

Open the /etc/passwd file in the text editor of your choice. As described in Chapter 3, you can do so with the **vipw** command. However, if you add users by directly editing the files of the shadow password suite, you'll have to do two more things:

- *Add a user home directory*. For example, for user donna, you'd have to add the /home/donna home directory, making sure that user donna and group donna both have ownership of that directory.

- *Populate the user home directory*. The default option is to copy the files from the /etc/skel directory, discussed later in this chapter. You'd also have to make sure that user donna and group donna have ownership of those files copied to the /home/donna directory.

Add Users to a Group Directly

Every Linux user is assigned to a group, at least his own private group. As implied in Chapter 3, the GID number listed in the /etc/group file should usually match that shown for that user in the /etc/passwd file. The user is the only member of that group.

Of course, users can be members of other groups as well. For example, to create a group named project, you could add the entries to the /etc/group and /etc/gshadow files. One way to do so in a text editor is with the **vigr** command. As an example, the following entry might be appropriate for a group named project:

```
project:x:60001:
```

The number 60001 is used, as that is beyond the limit of the **GID_MAX** directive from the /etc/login.defs file described earlier. But that's just arbitrary. There's no prohibition against a lower number, as long as it does not interfere with existing GIDs. However, it is convenient when the UID and GID numbers of regular users match.

Of course, for a group to be useful, you'd have to add users already configured in the /etc/passwd file at the end of the line. The following example assumes these users already exist:

```
project:x:60001:michael,elizabeth,stephanie,tim
```

You'd also have to add this group to the /etc/gshadow file. You could do so directly with the **vigr -s** command. Alternatively, to set up a group administrator with a password, you could run the **gpasswd** command. For example, the **gpasswd project** command would set up a password for administering the group, associated with the **newgrp** and **sg** commands described later in this chapter. It would automatically add the encrypted password with the given group name to the /etc/gshadow file.

Add Users at the Command Line

Alternatively, you can automate this process with the **useradd** command. The **useradd pm** command would add user pm to the /etc/passwd file. In addition, the **useradd** command creates the /home/pm home directory, adds the standard files from the /etc/skel directory, and assigns the default shell, /bin/bash. But **useradd** is versatile. It includes a number of command options, as shown in Table 8-6.

Assign a Password

Once a new user is created, you can use the **passwd** *username* command to assign a password to that user. For example, the **passwd pm** command prompts you to assign a new password to user pm. RHEL is configured to avoid passwords that are based on dictionary

TABLE 8-6	useradd Command Options

Option	Purpose
-u *UID*	Overrides the default assigned *UID.* By default, in RHEL this starts at 1000 and can continue sequentially to the maximum number of users supported by kernel 2.6, which is $2^{32}-1$, something over four billion users.
-g *GID*	Overrides the default assigned *GID.* If available, RHEL uses the same *GID* and *UID* numbers for each user. If you assign a *GID,* it must be either 100 (users) or already otherwise exist.
-c *info*	Enters the comment of your choice about the user, such as her name.
-d *dir*	Overrides the default home directory for the user, /home/*username.*
-e *YYYY-MM-DD*	Sets an expiration date for the user account.
-f *num*	Specifies a number of days after password expiration when the account is disabled.
-G *group1, group2*	Makes the user a member of *group1* and *group2,* based on their current names as defined in the /etc/group file. A space between *group1* and *group2* would lead to an error.
-s *shell*	Overrides the default shell for the user, /bin/bash.

words, shorter than eight characters, too simple, based on palindromes, and other, similar criteria for security reasons. Nevertheless, such passwords are legal and accepted if the **passwd** command is run by the root user.

Add or Delete a Group at the Command Line

When it's appropriate to add a special group to the shadow password suite, you may want to use the **groupadd** command. Generally, you'll want to use it with the **-g** switch. For example, the following command would set up a special project group with a GID of 60001:

```
# groupadd -g 60001 project
```

If you don't use the **-g** switch, the **groupadd** command takes the next available GID number. For example, if two regular users are configured on a system, they each have UID and GID numbers of 1000 and 1001, respectively. If you've run the **groupadd project** command without specifying a GID number, the project group is assigned a GID of 1002. The next regular user that's created would get a UID of 1002 and a GID of 1003, which could lead to confusion.

Fortunately, the command to delete a group is simpler. If the project group has completed its work, you can delete that group from the shadow password suite database with the following command:

```
# groupdel project
```

Delete a User

The removal of a user account is a straightforward process. The easiest way to delete a user account is with the **userdel** command. By default, this command does not delete that user's home directory, so administrators can transfer files from that user perhaps to an employee who has taken over the tasks of the deleted user. Alternatively, the **userdel -r** *username* command deletes that user's home directory along with all of the files stored in that home directory.

This is a lot faster than the GUI method, for which you open the Red Hat User Manager,

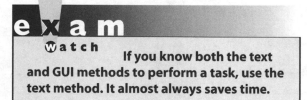

If you know both the text and GUI methods to perform a task, use the text method. It almost always saves time.

select the user, and then click Delete. Although it's probably easier for a less experienced user to remember the GUI method, text commands are faster.

Add a User with the Red Hat User Manager

If the GUI is available, one alternative to user management commands such as **useradd** and **usermod** is the Red Hat User Manager. If possible, try to open it remotely over an **ssh -X** connection, as described in Chapter 2. For example, if you've configured the server1 .example.com system as described in earlier chapters, connect to that system from a remote GUI with the **ssh -X root@192.168.122.50** command. Once logged in, enter the **system-config-users** command.

1. In the Red Hat User Manager, click the Add User button, or choose File | Add User. This will open the Add New User window, as shown here:

2. Complete the form. All entries are required, except Full Name. The entries are fairly self-explanatory (see the earlier discussions of each field). The password should be at least eight characters and should ideally contain a mix of upper- and lowercase letters, numbers, and punctuation to keep it more secure from the standard password-cracking programs.

3. Enter the identical password in the Confirm Password field.

4. Note the number associated with the Specify User ID Manually and Specify Group ID Manually options; those are the UID and GID numbers that will be assigned to the new user. Click OK when you are done.

5. Repeat the process as desired for any additional new users that may be required. Make sure to create at least one new user prior to running Exercise 8-2.

EXERCISE 8-2

Real and Fake Shells

Do not run this exercise unless a regular user has already been created on the local system. If desired, run Exercise 8-1 first, as that allows you to create a new regular user on the target system.

1. Open the /etc/passwd file. Find a current regular user, with a UID of 1000 or above.

2. Identify the default shell. It's specified in the last column, normally /bin/bash for regular users.

3. Change the default shell to /sbin/nologin, and save the changes to the /etc/passwd file.

4. Open a different virtual console. Press the CTRL-ALT-F2 keys to open a different console. (If you're already in the second virtual console, substitute F3, F4, F5, or F6 for F2. If you're in a KVM-based VM in the GUI, you can move to the second virtual console by clicking Send Key | CTRL-ALT-F2.)

5. Try logging in as the modified user. What happens?

6. Return to the original console. If it's the GUI, it should be accessible with the CTRL-ALT-F1 key combination. If that is not possible (such as when the GUI is not installed), you should still be able to log in as the root administrative user.

7. Reopen the /etc/passwd file. Restore the /bin/bash shell to the target regular user.

Modify an Account

As a Linux administrator, you may want to add some limitations to user accounts. The easiest way to illustrate some of the changes is with the User Manager tool. Start the User Manager, select a currently configured user, and then click Properties to open the User Properties dialog box.

FIGURE 8-1

Manage user
account life.

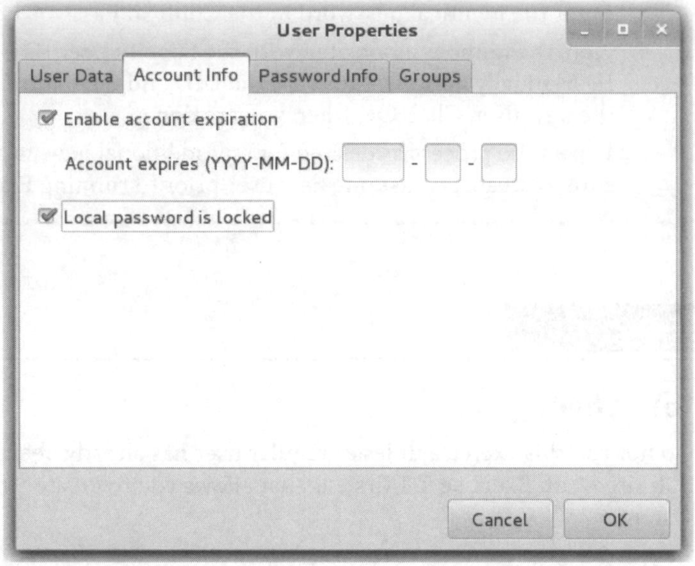

Click the Account Info tab for the account expiration information shown in Figure 8-1. As shown in the figure, you can limit the life of an account so that it expires on a specific date, or you can disable an account by locking it.

Click the Password Info tab. As shown in Figure 8-2, you can set several characteristics related to an individual user's password. Even when good passwords are set, frequent

FIGURE 8-2

Configure
password
information.

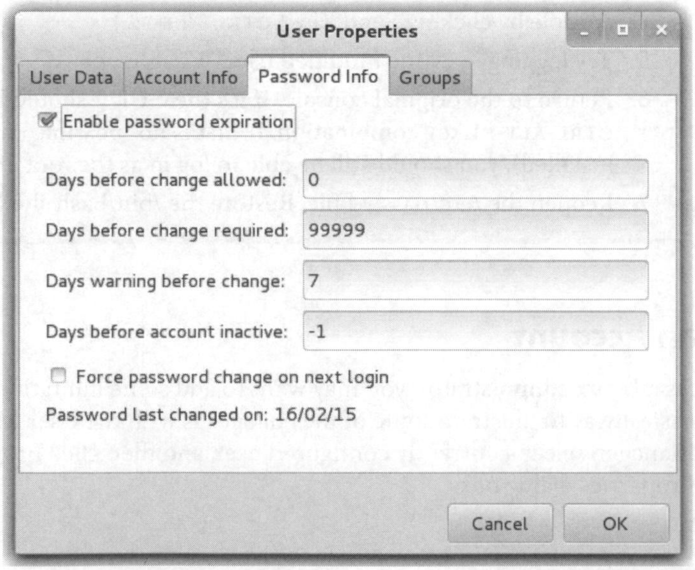

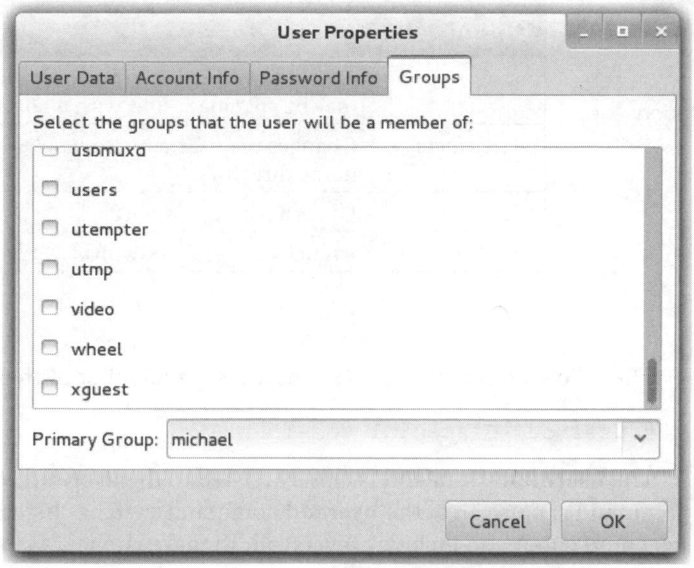

FIGURE 8-3

Assign a group.

password changes can help provide additional security. The categories shown in the figure are self-explanatory.

Click the Groups tab. Users can belong to more than one group in Linux. Under the Groups tab shown in Figure 8-3, you can assign the target user to other groups. For example, to share files and facilitate collaboration within a management team, you can assign appropriate users to a group named "managers." You can assign members of a team to the appropriate group through the Groups tab.

More User and Group Management Commands

While the Red Hat User Manager GUI utility is convenient, it's often faster to perform the associated administrative functions at the command-line interface. We've described some of these commands, such as **useradd**, **userdel**, **groupadd**, and **groupdel**. Three other key user administration commands are **usermod**, **groupmod**, and **chage**.

usermod

The **usermod** command modifies various settings in /etc/passwd. In addition, it allows you to set an expiration date for an account or an additional group. For example, the following command sets the account associated with user test1 to expire on June 8, 2016:

```
# usermod -e 2016-06-08 test1
```

TABLE 8-7	Option	Purpose
	-a -G *group1*	Appends to existing group memberships; multiple groups may be specified, split with a comma, with no spaces.
usermod Command Options	-l *newlogin*	Changes the username to *newlogin,* without changing the home directory.
	-L	Locks a user's password.
	-U	Unlocks a user's password.

The following command makes user test1 a member of the special group:

```
# usermod -G special test1
```

The **usermod** command is closely related to the **useradd** command; in fact, the **usermod** command can use all of the **useradd** command switches listed earlier in Table 8-6. The **usermod** command includes several additional switches, as listed in Table 8-7.

groupmod

The **groupmod** command is relatively simple. It has two practical uses. The following command changes the GID number of the group named project (in this case, to 60002):

```
# groupmod -g 60002 project
```

In contrast, the following command changes the name of the group named project to secret:

```
# groupmod -n secret project
```

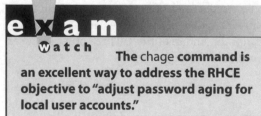

The chage **command is an excellent way to address the RHCE objective to "adjust password aging for local user accounts."**

chage

The **chage** command is primarily used to manage aging information for a password, as stored in the /etc/shadow file. While some of the parameters can also be set with the **useradd** and **usermod** commands, most of the switches are different, as described in Table 8-8.

TABLE 8-8	chage Command Options

Option	Purpose
-d YYYY-MM-DD	Sets the last change date for a password; output shown in /etc/shadow as the number of days after January 1, 1970.
-E YYYY-MM-DD	Assigns the expiration date for an account; output shown in /etc/shadow as the number of days after January 1, 1970.
-I *num*	Locks an account *num* days after a password has expired; can be set to -1 to make the account permanent.
-l	Lists all aging information.
-m *num*	Sets a minimum number of days that a user must keep a password.
-M *num*	Sets a maximum number of days that a user is allowed to keep a password; can be set to -1 to remove that limit.
-W *num*	Specifies when a user is warned to change her password, in number of days before the password expiration date.

CERTIFICATION OBJECTIVE 8.02

Administrative Control

It's important for administrators to execute most actions as regular users because the root administrative user has full privileges on a system. Limits on regular users can help protect Linux systems from accidents. Regular users who have the root administrative password can temporarily take root privileges with the **su** command. The **su** command can do more with other accounts. In contrast, the **sg** command is associated with privileges on special groups.

Although the **su** command is adequate for small networks, no administrator should work alone. With the help of the **sudo** command configured in the /etc/sudoers file, it's possible to set up dedicated administrators with partial or complete root administrative privileges, or to execute a command as another user.

The Ability to Log In as root

It's possible to keep users from logging in directly as the root administrative user. Local access is regulated in the /etc/securetty file. By default, it contains access directives for 11 virtual consoles. Although only six virtual consoles are enabled in the /etc/systemd/logind.conf file discussed in Chapter 5, it is possible to configure 12 (based on the number of function keys on a keyboard).

The virtual consoles listed in /etc/securetty determine the consoles where the root administrative user is allowed to log in. If the directives in this file were commented out, administrators would not be able to log in directly to the root account. They'd have to log in to a regular account and use either the **su** or **sudo** command for administration.

Although it's still possible to log in remotely as the root administrative user with the **ssh** command, that ability can also be regulated. The configuration of the SSH server in this manner is an RHCE skill described in Chapter 11.

EXERCISE 8-3

Limit root Logins

In this exercise, you'll examine the effect of eliminating the consoles in the /etc/securetty file. But first, you'll confirm that the root administrative user can log in to the standard consoles on virtual terminals 1 through 6. This exercise assumes that a regular account is available on the local system.

1. Move to the second virtual console. Press CTRL-ALT-F2; alternatively, in a KVM VM, click Send Key | CTRL-ALT-F2. At the *login:* prompt that appears, log in as the root user.

2. Repeat the process with the first, third, fourth, fifth, and sixth virtual consoles. Unless /etc/securetty has already been changed, you should be able to log in as the root user in all of these consoles.

3. Back up the current /etc/securetty file.

4. Open the /etc/securetty file in a text editor. Comment out all of the directives and then save the file.

5. Log out of the console. Try logging back in as the root administrative user. What happens? Repeat the process in other virtual consoles. What happens?

6. Log in to a console as a regular user. Does it work? Run the **su -** command to assume root privileges. Restore the original /etc/securetty file.

7. If a regular user account doesn't exist on the system, you'll have to reboot the system in the rescue target, as discussed in Chapter 5. You'll then be able to restore the /etc/securetty file from the prompt that appears.

The Ability to Log In

Beyond the /etc/securetty file is /etc/security/access.conf, which regulates access by all users. While the default version of this file is completely commented out, the comments provide useful examples. The first example would disallow (with the -) logins to the first virtual console (tty1) to *all* users but root:

```
-:ALL EXCEPT root:tty1
```

Jump ahead in the file. The following line is a slightly more complex example that would disallow access to all users, except users who are members of the wheel group, along with the shutdown and sync users, on *local* (non-networked) logins:

```
-:ALL EXCEPT (wheel) shutdown sync:LOCAL
```

Scroll down further in the file. The following lines (with the +) allow the root user to access the system from three specific remote IP addresses, along with the localhost address:

```
+ : root : 192.168.200.1 192.168.200.4 192.168.200.9
+ : root : 127.0.0.1
```

If you're protecting a system from outside networks, this type of limitation on direct root administrative access makes sense. As long as the **su** or **sudo** command allows it, users who log in remotely as regular users can still elevate their privileges accordingly.

Be aware, the directives in this file are considered in order. So if directives that allow access (with the +) come first, then the following directive denies access to all other users from all other local and remote logins:

```
- : ALL : ALL
```

The Proper Use of the su Command

In some cases, such as Red Hat exams, it's appropriate to log in as the root administrative user. But in real production systems, it's best to log in as a regular user. As a regular user, you can temporarily open a shell with root administrative privileges with the **su** command. Normally, that command prompts for the password of the root administrative user. After you've completed administrative tasks, it's best to log out of the root administrative account; the **exit** command would return to the regular account of that user.

The **su -** command is slightly different because it opens a login shell for the root administrative account. If the password is accepted, it navigates to the root user's home directory, /root, and sets an environment as if the root user had logged in directly.

If you have the password of a second user, you can use the **su -** *username* command to log in directly to that account. For example, if you wanted to log in to user dickens' account, you'd run the **su - dickens** command. When you enter her password successfully, the command takes you to the /home/dickens directory.

Finally, the **su -c** command can be used to assume administrative privileges for one command. For example, the following command can be used to modify the first virtual drive on a system (assuming the root administrative password is successfully entered in response to the prompt):

```
$ su -c '/sbin/fdisk /dev/vda'
```

Limit Access to su

As discussed earlier, the ability to log in directly as the root administrative user can be regulated. Further limitations on administrative access are possible. For example, you can limit the users who are allowed to run the **su** command. This requires two basic steps.

First, you'll need to list the users who should have access to the **su** command. Make them a part of the wheel group. By default, here is what this line in /etc/group looks like:

```
wheel:x:10:
```

You can add selected users to the end of this line directly with the **usermod -G wheel** *username* command or with the User Manager.

Second, this requires a change to the configuration of Pluggable Authentication Modules (PAM). While PAM, as described in Chapter 10, is an RHCE objective, there's a commented directive available in the /etc/pam.d/su file ready for this purpose:

```
# auth   required pam_wheel.so use_uid
```

If this line is activated, only users who are members of the wheel group are allowed to use the **su** command.

The Proper Use of the sg Command

With the **sg** command, you can execute another command with the rights associated with a special group. This assumes you're a member of the group or you've set up a group password for the project group with the **gpasswd project** command. Then the command **sg project -c** *command* allows you access to files and directories owned by the group named project. For example, if the /home/secret directory is owned by the project group, the following command copies the important.doc file to the noted directory:

```
$ sg project -c 'cp important.doc /home/project'
```

Custom Administrators with the sudo Command

You can limit access to the **sudo** command. Regular users who are authorized in /etc/sudoers can access administrative commands with their own password. You don't need to give out the administrative password to everyone who thinks they know as much as a Red Hat–certified professional.

To access /etc/sudoers with the editor specified in the /etc/environment file, run the **visudo** command. The **visudo** command locks the /etc/sudoers file against simultaneous edits and checks the syntax of the file before exiting. The following directive is active in the default version of the file. This allows the root user full access to administrative commands:

```
root     ALL=(ALL) ALL
```

Other users can be given administrative access. For example, if you want to allow user boris full administrative access, add the following directive to /etc/sudoers:

```
boris    ALL=(ALL) ALL
```

In this case, all boris needs to do to run an administrative command is to preface it with the **sudo** command. For example, if boris runs the following command, he's prompted for his own regular user password before the noted service is started:

```
$ sudo systemctl start vsftpd
Password:
```

Alternatively, you can allow special users administrative access without a password. As suggested by the comments, the following directive in /etc/sudoers would allow all users who are members of the wheel group to run administrative commands without a password:

```
%wheel   ALL=(ALL)   NOPASSWD: ALL
```

But you don't have to allow full administrative access. For example, if you want to allow users who are members of the %users group to shut down the local system, activate the following directive:

```
%users   localhost=/sbin/shutdown -h now
```

In many Linux configuration files, the % sign in front of a directive specifies a group. Even though the users group has a GID of 100, it's acceptable to make regular users members of that group. For example, another directive shown in comments specifies a group of commands that can be run by users who are members of the %sys group:

```
%sys ALL = NETWORKING, SOFTWARE, SERVICES, STORAGE, DELEGATING, ↵
PROCESSES, LOCATE, DRIVERS
```

Each of the directives can be associated with a set of commands. For example, users in the sys group, who are allowed to run PROCESSES directives, can run the commands associated with the following configuration line:

```
Cmnd_Alias PROCESSES = /bin/nice, /bin/kill, /usr/bin/kill, ↵
/usr/bin/killall
```

In a similar fashion, you could set up an admin group of users who are allowed to run these commands with the following directive:

```
%admin ALL = PROCESSES
```

This assumes that groups such as admin exist in the /etc/group and /etc/gshadow files.

Other Administrative Users

Various services may be configured with their own groups of administrative users. For example, examine the following directive from the /etc/cups/cups-files.conf file:

```
SystemGroup sys root
```

Members of groups listed with the **SystemGroup** get administrative privileges on the RHEL 7 print server.

 CUPS is no longer an acronym, to avoid concerns with the word "UNIX" as a trademark. CUPS is still the name of the default Linux print server, however.

CERTIFICATION OBJECTIVE 8.03

User and Shell Configuration

Each user on any Red Hat Enterprise Linux system has an *environment* when logged on to the system. The environment defines directories where Linux looks for programs to run, the look of the login prompt, the terminal type, and more. This section explains how you can configure the default environment for local users. All system-wide shell configuration files are kept in the /etc directory. These files are bashrc, profile, and the scripts in the /etc/profile.d directory. These files and scripts are supplemented by hidden files in each user's home directory, as just described. Let's take a look at these files.

Home Directories and /etc/skel

When a new user is created with standard commands such as **useradd** or utilities such as the User Manager, a default set of configuration files is copied to the user's home directory from the /etc/skel directory.

Home Directory

The home directory is where a user starts when logging in to a RHEL system. The home directory for most users is /home/*username,* where *username* is the user's login name. Every user should normally have write permission in his own home directory, so each user is free to read and write his own files.

/etc/skel

The /etc/skel directory contains default environment files for new accounts. The **useradd** command and the Red Hat User Manager copies these files to the home directory for new users. The contents of /etc/skel may vary. While the standard files in this directory are hidden, administrators are free to add more files for new users. Standard files from one copy of /etc/skel are described in Table 8-9.

e x a m

w a t c h   **Linux includes many hidden files that start with a dot (.). To list these files, run the** ls -a **command. For example, if you want to list all the files in the /etc/skel directory, run the** ls -a /etc/skel **command.**

| | |

TABLE 8-9   Standard Files in the /etc/skel Directory

File	Purpose
.bashrc	This basic bash configuration file may include a reference to the general /etc/bashrc configuration file. It can include commands to run when the bash shell is started. One example is an alias such as **rm='rm -i'**.
.bash_logout	This file is executed when you exit a bash shell, and it can include commands appropriate for this purpose, such as commands for clearing a screen.
.bash_profile	This file is sourced only when invoking a bash login shell, and it configures the bash startup environment. This is the appropriate place to add environment variables or modify the directories in your user account PATH.
.kde/	Specifies settings for the K Desktop Environment. It is not added to /etc/skel and not copied to user home directories if KDE is not installed.
.mozilla/	Includes options associated with the Firefox web browser, developed by the Mozilla project.

If you've installed more than a standard set of software packages on RHEL, additional configuration files and subdirectories may appear in the /etc/skel directory. For example, the installation of certain packages may include configuration files associated with emacs and the Z shell (zsh) in this directory.

As the system administrator, you can edit these files or place custom files in /etc/skel. When new users are created, these files are propagated to the new users' home directories.

/etc/bashrc

The /etc/bashrc file is used for aliases and functions on a system-wide basis. Open this file in the text editor of your choice. Read each line in this file. Even if you don't understand the programming commands, you can see that this file sets the following bash shell parameters for each user:

- It assigns a value of **umask**, which creates the default permissions for newly created files. It supports one set of permissions for root and system users (with user IDs below 200) and another for regular users. (Officially, RHEL reserves all user IDs above 1000 for regular users; however, that is not reflected in /etc/bashrc.)
- It assigns and defines a prompt, which is what you see just before the cursor at the command prompt.
- It includes settings from *.sh files in the /etc/profile.d/ directory.

The settings here are supplemented by the .bashrc file in each user's home directory and, for login shells, by the /etc/profile, .bash_profile, and .bash_logout files.

/etc/profile and /etc/profile.d

The /etc/profile file is used for system-wide environments and startup files, and is sourced when bash is invoked as a login shell.

The first part of the file sets the PATH for searching for commands. Additional directories are added to the PATH with the **pathmunge** command. (Unless you use the Korn shell, ignore the "ksh workaround" stanza.) Then it exports the PATH, USER, LOGNAME, MAIL, HOSTNAME, HISTSIZE, and HISTCONTROL variables and finally sets the umask and runs the scripts in the /etc/profile.d directory. You can check the current value of any of these variables with the **echo $*variable*** command.

/etc/profile.d

The /etc/profile.d directory is designed to contain scripts to be executed in a login or interactive shell (that is, not in a script or a command that is run as **bash -c *command***). If you performed a "Server with GUI" installation, the following is a partial listing of the files; those with .sh extensions apply to the default bash shell:

```
256term.csh                  colorls.csh   PackageKit.sh
256term.sh                   colorls.sh    vim.csh
abrt-cosole-notifiction.sh   lang.csh      vim.sh
bash_completion.sh           lang.sh       vte.sh
colorgrep.csh                less.csh      which2.csh
colorgrep.sh                 less.sh       which2.sh
```

In most cases, there are two versions of a script, customized for different shell environments. Look at the files in the /etc/profile.d script directory. You can see that any script in this directory that ends with .sh is included as part of the configuration with /etc/profile. Scripts with other extensions, such as .csh, relate to the C shell.

EXERCISE 8-4

Another Way to Secure a System

One more way to help secure a system is to change the default permissions for new files and directories. In this exercise, you'll reconfigure a system to remove access permissions for default files from other users or groups.

1. Back up the current version of the /etc/bashrc and /etc/profile files.
2. Open the /etc/bashrc file in a text editor. Two lines in the file set the umask. One of the two lines is selected, depending on the **if** statement above them. See if you can determine which value of umask is assigned to an average (non-root) user.
3. The **if** statement tests to see whether the username and group name are the same, and that the UID is greater than 199. In other words, the umask value of 002 is given to regular users. A umask value of 022 is given to system users.
4. Change the first **umask** statement to exclude all permissions for groups and others. In other words, replace the umask of 002 with a umask of 077.
5. Save and exit the file.
6. Repeat steps 2 to 5 for /etc/profile.
7. Log in as a regular, non-privileged user. Use the **touch** command to make a new empty file. Use **ls -l** to verify the permissions on that file.

8. Log in as root. Again, use the **touch** command to make a new empty file and use **ls -l** to verify the permissions on that new file.

You have just changed the default umask for all regular users. While this is an excellent option for security, it would affect the steps used in other chapters. Therefore, the final step is important.

9. Restore the original versions of /etc/bashrc and /etc/profile from the backup created in Step 1.

Shell Configuration Files in User Home Directories

As described earlier, each user gets a copy of all files from the /etc/skel directory, typically when the account is created. Most of them are hidden, revealed only with commands such as **ls -a**. As users start working with their accounts, more configuration files may be added to their home directories. Some users may work primarily with the default bash shell, whereas others will have additional configuration files related to their GUI desktop environments, such as GNOME.

The default Linux shell is bash, and until recently it was specifically included as the only shell described in associated Red Hat exam objectives. Although bash is no longer specifically included in the objectives, it is the default for RHEL 7.

Login, Logout, and User Switching

While this may seem like a "no-brainer" topic for Linux users with even a couple of days of experience, one of the RHCSA topics is "Log in and switch users in multi-user targets." It includes concepts from different chapters. As discussed in Chapter 5, the multi-user targets are multi-user.target and graphical.target. Virtual terminals are available at all of these targets. For the first RHEL 7 release, a text login prompt appears as follows:

```
Red Hat Enterprise Linux Server 7.0 (Maipo)
Kernel 3.10.0-123.el7.x86_64 on an x86_64

server1 login:
```

The hostname, as well as the versions of RHEL 7 and the kernel, will vary. But that's irrelevant to actual logins; all you need to do is type in a username, press ENTER, and type in a password when prompted.

Logouts from the command line are even simpler; the **exit**, **logout**, and CTRL-D commands all perform logouts from the command line. Of course, once you've logged out from a system, the login prompt just shown will appear.

As discussed earlier in this chapter, there's a different way to switch user accounts. For example, to switch from the current account to user donna's account, run the following command:

```
$ su - donna
```

The same **exit**, **logout**, and CTRL-D commands can be used to exit from user donna's account.

Of course, users can log in to and log out of the GUI. Although the steps vary a bit by desktop environment, they are as simple as the steps required to log in to and log out of any other operating system.

CERTIFICATION OBJECTIVE 8.04

Users and Network Authentication

By default, access to a Linux computer requires a valid username and password. One problem with a large network of Linux systems is that without some central database, each user would require an account on every Linux computer.

e x a m

w a t c h In the RHCSA exam objectives for RHEL 6, the only network authentication requirement was to be able to connect a client to an LDAP server. The corresponding objective for RHEL 7 is more generic and requires you to "configure a system to use an existing authentication service for user and group information." This may not include just LDAP, but also other services, such as Kerberos, Active Directory, and IPA. The authconfig **tool supports all of them and allows you to configure a client in a few easy steps.**

Several services are available that can be used as a central authentication database. One legacy option for Linux systems is the Network Information Service (NIS). In contrast, the Lightweight Directory Access Protocol (LDAP) offers more security and is now a de facto standard. Other services are available, such as Winbind, which can be configured to support access by Linux systems and users to networks governed by Microsoft Active Directory. Another option is IPA (and its free version FreeIPA), which is an Identity, Policy, and Auditing server that includes a certification authority, along with LDAP and Kerberos

TABLE 8-10 Common Network Authentication Services

Service	User and Group Information	Authentication
Local files	Retrieved from /etc/passwd and /etc/group	Hashed passwords in /etc/shadow
Network Information System (NIS) Server	Centralized /etc/passwd and /etc/group	Centralized /etc/shadow
Network Information System (NIS) Server with MIT Kerberos KDC	Centralized /etc/passwd and /etc/group	Kerberos
OpenLDAP, 389 Directory Server	LDAP/LDAPS protocol	LDAP/LDAPS protocol
OpenLDAP or 389 Directory Server with MIT Kerberos KDC	LDAP/LDAPS protocol	Kerberos
IPA, FreeIPA	LDAP/LDAPS against a 389 Directory Server	Kerberos
Microsoft Active Directory	LDAP/LDAPS protocol	Kerberos

services. In any of these cases, one database of passwords and usernames exists for a network.

Table 8-10 illustrates some of the common options available for centralized authentication as well as the protocols and resources that each solution relies on to retrieve user information and perform authentication.

As you can see from Table 8-10, different solutions can be used for user account information and authentication. As an example, you can use an LDAP server as a database for user and group information, while authentication can be provided by a Kerberos Key Distribution Center (KDC).

The focus of the next section is LDAP as a client. You'll configure a RHEL 7 system as an LDAP client, set up authentication in the name service switch file, and repeat the process with Red Hat network authentication tools. First, we'll show you how you can configure LDAP clients using the command-line interface and then use the Red Hat Authentication Configuration tool to repeat the process. This way, you'll know two methods for configuring LDAP clients.

In contrast to NIS, LDAP services can be configured on a variety of platforms. Of course, LDAP servers can be configured on RHEL 7, but they are not part of the current RHCSA or RHCE exam objectives. LDAP is also used by IPA and Microsoft-based Active Directory (AD) services.

on the job

LDAP directory services and authentication was one focus of the retired Red Hat's RH423 course, whereas the new RH413 course covers identity management with IPA. If you want to set up a centralized LDAP authentication server, explore the 389 Directory Server at http://directory.fedoraproject.org.

LDAP Client Configuration

To configure a RHEL computer as an LDAP client, you'll need the openldap-clients, openldap, and nss-pam-ldapd RPM packages. The openldap-clients and nss-pam-ldapd RPMs are both optional parts of the Directory Client package group. The openldap package should be installed by default on RHEL 7 systems that have the "Server with GUI" environment group selected at installation, as suggested in an earlier lab in this book.

To configure an LDAP client, you'll need to configure various LDAP configuration files—namely, /etc/nslcd.conf and /etc/openldap/ldap.conf. While the files can seem complex, you don't have to reconfigure a lot just to set up an LDAP client.

/etc/nslcd.conf

The default version of the /etc/nslcd.conf file includes a number of different commands and comments. Standard changes required to set up a basic LDAP client are based on several directives shown in Table 8-11. Encryption-related directives in this file may be

TABLE 8-11   Client Configuration Parameters in /etc/nslcd.conf

Directive	Description
uri	Configures the URI for the LDAP server, in the format ldap:// *hostname*. The URI scheme ldap:// specifies the use of the LDAP protocol in clear text (on TCP port 389), whereas ldaps:// is for LDAP over SSL (on TCP port 636).
base dc=example,dc=com	Sets the default **base** distinguished name to be used for LDAP searches to retrieve user and group objects (in this case, dc=example,dc=com).
ssl start_tls	Required if StartTLS is used to negotiate an encrypted communication over TCP port 389. As an alternative, encrypted communications can also be provided by turning off StartTLS (**ssl off**) and using LDAP over SSL via the ldaps:// URI scheme.
tls_cacertdir /etc/openldap/cacerts	Specifies the directory where the certificate of the Certification Authority (CA) is stored. This is required when using SSL or TLS for encryption.
nss_initgroups_ignoreusers root	Prevents group lookups for the specified users in the LDAP server.

associated with both the Secure Sockets Layer (SSL) and its successor, Transport Layer Security (TLS).

The nslcd.conf file applies Pluggable Authentication Modules to LDAP authentication. It is almost identical to the /etc/pam_ldap.conf file from RHEL 6; the differences do not affect the successful configuration of an LDAP client.

Related directives are included at the end of the file; they may include the following. First, the Uniform Resource Identifier, as specified by the **uri**, should redirect the client to the actual IP address of the LDAP server:

```
uri ldap://127.0.0.1/
```

If you want to enable secure communication via LDAP over SSL, you may change **ldap** to **ldaps**; when you configure the LDAP server, those protocols default to TCP/IP ports 389 and 636, respectively. An LDAP server won't work if a firewall blocks these ports. If LDAP over SSL is used, you must either specify the URI using the ldaps:// scheme or change the following to **ssl yes**:

```
ssl no
```

An alternative method to get encrypted communications to an LDAP server is to use StartTLS, which negotiates secure communications over TCP port 389. In this case, you would set **ssl start_tls** and type the URI using the ldap:// scheme.

Of course, to enable secure connections, LDAP needs access to appropriate certificates. While TLS is the successor to SSL, it's commonly used in concert with SSL directives. The following directive specifies the directory with those certificates:

```
tls_cacertdir /etc/openldap/cacerts
```

Finally, the nslcd service must be started and enabled at boot:

```
systemctl enable nslcd
systemctl start nscld
```

/etc/openldap/ldap.conf

You'll need to specify the **URI**, **BASE**, and **TLS_CACERTDIR** variables in this file, just as was done in the /etc/nslcd.conf configuration file. Given the parameters in the preceding section, you may even see a fourth directive in that file:

```
URI ldap://127.0.0.1
SASL_NOCANON    on
BASE dc=example,dc=com
TLS_CACERTDIR /etc/openldap/cacerts
```

If the LDAP server is not on the local system and the base distinguished name is not dc=example,dc=com, substitute accordingly. Individual users can supersede this file in a hidden .ldaprc file in their home directories.

The Name Service Switch File

The Name Service Switch (NSS) file, /etc/nsswitch.conf, governs how a computer searches for key files such as password databases. It can be configured to look through LDAP and other server databases. For example, when a client looks for a computer hostname, it might start with the following entry from /etc/nsswitch.conf:

```
hosts: files ldap dns
```

This line tells your computer to search through name databases in the following order:

1. Start with the database of hostnames and IP addresses in the local file /etc/hosts.
2. Search for the hostname by querying an LDAP server.
3. If none of these databases includes the desired hostname, refer to the DNS server.

You can configure the /etc/nsswitch.conf configuration file to look at an LDAP server for the desired databases. For example, to set up a centralized username and password database for your network, you'll need to configure at least the following commands in /etc/nsswitch.conf:

```
passwd:    files ldap
shadow:    files ldap
group:     files ldap
```

Other authentication databases can be configured; NIS is associated with the **nis** directive; Microsoft authentication can be configured either via LDAP-based AD services or by joining the Linux host to the AD domain with **winbind**. Another important client authentication service is **sssd**, which is the topic of the next section.

The System Security Service Daemon

The System Security Services Daemon (SSSD) provides caching and offline authentication services to allow users to authenticate even when a remote LDAP server is unavailable. SSSD can be used as a replacement for the nss-pam-ldapd daemon. It comes with several related RPM packages, such as sssd-ad, which SSSD can use to fetch identity data from an Active Directory server. You can install these packages, with dependencies, by installing the meta sssd RPM package:

```
yum -y install sssd
```

In a similar way to nss-pam-ldapd, SSSD provides an interface to NSS and PAM. However, SSSD is much more powerful and can also authenticate users with Kerberos, Active Directory, and IPA.

You can find the SSSD configuration file in /etc/sssd/sssd.conf. If the file is not present in your system, **authconfig** (the Red Hat Authentication Configuration tool, covered in the next section) can generate the file for you. A sample configuration for an LDAP client is shown here:

```
id_provider = ldap
auth_provider = ldap
chpass_provider = ldap
ldap_uri = ldap://127.0.0.1
ldap_id_use_start_tls = True
ldap_tls_cacertdir = /etc/openldap/cacerts
[sssd]
services = nss, pam
config_file_version = 1
domains = default
```

The first three lines tell SSSD to use LDAP for user information, authentication, and change-password operations. Then, an LDAP URI is specified, similar to the **uri** directive in /etc/nslcd.conf. The next two configuration options enable the use of TLS for encryption and the directory where the CA certificate is stored. Then, SSSD is instructed to work along with NSS and PAM. Finally, at least a default SSSD domain must be configured. A domain name is used to identify different user database information in such cases where more than an authentication method is available on the network.

When SSSD is used to retrieve remote user and authentication information, the entries in /etc/nsswitch.conf should look similar to the lines shown here:

```
passwd:     files sss
shadow:     files sss
group:      files sss
```

Whereas the **ldap** directive in /etc/nsswitch.conf tells the system to use the **nslcd** daemon to look up user information, the **sss** keyword uses SSSD instead. Of course, the SSSD daemon must be started and enabled at boot:

```
# systemctl enable sssd
# systemctl start sssd
```

Red Hat Network Authentication Tools

As you have seen in the previous sections, the configuration of an LDAP client requires you to edit several files. As such, the configuration process can be very error prone if you are not very familiar with all the configuration options. It is certainly easier to configure a client

FIGURE 8-4

Authentication
Configuration
options

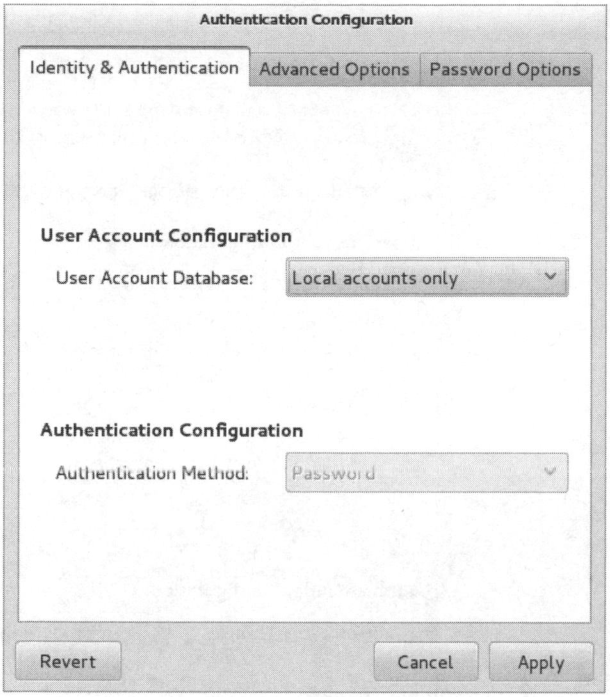

with the Red Hat Authentication Configuration tool. In RHEL 7, you can open it in the GUI
with the **system-config-authentication** command or with **authconfig-gtk**. There is also
a console version that can be started with the **authconfig-tui** command or the CLI tool
authconfig. Both the GUI and TUI tools are provided by the authconfig-gtk RPM package.
The GUI version is shown in Figure 8-4.

LDAP Client

The Authentication Configuration tool has changed. By default, it's set to look at only the
local authentication database, but if you click the drop-down text box, it presents five other
options. LDAP is one of the most common protocols for authentication services and user
information, but you should also become familiar with the settings of the other options.
When LDAP is selected, the window changes, as shown in Figure 8-5. It defaults to the
Kerberos Password Authentication Method.

FIGURE 8-5

LDAP
Authentication
Configuration
options

Note the warning in Figure 8-5. This tells us that in order to use Kerberos as a password authentication method, we need to install the pam_krb5 LDAP package. If a Kerberos server is not available for authentication, click the Authentication Method text box and select LDAP Password. The window changes again and should provide the following warning:

```
You must provide ldaps:// server address or use TLS for LDAP authentication.
```

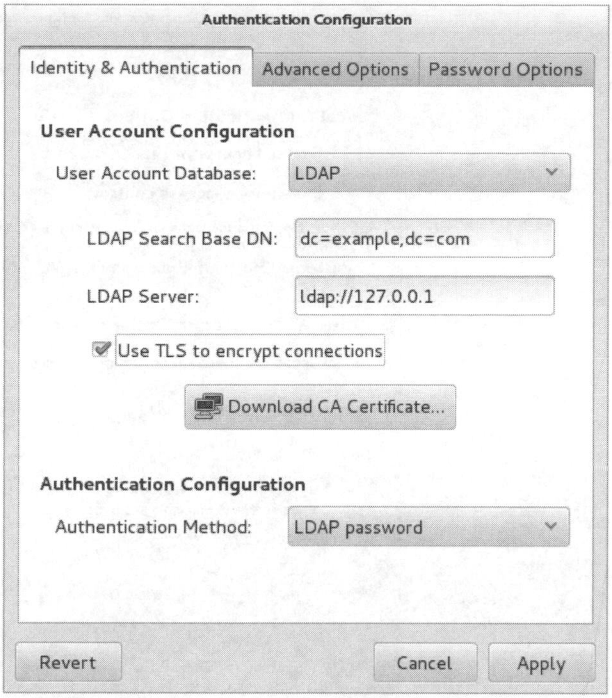

FIGURE 8-6

LDAP
authentication
with TLS
encryption

If you use LDAPS or StartTLS to encrypt traffic, the warning will disappear. In that case, what you see should resemble Figure 8-6.

The remaining options may vary:

1. The LDAP Search Base DN text box usually includes the domain name for the LDAP server and one or more Organizational Units (ou). For example, if the local system domain is example.com and the users are located under ou=People, the text box may contain the following:

   ```
   ou=People,dc=example,dc=com
   ```

2. The LDAP server text box should include the URI of that server. If your LDAP server is on the local computer, you can use the 127.0.0.1 IP address. But that's unlikely in production situations, which means that it is also unlikely during an exam. For standard LDAP communications, preface the URI with ldap://. For SSL-based LDAP communications, preface the URI with ldaps://. Alternatively, if you use StartTLS, preface the URI with ldap:// and select the Use TLS to Encrypt Connections check box.

3. If you configure secure LDAP, you need to include a Certification Authority (CA) certificate. Click Download CA Certificate. It opens a window where you can specify the URL with the CA certificate.

FIGURE 8-7

Advanced Options
tab

4. Now select the Advanced Options tab, shown in Figure 8-7. It's not related to the configuration of an LDAP client. In some configurations, you may want to select Create Home Directories on the First Login. That option enables the pam_mkhome-dir PAM module to automatically create a user's home directory at first logon, if it does not yet exist.

Once you've made desired changes, click OK; it may take a few seconds for the Authentication Configuration tool to write the changes to the noted configuration files.

IPA Client

IPA (and its free version FreeIPA) is an identity management suite that includes an LDAP 389 Directory Server, a MIT Kerberos KDC, a Dogtag certification authority, an NTP service, and an optional DNS service. While the configuration of an IPA server is outside the scope of this book and of the RHCSA exam, it is relatively easy to set up an IPA client.

First, install the ipa-client RPM package. This will also install needed dependent packages, such as krb5-workstation and sssd:

```
# yum install ipa-client
```

FIGURE 8-8

IPA Authentication
Configuration
options

Next, launch **authconfig-gtk**, which is shown in Figure 8-8.
The configuration options are straightforward:

- The domain is a DNS domain. As an IPA client, this should correspond to the
  domain for IPA Identity Management services. For example, if the client is
  server1.example.com, the corresponding domain would be example.com.
- The realm is a Kerberos realm, and usually is specified as a domain in capital letters,
  such as EXAMPLE.COM.
- The server text box should include the IP address or FQDN of the server.

Once all the settings have been entered, click Join Domain. You will be prompted for the
username and password of an IPA server account with privileges to add new clients to
the system.

on the **job**

**If you want to configure an IPA server, refer to the FreeIPA project at
www.freeipa.org.**

CERTIFICATION OBJECTIVE 8.05

Special Groups

In the past, Linux groups of regular users allowed their members to share files. Red Hat has helped change this with the way it assigns unique UID and GID numbers to each user. When regular users are all made members of the same primary group, that also means everyone in that group has access to the home directories of all other group members—and that's often not desirable. Users may not want to share the files in their home directories with others.

On the other hand, RHEL gives each user a unique user ID and group ID in /etc/passwd. This is known as the *user private group* scheme. Users get exclusive access to their own primary groups and don't have to worry about other users reading the files in their home directories.

Standard and Red Hat Groups

In RHEL, each user gets her own special private group by default. As noted earlier, UIDs and GIDs normally start at 1000, are assigned matching numbers, and proceed in ascending order. In addition, you can set up special groups of dedicated users, ideally with higher GIDs. For example, an administrator might configure accgrp for the accounting department, perhaps with a GID of 70000.

Shared Directories

Most people work in groups, and they may want to share files. However, there may be good reasons for people in those groups to keep their information hidden from others. To support such groups, you can set up a shared directory, with access limited to the members of the group.

Assume you want to set up a shared directory, /home/accshared, for a group of accountants. To that end, you can set up a shared directory with the following basic steps:

1. Create the shared directory:

   ```
   # mkdir /home/accshared
   ```

2. Create a group for the accountants. Call it accgrp. Give it a group ID that doesn't interfere with existing group or user IDs. One way to do this is to add a line such as the following to the /etc/group file or with the User Manager. Substitute the desired usernames.

   ```
   accgrp:x:70000:robertc,alanm,victorb,roberta,alano,charliew
   ```

3. Set up appropriate ownership for the new shared directory. The following commands prevent any specific user from taking control of the directory and assign group ownership to accgrp:

```
# chown nobody.accgrp /home/accshared
# chmod 2770 /home/accshared
```

Any user who is a member of the accgrp group can now create files in and copy files to the /home/accshared directory. Any files generated within or copied to that directory will be owned by the accgrp group.

This is made possible by the 2770 permissions assigned to the /home/accshared directory. Let's break that down into its component parts. The first digit (2) is the *set group ID bit*, also known as the *SGID bit*. When an SGID bit is set on a directory, any files created in that directory automatically have their group ownership set to be the same as the group owner of the directory. In addition, group ownership of files copied from other directories is reassigned (in this case, to the group named accgrp). There is a second way to set the SGID bit for the /home/accshared directory:

```
chmod g+s /home/accshared
```

The remaining digits are basic knowledge for any experienced Linux or Unix user. The **770** sets read, write, and execute permissions for the user and group that own the directory. Other users get no permissions to that directory. However, because the user owner of the directory is the non-privileged user named nobody, the group owner of the directory is most important. In this case, members of the accgrp group have read, write, and execute permissions to files created in this directory.

EXERCISE 8-5

Control Group Ownership with the SGID Bit

In this exercise, you will create new files in a directory designed to be shared by a group of users. You'll also see the difference in what happens before and after the SGID bit is set.

1. Add users called test1, test2, and test3. Specify passwords when prompted. Check the /etc/passwd and /etc/group files to verify that each user's private group was created:

```
# useradd test1; echo changeme | passwd --stdin test1
# useradd test2; echo changeme | passwd --stdin test2
# useradd test3; echo changeme | passwd --stdin test3
```

2. Edit the /etc/group file and add a group called tg1. Make the test1 and test2 accounts members of this group. You could add the following line to /etc/group directly or use the Red Hat User Manager:

```
tg1:x:99999:test1,test2
```

Before you proceed, make sure the group ID assigned to group tg1 (in this case, 99999) is not already in use. Make sure to add the following line to /etc/gshadow. A group password is not required.

```
tg1:!::test1,test2
```

3. Create a directory intended for use by the tg1 group:

```
# mkdir  /home/testshared
```

4. Change the user and group ownership of the shared directory:

```
# chown  nobody.tg1  /home/testshared
```

5. Log in as user test1. Make sure the login navigates to the /home/test1 directory. Run the **umask** command to confirm that files created from this account will have the appropriate permissions. (The output of the **umask** command for regular users such as test1 should be 0002.) If there's a problem with the home directory or the **umask** output, you may have made an error earlier in this chapter with user settings. If so, repeat Steps 1–5 on a different VM.

6. Run the **cd /home/testshared** command. Now try to create a file with the following commands. What happens?

```
$ date >> test.txt
$ touch abcd
```

7. Now as the root user, set group write permissions on the testshared directory:

```
# chmod 770 /home/testshared
```

8. Log in again as user test1, navigate back to the /home/testshared directory, and then try to create a file in the new directory. So far, so good.

```
$ cd /home/testshared
$ date >> test.txt
$ ls -l test.txt
```

9. Remove all permissions for other users on new files in the /home/testshared directory:

```
# chmod o-rwx /home/testshared/*
```

10. Now with the following command, check the ownership on the new file. Do you think other users in the tg1 group can access this file? If in doubt, log in as user test2 and see for yourself.

```
$ ls -l
```

11. From the root account, set the SGID bit on the directory:

```
# chmod g+s /home/testshared
```

(Yes, if you are efficiency minded, you may know that the **chmod 2770 /home/testshared** command combines the effect of this and the previous **chmod** commands.)

12. Switch back to the test1 account, navigate back to the /home/testshared directory, and create another file. Remove permissions for other users on the newly created file. Check the ownership on the newly created file. Do you think that user test2 can now access this file? (To see for yourself, try it from the test2 account.)

```
$ date >> testb.txt
$ chmod o-rwx /home/testshared/testb.txt
$ ls -l
```

13. Now log in as the test2 account. Go into the /home/testshared directory. Try accessing the testb.txt file. Create a different file and then use **ls -l** to check permissions and ownership again. (To see that it worked, try accessing this file from the test1 account.)

14. Switch to the test3 account and check whether that user can or cannot create files in this directory and whether that user can or cannot view the files in this directory.

CERTIFICATION SUMMARY

You can manage users and groups with the files of the shadow password suite. These files can be modified directly, with the help of commands such as **useradd** and **groupadd** or the User Manager tool. The way users are configured is based on the /etc/login.defs file. Any variables or system-wide settings are defined in /etc/bashrc or /etc/profile. They can be modified by files in user home directories.

There are several ways to limit the use of administrative privileges. The ability to log in can be regulated in files such as /etc/securetty and /etc/security/access.conf. Access to the **su** command can be limited with the help of PAM. Partial and complete administrative privileges can be configured for the **sudo** command in the /etc/sudoers file.

You can use centralized network account management with the LDAP service. RHEL 7 systems can be configured as an LDAP client with the help of the /etc/nslcd.conf, /etc/openldap/ldap.conf, and /etc/nsswitch.conf files.

By default, Red Hat Enterprise Linux assigns unique user and group ID numbers to each new user. This is known as the user private group scheme. This scheme supports the configuration of special groups for a specific set of users. The users in the group can be configured with read and write privileges in a dedicated directory, courtesy of the SGID bit.

✓ # TWO-MINUTE DRILL

Here are some of the key points from the certification objectives in Chapter 8.

User Account Management

❑ After installation, a system may have only a single login account: root. For everyday operation, it's best to create one or more regular accounts.

❑ The shadow password suite is configured in the /etc/passwd, /etc/shadow, /etc/group, and /etc/gshadow files.

❑ Administrators can add user and group accounts by directly editing the files of the shadow password suite, or with commands such as **useradd** and **groupadd**. The way accounts are added are defined by the /etc/login.defs file.

❑ Accounts can be added with the Red Hat User Manager tool. You can also use this tool or related commands such as **chage** and **usermod** to modify other account parameters.

Administrative Control

❑ Logins as the root user can be regulated by the /etc/securetty file.

❑ Logins in general can be regulated by the /etc/security/access.conf file.

❑ Access to the **su** command can be regulated through the /etc/pam.d/su file.

❑ Custom administrative privileges can be configured in the /etc/sudoers file.

User and Shell Configuration

❑ The home directory for new login accounts is populated from the /etc/skel directory.

❑ Each user has an environment when logged on to the system, based on /etc/bashrc, /etc/profile, and the scripts in /etc/profile.d/.

❑ All users have hidden shell configuration files in their home directories.

Users and Network Authentication

❑ LDAP allows you to configure one centrally managed username and password database with other Linux and Unix systems on a LAN.

❑ LDAP clients are configured in /etc/openldap/ldap.conf and either /etc/nslcd.conf (for the nslcd daemon) or /etc/sssd/sssd.conf (for SSSD).

❑ Changes are required to /etc/nsswitch.conf to make a system look for a remote authentication database such as LDAP.

❑ Red Hat includes **authconfig-gtk** and **authconfig-tui**, two GUI and console tools that can help you configure a system as an LDAP or IPA client.

Special Groups

❑ Red Hat's user private group scheme configures users with their own unique user and group ID numbers.

❑ With appropriate SGID permissions, you can configure a shared directory for a specific group of users.

❑ Setting the SGID bit is easy; use **chown** to set nobody as the user owner and the name of the group as the group owner. Then run the **chmod 2770** command on the shared directory.

SELF TEST

The following questions will help measure your understanding of the material presented in this chapter. As no multiple choice questions appear on the Red Hat exams, no multiple choice questions appear in this book. These questions exclusively test your understanding of the chapter. It is okay if you have another way of performing a task. Getting results, not memorizing trivia, is what counts on the Red Hat exams. There may be more than one answer to many of these questions.

User Account Management

1. What's the standard minimum user ID number for regular users on Red Hat distributions?

   _____

2. What command at a GUI-based text console starts the Red Hat User Manager?

   _____

Administrative Control

3. What file regulates the local consoles where the root user can log in?

_____

4. Which file controls the commands that a user can run with the privileges of root or of another user?

_____

5. When a regular user uses the **sudo** command to run an administrative command, what password is required?

_____

User and Shell Configuration

6. If you want to add files to every new user account, what directory should you use?

_____

7. What are the system-wide configuration files associated with the bash shell?

_____

Users and Network Authentication

8. If user objects are located in the Organizational Unit named "People," within another organizational Unit named "Global," which is part of the LDAP domain dc=example, dc=org, what is the LDAP Search Base DN?

_____

9. What's the full path to the file that refers to an LDAP database for authentication?

_____

Special Groups

10. What command would set the SGID bit on the /home/developer directory?

_____

11. What command would set up ownership of the developer group on the /home/developer directory?

_____

12. What command would add user alpha to the developer group? (This question assumes the alpha user and the developer group already exist and that alpha belongs to no group other than his own.)

_____

LAB QUESTIONS

Red Hat presents its exams electronically. For that reason, the labs in this chapter are available from the DVD that accompanies the book, in the Chapter8/ subdirectory. They're available in .doc, .html, and .txt formats, to reflect standard options associated with electronic delivery on a live RHEL 7 system. In case you haven't yet set up RHEL 7 on a system, refer to the first lab of Chapter 2 for installation instructions. The answers for these labs follow the Self Test answers for the fill-in-the-blank questions.

A SELF TEST ANSWERS

User Account Management

1. The minimum user ID number for regular users on Red Hat distributions is 1000.
2. The command in a GUI-based text console that starts the Red Hat User Manager is **authconfig-gtk** or **system-config-users**.

Administrative Control

3. The file that regulates the local consoles where the root user can log in is /etc/securetty.
4. The file that controls which commands a user can run with the privileges of root or of another user is /etc/sudoers.
5. When a regular user uses the **sudo** command to run an administrative command, the regular password of that user is required, unless the NOPASSWD directive was specified in /etc/sudoers.

User and Shell Configuration

6. To automatically add files to every new user account, you should use the /etc/skel directory.

7. The system-wide configuration files associated with the bash shell are /etc/bashrc, /etc/profile, and the scripts in /etc/profile.d/.

Users and Network Authentication

8. The LDAP Search Base DN is ou=People,ou=Global,dc=example,dc=org.

9. The full path to the file that points to an LDAP database for authentication is /etc/nsswitch.conf.

Special Groups

10. The command that would set the SGID bit on the /home/developer directory is **chmod g+s /home/developer**. Numeric options such as **chmod 2770 /home/developer** are not correct, as they go beyond just setting the SGID bit.

11. The command that sets up ownership of the developer group on the /home/developer directory is **chgrp developer /home/developer**.

12. The command that adds user alpha to the developer group is **usermod -aG developer alpha**.

LAB ANSWERS

Lab 1

While there are a number of methods available to create new users and groups, they should all come to the same result.

1. The output to the **ls -l /home** command should include the following output, substituting today's date:

```
drwx------.   4 newguy    newguy    4096 Jan 19 12:13 newguy
drwx------.   4 intern    intern    4096 Jan 19 12:13 intern
```

2. Run the **ls -la /etc/skel** command. The output should include a number of hidden files, owned by the user root and the group root.

3. Run the **ls -la /home/newguy** and **ls -la /home/intern** commands. The output should include the same hidden files as in /etc/skel, but owned by the users associated with each home directory.

4. The end of the /etc/passwd and /etc/shadow files should include entries for both users. If you've set up a password for these users, it should be in encrypted format in the second column of /etc/shadow.

5. The following entry should exist somewhere in the middle of the /etc/group file. It is acceptable if other users are included at the end of the line.

```
users:x:100:newguy
```

6. The following line should be near to or at the end of the /etc/group file; the order of the users in the fourth column does not matter.

```
peons:x:123456:newguy,intern
```

Lab 2

The simplest way to limit root logins to the sixth virtual console is in the /etc/securetty file. The only active directives in that file should be

```
vc/6
tty6
```

Of course, there are other ways to do just about anything in Linux. To try it out, press CTRL-ALT-F1 and try logging in as the root user. Press CTRL-ALT-F2, and repeat the process through virtual terminal 6.

Lab 3

Use the answer to the first part of Lab 1 as guidance to verify the ownership and permissions of the /home/senioradm directory, along with the files therein. With respect to **sudo** privileges, you should see the following line in the /etc/sudoers file:

```
senioradm    ALL=(ALL)        ALL
```

To test the result, log in as the senioradm user and run an administrative command, prefaced by a **sudo**. For example, try the following command:

```
# sudo firewall-config
```

Unless you've run the **sudo** command in the last few minutes, this action will prompt for a password. Enter the password created for user senioradm. It should open the Firewall Configuration tool.

Lab 4

Use the answer to Lab 1 as guidance to verify the ownership and permissions of the /home/junioradm directory, along with the files therein. With respect to **sudo** privileges, you should see the following line in the /etc/sudoers file:

```
junioradm    ALL=/usr/sbin/fdisk
```

Next, try running the **fdisk** command:

```
$ sudo /usr/sbin/fdisk -l
```

You'll be prompted for a password. Enter the password created for user junioradm. Unless the passwords are identical, the root password would not work. If successful, you should see a list of partitions for connected drives in the output.

Lab 5

Use the answer to Lab 1 as guidance to verify the ownership and permissions of the /home/infouser directory, along with the files therein. If you're successful, that directory will include an info-*/ subdirectory. In addition, the /etc/skel directory should include an info-*/ subdirectory. That subdirectory should have the same files as those shown in the /usr/share/doc/info-* directory. Of course, that works only if you copy the contents of the info-*/ subdirectory from the /usr/share/doc directory to /etc/skel.

Lab 6

This is a straightforward process, using the following basic steps:

1. Create accounts for mike, rick, terri, and maryam if required. You can use the **useradd** command, edit the /etc/passwd file directly, or work through the User Manager.

2. Set up a group for these users. Configure a group ID outside the range of regular users in /etc/group with a line such as this:

   ```
   galley:x:88888:mike,rick,terri,maryam
   ```

3. Create the /home/galley directory. Give it proper ownership and permissions with the following commands:

   ```
   # mkdir /home/galley
   # chown nobody.galley
   # chmod 2770 /home/galley
   ```

Chapter 9

RHCSA-Level System Administration Tasks

This final RHCSA chapter covers functional system administration tasks not already covered in other chapters. It starts with a discussion of process management and continues with the use of archive files.

In addition, this chapter helps you automate repetitive system administration tasks. Some of these tasks happen when you want to have a "life," others when you'd rather be asleep. In this chapter, you'll learn how to schedule both one-time and periodic execution of jobs. This is made possible with the **cron** and **at** daemons. In this case, "at" is not a preposition, but a service that monitors a system for one-time scheduled jobs. In a similar fashion, cron is a service that monitors a system for regularly scheduled jobs.

When you're troubleshooting, system logging often provides the clues you need to solve a lot of problems. The focus in this chapter is local logging.

INSIDE THE EXAM

System Administration

Administrators work on Linux systems in a number of ways. In this chapter, you'll learn various methods for meeting the following RHCSA objectives. The first of these objectives involves fundamental command skills:

■ Archive, compress, unpack, and uncompress files using **tar**, **star**, **gzip**, and **bzip2**

These other objectives are more closely related to system administration:

■ Identify CPU/memory-intensive processes, adjust process priority with **renice**, and **kill** processes

■ Schedule tasks using **at** and **cron**

Finally, you will look at where to find information logged by the systemd journal and rsyslog. The related RHCSA objective is

■ Locate and interpret system log files and journals

CERTIFICATION OBJECTIVE 9.01

Elementary System Administration Commands

Several system administration commands in the RHCSA objectives are not covered in previous chapters. They're associated with system resource management and archives. System resource management commands allow you to see what processes are running, to check the resources they're using, and to kill or restart those processes. Archive commands support the consolidation of a group of files in a single archive, which can then be compressed.

System Resource Management Commands

Linux includes a variety of commands that can help you identify those processes that are monopolizing a system. The most basic of those commands is **ps**, which provides a snapshot of currently running processes. Those processes can be ranked with the **top** command, which can display running Linux tasks in order of their resource usage. With **top**, you can identify those processes that are using the most CPU and RAM memory. Commands that can adjust process priority include **nice** and **renice**. Sometimes it's not enough to adjust process priority, at which point it may be appropriate to send a signal to a process with commands such as **kill** and **killall**. If you need to monitor system usage, the **sar** and **iostat** commands can also be helpful.

Process Management with the ps Command

It's important to know what's running on a Linux computer. To help with that task, the **ps** command has a number of useful switches. When you're trying to diagnose a problem, one common practice is to start with the complete list of running processes and then look for a specific program. For example, if the Firefox web browser were to suddenly crash, you'd want to kill any associated processes. The **ps aux | grep firefox** command could then help you identify the process(es) that you need to kill.

on the
job   **The** pgrep **command is also useful because it combines the features of** ps **and** grep. **In this case, the** pgrep -a firefox **command is functionally equivalent to** ps aux | grep firefox.

The **ps** command by itself is usually not enough. All it does is identify those processes running in the current terminal. This command typically returns just the process associated with the current shell, and the **ps** command process itself.

To identify those processes associated with a username, the **ps -u** *username* command can help. Sometimes there are specific users who may be problematic for various reasons. So if you're suspicious of user mjang, the following command can help you review every process currently associated with that user:

```
$ ps -u mjang
```

As an administrator, you may choose to focus on a specific account for various reasons, such as activity revealed by the **top** command, described in the next section. Alternatively, you may want to audit all currently running processes with a command such as the following:

```
$ ps aux
```

FIGURE 9-1   Output from the ps aux command

```
USER        PID %CPU %MEM    VSZ   RSS TTY      STAT START   TIME COMMAND
root          1  0.0  0.3 134996  6924 ?        Ss   Feb16   0:18 /usr/lib/system
d/systemd --switched-root --system --deserialize 23
root          2  0.0  0.0      0     0 ?        S    Feb16   0:00 [kthreadd]
root          3  0.0  0.0      0     0 ?        S    Feb16   0:00 [ksoftirqd/0]
root          5  0.0  0.0      0     0 ?        S<   Feb16   0:00 [kworker/0:0H]
root          7  0.0  0.0      0     0 ?        S    Feb16   0:00 [migration/0]
root          8  0.0  0.0      0     0 ?        S    Feb16   0:00 [rcu_bh]
root          9  0.0  0.0      0     0 ?        S    Feb16   0:00 [rcuob/0]
root         10  0.0  0.0      0     0 ?        R    Feb16   0:11 [rcu_sched]
root         11  0.0  0.0      0     0 ?        S    Feb16   0:20 [rcuos/0]
root         12  0.0  0.0      0     0 ?        S    Feb16   0:06 [watchdog/0]
root         13  0.0  0.0      0     0 ?        S<   Feb16   0:00 [khelper]
root         14  0.0  0.0      0     0 ?        S    Feb16   0:00 [kdevtmpfs]
root         15  0.0  0.0      0     0 ?        S<   Feb16   0:00 [netns]
root         16  0.0  0.0      0     0 ?        S<   Feb16   0:00 [writeback]
root         17  0.0  0.0      0     0 ?        S<   Feb16   0:00 [kintegrityd]
root         18  0.0  0.0      0     0 ?        S<   Feb16   0:00 [bioset]
root         19  0.0  0.0      0     0 ?        S<   Feb16   0:00 [kblockd]
root         20  0.0  0.0      0     0 ?        S    Feb16   0:00 [khubd]
root         21  0.0  0.0      0     0 ?        S<   Feb16   0:00 [md]
:
```

The **ps aux** command gives a more complete database of currently running processes, in order of their PIDs. The **a** option lists all running processes, the **u** displays the output in a user-oriented format, and the **x** lifts the standard limitation that listed processes must be associated with a terminal or console. One example is shown in Figure 9-1. While the output can include hundreds of processes and more, the output can be redirected for further analysis with commands such as **grep**. The output columns shown in Figure 9-1 are described in Table 9-1.

Incidentally, you may note that the **ps aux** command does not include the familiar dash in front of the **aux** switches. In this case, the command works with and without the dash (although slightly differently). Valid command options with the dash are also known as UNIX or POSIX style; in contrast, options without the dash are known as BSD style. The following alternative includes current environmental variables for each process:

```
$ ps eux
```

Processes can be organized in a tree format. Specifically, the first process, with a PID of 1, is systemd. That process is the base of the tree, which may be shown with the **pstree** command. In a few cases, it's not possible to use a standard **kill** command to kill a process. In such cases, look for the "parent" of the process in the tree. You can identify the parent of a process, known as the PPID, with the following command:

```
$ ps axl
```

TABLE 9-1	Columns of Output from ps aux

Column Title	Description
USER	The username associated with the process.
PID	Process identifier.
%CPU	CPU usage, as a percentage of time spent running during the entire lifetime of the process.
%MEM	Current RAM usage.
VSZ	Virtual memory size of the process in KiB.
RSS	Physical memory in use by the process, not including swap space, in KiB.
TTY	Associated terminal console.
STAT	Process state.
START	Start time of the process. If you just see a date, the process started more than 24 hours ago.
TIME	Cumulative CPU time used.
COMMAND	Command associated with the process, including all its arguments.

The **l** switch displays the output in long format and is not compatible with the **u** switch. You can view the PID and PPIDs of all running processes in Figure 9-2.

With the **-Z** switch (that's an uppercase Z), the **ps** command can also identify the SELinux contexts associated with a process. For example, the following command includes

FIGURE 9-2	Output from the ps axl command

```
F   UID   PID  PPID PRI  NI     VSZ    RSS WCHAN  STAT TTY       TIME COMMAND
4     0     1     0  20   0  134996   6924 ep_pol Ss   ?         0:19 /usr/lib/system
d/systemd --switched-root --system --deserialize 23
1     0     2     0  20   0       0      0 kthrea S    ?         0:00 [kthreadd]
1     0     3     2  20   0       0      0 smpboo S    ?         0:00 [ksoftirqd/0]
1     0     5     2   0 -20       0      0 worker S<   ?         0:00 [kworker/0:0H]
1     0     7     2 -100  -       0      0 smpboo S    ?         0:00 [migration/0]
1     0     8     2  20   0       0      0 rcu_gp S    ?         0:00 [rcu_bh]
1     0     9     2  20   0       0      0 rcu_no S    ?         0:00 [rcuob/0]
1     0    10     2  20   0       0      0 -      R    ?         0:11 [rcu_sched]
1     0    11     2  20   0       0      0 rcu_no S    ?         0:20 [rcuos/0]
5     0    12     2 -100  -       0      0 smpboo S    ?         0:06 [watchdog/0]
1     0    13     2   0 -20       0      0 rescue S<   ?         0:00 [khelper]
5     0    14     2  20   0       0      0 devtmp S    ?         0:00 [kdevtmpfs]
1     0    15     2   0 -20       0      0 rescue S<   ?         0:00 [netns]
1     0    16     2   0 -20       0      0 rescue S<   ?         0:00 [writeback]
1     0    17     2   0 -20       0      0 rescue S<   ?         0:00 [kintegrityd]
1     0    18     2   0 -20       0      0 rescue S<   ?         0:00 [bioset]
1     0    19     2   0 -20       0      0 rescue S<   ?         0:00 [kblockd]
1     0    20     2  20   0       0      0 hub_th S    ?         0:00 [khubd]
1     0    21     2   0 -20       0      0 rescue S<   ?         0:00 [md]
:
```

the SELinux contexts of each process at the start of the output. If you've read Chapter 4, the contexts should already seem familiar. For example, contrast the context of the vsFTP server process with the following excerpt:

```
system_u:system_r:ftpd_t:s0-s0:c0.c1023 2059 ? Ss 0:00 ↵
/usr/sbin/vsftpd /etc/vsftpd/vsftpd.conf
```

Contrast that with the context of the actual daemon. The object role works with the actual daemon; you can review it with other daemons in the /usr/sbin directory. The **vsftpd** daemon works with the associated configuration file with the etc_t type. In contrast, the **vsftpd** daemon alone is executable with the ftpd_exec_t type.

```
-rwxr-xr-x. root root system_u:object_r:ftpd_exec_t:s0 /usr/sbin/vsftpd
```

The role of different daemons and their corresponding processes should match and contrast in a similar fashion. If they don't, the daemon may not work, and the problem should be documented in the audit log, described in Chapter 4, in the /var/log/audit directory.

View Loads with the top Task Browser

The **top** command sorts active processes first by their CPU load and RAM memory usage. Take a look at Figure 9-3. It provides an overview of the current system status, starting with

---

FIGURE 9-3   Output from the top command

```
top - 21:19:27 up 26 days, 26 min,  5 users,  load average: 0.75, 0.24, 0.17
Tasks: 169 total,   2 running, 167 sleeping,   0 stopped,   0 zombie
%Cpu(s):  3.7 us,  0.3 sy,  0.0 ni, 95.7 id,  0.0 wa,  0.0 hi,  0.0 si,  0.3 st
KiB Mem:   2279972 total,  2100720 used,   179252 free,     2612 buffers
KiB Swap:  1679356 total,        0 used,  1679356 free.   873464 cached Mem

  PID USER      PR  NI    VIRT    RES    SHR S %CPU %MEM     TIME+ COMMAND
 2831 alex      20   0 1809068 467208  39644 S  4.0 20.5  70:33.07 gnome-shell
 3240 root      20   0  123648   1572   1092 R  0.3  0.1   0:00.29 top
    1 root      20   0  134996   6924   3752 S  0.0  0.3   0:19.12 systemd
    2 root      20   0       0      0      0 S  0.0  0.0   0:00.21 kthreadd
    3 root      20   0       0      0      0 S  0.0  0.0   0:00.29 ksoftirqd/0
    5 root       0 -20       0      0      0 S  0.0  0.0   0:00.00 kworker/0:0H
    7 root      rt   0       0      0      0 S  0.0  0.0   0:00.00 migration/0
    8 root      20   0       0      0      0 S  0.0  0.0   0:00.00 rcu_bh
    9 root      20   0       0      0      0 S  0.0  0.0   0:00.00 rcuob/0
   10 root      20   0       0      0      0 S  0.0  0.0   0:11.42 rcu_sched
   11 root      20   0       0      0      0 R  0.0  0.0   0:20.25 rcuos/0
   12 root      rt   0       0      0      0 S  0.0  0.0   0:06.64 watchdog/0
   13 root       0 -20       0      0      0 S  0.0  0.0   0:00.00 khelper
   14 root      20   0       0      0      0 S  0.0  0.0   0:00.00 kdevtmpfs
   15 root       0 -20       0      0      0 S  0.0  0.0   0:00.00 netns
   16 root       0 -20       0      0      0 S  0.0  0.0   0:00.00 writeback
   17 root       0 -20       0      0      0 S  0.0  0.0   0:00.00 kintegrityd
```

TABLE 9-2	Additional Columns of Output from top

Column Title	Description
PR	The priority of the task. For more information, see the **nice** and **renice** commands.
NI	The nice value of the task, an adjustment to the priority.
VIRT	The virtual memory in KiB used by the task.
RES	Physical memory in use by the process, not including swap space, in KiB (similar to RSS in the output to the **ps aux** command).
SHR	Shared memory in KiB available to a task.
S	Process status (same as STAT in the output to the **ps aux** command).
%CPU	CPU usage, as a percentage of time spent running since the last **top** screen update.

the current uptime, number of connected users, active and sleeping tasks, CPU load, and more. The output is, in effect, a task browser.

The default sort field is CPU usage. In other words, the process that's taking the most CPU resources is listed first. You can change the sort field with the help of the left and right directional (<, >) keys. Most of the columns are the same as shown in Figure 9-2, as detailed in Table 9-1. The additional columns are described in Table 9-2.

One problem with the **top** and **ps** commands is that they display the status of processes on a system as a snapshot in time. That may not be enough. Processes may load a system for just a blip of time, or even periodic blips in time. One way to find more information about the overall load on a system is with two commands from the sysstat package: **sar** and **iostat**. That system activity information is logged courtesy of the **sa1** and **sa2** commands associated with the /etc/cron.d/sysstat script, which will be described shortly.

System Activity Reports with the sar Command

The **sar** command, in essence, can be used to provide a system activity report. For example, Figure 9-4 shows the output of the **sar -A** command. As you can see, the output shows various CPU measures at different points in time. The default settings measure CPU load at 10-minute intervals. This system has eight logical CPUs (four cores with hyper-threading enabled), which are measured individually and as a whole. The large idle numbers shown in the figure are a good sign that the CPU is not being overloaded; however, the figure shows the load for less than an hour.

The 10-minute intervals associated with the **sar** command output are driven by a regular job in the /etc/cron.d directory. The output from those reports is collected in log files in the /var/log/sa directory. The filenames are associated with the numeric day of the month; for example, system activity report status for the 15th of the month can be found in the

```
Linux 3.10.0-123.el7.x86_64 (Maui)      14/03/15      _x86_64_      (8 CPU)

21:05:31       LINUX RESTART

21:10:01    CPU    %usr   %nice    %sys  %iowait  %steal    %irq   %soft  %guest  %gnice   %idle
21:20:01    all    0.10    0.31    0.26    0.06    0.00    0.00    0.00    0.24    0.00   99.02
21:20:01      0    0.12    0.04    0.16    0.04    0.00    0.00    0.00    0.34    0.00   99.30
21:20:01      1    0.12    0.03    0.12    0.10    0.00    0.00    0.00    0.35    0.00   99.27
21:20:01      2    0.14    0.08    0.13    0.03    0.00    0.00    0.00    0.21    0.00   99.41
21:20:01      3    0.16    0.05    0.09    0.01    0.00    0.00    0.00    0.22    0.00   99.47
21:20:01      4    0.01    0.68    0.64    0.00    0.00    0.00    0.00    0.15    0.00   98.52
21:20:01      5    0.04    1.44    0.79    0.01    0.00    0.00    0.00    0.01    0.00   97.72
21:20:01      6    0.06    0.08    0.05    0.01    0.00    0.00    0.00    0.39    0.00   99.41
21:20:01      7    0.14    0.13    0.09    0.30    0.00    0.00    0.00    0.26    0.00   99.08
21:30:01    all    0.01    0.00    0.02    0.03    0.00    0.00    0.00    0.03    0.00   99.90
21:30:01      0    0.01    0.00    0.03    0.03    0.00    0.00    0.00    0.10    0.00   99.83
21:30:01      1    0.01    0.00    0.03    0.09    0.00    0.00    0.00    0.03    0.00   99.85
21:30:01      2    0.01    0.00    0.05    0.01    0.00    0.00    0.00    0.11    0.00   99.82
21:30:01      3    0.02    0.00    0.02    0.00    0.00    0.00    0.00    0.02    0.00   99.95
21:30:01      4    0.01    0.00    0.02    0.01    0.00    0.00    0.00    0.00    0.00   99.96
21:30:01      5    0.01    0.00    0.01    0.01    0.00    0.00    0.00    0.00    0.00   99.97
21:30:01      6    0.00    0.00    0.01    0.01    0.00    0.00    0.00    0.00    0.00   99.98
21:30:01      7    0.04    0.00    0.02    0.08    0.00    0.00    0.00    0.00    0.00   99.87
:
```

sa15 file in the noted directory. However, such reports are normally stored at least for the last 28 days, based on the following default in the /etc/sysconfig/sysstat file:

```
HISTORY=28
```

CPU and Storage Device Statistics with iostat

In contrast to **sar**, the **iostat** command reports more general input/output statistics for the system, not only for the CPU, but also for connected storage devices, such as local drives and mounted shared NFS directories. The example shown in Figure 9-5 displays information for the CPU and the storage devices since system startup on server1.example.com.

Both the **sar** and the **iostat** command can capture statistics at regular intervals. As an example, the following command shows CPU and storage device statistics every five seconds and stops after a minute (12 reports):

```
# iostat 5 12
```

FIGURE 9-5

CPU and storage device statistics

```
[root@server1 ~]# iostat
Linux 3.10.0-123.13.2.el7.x86_64 (server1.example.com)   14/03/15      _x86_64_
(1 CPU)

avg-cpu:  %user   %nice %system %iowait  %steal   %idle
           0.88    0.01    0.18    0.00    0.02   98.92

Device:            tps    kB_read/s    kB_wrtn/s    kB_read    kB_wrtn
vda               0.85         1.99         4.56    1051023    2405632
dm-0              0.85         1.84         4.56     970234    2403513
dm-1              0.00         0.00         0.00       1464          0

[root@server1 ~]#
```

Variations on sar with sa1 and sa2

The **sa1** and **sa2** commands are often used to collect system activity report data. In the /etc/cron.d/sysstat script, the **sa1** command is used to gather system activity data every 10 minutes. In that same cron file, the **sa2** command writes a daily report in the /var/log/sa directory. As noted in the script, that report is processed every day, at seven minutes before midnight.

nice and renice

The **nice** and **renice** commands can be used to manage the priority of different processes. Whereas the **nice** command is used to start a process with a different priority, the **renice** command is used to change the priority of a currently running process.

Process priorities in Linux specify numbers that seem counterintuitive. The range of available nice numbers can vary from −20 to 19. The default nice number of a process is inherited from the parent and is usually 0. A process given a priority of 19 will have to wait until the system is almost completely free before taking any resources. In contrast, a process given a priority of −20 takes precedence over all other processes. In practice, this is true for almost all processes because "real-time" tasks take precedence over the lowest nice value of −20. But this is outside of the scope of the RHCSA exam, so ignore the existence of real-time processes for now, and for the sake of this discussion assume that all normal processes can be assigned a nice value from −20 to 19.

The **nice** command prefaces other commands. For example, if you have an intensive script to be run at night, you might choose to start it with a command like the following:

```
$ nice -n 19 ./intensivescript
```

This command starts the noted script with the lowest possible priority. If started at night (or at some other time when a system is not loaded by other programs), the script is run until just about any other job, such as a script in one of the /etc/cron.* directories, is scheduled for execution. Because such scripts are run on a schedule, they normally should take priority over some user-configured programs.

Sometimes a program is just taking up too many resources. If you don't want to kill a process, you can lower its priority with the **renice** command. Normally, the easiest way to identify a process that's taking up too many resources is with the **top** command. Identify the PID that's taking up too many resources. That PID number is in the left-hand column of the output.

If the PID of your target process is 1234, the following command would change the nice number of that process to 10, which gives that process a lower priority than the default of 0:

```
# renice -n 10 1234
```

If you want to decrease the nice level of a process, you must run **renice** as root. Even though the output of the command refers to the "priority," it really is just listing the old and new "nice" numbers for the process:

```
1234: old priority 0, new priority, 10
```

The new nice number is shown in the output to the **top** command, under the NI column.

Process Killing Commands

Sometimes, it's not enough to reprioritize a process. Some processes can just overwhelm a system. In most cases, you can stop such difficult processes with the **kill** and **killall** commands. In many cases, you can kill a process directly from the **top** task browser.

If there's a situation where a process is taking up a lot of memory or CPU, it's probably slowing down everything else running on that system. As shown in Figure 9-6, Firefox has loaded the CPU of the noted system pretty heavily. If it were unresponsive, we'd press **k** from the **top** task browser.

As shown in the figure, the **k** command reveals the PID To Signal/Kill: prompt, where we enter the PID of the Firefox process or accept the default of 4537, which appears to be Firefox. It applies the default signal (SIGTERM) to the process with that PID number.

Of course, you could apply the **kill** command directly to a PID number. For example, the following command is equivalent to the steps just described in the **top** task browser:

```
# kill 4537
```

FIGURE 9-6

The top task browser with heavy Firefox load

```
top - 13:57:44 up 10 min,  3 users,  load average: 0.29, 0.32, 0.25
Tasks: 257 total,   1 running, 256 sleeping,   0 stopped,   0 zombie
%Cpu(s):  9.6 us,  1.6 sy,  0.0 ni, 88.7 id,  0.0 wa,  0.0 hi,  0.0 si,  0.0 st
KiB Mem:  16153912 total,  3167324 used, 12986588 free,    1212 buffers
KiB Swap: 16383316 total,        0 used, 16383316 free.  915604 cached Mem
PID to signal/kill [default pid = 4537]
  PID USER      PR  NI    VIRT    RES    SHR S  %CPU %MEM     TIME+ COMMAND
 4537 alex      20   0 2357456 613972  57400 S  85.5  3.8   0:27.09 firefox
 3375 alex       9 -11 1147288  24136  17980 S   4.3  0.1   0:06.18 pulseaudio
 2867 root      20   0  213992  24264  12312 S   1.3  0.2   0:18.29 Xorg
 3443 alex      20   0 1800404 110844  34464 S   1.3  0.7   0:27.82 gnome-shell
 3762 alex      20   0  622768  21156  12856 S   0.7  0.1   0:00.82 gnome-term+
 2846 qemu      20   0 5688400 691360   7468 S   0.3  4.3   0:41.09 qemu-kvm
 3471 alex      20   0  461276   5672   3468 S   0.3  0.0   0:00.39 ibus-daemon
    1 root      20   0  134836   6900   3776 S   0.0  0.0   0:01.31 systemd
    2 root      20   0       0      0      0 S   0.0  0.0   0:00.00 kthreadd
    3 root      20   0       0      0      0 S   0.0  0.0   0:00.00 ksoftirqd/0
    5 root       0 -20       0      0      0 S   0.0  0.0   0:00.00 kworker/0:+
    7 root      rt   0       0      0      0 S   0.0  0.0   0:00.04 migration/0
    8 root      20   0       0      0      0 S   0.0  0.0   0:00.00 rcu_bh
    9 root      20   0       0      0      0 S   0.0  0.0   0:00.00 rcuob/0
   10 root      20   0       0      0      0 S   0.0  0.0   0:00.00 rcuob/1
   11 root      20   0       0      0      0 S   0.0  0.0   0:00.00 rcuob/2
   12 root      20   0       0      0      0 S   0.0  0.0   0:00.00 rcuob/3
```

TABLE 9-3		A List of Common POSIX Signals

Signal Name	Signal Number	Description
SIGHUP	1	Configuration reload.
SIGINT	2	Keyboard interrupt (CTRL-C). Causes program termination.
SIGKILL	9	Terminates a program immediately.
SIGQUIT	15	Similar to SIGKILL, but the program can ignore or handle the signal to release existing resources and perform a clean termination.
SIGCONT	18	Resumes a suspended process.
SIGSTOP	19	Temporarily suspends the execution of a process.

The **kill** command can be run by the owner of a process from his account. Thus, user alex could run the **kill 4537** command from his regular account because he has administrative privileges over processes associated with his username.

Despite its name, the **kill** command can send a wide variety of signals to different processes. For a full list, run the **kill -l** command or type **man 7 signal**. Table 9-3 lists some of the most common signals.

Before the advent of systemd and scripts in the /etc/init.d directory, the **kill -1** command was used to send a configuration reload signal to service daemons. For example, if the PID number of the main process associated with the Apache web server is 2059, the following command is functionally equivalent to the **systemctl reload httpd** command:

```
# kill -1 2059
```

Without the **-1** switch (and that's a dash number 1), the **kill** command, under normal circumstances, would terminate the given process. In this case, it would terminate the Apache web server. But sometimes, processes get stuck. In some such cases, the **kill** command does not work by itself. The process continues running. In that case, you can try two things.

First, you could try the **kill -9** command, which attempts to stop a process "uncleanly" by sending a SIGTERM signal. If it is successful, other related processes may still remain in operation.

Sometimes, a number of processes are running under the same name. For example, as you'll see in Chapter 14, the Apache web server starts several processes that run simultaneously. It's at best inefficient to kill just one process; the following command would kill all currently running server processes, assuming no other issues:

```
# killall httpd
```

Archives and Compression

Linux includes a variety of commands to archive groups of files. Some archives can be reprocessed into packages such as RPMs. Other archives are just used as backups. In either case, archives can be a terrific convenience, especially when compressed. This section explores the archive and compression commands specifically cited in the RHCSA objectives. These "essential tools" include the **gzip**, **bzip2**, **tar**, and **star** commands.

gzip and bzip2

The **gzip** and **bzip2** commands are functionally similar as they compress and decompress files, just using different algorithms. The **gzip** command uses the DEFLATE algorithm, whereas the **bzip2** command uses the Burrows-Wheeler block sorting algorithm. While they both work well, the **bzip2** command has a better compression ratio. For example, either of the two following commands could be used to compress a big document file named big.doc:

```
# gzip big.doc
# bzip2 big.doc
```

This adds a .gz or a .bz2 suffix to the file, compressed to the associated algorithms. With the **-d** switch, you can use the same commands to reverse the process:

```
# gzip -d big.doc.gz
# bzip2 -d big.doc.bz2
```

As an alternative, the **gunzip** and **bunzip2** commands can be used for the same purpose.

tar

The **tar** command was originally developed for archiving data to tape drives. However, it's commonly used today for collecting a series of files, especially from a directory, in a single archive file. For example, the following command backs up the information from the /home directory in the home.tar.gz file:

```
# tar czvf home.tar.gz /home
```

Like the **ps** command, this is one of the few commands that does not require a dash in front of the switch. This particular command creates (**c**) an archive, compresses (**z**) it, in verbose (**v**) mode, with the filename (**f**) that follows. Alternatively, you can extract (**x**) from that file with the following command:

```
# tar xzvf home.tar.gz /home
```

The compression specified (**z**) is associated with the **gzip** command; if you wanted to use **bzip2** compression, substitute the **j** switch. The **tar** command can store and extract access control list settings or SELinux attributes with the --**selinux** option.

If you have a tar archive created without the --**selinux** option, you can compensate. You can use commands such as **restorecon**, as described in Chapter 4, to restore the SELinux contexts of an archive.

star

The **star** command gained some popularity because it was the first to introduce support for archiving files in a SELinux system. As the **star** command is not normally installed, you'll need to install it; one method is with the following command:

```
# yum install star
```

Unfortunately, the **star** command doesn't quite work in the same fashion as **tar**. If you ever have to use the **star** command, do practice the command. For example, the following command would create an archive, with all SELinux contexts, from the current /home directory:

```
# star -xattr -H=exustar -c -f=home.star /home/
```

The -**xattr** switch saves the extended attributes associated with SELinux. The -**H=exustar** switch records the archive using the exustar format, which allows you to store ACLs if the **acl** option is specified. The -**c** creates a new archive file. The -**f** specifies the name of the archive file.

Once the archive is created, it can be unpacked with the following command, which extracts the archive:

```
# star -x -f=home.star
```

If desired, the archive can be compressed with the aforementioned **gzip** or **bzip2** command, or from **star** with the -**z** or -**bz** command-line option. The **star -x** command can detect and restore files from archives configured with various compression schemes. For example, based on a gzip-compressed archive, the **star** command unpacks that archive, as noted by the following log information message:

```
star: WARNING: Archive is 'gzip' compressed, trying to use the -z option.
```

CERTIFICATION OBJECTIVE 9.02

Automate System Administration: cron and at

The cron system is essentially a smart alarm clock. When the alarm sounds, Linux runs the commands of your choice automatically. You can set the alarm clock to run at all sorts of regular time intervals. Many cron jobs are scheduled to run during the middle of the night, when user activity is lower. Of course, that timing can be adjusted. Alternatively, the at system allows users to run the commands of their choice, once, at a specified time in the future.

RHEL 7 installs the **cron** daemon by default and incorporates the anacron system in cron. The **cron** daemon starts jobs on a regular schedule. The anacron system helps the **cron** daemon work on systems that are powered off at night. This ensures that important jobs are always run, even if a system was powered off for a period of time.

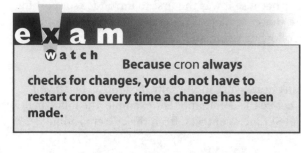

Because cron **always checks for changes, you do not have to restart cron every time a change has been made.**

The cron system is configured to check the /var/spool/cron directory for jobs by user. In addition, it incorporates jobs defined in the /etc/anacrontab file, based on the **0anacron** script in the /etc/cron.hourly directory. It also checks for scheduled jobs for the computer described in the /etc/crontab file and in the /etc/cron.d directory.

The System crontab and Components

The /etc/crontab file is set up in a specific format. Each line can be blank, a comment (which begins with #), a variable, or a configuration line. Naturally, blank lines and comments are ignored. In some Linux distributions, that file includes a schedule of jobs. In RHEL 7, the default crontab file just includes the format for other related configuration files.

Users run regular commands. Anyone who runs a new process, whether it be you or a daemon, inherits an "environment" that is made of various environmental variables. To see the environmental variables for the current user, run the **env** command. If that user is your account, some of the standard variables in RHEL include **HOME**, which should match your home directory, **SHELL**, which should match the default shell, and **LOGNAME** as the username.

Other variables can be set in the /etc/crontab and other cron files (in /etc/cron.d, /etc/cron.daily, and so on):

```
Variable=Value
```

Some variables are already set for you. For example, **MAIL** is /var/spool/mail/michael if your username is michael, **LANG** is en_US.UTF-8, and **PATH** is where the shell looks for commands. You can set these variables to different values in various cron configuration files. For example, the default /etc/crontab file includes the following variables:

```
SHELL=/bin/bash
PATH=/sbin:/bin:/usr/sbin:/usr/bin
MAILTO=root
```

Note that the values of **PATH** and **MAILTO** are different from standard environment variables. The **PATH** variable in a cron configuration file may be different from the **PATH** variable associated with a shell. In fact, the two variables are independent. Therefore, you'll want to specify the exact path of every command in each cron configuration file if it isn't in the crontab **PATH**.

on the **job**

The MAILTO variable can help you administer several Linux systems. The cron **daemon sends by e-mail any output that a job sends to** stdout **or** stderr. **Just add a line such as MAILTO=me@example.net to route all the output of cron jobs to that e-mail address.**

The format of a line in /etc/crontab is now detailed in comments, as shown in Figure 9-7. Each of these columns is explained in more detail in Table 9-4.

If you see an asterisk in any column, the **cron** daemon runs that command for all possible values of that column. For example, an * in the minute field means that the command is run every minute during the specified hour(s). Consider the example shown here:

```
1  5  3  4  *  ls
```

This line runs the **ls** command every April 3 at 5:01 A.M. The asterisk in the day of week column simply means that it does not matter what day of the week it is; **crontab** still runs the **ls** command at the specified time.

FIGURE 9-7

The format of a crontab

```
SHELL=/bin/bash
PATH=/sbin:/bin:/usr/sbin:/usr/bin
MAILTO=root

# For details see man 4 crontabs

# Example of job definition:
# .---------------- minute (0 - 59)
# |  .------------- hour (0 - 23)
# |  |  .---------- day of month (1 - 31)
# |  |  |  .------- month (1 - 12) OR jan,feb,mar,apr ...
# |  |  |  |  .---- day of week (0 - 6) (Sunday=0 or 7) OR sun,mon,tue,wed,thu,f
ri,sat
# |  |  |  |  |
# *  *  *  *  * user-name  command to be executed
```

TABLE 9-4	Field	Value
	minute	0–59.
Columns in a cron Configuration File	hour	Based on a 24-hour clock; for example, 23 = 11 P.M.
	day of month	1–31.
	month	1–12, or Jan, Feb, Mar, and so on.
	day of week	0–7 (where 0 and 7 are both Sunday), or Sun, Mon, Tue, and so on.
	command	The command to be executed; in a system cron job file, this is preceded by the username to run the command **as**.

The entries associated with the **cron** daemon are flexible. For example, a 7–10 entry in the hour field would run the specified command at 7:00 A.M., 8:00 A.M., 9:00 A.M., and 10:00 A.M. A list of entries in the minute field, such as 0,5,10,15,20,25,30,35,40,45,50,55, would run the specified command every five minutes. But that's a lot of numbers. The entry */5 in the minute field would lead to the same result. The **cron** daemon also recognizes abbreviations for months and the day of the week.

The actual command is the sixth field. You can set up new lines with a percent (**%**) symbol. All the text after the first percent sign is sent to the command as standard input. This is useful for formatting standard input. The following is an example of a cron file:

```
# crontab -l
# Sample crontab file
#
# Force /bin/bash to be my shell for all of my scripts.
SHELL=/bin/bash
# Run 15 minutes past Midnight every Saturday
15 0 * * sat    $HOME/scripts/scary.script
# Do routine cleanup on the first of every Month at 4:30 AM
30 4 1 * *      /usr/scripts/removecores >> /tmp/core.tmp 2>>&1
# Mail a message at 10:45 AM every Friday
45 10 * * Fri  mail -s "Project Update" employees@example.com
%Can I have a status
update on your project?%%Your Boss.%
# Every other hour check for alert messages
0 */2 * * * /usr/scripts/check.alerts
```

Hourly cron Jobs

Now it's time for some sample cron files. The files and scripts discussed are limited to those seen on the server1.example.com system. A number of different packages add their own cron jobs. Certain jobs associated with the **cron** daemon are run every hour, based on the 0hourly script in the /etc/cron.d directory. This file includes the same variables as the /etc/crontab file just described. For hourly jobs, it includes one line:

```
01 * * * * root run-parts /etc/cron.hourly
```

Given the information provided in the preceding section, you should be able to read this line. The **run-parts** command loads each script in the directory that follows; the scripts in that directory are executed as the root user. Of course, the first five columns specify the time; the scripts are run at one minute past the hour, every hour, every day, every month, on each day of the week.

The script of interest in the /etc/cron.hourly directory is 0anacron, which reviews the contents of the /var/spool/anacron/cron.daily file to see if the **anacron** command has been run in the current day. If not, and if the system is not running on battery (for example, on a laptop disconnected from main power), the **/usr/sbin/anacron -s** command is executed, which runs scripts defined in the /etc/anacrontab configuration file.

The system status script described earlier is stored in the /etc/cron.d/sysstat file. There are two active commands in that file. The first command, **sa1**, is run every 10 minutes, as depicted by */10. This command is run every hour, every day, and so on.

```
*/10 * * * * root /usr/lib64/sa/sa1 1 1
```

The second command, **sa2**, is run at 53 minutes after the hour, on the 23rd hour of each day. In other words, the system activity report is not collected until 11:53 P.M. at night.

```
53 23 * * * root /usr/lib64/sa/sa2 -A
```

Regular Anacron Jobs

The 0anacron script in the /etc/cron.hourly directory described earlier executes the **anacron** command after a system has been powered up. That command executes three scripts defined in the /etc/anacrontab file. This includes three environment variables that should seem familiar:

```
SHELL=/bin/sh
PATH=/sbin:/bin:/usr/sbin:/usr/bin
MAILTO=root
```

The **SHELL** directive may appear a bit different, but the **ls -l /bin/sh** command should confirm a soft link to the **/bin/bash** command, which starts the default bash shell. The following directive means that scripts are run at a random time of up to 45 minutes after the scheduled time:

```
RANDOM_DELAY=45
```

With the following directive, anacron jobs are run only between the hours of 3 A.M. and 10:59 P.M.

```
START_HOURS_RANGE=3-22
```

While the format of /etc/anacrontab is similar to the format listed in a script for a regular cron job, there are differences. The order of data in each line is specified by the following comment:

```
#period in days   delay in minutes   job-identifier   command
```

The period in days is 1, 7, or @monthly, because the number of days in a month varies. The delay in minutes is associated with the **RANDOM_DELAY** directive. Since the /etc/anacrontab file is executed through the /etc/cron.d/0hourly script, the clock starts one minute after the hour, after the system has been started. The delay in minutes comes before the **RANDOM_DELAY** directive.

In other words, based on the following line, the scripts in the /etc/cron.daily directory may be run anywhere from 5 to 50 minutes after the **anacron** command is run, or 6 to 51 minutes after the hour:

```
1  5  cron.daily      nice run-parts /etc/cron.daily
```

For more examples, review some of the scripts in the **/etc/cron.daily** directory. Here are three key scripts you should investigate:

- **logrotate**   Rotates log files
- **mlocate**   Updates the "locate" file database
- **man-db.cron**   Creates or updates the mandb database

Setting Up cron for Users

Each user can use the **crontab** command to create and manage cron jobs for their own accounts. Four switches are associated with the **crontab** command:

- **-u** *user*   Allows the root user to edit the crontab of another specific user.
- **-l**   Lists the current entries in the crontab file.
- **-r**   Removes cron entries.
- **-e**   Edits an existing **crontab** entry. By default, **crontab** uses vi, unless a different editor is specified via the **EDITOR** environment variable.

To set up cron entries on your own account, start with the **crontab -e** command. Normally, it opens a file in the vi editor, where you can add appropriate variables and commands, similar to what you've seen in other cron job files.

Once the cron job is saved, you can confirm the change with either the **crontab -l** command or, as the root user, by reading the contents of a file in the /var/spool/cron directory associated with a username. All current cron jobs for a user can be removed with the **crontab -r** command.

Create a cron Job

In this exercise, you will modify your crontab to read a text file at 1:05 P.M. every Monday in the month of January. To do this, use the following steps:

1. Log in as a regular user.
2. Create a ~/bin directory. Add a file called taxrem.sh, which reads a text file from your home directory. A command such as the following in the taxrem.sh file should suffice:

```
#!/bin/bash
cat /home/michael/reminder.txt
```

Make sure to add appropriate lines to the reminder.txt file in your home directory, such as "Don't forget to do your taxes!" Make sure the taxrem file is executable with the **chmod +x ~/bin/taxrem.sh** command.

3. Open up the crontab for your account with the **crontab -e** command.
4. Add an appropriate command to the crontab. Based on the conditions described, it would read as follows:

```
5 13 * 1 1 /home/michael/bin/taxrem.sh
```

5. Don't forget directives such as **MAILTO=user@example.com** at the start of the crontab.
6. Save and exit. Run **crontab -l** and confirm the existence of the user cron file in the /var/spool/cron directory. That file should have the same name as the user.

Running a Job with the at System

Like **cron**, the **at** daemon supports job processing. However, you can set an **at** job to be run once. Jobs in the cron system must be set to run on a regular basis. The **at** daemon works in a way similar to the print process; jobs are spooled in the /var/spool/at directory and run at the specified time.

TABLE 9-5	Time Period	Example	Start Time for Jobs
	Minutes	at now + 10 minutes	In 10 minutes
Examples of the at	Hours	at now + 2 hours	In 2 hours
Command	Days	at now + 1 day	In 24 hours
	Weeks	at now + 1 week	In 7 days
	n/a	at teatime	At 4:00 P.M.
	n/a	at 3:00 12/21/16	On December 21, 2016, at 3:00 A.M.

You can use the **at** daemon to run the command or script of your choice. For the purpose of this section, assume that user michael has created a script named 797.sh in his home directory to process some airplane sales database.

From the command line, you can run the **at** *time* command to start a job to be run at a specified time. Here, *time* can be now; in a specified number of minutes, hours, or days; or at the time of your choice. Several examples are illustrated in Table 9-5.

You can use one of the sample commands shown in Table 9-5 to open an **at** job. It opens a different command-line interface, where you can specify the command of your choice. For this example, assume you're about to leave work and want to start the job in an hour. From the conditions specified, run the following commands:

```
$ at now + 1 hour
at> /home/michael/797.sh
at> Ctrl-D
```

The CTRL-D command exits the **at** shell and returns to the original command-line interface. As an alternative, you can use input redirection, as follows:

```
$ at now + 1 hour < /home/michael/797.sh
```

The **atq** command, as shown here, checks the status of the current **at** jobs. All jobs that are pending are listed in the output to the **atq** command:

```
$ atq
1       2016-12-21 03:00 a michael
```

If there's a problem with the job, you can remove it with the **atrm** command. For example, you can remove the noted job, labeled job 1, with the following command:

```
$ atrm 1
```

Secure cron and at

You may not want everyone to be able to run a job in the middle of the night. You may also want to restrict this privilege for security reasons.

Users can be configured in /etc/cron.allow and /etc/cron.deny files. If neither of these files exist, **cron** usage is restricted to the root administrative user. If the /etc/cron.allow file exists, only users named in that file are allowed to use **cron**. If there is no /etc/cron.allow file, only users named in /etc/cron.deny can't use **cron**.

These files are formatted as one line per user; if you include the following entries in /etc/cron.deny, and the /etc/cron.allow file does not exist, users elizabeth and nancy aren't allowed to set up their own **cron** scripts:

```
elizabeth
nancy
```

However, if the /etc/cron.allow file does exist with the same list of users, it takes precedence. In that case, both users elizabeth and nancy are allowed to set up their own cron scripts. The range of possibilities is summarized in Table 9-6.

User security for the **at** system is almost identical. The corresponding security configuration files are /etc/at.allow and /etc/at.deny. The range of possibilities is summarized in Table 9-7.

If you're paranoid about security, it may be appropriate to include only desired users in the /etc/cron.allow and /etc/at.allow files. Otherwise, a security breach in a service account may allow a "black hat" hacker to run a **cron** or **at** script from the associated account.

TABLE 9-6   Security Effects of cron.allow and cron.deny

	/etc/cron.deny exists	/etc/cron.deny does not exist
/etc/cron.allow exists	Only users listed in /etc/cron.allow can run **crontab -e**; contents of /etc/cron.deny are ignored.	Only users listed in /etc/cron.allow can run **crontab -e**.
/etc/cron.allow does not exist	All users listed in /etc/cron.deny cannot use **crontab -e**.	Only the root user can run **crontab -e**.

TABLE 9-7   Security Effects of at.allow and at.deny

	/etc/at.deny exists	/etc/at.deny does not exist
/etc/at.allow exists	Only users listed in /etc/at.allow can run the **at** command; contents of /etc/at.deny are ignored.	Only users listed in /etc/at.allow can run the **at** command.
/etc/at.allow does not exist	All users listed in /etc/at.deny cannot run the **at** command.	Only the root user can run the **at** command.

CERTIFICATION OBJECTIVE 9.03

Local Log File Analysis

An important part of maintaining a secure system is monitoring those activities that take place on the system. If you know what usually happens, such as understanding when users log in to a system, you can use log files to spot unusual activity. Red Hat Enterprise Linux comes with new system-monitoring utilities that can help identify the culprit if there is a problem.

RHEL 7 comes with two logging systems: a traditional logging service, **rsyslog**, and an enhanced logging daemon known as **systemd-journald**. We briefly discussed systemd logging in Chapter 5. Thanks to its architecture, systemd can intercept and save all boot and syslog messages, along with the output that services send to standard error and to standard output. This is much more than what a traditional syslog server can do. By default, systemd journal logs are stored temporarily (in a RAM tmpfs filesystem) in the /run/log/journal directory.

The **rsyslog** daemon includes the functionality of the kernel and system logging services used through RHEL 7. You can use the log files thus generated to track activities on a system. The way rsyslog logs output to files is based on the configuration defined in the /etc/rsyslog.conf file and on the files in the /etc/rsyslog.d directory.

In many cases, services such as SELinux, Apache, and Samba have their own log files, defined within their own configuration files. Details are addressed in the chapters associated with those services.

System Log Configuration File

You can configure what is logged through the /etc/rsyslog.conf configuration file. As shown in Figure 9-8, it includes a set of rules for different facilities: authpriv, cron, kern, mail, news, user, and uucp.

Each facility is also associated with several different levels of logging, known as the priority. In ascending order, log priorities are **debug**, **info**, **notice**, **warn**, **err**, **crit**, **alert**, **emerg**. There's also a generic **none** priority that logs no messages of the specific facility; for example, an **authpriv.none** directive would omit all authentication messages.

For each facility and priority, log information is sent to a specific log file. For example, consider the following line from /etc/syslog.conf:

```
*.info;mail.none;authpriv.none;cron.none /var/log/messages
```

FIGURE 9-8

The rsyslog.conf
configuration file

```
#### RULES ####

# Log all kernel messages to the console.
# Logging much else clutters up the screen.
#kern.*                                                 /dev/console

# Log anything (except mail) of level info or higher.
# Don't log private authentication messages!
*.info;mail.none;authpriv.none;cron.none               /var/log/messages

# The authpriv file has restricted access.
authpriv.*                                             /var/log/secure

# Log all the mail messages in one place.
mail.*                                                 -/var/log/maillog


# Log cron stuff
cron.*                                                 /var/log/cron

# Everybody gets emergency messages
*.emerg                                                :omusrmsg:*

# Save news errors of level crit and higher in a special file.
uucp,news.crit                                         /var/log/spooler

# Save boot messages also to boot.log
local7.*                                               /var/log/boot.log
:
```

This line sends log information from all of the given facilities to the /var/log/messages file.
This includes all facility messages of **info** level and higher, except for log messages related to
the **mail**, **authpriv** (authentication), and **cron** services.

You can use the asterisk as a wildcard in /etc/syslog.conf. For example, a line that starts
with ***.*** tells the **rsyslogd** daemon to log everything. A line that starts with **authpriv.***
means you want to log all messages from the **authpriv** facility.

By default, **rsyslogd** logs all messages of a given priority or higher. In other words, a
cron.err line will include all log messages from the **cron** daemon at the **err**, **crit**, **alert**, and
emerg levels.

Most messages from the **rsyslogd** daemon are written to files in the /var/log directory.
You should scan these logs on a regular basis and look for patterns that could indicate a
security breach. It's also possible to set up cron jobs to look for such patterns.

Log File Management

Logs can easily become very large and difficult to read. By default, the **logrotate** utility creates
a new log file on a weekly basis, using the directives in the /etc/logrotate.conf file, which also
pulls in directives from files in the /etc/logrotate.d directory. As shown in Figure 9-9, the
directives in the file are straightforward and well explained by the comments.

FIGURE 9-9

Log rotation
configured in
/etc/logrotate.conf

```
# see "man logrotate" for details
# rotate log files weekly
weekly

# keep 4 weeks worth of backlogs
rotate 4

# create new (empty) log files after rotating old ones
create

# use date as a suffix of the rotated file
dateext

# uncomment this if you want your log files compressed
#compress

# RPM packages drop log rotation information into this directory
include /etc/logrotate.d

# no packages own wtmp and btmp -- we'll rotate them here
/var/log/wtmp {
    monthly
    create 0664 root utmp
        minsize 1M
    rotate 1
}

/var/log/btmp {
    missingok
    monthly
    create 0600 root utmp
    rotate 1
}

# system-specific logs may be also be configured here.
```

Specifically, the default settings rotate log files on a weekly basis, storing the past four weeks of logs. New log files are created during the rotation, and older files have the date of rotation as a suffix. Different provisions are given to **wtmp** and **btmp** logs, related to user login records.

A Variety of Log Files

Various log files and their functionality are described in Table 9-8. These files are created based on the previously described configuration of the /etc/rsyslog.conf file and of service configuration files in the /etc/rsyslog.d directory. Some of the log files (such as those in /var/log/httpd) are created directly by applications. All files shown are in the /var/log directory. If you haven't installed, activated, or used the noted service, the associated log file may not appear. In contrast, you may see log files not shown here based on additional installed services.

TABLE 9-8   Standard Red Hat Log Files

Log Files	Description
anaconda/*	Includes at least five log files: anaconda.log for general installation messages; anaconda .packaging.log for package installation; anaconda.program.log for calls to external programs; anaconda.storage.log for storage device configuration and partitioning; anaconda.ifcfg.log for network adapter initialization; and sometimes, syslog for kernel messages; and anaconda.xlog for the first start of the GUI server.
audit/	Includes the audit.log file, which collects messages from the kernel audit subsystem.
boot.log	Associated with services that start and shut down processes.
btmp	Lists failed login attempts; readable with the **utmpdump btmp** command.
cron	Collects information from scripts run by the **cron** daemon.
cups/	Directory of printer access, page, and error logs.
dmesg	Includes basic boot messages.
gdm/	Directory of messages associated with starting via the GNOME Display Manager; includes login failures.
httpd/	Directory of log files associated with the Apache web server.
lastlog	Lists login records; readable with the **lastlog** command.
maillog	Collects log messages related to e-mail servers.
messages	Includes kernel logs and messages from other services, as defined in /etc/rsyslog.conf.
pm-powersave.log	Log messages related to power management.
ppp/	Directory with Point to Point Protocol logs; usually associated with telephone modems.
rhsm/	Directory with logs from the Red Hat Subscription Manager plugin.
sa/	Directory with system activity reports.
samba/	Directory of access and service logs for the Samba server.
secure	Authentication and access messages.
spooler	Shows a log file that might include critical messages.
sssd/	Directory of messages associated with the System Security Services daemon.
tallylog	Supports **pam_tally**, which locks out a user after excessive login failure attempts.
up2date	Includes log messages from the Red Hat Update Agent.
wtmp	List of logins, in binary format; can be read with the **utmpdump** command.
xferlog	Adds messages associated with file transfers from a local FTP server.
Xorg.0.log	Notes setup messages for the X Window System; may include configuration problems.
yum.log	Logs packages installed, updated, and erased with **yum**.

Service-Specific Logs

As suggested earlier, a number of services control their own log files. The log files for the vsFTP server, for example, are configured in the vsftpd.conf file in the /etc/vsftpd directory. As noted from that file, the following directive enables the logging of both uploads and downloads in the /var/log/xferlog file:

```
xferlog_enable=YES
```

The logging of other services may be more complex. For example, separate log files are configured for access and errors in the Apache web server in the /var/log/httpd directory.

EXERCISE 9-2

Learn the Log Files

In this exercise, you'll inspect the log files on a local system to try to identify different problems.

1. Restart the Linux computer. Log in as the root user. Use the wrong password once.

2. Log in properly with the correct password as the root user.

3. In a console, navigate to the /var/log directory and open the file named "secure." Navigate to the "Failed password" message closest to the end of the file. Review what happened. Close the file.

4. Review other logs in the /var/log directory. Use Table 9-8 for guidance. Look for messages associated with hardware. What log files are they in? Does that make sense?

5. Most, but not all, log files are text files. Try reading the lastlog file in the /var/log directory as a text file. What happens? Try the **lastlog** command. Are you now reading the contents of the /var/log/lastlog file? Can you confirm this from the associated man page?

View systemd Journal Log Entries

Aside from initializing the system and managing services, systemd also implements a powerful logging system. By default, logs are stored in a ring buffer using a binary format inside the directory /run/log/journal, and they do not persist a system reboot. In Chapter 5 we briefly introduced **journalctl** and explained how to enable persistent logging. In this section, we will review some of the basic functionalities of the **journalctl** command and show how to perform advanced searches.

One of the main advantages of the systemd journal over rsyslog is that it can store not just kernel and syslog messages, but also any other output that services send to their standard output or standard error. You don't need to know where a daemon sends its logs because everything is captured by systemd and logged into the journal. The journal is indexed so that it can be easily searched using different options.

By default, the **journalctl** command shows all the messages in the journal in a paged format, chronologically. It displays messages of **err** and **crit** severity in bold, and it shows **alert** and **emerg** lines in red. A useful command switch is **-f**, which works in a similar way to the **tail -f** command, by displaying the last 10 log entries and continuously printing any new log entries as they are appended to the journal.

You can filter the output of **journalctl** in several ways. You can use the **-p** switch to display messages whose priority is the same or higher than the one specified. As an example, the following command shows only entries of priority **err** or above:

```
# journalctl -p err
```

The command switches **--since** and **--until** can restrict the output to a specified time range. The next examples should be self-explanatory:

```
# journalctl --since yesterday
# journalctl --until "2015-03-28 11:59:59"
# journalctl --since 04:00 --until 10:59
```

You can also filter the output by looking at the most recent journal entries via the **-n** option. For example, you can run the next command to show the last 20 lines in the journal:

```
# journalctl -n 20
```

But there's more. Each entry in the systemd journal has a set of metadata that you can display with the **-o verbose** switch. Figure 9-10 shows how a journal entry looks when enabling verbose output.

The **journalctl** command can filter the output using any of the fields listed in Figure 9-10. For example, the following command shows all log entries associated with user ID 1000:

```
# journalctl _UID=1000
```

Similarly, the next example displays all journal entries related to the **nslcd** daemon:

```
# journalctl _COMM=nslcd
```

You can also specify multiple conditions on the same line. As you get more practice with the **journalctl** command, you will find that the systemd journal is very robust and flexible, and can be queried using a myriad of different options.

FIGURE 9-10   A journal entry with metadata

```
Sun 2015-03-08 22:01:03.074289 GMT [s=6b28fd9c29aa4618ba499fc63109198e;i=31c97;b
=7afe9ed7d1c04a00ad954c9cb7cbff99;m=220188bce86;t=5115ade9c68dd;x=825a08f554ea90
65]
    _TRANSPORT=syslog
    PRIORITY=3
    SYSLOG_FACILITY=3
    SYSLOG_IDENTIFIER=nslcd
    SYSLOG_PID=11103
    _PID=11103
    _UID=65
    _GID=55
    _COMM=nslcd
    _EXE=/usr/sbin/nslcd
    _CMDLINE=/usr/sbin/nslcd
    _CAP_EFFECTIVE=0
    _SYSTEMD_CGROUP=/system.slice/nslcd.service
    _SYSTEMD_UNIT=nslcd.service
    _SYSTEMD_SLICE=system.slice
    _SELINUX_CONTEXT=system_u:system_r:nslcd_t:s0
    _BOOT_ID=7afe9ed7d1c04a00ad954c9cb7cbff99
    _MACHINE_ID=b37be8dd26f97ac4ba4a6152f5e92b44
    _HOSTNAME=server1.example.com
    MESSAGE=[7721c9] <group/member="alex"> no available LDAP server found: Serve
r is unavailable: Transport endpoint is not connected
    _SOURCE_REALTIME_TIMESTAMP=1426456863074289
```

SCENARIO & SOLUTION

A script in a crontab file is not executed.	Check /var/log/cron. Ensure that the script has executable permissions.
Regular users can't access the **crontab** command or the **at** prompt.	Review the cron.allow and cron.deny files in the /etc directory to ensure that users can run the **crontab** command. Similarly, to grant users permission to schedule **at** jobs, review the at.allow and at.deny files.
Log files don't include sufficient information.	Revise /etc/rsyslog.conf. Focus on the desired facility, such as authpriv, mail, or cron, and revise the priority to include more detailed information. Look for log entries in the systemd journal.

CERTIFICATION SUMMARY

RHEL 7 includes a variety of system administration commands that can help you monitor and manage the resources used on a system. These commands include **ps**, **top**, **kill**, **nice**, and **renice**. In addition, with the right commands, you can create archives. However, special command options are required to back up files with specialized attributes such as those based on ACLs and SELinux.

The **cron** and **at** daemons can help you manage what jobs are run on a system on a schedule. With related configuration files, access to these daemons can be limited to certain users. While cron configuration files follow a specific format documented in /etc/crontab, those configuration directives have been integrated with the anacron system that supports job management on systems that are powered off on a regular basis.

RHEL 7 includes two logging systems—the **systemd journal** and the **rsyslog** daemon— that are configured primarily for local systems in the /etc/rsyslog.conf file. Log entries are normally collected by systemd in the /run/log/journal directory, whereas rsyslog stores log files permanently in the /var/log directory. The **rsyslog** daemon also supports the creation of a logging server that can collect log file information from a variety of systems.

TWO-MINUTE DRILL

Here are some of the key points from the certification objectives in Chapter 9.

Elementary System Administration Commands

❑ The **ps** command can identify currently running processes.

❑ The **top** command starts a task browser that can identify processes utilizing excessive resources on the system.

❑ The **sar** and related commands provide system activity reports.

❑ The **iostat** command can provide CPU and storage device statistics.

❑ The **nice** and **renice** commands can be used to reprioritize processes.

❑ The **kill** and **killall** commands can be used to stop currently running processes and even daemons with a variety of signals.

❑ Archives can be created, extracted, and compressed with the **gzip**, **bzip2**, **tar**, and **star** commands.

Automate System Administration: cron and at

❑ The cron system allows users to schedule jobs so they run at given intervals.

❑ The at system allows users to configure jobs to run once at a scheduled time.

❏ The **crontab** command is used to work with cron files. Use **crontab -e** to edit, **crontab -l** to list, and **crontab -r** to delete cron files.

❏ The /etc/cron.allow and /etc/cron.deny files are used to control access to the cron job scheduler; the /etc/at.allow and /etc/at.deny files are used to control access to the at job scheduler in a similar fashion.

Local Log File Analysis

❏ Red Hat Enterprise Linux includes the **rsyslog** daemon, which monitors a system for kernel messages as well as other process activity, as configured in /etc/rsyslog.conf.

❏ You can use log files generated in the /var/log directory to track activities on a system.

❏ Other log files may be created and configured through service configuration files.

❏ Log files may be rotated on a regular basis, as configured in the /etc/logrotate.conf file.

❏ The systemd journal logs all boot, kernel, and service messages in a ring buffer inside the /run/log/journal directory.

❏ The **journalctl** command is used to display and filter journal entries.

SELF TEST

The following questions will help measure your understanding of the material presented in this chapter. As no multiple choice questions appear on the Red Hat exams, no multiple choice questions appear in this book. These questions exclusively test your understanding of the chapter. It is okay if you have another way of performing a task. Getting results, not memorizing trivia, is what counts on the Red Hat exams.

Elementary System Administration Commands

1. What command identifies all running processes in the current terminal console?

   _____

2. What is the highest priority number you can set for a process with the **nice** command?

   _____

3. What **tar** command option can be used to archive the files of an existing directory while saving its SELinux contexts?

_____

4. You want to create an archive of the /etc directory. What command do you need to run to create a compressed bzip2 archive of that directory? Assume that archive is named /tmp/etc.tar.bz2

_____

Automate System Administration: cron and at

5. You want to schedule a maintenance job, maintenance.pl, to run from your home directory on the first of every month at 4:00 A.M. You've run the **crontab -e** command to open your personal crontab file. Assume you've added appropriate **PATH** and **SHELL** directives. What directive would you add to run the specified job at the specified time?

_____

6. Suppose you see the following entry in the output to the **crontab -l** command:

```
42 4 1 * * root run-parts /etc/cron.monthly
```

When is the next time Linux will run the jobs in the /etc/cron.monthly directory?

_____

7. If the users tim and stephanie are listed in both the /etc/cron.allow and the /etc/cron.deny files, and users donna and elizabeth are listed only in the /etc/cron.allow file, which of those users is allowed to run the **crontab -e** command?

_____

8. What file is used to configure log file rotation?

_____

Local Log File Analysis

9. What entry in the /etc/rsyslog.conf file would notify logged-in users whenever there is a critical problem with the kernel?

_____

10. There are several files in the /var/log directory related to what happened during the installation process. What is the first word shared by the name of these log files?

_____

11. What command displays all systemd journal entries with a priority equal to alert or higher?

_____

12. How you can show the systemd journal entries related to the **httpd** daemon logged since the 16th of March 2015?

_____

LAB QUESTIONS

Several of these labs involve exercises that can seriously affect a system. You should do these exercises on test machines only. The second lab of Chapter 1 sets up KVM for this purpose.

Red Hat presents its exams electronically. For that reason, the labs for this chapter are available on the DVD that accompanies the book, in the Chapter9/ subdirectory. They're available in .doc, .html, and .txt formats. In case you haven't yet set up RHEL 7 on a system, refer to the first lab of Chapter 2 for installation instructions. However, the answers for each lab follow the Self Test answers for the fill-in-the-blank questions.

SELF TEST ANSWERS

Elementary System Administration Commands

1. This is a bit of a trick question because the **ps** command by itself identifies any currently running processes in the current console.

2. The highest priority number that can be used with the **nice** command is -20. Remember, priority numbers for processes are counterintuitive.

3. The **tar** command option that preserves SELinux contexts in an archive is **--selinux**.

4. The command that creates a compressed bzip2 archive of the /etc directory is

```
# tar cvfj /tmp/etc.tar.bz2 /etc
```

Automate System Administration: cron and at

5. The directive that runs the maintenance.pl script from a home directory at the noted time is

```
0 4 1 * * ~/maintenance.pl
```

6. Based on the noted entry in /etc/crontab, the next time Linux will run the jobs in the /etc/cron.monthly directory is on the first of the upcoming month, at 4:42 A.M.

7. When usernames exist in both the /etc/cron.allow and /etc/cron.deny files, users listed in /etc/cron.deny are ignored. Thus, all four users listed are allowed to run various **crontab** commands.

8. The configuration file associated with the rotation of log files over time is /etc/logrotate.conf. Additional service-specific configuration files can be created in the /etc/logrotate.d directory.

Local Log File Analysis

9. There's a commented entry in the /etc/rsyslog.conf file that meets the requirements of the question. Just activate it and change the priority to **crit** to notify you (and everyone) whenever a serious problem with the kernel logs occurs:

```
kern.crit        /dev/console
```

Of course, that means there are other acceptable ways to meet the requirements of the question.

10. The log files in /var/log that are most relevant to the installation process start with **anaconda**.

11. The command that displays all systemd journal entries with a priority equal to alert or higher is **journalctl -p alert**.

12. To show all systemd journal entries related to the **httpd** daemon and logged since the 16th of March 2015, run the command **journalctl _COMM=httpd --since 2015-03-16**.

LAB ANSWERS

Lab 1

One way to modify the login messages as noted is with the following steps (there is at least one other method, related to the /etc/cron.d directory):

1. Log in as the root user.

2. Run the **crontab -e** command.

3. Add the appropriate environment variables, at least the following:

```
SHELL=/bin/bash
```

4. Add the following commands to the file to overwrite /etc/motd at the appropriate times:

```
0 7  * * * /bin/echo 'Coffee time' > /etc/motd
0 13 * * * /bin/echo 'Want some ice cream?' > /etc/motd
0 18 * * * /bin/echo 'Shouldn\'t you be doing something else?' > /etc/motd
```

5. Save the file. As long as the **cron** daemon is active (which it is by default), the next user who logs in to the console after one of the specified times should see the message upon a successful login. If you want to test the result immediately, the **date** command can help. For example, the command

```
# date 06120659
```

sets a date of June 12, at 6:59 A.M., just before the **cron** daemon should execute the first command in the list. (Of course, you'll want to substitute today's date and wait one minute before logging in to this system from another console.)

Lab 2

To set up an at job to start 5 minutes from now, start with the **at** command. It'll take you to an at> prompt.

Currently installed RPMs are shown in the output to the **rpm -qa** command. Since there is no PATH defined at the at> prompt, you should include the full path. So one way to create a list of currently installed RPMs in the /root/rpms.txt file in a one-time job starting five minutes from now is with the following commands:

```
# at now + 5 min
at> /bin/rpm -qa > /root/rpms.txt
at> Ctrl+d
#
```

Within five minutes, you should see an rpms.txt file in the home directory of the root user, /root. If five minutes is too long to wait (as it might be during the RHCSA exam), proceed to Lab 3 and come back to this problem afterward. Don't forget to set up the other at job to be run in 24 hours.

Lab 3

One way to set up the cron job specified in the lab requirements is detailed here:

1. Log in as the root user.

2. The lab requirements don't allow you to use the **crontab -e** command to edit the root crontab file. Hence, create a system crontab in the /etc/cron.d directory, using the following command:

```
# cat > /etc/cron.d/etc-backup << EOF
```

3. Type the following line to set up the cron job:

```
5 2 * * 6 root /usr/bin/tar --selinux -czf /tmp/etc-backup-\$(/bin/date ↵
+\%m\%d).tar.gz /etc > /dev/null
```

4. Don't forget to escape the % characters in the crontab entry; otherwise, they will be interpreted as newlines.

5. Type the EOF sequence:

   ```
   EOF
   ```

6. To test the job, modify the crontab entry so that it runs a few minutes from now. Then, change the directory to /tmp and extract the generated archive using the following command:

   ```
   # tar --selinux -xzf etc-backup-$(date +%m%d).tar.gz
   ```

7. Confirm that SELinux contexts have been preserved by running the following command:

   ```
   # ls -lRZ /tmp/etc
   ```

Lab 4

There are no secret solutions in this lab; the intent is to get you to review the contents of key log files to understand what should be there.

When you review the anaconda.* files in /var/log and compare them to other files, you may gain some insight on how to diagnose installation problems. In future chapters, you'll examine some of the log files associated with specific services; many are located in subdirectories such as /var/log/samba and /var/log/httpd.

The failed login should be readily apparent in the /var/log/secure file. You may be able to get hints in the output to the **utmpdump btmp** command.

When you review the /var/log/cron file, you'll see when standard cron jobs were run. Most of the file should be filled (by default) by the standard hourly job, **run-parts** /etc/cron.hourly, from the /etc/cron.d/0hourly configuration file. If you've rebooted, you may see the anacron service, and you should be able to search for the job of the same name.

While /var/log/dmesg includes the currently booted kernel, it may be the same kernel as the one associated with /var/log/anaconda/syslog, if you haven't upgraded kernels. At the end of /var/log/dmesg, you can find the filesystems mounted to the XFS format, as well as currently mounted swap partitions. For example, the following lists the partitions from a KVM-based virtual drive:

```
XFS (vda1): Mounting Filesystem
Adding 1023996k swap on /dev/mapper/rhel-swap.
Priority:-1 extents:1 across:1023996k
XFS (vda1): Ending clean mount
SELinux: initialized (dev vda1, type xfs), uses xattr
```

As you've hopefully discovered, the /var/log/maillog file does not include any information on mail clients, only servers.

Red Hat has included a GUI configuration tool in RHEL 7. The automatic configuration for hardware graphics is now sufficiently reliable, but in case you face any problems, you can look into /var/log/Xorg.0.log.

Chapter 10

A Security Primer

As you start the first chapter of the RHCE section of this book, you'll start with security. Many administrators and enterprises move toward Linux because they believe it's more secure. Since most Linux software is released under open-source licenses, the source code is available to all. Some believe that provides advantages for black hat hackers who want to break into a system.

However, Linux developers are believers in collaboration. "Linus's Law," according to the open-source luminary Eric Raymond, is that "given enough eyeballs, all bugs are shallow." Some of those eyes are from the U.S. National Security Agency (NSA), which has contributed a lot of code to Linux, including the foundations of SELinux.

The NSA has also contributed a number of other concepts adapted by Red Hat that have been integrated into a layered security strategy. These include guidelines to set up firewalls, wrappers on packets, and security by service. They cover both user- and host-based security. They include access controls such as ownership, permissions, and SELinux. (A number of these layers were covered in earlier chapters.) The fundamentals of these layers of security, as they apply to the RHCE objectives, are also covered here.

In this chapter, you'll examine some of the tools provided by RHEL for managing security. You'll start with some fundamentals and continue with detailed analysis of zone-based firewalls, Pluggable Authentication Modules (PAM), TCP Wrappers, and more.

This is not the only chapter to focus on security. Strictly speaking, it covers only two of the RHCE objectives. However, this chapter covers the themes associated with security on Linux systems, and those themes can help you understand the security options associated with every service in this book.

CERTIFICATION OBJECTIVE 10.01

The Layers of Linux Security

The best computer security comes in layers. If there's a breach in one layer, such as penetration through a firewall, a compromised user account, or a buffer overflow that messes up a service, there's almost always some other security measure that prevents or at least minimizes further damage.

INSIDE THE EXAM

Inside the Exam

This chapter is the first one in this book focused on the RHCE requirements. As described in the RHCE objectives, security starts with packet filtering and NAT developed with the firewalld zone-based firewall. The related objective is

- Use firewalld and associated mechanisms, such as rich rules, zones, and custom rules, to implement packet filtering and configure Network Address Translation (NAT)

But as suggested in the introduction, security is an issue for all services covered in the RHCE objectives. This chapter provides a foundation for a discussion of security, including several methods to

- Configure host-based and user-based security for the service

Whereas host-based security can start with zone-based firewalls, host- and user-based security measures can involve TCP Wrappers and Pluggable Authentication Modules.

These options start with minimally configured bastion hosts, which minimize the functionality associated with an individual Linux system. Beyond the firewall and SELinux come security options associated with individual services. Isolation options such as chroot jails are generally configured as part of a service. A number of these options are based on recommendations from the NSA.

While the sections on bastion systems are intended to be a lead-in to the security measures used for RHCE-level services, they also incorporate those security options often associated with the RHCSA exam, which are described in earlier chapters.

Bastion Systems

Properly configured, a bastion system minimizes the risk of a security breach. It's based on a minimal installation, with less software than was installed on the systems configured in Chapters 1 and 2. A bastion system is configured with two services. One service defines the functionality of the system. It could be a web server, a file server, an authentication server, or something similar. The other service supports remote access, such as SSH, or perhaps VNC over SSH.

Before virtualization, the use of bastion systems was frequently limited. Only the wealthiest enterprises could afford to dedicate different physical systems to each service. If redundancy was required, the costs only increased further.

With virtualization, bastion systems are within reach of even smaller businesses. All that's needed is a standard minimal installation. With a few Kickstart files, you as an administrator of such a network could easily create a whole group of bastion systems. Each system could then be customized with and dedicated to a single server.

Well-constructed bastion systems follow two principles:

- If you don't need the software, uninstall it.
- If you need the software but aren't using it, make sure it's not active.

In general, black hat hackers can't take advantage of a security flaw if the associated service isn't installed. If you do have to install the service for test purposes, keep that service inactive. That can help keep risks to a minimum. Of course, firewalls configured for each bastion system should allow traffic through only for the dedicated service and the remote access method.

Best Defenses with Security Updates

Security updates are extremely important. You can review available updates with the Software Update tool. You can start that tool in a GUI with the **gpk-update-viewer** command. As discussed in Chapter 7, you can set up automatic security updates with the Software Updates Preferences tool, which you can start in a GUI with the **gpk-prefs** command.

In practice, security is often a race, between when a vulnerability is discovered and when an update is made available. Until those updates are installed, any affected services might be vulnerable.

As a Linux professional, it's your job to know these vulnerabilities. If you maintain servers such as Apache, vsFTP, and Samba, monitor the information feeds from these developers. Security news may come in various forms, from message board updates to RSS feeds. Normally, Red Hat also keeps up to speed on such issues. However, if you've subscribed to the forums maintained by the developers of a service, it's best to hear about problems and planned solutions directly from the source. To some extent, that is a province of service-specific security.

Information security vulnerabilities are tracked in a standardized format system known as Common Vulnerabilities and Exposures (CVE), which is maintained by MITRE Corporation (http://cve.mitre.org). In its "Errata" security advisories, Red Hat always references the corresponding CVE identifiers. You should familiarize yourself with the CVE format and monitor the Red Hat CVE database and Errata announcement websites for updates, available at https://access.redhat.com/security/cve and https://rhn.redhat.com/errata, respectively.

Service-Specific Security

Most major services have some level of security that can be configured within. In many cases, you can configure a service to limit access by host, by network, by user, and by group. As listed in the RHCE objectives, you need to know how to configure host- and user-based security for each listed service. SELinux options that can help secure each of these services are also available. While details are discussed in appropriate upcoming chapters, the following is a brief overview of service-specific security options.

HTTP/HTTPS Service-Specific Security

Although there are alternatives, the primary service for the HTTP and HTTPS protocols on Linux is the Apache web server. In fact, Apache is the dominant web server on the Internet. No question, Apache configuration files are complex, but they need to be, because the security challenges on the Internet are substantial. Some options for responding to these challenges are covered in Chapter 14.

Apache includes numerous optional software components. Don't install more than is absolutely necessary. If there's a security breach in a Common Gateway Interface (CGI) script and you haven't installed Apache support for CGI scripts, that security issue doesn't affect you. However, because the RHCE specifies an objective to deploy a "basic CGI application," you don't have that luxury for the exam.

Fortunately, with Apache, you can limit access in a number of ways. Limits can be created on the server or on individual virtual hosts. Different limits can be created on regular and secure websites. In addition, Apache supports the use of secure certificates.

DNS Service-Specific Security

Domain Name Service (DNS) servers are a big target for black hat hackers. With that in mind, RHEL 7 includes the bind-chroot package, which configures the necessary files, devices, and libraries in an isolated subdirectory. That subdirectory provides a limit for any user who breaks through DNS security known as a chroot jail. It's designed to limit the directories where a black hat hacker can navigate if he does break into the service. In other words, if someone breaks into a RHEL 7 DNS server, they should not be able to "escape" the subdirectory configured as a chroot jail.

Since RHCE exam candidates are not expected to create a master or a slave DNS server, the challenges and risks are somewhat limited. Nevertheless, in Chapter 13, you'll see how to limit access to the configured DNS server by host.

NFS Service-Specific Security

With the move to the Network File System version 4, it is now possible to set up Kerberos authentication to support user-based security. Although the configuration of Kerberos and LDAP servers is beyond the scope of the RHCE objectives, for the RHCE exam you need to control access to NFS shares using Kerberos. Chapter 16 will cover this topic, along with host-based security options.

SMB Service-Specific Security

The SMB listed in the RHCE objectives stands for the Server Message Block protocol. It's the networking protocol originally developed by IBM, and later modified by Microsoft, as the network protocol for its operating systems. While Microsoft now refers to it as the Common Internet File System (CIFS), the Linux implementation of this networking protocol is still known as Samba.

As implemented for RHEL 7, you can use Samba to authenticate via Microsoft Active Directory. Samba supports the mapping of such users and groups into a Linux authentication database. Samba also supports both user- and host-based security on the global and shared directory levels, as discussed in Chapter 15.

The standard version of Samba for RHEL 7 is 4.1. With the release of version 4, Samba can also act as a Domain Controller compatible with Microsoft Active Directory. However, this configuration is outside of the scope of the RHCE exam.

SMTP Service-Specific Security

RHEL supports two different services for e-mail communication through the Simple Mail Transport Protocol (SMTP): Postfix and Sendmail. Both are released under open-source licenses.

The default SMTP e-mail service for RHEL 7 is Postfix, although you can configure either service to meet the associated RHCE objective. In either case, the service normally only listens on the localhost address, which is one level of security. Other levels of security are possible based on hosts, usernames, and more. For more information, see Chapter 13.

SSH Service-Specific Security

The SSH service is installed by default even in the minimal installation of RHEL 7. That encourages its use as a remote administration tool. However, there are risks associated with the SSH server that can be minimized. For example, remote logins to the root account do not have to be allowed. Security can be further regulated by user.

Host-Based Security

Host-based security refers to access limits, not only by the system hostnames, but also by their fully qualified domain names and IP addresses. The syntax associated with host-based security can vary. For example, while every system recognizes a specific IP address such as 192.168.122.50, not all services recognize wildcards or Classless Inter-Domain Routing (CIDR) notation for a range of IP addresses. Depending on the service, you may use one or more of the following options for the noted range of network addresses:

```
192.168.122.0/255.255.255.0
192.168.122.0/24
192.168.122.*
192.168.122.
192.168.122
```

Just be careful, because some of these options may lead to syntax errors on some network services. In a similar fashion, any of the following options may or may not work to represent all of the systems on an example.com network:

```
*.example.com
.example.com
example.com
```

User-Based Security

User-based security includes users and groups. Generally, users and groups who are allowed or denied access to a service are collected in a list. That list could include a user on each line, as in a file such as /etc/cron.allow, or it could be in a list that follows a directive, such as

```
valid users = michael donna @book
```

Sometimes the syntax of a user list is unforgiving; in some cases, an extra space after a comma or at the end of a line may result in an authentication failure.

Groups are frequently included in a list of users, with a special symbol in front, such as @ or +.

Sometimes, users who are allowed access to a system are configured in a separate authentication database, such as that associated with the Samba server, configured with the **smbpasswd** command.

Console Security

As discussed in Chapter 5, console security is managed by the /etc/securetty file. It can help you regulate local console access to root and regular users.

However, console access is not just local. For a full view of console security, you need to be able to configure limits on remote console access. Two primary options are SSH, as discussed earlier, and Telnet. While the **telnet** command has its uses, as described in Chapter 2, communications to Telnet servers are inherently insecure. Usernames, passwords, and other communication to and from a Telnet server are transmitted in clear text. That means a network protocol analyzer such as Wireshark could be used to read those usernames, passwords, and any other critical information.

Even though Kerberos-based options are available for Telnet servers, most security professionals avoid Telnet for remote consoles at almost all costs—and that's consistent with the recommendations from the NSA.

Recommendations from the U.S. National Security Agency

The NSA has taken a special interest in Linux, and specifically Red Hat Enterprise Linux. Not only has the NSA taken the time to develop SELinux, but it also has created guides to help administrators like you create a more secure RHEL configuration. (Yes, the "super-secret" NSA has released SELinux code under open-source licenses for all to see.) They recognize the importance of Linux in the infrastructure of computer networks. Observers of RHEL may notice how changes between RHEL 5, RHEL 6, and RHEL 7 follow NSA recommendations.

The NSA includes five general principles for securing operating systems in general and RHEL in particular:

- *Encrypt transmitted data whenever possible.* NSA recommendations for encryption include communications over what should be private and secure networks. The use of SSH, with the security options described in Chapter 11, is an excellent step in this process.

- *Minimize software to minimize vulnerability.* As suggested by the NSA, "The simplest way to avoid vulnerabilities in software is to avoid installing that software." The NSA pays special attention to any software that can communicate over a network, including the Linux GUI. The minimal installation of RHEL 7 includes far fewer packages than the comparable installation of RHEL 5.

■ *Run different network services on separate systems.* This is consistent with the concept of bastion servers described earlier in this chapter. Implementation is made easier by the flexibility afforded by virtual machine technologies such as KVM.

■ *Configure security tools to improve system robustness.* The RHCSA and RHCE objectives have this well covered, with the use of zone-based firewalls, SELinux, and appropriate log collection services.

■ *Use the principle of least privilege.* In principle, you should give users the minimum privileges required to accomplish their tasks. Not only does that mean minimize access to the root administrative account, but also careful use of the **sudo** command privileges. SELinux options such as the user_u role for confinement (described in Chapter 4) may also be helpful to that end.

The PolicyKit

The PolicyKit is one more security mechanism designed to help protect different administrative tools. Most administrative tools started in the GUI from a regular account will prompt for the root administrative password with a window similar to the one shown in Figure 10-1.

Alternatively, you might see a slightly different window similar to that shown in Figure 10-2. Functionally, the effect is the same. As described in the window, authentication by the superuser is required. In this case, you'd still have to enter the root administrative password.

PolicyKit stores its policies in the /usr/share/polkit-1/actions directory. The corresponding file for the **system-config-date** tool is org.fedoraproject.config.date.policy.

FIGURE 10-1

Access to administrative tools in the GUI requires the root password.

Query

You are attempting to run "system-config-language" which requires administrative privileges, but more information is needed in order to do so.

Authenticating as "alex"

Password: [_____]

Cancel   OK

FIGURE 10-2

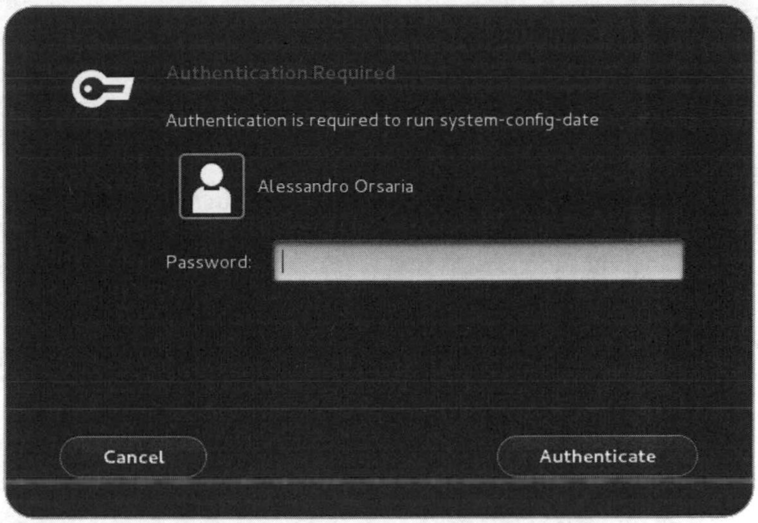

Access to
administrative
tools may be
limited by the
PolicyKit.

These policy files are configured in XML format and may be modified further to support fine-grained control by individual users. Although PolicyKit provides an API that can also be used by text-based programs, it is typically used to authorize the execution of GUI-based tools.

One alternative that also provides fine-grained control is the /etc/sudoers file described in Chapter 8.

CERTIFICATION OBJECTIVE 10.02

Firewalls and Network Address Translation

Typically, firewalls reside between internal LANs and outside insecure networks such as the Internet. A firewall can be configured to examine every network packet that passes into or out of your LAN. When configured with appropriate rules, it can filter out those packets that may pose a security risk to the systems on the LAN.

However, to follow the spirit of the recommendations from the NSA, you'll configure a firewall on every system.

Although network address translation (NAT) can be implemented on every system in the LAN, it is more commonly used on those systems configured as a gateway or router between a LAN and an outside network.

Definitions

Firewalls based on the firewalld service read the headers of each network packet. Based on the information contained in the headers, you can configure firewalld rules to filter each packet. To understand how *packet filtering* works, you have to understand a little bit about how information is sent across networks.

Before a message is sent over a network, that message is broken down into smaller units called *packets.* Administrative information, including the type of data, the source, and the destination addresses, as well as the source and destination ports (for TCP and UDP traffic), is added to the header of each packet. The packets are sent over the network and reach the destination Linux host. A firewall can examine the fields in each header. Based on existing rules, the firewall may then take one of the following actions with that packet:

- Allow the packet into the system.
- Forward the packet to other systems if the current system is a gateway or router between networks.
- Rate-limit the traffic.
- Reject the packet with a message sent to the originating IP address.
- Drop the packet without sending any sort of message.

Whatever the result, the decision can be logged to syslog or to the auditd subsystem. If a substantial number of packets are rejected or dropped, a log file may be useful.

RHEL 7 comes with everything you need to configure a system to be a firewall, for both IPv4 and IPv6 networks.

NAT can hide the IP address of the computers of a LAN that connect to outside networks. NAT replaces the internal source address with the IP address of the firewall interface connected to the outside network. The internal source address, along with other information that identifies the connection, is stored on the firewall connection table to keep note of which host made the request.

When the firewall receives a response, such as the content of a web page, the process is reversed. As the packets pass through the firewall, the destination host is identified in the connection table. The firewall modifies the IP header of each packet before sending the packets on their way.

This approach is useful for several reasons. Hiding internal IP addresses makes it harder for a black hat hacker to break into an internal network. NAT supports connections between systems with private IP addresses and external networks such as the Internet. It's the reason why IPv4 addressing has survived for so long. In the Linux world, this process is also known as *IP masquerading.*

While IP masquerading is usually referred to as "source NAT," there is also another form of NAT that works in the reverse direction, and is known as *port forwarding* or *destination NAT.* Port forwarding can hide the internal port and IP address of a service. As an example,

TABLE 10-1	Elements of a firewalld Zone

Zone Element	Description
Interfaces	Network interfaces associated with a zone
Sources	Source IP addresses associated with a zone
Services	Inbound services that are allowed through a zone, such as http
Ports	Destination TCP or UDP ports that are allowed through a zone, such as 8080/tcp
Masquerade	Specifies whether source network address translation (masquerading) is enabled
Forward ports	Port forwarding rules (map traffic sent to a local port onto another port on the same or another host)
ICMP blocks	Used to block ICMP messages
Rich rules	Advanced firewall rules

suppose you have an internal server with IP address 192.168.122.50, running a web service on TCP port 8080. With port forwarding, you can have clients connecting to a different IP address and port, such as a public IP on port 80, and forward traffic to the host and port on the internal network.

The Structure of firewalld

In Chapter 4 we introduced some of the basic concepts of firewalld. In this section, we will explore its advanced features, such as zone configuration and rich rules.

As you already know, firewalld is based on zones. A *zone* defines the level of trust of network connections. The basic elements that define a zone are illustrated in Table 10-1.

You can list all firewalld zones by typing the following command:

```
# firewall-cmd --get-zones
block dmz drop external home internal public trusted work
```

These correspond to the zones you have already encountered in Table 4-8 of Chapter 4. Take a few minutes to review the contents of that table.

To display the settings associated with a zone, use the **--list-all** command switch. As an example, let's show all the configuration settings of the *public* zone:

```
# firewall-cmd --list-all --zone=public
public (default, active)
  interfaces: eth0
  sources:
  services: dhcpv6-client ssh
```

```
ports:
masquerade: no
forward-ports:
icmp-blocks:
rich-rules:
```

As you can see from the output, the *public* zone is associated with interface eth0. Incoming traffic for the DHCPv6 and SSH services is allowed through the zone, whereas masquerading is disabled. Note that on the first line of the command output, the public zone is marked as "default" and "active."

An *active zone* is a zone associated with at least one network interface or source IP address in firewalld. We introduced the concept of a *default zone* in Chapter 4: Only one zone can be marked as the "default" zone, and this special status means that any network interfaces added to the system will be automatically assigned to that zone.

Additionally, the default zone acts like a sort of "catch-all." This is related to how firewalld assigns incoming packets to a zone, based on the following rules:

- If the *source address* of the packet matches the source addresses associated with a zone, then the packet is processed according to the rules of that zone.
- If the packet comes from a *network interface* associated with a zone, then the packet is processed according to the rules of that zone.
- Otherwise, the packet is processed according to the rules of the default zone.

Once an incoming packet is matched to a zone, firewalld processes it according to the rules of that zone. As an example, based on the previous listed **firewall-cmd** output, incoming packets that reach the eth0 interface will be processed using the settings of the firewalld public zone. According to the rules of that zone, traffic will be allowed only if it belongs to the DHCPv6 or SSH protocol.

The most common **firewall-cmd** options related with zone configuration are shown in Table 10-2. Some of the listed options relate to the **--zone** command switch for non-default zones.

The following example shows how to set the default zone to the "work" zone:

```
# firewall-cmd --get-default-zone
public
# firewall-cmd --get-active-zones
public
  interfaces: virbr0 virbr1 wlp4s0
# firewall-cmd --set-default-zone=work
# firewall-cmd --get-default-zone
work
# firewall-cmd -get-active-zones
work
  interfaces: virbr0 virbr1 wlp4s0
```

TABLE 10-2	The firewall-cmd Zone Configuration Options

Command Option	Description
--get-default-zone	Lists the default zone
--set-default-zone=ZONE	Sets the default zone to ZONE
--get-zones	List all zones
--get-active-zones	List only the active zones—that is, the zones associated with at least one source interface or address in firewalld
--list-all-zones	Lists all the settings for all zones
--list-all [--zone=ZONE]	Lists all the settings for a specific ZONE or for the default zone
--add-source=NETWORK [zone=ZONE]	Binds a source network to a ZONE or to the default zone
--change-source=NETWORK [--zone=ZONE]	Changes a source network currently assigned to a zone to a different ZONE or to the default zone
--remove-source=NETWORK [--zone=ZONE]	Removes a source network from a ZONE or from the default zone
--add-interface=INTERFACE [--zone=ZONE]	Adds an interface to a ZONE or to the default zone
--change-interface=INTERFACE [zone=ZONE]	Changes an interface currently assigned to a zone into a different ZONE or into the default zone
--remove-interface=INTERFACE [--zone=ZONE]	Removes an interface from a ZONE or from the default zone

Observe how all interfaces that were assigned to the "public" zone have been moved to the "work" zone after the change. Also, note the **--set-default-zone** option makes a permanent change that survives after a system reboot. This is one of the few options in firewalld that does not require the **--permanent** switch, as you will see in a moment.

The next example associates the virbr1 interface with the "dmz" zone and adds the source IP range 192.168.99.0/24 to the "public" zone:

```
# firewall-cmd --change-interface=virbr1 --zone dmz
success
# firewall-cmd --add-source 192.168.99.0/24 --zone=public
success
# firewall-cmd --get-active-zones
dmz
  interfaces: virbr1
work
  interfaces: virbr0 wlp4s0
public
  sources: 192.168.99.0/24
```

The configuration change made to the public zone in the previous example won't survive a reboot. As was noted in Chapter 4, to make permanent configuration changes, most **firewall-cmd** actions require the --**permanent** option. Once the new settings are saved into the permanent configuration, run **firewall-cmd** --**reload** to apply the settings immediately into the run-time configuration.

Services and Ports Configuration

To configure an effective firewalld zone, you need to give it the ability to allow or block traffic. You can do so by making appropriate changes to the services and port configuration. Before we dig into the details, examine Table 10-3, which provides a list of the service and port configuration options.

Two common ways to allow traffic through firewalld is by adding to a zone a pre-defined service, or a port and protocol combination, such as 8080/tcp. By default, all but one zone contains an implicit "deny all traffic" rule. The exception is the "trusted" zone, which allows all traffic by default. Hence, except for the "trusted" zone, you must explicitly allow a service or port; otherwise, the corresponding traffic will be blocked by the firewall.

TABLE 10-3 The firewall-cmd Service and Port Configuration Options

Command Option	Description
--get-services	Lists all predefined services
--list-services [--zone=ZONE]	Lists all services allowed for the specified ZONE or for the default zone
--add-service=SERVICE [--zone=ZONE]	Allows traffic for the specified SERVICE through a ZONE or the default zone
--remove-service=SERVICE [--zone=ZONE]	Removes a SERVICE from a ZONE or from the default zone
--list-ports [--zone=ZONE]	Lists TCP and UDP destination ports allowed through a ZONE or the default zone
--add-port=PORT/PROTOCOL [--zone=ZONE]	Allows traffic for the specified PORT/PROTOCOL through a ZONE or the default zone
--remove-port=PORT/PROTOCOL [--zone=ZONE]	Removes a PORT/PROTOCOL from a ZONE or from the default zone

on the
ǃob
Making configuration changes to firewalld on a production server may be dangerous and result in a loss of administrative access to the host. To avoid this problem, you can include the --timeout=*SECONDS* **option with your** firewall-cmd **command, which applies a configuration change only for the specified number of seconds.**

Take a look at the firewall services defined by default by running the following command:

```
# firewall-cmd --get-services
amanda-client bacula bacula-client dhcp dhcpv6 dhcpv6-client dns ftp
high-availability http https imaps ipp ipp-client ipsec kerberos kpasswd
ldap ldaps libvirt libvirt-tls mdns mountd ms-wbt mysql nfs ntp openvpn
pmcd pmproxy pmwebapi pmwebapis pop3s postgresql proxy-dhcp radius rpc-bind
samba samba-client smtp ssh telnet tftp tftp-client transmission-client
vnc-server wbem-https
```

These services are configured in XML files in the /usr/lib/firewalld/services/ directory. You can add services to the /etc/firewalld/services/ directory.

To see how this works, look at Figure 10-3. Note how the contents of the file http.xml contain an XML declaration and a <service> block, with three additional elements: the service short name, a description, and the corresponding protocol and port associated with the service (in this case, TCP/80).

Review the services associated with the default zone. If you had set the default to a different zone, revert your changes by running the command **firewall-cmd --set-default-zone=public**. Next, list the services associated with the zone with the following command:

```
# firewall-cmd --list-services
dhcpv6-client ftp http ssh
```

If you have completed the labs in Chapters 1 and 2 on your physical workstation, you should see the FTP and HTTP protocols in the list of services associated with the default

FIGURE 10-3   The firewalld configuration for the http service

```
[root@server1 ~]# cat /usr/lib/firewalld/services/http.xml
<?xml version="1.0" encoding="utf-8"?>
<service>
  <short>WWW (HTTP)</short>
  <description>HTTP is the protocol used to serve Web pages. If you plan to make
your Web server publicly available, enable this option. This option is not requ
ired for viewing pages locally or developing Web pages.</description>
  <port protocol="tcp" port="80"/>
</service>
[root@server1 ~]# █
```

zone. If a service is missing, you can permanently add it to the zone configuration using the following commands:

```
# firewall-cmd --permanent --add-service=ftp
# firewall-cmd --reload
```

You can also specify the traffic to be allowed through a zone using a port/protocol pair. As an example, suppose you have a web server running on a nonstandard port, such as TCP port 81. To allow connections to this port through the default firewalld zone, run the following command:

```
# firewall-cmd --permanent --add-port=81/tcp
# firewall-cmd --reload
```

The next command confirms the change:

```
# firewall-cmd --list-ports
81/tcp
```

To add a new service or port onto a different zone, the syntax of these commands is the same. You just need to specify the desired zone with the **--zone** command switch.

When you run a service on a nonstandard port, you may need to change the default SELinux port label configuration. This is not required for a web server running on TCP port 81, but it may be required in other situations, as you will see in Chapter 11.

Rich Rules

Adding services and ports to a zone is the most common way to allow traffic through a firewall. However, in some situations you may need the flexibility to create more complex rules. As an example, you may want to allow connections from all the IP addresses in a subnet, except for one specific host. With rich rules, you can satisfy this type of requirement and set up firewall rules that match a more complex logic. But there's more. You can also rate-limit incoming connections and log any connection attempts to syslog or to the audit service.

The common **firewall-cmd** options associated with rich rules are listed in Table 10-4. A rich rule does two things: it specifies the conditions a packet must meet to match the rule, and it specifies the action to execute if the packet matches.

A rich rule uses the following basic format:

```
rule [family=<rule_family>]
[source address=<address> [invert=true]]
[destination address=<address> [invert=true]]
service|port|protocol|icmp-block|masquerade|forward-port
[log] [audit] [accept|reject|drop]
```

TABLE 10-4	The firewall-cmd Rich Rule Configuration Options

Command Option	Description
--list-rich-rules [--zone=ZONE]	Lists all rich rules for the specified ZONE or for the default zone
--add-rich-rule='RULE' [--zone=ZONE]	Adds a rich rule for the specified ZONE or for the default zone
--remove-rich-rule='RULE' [--zone=ZONE]	Removes a rich rule for the specified ZONE or for the default zone
--query-rich-rule='RULE' [--zone=ZONE]	Checks whether a rich rule has been added for the specified ZONE or for the default zone

Now let's analyze this command, item by item. The first item is the **rule** keyword, followed by an optional family type. There are two family options for a rule:

- **family="ipv4"**   Limits the action of the rule to IPv4 packets
- **family="ipv6"**   Limits the action of the rule to IPv6 packets

Without the **family** keyword, the rule applies to both IPv4 and IPv6 packets.

The next two optional items are the source and destination addresses. You may specify them using the following format:

- **source address=*address[/mask]* [invert=true]**   Matches all source IP addresses within the address/mask range. If you add **invert=true**, the rich rule applies to all but the specified address(es).
- **destination address=*address[/mask]* [invert=true]**   Matches all destination IP addresses within the address/mask range. If you add **invert=true**, the rich rule applies to all but the specified address(es).

Packet patterns can be more complex. In TCP/IP, most packets are sent using the Transport Control Protocol (TCP), the User Datagram Protocol (UDP), or the Internet Control Message Protocol (ICMP) protocols. The associated packet patterns are listed here:

- **service name=*service_name***   All packets are checked for a specific service.
- **port=*port_number* protocol=tcp|udp**   All packets are checked for a specific port number and protocol.
- **icmp-block name=*icmptype_name***   All packets are checked for a specific ICMP type. To display a list of supported ICMP types, run the command **firewall-cmd --get-icmptypes**.

The **masquerade** and **forward-port** options will be covered in the next sections of the chapter.

Once a rich rule finds a packet pattern match, it needs to know what to do with that packet. The last part of the rich rule options determines what happens to matched packets. There are five basic options:

- **drop** The packet is dropped. No message is sent to the source host.
- **reject** The packet is dropped. An ICMP error message is sent to the source host.
- **accept** The packet is allowed through the firewall.
- **log** The packet is logged to syslog.
- **audit** The packet is logged to the audit system.

The **limit value=*rate/duration*** directive is used to limit the amount of connections and packets logged in a time interval. For example, **limit value=5/m** specifies that a maximum of five log messages per minute will be logged or accepted, **limit value=10/h** sets the limit to 10 per hour, and so on. For a syntax reference of the firewalld rich language, refer to the **firewalld.richlanguage** man page.

EXERCISE 10-1

Configure Rich Rules

In this exercise, you will create a rich rule to allow all web traffic from all hosts in the network, except the tester1.example.com host. The rule you create will deny access to that host with an ICMP error message. In addition, the host oustider1.example.org should be allowed to connect to the web server, with all its connection attempts logged to syslog, at a rate limited to two messages per minute. Use the default (public zone) for all traffic. Assign the 192.168.100.0/24 network segment to the dmz zone.

This exercise assumes that you have installed the virtual machines and configured a default Apache server on your physical workstation, as explained in the labs of Chapters 1 and 2.

1. On your physical host, make sure that Apache is running and that you can access the Apache home page by navigating to the following URL: http://127.0.0.1.

```
# systemctl status httpd
# elinks --dump http://127.0.0.1
```

2. Check that the default zone is set to the public zone.

```
# firewall-cmd --get-default-zone
# firewall-cmd --set-default-zone=public
```

3. List the settings associated with the default zone. You should see the two virbr0 and virbr1 virtual bridges in the list of interfaces.

```
# firewall-cmd --list-all
```

4. Confirm that virbr1 is associated with the 192.168.100.0/24 network and move this interface to the dmz zone.

```
# ip addr show virbr1
# firewall-cmd --permanent --change-interface=virbr1 --zone=dmz
```

5. If the HTTP service is not allowed through the default zone, add it to the firewalld configuration.

```
# firewall-cmd --permanent --add-service-http
```

6. Create a rich rule to reject web connections from server1.example.com (192.168.122.50):

```
# firewall-cmd --permanent--add-rich-rule='rule family=ipv4 source ↵
address=192.168.122.50 service name=http reject'
```

7. Create a rich rule to log all connection attempts from outsider1.example.org (192.168.100.100) and rate-limit the logs to two messages per minute.

```
# firewall-cmd --permanent --zone=dmz --add-rich-rule='rule ↵
family=ipv4 source address=192.168.100.100 service name=http log limit ↵
value=2/m'
```

8. Reload the firewall configuration to apply the permanent changes to the run-time configuration.

```
# firewall-cmd --reload
```

9. Test from server1 and point the ELinks browser to 192.168.122.1. Is the host allowed to connect?

```
# elinks --dump http://192.168.122.1
```

10. Test from outsider1 and point the ELinks browser to 192.168.100.1. Is the host allowed to connect? Do you see any connection attempts logged to /var/log/messages?

```
# elinks --dump http://192.168.100.1
```

11. Revert the firewalld configuration to the initial settings.

Further Recommendations from the NSA

Simple firewalls are frequently the most secure. On an exam, it's best to keep everything, firewalls included, as simple as possible. But the NSA would go further. It has recommendations for the default rules, for limitations on the **ping** command, and for blocking suspicious groups of IP addresses. To those recommendations, we add a couple more suggestions to reduce risks to a system. Although these recommendations go beyond what's suggested by the RHCE objectives, read this section. If you're less than comfortable with the **firewall-cmd** command, this section can help. While you could implement these changes with the Rich Rules option in the Firewall Configuration tool, that is less efficient than with **firewall-cmd**.

You can test any of these suggestions on a system like the server1.example.com VM created in Chapter 2.

Regulate the ping Command

One earlier attack on various Internet systems involved the **ping** command. From Linux, it's possible to flood another system with the -**f** switch. If the attacker uses multiple systems, it may transmit thousands or millions of packets per second. It's important to be able to defend a system from such attacks or to limit their impact because they can prevent others from accessing your websites and more.

The -f **switch to the** ping **command was described solely to point out one of the major risks on a network. On most Linux distributions, only root is allowed to specify the** -f **switch. In many cases, it is illegal to run such a command on or against someone else's system. For example, one article suggests that such an attack could be a violation of the Police and Justice Act in the United Kingdom with a penalty of up to 10 years in prison. Similar laws exist in other countries.**

One potentially troublesome rule in the default firewall is that all ICMP traffic is allowed by default. ICMP messages go both ways. If you run the **ping** command on a remote system, the remote system responds with an ICMP Echo Reply packet. So if you want to limit ICMP messages, use the following rules to filter ICMP Echo Requests:

```
# firewall-cmd --add-icmp-block=echo-request
```

Add this rule to the server1.example.com VM, and measure the amount of packets sent and received from your physical host to server1 with the **ping -f** command. Then, do the same after removing the ICMP block and compare your results.

Block Suspicious IP Addresses

Black hat hackers who want to break into a system may hide their source IP address. As nobody is supposed to use a private or experimental IPv4 address on the public Internet, such addresses are one way to hide. The following additions to firewalld would drop packets sourced from the specified IPv4 network address blocks:

```
# firewall-cmd --add-rich-rule='rule family=ipv4 source↵
address=10.0.0.0/8 drop'
# firewall-cmd --add-rich-rule='rule family=ipv4 source↵
address=172.16.0.0/12 drop'
# firewall-cmd --add-rich-rule='rule family=ipv4 source↵
address=192.168.0.0/16 drop'
# firewall-cmd --add-rich-rule='rule family=ipv4 source↵
address=169.254.0.0/16 drop'
```

Regulate Access to SSH

Since SSH is important for the administration of remote systems, additional measures to protect this service are appropriate. It's certainly possible to set up a nonstandard port for SSH communication. Such a measure can be a part of a layered security strategy. However, tools such as **nmap** can detect the use of SSH on such nonstandard ports. So it's generally better to set up the configuration of the SSH server as discussed in Chapter 11 along with firewall rules such as the following. The following rich rule allows all SSH traffic, but limits incoming connections to three per minute:

```
# firewall-cmd --add-rich-rule='rule service name=ssh accept↵
limit value=3/m'
```

Make Sure That firewalld Is Running

Once desired changes are saved with the **--permanent** option, make sure that firewalld is in operation with the new rules. Don't forget to reload the configuration with the following command:

```
# firewall-cmd --reload
```

To avoid starting the old iptables firewall (which was the default in RHEL 6), it is a good idea to mask the corresponding service units, as shown here:

```
# systemctl mask iptables
# systemctl mask ip6tables
```

These commands link the **iptables** and **ip6tables** service units to /dev/null, preventing a system administrator from accidentally starting those services.

IP Masquerading

Red Hat Enterprise Linux supports a variation of NAT called *IP masquerading.* IP masquerading is often used to allow Internet access from multiple internal hosts, while sharing only a single public IP address. IP masquerading maps multiple internal IP addresses to that single valid external IP address. That helps, because all public IPv4 address blocks have now been allocated. IPv4 addresses are often still available from third parties, but at a cost. That cost is one more reason for IP masquerading. On the other hand, you may think that systems on IPv6 networks do not need masquerading, as it's relatively easy for many requesting users to get their own subnet of public IPv6 addresses. Nevertheless, even on IPv6 networks, masquerading can help keep that system secure.

IP masquerading is a fairly straightforward process. It's implemented on a gateway or router, which, by definition, has two or more network interfaces. One network interface is typically connected to an outside network such as the Internet, and the second network interface is connected to a LAN. In a small office, the interface connected to the outside network may connect through an external device such as a cable "modem" or Digital Subscriber Line (DSL) adapter. The following assumptions are made for the configuration:

- The public IP address is assigned to the network interface that is directly connected to the outside network.
- Network interfaces on the LAN get IP addresses associated with a single private network.
- One network interface on the gateway or router system gets an IP address on that same private network.
- IP forwarding is enabled on the router or gateway system, as discussed later in this chapter.
- Each system on the LAN is configured with the private IP address of the router or gateway system as the default gateway address.

When a computer on a LAN wants a web page on the Internet, packets are routed to the firewall. The firewall replaces the source IP address on each packet with the firewall's public IP address. It then assigns a new port number to the packet. The firewall caches the original source IP address and port number.

exam

⚙atch It's critical to understand how to secure a Red Hat Enterprise Linux system against unauthorized access.

exam

⚙atch The RHCE objectives specify the use of firewalld to configure network address translation.

When a packet comes back from the Internet to the firewall, it should include a port number. If the firewall can match an associated rule with the port number assigned to a previous outgoing packet, the process is reversed. The firewall replaces the destination IP address and port number with the internal computer's private IP address and then forwards the packet back to the original client on the LAN.

In practice, the following command enables masquerading. The noted command assumes that the zone that is directly connected to the Internet is the "dmz":

```
# firewall-cmd --permanent --zone=dmz --add-masquerade
```

You can also use a rich rule to enable masquerading. This offers the option to control which source IP addresses should be masqueraded:

```
# firewall-cmd --permanent --zone=dmz --add-rich-rule='rule family-ipv4↵
source address=192.168.0.0/24 masquerade'
```

In most cases, the private IP network address is not required because most LANs protected by a masquerade are configured on a single private IP network.

on the

Job

On the "external" zone, masquerading is enabled by default. Assigning the Internet-facing network interface to this zone would automatically masquerade all internal clients that establish a connection to the Internet.

IP Forwarding

IP forwarding is more commonly referred to as *routing*. Routing is critical to the operation of the Internet or any IP network. Routers connect and facilitate communication between multiple networks. When you set up a computer to find a site on an outside network, it needs a gateway address. This corresponds to the IP address of a router on the LAN.

A router looks at the destination IP address of each packet. If the IP address is on one of the router's LANs, it routes the packet directly to the proper computer. Otherwise, it sends the packet to another router closer to its final destination. To use a Red Hat Enterprise Linux system as a router, you should enable IP forwarding in the /etc/sysctl.conf configuration file by adding this line:

```
net.ipv4.ip_forward = 1
```

These settings take effect on the next reboot. Until then, the new settings in sysctl.conf can be enabled with the following command:

```
# sysctl -p
```

On a physical host running the KVM hypervisor, IP forwarding is usually enabled by default, as you can verify with the following command:

```
# sysctl net.ipv4.ip_forward
```

The Red Hat Firewall Configuration Tool

Chapter 4 introduced the RHCSA elements of the Red Hat Firewall Configuration tool. In this section, we will explain how you can implement the RHCE objectives related to firewalld using the Firewall Configuration tool.

Start the Firewall Configuration tool with the **firewall-config** command or by clicking Applications | Sundry | Firewall. The Firewall Configuration tool has a number of capabilities, as shown in Figure 10-4. In general, if you have selected the run-time configuration mode, it implements changes immediately, but those won't persist a system reboot. In most cases, you will want to select Permanent mode, which writes changes that survive system reboot.

After you make a change, you can apply the saved configuration immediately by clicking Options | Reload Firewalld.

Default Zone and Interfaces

In the Firewall Configuration tool, the left pane lists zones; the default zone is marked in bold. You can do everything in the Firewall Configuration tool that you can do with the

FIGURE 10-4   The Firewall Configuration tool

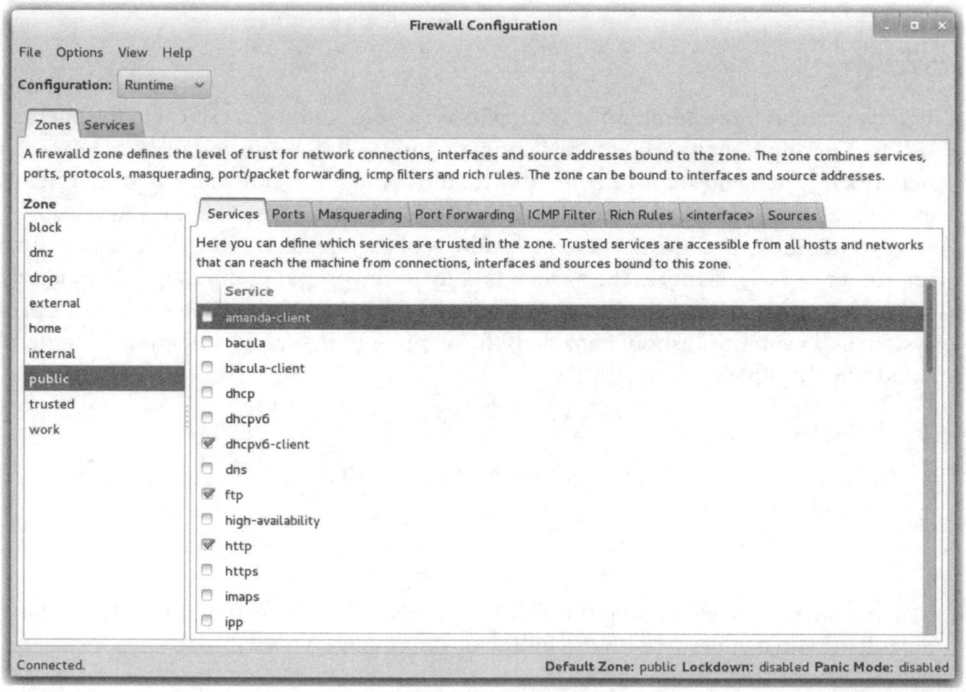

firewall-cmd command. You can assign interfaces to zones, select which services and ports are allowed through a zone, enable masquerading, and so on.

To bind interfaces to a zone, click the Interface tab to reveal the window shown in Figure 10-5. Routers have two or more network interfaces. Administrators who trust the systems on the internal network may click Add to assign internal interfaces to the "trusted" zone. However, this can be a risky practice. Threats can come from within as well as from outside a network.

In most cases, the gateway or router system has two or more Ethernet devices. Assume you are configuring a system with three devices: eth0, eth1, and eth2, where eth0 is connected to an external network, eth1 to a DMZ, and eth2 to the internal network. If you trust all systems on a local network, you might assign device eth2 as part of the trusted zone.

Sometimes a device may be listed using a different naming convention. As an example, a wireless adapter can be named wlan0 or even ath0. In other cases, it may be named wlp4s0, where p4 and s0 indicate the PCI bus and slot number, respectively. So it's important to know the device files associated with each network device on a system.

FIGURE 10-5   Zone interfaces

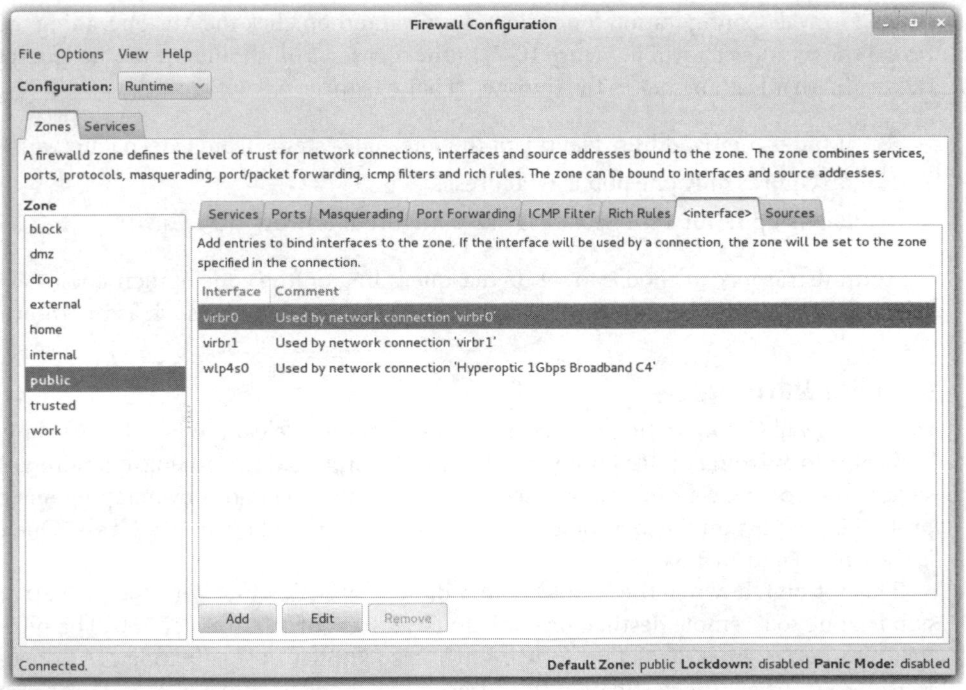

FIGURE 10-6

A source IP address
range assigned to
a zone

Address

Please enter an ipv4 or ipv6 address with the form address[/mask].
The mask can be a network mask or a number for ipv4.
The mask is a number for ipv6.

192.168.200.0/24

Cancel   OK

In the Firewall Configuration tool, you can bind source IP addresses to a zone. To do so, select the Source tab and click the Add button. This opens the Address window shown in Figure 10-6. Then, enter the source IP address range, such as 192.168.200.0/16.

Similarly, you can enable services and ports from the corresponding tabs. Once the configuration is applied, traffic matching the selected services and ports will be trusted through the interfaces and source IP addresses bound to the zone.

Masquerading

In the Firewall Configuration tool, select a zone and then click the Masquerading tab to reveal the window shown in Figure 10-7. In most cases, you should set up masquerading for the traffic that is going out to the Internet. That has three advantages:

- It hides the IP address identity of the internal systems from external networks.
- It requires only one public IP address.
- It sets up IP forwarding across the configured network devices.

Administrators can choose to set up masquerading on the zone of their choice. The selected zone should be the one connected to an external network such as the Internet.

Port Forwarding

In the Firewall Configuration tool, select a zone and then select the Port Forwarding tab. Typically, forwarding in this fashion works only in combination with masquerading. With such rules, port forwarding can be used to set up communications by mapping one port and protocol to a port on the local or a remote system, as defined by its IP address. One example is shown in Figure 10-8.

The options shown in the figure would redirect traffic destined for TCP port 80 on the public zone to a remote destination, with an IP address of 192.168.122.150. The port on that remote system is 8008. Port forwarding is also known as "destination NAT" because it is used to translate the destination IP address and service port of a packet. Port forwarding is typically used to make an internal service visible to other machines on the Internet, while hiding all the other services running on the internal host.

FIGURE 10-7   Masquerading with the Firewall Configuration tool

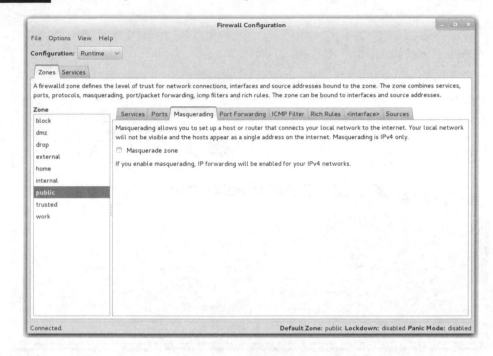

FIGURE 10-8

Port forwarding
with the Firewall
Configuration tool

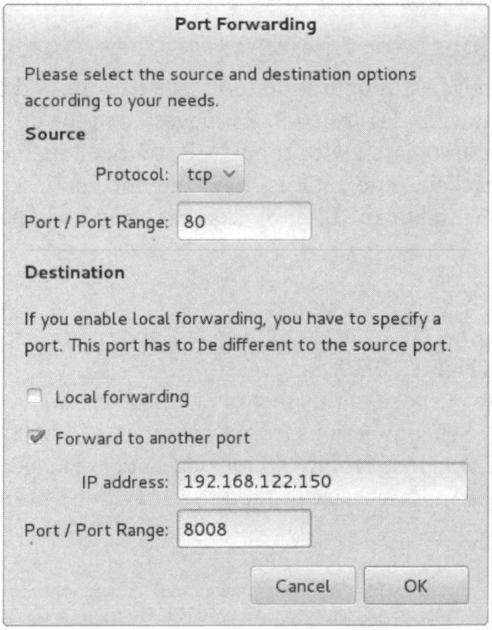

FIGURE 10-9 ICMP Filter with the Firewall Configuration tool

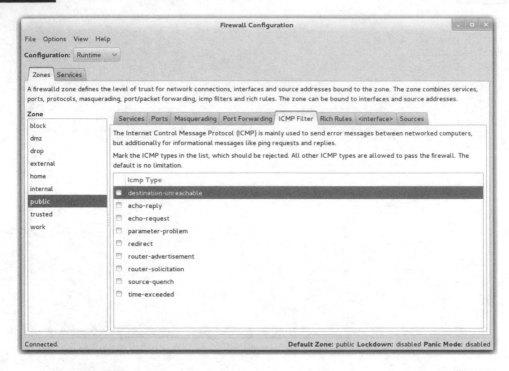

ICMP Filter

In the Firewall Configuration tool, select a zone and click the ICMP Filter tab to open the screen shown in Figure 10-9. As suggested in the description, the options relate to different messages associated with the ICMP protocol, including but not limited to, the **ping**-related packets. The options shown are further described in Table 10-5. If you activate a filter in that table, the filter blocks that category of packets.

Rich Rules

Select a zone, click the Rich Rules tab, and then click Add to open the Rich Rule window shown in Figure 10-10.

For the purpose of this section, we have created a new rule, as shown in Figure 10-10, to block all SSH connections from the host 192.168.100.50. Connection attempts are rejected with a ICMP Host Prohibited message and are logged to /var/log/messages with an "SSH" prefix. Log messages are limited to a maximum of five per minute.

TABLE 10-5   ICMP Filter Options

Filter	Description
Destination Unreachable	A message generated by a router to inform that a destination address is unreachable
Echo Reply	Regular response messages to Echo Requests
Echo Request	A message that can be generated with the **ping** command
Parameter Problem	Error messages not otherwise defined by other ICMP messages
Redirect	A message to notify the source host to send packets via an alternative route
Router Advertisement	Periodic message multicasted to other routers to announce the IP addresses assigned to an interface
Router Solicitation	A request for a router advertisement
Source Quench	Response to a host to slow down packet transfers
Time Exceeded	Error message if a "Time To Live" field in a packet is exceeded

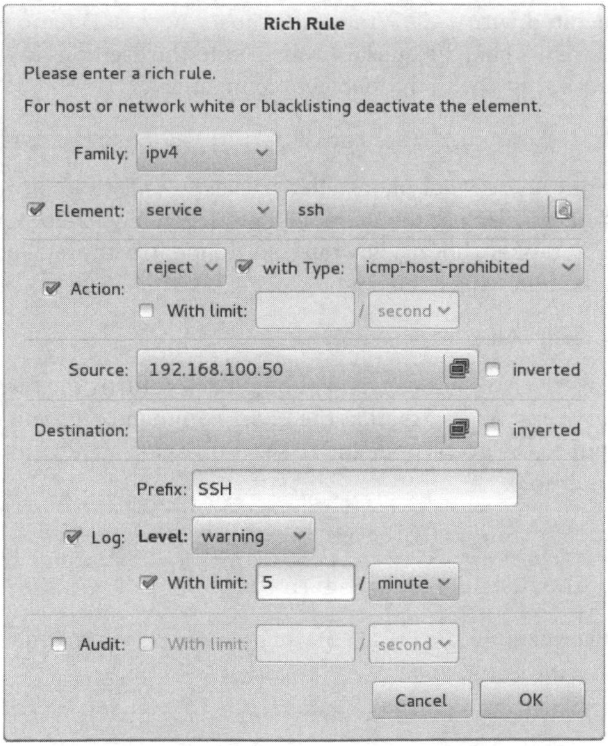

FIGURE 10-10

Take advantage of rich rules.

CERTIFICATION OBJECTIVE 10.03

TCP Wrappers

As suggested by its name, TCP Wrappers protects those services that communicate using the TCP protocol. It was originally designed to help protect services configured through the Extended Internet Super-Server daemon (xinted). However, TCP Wrappers' protection is no longer limited to such services; the protection can apply to all services statically and dynamically linked to the associated library wrapper file, libwrap.so.0.

The way TCP Wrappers protects a service is defined in the /etc/hosts.allow and /etc/hosts.deny configuration files.

Is a Service Protected by TCP Wrappers?

The **strings** command can be used to identify those daemons protected by TCP Wrappers. It does so by listing the printable character sequences included in a binary. The string associated with TCP Wrappers is hosts_access. Daemons can be found in the /usr/sbin directory. Thus, the quickest way to scan the daemons in these directories for the hosts_access string is with the following command:

```
# strings -f /usr/sbin/* | grep hosts_access
```

The output depends on installed packages. One example is the SSH daemon, /usr/sbin/sshd.

You can also use the shared library dependencies command, **ldd**, to confirm a link to the TCP Wrappers library, libwrap.0.so. To identify those dependencies for the **sshd** daemon, run the following command:

```
# ldd /usr/sbin/sshd
```

However, that's not convenient because it returns the files for more than a couple of dozen library files. As an expert at the Linux command line, you should know how to pipe that output to the **grep** command to see if it's associated with the TCP Wrappers library file, libwrap.so.0:

```
# ldd /usr/sbin/sshd | grep libwrap.so.0
```

And from the output, it's confirmed:

```
libwrap.so.0 => /lib64/libwrap.so.0 (0x00007f13b94380000)
```

The TCP Wrappers configuration files can help you protect the SSH service. That protection comes over and above any settings included in the standard zone-based firewalld, the SSH server configuration file, SELinux, and so on. However, such redundant protection is important in a layered security strategy.

TCP Wrappers Configuration Files

When a system receives a network request for a service linked to the libwrap.so.0 library, it passes the request on to TCP Wrappers. This system logs the request and then checks its access rules. If there are no limits on the particular host or IP address, TCP Wrappers passes control back to the service.

The key files are hosts.allow and hosts.deny in the /etc directory. The philosophy is fairly straightforward: users and clients listed in hosts.allow are allowed access; users and clients listed in hosts.deny are denied access. As users and/or clients may be listed in both files, the TCP Wrappers system takes the following steps:

1. It searches /etc/hosts.allow. If TCP Wrappers finds a match, it grants access. No additional searches are required.
2. It searches /etc/hosts.deny. If TCP Wrappers finds a match, it denies access.
3. If the host isn't found in either file, access is automatically granted to the client.

You use the same access control language in both /etc/hosts.allow and /etc/hosts.deny files. The basic format for commands in each file is as follows:

```
daemon_list : client_list
```

The simplest version of this format is

```
ALL : ALL
```

This specifies all services and makes the rule applicable to all hosts on all IP addresses. If you set this line in /etc/hosts.deny, access is prohibited to all services. Of course, since that is read after /etc/hosts.allow, services in that file are allowed.

You can create finer-grained filters than just prohibiting access to *all* daemons from *all* systems. For example, the following line in /etc/hosts.allow allows the client with an IP address of 192.168.122.50 to connect to the local system through the Secure Shell:

```
sshd : 192.168.122.50
```

The same line in /etc/hosts.deny would prevent the computer with that IP address from using SSH to connect. If the same line exists in both files, /etc/hosts.allow takes precedence, and users from the noted IP address will be able to connect through SSH, assuming other

| TABLE 10-6 | Sample Client Lists in /etc/hosts.allow and /etc/hosts.deny |

Client	Description
.example.com	Domain name. Since this domain name begins with a dot, it specifies all clients on the example.com domain.
172.16.	IP address. Since this address ends with a dot, it specifies all clients with an IP address of 172.16.*x.y.*
172.16.72.0/255.255.254.0	IP network address with subnet mask.
172.16.72.0/23	IP network address with subnet mask, but using CIDR notation.
ALL	Any client, any daemon.

security settings such as zone-based firewalls allow it. You can specify clients a number of different ways, as shown in Table 10-6.

As you can see in Table 10-6, there are two different types of wildcards. **ALL** can be used to represent any client or service, and the dot (.) specifies all hosts with the specified domain name or IP network address.

You can set up multiple services and addresses with commas. Exceptions are easy to make with the **EXCEPT** operator. Review the following excerpt from the /etc/hosts.allow file:

```
ALL : .example.com
sshd : 192.168.122.0/24 EXCEPT 192.168.122.150
vsftpd : 192.168.100.100
```

The first line in this file opens **ALL** services to all computers in the example.com domain. The following line opens the SSH service to any computer on the 192.168.122.0/24 network, except the one with an IP address of 192.168.122.150. Then the vsFTP service is opened to the computer with an IP address of 192.168.100.100. You may want to add the localhost IP address network to the noted daemons in the /etc/hosts.allow file, as follows:

```
sshd : 127. 192.168.122.0/24 EXCEPT 192.168.122.150
vsftpd : 127. 192.168.100.100
```

Otherwise, attempts to connect from the local system may be denied based on other directives in the /etc/hosts.deny file.

The configuration that follows contains a hosts.deny file to see how lists can be built to control access:

```
ALL EXCEPT vsftpd : .example.org
sshd : ALL EXCEPT 192.168.122.150
ALL : ALL
```

The first line in the hosts.deny file denies all services except vsFTP to computers in the example.org domain. The second line states that the only computer allowed to access the local SSH server has an IP address of 192.168.122.100. Finally, the last line is a blanket denial; all other computers are denied access to all services controlled by TCP Wrappers.

EXERCISE 10-2

Configure TCP Wrappers

In this exercise, you will use TCP Wrappers to control access to network resources. Since such controls are enabled by default, you shouldn't have to make any modifications to installed services.

1. Try to connect to the local vsFTP server using the address localhost. You may need to do several things first:
   A. Install the Very Secure FTP daemon from the vsftpd RPM.
   B. Install the **lftp** client from the lftp RPM.
   C. Activate the vsFTP service with the **systemctl start vsftpd** command.
   D. Configure the service to start at boot with the **systemctl enable vsftpd** command.
   E. Allow the FTP protocol through firewalld.
2. Edit /etc/hosts.deny and add the following line (don't forget to write the file):

   ```
   ALL : ALL
   ```
3. What happens when you try to run **lftp 127.0.0.1**? And what if you run a command such as **ls** after logging into the FTP server?
4. Edit /etc/hosts.allow and add the following line:

   ```
   vsftpd : 127.0.0.1
   ```
5. Now what happens when you try to run **lftp 127.0.0.1**? Does the **ls** command return any output from the FTP server?
6. Undo any changes made when you are finished.

CERTIFICATION OBJECTIVE 10.04

Pluggable Authentication Modules

RHEL uses the Pluggable Authentication Modules (PAM) system as another layer of security primarily for administrative tools and related commands. PAM includes a group of dynamically loadable library modules that govern how individual applications verify their users. You can modify PAM configuration files to customize security requirements for different administrative utilities. Most PAM configuration files are stored in the /etc/pam.d directory.

PAM modules also standardize the user authentication process. For example, the login program uses PAM to require usernames and passwords at login. Open the /etc/pam.d/login file. Take a look at the first line:

```
auth [user_unknown=ignore success=ok ignore=ignore default=bad] ↵
pam_securetty.so
```

To interpret, this line means that the root user can log in only from secure terminals as defined in the /etc/securetty file, and unknown users are ignored.

The configuration files shown in the /etc/pam.d directory often have the same name as the command that starts the administrative utility. These utilities are "PAM aware." In other words, you can change the way users are verified for applications such as the console login program. Just modify the appropriate configuration file in the /etc/pam.d directory.

Configuration Files

Take a look at the configuration files in a typical /etc/pam.d directory, as shown in Figure 10-11. Depending on what's installed, you may see a somewhat different list of files.

As suggested earlier, most of the filenames in the /etc/pam.d directory are descriptive. Take a look at some of these files. In most cases, they refer to PAM modules. These modules can be found in the /usr/lib64/security directory. Excellent descriptions of each module can be found in the /usr/share/doc/pam-*versionnumber* directory, in the txts/ and html/ subdirectories. For example, the functionality of the pam_securetty.so module is described in the README.pam_securetty file.

You can also refer to the HTML version of the Linux-PAM System Administrators' Guide available in the /usr/share/doc/pam-*versionnumber*/html directory, starting with the Linux-PAM_SAG.html file.

```
[root@server1 ~]# \ls /etc/pam.d
atd                      login                smtp
authconfig               newrole              smtp.postfix
authconfig-gtk           other                sshd
authconfig-tui           passwd               su
chfn                     password-auth        subscription-manager
chsh                     password-auth-ac     subscription-manager-gui
config-util              pluto                sudo
crond                    polkit-1             sudo-i
cups                     postlogin            su-l
fingerprint-auth         postlogin-ac         system-auth
fingerprint-auth-ac      ppp                  system-auth-ac
gdm-autologin            remote               system-config-authentication
gdm-fingerprint          rhn_register         system-config-language
gdm-launch-environment   runuser              systemd-user
gdm-password             runuser-l            vlock
gdm-pin                  setup                vmtoolsd
gdm-smartcard            smartcard-auth       vsftpd
liveinst                 smartcard-auth-ac    xserver
[root@server1 ~]#
```

Control Flags

The PAM system provides four different types of services. These are associated with four different types of PAM rules:

- **Authentication management (auth)**   Validates the identity of a user. For example, a PAM **auth** rule verifies whether a user has provided valid username and password credentials.

- **Account management (account)**   Allows or denies access according to the account policies. For example, a PAM **account** rule may deny access according to time, password expiration, or a specific list of restricted users.

- **Password management (password)**   Manages password change policies. For example, a PAM **password** rule may enforce a minimum password length when a user tries to change her password.

- **Session management (session)**   Applies settings for an application session. For example, a PAM **session** rule may set default settings for a login console.

The configuration shown in Figure 10-12 is from a sample PAM configuration file, /etc/pam.d/login. Every line in all PAM configuration files is written in the following format:

```
type  control_flag  module_name  [arguments]
```

The **type**, as described previously, can be **auth**, **account**, **password**, or **session**. The **control_flag** determines what PAM does if the module succeeds or fails.

FIGURE 10-12   The PAM /etc/pam.d/login configuration file

```
#%PAM-1.0
auth [user_unknown=ignore success=ok ignore=ignore default=bad] pam_securetty.so
auth       substack     system-auth
auth       include      postlogin
account    required     pam_nologin.so
account    include      system-auth
password   include      system-auth
# pam_selinux.so close should be the first session rule
session    required     pam_selinux.so close
session    required     pam_loginuid.so
session    optional     pam_console.so
# pam_selinux.so open should only be followed by sessions to be executed in the
user context
session    required     pam_selinux.so open
session    required     pam_namespace.so
session    optional     pam_keyinit.so force revoke
session    include      system-auth
session    include      postlogin
-session   optional     pam_ck_connector.so
~
~
~
~
"/etc/pam.d/login" 18L, 796C
```

The **module_name** specifies the name of the actual PAM module file. Finally, you can specify options for each module.

The **control_flag** field requires additional explanation. It determines how PAM reacts when a module returns success or failure. The five most common control flags are described in Table 10-7.

TABLE 10-7   PAM Control Flags

control_flag	Description
required	If this module returns success, PAM proceeds to the next rule of this type. If it fails, PAM proceeds to the next rule in the configuration file—but the final result is failure.
requisite	If this module fails, PAM does not check any additional rules and returns a failure.
sufficient	If this module passes, no other rules of this type need to be processed, and the result is success. Otherwise, if the check fails, PAM continues processing the remaining rules.
optional	PAM ignores the success or failure of this rule.
include	Includes all directives of the same **type** from the noted configuration file; for example, if the directive is **password include system-auth**, this includes all password directives from the PAM system-auth file.

To see how control flags work, take a look at the rules from the /etc/pam.d/runuser configuration file:

```
auth    sufficient    pam_rootok.so
```

The first **auth** command checks the pam_rootok.so module. In other words, if the root user tries to run the **runuser** command, the rule will return a pass and the **runuser** command will be executed. As the **control_flag** is **sufficient**, if there were other **auth** commands in this file, they would be ignored.

```
session    optional    pam_keyinit.so ignore
```

The purpose of the second line is to clear the session key ring of the **runuser** process when this exits. In this case, the **control_flag** is **optional**, meaning that the outcome of this rule does not have any effect on the other **session** rules.

```
session    required    pam_limits.so
```

The third line sets the resource limits defined in /etc/security/limits.conf when invoking an instance of the **runuser** application. The **control_flag** is **required**, which will cause the command session to fail if the limits cannot be set.

```
session    required    pam_unix.so
```

The module associated with the last **session** type (pam_unix.so) logs the username and service type at the beginning and end of each command session.

The Format of a PAM File

This section is a little complex. It starts with the /etc/pam.d/login configuration file shown in Figure 10-12. In addition, as the file includes references to the /etc/pam.d/system-auth configuration file, shown in Figure 10-13, you'll need to go back and forth between files to follow along with this section.

You don't have to memorize the content in this section. Instead, you should use it to become more familiar with PAM configuration files. While you read this section, familiarize yourself with each PAM module by reading the corresponding man page. The **rpm -qd pam** command gives a full list of the installed PAM man pages in your system.

When a user opens a text console and logs in, Linux goes through the /etc/pam.d/login configuration file line by line. As previously noted, the first line in /etc/pam.d/login limits root user access to secure terminals as defined in the /etc/securetty file:

```
auth [user_unknown=ignore success=ok ignore=ignore default=bad] ↵
pam_securetty.so
```

FIGURE 10-13 The PAM /etc/pam.d/system-auth configuration file

```
#%PAM-1.0
# This file is auto-generated.
# User changes will be destroyed the next time authconfig is run.
auth        required      pam_env.so
auth        sufficient    pam_unix.so nullok try_first_pass
auth        requisite     pam_succeed_if.so uid >= 1000 quiet_success
auth        required      pam_deny.so

account     required      pam_unix.so
account     sufficient    pam_localuser.so
account     sufficient    pam_succeed_if.so uid < 1000 quiet
account     required      pam_permit.so

password    requisite     pam_pwquality.so try_first_pass local_users_only retry
=3 authtok_type=
password    sufficient    pam_unix.so sha512 shadow nullok try_first_pass use_au
thtok
password    required      pam_deny.so

session     optional      pam_keyinit.so revoke
session     required      pam_limits.so
-session    optional      pam_systemd.so
session     [success=1 default=ignore] pam_succeed_if.so service in crond quiet
use_uid
session     required      pam_unix.so
~
"/etc/pam.d/system-auth" 22L, 974C
```

The next line includes the **auth** commands from the system-auth PAM configuration file:

```
auth    substack      system-auth
```

For the purpose of this example, you can assume that the **substack** control flag is equivalent to an **include** directive. The system-auth configuration file shown in Figure 10-13 includes four **auth** directives. On your system, you may see additional lines—for example, if you configured the machine as an LDAP or Kerberos client. In that case, your configuration will reference additional PAM modules, such as pam_ldap or pam_krb5.

```
auth        required      pam_env.so
auth        sufficient    pam_unix.so nullok try_first_pass
auth        requisite     pam_succeed_if.so uid >= 1000 quiet_success
auth        required      pam_deny.so
```

In order, the preceding lines set up environment variables and check password authentication against the local /etc/passwd and /etc/shadow databases (pam_unix.so). The **sufficient** flag associated with the second module means that authentication succeeds if a valid password has been entered, and no further rules from the **auth** section are processed.

If the pam_unix.so module returns a fail, PAM
will process the next rule, which disables logging
if the user ID of the account is 1000 and above.
Then, if PAM gets to the last rule, the user is
denied access (pam_deny.so).

Now return to the /etc/pam.d/login file. The
next line includes the directive in the postlogin
file, which does not contain any **auth** rules.
Moving to the subsequent line, this invokes the
account type of the pam_login.so module. This
module disables user logins if the file /etc/nologin
exists:

```
account  required   pam_nologin.so
```

The following rule includes the **account** rules from the /etc/pam.d/system-auth
configuration file:

```
account  include    system-auth
```

These are the **account** type rules lines from the default /etc/pam.d/system-auth:

```
account  required    pam_unix.so
account  sufficient  pam_localuser.so
account  sufficient  pam_succeed_if.so uid < 1000 quiet
account  required    pam_permit.so
```

The first line refers to the pam_unix.so module in the /usr/lib64/security directory, which
checks in /etc/shadow whether the account is valid and has not expired. Based on the
pam_localuser.so module and on the **sufficient** control type, if the username is listed in
/etc/passwd, no further directives are processed. The pam_succeed_if.so module disables
logging for service users (with user IDs less than 1000). Then, the pam_permit.so module
always returns success.

Now return to the /etc/pam.d/login file. The next line is a **password** directive, which
includes other password rules from the /etc/pam.d/system-auth file:

```
password  include    system-auth
```

These are the **password** type rules from the default /etc/pam.d/system-auth:

```
password requisite   pam_pwquality.so try_first_pass ↵
local_users_only retry=3 authok_type=
password sufficient  pam_unix.so sha512 shadow nullok try_first_pass ↵
use_authok
password required    pam_deny.so
```

The first rule from this output performs a password strength check. It allows the use of the password collected by the application that called PAM (**try_first_pass**) and applies its checks to local users only, with a maximum of three password change attempts.

The next rule updates the user's password using the SHA512 encryption hash, supports the Shadow Password Suite described in Chapter 8, allows the use of an existing null (zero-length) password, and forces the module to set the new password to the value provided by the previous module (**use_authok**).

The **password required pam_deny.so** directive is trivial; as noted in README.pam_deny in the /usr/share/doc/pam-*versionlevel*/txt directory, this module always fails.

Finally, there are six **session** rules in the default /etc/pam.d/login file. Let's take them three at a time:

```
session     required    pam_selinux.so open
session     required    pam_namespace.so
session     optional    pam_keyinit.so force revoke
```

The first line (**pam_selinux.so open**) sets up a few SELinux security contexts. The second line (**pam_namespace.so**) creates separate namespaces for users at logon. The third line initializes the key ring of the login session (**pam_keyring.so**).

```
session     include     system-auth
session     include     postlogin
-session    optional    pam_ck_connector.so
```

Jumping ahead, the last of this group of rules registers a login session with the ConsoleKit daemon. Note the minus character in front of the line: this tells PAM not to send any error message to syslog if the module is missing. The preceding rules include the following **session** type lines from the system-auth and postlogin files:

```
session     optional    pam_keyinit.so revoke
session     required    pam_limits.so
-session    optional    pam_systemd.so
session     [success=1 default=ignore] pam_succeed_if.so service in ↵
crond quiet use_uid
session     required    pam_unix.so
```

The first of these rules is identical to the line in the main /etc/pam.d/login file that revokes the session key ring of the invoking process. The next rule sets limits (pam_limits.so) on individual user resources through /etc/security/limits.conf. The next rule registers the user session with the systemd login manager. The fourth rule will skip the next rule (**success=1**) for cron jobs. The final rule logs the result when the user logs in.

Finally, the next three rules included from the postlogin file invoke the pam_lastlogin.so module with different options, depending on whether the requesting service is the graphical login, the **su** command, or another process. The pam_lastlogin.so module shows the amount of previous failed login attempts to the user, and is also commonly used to record the date of the last login in /var/log/lastlog.

```
session     [success=1 default=ignore] pam_succeed_if.so ↵
service !~ gdm* service !~ su* quiet
session     [default=1]   pam_lastlog.so nowtmp showfailed
session     optional      pam_lastlog.so silent noupdate showfailed
```

EXERCISE 10-3

Configure PAM to Limit root Access

In this exercise, you can experiment with some of the PAM security features of Red Hat Enterprise Linux 7.

1. Make a backup copy of /etc/securetty with the following command:

   `# cp /etc/securetty /etc/securetty.bak`

2. Edit /etc/securetty and remove the lines for tty3 through tty11. Save the changes and exit.

3. Use ALT-F3 (CTRL-ALT-F3 if you're running X Window) to switch to virtual console number 3. Try to log in as root. What happens?

4. Repeat Step 3 as a regular user. What happens? Do you know why?

5. Use ALT-F2 to switch to virtual console number 2 and try to log in as root.

6. Review the messages in /var/log/secure. Do you see where you tried to log in as root in virtual console number 3?

7. Restore the original /etc/securetty file with the following command:

   `# mv /etc/securetty.bak /etc/securetty`

One thing to remember is that the /etc/securetty file governs the consoles from which you can log in as the root user. Therefore, the changes that were made do not affect regular (non-root) users.

PAM and User-Based Security

In this section, you'll learn how to configure PAM to limit access to specific users. The key to this security feature is the pam_listfile.so module, which is located in the /usr/lib64/ security directory. If you've installed the vsFTP server, the /etc/pam.d/vsftpd file includes an example of this module.

First, the following line in the vsftpd file initializes and clears out any existing key rings when the session is closed:.

```
session optional pam_keyinit.so  force revoke
```

The way PAM can limit user access is shown in the next rule:

```
auth required pam_listfile.so item=user sense=deny ↵
file=/etc/vsftpd/ftpusers onerr=succeed
```

To understand how this works, let's break this rule into its component parts. You already know the first three parts of the rule from the previous section. The options that are shown are associated with the pam_listfile.so module, as described in the pam_listfile man page and in Table 10-8.

Thus, for the specified rule (**onerr=succeed**), an error, strangely enough, returns success (**item=user**). If the user is in the specified list (**file=/etc/vsftpd/ftpusers**), the rule allows that user (**sense=allow**) to access the specified tool.

e x a m

ⓦ a t c h   **Make sure you understand how Red Hat Enterprise Linux handles user authorization through the /etc/pam.d configuration files. When you test these files, make sure you create a backup of everything** **in PAM before making any changes, because any errors that you make on a PAM configuration file can disable access to your system completely (PAM is that secure).**

TABLE 10-8   Options for the pam_listfile.so Module

pam_listfile Option	Description
item	This option can be used to limit access to a terminal (**tty**), user (**user**), group (**group**), or more.
sense	If the item is found in the specified **file**, take the noted action. For example, if the user is listed in /etc/special and **sense=allow**, then this command grants the user permission for the specified tool.
file	The path of the file with a list of users, groups, and so on, such as **file = /etc/special**.
onerr	If there is a problem, tell the module what to do. The options are **onerr=succeed** or **onerr=fail**.

EXERCISE 10-4

Use PAM to Limit User Access

You can also use the PAM system to limit access to all non-root users. In this exercise, you'll limit access using the pam_nologin.so module. It should work hand in hand with the default /etc/pam.d/login security configuration file, specifically the following line:

```
account   required   pam_nologin.so
```

1. Look for an /etc/nologin file. If it doesn't already exist, create one with a message such as the following:

```
I'm sorry, access is limited to the root user
```

2. Access another terminal with a command such as CTRL-ALT-F2. Try logging in as a regular user. What do you see?

3. Log in as the root user. You'll see the same message; but as the root user, you're allowed access.

4. Inspect the /var/log/secure file. Did your system reject the attempted login from the regular user? What were the associated messages for the root user?

SCENARIO & SOLUTION

You have only one public IP address, but you need to provide Internet access to all of the systems on your LAN. Each computer on the LAN has its own private IP address.	Use firewalld to implement IP masquerading. Make sure IP forwarding is active.
You have installed an SSH server on a corporate network and want to restrict access to certain departments. Each department has its own subnet.	Use the /etc/hosts.deny file in the tcp_wrappers package to block SSH access to the unwanted subnets. A better alternative would be to use /etc/hosts.allow to support access to desired departments, and then use /etc/hosts.deny to deny access to everyone else. Similar options are possible using firewalld rich rules.
You want to restrict access to a service, such as SSH, only to certain users.	Add a line in the appropriate Pluggable Authentication Module configuration files in /etc/pam.d to use the **pam_listfile.so** module.
You want to modify the local firewall to defend against ICMP attacks such as **ping** command floods.	Modify the firewall to reject or deny certain types of ICMP packets.

CERTIFICATION OBJECTIVE 10.05

Secure Files and More with GPG2

With the importance of network security, you should know how to encrypt files for secure transmission. The computer standard for file encryption and signature services is known as Pretty Good Privacy (PGP). The open-source implementation of PGP is known as the GNU Privacy Guard (GPG). The version released for RHEL 7 is more advanced and capable, documented as GPG version 2 (GPG2) You've likely already used GPG2 to verify the authenticity of RPM packages, as discussed in Chapter 7. This section takes such checks one step further; you'll generate private and public keys and then use those keys to encrypt and decrypt selected files.

Although GPG is not listed in the RHCE objectives, it's a security topic consistent with other security objectives discussed in this book. We believe it's an excellent topic that might be included in future versions of the RHCE exam.

GPG2 Commands

The GPG version 2 included in RHEL 7 has a more modular approach to encryption and authentication. There's even a related package used for smartcard authentication. But that's not the point of the new **gpg2** commands. Available GPG commands are briefly described in Table 10-9.

Table 10-9 is just intended to describe the range of capabilities associated with the RHEL 7 GPG2 packages. The focus of this section is on the encryption and decryption of files.

TABLE 10-9   GPG2 Commands

Command	Description
gpg	Symbolic link to the **gpg2** command
gpg2	The GPG2 encryption and signing tool
gpg-agent	GPG2 key management daemon
gpgconf	Provides access and modifies configuration files in ~/.gnupg
gpg-connect-agent	Utility to communicate with an active GPG2 agent
gpg-error	Command to interpret a GPG2 error number
gpgsplit	Command to split a GPG2 message into packets
gpgv	Symbolic link to the **gpg2v** command
gpgv2	Command to verify GPG signatures; requires a signature file
gpg-zip	Command to encrypt or sign files into an archive

Current GPG2 Configuration

While the man page for the **gpgconf** command suggests that it's just used to modify the directory with associated configuration files, that command does more. By itself, it defaults to the --**list-components** switch, which specifies the full path to related executable files. With the --**check-programs** switch, it makes sure all related programs can be executed. **gpgconf** can also be used to check the syntax of a GPG2 configuration file. One typical option is in the current user's home directory, in the .gnupg/ subdirectory. Another typical option is in the /etc/gnupg directory.

GPG2 Encryption Options

The generation of a GPG2 key includes a choice of three different cryptographic algorithms, as listed next. Each of these algorithms includes a public and a private key. The public key can be distributed to others for use in encrypting files and messages. The private key is used by the owner, and is the only way to decrypt the file or message.

- **RSA**   Named for its developers, Rivest, Shamir, and Adleman. Although typical RSA keys are 1024 or 2048 bits in length, they can be larger. Shorter keys of 512 bits have been cracked. RSA is in the public domain.

- **DSA**   The Digital Signature Algorithm. Proposed by the U.S. National Institute of Science and Technology, DSA has been made available for worldwide use, royalty free. This is a U.S. government standard that uses Secure Hash Algorithm (SHA) versions SHA-1 and SHA-2 as message digest hash functions. SHA-1 is being phased out; SHA-2 includes six hash functions with message digests of up to 512 bits, also known as SHA-512, the same hash as is now used for the RHEL 7 shadow password suite.

- **ElGamal**   Developed by Taher Elgamal, this probabilistic encryption algorithm is used in GPG in combination with DSA, with an ElGamal key pair used for encryption and another DSA key pair for making signatures. ElGamal is the first encryption scheme based on the Diffie-Hellman key exchange method.

Generate a GPG2 Key

The **gpg --gen-key** command can be used to set up key pairs with different types of encryption schemes. Before running the command, be prepared with answers to the following questions:

- The number of bits for the encryption keys. Normally, the maximum number of bits is 4096, but an encryption key that complex may take a number of minutes to develop.

- The desired lifetime of the keys. Especially if you set up keys with a smaller number of bits, you should assume that a determined black hat hacker would be able to decrypt the key within some number of months or weeks.

- A name, an e-mail address, and a comment. Although the name and e-mail address do not have to be real, they will be seen by others as part of the public key.

- A passphrase. Good passphrases should include spaces, lower- and uppercase letters, numbers, and punctuation.

As given, the **gpg --gen-key** command prompts for one of four different encryption schemes. As suggested by the (sign only) label associated with choices 3 and 4, those options work just as digital signatures, not for encryption.

```
Please select what kind of key you want:
   (1) RSA and RSA (default)
   (2) DSA and Elgamal
   (3) DSA (sign only)
   (4) RSA (sign only)
Your selection?
```

All four options follow a similar sequence of steps. For example, if you select option 2, the following output appears:

```
DSA keys may be between 1024 and 3072 bits long.
What keysize do you want? (2048)
```

The default is 2048 bits, which is selected if you just press ENTER. The command then prompts for a key lifetime:

```
Requested keysize is 2048 bits
Please specify how long the key should be valid.
        0 = key does not expire
     <n>  = key expires in n days
     <n>w = key expires in n weeks
     <n>m = key expires in n months
     <n>y = key expires in n years
Key is valid for? (0) 2m
```

In this case, we've selected two months. The command responds with a date and time two months into the future and prompts for confirmation.

```
Key expires at Sat 27 Apr 2015 11:14:17 AM BST
Is this correct? (y/N) y
```

At this point, the **gpg** command prompts for identifying information for the key. The "User ID" requested here is not related to the UID in the standard Linux authentication database. In this example, the responses are shown in bold:

```
Real name: Michael Jang
Email address: michael@example.com
Comment: DSA and Elgamal key
```

```
You selected this USER-ID:
    "Michael Jang (DSA and Elgamal key) <michael@example.com>"

Change (N)ame, (C)omment, (E)mail or (O)kay/(Q)uit? o
```

The system should now prompt for a passphrase. Then, the **gpg** command goes to work. Especially with larger keys, it may seem to pause for a few minutes with a message about creating random bytes. You might need to run some other programs to stimulate the process. When complete, it displays a message similar to the following:

```
gpg: key D385AFDD marked as ultimately trusted
public and secret key created and signed.
```

To make sure the public and private keys were actually written, run the following command:

```
$ gpg --list-key
```

The output should include the latest key, along with any others created from the user's home directory, in the .gnupg/ subdirectory. For the given options, if this is the only key pair on the local account, you'll see something similar to the following output:

```
/home/michael/.gnupg/pubring.gpg
--------------------------------
pub   2048D/9F688440 2015-04-28 [expires: 2015-06-27]
uid   Michael Jang (DSA and ElGamal) <michael@example.com>
sub   2048g/306A91C0 2015-04-28 [expires: 2015-06-27]
```

Use a GPG2 Key to Encrypt a File

Now you can send the public key to a remote system. To start the process, you'll need to export the public key. For the key pair just created, you could do so with the following command (substitute your name for "Michael Jang"):

```
$ gpg --export Michael Jang > gpg.pub
```

Now copy that key to a remote system. The delivery vehicle, such as e-mail, a USB stick, or the **scp** command shown here, is not important. This particular command from user michael's account would copy the gpg.pub key to user michael's home directory on the tester1.example.com system. If you prefer, substitute the IP address, like so:

```
$ scp gpg.pub tester1.example.com:
```

Now go to the remote system (in this case, tester1.example.com). Log in to user michael's account (or the account home directory to which you copied the gpg.pub key). Once connected to that system, first check for existing GPG keys with the following command:

```
$ gpg --list-key
```

If this is a system without previous GPG keys, the list should be empty, and nothing will appear in the output to this command. Now import the gpg.pub file into the list of local GPG keys with the following command:

```
$ gpg --import gpg.pub
```

Confirm the import by running the **gpg --list-key** command again.

Now on the remote system, you can encrypt a file with the **gpg** command. The following example encrypts the local keepthis.secret file:

```
$ gpg --out underthe.radar --recipient 'Michael Jang' ↵
--encrypt keepthis.secret
```

The username in this case is Michael Jang. If you've just imported a private key, the username as shown in the output to the **gpg --list-key** command may be different. Substitute as appropriate.

Now when the underthe.radar file is copied to the original system, server1.example.com, you can start the decryption process with the private key with the following command:

```
$ gpg --out keepthis.secret --decrypt underthe.radar
```

In a console, you'd be prompted for the passphrase created earlier, with a screen similar to that shown in Figure 10-14.

FIGURE 10-14

Prompting for a passphrase for decryption

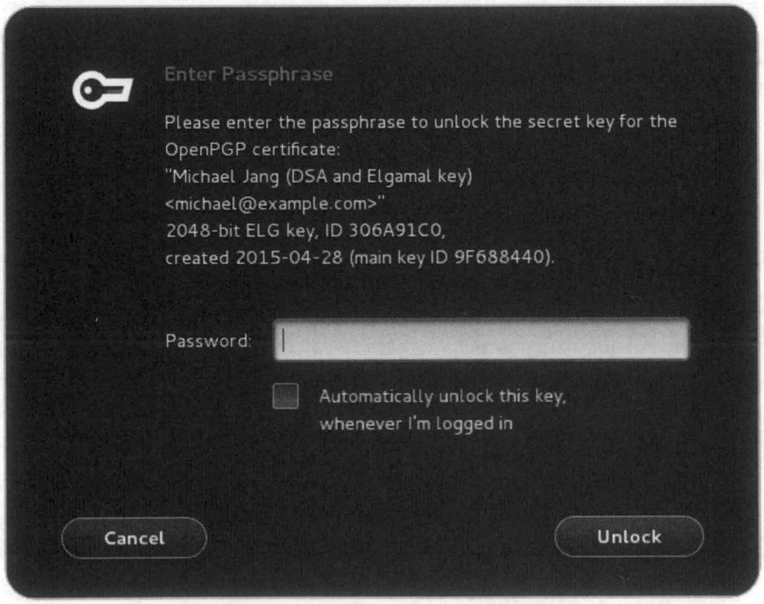

Enter Passphrase

Please enter the passphrase to unlock the secret key for the OpenPGP certificate:
"Michael Jang (DSA and Elgamal key)
<michael@example.com>"
2048-bit ELG key, ID 306A91C0,
created 2015-04-28 (main key ID 9F688440).

Password:

☐ Automatically unlock this key, whenever I'm logged in

Cancel   Unlock

CERTIFICATION SUMMARY

To help defend the data, the services, and the systems on a network, Linux provides layers of security. If a service is not installed, a black hat hacker can't use it to break into a system. Those systems that are installed should be kept up to date. Such services can be protected by firewalls, along with host- and user-based security options. Many services include their own layers of security. RHEL 7 incorporates several recommendations from the NSA, including SELinux.

Zone-based firewalls can regulate and protect gateways as well as individual systems. That same firewalld daemon can be used to set up packet forwarding, as well as masquerading of private networks. Such options can be configured directly via the CLI using **firewall-cmd**, or set up with the help of the Firewall Configuration tool.

Those daemons linked to the TCP Wrappers library can be protected by appropriate settings in the /etc/hosts.allow and /etc/hosts.deny files. If there is a conflict, /etc/hosts .allow is read first. Regulation through TCP Wrappers is possible by user or host.

PAM supports user-based security for a number of administrative tools. They're configured individually through files in the /etc/pam.d directory. These files refer to modules in the /usr/lib64/security directory.

Linux supports encryption with the help of GPG. RHEL 7 includes GPG2 for this purpose as well as commands such as **gpg** to set up private/public key pairs using the RSA, DSA, or ElGamal scheme.

✔ # TWO-MINUTE DRILL

The following are some of the key points from the certification objectives in Chapter 10.

The Layers of Linux Security

❑ Bastion systems are more secure because they're configured with a single service. With virtualization, bastion systems are now a practical option even for smaller organizations.

❑ You may choose to automate at least security updates with the Software Updates Preference tool.

❑ Many services include their own security options in their configuration files.

❑ Host-based security can be configured by domain name or IP address.

❑ User-based security includes specified users and groups.

❑ The PolicyKit can regulate security of administrative tools run from the GNOME desktop environment.

Firewalls and Network Address Translation

❑ The firewalld configuration command is **firewall-cmd**.

❑ With firewalld, you can assign interfaces and source IP ranges to different zones as well as control which traffic is allowed into a zone.

❑ With firewalld, you can also masquerade the IP addresses from one network on an outside network such as the Internet.

❑ firewalld can also be configured with the help of the Firewall Configuration tool, which you can start with the **firewall-config** command.

TCP Wrappers

❑ The **strings -f /usr/sbin/*** command can identify services that can be regulated by TCP Wrappers.

❑ Clients and users listed in /etc/hosts.allow are allowed access; clients and users listed in /etc/hosts.deny are denied access.

❑ Remember to use the actual executable name of the daemon in /etc/hosts.allow and /etc/hosts.deny (normally in /usr/sbin), such as **vsftpd**.

Pluggable Authentication Modules

❑ RHEL 7 uses the Pluggable Authentication Modules (PAM) system to provide a common application programming interface for authentication services.

❑ PAM modules are called by configuration files in the /etc/pam.d directory. These configuration files are usually named after the service or command they control.

❑ There are four main types of PAM rules: authentication, account, password, and session management.

❑ PAM configuration files include lines that list the type, the control_flag, and the name of the actual module, followed by optional arguments.

❑ PAM modules are well documented in the /usr/share/doc/pam-*versionnumber*/txts directory and in the man pages.

Secure Files and More with GPG2

❑ GPG is the open-source implementation of PGP.

❑ RHEL 7 includes version 2 of GPG, known as GPG2.

❑ GPG2 encryption and signature can use the DSA, RSA, and ElGamal keys.

❑ GPG2 keys can be created with the **gpg --gen-key** command and listed with the **gpg --list-key** command.

SELF TEST

The following questions will help measure your understanding of the material presented in this chapter. As no multiple choice questions appear on the Red Hat exams, no multiple choice questions appear in this book. These questions exclusively test your understanding of the chapter. It is okay if you have another way of performing a task. Getting results, not memorizing trivia, is what counts on the Red Hat exams. There may be more than one answer to many of these questions.

The Layers of Linux Security

1. What security option is best for a service that isn't currently required on a system?

_____

Firewalls and Network Address Translation

2. Consider a system with the default firewalld settings, where the following commands have been entered:

```
# firewall-cmd --zone=dmz --add-source=192.168.77.77
# firewall-cmd --zone=dmz --remove-service=ssh
```

Once these are entered, and before a reboot, what effect will they have when a client with an IP address of 192.168.77.77 tries to connect to this system?

_____

3. What directories include the configuration files that define the firewalld services?

_____

4. You are setting up a small office and would like to provide Internet access to a small number of users but don't have enough dedicated public IPv4 addresses for each system on the network. What can you do?

_____

5. What **firewall-cmd** command switch sets up masquerading?

_____

6. What **firewall-cmd** command adds a rich rule to the default zone to allow HTTP connections only from the 192.168.122.50 host?

   _____

7. What **firewall-cmd** command option is used to make permanent configuration changes?

   _____

TCP Wrappers

8. With TCP Wrappers configuration files, how could you limit FTP access to clients on the 192.168.170.0/24 network? Hint: the vsFTP daemon, when installed, is in /usr/sbin/vsftpd.

   _____

9. What happens to a service if you allow the service in /etc/hosts.allow and prohibit it in /etc/hosts.deny?

   _____

Pluggable Authentication Modules

10. What are the four basic PAM rule types?

    _____

    _____

    _____

    _____

11. You are editing a PAM configuration file by adding a module. Which control flag immediately terminates the authentication process if the module succeeds?

    _____

Secure Files and More with GPG2

12. What command lists the GPG public keys loaded on the current local account?

    _____

LAB QUESTIONS

Several of these labs involve exercises that can seriously affect a system. You should do these exercises on test machines only. The second lab of Chapter 1 sets up KVM for this purpose.

Red Hat presents its exams electronically. For that reason, the labs for this chapter are available from the media that accompanies the book, in the Chapter10/ subdirectory. They're available in .doc, .html, and .txt formats. In case you haven't yet set up RHEL 7 on a system, refer to the first lab of Chapter 2 for installation instructions. The answers for each lab follow the Self Test answers for the fill-in-the-blank questions.

SELF TEST ANSWERS

The Layers of Linux Security

1. The security option that is best for a service that isn't currently required on a system is to not install that service.

Firewalls and Network Address Translation

2. Based on the given commands, any connection attempt to the SSH service from the 192.168.77.77 system is rejected.

3. The configuration of firewalld services is stored in the /usr/lib/firewalld/services/ and /etc/firewalld/services/ directories.

4. To set up a small office while providing Internet access to a small number of users, all you need is one dedicated IP address. The other addresses can be on a private network. Masquerading makes this possible.

5. The **firewall-cmd** command switch that sets up masquerading is **--add-masquerade**.

6. The following rich rule allows HTTP traffic from 192.168.122.50 for the default zone:

```
# firewall-cmd --add-rich-rule='rule family=ipv4 source ↵
address=192.168.122.50 service name=http accept'
```

7. The **--permanent** option of **firewall-cmd** is used to make permanent configuration changes. Don't forget to load the saved configuration into the run-time configuration using the **firewall-cmd --reload** command.

TCP Wrappers

8. To limit FTP access to clients on the 192.168.170.0 network, you'd allow access to the network in /etc/hosts.allow and deny it to all others in /etc/hosts.deny. As /usr/sbin is in the root user path, you can cite the **vsftpd** daemon directly and add the following directive to /etc/hosts.allow:

```
vsftpd : 192.168.170.0/255.255.255.0
```

Then you would add the following to /etc/hosts.deny:

```
vsftpd : ALL
```

9. If you allow a service in /etc/hosts.allow and prohibit it in /etc/hosts.deny, the service is allowed.

Pluggable Authentication Modules

10. The four basic PAM rule types are **auth**, **account**, **password**, and **session**. The **include** type refers to one or more of the other PAM types in a different file.

11. The **sufficient** control flag immediately terminates the authentication process if the module succeeds.

Secure Files and More with GPG2

12. The command that lists currently loaded public keys is **gpg --list-key**. The **gpg2 --list-key** command is also acceptable.

LAB ANSWERS

Lab 1

Verifying this lab should be straightforward. If it works, you should be able to confirm with the following command on the tester1.example.com system:

```
$ gpg --list-keys
```

It should include the GPG2 public key just imported to that system. Of course, if the encryption, file transfer, and decryption worked, you should also be able to read the decrypted text file in a local text editor.

Lab 2

This lab is somewhat self-explanatory, in that it can help you think about how to make a system more secure. As discussed in the chapter, you can start with a minimal installation. The minimal installation of RHEL 7 happens to include the SSH server for remote administrative access.

While RHEL 7 has greatly reduced the number of standard services installed, most users will find some services that are not required. For example, how many administrators actually need Bluetooth services for a RHEL 7 system installed on a virtual machine?

Lab 3

If you want to set up a RHEL computer as a secure web server, it's a straightforward process that's described in Chapter 14. However, firewall configuration is part of the process covered in this chapter. To that end, you'll want to set up a firewall to block all but the most essential ports. This should include TCP/IP ports 80 and 443, which allow outside computers to access local regular and secure web services. Open ports should also include port 22 for SSH communication.

The easiest way to set this up is with the Red Hat Firewall Configuration tool, which you can start with the **firewall-config** command. Once in the Firewall Configuration tool, take the following steps, which vary slightly between the GUI- and console-based versions of the tool:

1. Set the Configuration mode to Permanent.
2. Select the "public" zone. Click the <interface> tab and ensure that the system network interfaces are listed under this zone.
3. Select the Services tab and enable the http service. This allows access from outside the local computer to the local regular website. Activate the https option as well. Make sure the ssh option remains active.
4. Click Options | Reload Firewalld to apply the changes to the run-time configuration.
5. Enter the following command to check the resulting firewall:

   ```
   # firewall-cmd --list-all
   ```

6. Once you've configured a web service as described in Chapter 14, users will be able to access both the regular and secure web servers from remote systems.

Lab 4

The following steps demonstrate two different methods to limit access to the noted system on IP address 192.168.122.150. Any of the two methods would be acceptable. These methods secure vsFTP in two ways: through TCP Wrappers and with the appropriate firewall commands. In a "real-world" scenario, you might use all methods in a layered security strategy. These steps assume you're performing this lab on the server1.example.com system.

1. Make sure that the vsftpd RPM is installed.
2. Start the FTP service. Use the **systemctl start vsftpd** command.
3. Back up the current version of the /etc/hosts.deny file. Open that file in a text editor. Add the **vsftpd : ALL EXCEPT 192.168.122.150** line.
4. Try accessing the FTP service from the computer with the IP address of 192.168.122.50. What happens? Try again from a different computer on your LAN.
5. Restore the previous /etc/hosts.deny file.
6. Block the FTP service for all IP addresses except 192.168.122.150 with the following commands:

```
# firewall-cmd --permanent --add-rich-rule='rule family=ipv4 source ↵
address=192.168.122.150 service name=ftp drop'
# firewall-cmd --permanent --add-service=ftp
```

7. Promote the permanent configuration into the run-time configuration with the **firewall-cmd --reload** command.
8. Try accessing the FTP server from the computer with the IP address of 192.168.122.150. What happens? Try again from a different computer on the LAN.
9. Remove the firewall rules you have added.
10. Bonus: Repeat these commands for the SSH service on port 22.

Lab 5

To confirm that TCP Wrappers can be used to help protect the SSH service, run the following command:

```
# ldd /usr/sbin/sshd | grep libwrap
```

Output, which includes a reference to the libwrap.so.0 library, confirms a link to the TCP Wrappers library. In general, it's safest to deny access to all services by including the following entry in the /etc/hosts.deny file:

```
ALL : ALL
```

You can then set up access to the SSH service with a line like the following in the /etc/hosts.allow file:

```
sshd : 192.168.122.50
```

While in most cases the use of the fully qualified domain name for the noted IP address (server1 .example.com) should work too, the use of the IP address is often appropriate. Limits by IP address don't depend on connections to DNS servers or reverse DNS being accurate.

Of course, this is not the only way to limit access to the SSH service to one system. It's possible within the /etc/hosts.deny file with a directive such as the following:

```
sshd : ALL EXCEPT 192.168.122.50
```

It's possible to set this up with other security options such as the firewalld zone–based service.

Lab 6

Before this lab can work, you'll need to activate one SELinux boolean: **ftp_home_dir**. It's listed in the SELinux Administration tool as "Determine whether ftpd can read and write files in user home directories." Therefore, with the key boolean identified, you should be able to set up vsFTP as described.

The description in this lab should point you to the /etc/pam.d/vsftpd configuration file. The model command line in this file is

```
auth required  pam_listfile.so item=user sense=deny ↵
file=/etc/vsftpd/ftpusers onerr=succeed
```

which points to the /etc/vsftpd/ftpusers file, a list of users to "deny" access to. As the conditions in the lab suggest that you need a list of (one) user to which access is to be allowed, a second line of a similar type in this file is appropriate. For example,

```
auth required  pam_listfile.so item=user sense=allow ↵
file=/etc/vsftpd/testusers onerr=succeed
```

allows all users listed in the /etc/vsftpd/testusers file. The **onerr=succeed** directive means that the vsFTP server still works if there's an error elsewhere. For example, if there is no testusers file in the /etc/vsftpd directory, the directives in this line are forgiving, allowing the conditions for the **auth** module type to succeed.

As an experiment, try this lab with the boolean **ftp_home_dir** variable set and unset. That should demonstrate the power of SELinux and serve as an appropriate preview of Chapter 11.

Chapter 11

System Services
and SELinux

This is a "big picture" chapter, focused on common tasks you'll perform on the job. These tasks relate to the detailed configuration of RHCE-level services.

RHEL 7 incorporates basic system configuration files in the /etc/sysconfig directory, called by various services and cron jobs. Integral to this approach is the configuration of SELinux, as it includes a substantial number of custom options for various services.

You will test these tools on the one service that you might install on all bastion systems: SSH. As it is the common service for all such systems, "black hat" hackers want to find a weakness in SSH. Therefore, this chapter describes how you can make SSH services more secure. This is the first chapter where you will use the three virtual machines created in Chapters 1 and 2.

In this chapter, you'll also configure the boolean options used by SELinux to secure various services. While SELinux is a common source of frustration, it is easier to handle when you know the options that support the desired features.

In addition, this chapter covers the basic procedure to make sure various services are operational, accessible from remote systems, and started the next time the system is rebooted.

INSIDE THE EXAM

Inside the Exam

This section includes tasks that will be repeated in the remainder of the book:

- Install the packages needed to provide the service

Whether you're installing the Samba file server or a DNS caching-only name server, you will use the same tools. Yes, these are the same **rpm** and **yum** commands, along with the Package Management tools described in Chapter 7. To save time, you might use these commands to install the services described in Chapters 12 through 17.

- Configure the service to start when the system is booted
- Configure SELinux to support the service
- Configure SELinux port-labeling to allow services to use nonstandard ports

While the detailed configuration of individual services is the province of each chapter, the steps required to configure a service to start during the boot process are based on common commands such as **systemctl**. In addition, the configuration of SELinux to support a service requires access to and the configuration of similar options.

As suggested in the introduction, there's a special focus on the SSH service.

- Configure key-based authentication

Key-based authentication is a requirement for both the RHCSA and RHCE exams, covered in Chapter 4. You may want to review that chapter's section titled "Securing SSH with Key-Based Authentication." Given the importance of SSH security, in this chapter we also cover the following task:

- Configure additional options described in documentation

CERTIFICATION OBJECTIVE 11.01

Red Hat System Configuration

In this section, you'll review basic information on how services are configured on Red Hat systems. The actual process associated with a service is a daemon. Such daemons are executable files, normally stored in the /usr/sbin directory. Red Hat configures custom parameters and more in the /etc/sysconfig directory. These files are referenced by cron jobs or systemd units.

Service Management

As discussed throughout the book, services are controlled by systemd service unit configuration files. As described in Chapter 4, you can use **systemctl** to start, stop, or restart a service. In many cases, you can use **systemctl** to reload a service with modified configuration files, without kicking off currently connected users.

Although the real daemons are in the /usr/sbin directories, the systemd unit files do more. They call the daemons with parameters configured in their unit files in the /lib/systemd/system directory. The unit files then reference service-specific configuration files.

RHEL 7 maintains compatibility with the traditional init-script system that was found in earlier versions of Red Hat Enterprise Linux. Old-style init scripts are still located in the /etc/rc.d/init.d directory and referenced by symbolic links in the /etc/rc.d/rc*X*.d subdirectories. And the old **service** command in the /usr/sbin directory is a wrapper to the **systemctl** command. In other words, the following commands are functionally identical:

```
# systemctl restart sshd
# service sshd restart
```

System Services

The files in the /etc/sysconfig directory are normally used with cron jobs and systemd units. They're as varied as the unit configuration files included in the /lib/systemd/system directory. As they include basic configuration options for each daemon, they drive the basic operation of each service.

In most cases, each of these files supports the use of switches as described in the associated man pages. For example, the /etc/sysconfig/httpd file can be used to set up custom options for starting the Apache web server. In that file, the **OPTIONS** directive would pass switches to the /usr/sbin/httpd daemon, as defined in the httpd man page.

Bigger Picture Configuration Process

In general, when you configure a network service on Linux, run the general steps described in this section. The actual steps you take may vary; for example, you may sometimes modify SELinux options first. Sometimes, you'll want to test a service locally and remotely before making sure the service starts automatically upon the next reboot.

1. Install the service with a command such as **rpm** or **yum**. In some cases, you may need to install additional packages.

2. Edit appropriate service configuration files. Usually, you have to modify and customize several configuration files, such as for the Postfix e-mail server in the /etc/postfix directory.

3. Modify SELinux booleans. As discussed later in this chapter, most services have more than one SELinux boolean. For example, you may modify different SELinux booleans to allow the Samba file server to share files in read/write or read-only mode.

4. Start the service. You'll also need to make sure the service starts the next time the system is booted, as discussed later in this chapter.

5. Test the service locally. Make sure it works from the appropriate client(s) and on the local system.

6. Set appropriate firewall policies, based on firewalld, TCP Wrappers, and service-specific configuration files. Configure access to desired users and systems.

7. Test the service remotely. If the right ports are open, the service should work as well as when you connect locally. With the right limits, the service should not be accessible to undesired users or systems.

Available Configuration Tools

In general, it's most efficient to configure various services from the command line. An administrator who knows a service can set up basic operation in just a few minutes. However, most administrators can't specialize in everything. To that end, Red Hat has developed a number of configuration tools. When used properly, these tools will modify the right configuration files. Some are installed with each service; others have to be installed separately. Most of these tools are accessible from a GUI command-line interface with a **system-config-*** command.

The tools used in this book (and a couple more) are summarized in Table 11-1.

TABLE 11-1	Red Hat Configuration Tools	

Tool	Command	Function
Add/Remove Software	gpk-application	Front end to the **yum** command; manages current software configuration
Authentication Configuration	authconfig*, system-config-authentication	Configuration of user/group databases and client authentication
Date/Time Properties	system-config-date	Management of the current time zone, NTP client
Firewall Configuration	firewall-config	Configuration of firewalld-based firewalls, masquerading, and forwarding
Language Selection	system-config-language	Language selection within the GUI
Network Connections	nm-connection-editor	Detailed network device configuration tool
Network Management	nmtui	Network device/DNS client configuration at the console
Printer Configuration	system-config-printer	Management of the CUPS print server
SELinux Management	system-config-selinux	Configuration of SELinux booleans, labels, users, and so on
Software Update	gpk-update-viewer	Used to review and install available updates to installed packages
User Manager	system-config-users	Management and configuration of users and groups

CERTIFICATION OBJECTIVE 11.02

Security-Enhanced Linux

Security-Enhanced Linux (SELinux) provides one more layer of security. Developed by the U.S. National Security Agency, SELinux makes it more difficult for "black hat" hackers to use or access files or services, even on compromised systems. SELinux assigns a *context* to each *object,* such as a file, a device, or a network socket. The context of the object tells which *actions* a process (or *subject,* in SELinux jargon) can perform.

Basic SELinux options were covered in Chapter 4, as this is also a requirement for the RHCSA certification. For the RHCE, the focus of SELinux relates to various services. Specifically, you need to know how to configure SELinux to support the Apache web server, the Domain Name System (DNS) service, the MariaDB database management system, the Samba file server, the Simple Mail Transport Protocol (SMTP) service, the Secure Shell (SSH) daemon, and the Network Time Protocol (NTP) service.

The requirements for each of these services are covered in this and later chapters of this book. As the SELinux configuration for each service requires the use of the same commands and tools, they're covered here.

The key commands and tools discussed in this section are **getsebool**, **setsebool**, **chcon**, **restorecon**, **ls -Z**, and the SELinux Management Tool. While these are the same tools used in Chapter 4, the focus is different. To review, the **getsebool** and **setsebool** commands set boolean options in the files of the /sys/fs/selinux/booleans directory. A boolean is a binary option, 1 or 0, which corresponds to yes or no.

Options in the SELinux Booleans Directory

When configuring SELinux for a service, you'll generally make changes to boolean settings in the /sys virtual filesystem. Take a look at the files in the /sys/fs/selinux/booleans directory. The filenames are somewhat descriptive.

For example, the http_enable_homedirs boolean either allows or denies access to user home directories via an Apache server. It is disabled by default. In other words, if you configured the Apache server in Chapter 14 to serve files from user home directories without changes to SELinux, the web server wouldn't be able to access the files.

Problems like this are a common source of frustration for administrators of RHEL systems. They do all the work to configure a service, they test out the configuration, they check their documentation, they think they've done everything right, and yet the service doesn't work as they want. The solution is to make SELinux a part of what you do to configure a service.

As an example, run the following command:

```
$ cat /sys/fs/selinux/booleans/httpd_enable_homedirs
```

By default, the output should be

```
0 0
```

That's two zeros. Supposedly one boolean is for the current setting, and the other is for the permanent setting. In practice, the numbers don't reflect the differences, at least for RHEL 7, but the differences are still there. Because of this issue, the best way to see the current state of a boolean is the **getsebool** command. For example, the command

```
$ getsebool httpd_enable_homedirs
```

leads to the following output:

```
httpd_enable_homedirs --> off
```

Bottom line, if the current setting is 0, the following command would activate httpd_enable_homedirs only until the system is rebooted:

```
# setsebool httpd_enable_homedirs 1
```

To repeat from Chapter 4, the way to make the change permanent from the command line is with the **setsebool -P** command, which in this case is

```
# setsebool -P httpd_enable_homedirs 1
```

e x a m
w a t c h   **Many service-related SELinux booleans are described in local documentation; for a list of associated man pages, run the** man -k selinux **command.**

Service Categories of SELinux Booleans

There are nearly 300 pseudo-files in the /sys/fs/selinux/booleans directory. As the filenames in this directory are descriptive, you can use database filter commands such as **grep** to help classify those booleans. Based on some of the services discussed in this book, the following would be some appropriate filtering commands:

```
$ ls /sys/fs/selinux/booleans | grep http
$ ls /sys/fs/selinux/booleans | grep samba
$ ls /sys/fs/selinux/booleans | grep nfs
```

You'll explore each of these categories of booleans in more detail shortly. For a brief description of available booleans with their current status, run the **semanage boolean -l** command. The **semanage** command is part of the policycoreutils-python package.

Boolean Configuration with the SELinux Management Tool

One of the benefits of GUI tools is a view of the "big picture." With the SELinux Management tool, you can review the active booleans and quickly get a sense of whether SELinux is set to allow few or many options associated with a service. As discussed in Chapter 4, you can start the SELinux Management tool in a GUI desktop environment with the **system-config-selinux** command. In the left pane, click Boolean. This opens access to a

FIGURE 11-1   Filter booleans with the SELinux Management tool.

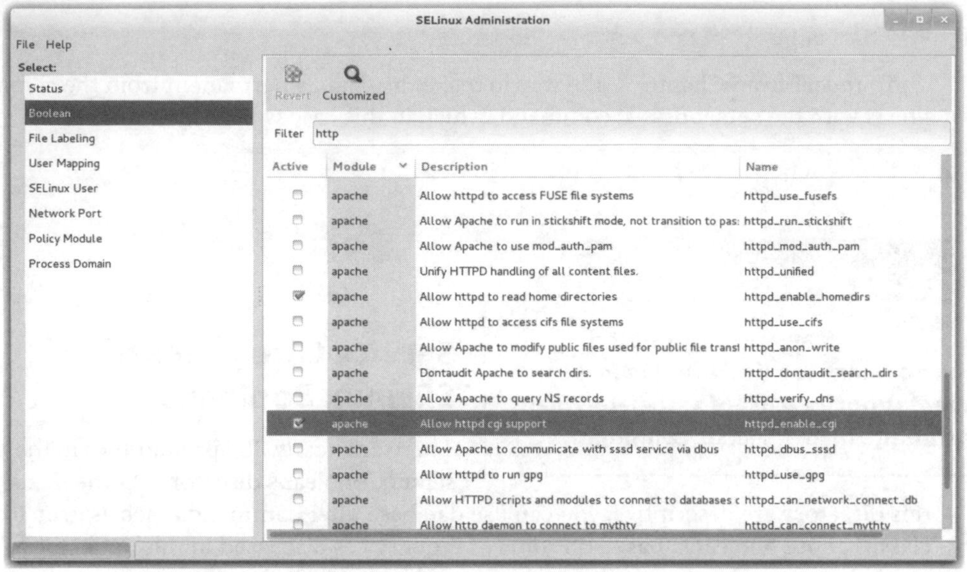

group of booleans in the right side of the window. Note the **http** filter added in Figure 11-1. It filters the system for all booleans related to the Apache web server.

Compare the list to the output of the **ls /sys/fs/selinux/booleans | grep http** command described earlier. Note the differences. You'll actually see more Apache-related booleans in the GUI tool because the filter in the SELinux Management tool filters by SELinux boolean names and descriptions.

A number of categories are shown in the left pane of the SELinux Management Tool window; they are described in the following sections. Most of the focus here will be on the boolean category, where most of the SELinux policies are customized.

In some cases, a boolean is associated with a requirement for a SELinux file context. For example, the httpd_anon_write boolean works only if associated files and directories are labeled with the public_content_rw_t type. To set that type on, say, the /var/www/html/files directory (and subdirectories), you would run the following command:

```
# chcon -R -t public_content_rw_t /var/www/html/files
```

Boolean Settings

The boolean settings discussed in the following sections fall into several categories. They're based on the services defined in the RHCE objectives. The SELinux settings do not stand alone. For example, if you enable the httpd_enable_homedirs boolean, you'll still have to configure the /etc/httpd/conf.d/userdir.conf file to support access to user home directories. Only after both SELinux and Apache are configured with such support can users connect to their home directories through that Apache server.

As there are no current SELinux booleans related to the Network Time Protocol (NTP) service, there is no separate section for NTP booleans in this discussion.

Regular and Secure HTTP Services

A number of SELinux directives are available to help secure the Apache web server, as summarized in the following list. Most are straightforward and self-explanatory. They are ordered by the filename of the boolean, as shown in the /sys/fs/selinux/booleans directory. While these booleans can apply to other web servers, Red Hat assumes the use of the Apache web server. The descriptions specify the configuration if the boolean is active.

- **httpd_anon_write**   Allows the web service to write to files labeled with the public_ content_rw_t type.
- **httpd_builtin_scripting**   Permits access to scripts, normally associated with PHP. Enabled by default.
- **httpd_can_check_spam**   Supports the use of SpamAssassin for web-based e-mail applications.
- **httpd_can_network_connect**   Allows Apache scripts and modules access to external systems over the network; normally disabled to minimize risks to other systems.
- **httpd_can_network_connect_cobbler**   Allows Apache scripts and modules to access an external Cobbler installation server. If you don't need to connect to any services other than Cobbler, you should disable the httpd_can_network_connect boolean.
- **httpd_can_network_connect_db**   Allows connections to database server ports; more specific than httpd_can_network_connect.
- **httpd_can_network_memcache**   Enables access to a memcache server over the network.
- **httpd_can_network_relay**   Supports the use of the HTTP service as a forward or reverse proxy.
- **httpd_can_sendmail**   Allows Apache to send e-mails.
- **httpd_dbus_avahi**   Supports access to the avahi service via the D-bus message system. Disabled by default.
- **httpd_enable_cgi**   Allows the running of Common Gateway Interface (CGI) scripts. Enabled by default; requires scripts to be labeled with the httpd_sys_script_ exec_t file type.

- **httpd_enable_ftp_server**   Allows Apache to listen on the FTP port (normally 21) and work as an FTP server.
- **httpd_enable_homedirs**   Allows Apache to serve content from user home directories via the UserDir directive.
- **httpd_execmem**   Supports programs such as those written in Java or Mono that require memory addresses that are executable and writable.
- **httpd_mod_auth_ntlm_winbind**   Permits access to the Microsoft NT LAN Manager (NTLM) and Winbind authentication databases; requires an installed and active mod_auth_ntlm_winbind module for Apache.
- **httpd_mod_auth_pam**   Supports PAM access for user authentication; requires an installed and active mod_auth_pam module for Apache.
- **httpd_read_user_content**   Allows the Apache web server to read all files in user home directories.
- **httpd_setrlimit**   Allows changes to Apache file descriptor limits.
- **httpd_ssi_exec**   Supports executable Server Side Includes (SSIs).
- **httpd_sys_script_anon_write**   Allows HTTP scripts to write to files labeled with the public_content_rw_t type.
- **httpd_tmp_exec**   Lets Apache run executable files from the /tmp directory.
- **httpd_tty_comm**   Supports access to a terminal; needed by Apache to prompt for a password if the private key of a TLS certificate is password-protected.
- **httpd_unified**   Enables access to all httpd_*_t labeled files, whether they are read-only, writable, or executable. Disabled by default.
- **httpd_use_cifs**   Supports access from Apache to shared Samba files and directories labeled with the cifs_t file type.
- **httpd_use_fuse**   Supports access from Apache to FUSE filesystems, such as GlusterFS volumes.
- **httpd_use_gpg**   Allows Apache to use GPG for encryption.
- **httpd_use_nfs**   Supports access from Apache to shared NFS files and directories labeled with the nfs_t file type.
- **httpd_use_openstack**   Allows Apache to access OpenStack ports.

Name Service

The name service daemon (**named**) is based on the Berkeley Internet Name Domain (BIND) software, which is the default RHEL 7 DNS service. If you maintain an authoritative DNS zone, activate the named_write_master_zones boolean. Then local DNS software can overwrite master zone files.

In general, this section does not apply to the RHCE because the objectives state that all you need to do with DNS is to configure a caching-only name server. Such servers are not authoritative for a specific domain. Therefore, the noted DNS boolean does not apply because such DNS servers do not have master zone files.

RHEL includes the Unbound DNS resolver, a small service that you can install in place of BIND to provide a caching name server.

MariaDB

Two SELinux booleans are solely related to the MariaDB database service. Typically, you don't need to change their default values.

- **mysql_connect_any**   Allows MariaDB/MySQL to connect to all ports. Disabled by default.
- **selinuxuser_mysql_connect_enabled**   Allows SELinux users to connect to a local MariaDB/MySQL server using a Unix domain socket. Disabled by default.

NFS

Some of the basic SELinux booleans associated with the Network File System (NFS) servers are enabled by default, which allows you to share directories with the NFS server.

- **nfs_export_all_ro**   Allows shared NFS directories to be exported with read-only permissions. Enabled by default.
- **nfs_export_all_rw**   Allows shared NFS directories to be exported with read/write permissions. Enabled by default.
- **use_nfs_home_dirs**   Supports access of home directories from remote NFS systems. Disabled by default.
- **virt_use_nfs**   Enables access from virtual guests to NFS mounted filesystems.

Samba

Samba booleans are generally not enabled by default. So in most configurations, you'll need to activate one or more SELinux booleans to match changes to the Samba configuration files. These booleans include the following:

- **samba_create_home_dirs**   Allows Samba to create new home directories, such as for users who connect from other systems, normally via the pam_mkhomedir.so PAM module.
- **samba_domain_controller**   Enables the configuration of the local Samba server as a local domain controller on a Microsoft Windows–style network.
- **samba_enable_home_dirs**   Supports the sharing of user home directories.

- **samba_export_all_ro**   Allows files and directories to be shared in read-only mode.
- **samba_export_all_rw**   Allows files and directories to be shared in read/write mode.
- **samba_run_unconfined**   Allows Samba to run unconfined scripts stored in the /var/lib/samba/scripts directory.
- **samba_share_fusefs**   Supports sharing of filesystems mounted under FUSE filesystems (fusefs).
- **samba_share_nfs**   Supports sharing of filesystems mounted under NFS.
- **smbd_anon_write**   Allows Samba to modify files on public directories configured with the public_content_rw_t and public_content_r_t SELinux contexts.
- **use_samba_home_dirs**   Supports the use of a remote Samba server for local home directories.
- **virt_use_samba**   Allows virtual machines to use files shared from Samba.

SMTP

The two SELinux booleans associated with SMTP services both work with the default Postfix server. The httpd_can_sendmail boolean was previously described. The other Postfix boolean is enabled by default:

- **postfix_local_write_mail_spool**   Allows Postfix to write to the local mail spool directories

SSH

The SELinux booleans associated with SSH connections are listed next. All are disabled by default:

- **ssh_chroot_rw_homedirs**   Allows a **chroot**-enabled SSH service to read and write files from user home directories.
- **allow_ssh_keysign**   Allows host-based authentication; would not require usernames or public/private passphrase-based authentication.
- **ssh_sysadm_login**   Supports access by users configured with the sysadm_r role. This does not include the root administrative user; in general, it's more secure to log in as a regular user, connecting with passphrases, before authenticating with administrative privileges.

SELinux File Contexts

Changes made with the **chcon** command are not permanent. While they do survive a reboot, they do not survive a *relabel*. SELinux relabels of a system can happen when

SELinux is disabled and then re-enabled. The **restorecon** command relabels a target directory. The configured SELinux contexts are stored in the /etc/selinux/targeted/contexts/files directory.

The default version of this directory includes, among the others, three important files:

- **file_contexts** Baseline file contexts for the entire system
- **file_contexts.homedirs** File contexts for the /home directory and all subdirectories
- **media** File contexts for removable devices that may be mounted after installation

If you need a change to file system contexts to survive a relabel, the **semanage** command can help. For example, if you need to set up the /www directory for virtual websites, the following command makes sure the file contexts are appropriate for that directory (and subdirectories) even after a relabel:

```
# semanage fcontext -a -t httpd_sys_content_t "/www(/.*)?"
```

The noted command adds a file context rule to the file_contexts.local file in the /etc/selinux/targeted/contexts/files directory. For a discussion of the meaning of the **(/.*)?** regular expression, refer to Chapter 4.

While the **semanage** command manages a variety of SELinux policies, the focus here is on file contexts, as represented by the **fcontext** option. The command switches available are described in Table 11-2.

TABLE 11-2	Switch	Description
	-a	Add
Command	-d	Delete
Switches for	-D	Delete all
semanage fcontext	-f	File type
	-l	List
	-m	Modify
	-n	No heading
	-r	Range
	-s	SELinux user name (used for user roles)
	-t	SELinux file type

SELinux Port Labeling

The SELinux policy controls every action that a process can execute on a certain object, such as a file, a device, or a network socket. Opening a TCP socket and listening to a network port is one of those actions you can control and restrict via the SELinux policy.

If one of the services covered in the previous section is configured to listen to a nonstandard port, by default the SELinux targeted policy will deny this action. In fact, SELinux uses labels to control not only access to files or devices, but also to network ports. You can list all SELinux port labels by running the **semanage** command:

```
# semanage port -l
```

Filtering for a certain string can help in identifying which ports a service is allowed to listen to. As shown in the following example, the SSH service is restricted to listening to port 22:

```
# semanage port -l | grep ssh
ssh_port_t              tcp        22
```

Similarly, the http_port_t label regulates the ports that Apache can listen to, whereas http_cache_port_t identifies the ports allowed by web proxies:

```
# semanage port -l | grep http
http_cache_port_t       tcp        8080, 8118, 8123, 10001-10010
http_cache_port_T       udp        3130
http_port_t             tcp        80, 81, 443, 488, 8008, 8009, 8443, 9000
```

If you need to change a label to allow a service to listen to a nonstandard port, use the **semanage** command. In the following example, the SELinux policy is modified to allow Apache to listen to port 444:

```
# semanage port -a -t http_port_t -p tcp 444
```

Needless to say, you can achieve the same result from the SELinux Management tool, as shown in Figure 11-2.

EXERCISE 11-1

Configure a New Directory with Appropriate SELinux Contexts

In this exercise, you'll set up a new directory, /ftp, with SELinux contexts that match the standard directory for FTP servers. This exercise demonstrates how this is done with the **chcon** command, along with the effect of the **restorecon** and **semanage** commands.

1. Create the /ftp directory. Use the **ls -Zd /ftp** command to identify the SELinux contexts on that directory. Contrast that with the contexts on the /var/ftp directory.

FIGURE 11-2   Adding a network port with the SELinux Management Tool

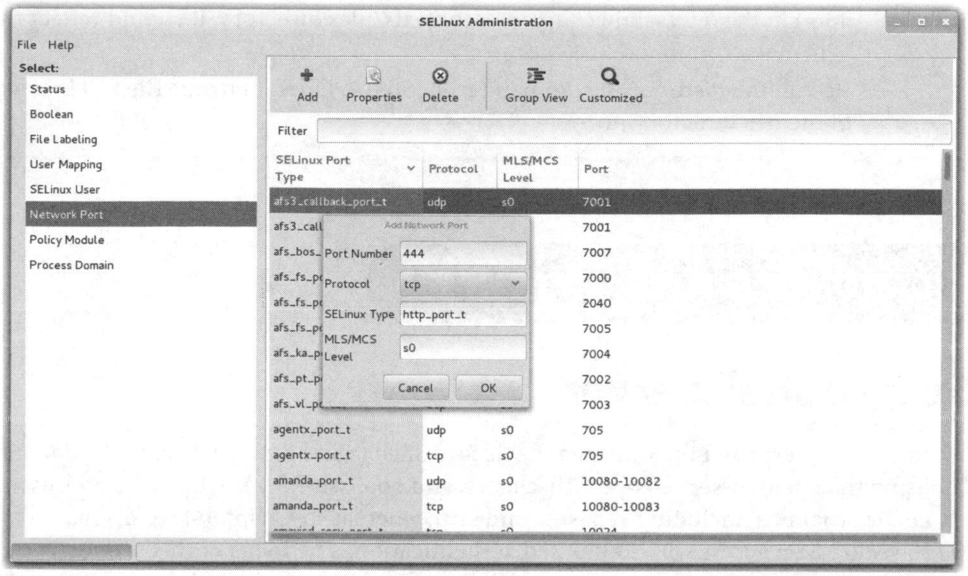

2. Change the contexts on the /ftp directory to match those on the /var/ftp directory. The most efficient method is with the following command:

```
# chcon -R --reference /var/ftp /ftp
```

While the **-R** switch is not required, we include it to help you get used to the idea of changing contexts recursively.

3. Run the **ls -Zd /ftp** command to review the changed contexts on that directory. It should now match the contexts on the /var/ftp directory.

4. Run the following command to see what happens when SELinux is relabeled:

```
# restorecon -Rv /ftp
```

What did this command do to the contexts of the /ftp directory?

5. To make changes to the /ftp directory permanent, you need help from the **semanage** command, with the **fcontext** option. As there is no analog to the **chcon --reference** command switch, the following command specifies the user role and file type, based on the default settings for the /var/ftp directory:

```
# semanage fcontext -a -s system_u -t public_content_t "/ftp(/.*)?"
```

6. Review the results. First, the **semanage** command does not change the current SELinux contexts of the /ftp directory. Next, review the contents of file_contexts .local in the /etc/selinux/targeted/contexts/files directory. It should reflect the **semanage** command just executed.

7. Re-run the **restorecon** command from Step 4. Does it change the SELinux contexts of the /ftp directory now?

CERTIFICATION OBJECTIVE 11.03

The Secure Shell Server

Red Hat Enterprise Linux installs the Secure Shell (SSH) server packages by default, using the openssh-server, openssh-clients, and openssh RPMs. Chapter 2 addressed SSH client programs, including **ssh**, **scp**, and **sftp**, whereas in Chapter 4 we discussed how to secure SSH access with key-based authentication. The focus of this section is on the SSH server. The secure daemon, **sshd**, listens for all inbound traffic on TCP port 22. The SSH server configuration files are located in the /etc/ssh directory.

SSH Server Configuration Files

The configuration files of the SSH server are stored in the /etc/ssh directory. The functionality of these files is summarized here:

- **moduli**   Supports the Diffie-Hellman Group Exchange key method with prime numbers and random key generators
- **ssh_config**   Includes the configuration for the local SSH client, discussed in Chapter 2
- **sshd_config**   Specifies the configuration of the SSH server, which is discussed in detail later in this chapter
- **ssh_host_ecdsa_key**   Includes the host private key for the local system, based on the ECDSA algorithm
- **ssh_host_ecdsa_key.pub**   Includes the host public key for the local system, based on the ECDSA algorithm
- **ssh_host_rsa_key**   Includes the host private key for the local system, based on the RSA algorithm
- **ssh_host_rsa_key.pub**   Includes the host public key for the local system, based on the RSA algorithm

Configure an SSH Server

You don't have to do much to configure an SSH server for basic operation. Install the packages described earlier, activate the service, and make sure it's active the next time the system is rebooted. As discussed in Chapter 1, the standard SSH port (TCP 22) is open in the default RHEL 7 firewall.

However, the RHCE objectives specify that you should be prepared to "configure additional options described in the documentation." Because of the general nature of that objective, this section will address every active and commented option in the default version of the SSH server configuration file.

The SSH server configuration file is /etc/ssh/sshd_config. The commands in comments are generally defaults. So if you want to set a nonstandard port for the SSH service, you could change the commented directive

```
#Port 22
```

to something like this:

```
Port 2222
```

Assuming the firewall and SELinux allow access through this port, you'd then be able to connect from a remote system with the **ssh -p 2222 server1.example.com** command. If the SSH server is different, substitute for server1.example.com.

While the next commented line (**#AddressFamily any**) implies that the SSH server uses both IPv4 and IPv6 addresses, it's possible to limit access to one of these types of addresses with the **inet** and **inet6** keywords, which correspond to IPv4 and IPv6, respectively:

```
AddressFamily inet
AddressFamily inet6
```

The default shown with the following **ListenAddress** directives is to listen for SSH communications on all local IPv4 and IPv6 addresses:

```
#ListenAddress 0.0.0.0
#ListenAddress ::
```

You can limit SSH to listening on the IPv4 or IPv6 addresses of certain network cards. That can help limit access to the SSH server to certain networks.

The next commented directive configures the SSH version. As noted earlier, SSH version 1 is considered insecure. Version 2 is used by default:

```
#Protocol 2
```

Since SSH version 1 is disabled, you should not have to activate the following directive, which sets the host key for version 1:

```
#HostKey /etc/ssh/ssh_host_key
```

The standard RSA and ECDSA keys are documented in the next lines. ECDSA (Elliptic Curve DSA) is considered more secure than the standard DSA protocol. Generally, there's no reason to change the locations of the keys:

```
HostKey /etc/ssh/ssh_host_rsa_key
#HostKey /etc/ssh/ssh_host_dsa_key
HostKey /etc/ssh/ssh_host_ecdsa_key
```

The commented directives that follow relate to an SSH version 1 ephemeral key. Such a server key would be regenerated every hour, with 1024 bits, but that would still be insecure.

```
#KeyRegenerationInterval 1h
#ServerKeyBits 1024
```

The next line specifies how often a session key is renegotiated. The default is to renegotiate after the cipher's default amount of data has been transmitted ("default"), with no time-based limits ("none").

```
#RekeyLimit default none
```

In the following lines, the first uncommented directive sends all log messages to the appropriate log facility. Based on the configuration of the /etc/rsyslog.conf file, all messages associated with the AUTHPRIV facility are logged to the /var/log/secure file. The level of information is INFO and above.

```
#SyslogFacility AUTH
SyslogFacility AUTHPRIV
#LogLevel INFO
```

To limit denial-of-service (DOS) attacks, the default **LoginGraceTime** shown here is two minutes. In other words, if a login process has not been completed in that time, the SSH server automatically disconnects from the remote client.

```
#LoginGraceTime 2m
```

The directive that follows documents that the root administrative user can log in using SSH:

```
#PermitRootLogin yes
```

Direct root logins over SSH can be inherently insecure. If you've set up private/public key–based passphrase authentication from an administrative account on a laptop system, that's a risk. A "black hat" hacker who gets a hold of that laptop system might then be able to connect to the remote server with administrative privileges. For that reason, it's usually recommended to change that directive to the following:

```
PermitRootLogin no
```

Administrators who log in as regular users can use the **su** or **sudo** command as appropriate to take administrative privileges with fewer risks. But if that's not a requirement when you take the RHCE exam, don't make that change. In fact, it could be counted as an error on the exam.

Next, it's more secure to retain the following directive, especially with respect to private and public keys:

```
#StrictModes yes
```

This directive checks that appropriate permissions are set on the user's home directory and SSH keys, before authorizing a login.

As noted with the following directive, the default number of authentication attempts per connection is six. You could reduce that number for additional security, but the downside is that you may get more false positives in the logs related to legitimate users who have mistyped their password:

```
#MaxAuthTries 6
```

The following directive suggests that you could open up to 10 SSH sessions on a connection:

```
#MaxSesssions 10
```

The following directive is used only with SSH version 1. Hopefully, you didn't activate that version of SSH.

```
#RSAAuthentication yes
```

On the other hand, the following directive is critical if you want to set up private/public key–based authentication on the standard SSH protocol version 2:

```
#PubkeyAuthentication yes
```

The following directive confirms the use of the authorized_keys file on the system to specify the public keys that can be used for authentication:

```
#AuthorizedKeysFile .ssh/authorized_keys
```

The next directive applies only when a Certification Authority is used in the authentication process:

```
#AuthorizedPrincipalsFile none
```

The two directives that follow are typically ignored:

```
#AuthorizedKeysCommand none
#AuthorizedKeysCommandRunAs nobody
```

The following Rhosts directive is generally not used because it applies to SSH version 1 and the less secure Remote Shell (RSH):

```
#RhostsRSAAuthentication no
```

While the following directive could support the use of the /etc/hosts.equiv file to limit hosts that connect, that's not normally encouraged. Nevertheless, it is one method for SSH host-based security beyond what's possible with an alternative such as TCP Wrappers, as discussed in Chapter 10.

```
#HostbasedAuthentication no
```

As described in Chapter 4, the .ssh/known_hosts file stores public keys from remote systems, and is read because of the following default:

```
#IgnoreUserKnownHosts no
```

The following directive may help administrators who are converting from RSH to SSH, as they use .rhosts and .shosts files. However, because it's not used by default, the following option is sensible:

```
#IgnoreRhosts yes
```

For systems and users where private/public passphrases aren't used, password-based authentication is needed, as enabled by this default:

```
#PasswordAuthentication yes
```

In general, you should never permit empty passwords due to security risks:

```
#PermitEmptyPasswords no
```

Challenge-response authentication is normally associated with one-time passwords common with remote terminals. While it can also work with PAM, it is normally disabled on SSH:

```
ChallengeResponseAuthentication no
```

If you did set up a Kerberos system for the local network using SSH version 1, you would have used some of the following options. The first two are almost self-explanatory, as they can enable Kerberos verification of a user and set up alternative Kerberos or local password authentication.

```
#KerberosAuthentication no
#KerberosOrLocalPasswd yes
#KerberosTicketCleanup yes
#KerberosGetAFSToken no
```

With SSH version 2, the Generic Security Services Application Programming Interface (GSSAPI) library is used for Kerberos authentication:

```
GSSAPIAuthentication = yes
```

The following directive destroys GSSAPI credentials upon logout:

```
GSSAPICleanupCredentials = yes
```

Normally, hostname checks are strict:

```
GSSAPIStrictAcceptorCheck = yes
```

Also, GSSAPI key exchange is allowed:

```
GSSAPIKeyExchange = yes
```

Authentication via PAM modules is supported:

```
UsePAM yes
```

With the following setting, the **ssh-agent** command can be used to forward private keys to other remote systems:

```
#AllowAgentForwarding yes
```

With the next configuration line, TCP communications can be forwarded over an SSH connection:

```
#AllowTCPForwarding yes
```

The **GatewayPorts** directive is normally disabled to keep remote hosts from connecting to forwarded ports:

```
#GatewayPorts no
```

The following directive is important for anyone who needs remote access to a GUI tool via X forwarding:

```
X11Forwarding yes
```

For example, when you are working from a remote location, you can connect to and open GUI tools from your Red Hat system at home or in our office via SSH, using a command similar to the following:

```
# ssh -X michael@Maui.example.com
```

The next directive helps avoid conflicts between local and remote GUI displays. The default should be adequate, unless there are more than 10 X11 displays in use.

```
#X11DisplayOffset 10
```

Normally, no changes are required to the following default, related to how the GUI display is bound on the SSH server:

```
#X11UseLocalhost yes
```

When SSH users log in remotely, the following setting means they see the contents of the /etc/motd file. Different messages are possible, based on the cron script configured in Chapter 9.

```
#PrintMotd yes
```

This is one useful setting for administrators because it documents the date and time of the last login to the noted system:

```
#PrintLastLog yes
```

The **TCPKeepAlive** directive enables TCP keepalive messages, to avoid a session hanging forever if a network connection, the SSH server, or any connected SSH client goes down:

```
#TCPKeepAlive yes
```

Generally, you should not enable this option because it is incompatible with **X11Forwarding**:

```
#UseLogin no
```

The privilege separation associated with the following directive sets up a separate process after successful authentication, with the privileges of the authenticated user:

```
UsePrivilegeSeparation sandbox
```

The following directive does not supersede the default **AuthorizedKeysFile** setting earlier in the file:

```
#PermitUserEnvironment no
```

Compression often helps speed communications over an SSH connection. The default is to delay compression until the password is accepted or the private/public key pair is matched to authenticate the user:

```
#Compression delayed
```

Sometimes, it's important to have the SSH server make sure the user still wants to transmit data. It's how clients are disconnected from sensitive systems such as bank accounts. But for an administrative connection, the following option disables such checks:

```
#ClientAliveInterval 0
```

If the **ClientAliveInterval** is set to some number, the following directive specifies the number of messages that may be sent before that client is automatically disconnected:

```
#ClientAliveCountMax 3
```

The following option for a patch level applies only to SSH version 1:

```
#ShowPatchLevel no
```

To minimize the risks of spoofing, the following directive checks remote hostnames against a DNS server or an /etc/hosts file:

```
#UseDNS yes
```

The PID file listed here contains the process ID number of the running SSH server process:

```
#PidFile /var/run/sshd.pid
```

When a "black hat" hacker tries to break into an SSH server, he may try to set up a bunch of connections, all attempting to log in simultaneously. The following directive limits the number of unauthenticated connections that the SSH server will work with. For an SSH server on an administrative system, it's something that you might consider reducing.

```
#MaxStartups 10
```

The following directive, if activated, would support device forwarding:

```
#PermitTunnel no
```

The following directive may seem like a good idea, but could be difficult to put into practice. Any directory specified should contain all of the commands and configuration files within that directory tree because the SSH session will be chroot'ed to the noted directory:

```
#ChrootDirectory none
```

The next directives can be used to specify additional text to append to the SSH protocol banner and to set a default banner:

```
#VersionAddendum none
#Banner none
```

The following directives allow the client to set several environmental variables. The details are normally trivial between two Red Hat Enterprise Linux systems:

```
AcceptEnv LANG LC_CTYPE LC_NUMERIC LC_TIME LC_COLLATE LC_MONETARY LC_MESSAGES
AcceptEnv LC_PAPER LC_NAME LC_ADDRESS LC_TELEPHONE LC_MEASUREMENT
AcceptEnv LC_IDENTIFICATION LC_ALL LANGUAGE
AcceptEnv XMODIFIERS
```

The final directive supports the use of SSH encryption for SFTP file transfers:

```
Subsystem    sftp    /usr/libexec/openssh/sftp-server
```

EXERCISE 11-2

Run an SSH Server on a Nonstandard Port

In this exercise, you'll configure the OpenSSH server to listen to TCP port 2222. To complete this objective, you'll have to modify not just the SELinux policy, but also the SSH service and the firewall configuration.

1. Show which ports the SSH service is allowed to listen to, based on the current SELinux policy:

   ```
   # semanage port -l | grep ssh
   ```

2. Run the following command to allow OpenSSH to listen to TCP port 2222:

   ```
   # semanage port -a -t ssh_port_t -p tcp 2222
   ```

3. Open the /etc/ssh/sshd_config file and change the line

   ```
   #Port 22
   ```

   to

   ```
   Port 2222
   ```

4. Don't forget to allow TCP port 2222 through the default zone of the firewall, as shown here:

   ```
   # firewall-cmd --permanent --add-port 2222/tcp
   # firewall-cmd --reload
   ```

5. Reload the SSH service to apply the change:

   ```
   # systemctl reload sshd
   ```

6. If you have successfully completed the previous steps, you should be able to log in from a remote system by running a command similar to the following:

   ```
   $ ssh -p 2222 alex@192.168.122.50
   ```

7. Finally, restore the SSH configuration to its original settings.

User-Based Security for SSH

User-based security can be configured in the /etc/ssh/sshd_config file. To that end, we like to add directives that limit the users allowed to access a system via SSH. The key is the **AllowUsers** directive. You can limit by user with a directive such as

```
AllowUsers michael donna
```

Alternatively, you can limit access by each user from certain hosts with a directive such as the following, which combines aspects of both user- and host-based security:

```
AllowUsers michael@192.168.122.50 donna@192.168.122.150
```

Be aware, if an access request is coming from a remote network, a masquerading firewall may assign the IP address of the router to the remote system. In that case, you won't be able to block a single system on a remote network.

You can include several related directives in the /etc/ssh/sshd_config file: **AllowGroups**, **DenyUsers**, and **DenyGroups**.

If you want to limit access to SSH to a very few users, the **AllowUsers** directive is the simplest solution. For the first **AllowUsers** directive just shown, only users michael and donna can connect to this SSH server. A corresponding **DenyUsers** or **DenyGroups** directive is not required. Even the root user can't connect via SSH under those circumstances.

Although the SSH server would prompt other users for a password, access is denied even when the remote user enters the correct password. The /var/log/secure log file would reflect that with a message similar to the following:

```
User alex from 192.168.122.150 not allowed because not listed in AllowUsers.
```

Host-Based Security for SSH

Although there are methods for configuring host-based security through the SSH configuration files, the process is complex. It requires changes to both servers and clients, and involves risks that we believe are not necessary. It's also possible to set up host-based security through the local firewalld zone-based firewall.

The simplest method for host-based SSH security is based on TCP Wrappers, as discussed in Chapter 10. For the purpose of this chapter, we've included the following directive in /etc/hosts.allow, which accepts SSH connections from the noted network addresses:

```
sshd : 127. 192.168.122.
```

To make sure access is limited to systems on the noted networks, you would also include the following line in /etc/hosts.deny:

```
sshd : ALL
```

Of course, it would be more secure to include **ALL : ALL** in /etc/hosts.deny, but that may block communications to legitimate services that you've configured. In addition, other ports should already be protected by an appropriate firewall rule. So it may be an option to avoid during a Red Hat exam.

CERTIFICATION OBJECTIVE 11.04

A Security and Configuration Checklist

A number of steps required to install, configure, and secure a service are repetitive. We therefore summarize them in this section. If desired, you can use this section to help prepare for Chapters 12 through 17. It will help you install required services, as well as make sure those services are active and accessible through a firewall configured with the appropriate open ports.

Installation of Server Services

The RHCE objectives directly address eight different services. This section addresses some of the different ways you can install these services. If you've read Chapter 7, this should be mostly review, but it will also give you an opportunity to prepare a system such as the server1.example.com virtual machine for testing in Chapters 12 through 17.

In this section, you'll review commands such as **rpm** and **yum** in the context of the server services needed for upcoming chapters. If you prefer to use the GNOME Software tool, refer to Chapter 7. Generally, you can use any of these options to install desired services.

Install the vsFTP Server with the rpm Command

In general, the installation of a service requires more than one RPM package. One exception is the RPM package associated with the vsFTP server. To that end, if you've mounted the RHEL 7 DVD on the /media directory, you can install the vsFTP server with the following command (the version number may vary):

```
# rpm -ivh /media/Packages/vsftpd-3.0.2-9.el7.x86_64.rpm
```

Install Server Services with the yum Command

As discussed in Chapter 7, the **yum** command can be used to install packages with dependencies. Sometimes, dependencies are simple. For example, for the DNS services configured in Chapter 13, you may be more familiar with BIND, as opposed to the Unbound DNS service.

One way to install the bind package with dependencies is with the following command:

```
# yum install bind
```

As needed, you can use the **yum install** command to install a package in a way that automatically identifies and installs all dependent packages.

TABLE 11-3	RHCE-Related Server Package Groups

Package Group	Description
File and Storage Server	Package group for the Samba, NFS, and iSCSI storage servers.
E-mail Server	Support packages for SMTP and Internet Message Access Protocol (IMAP) services; the default services are Postfix and Dovecot. The sendmail server is an optional package in this group.
Network Infrastructure Server	Environment group for the DNS, rsyslog, Samba, FTP, and other services; all packages in this group are optional.
Network File System Client	Includes clients for the automounter, Samba, and NFS.
Web Server	Includes basic Apache web server packages.
MariaDB Database Server	Includes only one mandatory package, mariadb-server.

Install Server Package Groups with the yum Command

Chapter 7 also describes how RHEL 7 packages are organized in groups. Each of those groups have names, which can be identified with the **yum group list** command. The relevant groups for the RHCE exam are listed in Table 11-3.

You can identify different packages and subgroups in each group with the **group list** switch; for example, the following command lists the subgroups that are part of the Basic Web Server environment group:

```
# yum group info "Basic Web Server"
```

The output for RHEL 7 is shown in Figure 11-3. From there, you can identify the packages included in each subgroup. For example, the following command lists the packages in the web-server group:

```
# yum group info web-server
```

The output is shown in Figure 11-4. Note that packages are classified in three categories: mandatory, default, and optional. If you run the following command, only packages and groups in the mandatory and default categories are installed:

```
# yum group install "Web Server"
```

In most cases, that's not a problem. However, sometimes you may need to install packages that are listed as optional. Although there are ways to set up the installation of optional packages with the **group install** switch, it's easier for our purposes to just install the needed packages separately by name.

| FIGURE 11-3 | Packages in the Basic Web Server environment group |

```
[root@server1 ~]# yum group info "Basic Web Server"
Loaded plugins: langpacks, product-id

Environment Group: Basic Web Server
 Environment-Id: web-server-environment
 Description: Server for serving static and dynamic internet content.
 Mandatory Groups:
    base
    core
    web-server
 Optional Groups:
   +backup-client
   +directory-client
    guest-agents
   +hardware-monitoring
   +java-platform
   +large-systems
   +load-balancer
   +mariadb-client
   +network-file-system-client
   +performance
   +perl-web
   +php
   +postgresql-client
   +python-web
   +remote-system-management
   +web-servlet
```

In a similar fashion, you can install the Samba File Server (covered in Chapter 15) and NFS (covered in Chapter 16) with the following command:

```
# yum groupinstall "File and Storage Server"
```

For Chapter 13, the Network Infrastructure Server package group includes packages associated with logging and DNS. However, as all packages in this group are optional, the **yum group install** command would not install any packages from that group. Fortunately, the rsyslog package is already installed by default, even in a minimal RHEL 7 installation, but you will want to install DNS to address one of the RHCE objectives. One way to set up a DNS caching service for Chapter 13 is to install the Unbound DNS resolver with the following command:

```
# yum install unbound
```

FIGURE 11-4

```
[root@server1 ~]# yum group info web-server
Loaded plugins: langpacks, product-id

Group: Web Server
 Group-Id: web-server
 Description: Allows the system to act as a web server, and run Perl and Python
web applications.
 Mandatory Packages:
   httpd
 Default Packages:
  =crypto-utils
   httpd-manual
   mod_fcgid
   mod_ssl
 Optional Packages:
  certmonger
  libmemcached
  memcached
  mod_auth_kerb
  mod_nss
  mod_revocator
  mod_security
  mod_security_crs
  perl-CGI
  perl-CGI-Session
  python-memcached
  squid
[root@server1 ~]# ▉
```

Packages in
the Web Server
package group

For a number of server services, you should make sure that appropriate client packages are installed. The Network File System client package group can help in that respect; the following command would install clients for the automounter, Samba, and NFS:

```
# yum group install "Network File System Client"
```

A different kind of network server relates to iSCSI storage. There are two package groups of interest: the File and Storage Server already mentioned earlier, and the iSCSI Storage Client.

Finally, a couple of packages of interest are not included in standard package groups. They set up the NTP server and authentication to remote user directories. If they're not already installed, you'll need to install them. One method is with the following command:

```
# yum install ntp sssd
```

We focus on command-line installation methods because they are generally fastest. Of course, you could install packages with the GUI Add/Remove Software tool discussed in Chapter 7.

Basic Configuration

While the current RHCE objectives are more specific than ever, it's best to keep what you change as simple as possible. As noted in the objectives, you'll be asked to "configure the service for basic operation." Basic operation is easier to set up. It is frequently more secure. If you do less to configure a service, it takes less time. You'll have a better chance to finish the exam. You'll be able to do more on the job.

The details associated with basic configuration are covered in upcoming chapters.

Make Sure the Service Survives a Reboot

In Chapter 5, you looked at when a service starts or does not start during the boot process. The simplest method is associated with the **systemctl** command. To review, the **systemctl list-unit-files --type=service** command lists all service units and whether they are activated at boot. For the services discussed in the following chapters, once the appropriate packages have been installed, you'll want to make sure they start during the boot process with the following commands:

```
# systemctl enable httpd
# systemctl enable iscsi
# systemctl enable mariadb
# systemctl enable nfs-server
# systemctl enable nmb
# systemctl enable ntpd
# systemctl enable rsyslog
# systemctl enable smb
# systemctl enable sshd
# systemctl enable target
# systemctl enable unbound
```

This is just a list. On an actual exam, install just the services you're asked to install.

Of course, during an exam, you might be told to make sure a service does *not* start during the boot process. Also, keep in mind that in a production environment the installation of so many services on a single system is rare because of the security risks.

Review Access Through Layers of Security

The first place to check a service is from the local system. For example, if you can connect to an Apache server from that system, you've set up basic configuration of Apache.

If you have problems connecting locally or remotely, you may have issues related to SELinux or various user- and host-based firewalls. For issues beyond SELinux, refer to the network command tools installed in Chapter 2: **telnet**, **elinks**, and **nmap**.

Troubleshoot SELinux Issues

If the configuration is good but still does not work, that suggests a SELinux issue, typically in one of the two following areas:

- **Boolean settings**   For example, to enable Apache server access to user home directories, enable the SELinux boolean **httpd_enable_homedirs**.
- **SELinux file contexts**   Make sure the contexts of files and directories match those of default directories. Assume you've set up a virtual web host on the /virtual/host directory. Run the **ls -Z /virtual/host** command. The file contexts you see in that output should match what you see from the **ls -Z /var/www/html** command.

Next, test the connection from a remote system:

Troubleshoot Zone-Based Firewall Issues

If a system allows access for server communications to the default zone, you'll see it in the output to the **firewall-cmd --list-all** command. To review the configuration for all zones, run **firewall-cmd --list-all-zones**.

While you can use the Firewall Configuration tool described in Chapters 4 and 10, you need to know how to configure firewalls from the command line.

If a port or server is not open in the firewall, an attempt to connect to a service is rejected. For example, for the SSH server you may get a message like the following:

```
ssh: connect to host server1.example.com port 22: No route to host
```

To verify whether connectivity to a remote service is operational, you can use the **telnet** or **nmap** command. For example, run the following command to verify connectivity to the HTTP port on the server 192.168.122.50:

```
$ telnet 192.168.122.50 80
```

If you can successfully connect to the server, you will see the following reply:

```
Escape character is '^]'
```

Similarly, you can use **nmap**, as shown next, to verify connectivity to the HTTP service on TCP port 80:

```
$ nmap -p 80 192.168.122.50
```

If you can successfully connect to the service, you will see the following output:

```
PORT    STATE SERVICE
80/tcp open  http
```

EXERCISE 11-3

Practice Troubleshooting Network Connectivity Issues

In this exercise we explore the effects of different network and firewalld misconfigurations on a running service. We assume that you have a working SSH service running on server1 .example.com.

1. From another host, run the **ping 192.168.122.50** command to test the connection to the server.
2. Now run the following command on server1:

   ```
   # systemctl stop network
   ```

   Run the **ping** command again. What is the output?
3. Restore network connectivity with **systemctl start network**.
4. From the client, use the **telnet** or **nmap** command to check the connection on the SSH server port:

   ```
   $ telnet 192.168.122.50 22
   ```

   If successful, you'll see the following output:

   ```
   Escape character is '^]'
   ```

   Type in the **quit** command. You should see an error message from the OpenSSH server, followed by this message:

   ```
   Connection closed by foreign host.
   ```

   Block connectivity to the SSH service on server1 with the following command:

   ```
   # firewall-cmd --remove-service=ssh
   ```

5. Try the **ping** and **telnet** commands again. What output do you see?
6. Restore connectivity on the firewall by running **firewall-cmd --reload**.
7. Block the IP address of the client (assuming it is 192.168.122.1), as shown here:

   ```
   # firewall-cmd --add-rich-rule='rule family=ipv4 source ↵
   address=192.168.122.1 drop'
   ```

8. Try the **ping** and **telnet** commands again. What output do you see?

In general, if the **telnet** or **nmap** command does not connect to the specified port, you may have one of the following firewall issues:

- The firewalld zone-based firewall may be blocking the desired port.
- The firewalld zone-based firewall may be limiting access to the client.
- The TCP Wrappers system discussed in this chapter may also be limiting access to specific clients and users, by service.
- Some servers include configuration files that also limit access based on users, IP addresses, and hostnames.

Troubleshoot TCP Wrappers Firewall Issues

In contrast, if the service is protected by TCP Wrappers, the error message behavior is different. For this section, we configured the /etc/hosts.allow and /etc/hosts.deny files on the server1.example.com system to allow access only from .example.com systems on the 192.168.122.0/24 network. That means access is not allowed from systems such as outsider1.example.org on IP address 192.168.100.100.

In that case, when we tried accessing the server1.example.com system with the **ssh** command, we received the following error message:

```
ssh_exchange_identification: Connection closed by remote host
```

In contrast, the **telnet server1.example.com 22** command from the same system returns the following messages, which stops for a moment:

```
Trying 192.168.122.50
Connected to server1.example.com.
Escape character is '^]'
```

For a few moments, it appears the system is about to connect, but then the block from TCP Wrappers results in the following message:

```
Connection closed by foreign host.
```

EXERCISE 11-4

Review the Different Effects of firewalld and TCP Wrappers

This exercise assumes an operational vsFTP server, similar to the one configured in Chapter 1 for installations. Configure that vsFTP server on the server1.example.com system. Make sure the firewall blocks traffic on the standard FTP port, TCP 21, and then check the connection from a blocked system, outsider1.example.org. To review, these systems as configured in Chapters 1 and 2 are on IP addresses 192.168.122.50 and 192.168.100.100, respectively.

Next, open TCP port 21 on the firewall. In addition, limit access using TCP Wrappers. This exercise is complex; each numbered step requires several commands or actions. In some cases, the required command is implied.

1. If it is not already installed, install the vsFTP server, as discussed in the chapter. Make sure that server is active with the **systemctl start vsftpd** command.

2. Start the Firewall Configuration tool with the **firewall-config** command. Make sure FTP is not activated in the list of services in the default zone. Make sure the changes are applied and then exit from the Firewall Configuration tool.

3. Try connecting to the vsFTP server from the local system with a command such as **lftp localhost**. It should work, which you can confirm from the lftp localhost:/> prompt with the **ls** command. Exit from the vsFTP server with the **quit** command.

4. Move to the outsider1.example.org system. It's acceptable to connect to it via SSH; in fact, that may be the only method available to connect to that system on the exam (and in real life).

5. Try pinging the system running the vsFTP server with the **ping 192.168.122.50** command. Remember to press CTRL-C to stop the process. Try connecting to the vsFTP server with the **lftp 192.168.122.50** command. What happens? Try to connect to the system with the **telnet 192.168.122.50 21** command. What happens?

6. Return to the server1.example.com system. Open the Firewall Configuration tool again, and this time make FTP a trusted service. Don't forget to apply the change before exiting from the Firewall Configuration tool.

7. Open the /etc/hosts.allow file and include the following entry:

```
vsftpd : localhost 127. 192.168.122.50
```

8. Open the /etc/hosts.deny file and include the following entry:

```
vsftpd : ALL
```

9. Return to the outsider1.example.com system as discussed in Step 4. Repeat Step 5. What happens after each attempt to connect?

10. Go back to the server1.example.com system. Open the /etc/hosts.allow and /etc/hosts.deny files and delete the lines created in Steps 7 and 8.

11. Once again, move to the outsider1.example.org system. Repeat Step 5. Both commands should result in a successful connection. The **quit** command should exit in both cases.

12. BONUS: Review connections via the contents of the /var/log/secure file. Review the originating IP addresses in that file. Use that information to configure firewalld to deny access to all but one IP address.

SCENARIO & SOLUTION	
You want to limit SSH access to two users.	Specify the desired usernames in the SSH server configuration file, /etc/ssh/sshd_config, with the **AllowUsers** directive.
You're told to limit SSH access to systems on the 192.168.122.0/24 network.	You can use TCP Wrappers. Configure /etc/hosts .allow to allow access to the **sshd** daemon from systems on the noted network. Configure /etc/hosts .deny to restrict access to **sshd** from **ALL** systems.
You need to make sure SELinux user and file types survive a relabel.	Use the **semanage fcontext -a** command to specify the desired user and file types for desired directories.
You need to run Apache on a nonstandard network port.	Change the port definition with **semanage port -a**. Don't forget to configure the service to run on a different port and to check firewall rules.
A server is accessible only locally.	Check security options for firewalld rules and TCP Wrappers; make sure the service allows remote access.
A server is properly configured but still is not accessible.	Check for SELinux booleans and file label types.

CERTIFICATION SUMMARY

This chapter focused on the general steps required to configure, secure, and access various services. Daemons are controlled by unit files in the /lib/systemd/system directory, and by configuration files in /etc/sysconfig. Access to various aspects of server services may be controlled by different SELinux booleans.

The SSH server configuration files are located in the /etc/ssh directory. The sshd_config configuration file includes a substantial number of options for configuring that service.

To configure a service, you'll need to install the right packages and make sure the service is active after the next reboot. You'll also need to navigate through a variety of available security options, including SELinux, zone-based firewalls, and TCP Wrappers—based security in the /etc/hosts.allow and /etc/hosts.deny files.

✓ # TWO-MINUTE DRILL

The following are some of the key points from the certification objectives in Chapter 11.

Red Hat System Configuration

❑ System services can be started by **systemctl**, based on unit configuration files in the /lib/systemd/system and /etc/systemd/system directories.

❑ System services use basic configuration files in the /etc/sysconfig directory. Such files often include basic parameters for service daemons.

❑ When configuring a network server, you'll need to be concerned about SELinux booleans, zone-based firewalls, TCP Wrappers, and more.

❑ Services should be tested locally and remotely.

Security-Enhanced Linux

❑ Individual services are frequently protected by multiple SELinux booleans.

❑ SELinux booleans are stored in the /sys/fs/selinux/booleans directory, with descriptive filenames.

❑ SELinux booleans can be changed with the **setsebool -P** command or the SELinux Management tool. From the command line, make sure to use the **-P** switch; otherwise, the change won't survive a reboot.

❑ SELinux file contexts can be changed with the **chcon** command. However, the change does not survive a relabel unless the new context rule is made persistent with the **semanage fcontext -a** command. Changes are documented in the file_contexts .local file, in the /etc/selinux/targeted/contexts/files directory.

❑ SELinux port labels can be modified with the **semanage port -a** command to allow services to listen to nonstandard network ports.

The Secure Shell Package

❑ SSH server configuration files in the /etc/ssh directory include client and server files, along with public and private RSA and ECDSA host key pairs.

❑ The SSH server configuration file, sshd_config, can be set up with user-based security.

❑ The **AllowUsers** directive in sshd_config specifies which users are allowed to log in via SSH.

❑ The easiest way to set up host-based SSH security is through TCP Wrappers.

A Security and Configuration Checklist

❑ You'll need to install a number of services to prepare for the RHCE exam with commands such as **rpm** and **yum**.

❑ One way to make sure services survive a reboot is with the **systemctl** command; a full list of such commands related to RHCE services is provided in the chapter.

❑ You'll need to configure access to a service through layers of security, including SELinux, zone-based firewalls, and TCP Wrappers.

SELF TEST

The following questions will help measure your understanding of the material presented in this chapter. As no multiple choice questions appear on the Red Hat exams, no multiple choice questions appear in this book. These questions exclusively test your understanding of the chapter. It is okay if you have another way of performing a task. Getting results, not memorizing trivia, is what counts on the Red Hat exams. There may be more than one answer to many of these questions.

Red Hat System Configuration

1. Which directory includes configuration files that specify startup options for various service daemons?

   _____

2. What command reloads the configuration of the SSH server without stopping the service?

   _____

Security-Enhanced Linux

3. What directory contains boolean options associated with SELinux? Specify the full path.

   _____

4. What man page contains SELinux options associated with NFS daemons?

   _____

5. What command restores the default SELinux file context on a given directory?

   _____

6. What file is modified when you run the **semanage fcontext -a** command? Hint: it's in the /etc/selinux/targeted/contexts/files directory.

   _____

7. Which command lists the current SELinux port label configuration for the MariaDB (MySQL) service?

   _____

The Secure Shell Server

8. What directory contains the OpenSSH server configuration file and host keys?

   _____

9. What directive specifies the port number of the local SSH server in the associated configuration file?

   _____

10. What directive specifies a list of allowed users in the SSH server configuration file?

   _____

A Security and Configuration Checklist

11. What command displays a list of available environment groups?

   _____

12. What command can help the abcd service survive a reboot?

   _____

LAB QUESTIONS

Several of these labs involve configuration exercises. You should do these exercises on test machines only. It's assumed that you're running these exercises on KVM-based virtual machines.

Red Hat presents its exams electronically. For that reason, the labs in this and future chapters are available from the media that accompanies the book, in the Chapter11/ subdirectory. In case you haven't yet set up RHEL 7 on a system, refer to Chapter 1 for installation instructions.

The answers for the labs follow the Self Test answers for the fill-in-the-blank questions.

A SELF TEST ANSWERS

Red Hat System Configuration

1. Slight trick question: the file in the /etc/sysconfig directory, as well as unit files in /lib/systemd/system and /etc/systemd/system, can specify options for various service daemons at startup.

2. The command to reload the configuration of the SSH service is

```
# systemctl reload sshd
```

Security-Enhanced Linux

3. The directory with SELinux booleans is /sys/fs/selinux/booleans.

4. The nfsd_selinux man page contains some SELinux booleans for that service.

5. The command that restores the default file context on a given directory is **restorecon**.

6. The name of the file that is modified by the noted command is file_contexts.local.

7. One acceptable answer is

```
# semanage port -l | grep mysql
```

The Secure Shell Server

8. The OpenSSH server configuration file and host keys are included in the /etc/ssh directory.

9. The directive is **Port**.

10. The directive is **AllowUsers**.

A Security and Configuration Checklist

11. The command that lists all available environment groups is **yum group list**.

12. Assuming the abcd service is also associated with a service unit in the /lib/systemd/system directory, the command that would help it survive a reboot is **systemctl enable abcd**.

LAB ANSWERS

Lab 1

This lab should give you an idea of what can be done with /etc/sysconfig files and how those files change the way a daemon is started. This lab should also demonstrate the risks; the wrong change, such as that shown in the lab, means that the service won't work.

Lab 2

Although SSH key-based authentication was covered in the first part of this book, it is also a requirement for the RHCE exam. If you don't remember how to configure key-based authentication, review Chapter 4. There are three measures of success in this lab:

- There will be an id_rsa file and an id_rsa.pub file in the client /home/hawaii/.ssh directory.
- You'll be able to connect to the remote system without a password. Just enter the "I love Linux!" passphrase (without quotes) when prompted.
- You'll find the contents of the user's id_rsa.pub file in the remote authorized_keys file in the /home/hawaii/.ssh directory.

Unsecure permissions are one of the most common reasons of failure for SSH key-based authentication. Your ~/.ssh directory should have octal permissions 0700, whereas the private key and the authorized_keys files should have the permissions bits set to 0600.

Lab 3

Much as in Lab 2, there are three measures of success in this lab:

- There will be an id_ecdsa and an id_ecdsa.pub file in the client /home/tonga/.ssh directory.
- You'll be able to connect to the remote system without a password. Just enter the "I love Linux!" passphrase when prompted.
- You'll find the contents of the client's id_ecdsa.pub file in the remote authorized_keys file in the /home/hawaii/.ssh directory.

Lab 4

The simplest way to implement this lab is to add the following directive to the /etc/ssh/sshd_config file:

```
AllowUsers hawaii
```

Just don't forget to reload or restart the SSH service after making the change; otherwise, other users will still have access.

In case you're curious, user tonga on the client is still able to access the hawaii account on the SSH server with the passphrase because connections to the user hawaii account are being allowed. The identity of the remote account does not matter to the **AllowUsers** directive.

If you've made too many changes to the /etc/ssh/sshd_config file and want to start fresh, move that file and run the **yum reinstall openssh-server** command. It'll set up a fresh copy of that configuration file. If you want to connect from other accounts in the future, make sure the **AllowUsers hawaii** directive is disabled.

Oh yes, did you need to activate the **PermitRootLogin no** directive to prevent SSH logins to the root account?

Lab 5

Success in this lab is confirmed by a good SSH connection from client to server. If you just want to make sure, use the **ssh -p 8122** command from the client. If you haven't disabled the **AllowUsers** directive on the server, that connection would have to be to the hawaii account.

In addition, this lab should give you a sense of the effort required to set up obscure ports. However, although the **nmap** command would detect a listening application on port 8122, it would be obscure; the relevant output would be

```
PORT        STATE       SERVICE
8122/tcp    open        unknown
```

Go to the client system and try connecting to the SSH server. Remember, you'll also need to open port 8122 in the firewall of the SSH server.

Although repeating this lab with port 8022 may look similar to using port 8122, there is a little problem when you try to add port 8022 to the ssh_port_t label:

```
# semanage port -a -t ssh_port_t -p tcp 8022
ValueError: Port tcp/8022 already defined
```

This error occurs because port 8022 is already in use by another service:

```
# semanage port -l | grep 8022
oa_system_port_t        tcp         8022
oa_system_port_t        udp         8022
```

There is not an easy way to add port 8022 to the ssh_port_t type without recompiling the policy. When this lab is complete, restore the original port numbers on the SSH client and server.

Lab 6

Confirmation of success in this lab is straightforward. Run the **ls -Zd** commands on the noted directories. The SELinux contexts for the /virtual/web and /var/www directories should match with the following contexts:

```
system_u:object_r:httpd_sys_content_t:s0
```

The contexts for the /virtual/web/cgi-bin and /var/www/cgi-bin directories should also match:

```
system_u:object_r:httpd_sys_script_exec_t:s0
```

It should go without saying that any changes you make should survive a SELinux relabel. Otherwise, how do you expect to get credit for your work? If you've run the **semanage fcontext -a** command on the correct directories, you'll see these contexts listed in the file_contexts.local file, in the /etc/selinux/targeted/contexts/files directory:

```
/virtual/web(/.*)?      system_u:object_r:httpd_sys_content_t:s0
/virtual/web/cgi-bin(/.*)?   system_u:object_r:httpd_sys_script_exec_t:s0
```

Chapter 12

RHCE Administrative Tasks

T he automation of system maintenance is an objective for both the RHCSA and RHCE exams. For the RHCE, you need to know how to create a shell script. You'll study some sample scripts used on RHEL 7 to automate system maintenance. You can automate those scripts on a schedule: hourly, daily, or even weekly.

Linux system utilization reports are associated with the **sar** command, which is configured as a cron job. Once you have identified the most utilized system resources, you can tune a system. This process starts from the Linux kernel, which is highly customizable. With different run-time parameters configured in the /proc/sys directory, kernels can be tuned to meet the needs of your applications.

The RHCE objectives also include a number of additional network requirements. You need to know how to set up static routes and configure IPv6. You will also learn how to configure network teaming and to provide bandwidth aggregation and link redundancy from multiple network interfaces. Finally, you should know how to set up a system as a Kerberos client.

INSIDE THE EXAM

This chapter directly addresses seven RHCE objectives. The first is an essential skill for systems administration; specifically, to

- Use shell scripting to automate system maintenance tasks

Shell scripts combine a series of commands in a single executable file. Automated scripts are normally run on a regular schedule, which the **cron** daemon is perfectly designed to handle.

System utilization reporting is an important skill for all computer professionals. RHEL 7 includes the sysstat package for such reports. The related objective is

- Produce and deliver reports on system utilization (processor, memory, disk, and network)

As this is not a traditional network service, there is no need to configure a firewall. There are no current SELinux-related booleans.

Some Linux tuning tasks can be met through kernel run-time parameters. That's made possible by the virtual files in the /proc/sys directory and by the **sysctl** command. The corresponding objective is

- Use /proc/sys and sysctl to modify and set kernel run-time parameters

This chapter also addresses several network tasks from the RHCE objectives. The configuration of static routes, as described in the following objective, is an essential task in enterprise networking:

- Route IP traffic and create static routes

Now that we are running out of IPv4 addresses, the RHCE for RHEL 7 includes a related objective:

- Configure IPv6 addresses and perform basic IPv6 troubleshooting

In an enterprise network, it is common to aggregate multiple network interfaces for increased resiliency or higher through-put. In RHEL 7, you can aggregate multiple network interfaces either through interface bonding or network teaming, as addressed by the following objective:

■ Use network teaming or bonding to configure aggregated network links between two Red Hat Enterprise Linux systems

For the final objective in this chapter, you will learn to configure a RHEL 7 system as a Kerberos client. Kerberos provides secure authentication services on insecure networks. For the RHCE exam you must be able to

■ Configure a system to authenticate using Kerberos

To prepare for these requirements, you will learn to configure a Kerberos Key Distribution Center (KDC). For a more detailed background about Kerberos, refer to the Red Hat System-Level Authentication Guide, available at https://access.redhat.com/Documentation/en-US/Red_Hat_Enterprise_Linux/7.

CERTIFICATION OBJECTIVE 12.01

Automate System Maintenance

As discussed in Chapter 9, RHEL 7 includes standard system maintenance scripts, scheduled by the /etc/crontab and the /etc/anacrontab configuration files, as well as various files in the /etc/cron.* directories. In this chapter, you'll analyze some scripts and some related bash internal commands. You'll then have the skills you need to create basic administrative scripts.

Standard Administrative Scripts

Review the scripts in the /etc/cron.daily directory, starting with **rhsmd**, part of Red Hat Subscription Manager. It logs information about the current entitlement status of the system. That script has two lines. Normally, lines that start with the hash symbol (#) are comments. The first line starts with a "shebang" (**#!**), followed by **/bin/sh**, which is a standard first line for bash scripts. On RHEL 7, since **/bin/sh** is symbolically linked to **/bin/bash**, it tells RHEL 7 to interpret the commands that follow with the bash shell:

```
#!/bin/sh
```

```
[root@server1 ~]# cat /etc/cron.daily/logrotate
#!/bin/sh

/usr/sbin/logrotate /etc/logrotate.conf
EXITVALUE=$?
if [ $EXITVALUE != 0 ]; then
    /usr/bin/logger -t logrotate "ALERT exited abnormally with [$EXITVALUE]"
fi
exit 0
[root@server1 ~]#
```

The logrotate
script

on the

job **Some Linux distributions (not Red Hat) link the** /bin/sh **command to a shell other than bash. Unless** #!/bin/bash **is specified in the script, it may not be transferable to other distributions.**

The second line runs the **rhsmd** command, logging all results (**-s**) to syslog:

```
/usr/libexec/rhsmd -s
```

Next, examine the contents of the /etc/cron.daily directory. A slightly more complex script is logrotate. A copy of the script is shown in Figure 12-1.

The script starts with a shebang and the path of the program interpreter that will parse the rest of the script:

```
#!/bin/sh
```

The next line in the file is executed automatically. The **logrotate** command rotates logs as defined in the /etc/logrotate.conf file, described in Chapter 9:

```
/usr/sbin/logrotate /etc/logrotate.conf
```

The following line assigns the exit value returned by the last command to a variable named **EXITVALUE**:

```
EXITVALUE=$?
```

If the **logrotate** command is successful, **EXITVALUE** is set to 0.

The next **if** command starts a conditional statement. The **!=** character sequence means "not equal." Therefore, the following **if** conditional is true when the value of **EXITVALUE** is something other than 0:

```
if [ $EXITVALUE != 0 ]; then
```

If **EXITVALUE** is not 0, bash executes the commands inside the **if** conditional, which tells the administrator that there is a problem with the logrotate script or related log files.

```
/usr/bin/logger -t logrotate "ALERT exited abnormally with [$EXITVALUE]"
```

The **fi** command that follows ends the conditional statement. The last directive returns 0, an indication of success:

```
exit 0
```

With this introduction to scripts, you are ready to examine some bash variables and commands.

Bash Variables

You can use variables in bash to store data. Although it's common to write variable names in uppercase letters, you cannot start a variable name with a number.

The following example illustrates how you can assign a variable from the command line:

```
# today=4
```

Take care when assigning a variable to not add spaces around the equal (=) character. To display the value of a variable, use the **echo** command and add a dollar sign in front of the variable:

```
# echo $today
4
```

You can also add braces around the variable name to avoid ambiguous expressions. For example, without braces, the following command would retrieve the value of the variable **$todayth**, rather than **$today**:

```
# echo "Today is the ${today}th of June"
Today is the 4th of June
```

You can use variables as part of arithmetic expressions. In bash, arithmetic expressions are enclosed in the **$((*expression*))** syntax. Here's an example:

```
# tomorrow=$(($today + 1))
# echo "Tomorrow is the ${tomorrow}th of June"
Tomorrow is the 5th of June
```

But there's more. Variables can also store the output of a command. There are two ways to do so: using the **$(*command*)** syntax and with backticks `` `*command*` ``. Here's an example of each:

```
# day=$(date +%d)
# month=`date +%b`
# echo "The current date is $month, $day"
The current date is Jun, 29
```

Bash Commands

Scripts are filled with various command constructs. Some groups of commands are executed only if a condition is met. Others are organized in a loop, which continues to run as long as a condition is satisfied. These command constructs are also known as *conditional and control structures.* Common commands include **for**, **if**, and **test**. The end of a loop may be labeled with a keyword such as **done** or **fi**. Some commands only exist in the context of others, which will be described in the subsections that follow.

Test Operators with if

The **if** operator is primarily used to check if a condition is met, such as if a file exists. For example, the following command checks if the /etc/sysconfig/network file exists and is a regular file:

```
if [ ! -f /etc/sysconfig/network ]; then
```

The exclamation mark (!) is the "not" operator and negates the result of the test. The **-f** checks to see if the filename that follows is a currently existing regular file. Test operators are very common in bash shell scripts. Some of these operators are listed in Table 12-1.

TABLE 12-1 Test Operators for bash Scripts

Operator	Description
STRING1 = STRING2	True if the two strings are equal
STRING1 != STRING2	True if the two strings are not equal
INTEGER1 **-eq** *INTEGER2*	True if the two integers are equal
INTEGER1 **-ne** *INTEGER2*	True if the two integers are not equal
INTEGER1 **-ge** *INTEGER2*	True if *INTEGER1* is greater than or equal to *INTEGER2*
INTEGER1 **-gt** *INTEGER2*	True if *INTEGER1* is greater than *INTEGER2*
INTEGER1 **-le** *INTEGER2*	True if *INTEGER1* is less than or equal to *INTEGER2*
INTEGER1 **-lt** *INTEGER2*	True if *INTEGER1* is less than *INTEGER2*
-d *FILE*	True if *FILE* is a directory
-e *FILE*	True if *FILE* exists
-f *FILE*	True if *FILE* exists and is a regular file
-r *FILE*	True if *FILE* exists and is granted read permissions
-w *FILE*	True if *FILE* exists and is granted write permissions
-x *FILE*	True if *FILE* exists and is granted execute permissions

The **if** operator normally is associated with a **then**, and possibly an **else** operator. For example, take the following hypothetical block:

```
if [ -e /etc/fstab];
then
     cp /etc/fstab /etc/fstab.bak
else
     echo "Don't reboot, /etc/fstab is missing!"
fi
```

In this code, if the /etc/fstab file exists (courtesy of the **-e**), the command associated with the **then** operator is run. If that file is missing, the noted message is displayed.

An Example: The 0anacron Script

We summarized the intent of the 0anacron script in Chapter 9, but you'll analyze it in detail here. You can find the script in the /etc/cron.hourly directory. A copy of the script is shown in Figure 12-2.

The script starts with a shebang line, which tells Linux that this is a bash script. Then, there is the following **if** block:

```
if test -r /var/spool/anacron/cron.daily; then
     day=`cat /var/spool/anacron/cron.daily`
fi
```

The **test** operator is sometimes used as a conditional within the **if**. For example, the line

```
if test -r /var/spool/anacron/cron.daily;
```

FIGURE 12-2

The 0anacron script

```
[root@server1 ~]# cat /etc/cron.hourly/0anacron
#!/bin/sh
# Check whether 0anacron was run today already
if test -r /var/spool/anacron/cron.daily; then
     day=`cat /var/spool/anacron/cron.daily`
fi
if [ `date +%Y%m%d` = "$day" ]; then
     exit 0;
fi

# Do not run jobs when on battery power
if test -x /usr/bin/on_ac_power; then
     /usr/bin/on_ac_power >/dev/null 2>&1
     if test $? -eq 1; then
     exit 0
     fi
fi
/usr/sbin/anacron -s
[root@server1 ~]#
```

is functionally equivalent to

```
if [ -r /var/spool/anacron/cron.daily ];
```

This **if** block verifies whether the file /var/spool/anacron/cron.daily exists and is readable. If the test is successful, the content of the cron.daily file is saved into the **day** variable. In fact, the cron.daily file contains the last date (in YYYYMMDD format) that **anacron** was run.

The next lines contain another **if** block:

```
if [ `date +%Y%m%d` = "$day" ]; then
    exit 0
fi
```

This code compares two strings: the current date, as returned by the **date** command in YYYYMMDD format (note the backticks, to substitute the output of the **date** command as the first operand in the test comparison), and the content of the **day** variable. As a good practice, the name of the **day** variable is enclosed in double quotes to prevent any special characters within the quoted string, apart from the dollar sign, to be interpreted by bash.

If the two dates are equal, the script exits immediately with a value of 0, indicating no errors. In other words, if **anacron** was already run today, the content of the /var/spool/anacron/cron.daily file would include today's date. In this case, the script won't run a second time and will exit with a value of 0.

The next section of code contains two nested **if** blocks:

```
if test -x /usr/bin/on_ac_power; then
    /usr/bin/on_ac_power >/dev/null 2>&1
    if test $? -eq 1; then
    exit 0
    fi
fi
```

The first **if** instruction checks if the /usr/bin/on_ac_power file exists and is executable. If so, it runs the program and suppresses all its output by redirecting the standard output and standard error to /dev/null. As indicated in the man page of **on_ac_power**, this command returns an exit code of 0 if the system is on line power, and 1 otherwise.

Next, the script checks the exit code (**$?**) of the last command. If this is 1 (that is, if the system is not on AC power), the scripts exits with a value of 0.

Finally, if all the previous tests are passed, the script runs the **anacron** command:

```
/usr/bin/anacron -s
```

In turn, **anacron** will read a list of jobs from /etc/anacrontab and execute them in sequential (**-s**) order.

The for Loop

The **for** loop executes a list of commands for all the items specified in a list. It's fairly simple and has different forms. In the following example, the command in the **for** loop is executed three times, for each value of the variable **n** in the list 1, 2, 3:

```
for n in 1 2 3; do
    echo "I love Linux #$n"
done
```

The output of the previous snippet of code is

```
I love Linux #1
I love Linux #2
I love Linux #3
```

A different example exists within the certwatch script in the /etc/cron.daily directory. If you don't see it on your system, install the crypto-utils package.

Here, the list in the **for** loop is replaced by the value of a variable:

```
for c in $certs; do
  # Check whether a warning message is needed, then issue one if so.
  /usr/bin/certwatch $CERTWATCH_OPTS -q "$c" &&
    /usr/bin/certwatch $CERTWATCH_OPTS "$c" | /usr/bin/sendmail -oem↵
  -oi -t 2>/dev/null
done
```

The **$certs** variable contains a list of all the certificate files used by the Apache web server. The **for** goes through each certificate and checks whether it is about to expire. If so, it sends an alert.

Note the **&&** operator between the two **certwatch** commands. It tells bash to execute the second command only if the first is successful (that is, if it returns a state of 0).

A more complex example is shown next. The **for** loop is executed for all the users in the system, as returned by the **getent passwd** command:

```
for username in $(getent passwd | cut -f 1 -d ":"); do
    usergroups=$(groups $username | cut -f 2 -d ":")
    echo "User $username is a member of the following groups: $usergroups"
done
```

In the first line, the **getent passwd** command returns all the users in the system. This may include users defined locally in /etc/passwd, as well as users defined in a central directory service such as LDAP. The output of the command is truncated to the first column (**-f 1**), defined by a separator character (**-d ":"**). This gives a list of usernames that the **for** loop can cycle through and assign to the **username** variable at each iteration.

Then, the previous code snippet executes the **groups** command, with each username as an argument. This command returns the groups that a user is part of, in the following format:

```
user : group1 group2 ...
```

The **cut -f 1 -d ":"** command extracts all the output after the column separator, and the result is saved in the **usergroups** variable. Finally, the result is displayed by the **echo** command.

Script Arguments

You can use arguments to pass information to a script, in the same fashion that you would do with normal commands. In a bash script, the first command argument is saved in the special variable **$1**, the second in **$2**, and so forth. The total number of arguments is saved in the $# special variable. As an example, consider the following script:

```
#!/bin/bash
echo "The number of arguments is $#"
if [ $# -ge 1 ]; then
     echo "The first argument is $1"
fi
```

Save the code in a file named args.sh and make it executable with the **chmod +x args.sh** command. Then, run the program as shown:

```
# ./args.sh orange
```

You should see the following output:

```
The number of arguments is 1
The first argument is orange
```

In Exercise 12-1, you will have a chance to put these lessons into practice.

EXERCISE 12-1

Create a Script

In this lab, you'll create a script named get-shell.sh. The script takes a username as the first argument and displays the default shell of the indicated user, using the following format:

```
# ./get-shell.sh mike
mike's default shell is /bin/bash
```

If no argument is provided, the script must display the default shell of the current user. If more than one argument is given, the script must print the following error message and exit with a value of 1:

```
Error: too many arguments
```

If the user given as an argument does not exist, the script must display the following error message and exit with a value of 2:

```
Error: cannot retrieve information for user <user>
```

1. Create a file named get-shell.sh and assign execute permissions to that file:

   ```
   $ touch get-shell.sh
   $ chmod +x get-shell.sh
   ```

2. Open the file with your favorite editor. Start the script with the following line:

   ```
   #!/bin/sh
   ```

3. Add the following lines that check if the number of arguments (**$#**) is greater than one. If so, print an error message and exit with a value of 1:

   ```
   if [ $# -gt 1 ]; then
       echo "Error: too many arguments"
       exit 1
   fi
   ```

4. Add the lines that follow. If no arguments have been passed, the script saves the name of the current user (**$USER**) in the **username** variable. Otherwise, the **username** variable takes the value of the first argument (**$1**). To express this logic, we use the **if-then-else** construct:

   ```
   if [ $# -eq 0 ]; then
       username=$USER
   else
       username=$1
   fi
   ```

5. Retrieve the user's information. You can query the user database with the **getent passwd** command. This command returns user information from the local /etc/passwd file and from any configured directory systems:

   ```
   userinfo=$(getent passwd $username)
   ```

6. Check the exit value of the previous command. Any nonzero exit value means that an error has occurred. If so, exit the program immediately with an exit status of 2:

   ```
   if [ $? -ne 0 ]; then
       echo "Error: cannot retrieve information for user $username"
       exit 2
   fi
   ```

7. Extract the user's shell from the **userinfo** variable. This is the seventh field (**-f 7**) of /etc/passwd, where each field is separated by a column character (**-d ":"**):

```
usershell=$(echo $userinfo | cut -f 7 -d ":")
```

8. Print the result. As a good practice, exit with a value of 0 to indicate that no errors have occurred:

```
echo "$username's shell is $usershell"
exit 0
```

9. Save your changes. Execute the script with different arguments to test every possible condition:

```
$ ./get-shell.sh alex
alex's shell is /bin/bash
$ ./get-shell.sh mike
mike's shell is /bin/bash
$ ./get-shell.sh daemon
daemon's shell is /sbin/nologin
$ ./get-shell.sh mikes
Error: cannot retrieve information for user mikes
$ ./get-shell.sh alex mike
Error: too many arguments
```

CERTIFICATION OBJECTIVE 12.02

Set Up System Utilization Reports

As an administrator, it's helpful to know when a system is overloaded. To help you, RHEL 7 includes the sysstat package. In addition, there are other commands related to measuring system utilization—specifically **top**. Of course, you can identify current disk usage with commands such as **df** and **fdisk**. Once system utilization reports are collected, you can review the results to help identify times when a system is in heavier use.

To paraphrase the relevant RHCE objective, there are other important commands that can help you "produce and deliver reports" on the load on the CPU, RAM, hard drives, and the network. While they collect data similar to commands such as **top**, **df**, and **fdisk**, the commands associated with the sysstat package collect such data on each of the noted components. Performance data is collected in log files. Then, the **sadf** command is designed to actually use that log data to prepare a report. When written to an appropriate text or database file, such reports can then be delivered for evaluation and processing.

FIGURE 12-3 The top command displays system utilization.

```
top - 18:48:03 up 4 days, 22:01,  2 users,  load average: 0.34, 0.10, 0.06
Tasks: 164 total,   2 running, 162 sleeping,   0 stopped,   0 zombie
%Cpu(s):  7.0 us,  0.3 sy,  0.0 ni, 92.7 id,  0.0 wa,  0.0 hi,  0.0 si,  0.0 st
KiB Mem:   2279980 total,  1332628 used,   947352 free,      824 buffers
KiB Swap:  1679356 total,        0 used,  1679356 free.   483256 cached Mem

  PID USER      PR  NI    VIRT    RES    SHR S  %CPU %MEM     TIME+ COMMAND
 3791 alex      20   0 1694336 355552  38596 S   6.0 15.6  29:15.84 gnome-shell
  753 root      20   0  196608  44980  11284 S   0.7  2.0   2:47.81 Xorg
    1 root      20   0  137248   7056   3848 S   0.0  0.3   0:06.92 systemd
    2 root      20   0       0      0      0 S   0.0  0.0   0:00.05 kthreadd
    3 root      20   0       0      0      0 S   0.0  0.0   0:00.07 ksoftirqd/0
    5 root       0 -20       0      0      0 S   0.0  0.0   0:00.00 kworker/0:0H
    6 root      20   0       0      0      0 S   0.0  0.0   0:00.00 kworker/u2:0
    7 root      rt   0       0      0      0 S   0.0  0.0   0:00.00 migration/0
    8 root      20   0       0      0      0 S   0.0  0.0   0:00.00 rcu_bh
    9 root      20   0       0      0      0 S   0.0  0.0   0:00.00 rcuob/0
   10 root      20   0       0      0      0 S   0.0  0.0   0:02.40 rcu_sched
   11 root      20   0       0      0      0 R   0.0  0.0   0:03.34 rcuos/0
   12 root      rt   0       0      0      0 S   0.0  0.0   0:01.06 watchdog/0
   13 root       0 -20       0      0      0 S   0.0  0.0   0:00.00 khelper
   14 root      20   0       0      0      0 S   0.0  0.0   0:00.00 kdevtmpfs
   15 root       0 -20       0      0      0 S   0.0  0.0   0:00.00 netns
   16 root       0 -20       0      0      0 S   0.0  0.0   0:00.00 writeback
   17 root       0 -20       0      0      0 S   0.0  0.0   0:00.00 kintegrityd
```

System Utilization Commands

Basic system utilization commands are already available for Linux. For example, the **top** command provides a current view of three important items: CPU, RAM, and processes. Examine the output of the **top** command, shown in Figure 12-3. Current CPU, RAM, and swap space use is shown atop the display; currently running processes are shown below the bar. Processes that take a lot of CPU and RAM are shown first. By default, the view is refreshed every three seconds.

Alternatively, there's the **dstat** command, part of the dstat package. As shown in Figure 12-4, it lists a variety of statistics, refreshed every second. The one item added here relative to the **top** command is network traffic, which can help you view current network usage.

Of course, these are real-time statistics and something that you can't stare at all the time. That's the reason behind the System Activity Report tool, or **sar**.

The System Activity Report Tool

To set up the System Activity Report tool, install the sysstat package. The package includes a systemd service, as well as a cron job that runs on a regular basis, as defined in the

FIGURE 12-4

The dstat
command displays
system utilization.

```
[root@server1 ~]# dstat
You did not select any stats, using -cdngy by default.
----total-cpu-usage----  -dsk/total-  -net/total-  ---paging--  ---system--
usr sys idl wai hiq siq|  read  writ|  recv  send|   in   out |  int   csw
  1   0  99   0   0   0|3019B  989B|    0     0 |    0     0 |    5    11
 42   1  57   0   0   0|    0     0 |    0     0 |    0     0 |  519   667
 43   1  56   0   0   0| 120k    0 | 104B     0 |    0     0 |  519   919
 88   3   9   0   0   0|    0     0 |  66B  163B|    0     0 | 1003  1841
 77   2  21   0   0   0|    0  1956k| 104B     0 |    0     0 |  918  1641
 73   2  24   0   0   0|  24k    0 |2346B 1862B|    0     0 |  885  1145
 17   2  81   0   0   0|    0     0 | 104B     0 |    0     0 |  345  1050
 27   2  71   0   0   0|    0     0 |    0     0 |    0     0 |  442   827
 47   1  52   0   0   0|    0     0 | 104B     0 |    0     0 |  587   874
 22   1  77   0   0   0|    0     0 |    0     0 |    0     0 |  285   335
 26   0  74   0   0   0|    0     0 | 104B     0 |    0     0 |  322   376
 92   3   5   0   0   0|  84k   68k|2092B 1224B|    0     0 | 1037  1414
 95   4   0   0   0   1|1288k  452k| 237k   10k|    0     0 | 1203  1508
 95   4   1   0   0   0|8192B    0 | 163k   15k|    0     0 | 1214  1595
 40   3  56   1   0   0| 128k    0 | 190B  173B|    0     0 |  666  1279
 38   2  60   0   0   0|    0     0 |3917B 6707B|    0     0 |  649  1112
 39   1  60   0   0   0|    0   27k| 146B  156B|    0     0 |  637  1099
 57   3  40   0   0   0|    0     0 |    0     0 |    0     0 |  772  1274
 41   1  58   0   0   0|    0     0 | 104B     0 |    0     0 |  604   966
 39   2  59   0   0   0|    0     0 |    0     0 |    0     0 |  565   902
```

/etc/cron.d/sysstat file. The package also contains a series of related commands, which are covered here.

The commands that are part of sysstat use the parameters shown in the sysstat and sysstat.ioconf files, in the /etc/sysconfig directory. The sysstat file is relatively simple; the following directive specifies that log files should be kept for 28 days:

```
HISTORY=28
```

And this directive specifies that log files that are more than 31 days old should be compressed:

```
COMPRESSAFTER=31
```

Of course, that means that log files are erased before they can be compressed. Naturally, you can change either variable as needed. The meaty /etc/sysconfig file is sysstat.ioconf because it helps collect activity data from a variety of storage devices. It helps some of the commands of the sysstat package collect data from disk devices. While the sysstat.ioconf file is large, changes should not be required to that file unless there's new disk storage hardware—and the Red Hat exams are not hardware exams.

Collect System Status into Logs

The sysstat package includes a regular cron job. Available in the /etc/cron.d directory, that job collects information on system utilization and sends it to log files in the /var/log/sa directory. Examine the sysstat file in the /etc/cron.d directory. The first line defines a job that's run every 10 minutes by the root administrative user:

```
*/10 * * * * root /usr/lib64/sa/sa1 1 1
```

The **sa1** command, with the 1 and 1 at the end, specifies that the command should run once, one second after the job is started. Information from this command is collected in the file named sa*dd* in the /var/log/sa directory, where *dd* represents the day of the month.

The next line is more powerful than it looks. On a daily basis, at seven minutes before midnight, with the privileges of the root administrative user, the **sa2** command writes a daily report on most system activity.

```
53 23 * * * root /usr/lib64/sa/sa2 -A
```

The **-A** switch is associated with the **sar** command. As suggested by the following excerpt from the **sar** man page, it essentially collects every reasonable bit on system utilization:

```
-A      This is equivalent to specifying -bBdqrRSuvwWy
-I SUM -I XALL -n ALL -u ALL -P ALL.
```

Prepare a System Status Report

This section will not prepare a report for a presentation. It's simply an analysis of the **sadf** command and how it can be used to specify information to filter from the log files in the /var/log/sa directory. The binary log files with names such as sa10 (for the 10th day of the month) can be processed in a number of ways by the **sadf** command. Some of the more important **sadf** switches are listed in Table 12-2.

For example, the following command sets up a report with data between the start and end of the 10th of the month:

```
# sadf -s 00:00:01 -e 23:59:59 /var/log/sa/sa10 > activity10
```

The data is redirected to the activity10 file for later processing. But the power of the sysstat package comes from the way it interacts with the **sar** command. However, only some of the options of the **sar** command work with **sadf**. As suggested in the **sadf** man page, the following command prepares a report based on "memory, swap space, and network statistics" from the /var/log/sa/sa21 file in a format that can be processed by a database:

```
# sadf -d /var/log/sa/sa21 -- -r -n DEV
```

| TABLE 12-2 | Options for the sadf Command |

Switch	Description
-d	Displays contents in a format usable by a relational database system.
-e hh:mm:ss	Lists the end time of the report in 24-hour format.
-p	Displays contents in a format usable by the **awk** command; do not use with **-d** or **-x**.
-s hh:mm:ss	Lists the start time of report in 24-hour format.
-x	Displays contents in XML format; do not use with **-d** or **-p**.

While the **-d** switch is associated with the **sadf** command, the double-dash (--) points to options associated with the **sar** command. So the **-r** switch reports memory usage, and **-n DEV** reports statistics from network devices.

The **sadf** man page is an excellent reference for the command options required to create a report while on the job, or even during a Red Hat exam. As with many other commands, you can find examples in the EXAMPLES section of the man page.

Of course, there are other important **sar** command switches. Those that may be relevant when you prepare a report on "processor, memory, disk, and network" utilization are described in Table 12-3.

With the switches listed in Table 12-3, you might modify the previous **sadf** command to meet all four items listed in the related RHCE objective:

```
# sadf -d /var/log/sa/sa21 -- -u -r -dp -n DEV
```

| TABLE 12-3 | System Utilization Options for the sar Command |

Switch	Description
-d	Lists block device activity. Normally used with **-p** to specify common drive device filenames such as sda and sdb.
-n DEV	Reports statistics from network devices.
-P *cpu*	Lists statistics on a per-processor (or core) basis; for example, **-P 0** specifies the first CPU.
-r	Reports memory utilization statistics.
-S	Shows swap space utilization statistics.
-u	Reports CPU utilization, including categories related, user, system and idle time, and more.
-W	Reports swapping statistics.

In other words, the **sadf** command specifies output usable by a database (**-d**) from the database file in the /var/log/sa directory associated with the 21st of the month. The double dash (**--**) points to **sar** command switches, with CPU utilization (**-u**), RAM utilization (**-r**), and activity by block device (**-d**) presented in more familiar block device names such as sda (**-p**), and with statistics from network devices (**-n DEV**).

CERTIFICATION OBJECTIVE 12.03

Kernel Run-time Parameters

Kernel run-time parameters, as defined in the RHCE objectives, relate to files in the /proc/sys directory and the **sysctl** command. Closely related is the /etc/sysctl.conf configuration file, which is used by the **sysctl** command during the boot process to tune parameters to various files in the /proc/sys directory. Therefore, it's appropriate to start this section with a look at that sysctl.conf file.

How sysctl Works with /etc/sysctl.conf

You can enable IPv4 forwarding in two steps. First, add the following boolean directive to activate IPv4 forwarding in the configuration:

```
net.ipv4.ip_forward = 1
```

Then make the system re-read the configuration file with the following command:

```
# sysctl -p
```

Let's examine this process in a bit more detail. First, kernel run-time parameters are documented in various files in the /proc/sys directory. The content of the **net.ipv4 .ip_forward** variable is stored in the ip_forward file, in the net/ipv4/ subdirectory. In other words, IPv4 forwarding is documented in the ip_forward file, in the /proc/sys/net/ipv4 directory.

As that file contains either a 0 or a 1, it is a boolean variable. So the value 1 for the **net.ipv4.ip_forward** variable activates IPv4 forwarding.

What if you want to add IPv6 forwarding? While that's not configured in the /etc/sysctl.conf file, it's a feature that you can add. IPv6 forwarding can be set in a file named forwarding, in the /proc/sys/net/ipv6/conf/all directory. In other words, to set IPv6 forwarding on reboot, you'd include the following directive in /etc/sysctl.conf:

```
net.ipv6.conf.all.forwarding=1
```

Similar directives would work for other settings associated with files in the /proc/sys directory. Look at the icmp_* directives in the /proc/sys/net/ipv4 directory. You might recognize that the Internet Control Message Protocol (ICMP) is sometimes associated with the **ping** command. In fact, a **ping** command is a request for an echo. Thus, **icmp_echo_ignore_all** and **icmp_echo_ignore_broadcasts** relate to a direct **ping** command, as well as a **ping** command associated with the broadcast address.

In other words, if you add the directives

```
net.ipv4.icmp_echo_ignore_all = 1
net.ipv4.icmp_echo_ignore_broadcasts = 1
```

to the /etc/sysctl.conf file, the local system won't respond to a direct **ping** command, nor will it respond to a request made by a **ping** to the broadcast address for the network.

Settings in the /etc/sysctl.conf File

The settings in the /etc/sysctl.conf file are a small fraction of what can be configured. In RHEL 7, /etc/sysctl.conf contains only comments, while the default configuration has been moved to files within the /usr/lib/sysctl.d directory. Have a look at those files. It's fair to assume that RHEL 7 includes the options in those files for a reason, and those settings are most likely to be addressed in a RHCE exam. You've already examined the first directive for IPv4 forwarding. The next directive is included in the 50-default.conf file in the /usr/lib/sysctl.d directory. If active, it makes sure that packets that come in from an external network are in fact external by doing a reverse path forwarding check:

```
net.ipv4.conf.default.rp_filter = 1
```

The following directive is normally disabled as a security measure to avoid a potential attack using source routing:

```
net.ipv4.conf.default.accept_source_route = 0
```

Also known as the kernel magic sysrq key, developers may change the value of this directive for development purposes. Generally, you should retain the default setting:

```
kernel.sysrq = 16
```

If there's a crash of the Linux kernel, this option includes the PID number with the kernel core dump file to help identify the culprit:

```
kernel.core_uses_pid = 1
```

Another standard method used by white-hat hackers to overload a system is a flood of SYN packets. It's similar to the so-called "ping of death." The following setting avoids the overload:

```
net.ipv4.tcp_syncookies = 1
```

A bridge is an older term for a switch that can forward traffic between different network segments. The following directives, included in the 00-system.conf file in the /usr/lib/sysctl.d directory, disable the use of the noted **iptables**, **ip6tables**, and **arptables** filters on such bridges:

```
net.bridge.bridge-nf-call-ip6tables = 0
net.bridge.bridge-nf-call-iptables = 0
net.bridge.bridge-nf-call-arptables = 0
```

Such bridges are usually related to virtual networks on a KVM host.

EXERCISE 12-2

Disable Responses to the ping Command

In this exercise, you'll use kernel parameters to disable responses to the **ping** command. While this exercise can be run on any two connected systems, it assumes that you'll be configuring the server1.example.com system and testing the result from the tester1.example.com system.

1. On the server1.example.com system, review the current setting related to responses to **ping** messages with the following command:

   ```
   # cat /proc/sys/net/ipv4/icmp_echo_ignore_all
   ```

2. Assuming the output is a 0, try the **ping localhost** command. What happens? Don't forget to press CTRL-C to exit from the output stream. If the output is 1, skip to Step 5.

3. Confirm the result from a remote system such as tester1.example.com. In some situations, you may not have physical access to that system, so connect with the appropriate **ssh** command. From the remote system, try the **ping server1.example.com** or **ping 192.168.122.50** command.

4. Return to the server1.example.com system. Change the kernel setting described in Step 1 with the following command:

   ```
   # echo "1" > /proc/sys/net/ipv4/icmp_echo_ignore_all
   ```

   Confirm by repeating the command from Step 1. Try the **ping localhost** command again. What happens?

5. Restore the original 0 setting to the **icmp_echo_ignore_all** option.

CERTIFICATION OBJECTIVE 12.04

IP Routes

As described in the RHCE objectives, you need to know how to "route IP traffic and create static routes." That's really two tasks. First, it's a standard part of network configuration to set up a default route to an outside network. But there's also the related task, when a system has two or more network devices, of setting up a static route to a specific network.

Configure a Default Route

The default route is the path taken by a network packet when there aren't any other more specific routes for that destination address. When a Dynamic Host Configuration Protocol (DHCP) server is working and is configured to provide a default gateway with IP addresses, a default route is assigned with the IP address received by the DHCP server. That's normally evident in the output to the **ip route** command discussed in Chapter 3. One sample of such output for a system that uses a DHCP server is shown here:

```
default via 192.168.122.1 dev eth0  proto static  metric 1024
192.168.122.0/24 dev eth0  proto kernel  scope link  src ↵
192.168.122.50
```

To review, the default route goes through the gateway address of 192.168.122.1. In a similar fashion, the default route for a statically configured network system is configured with the **GATEWAY** directive in its configuration file. Such configuration files are stored in the /etc/sysconfig/network-scripts directory, with names such as ifcfg-eth0.

But there are situations, such as a temporary network issue, where the default route is not given by a DHCP server. Perhaps the DHCP server has to be replaced and you'll have to set up static IP address information. In such cases, a default route can be added temporarily with the **ip route** command. For example, the following command would restore the default route shown earlier:

```
# ip route add default via 192.168.122.1 dev eth0
```

To make sure that default route survives a reboot, you'll need to ensure either the system configures that default gateway IP address as part of a static network configuration, or the DHCP server used for the network can assign that gateway IP address. To review, Figure 12-5 reflects the way the default gateway IPv4 address is configured with the Network Manager tool. Alternatively, you can make sure the added default route survives a reboot by a direct change to the ifcfg-eth*x* configuration file.

Some systems may have multiple network devices. In that case, you may need to configure a static route.

FIGURE 12-5   A static network configuration with a default gateway

```
|------------------------------------| Edit connection |------------------------------------|
                                                                                           ↑
                  Profile name  eth0                                                       ▓
                        Device  52:54:00:85:61:C0 (eth0)                                    ▓
                                                                                           ▓
  = ETHERNET                                                                <Show>          ▓
                                                                                           ▓
  = IPv4 CONFIGURATION  <Manual>                                            <Hide>          ▓
                    Addresses  192.168.122.50/24            <Remove>                        ▓
                               <Add...>                                                     ▓
                      Gateway  192.168.122.1                                                ▓
                  DNS servers  192.168.122.1               <Remove>                         ▓
                               <Add...>                                                     ▓
               Search domains  example.com                <Remove>                         ▓
                               <Add...>                                                     ▓
                                                                                           ▓
                    Routing (No custom routes) <Edit...>                                    ▓
              [ ] Never use this network for default route                                  ▓
                                                                                           ▓
              [X] Require IPv4 addressing for this connection                               ▓
                                                                                           ↓
```

Configure a Static Route

One way to configure a special route is with the Network Manager Connection Editor tool.
As discussed in Chapter 3, you can start it from a GUI console with the **nm-connection-editor** command. Select an existing wired or wireless network device and then click Edit.
Under either the IPv4 or IPv6 tab, there's a Routes button to add static routes. Click it to see
the window shown in Figure 12-6.

When you save the configuration, Network Manager creates a route-eth0 file in the
/etc/sysconfig/network-scripts directory. The following is the complete contents of that file:

```
ADDRESS0=192.168.0.0
NETMASK0=255.255.255.0
GATEWAY0=192.168.122.1
```

When the NetworkManager service is restarted, the new route is added to the routing
table. Based on the previously configured routing table, the following is the output of the **ip
route** command:

```
default via 192.168.122.1 dev eth0  proto static  metric 1024
192.168.0.0/24 via 192.168.122.1 dev eth0  proto static  metric 1
192.168.122.0/24 dev eth0  proto kernel  scope link  src ↵
192.168.122.50
```

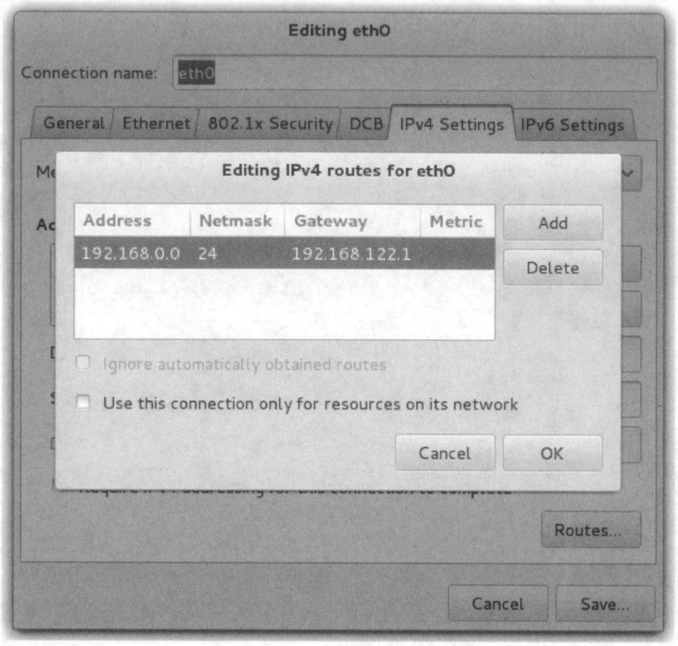

FIGURE 12-6

A static route for
a specific network
destination

exam

ⓦatch A dummy interface is a special type of virtual interface that is not associated with any network adapters on the system. You can use a dummy interface to practice with certain network scenarios when you don't have access to a physical network or your system is offline.

EXERCISE 12-3

Practice with Static Routes

In this exercise, you'll create a dummy interface to practice the configuration of static routes. A dummy interface is a virtual interface that is not associated with any adapter on the host. This exercise assumes you'll be configuring the dummy interface on the server1.example.com system, while the static route will be added to the physical host system.

1. On server1.example.com, run the following commands to add a dummy interface. Check that the IP range 192.168.123.0/24 is not already in use in your network. If so, choose a different network range:

```
# modprobe dummy
# ip link set name eth2 dev dummy0
# ip address add 192.168.123.123/24 dev eth2
# ip link set eth2 up
```

2. Run the **ping 192.168.123.123** command on server1.example.com. If you have correctly set up the dummy interface, you should get a reply to your ping requests. Don't forget to press CTRL-C to exit from the output stream.

3. Run the **ip route** command on server1.example.com. You will see a valid route to 192.168.123.0/24 because this network segment is directly connected to the dummy interface eth2:

```
192.168.123.0/24 dev eth2  proto kernel  scope link  src ↵
192.168.123.123
```

4. Rerun the **ping 192.168.123.123** command from the physical host. As your physical host probably doesn't have a route to 192.168.123.0/24 via server1, your **ping** command won't receive a response.

5. Add a static route to 192.168.123.0/24 on your physical host. To do so, open the Network Manager Connection Editor tool. Select the virbr0 bridge device and then click Edit. Under the IPv4 Settings tab, click the Routes button to add a static route. Set 192.168.123.0 as the network address, 24 as the netmask, and 192.168.122.50 (the IP address of server1) as the gateway.

6. Restart Network Manager, like so:

```
# systemctl restart NetworkManager
```

7. Confirm that the route to 192.168.123.0/24 is installed in the routing table by running the **ip route** command.

8. Try the **ping 192.168.123.123** command again from your physical host. What happens?

9. Remove the static route on the physical host.

10. Delete the dummy interface on server1:

```
# ip link delete eth2
```

CERTIFICATION OBJECTIVE 12.05

An Introduction to IPv6

One of the special challenges of the RHCE exam is IPv6 networking. While most current networks are configured with IPv4 addresses, several regions have run out of public IPv4 addresses.

Internet Protocol Version 6 (IPv6) was introduced in the late 1990s as a replacement for IPv4. It turns out that the 4 billion (2^{32}) IPv4 addresses are not enough. IPv6 supports many more addresses, potentially up to 2^{128}, or 3.4×10^{38} (340 undecillion) addresses.

Basic IPv6 Addressing

In Chapter 3, we introduced the "dot-decimal" notation for IPv4 addresses, where each decimal octet represents 8 bits of the 32-bit address (for example, 192.168.122.50). IPv6 addresses are made of 128 bits and are set up in hexadecimal notation, also known as base 16. In other words, an IPv6 address may include the following "digits":

```
0, 1, 2, 3, 4, 5, 6, 7, 8, 9, a, b, c, d, e, f
```

An IPv6 address is normally organized in eight groups of four hexadecimal numbers each, called "nibbles," in the following format:

```
2001:0db8:3dab:0001:0000:0000:0000:0072
```

You can simplify IPv6 addressing further:

- ■ Remove any leading zeros in a nibble. For example, you can write 0db8 as db8, 0072 as 72, 0000 as 0, and so on.

- ■ Replace any sequence of 0000 nibbles with a pair of colons (::). As an example, you can abbreviate 0000:0000:0000 with a pair of colons. However, to avoid ambiguity, you can apply this rule only once in an IPv6 address.

Hence, we can rewrite the previous address in a much more compact form:

```
2001:db8:3dab:1::72
```

Similarly to IPv4, IPv6 addresses are made of two parts: a host and a network address. The host portion of an IPv6 address is known as the "interface identifier." In IPv6, subnet masks are typically specified in prefix notation (such as /48).

As an example, assume that the IPv6 address 2001:db8:3dab:1::72 has a network prefix of /64. In other words, the network part of that IPv6 address includes the first 64 bits of that address. In this case, that network prefix is 2001:db8:3dab:1. The interface identifier includes the last 64 bits, shown as the hexadecimal number 72.

IPv6 addresses are classified in several categories. First, there are three address formats:

- **Unicast**   A unicast address is associated with a single network adapter.
- **Anycast**   An anycast address can be assigned to multiple hosts simultaneously. It can be used for load balancing and redundancy. Anycast addresses are organized in the same way as unicast addresses.
- **Multicast**   A multicast address is used to send a message to multiple destinations simultaneously.

With that diversity of address formats, IPv4-style broadcast addresses aren't needed. If you want to send a message to multiple systems, use IPv6 multicast addresses.

IPv6 addresses are also organized in several different ranges, as described in Table 12-4. The default route in IPv4 (0.0.0.0/0) is shown as ::/0 in IPv6.

The link-local address range requires explanation. Every interface in an IPv6 network is automatically configured with a link-local address. These addresses are not routable; as such communication is limited to the local network segment. Link-local addresses are needed for various IPv6 operations.

Even if you haven't configured IPv6 in your RHEL 7 servers, each network interface is automatically assigned a link-local address, as shown in the following output:

```
# ip addr show eth0
2: eth0: <BROADCAST,MULTICAST,UP,LOWER_UP> mtu 1500 qdisc pfifo_fast ↵
state UP qlen 1000
    link/ether 52:54:00:85:61:c0 brd ff:ff:ff:ff:ff:ff
    inet 192.168.122.50/24 brd 192.168.122.255 scope global eth0
      valid_lft forever preferred_lft forever
    inet6 fe80::5054:ff:fe85:61c0/64 scope link
      valid_lft forever preferred_lft forever
```

TABLE 12-4   IPv6 Address Types

IPv6 Address Type	Address Range	Description
Global unicast	2000::/3	Used for host-to-host communications.
Anycast	Same as unicast	Assigned to any number of hosts.
Multicast	ff00::/8	Used for one-to-many and many-to-many communications.
Link-local	fe80::/10	Reserved for link-local communications.
Unique local	fc00::/7	It is the equivalent of RFC 1918 private addresses in IPv4.

To identify a link-local address, look for an address that starts with fe80. Note the "scope link" entry. As you can see, interface eth0 has the following IPv6 link-local address: fe80::5054:ff:fe85:61c0/64.

Troubleshooting Tools

Most of the network tools that we introduced in Chapter 3 work seamlessly with both IPv4 and IPv6 addresses. There are two notable exceptions: the **ping** and **traceroute** commands. For IPv6 networking, you would use the **ping6** and **traceroute6** commands.

The **ping6** command works in a similar way to **ping**. Even before you configure an IPv6 address, you can run the **ping6** command on the link-local address of the server1.example.com system:

```
# ping6 -I virbr0 fe80::5054:ff:fe85:61c0
```

Since link-local addresses are not routable, you must specify the outbound interface (**-I**) in the **ping6** command when you ping a remote link-local address.

Configure IPv6 Addresses

As with IPv4 networking, you can configure an IPv6 address with the Network Manager command-line tool **nmcli**, the text-based graphical tool **nmtui**, or the Network Manager Connections Editor.

Start the Network Manager Connections Editor from the GUI with the **nm-connection-editor** command.

Highlight the connection profile of the first Ethernet device (eth0 in our system) and click Edit; then click the IPv6 Settings tab. It'll open the window shown in Figure 12-7.

Click the Method drop-down text box and select Manual. You can now add IP address information for the system. For example, on server1.example.com we added the following settings:

- **IP Address** 2001:db8:3dab:2
- **Prefix** 64
- **Gateway Address** 2001:db8:3dab:1

Similarly, we have associated the IPv6 address 2001:db8:3dab:1 with the virbr0 interface on our physical system. You can verify the configuration with the following command:

```
# ip addr show eth0
2: eth0: <BROADCAST,MULTICAST,UP,LOWER_UP> mtu 1500 qdisc pfifo_fast ↵
state UP qlen 1000
    link/ether 52:54:00:85:61:c0 brd ff:ff:ff:ff:ff:ff
    inet 192.168.122.50/24 brd 192.168.122.255 scope global eth0
      valid_lft forever preferred_lft forever
```

FIGURE 12-7

Editing an IPv6 address in the Network Manager Connections Editor

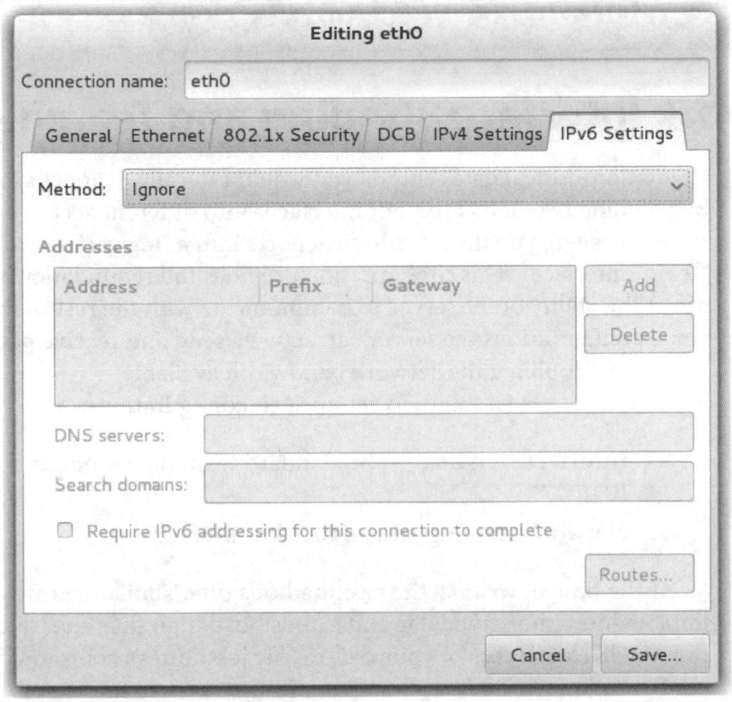

```
inet6 2001:db8:3dab::2/64 scope global
    valid_lft forever preferred_lft forever
inet6 fe80::5054:ff:fe85:61c0/64 scope link
    valid_lft forever preferred_lft forever
```

The configuration is saved in the ifcfg-eth0 file in the /etc/sysconfig/network-scripts directory. Open that file. You will notice that the Network Manager Connections Editor added the following configuration lines:

```
IPV6_AUTOCONF=no
IPV6ADDR=2001:db8:3dab::2/64
IPV6_DEFAULTGW=2001:db8:3dab::1
IPV6_DEFROUTE=yes
IPV6_FAILURE_FATAL=no
```

The **IPV6_AUTOCONF** directive disables auto-configured IPv6 addresses. The next variables, **IPV6ADDR** and **IPV6_DEFAULTGW**, set the IP addresses of the interface and the default gateway, respectively, whereas **IPV6_DEFROUTE** installs a default route in the routing table. Finally, if the **IPV6_FAILURE_FATAL** directive is enabled, then a failure with the IPv6 configuration would result in the interface being down, even if the IPv4 configuration succeeded.

CERTIFICATION OBJECTIVE 12.06

Network Interface Bonding and Teaming

In mission-critical data centers, you would typically connect a Linux server to the network by patching two of its Ethernet interfaces into different access switches. You would also normally aggregate the two physical ports into a "logical" network interface (the "bond" or "team" interface). This configuration provides full redundancy because a single failure won't affect the ability of the server to communicate with the rest of the network. In addition, in some configurations the server can actively send and receive packets through both network interfaces, doubling the network bandwidth available.

RHEL 7 offers two ways to set up such configurations:

- **Interface bonding** The standard teaming method in RHEL 6 and still available on RHEL 7
- **Network teaming** Introduced in RHEL 7

At the time of writing, the two methods offer similar features, but network teaming implements a more modular and extensible design than the traditional bond driver. For the RHCE exam (and for your day-to-day job duties), you should be familiar with both configuration methods.

To practice with interface bonding and teaming, start with two Ethernet interfaces. For this purpose, power off the server1.example.com virtual machine and add a second Ethernet adapter. To do so, start the Virtual Machine Manager, open the virtual machine console and details window, and click the virtual hardware details button. Click Add Hardware and select a network device, as shown in Figure 12-8. Set "virtio" as the device model and then click Finish. Power on the virtual machine and run the **ip link show** command to confirm that the new virtual adapter is recognized by the system. You should see one loopback and two Ethernet adapters installed on your system, as shown in the next output:

```
# ip link show
1: lo: <LOOPBACK,UP,LOWER_UP> mtu 65536 qdisc noqueue state UNKNOWN
mode DEFAULT
    link/loopback 00:00:00:00:00:00 brd 00:00:00:00:00:00
2: eth0: <BROADCAST,MULTICAST,UP,LOWER_UP> mtu 1500 qdisc pfifo_fast ↵
state UP mode DEFAULT qlen 1000
    link/ether 52:54:00:b6:0d:ce brd ff:ff:ff:ff:ff:ff
3: eth1: <BROADCAST,MULTICAST,UP,LOWER_UP> mtu 1500 qdisc pfifo_fast ↵
state UP mode DEFAULT qlen 1000
    link/ether 52:54:00:a1:48:6c brd ff:ff:ff:ff:ff:ff
```

FIGURE 12-8   Add a new network device to a virtual machine.

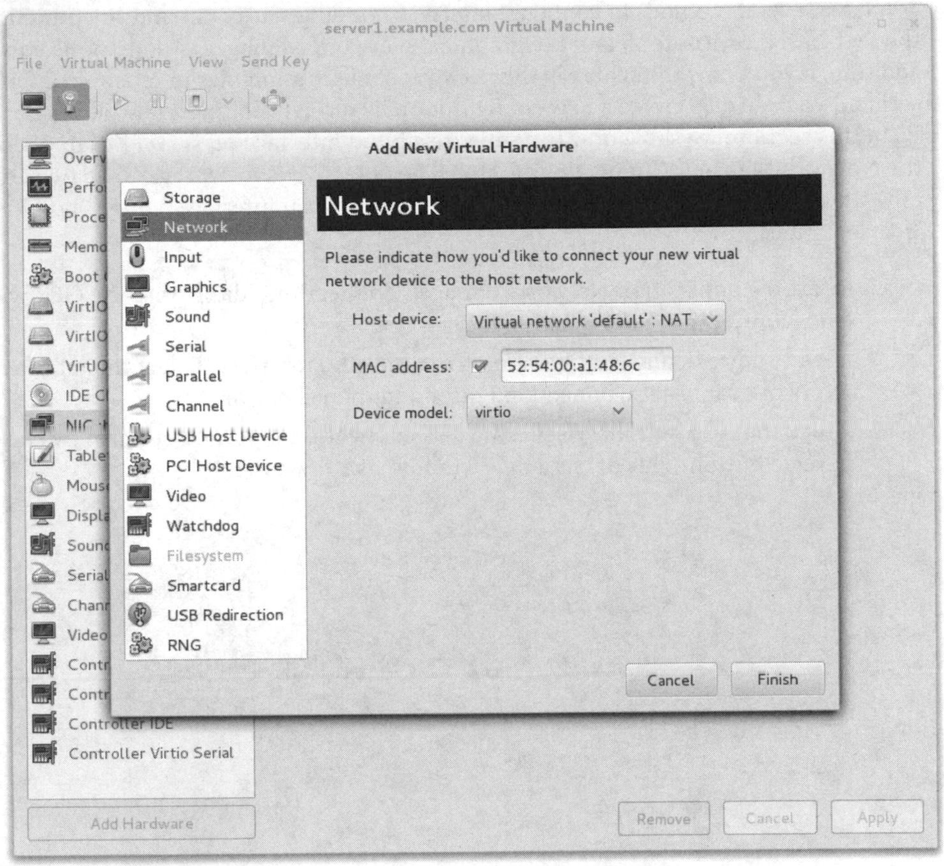

on the

j o b

As noted in Chapter 3, RHEL 7 tries to name network interfaces based on their physical location (for example, "enoX" or "emX" for the onboard network interfaces). If you have configured the virtual adapters on a systems using the "virtio" type, as discussed in this chapter, RHEL 7 should fail back to the traditional interface enumeration method of eth0, eth1.... If you want to force your system to use the traditional ethX naming style, you can apply the procedure described in KB article 283233 at https://access.redhat.com/solutions/283233.

Configure Interface Bonding

You have several methods to configure interface bonding: the command-line **nmcli** program, the text-based **nmtui** tool, and the graphical Network Manager Connections editor. In addition, if you know the syntax of the network configuration files in /etc/sysconfig/network-scripts/, you can also create a new configuration by directly editing a few files.

In this section, we show how to configure a bond interface on server1.example.com using the Network Manager Connections Editor. The objective is to aggregate the two eth0 and eth1 interfaces (the "slave" interfaces) into a single, logical interface named "bond0" (the "master" interface).

1. Start the application Network Manager Connection Editor from the GUI with the **nm-connection-editor** command.

2. Delete any existing configuration from the eth0 interface. Select the interface in the Network Manager Connection Editor and then click Delete.

3. Click the Add button, select Bond as a connection type, and confirm by clicking the Create button. This opens a new window, as shown here:

4. This next step consists of adding the "slave" interface eth0 to the bond configuration. Click the Add button, select Ethernet as a connection type, and click Create.

5. The Editing bond0 slave 1 window will appear. Set the Connection name to eth0 and set the Device MAC address to the address of the eth0 interface from the drop-down menu, as shown here. Click Save.

6. Move to the General tab and select the option "Automatically connect to this network when it is available." Click Save. This will ensure that the device is activated at boot.

7. Repeat Steps 4, 5, and 6 for the other slave interface eth1.

8. Back to the main window in the first illustration, select Active-backup as the failover mode. The available modes for the bonding driver are discussed in Table 12-5.

9. Optionally, you can set the name of the primary interface in the Primary field.

10. Leave the other settings in this window at their default value.

11. Move to the IPv4 Settings tab. Configure the IP address, netmask, and gateway for the system with the settings from Table 1-2 in Chapter 1.

12. Click Save.

TABLE 12-5	Bonding Modes
Bonding Mode	**Description**
Round-robin	Packets are transmitted in a round-robin fashion across the slave interfaces. Provides load balancing and fault tolerance. Requires support on the network switches (for example, the configuration of a "port channel" on Cisco devices).
Active-backup	Only one slave interface is active. If this active interface fails, a different slave becomes active. Provides fault tolerance and does not require any special switch support.
XOR	Packets are transmitted across slave interfaces using a XOR hash policy. Provides per-flow load balancing and fault tolerance.
Broadcast	Packets are transmitted on all slave interfaces. Rarely used.
802.3ad	Uses IEEE 802.3ad link aggregation, which must be supported on the network switches. Provides load balancing and fault tolerance.
Adaptive transmit load balancing	Packets are transmitted across interfaces based on their current load. Provides load balancing and fault tolerance.
Adaptive load balancing	Similar to adaptive transmit load balancing, but also provides inbound load balancing via ARP negotiation.

When configuration is complete, you should have a bond0 interface configured in active-backup mode, with two slave interfaces: eth0 and eth1. The following command confirms the current IP configuration settings:

```
# ip addr show bond0
4: bond0: <BROADCAST,MULTICAST,MASTER,UP,LOWER_UP> mtu 1500 qdisc noqueue ↵
 state UNKNOWN
    link/ether 52:54:00:b6:0d:ce brd ff:ff:ff:ff:ff:ff
    inet 192.168.122.50/24 brd 192.168.122.255 scope global dynamic bond0
       valid_lft 3367sec preferred_lft 3367sec
    inet6 fe80::5054:ff:feb6:dce/64 scope link
       valid_lft forever preferred_lft forever
```

To show the status of the bond0 interface and its slaves from the link-layer perspective, run the **cat /proc/net/bonding/bond0** command. The output is shown in Figure 12-9 and indicates that both slave interfaces are up, with the eth0 interface being the active slave.

Showing the
status of the
bond0 interface

```
[root@server1 ~]# cat /proc/net/bonding/bond0
Ethernet Channel Bonding Driver: v3.7.1 (April 27, 2011)

Bonding Mode: fault-tolerance (active-backup)
Primary Slave: None
Currently Active Slave: eth0
MII Status: up
MII Polling Interval (ms): 1
Up Delay (ms): 0
Down Delay (ms): 0

Slave Interface: eth0
MII Status: up
Speed: Unknown
Duplex: Unknown
Link Failure Count: 0
Permanent HW addr: 52:54:00:b6:0d:ce
Slave queue ID: 0

Slave Interface: eth1
MII Status: up
Speed: Unknown
Duplex: Unknown
Link Failure Count: 0
Permanent HW addr: 52:54:00:a1:48:6c
Slave queue ID: 0
[root@server1 ~]# █
```

EXERCISE 12-4

Test Bonding Failover

In this exercise, you will test bonding failover. We assume that you have configured an active-backup bonding interface with two slaves, as explained in the previous section.

1. Run a continuous **ping** command from your physical host to server1.example.com to confirm that IP connectivity is operational:

   `# ping 192.168.122.50`

2. Shut down the active interface on server1 with the **ifdown eth0** command. Is server1 still replying to ping requests?

3. Confirm the status of the active slave interface with the following command:

   `# cat /proc/net/bonding/bond0`

4. Bring back the eth0 interface with the **ifup eth0** command. Is server1 still replying to ping requests? Which is the active interface of the bond master interface?

5. Repeat Steps 2–4 for the eth1 interface. As long as you have one slave interface active, IP connectivity should always be operational.

6. Bring down both eth0 and eth1 interfaces. What happens?

Configure Interface Teaming

Network teaming is a new method of link aggregation available in RHEL 7. Functionally, it is similar to interface bonding. However, its architecture differs significantly. Whereas bonding is implemented in the Linux kernel, interface teaming relies on a very small kernel driver. All the rest of the code runs in user space as part of a user service daemon (**teamd**). This approach guarantees a more modular and extensible design that facilitates the introduction of new features.

To create a new team interface, start the Network Manager Connection Editor, click the Add button, and select Team as a connection type. Once you click the Create button, a window similar to the one shown next will be displayed.

From this point, the configuration for the basic aspects is similar to that of a bonding interface. As such, you can refer to the previous section for details.

Once a new team interface is set up, you can confirm its status with the following command:

```
# teamdctl team0 state
setup:
    runner: roundrobin
ports:
  eth0
    link watches:
```

```
        link summary: up
        instance[link_watch_0]:
          name: ethtool
          link: up
    eth1
      link watches:
        link summary: up
        instance[link_watch_0]:
          name: ethtool
          link: up
```

Authentication with Kerberos

Two systems configured with and authenticated by Kerberos can communicate in encrypted format with a symmetric key. That key is granted by a Key Distribution Center (KDC). Although there is no RHCE objective related to the configuration of a Kerberos KDC, you need a KDC to practice with the configurations covered in this section and in Chapter 16. In the following sections, we start with the basics of Kerberos and then practice with the configuration of a KDC and a simple client.

A Kerberos Primer

Kerberos is a network authentication protocol, originally developed at the Massachusetts Institute of Technology (MIT), that supports secure identification of networked systems. RHEL 7 includes the Kerberos 5 client and software packages developed by MIT.

Kerberos is not a directory service like LDAP. In other words, for a valid client to authenticate to a Kerberos server, it'll also need a connection to a network authentication database such as LDAP, NIS, or the user database in the /etc/passwd file. Directory services contain the user and group identifiers, users' home directories, and default shell information. Kerberos was not designed to store this information, but to provide authentication services.

Every participant in a Kerberos network (also known as *realm)* is identified by a *principal*. A principal for a user has the form *username/instance@REALM*. The instance part is optional and normally qualifies the type of user. The realm indicates the scope of the Kerberos domain and is normally indicated by a capitalized version of the DNS domain name. For example, the Kerberos realm for the DNS domain example.com is normally EXAMPLE.COM.

According to these rules, the Kerberos principals for the users mike, alex, and root (with an admin instance) are as follows:

```
mike@EXAMPLE.COM
alex@EXAMPLE.COM
root/admin@EXAMPLE.COM
```

Kerberos principals are not limited to users. You can create principals to identify a computer host or a service. For example, you can represent a host principal in the following format: host/*hostname@REALM*. As an example, the host principal for server1.example.com would be represented by the following string:

```
host/server1.example.com@EXAMPLE.COM
```

In a similar fashion, you can set up a Kerberos service principal in the following format: *service/hostname@REALM*. For example, you can set up the following principals for the NFS and FTP services on the host server1.example.com:

```
nfs/server1.example.com@EXAMPLE.COM
ftp/server1.example.com@EXAMPLE.COM
```

In a Kerberos-based network, after a user has typed her username and password, the login program converts the username into a Kerberos principal and sends this information to the KDC, which consists of an authentication server (AS) and a ticket-granting server (TGS). Then, the KDC verifies the user's access rights and sends back to the client a special message known as a *ticket-granting ticket* (TGT), encrypted using the password that belongs to the user's principal. If the user has supplied the correct password to the login program, the client will be able to decrypt the TGT message and authenticate successfully.

When authentication is confirmed, the Kerberos client gets a ticket good for a limited time, typically 24 hours. Besides the maximum ticket lifetime, a TGT also contains the principal name, a session key to encrypt communications, and a timestamp.

Once an account has a valid TGT, that account can authenticate to other network services by providing the same TGT, which takes the place of re-entering authentication credentials for the life of the TGT. This feature is known as *single sign-on* (SSO).

Prerequisites for Kerberos Servers and Clients

Kerberos relies on accurate timestamps. If the time on the servers and clients is more than five minutes apart, this will result in authentication failures. To avoid this problem, in a production network usually all the hosts keep their time in sync via NTP (Network Time Protocol).

Kerberos also relies on a name resolution service. You can make it work with either a local DNS server or a complete /etc/hosts file on each host of your network.

For this book, we've set up a physical workstation named maui.example.com. This host runs the virtual machines server1.example.com, tester1.example.com, and outsider1.example.com. The /etc/hosts file for this lab environment is shown in Figure 12-10.

FIGURE 12-10

The contents of
the file /etc/hosts

```
127.0.0.1     localhost localhost.localdomain localhost4 localhost4.localdomain4
::1           localhost localhost.localdomain localhost6 localhost6.localdomain6
192.168.122.1    maui.example.com maui
192.168.122.50   server1.example.com server1
192.168.122.150  tester1.example.com tester1
192.168.100.100  outsider1.example.com outsider1
```

EXERCISE 12-5

Install a Kerberos KDC

In this guided exercise, we'll show how to set up a Key Distribution Center. Although this is not an RHCE requirement, you need a KDC to practice with Exercise 12-6 and the labs at the end of the chapter. You can install a KDC either on the workstation that runs the virtual machines that you deployed in Chapter 1 or on a dedicated virtual machine.

1. Install the krb5-server and krb5-workstation RPM packages:

   ```
   # yum install -y krb5-server krb5-workstation
   ```

2. Edit the /etc/krb5.conf file. Uncomment the **default_realm** = **EXAMPLE.COM** line and the four lines in the [**realms**] stanza. Replace the **kdc** and **admin_server** defaults with the fully qualified domain name of your server (maui.example.com, in our case). The result is shown here.

   ```
   [logging]
    default = FILE:/var/log/krb5libs.log
    kdc = FILE:/var/log/krb5kdc.log
    admin_server = FILE:/var/log/kadmind.log

   [libdefaults]
    dns_lookup_realm = false
    ticket_lifetime = 24h
    renew_lifetime = 7d
    forwardable = true
    rdns = false
    default_realm = EXAMPLE.COM
    default_ccache_name = KEYRING:persistent:%{uid}

   [realms]
    EXAMPLE.COM = {
     kdc = maui.example.com
     admin_server = maui.example.com
    }

   [domain_realm]
   .example.com = EXAMPLE.COM
   example.com = EXAMPLE.COM
   ```

3. Review the contents of the file /var/kerberos/krb5kdc/kdc.conf. By default, this file is configured for the Kerberos realm EXAMPLE.COM, as illustrated next. You don't have to modify this file, unless you want to configure a different Kerberos realm name than the default.

```
[kdcdefaults]
 kdc_ports = 88
 kdc_tcp_ports = 88

[realms]
 EXAMPLE.COM = {
  #master_key_type = aes256-cts
  acl_file = /var/kerberos/krb5kdc/kadm5.acl
  dict_file = /usr/share/dict/words
  admin_keytab = /var/kerberos/krb5kdc/kadm5.keytab
  supported_enctypes = aes256-cts:normal aes128-cts:normal des3-hmac-sha1:normal
 arcfour-hmac:normal camellia256-cts:normal camellia128-cts:normal des-hmac-sha1
:normal des-cbc-md5:normal des-cbc-crc:normal
  }
```

4. Create a new Kerberos database by running the following command. You will be prompted for a master key (password), which the KDC uses to encrypt the database:

```
# kdb5_util create -s
Loading random data
Initializing database '/var/kerberos/krb5kdc/principal' for realm ↵
 'EXAMPLE.COM',
master key name 'K/M@EXAMPLE.COM'
You will be prompted for the database Master Password.
It is important that you NOT FORGET this password.
Enter KDC database master key:
Re-enter KDC database master key to verify:
```

The **-s** option saves the master key in a stash file so that you don't have to manually enter the master key every time the Kerberos service is started.

5. Start and enable the Kerberos services to start at boot:

```
# systemctl start krb5kdc kadmin
# systemctl enable krb5kdc kadmin
```

6. Allow connections to the Kerberos server through the default zone on the firewall:

```
# firewall-cmd --permanent --add-service=kerberos
# firewall-cmd --reload
```

7. Run the **kadmin.local** command to administer the KDC and create, list, or delete principals, as shown in the following example:

```
# kadmin.local
Authenticating as principal root/admin@EXAMPLE.COM with password
```

```
kadmin.local:  listprincs
K/M@EXAMPLE.COM
kadmin/admin@EXAMPLE.COM
kadmin/changepw@EXAMPLE.COM
kadmin/maui.example.com@EXAMPLE.COM
krbtgt/EXAMPLE.COM@EXAMPLE.COM

kadmin.local:  addprinc mike
Enter password for principal "mike@EXAMPLE.COM":
Re-enter password for principal "mike@EXAMPLE.COM":
Principal "mike@EXAMPLE.COM" created.

kadmin.local:  addprinc alex
Enter password for principal "alex@EXAMPLE.COM":
Re-enter password for principal "alex@EXAMPLE.COM":
Principal "alex@EXAMPLE.COM" created

kadmin.local:  delprinc alex
Are you sure you want to delete the principal "alex@EXAMPLE.COM"? ↵
  (yes/no): yes
Principal "alex@EXAMPLE.COM" deleted.
Make sure that you have removed this principal from all ACLs before ↵
  reusing.
kadmin.local
```

Set Up a Kerberos Client

For the purpose of an exam, as well as on the job, it's almost always best to keep the solutions as simple as possible. That's where the Authentication Configuration tool can help. To see what this tool does to help configure a Kerberos client, you could back up the files in the /etc/sssd directory, along with the /etc/nsswitch.conf configuration file. This file is related to the System Security Services Daemon.

The Graphical Authentication Configuration Tool

One way to open the GUI version of the Authentication Configuration tool is with the **authconfig-gtk** command. That should open the Authentication Configuration tool with the two tabs shown in Figure 12-11. Although other authentication databases are supported, the focus is on LDAP. The options in the LDAP section of the Identity & Authentication tab were discussed in Chapter 8.

FIGURE 12-11

Configure a
Kerberos-based
client with
the graphical
Authentication
Configuration tool.

The focus of this section is on the second half of the tab. For a Kerberos-based client, you'd retain Kerberos Password as the Authentication Method setting. Here are the other options:

- **Realm** By convention, the Kerberos realm is the same as the domain name for the network, in uppercase letters.
- **KDCs** The KDC is the Kerberos Key Distribution Center. The entry here should correspond either to the fully qualified domain name (FQDN) or the IP address of the actual Kerberos server.

■ **Admin Servers**   The administrative server associated with the KDC is frequently located on the same system. On the Kerberos administrative server, the kadmind daemon is running.

■ **Use DNS to Resolve Hosts to Realms**   Where a trusted DNS server exists for the local network, you can allow the local system to use a DNS server to find the realm. If this option is activated, the Realm text box will be blanked out.

■ **Use DNS to Locate KDCs for Realms**   Where a trusted DNS server exists for the local network, you can allow the local system to use a DNS server to find the KDC and administrative server. If this option is activated, the KDCs and Admin Servers text boxes will be blanked out.

For the purpose of this section, accept the default options, as shown in Figure 12-11. Click Apply. After a few moments, the Authentication Configuration window will close and changes will be made to the configuration files.

The Console Authentication Configuration Tool

To start the text-mode version of the Authentication Configuration tool, run the **authconfig-tui** command. As shown in Figure 12-12, you don't need to activate LDAP, at least for authentication.

After you select Next, the tool prompts for the Kerberos Settings screen shown in Figure 12-13. The default options shown here are the same as those shown in the graphical version of the tool from Figure 12-11.

You may also need to set up changes to configuration files, as described next.

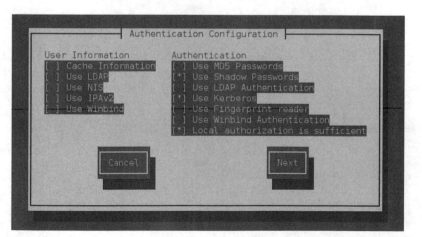

FIGURE 12-12

Configure a Kerberos-based client with the console Authentication Configuration tool.

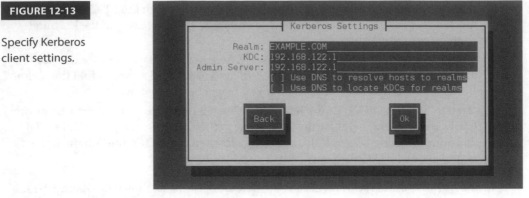

FIGURE 12-13

Specify Kerberos
client settings.

EXERCISE 12-6

Configure Kerberos Authentication

In this exercise you will set up a user with an associated Kerberos principal for authentication. We assume that you have a KDC installed on your physical system listening to the IP address 192.168.122.1, and that you want to set up a user on the virtual machine server1.example.com to authenticate against the KDC. Follow these steps:

1. Install the RPM packages krb5-workstation and pam_krb5 on the Kerberos client server1.example.com:

   ```
   # yum -y install krb5-workstation pam_krb5
   ```

2. Add a new user on server1.example.com to test Kerberos authentication. For example:

   ```
   # useradd mike
   ```

3. From a GNOME terminal, run the command **authconfig-tui** and set up server1 .example.com to use Kerberos for authentication, as illustrated previously in Figures 12-11 and 12-12. Alternatively, you could run the following command:

   ```
   # authconfig --update --enablekrb5 --krb5kdc=192.168.122.1 \
   > --krb5adminserver=192.168.122.1 --krb5realm=EXAMPLE.COM
   ```

4. On the KDC, run **kadmin.local** and add a principal for the user mike:

   ```
   # kadmin.local
   Authenticating as principal root/admin@EXAMPLE.COM with password
   kadmin.local:  addprinc mike
   Enter password for principal "mike@EXAMPLE.COM":
   Re-enter password for principal "mike@EXAMPLE.COM":
   Principal "mike@EXAMPLE.COM" created.
   ```

5. Test authentication by logging into server1 as mike via SSH.

6. If successful, the **klist** command will show the TGT for the user mike:

```
[mike@server1 ~]$ klist
Ticket cache: KEYRING:persistent:1001:krb_ccache_0YxfosR
Default principal: mike@EXAMPLE.COM

Valid starting       Expires             Service principal
12/08/15 17:42:53   13/08/15 17:42:53   krbtgt/EXAMPLE.COM@EXAMPLE.COM
```

SCENARIO & SOLUTION

You need to set up a system utilization report for various system resources.	Start with the man page for the **sadf** command; use the options associated with the **sar** command for the desired resources.
You've been told to set up IPv6 forwarding on a system.	Include the **net.ipv6.conf.all.forwarding=1** setting in /etc/sysctl.conf, and activate it with the **sysctl -p** command.
You need to set up a special static route over device eth1.	Use the Network Connections Editor tool to set up that special route, given the network address, subnet mask, and desired gateway IP address.
You need network redundancy on your system.	Add a second network interface. Aggregate together the two interfaces using the bond or team driver.
You need to set up a system as a Kerberos client.	Use the GUI Authentication Configuration tool; the realm should be the uppercase listing for the domain. You'll also need the FQDN for the KDC and Kerberos administration servers (which may be the same).

CERTIFICATION SUMMARY

Linux administrators need to configure scripts on a regular basis. Sample scripts are already available in different /etc/cron.* directories. Normally, bash scripts start with the **#!/bin/sh** line, which sets up the interpreter. Administrative scripts can use Linux commands, along with internal bash commands such as **for**, **if**, **do**, and **test**.

As an RHCE, you need to be able to monitor the performance of administered systems. That's the province of the sysstat service. While commands such as **df**, **top**, and **dstat** can display CPU, RAM, disk, and network utilization data, actual reports can be prepared with the help of the **sadf** command. An example of how this collects RAM and network data is available in the **sadf** man page; you can then add CPU and disk use data from related **sar** command switches.

Kernel run-time parameters can be found in the /proc/sys directory, but changes to such files are temporary. For more permanent changes, you'd set up options in the /etc/sysctl.conf file. Changes to that file can be implemented with the **sysctl -p** command. Many standard kernel options relate to networking.

The RHCE objectives include requirements for several special network configurations. With the help of the Network Connections Editor tool, static IP routes can be configured in a file in the /etc/sysconfig/network-scripts directory. Using the same tool, you can also configure IPv6 addresses, as well as bonding and team interfaces.

Kerberos clients can be configured with the **authconfig-gtk** command. To practice with Kerberos, you need to configure a Key Distribution Center (KDC), as explained in this chapter.

✓ TWO-MINUTE DRILL

Here are some of the key points from the certification objectives in Chapter 12.

Automate System Maintenance

❑ Standard administrative scripts can provide a model for custom scripts to automate system maintenance tasks.

❑ Various commands within scripts include **do**, **for**, **if**, and **test**.

❑ Bash scripts start with the **#!/bin/sh** or **#!/bin/bash** shebang line.

Set Up System Utilization Reports

❑ Several system utilization commands are available in RHEL 7 with the help of the sysstat package.

❑ The **sa1** command regularly collects data in the /var/log/sa directory.

❑ System status reports can be created with the **sadf** command, with an assist from **sar** command switches.

❑ One example of a system status report command is shown in the **sadf** man page.

Kernel Run-time Parameters

❑ Kernel run-time parameters are located in the /proc/sys directory.

❑ Many kernel run-time parameters relate to network options such as IP forwarding and security.

❑ Kernel run-time parameters can be configured on a permanent basis with the help of the /etc/sysctl.conf file.

IP Routes

❏ The configuration of a default route requires a gateway IP address.

❏ Static routes to different networks can be configured with the help of the Network Connections Editor tool and its text-based counterpart **nmtui**.

An Introduction to IPv6

❏ IPv6 addresses have 128 bits organized in nibbles of 16 bits.

❏ The three different types of IPv6 addresses are unicast, anycast, and multicast.

❏ IPv6 addresses can be limited to local network segments (link-local) or routable.

Network Interface Bonding and Teaming

❏ Network bonding and teaming provide link redundancy and optionally higher network throughput through various configuration modes, such as round-robin and active-backup.

Authentication with Kerberos

❏ To authenticate with Kerberos, you need a Key Distribution Center (KDC).

❏ To configure a Kerberos client, you can use the **authconfig-gtk** command.

Q SELF TEST

The following questions will help measure your understanding of the material presented in this chapter. As no multiple choice questions appear on the Red Hat exams, no multiple choice questions appear in this book. These questions exclusively test your understanding of the chapter. It is okay if you have another way of performing a task. Getting results, not memorizing trivia, is what counts on the Red Hat exams.

Automate System Maintenance

1. What exit code is associated with success in a script?

_____

2. Write a bash **test** command to check if a file exists and is executable.

_____

3. Write a bash **for** statement to cycle through all the users in a system.

_____

Set Up System Utilization Reports

4. What directory includes a cron job that logs system activity? Assume the appropriate package is installed.

_____

5. On a RHEL 7 system, where can you find a sample command to create a system utilization report? Where can you find additional switches for that report?

_____

Kernel Run-time Parameters

6. What's the full path to the /proc file associated with the **net.ipv4.ip_forward** parameter?

_____

IP Routes

7. What are the configuration parameters associated with a static route?

_____

An Introduction to IPv6

8. What is the shortest representation of the 2001:0db8:00aa:0000:04ba:0000:0000:00cd IPv6 address?

_____

9. What command can you use to ping an IPv6 address?

_____

Network Interface Bonding and Teaming

10. What command can you run to check the status of a bond0 interface and of its slave interfaces?

_____

Authentication with Kerberos

11. What is the standard Kerberos realm for the server1.example.com system?

_____

12. Which command do you run to list the Kerberos tickets for the current user?

_____

LAB QUESTIONS

Several of these labs involve configuration exercises. You should do these exercises on test machines only. It's assumed that you're running these exercises on virtual machines such as KVM.

Red Hat presents its exams electronically. For that reason, the labs for this chapter are available from the media that accompanies the book in the Chapter12/ subdirectory. In case you haven't yet set up RHEL 7 on a system, refer to Chapter 1 for installation instructions.

The answers for the labs follow the Self Test answers for the fill-in-the-blank questions.

SELF TEST ANSWERS

Automate System Maintenance

1. The exit code associated with success in a script is 0.

2. A bash **test** command to check if a file exists and is executable can be written as follows:

```
test -x /path/to/file
```

3. A **for** statement to cycle through all the usernames in a system can be written as follows:

```
for username in $(getent passwd | cut -f 1 -d ":")
```

Set Up System Utilization Reports

4. The directory with the standard sysstat job is /etc/cron.d.

5. On a RHEL 7 system, one place where you can find a command example of a system utilization report is the **sadf** man page. Additional switches can be found in the **sar** man page.

Kernel Run-time Parameters

6. The full path to the file associated with the **net.ipv4.ip_forward** parameter is /proc/sys/net/ipv4/ip_forward.

IP Routes

7. The configuration parameters associated with a static route are the network address, the subnet mask, and the gateway address.

An Introduction to IPv6

8. The shortest representation of the 2001:0db8:00aa:0000:04ba:0000:0000:00cd IPv6 address is 2001:db8:aa:0:4ba::cd.

9. You can use the **ping6** command to ping an IPv6 address. If this is a link-local address, you need to specify the outbound interface with the **-I** switch.

Network Interface Bonding and Teaming

10. To check the status of the bond0 interface and its slave interfaces, run the following command:

```
# cat /proc/net/bonding/bond0
```

Authentication with Kerberos

11. The standard Kerberos realm for the server1.example.com system is EXAMPLE.COM.

12. The command that lists the Kerberos tickets for the current user is **klist**.

LAB ANSWERS

Lab 1

Success in this lab should be straightforward. The simplest way to set up the script is to start with the fundamental requirements and then add the other functionalities. For example, the following script saves the current date in MMDDHHSS format in the **$TODAY** variable. Then, it runs the **tar** command to back up the directory passed as the first argument into the backup-MMDDHHSS.tar file within the directory given as the second argument:

```
#!/bin/bash
TODAY=$(date +%m%d%H%S)
tar cf "$2/backup-$TODAY.tar" "$1"
```

The next step is to add the other non-core functionalities. You will need a test to check whether the number of arguments is not equal to two:

```
if [ $# -ne 2 ]; then
    echo "Usage: backup.sh <source> <destination>"
    exit 1
fi
```

You will also need to add another test to confirm that the arguments passed to the script are regular directories:

```
if [ ! -d "$1" ]; then
    echo "Error: directory $1 does not exist"
    exit 2
fi
```

In addition, another test is required to check if the second argument is a directory. If the test fails, the script must create the directory:

```
if [ ! -d "$2" ]; then
    mkdir -p "$2"
fi
```

Note that if the second argument is a file but not a directory, the script will return an error. However, this is not an error condition that the exercise asks you to take into consideration.

If you put together all the blocks of code, you will have a working script. Test the script with different arguments to verify that all the exception conditions are recognized and successfully processed.

Lab 2

If you understood the requirements of this lab, the answer should be easy. While there are other methods, one appropriate command that meets the given requirements is available on the man page for the **sadf** command:

```
# sadf -d /var/log/sa/sa21 -- -r -n DEV
```

Of course, to get that information into the noted file, the output must be redirected:

```
# sadf -d /var/log/sa/sa21 -- -r -n DEV > sysstat_report.txt
```

Lab 3

This lab builds upon what you did in Lab 2. If you haven't memorized the additional command options that specify information on CPU and disk usage, you can find those options in the man page for the **sar** command. As suggested in the man page, the **-u** switch can be used to report CPU usage, whereas the **-d** switch reports activity by block device. It can help users read the output if the **-p** switch is combined with **-d**.

But there's one more requirement: the **-p** switch next to the **sadf** command leads to output in a format usable by the **awk** command utility. The following is one method to meet the requirements of the lab:

```
# sadf -p /var/log/sa/sa21 -- -u -r -dp -n DEV > morestat_report.txt
```

Lab 4

If you've successfully completed this lab, the /etc/sysctl.conf file (or a file in the /etc/sysctl.d directory) should now have the following entry:

```
net.ipv4.icmp_echo_ignore_all = 1
```

That just makes sure the new setting survives a reboot. You may have also set the associated file, /proc/sys/net/ipv4/icmp_echo_ignore_all, to 1, or run the **sysctl -p** command to implement the change before the system is rebooted.

Of course, success can be confirmed with a **ping** command, both from local and remote systems. If you want to restore the original configuration, return to the server1.example.com system and then remove the **net.ipv4.icmp_echo_ignore_all** option from the /etc/sysctl.conf file.

Lab 5

If you used the Network Connections tool to set up a special route, it should set up a new file in the /etc/sysconfig/network-scripts directory. If the specified network adapter is eth0, that special file would be route-eth0. Given the parameters used for the outsider1.example.org network, as discussed in Chapter 1, that file would contain the following three lines:

```
ADDRESS0=192.168.100.0
NETMASK0=255.255.255.0
GATEWAY0=192.168.122.1
```

Of course, if the outsider1.example.org system is on a different network, the contents of the route-eth0 file would change accordingly.

Lab 6

To complete this lab, use the Network Manager Connection Editor and add the IPv6 addresses indicated to the interfaces. The network prefix is /64. You don't need to set an IPv6 default gateway because all the IPv6 addresses indicated are on the same subnet.

Then, test connectivity between the hosts with the **ping6** command. For example, run the following command from server1 and tester1 to ping the physical host:

```
# ping6 2001:db8:7a::1
```

Lab 7

Start this lab by shutting down tester1. Add a new network adapter using the virtio device model and then power on the machine. You can confirm that the new adapter is available on the system with the **ip link show** command.

Use the Network Manager Connection Editor tool to create the team0 adapter. Before creating the new interface, ensure that the existing configuration on eth0 is removed.

Success in this lab means the following:

- You have full network connectivity, as demonstrated by running the **ping** command to verify that other hosts are reachable.
- The team0 interface is up and aggregates together eth0 and eth1. You can verify this by running the **teamdctl team0 state** command.
- If you disable the eth0 or eth1 interface with the **ifdown** command, the system still has network connectivity.

Chapter 13

Network Services: DNS, SMTP, iSCSI, and NTP

CERTIFICATION OBJECTIVES

T his chapter examines four system services: the Domain Name System (DNS), the Simple Mail Transfer Protocol (SMTP), the Internet Small Computer System Interface (iSCSI), and the Network Time Protocol (NTP) service.

For DNS, the RHCE objectives require the configuration of a caching-only name server. So in this book, we do not cover the configuration of a master or secondary DNS server. Next, we'll cover SMTP e-mail services. Linux offers a number of alternative methods for handling incoming and outgoing e-mail. RHEL 7 includes two SMTP services: sendmail and

Postfix. We focus on Postfix, the default RHEL 7 mail transfer agent. Postfix was originally developed in the late 1990s as an alternative to sendmail. It is modular and relatively easy to configure.

You will also learn how to configure a storage device and persistent mount that via the Internet Small Computer Systems Interface (iSCSI) protocol. The storage device is known as an iSCSI target, whereas clients are known as iSCSI initiators.

Finally, whereas you learned about the default NTP server in Chapter 5, you'll learn about the configuration of NTP peers in this chapter.

INSIDE THE EXAM

Domain Name Service

Examine the RHCE objectives associated with DNS:

- Configure a caching-only name server
- Troubleshoot DNS client issues

You'll learn how to troubleshoot DNS client issues with the help of the **dig** and **host** commands.

The SMTP Service

The objective related to e-mail services on the RHCE exam is relatively simple:

- Configure a system to forward all email to a central mail server

The focus of this objective is to configure a null client—that is, a system that can only forward e-mails to a remote server. However, for testing purposes in our lab environment we would need a second system configured to accept inbound e-mails. Although this is not a specific RHCE requirement (it was on the RHCE objectives for RHEL 6), we will cover

some of the more general configuration of mail transfer agents (MTAs).

iSCSI Targets and Clients

This chapter also addresses the configuration of iSCSI targets and clients (initiators), as described in the following objective:

- Configure a system as either an iSCSI target or a initiator that persistently mounts an iSCSI target

The Network Time Service

Finally, one service that was partially covered in the RHCSA objectives is based on the NTP protocol. Whereas the focus on the RHCSA was to "configure a system to use time services," the RHCE objective suggests that you need a more in-depth knowledge of the configuration of NTP servers:

- Synchronize time using other NTP peers

In addition, you need to meet the basic RHCE objectives that apply to all network services, as discussed in Chapter 11.

An Introduction to Domain Name Services

DNS is a service that translates human-readable hostnames such as www.mheducation .com to IP addresses such as 192.0.2.101, and vice versa. DNS is a distributed database; each server has its own delegated zone of authority for one or more domains. The DNS service associated with RHEL is the Berkeley Internet Name Domain (BIND). As no individual DNS server is large enough to keep a database for the entire Internet, each server can refer requests to other DNS servers.

RHEL 7 includes another DNS service, Unbound. The Unbound package does not include all the features of BIND, but it is simple and easy to configure if you need just a secure caching DNS resolver. In this chapter, we will cover the configuration of both BIND and Unbound. You can use either of them to meet the RHCE objective related to DNS configuration.

The BIND Name Server

The default DNS service on RHEL 7 is based on the **named** daemon, included with the BIND 9.9 software package developed through the Internet Systems Consortium. This package includes the **rndc** command, which you can use to manage DNS operations.

DNS Package Options

To configure a system as a BIND DNS server, start with the RPMs associated with the DNS Name Server package group, shown here:

- **bind**   Includes the basic name server software and extensive documentation
- **bind-chroot**   Adds directories that isolate BIND in a so-called "chroot jail," which limits access if DNS is compromised
- **bind-dyndb-ldap**   Provides an LDAP back-end plug-in for BIND
- **bind-libs**   Adds library files used by the bind and bind-utils RPMs
- **bind-libs-lite**   Includes a lite version of the BIND libraries for client utilities
- **bind-license**   Contains the license file of BIND
- **bind-utils**   Includes tools such as **dig** and **host** to query DNS servers and retrieve information about hostnames and domains

By now, you should be comfortable installing these packages with commands such as **yum** from software repositories, as discussed in Chapter 7.

RHEL 7 also supports the dnsmasq package, which can be used to set up a forwarding DNS server with an integrated DHCP service in a small network.

Different Types of DNS Servers

While additional options are available, there are four basic types of DNS servers:

- A master DNS server, authoritative for one or more domains, includes host records for that domain.
- A slave DNS server, which relies on a master DNS server for data, can be used in place of that master DNS server.
- A caching-only DNS server stores recent requests like a proxy server. If configured with forwarding features, it refers to other DNS servers for requests not in its current cache.
- A forwarding-only DNS server refers all requests to other DNS servers.

As described earlier, all you need to know for the RHCE exam is how to configure a caching-only DNS server.

Each of these servers can be configured with access limited to internal networks, or even just a local system. Alternatively, they can be configured as public DNS servers, accessible to the entire Internet. But such access comes with risks, as a successful attack against an authoritative corporate DNS server could easily keep their websites hidden from customers' web browsers. This attack is a form of denial of service.

CERTIFICATION OBJECTIVE 13.02

Minimal DNS Server Configurations

You can configure DNS servers by directly editing the associated configuration files. In this section, we'll briefly review the configuration files installed with the BIND and Unbound software packages. You'll then learn how to configure a caching-only name server, as well as a name server that includes forwarding to specified DNS servers.

BIND Configuration Files

DNS configuration files can help you configure a Linux system as a database of hostnames and IP addresses. That database can be cached, listed in a local database, or the request can

TABLE 13-1	DNS Server Configuration Files

DNS Configuration File	Description
/etc/sysconfig/named	Specifies options to be passed to the named daemon at startup.
/etc/named.conf	The main DNS configuration file. Includes the location of the zone files. Can incorporate data from other files, normally in the /etc/named directory, with the **include** directive.
/etc/named.rfc1912.zones	Adds appropriate zones for localhost names and addresses.
/var/named/named.empty	Includes a template zone file.
/var/named/named.localhost	Lists the zone file for the localhost computer.
/var/named/named.loopback	Lists the zone file for the loopback address.

be forwarded to a different system. The configuration files that support the use of DNS as a server are described in Table 13-1. While the table includes references to standard /var/named database files, changes to such files are not required to configure a caching-only or forwarding DNS server.

If you've installed the bind-chroot package, a tree of directories and files will also be available in the /var/named/chroot directory to run BIND in a confined chroot jail. If you wish to run BIND in a chroot jail, you'll have to move the configuration files and DNS zones to /var/named/chroot/etc and /var/named/chroot/var/named and then enable the named-chroot service unit.

In the following sections, you'll experiment with the /etc/named.conf file. You should back it up in some fashion. Just be aware of the ownership and, yes, the SELinux contexts of the file, as shown in this output:

```
# ls -Z /etc/named.conf
-rw-r-----. root named system_u:object_r:named_conf_t:s0 /etc/named.conf
```

If backups are restored haphazardly, even by the root user, the group ownership and/or the SELinux contexts may be lost. So if there's ever a failure in starting or restarting the named service, check the ownership and SELinux contexts of the /etc/named.conf file. If necessary, apply the following commands to that file:

```
# chgrp named /etc/named.conf
# restorecon -F /etc/named.conf
```

In addition, after a DNS configuration is tested, some information may remain in a cache. That's the nature of a caching DNS server. If that cache still exists after a change to DNS configuration files, it could affect the results. Therefore, it's wise to flush the DNS cache after each configuration change with the following command:

```
# rndc flush
```

A BIND Caching-Only Name Server

When you request a web page such as www.mcgraw-hill.com, a request to resolve the hostname is sent to the configured DNS server. The response is the associated IP address. The request is also known as a *name query.* For requests to external DNS servers, responses can take time. That's where a caching-only name server can help, as repeated requests are stored locally.

When you are configuring a caching-only name server, the first step is to look at the default version of the /etc/named.conf configuration file. The directives in the default version of this file are organized to set up a caching-only name server. One view of this file is shown in Figure 13-1.

■ The **options** directive encompasses several basic DNS directives, including the following:

　■ The **listen-on port** (and **listen-on-v6 port**) directives specify the port number to listen on (for IPv4 and IPv6).

　To extend this to a local network, you'll need to include the IP address of the local network interface. For example, if you want the server to respond to queries on the local IPv4 address of 192.168.122.50, you'd change the directive to read as follows (don't forget the semicolon followed by a space after each IP address):

```
listen-on port 53 { 127.0.0.1; 192.168.122.50; };
```

If IPv6 networking is active on the local network, you would need to configure similar IPv6 addresses for the **listen-on-v6** directive. If IPv6 networking is not active, the default **listen-on-v6** directive is sufficient.

　■ The **directory** directive specifies where the DNS server looks for data files. Be aware, if the bind-chroot RPM is installed, these file paths are relative to the /var/named/chroot path.

　■ The **dump-file** directive specifies the file on which BIND dumps the cache for the current DNS database when the **rndc dumpdb** command is issued.

| FIGURE 13-1 | The /etc/named.conf configuration file for a caching-only name server |

```
options {
        listen-on port 53 { 127.0.0.1; };
        listen-on-v6 port 53 { ::1; };
        directory       "/var/named";
        dump-file       "/var/named/data/cache_dump.db";
        statistics-file "/var/named/data/named_stats.txt";
        memstatistics-file "/var/named/data/named_mem_stats.txt";
        allow-query     { localhost; };

        /*
         -- If you are building an AUTHORITATIVE DNS server, do NOT enable recursion.
         - If you are building a RECURSIVE (caching) DNS server, you need to enable
           recursion.
         - If your recursive DNS server has a public IP address, you MUST enable access
           control to limit queries to your legitimate users. Failing to do so will
           cause your server to become part of large scale DNS amplification
           attacks. Implementing BCP38 within your network would greatly
           reduce such attack surface
        */
        recursion yes;

        dnssec-enable yes;
        dnssec-validation yes;
        dnssec-lookaside auto;

        /* Path to ISC DLV key */
        bindkeys-file "/etc/named.iscdlv.key";

        managed-keys-directory "/var/named/dynamic";

        pid-file "/run/named/named.pid";
        session-keyfile "/run/named/session.key";
};

logging {
        channel default_debug {
                file "data/named.run";
                severity dynamic;
        };
};

zone "." IN {
        type hint;
        file "named.ca";
};

include "/etc/named.rfc1912.zones";
include "/etc/named.root.key";
```

- The **statistics-file** directive specifies the file to write statistics data when the **rndc stats** command is issued.

- The **memstatistics-file** directive specifies the location to save memory usage statistics when BIND exits.

- The **allow-query** directive lists the IP addresses allowed to get information from this server. By default, access is limited to the local system. To extend this to another network such as 192.168.122.0/24, you'd change the directive to this:

```
allow-query { 127.0.0.1; 192.168.122.0/24; };
```

- The **recursion** directive enables recursive queries. A recursive query will interrogate the authoritative name servers for the requested domain and always provide an answer to clients. This is the behavior that you would expect from a caching name server. As shown in the comments of the named.conf file in Figure 13-1, if the server has a public IP address, you must restrict access to legitimate clients with the **allow-query** directive.

- Since BIND version 9.5, the software has included support for DNS Security Extension (DNSSEC), with **dnssec-*** directives. DNSSEC protects a caching name server from spoofing and cache poisoning attacks by validating the integrity and authenticity of responses received from other name servers. The following directives enable DNSSEC security, validation (to check authenticity), and querying, with the noted **bindkeys-file**:

```
dnssec-enable yes;
dnssec-validation yes;
dnssec-lookaside auto;
bindkeys-file "/etc/named.iscdlv.key";
managed-keys-directory "/var/named/dynamic";
```

- The **logging** directive specifies several more parameters; the **channel** directive specifies output methods, in this case to **default_debug**, activated in the named.run file in the /var/named/data directory, logging only **dynamic** issues.
- The **zone "."** directive specifies the root zone for the Internet, along with the root DNS servers as specified in the /var/named/named.ca file.
- Finally, the **include** directives include the localhost settings described in the /etc/named.rfc1912.zones file, along with a key for the DNSSEC security protocol stored in the /etc/named.root.key file.

No changes are required to create a caching DNS server. All you need to do is install the aforementioned **bind-*** packages and start the **named** service with the following command:

```
# systemctl start named
```

Next, run the **rndc status** command. If successful, you'll see output similar to that shown in Figure 13-2. The **rndc** command is the name server control utility.

FIGURE 13-2

The status of an
operational DNS
server

```
[root@server1 ~]# rndc status
version: 9.9.4-RedHat-9.9.4-14.el7_0.1 <id:8f9657aa>
CPUs found: 1
worker threads: 1
UDP listeners per interface: 1
number of zones: 101
debug level: 0
xfers running: 0
xfers deferred: 0
soa queries in progress: 0
query logging is OFF
recursive clients: 0/0/1000
tcp clients: 0/100
server is up and running
[root@server1 ~]#
```

Starting named

After starting the DNS server with the **systemctl start named** command, view the
systemd journal with the **journalctl -u named** command. If there are problems, you'll see
error messages. The journal will usually display the file with the error. You can then stop
the service with the **rndc stop** or **systemctl stop named** command and then check the
applicable configuration files.

Once you are satisfied with the new configuration, make sure that DNS starts the next
time you reboot Linux. As noted in other chapters, the following command makes sure that
the **named** daemon starts the next time you boot Linux in the default target:

```
# systemctl enable named
```

A Forwarding Name Server

This type of DNS server is simple. It requires a single configuration line in the /etc/named
.conf configuration file. As you can see, it's straightforward; we've set it to refer to a couple
of other DNS servers on our network:

```
options {
      listen-on port 53 { 127.0.0.1; };
      listen-on-v6 port 53 { ::1; };
      directory "/var/named";
      forward only;
      forwarders {
          192.168.122.1;
          192.168.0.1;
      };
};
```

With this configuration, queries to the local name server are forwarded to DNS servers on the IP addresses shown. In a home lab, these are usually the name servers of your Internet service provider.

If you want to open up this server to external queries, a couple of more changes are required. The changes are the same as made earlier to the caching-only name server configuration. As an example, if the local network card has an address of 192.168.122.50, you'd change the **listen-on** directive to

```
listen-on port 53 { 127.0.0.1; 192.168.122.50; };
```

You should also include the **allow-query** directive described earlier, with references to the localhost system and the local network address:

```
allow-query    { localhost; 192.168.122.0/24; };
```

Don't forget to enable the DNS service on the local firewall:

```
# firewall-cmd --permanent --add-service=dns
# firewall-cmd --reload
```

Forwarding from a Caching-Only Name Server

As suggested earlier, the caching-only name server configured in the default version of the /etc/named.conf file is enabled for recursive queries. Otherwise, it would not be able to return any results from DNS requests for zones for which it is not an authoritative server.

However, you can combine aspects of the caching-only and forwarding name servers just described. Requests not in the local cache would be forwarded to the name servers specified with the **forwarders** directive. Figure 13-3 displays the relevant excerpt of a /etc/named .conf file where the forwarding directives have been included.

BIND Commands

Two useful commands associated with the BIND service are **named-checkconf** and **rndc**. The **named-checkconf** command checks the /etc/named.conf file for syntax errors. If no errors are found, it exits with a status of 0; otherwise, it shows onscreen the problematic configuration lines.

The **rndc** command arguments are straightforward. Try **rndc** by itself. The output guides you through the available options. The options we use are straightforward: **rndc status**, **rndc flush**, **rndc reload**, and **rndc stop**. If the DNS server is running correctly, the **rndc status** command should display the results shown in Figure 13-2. The **rndc flush** command flushes the server cache. The **rndc reload** command rereads any changes made to the configuration or DNS zone files. Finally, the **rndc stop** command stops the operation of the DNS server.

FIGURE 13-3

A caching
name server
that forwards
to specific DNS
servers

```
//
// named.conf
//
// Provided by Red Hat bind package to configure the ISC BIND named(8) DNS
// server as a caching only nameserver (as a localhost DNS resolver only).
//
// See /usr/share/doc/bind*/sample/ for example named configuration files.
//

options {
        listen-on port 53 { 127.0.0.1; 192.168.122.50; };
        listen-on-v6 port 53 { ::1; };
        directory       "/var/named";
        dump-file       "/var/named/data/cache_dump.db";
        statistics-file "/var/named/data/named_stats.txt";
        memstatistics-file "/var/named/data/named_mem_stats.txt";
        allow-query     { localhost; };

        forwarders {
             192.168.122.1;
             192.168.0.1;
        };
```

Unbound as a Caching-Only Name Server

If you don't need a full-featured name server such as BIND, you can opt for the Unbound
DNS resolver. This is a small package that provides a caching and forwarding name server.

The Unbound project was initially funded
by VeriSign. The software is currently
maintained by NLnet Labs and distributed
under the BSD license. It was developed with
security and modularity in mind, and as such
it is a viable alternative to BIND as a local DNS
resolver.

To install Unbound, run the following
command:

```
# yum install unbound
```

The default configuration file is /etc/unbound/
unbound.conf. Although the file contains
more than 500 lines, it includes lots of comments and examples. The **man unbound.conf**
command provides additional information and some configuration examples.

exam

w a t c h   **Red Hat exams are lab
based, so results do matter, rather than the
way in which you achieve them. Therefore,
unless a lab question specifically asks you
to install BIND or Unbound, feel free to
choose either of them to set up a caching
name server.**

To set up a caching/forwarding name server, you only need to enable three directives in the unbound.conf file. First, you should specify which interfaces Unbound should be listening on:

```
interface: 0.0.0.0
```

If you don't include the **interface** directive in the configuration file, Unbound listens only on the localhost interface. The **interface** directive is similar to the **listen-on port** and **listen-on-v6 port** configuration options of BIND. You can specify the IP address of a local interface or 0.0.0.0 to bind to all IPv4 interfaces. If Unbound listens on an interface other than the localhost, enable the DNS service on the local firewall.

Next, specify which clients are allowed to send queries to the server:

```
access-control: 192.168.122.0/24 allow
```

The **access-control** directive has the same function of **allow-query** in BIND. The unbound.conf file provides several commented examples of valid configuration lines:

```
# access-control: 0.0.0.0/0 refuse
# access-control: 127.0.0.0/8 allow
# access-control: ::0/0 refuse
# access-control: ::1 allow
# access-control: ::ffff:127.0.0.1 allow
```

With no **access-control** directive, Unbound allows client queries only from the localhost. Optionally, configure forwarding to send DNS requests to another name server. Similar to the BIND configuration, you need to define a zone with **name "."** to forward all queries to a name server:

```
forward-zone:
    name: "."
    forward-addr: 192.168.0.1
```

Finally, check the syntax of the configuration with the **unbound-checkconf** command. Start and enable the unbound service with the commands listed here:

```
# systemctl start unbound
# systemctl enable unbound
```

DNS Client Troubleshooting

After you configure a DNS resolver, examine the results with a command such as the **host mheducation.com localhost** command. The output confirms the use of the local system as a DNS server and then provides a straightforward view of the IP address of the host and the hostname of the mail server:

```
Using domain server:
Name: localhost
Address: 127.0.0.1#53
Aliases:

mheducation.com has address 204.74.99.100
mheducation.com mail is handled by 20 ↵
mheducation-com.mail.protection.outlook.com.
```

You can use the **dig** or **host** command to examine your work. For example, with the command **dig @127.0.0.1 www.mheducation.com**, you'll see something like the output shown in Figure 13-4.

The **dig** command shown in the figure asks the local DNS server to look for the "A record" of www.mheducation.com. An A record maps a hostname to an IP address. Assuming the IP address information for www.mheducation.com isn't cached locally,

FIGURE 13-4	``` ; <<>> DiG 9.9.4-RedHat-9.9.4-14.el7_0.1 <<>> @127.0.0.1 www.mheducation.com ; (1 server found) ;; global options: +cmd ;; Got answer: ;; ->>HEADER<<- opcode: QUERY, status: NOERROR, id: 53296 ;; flags: qr rd ra; QUERY: 1, ANSWER: 4, AUTHORITY: 4, ADDITIONAL: 1 ```
Test a local DNS server with the dig command.	``` ;; OPT PSEUDOSECTION: ; EDNS: version: 0, flags:; udp: 4096 ;; QUESTION SECTION: ;www.mheducation.com. IN A ;; ANSWER SECTION: www.mheducation.com. 600 IN CNAME ecom-prod-ext-460002190.us-east 1.elb.amazonaws.com. ecom-prod-ext-460002190.us-east-1.elb.amazonaws.com. 60 IN A 52.1.15.205 ecom-prod-ext-460002190.us-east-1.elb.amazonaws.com. 60 IN A 54.175.172.124 ecom-prod-ext-460002190.us-east-1.elb.amazonaws.com. 60 IN A 52.0.232.222 ;; AUTHORITY SECTION: us-east-1.elb.amazonaws.com. 299 IN NS ns-1119.awsdns-11.org. us-east-1.elb.amazonaws.com. 299 IN NS ns-934.awsdns-52.net. us-east-1.elb.amazonaws.com. 299 IN NS ns-235.awsdns-29.com. us-east-1.elb.amazonaws.com. 299 IN NS ns-1793.awsdns-32.co.uk. ;; Query time: 4901 msec ;; SERVER: 127.0.0.1#53(127.0.0.1) ;; WHEN: Mon Nov 30 00:25:17 GMT 2015 ;; MSG SIZE rcvd: 295 ```

| TABLE 13-2 | The Most Common DNS Resource Records |

DNS Resource Record	Description
A	Maps a hostname to an IPv4 address
AAAA	Maps a hostname to an IPv6 address
PTR	Maps an IP address to a hostname
CNAME	An alias; maps a hostname to another hostname
NS	Returns the name servers that are authoritative for a DNS zone
MX	Returns the mail servers for a DNS zone
SOA	Returns information about a DNS zone

it then contacts one of the forward DNS systems listed in the named.conf file. If those systems are down or otherwise inaccessible, the local DNS server proceeds to forward the request to one of the name servers listed in the named.ca file. As though those are the root name servers for the Internet, the request will be passed on to another DNS server that is authoritative for the mheducation.com domain. Therefore, it may take a number of seconds before you see an answer.

In the answer section shown in Figure 13-4, it looks like www.mheducation.com is actually an alias (CNAME) that points to another hostname. The **dig** command can query all types of DNS resource records with the help of the **-t** switch. For example, to identify the mail servers for the mheducation.com domain, ask for the MX (mail exchange) record with the following command:

```
# dig -t MX mheducation.com
```

As you have noticed, there are different types of DNS resource records. The most common are summarized in Table 13-2.

EXERCISE 13-1

Set Up Your Own BIND DNS Server

Following the example files shown previously, set up a local caching DNS server using the BIND name server. Access will be limited to the local system.

1. Install the bind RPM package.

2. Review the contents of the /etc/named.conf file, based on the discussion so far in this chapter. Do not make any changes.

3. Start the DNS server with the following command:

```
# systemctl start named
```

4. To make sure the DNS server is running, run the **rndc status** command. The output should be similar to that shown in Figure 13-2. Compare the output with the **systemctl status named** command.

5. Flush the current cache with the **rndc flush** command.

6. Test the DNS server. Try the **dig @127.0.0.1 www.mheducation.com** command.

7. Stop the BIND service with the **systemctl stop named** command

EXERCISE 13-2

Set Up Your Own Unbound DNS Server

The requirements for this exercise are identical to the previous one. However, you will be using the Unbound name server, rather than BIND.

1. Install the unbound RPM package.

2. Review the /etc/unbound/unbound.conf configuration file. Do not make any changes.

3. Start the DNS server with the following command:

```
# systemctl start unbound
```

4. Test the DNS server. Try the **dig @127.0.0.1 www.mheducation.com** command.

CERTIFICATION OBJECTIVE 13.03

A Variety of E-Mail Agents

The Postfix configuration files may seem verbose to Linux engineers who are newer to e-mail administration. Do not let the size of the configuration files intimidate you. Just a few changes are required to meet the requirements associated with the RHCE objective. In this section, you'll explore where SMTP services fit in the hierarchy of e-mail services.

TABLE 13-3 Mail Server Components

Abbreviation	Meaning	Examples
MTA	Mail transfer agent	Postfix, sendmail, Dovecot
MUA	Mail user agent	mutt, Evolution, mail, Thunderbird
MDA	Mail delivery agent	procmail
MSA	Mail submission agent	Postfix, sendmail

Definitions and Protocols

A mail server has four major components, as described in Table 13-3. On any Linux computer, you can configure a mail transfer agent (MTA) such as Postfix or sendmail for various outbound services, such as forwarding, relaying, smart host communication with other MTAs, aliases, and spooling directories. Other MTAs, such as Dovecot, are designed to handle only incoming e-mail services, based on the protocols they serve, POP3 (Post Office Protocol, version 3) and IMAP4 (Internet Message Access Protocol, version 4).

E-mail systems are heavily dependent on name resolution. While you could handle name resolution through /etc/hosts on a small network, any mail system that is connected to the Internet needs access to a fully functional DNS server. For spam protection and more, it's important to make sure that the system that intends to send an e-mail has a valid reverse DNS record (PTR) and is actually transmitting with that IP address.

But that is only one component of how e-mail works, from transmission to delivery. E-mail messages start with a mail user agent (MUA), a client system for sending and receiving e-mail such as mutt, Evolution, or Thunderbird. With the help of a mail submission agent (MSA), such mail is normally sent to an MTA such as Postfix or sendmail. A mail delivery agent (MDA) such as procmail works locally to transfer e-mail from a server to an inbox folder. procmail can also be used to filter e-mail. Red Hat supports additional MTA services such as Dovecot to enable POP3 and/or IMAP (or the secure cousins, POP3s and IMAPs) to receive e-mail.

SMTP, the Simple Mail Transfer Protocol, has become one of the most important service protocols of the modern era. Much of the Internet-connected world lives and dies by e-mail and relies on SMTP to deliver it. Like POP3 and IMAP, SMTP is a *protocol*, a set of rules for transferring data used by various mail transfer agents.

Relevant Mail Server Packages

The packages associated with Postfix are part of the "E-mail Server" package group. Key packages are listed in Table 13-4. You can install them with the **rpm** or **yum** command. Just remember that you do not need to install everything in this table.

TABLE 13-4   Mail Server Packages

RPM Package	Description
cyrus-imapd-*	Installs the Cyrus IMAP enterprise e-mail system.
cyrus-sasl	Adds the Cyrus implementation of the Simple Authentication and Security Layer (SASL).
dovecot	Supports both the IMAP and the POP incoming e-mail protocols.
dovecot-mysql, dovecot-pgsql, dovecot-pigeonhole	Includes database back ends and related plug-ins for Dovecot.
mailman	Supports e-mail discussion lists.
postfix	The default mail server on RHEL 7. It is an alternative to sendmail.
sendmail	Installs the most popular open-source mail server of the same name.
sendmail-cf	Adds a number of templates that you can use to generate your sendmail configuration file; required to process several sendmail configuration files.
spamassassin	Includes the spam filter package of the same name.

When installed, the default E-mail Server package group includes software packages for the Postfix and Dovecot servers, along with the SpamAssassin filter. For the purpose of the RHCE exam, you do not need all of these packages, just Postfix. Install Postfix with the **rpm** or **yum** command, if it is not installed by default.

Use the alternatives Command to Select an E-Mail System

The **alternatives** command, with the **--config** switch, supports choices between different services such as Postfix and sendmail:

```
# alternatives --config mta
```

The command leads to the following output, which allows you to choose from installed SMTP e-mail servers. Other SMTP services, if installed, would be included in the list that follows:

```
There are 2 programs which provide 'mta'.

  Selection    Command
-----------------------------------------------
*+ 1           /usr/sbin/sendmail.postfix
   2           /usr/sbin/sendmail.sendmail
```

Enter to keep the current selection[+], or type selection number:

The preceding output assumes that both Postfix and sendmail are installed in the system.

The **alternatives** command does not by itself stop or start a service. If you do not stop the original mail service, the daemon will still be running. It's important to have only one SMTP service running on a system. Interactions between sendmail and Postfix would lead to errors.

In this chapter, we assume that you are running the Postfix mail transfer agent. You can confirm that Postfix is the default MTA with the following command:

```
# alternatives --list | grep mta
mta      auto      /usr/sbin/sendmail.postfix
```

General User Security

By default, all users are allowed to use locally configured SMTP services, without passwords. You'll see how this can be changed for Postfix later in this chapter.

In some cases, you may want to set up local users just so they have access to such services. If you don't want such users to log in to the server with regular accounts, one option is to make sure that such users don't have a login shell. For example, the following command can set up a user named tempworker on a local system without a login shell:

```
# useradd tempworker -s /sbin/nologin
```

That tempworker user can then set up his own e-mail manager, such as Evolution, Thunderbird, or even Outlook Express, to connect to networked Postfix or sendmail SMTP services. Any attempts by that user to open an SSH session to the server are rejected.

Of course, access is limited to configured users, whether or not their accounts are configured with a login shell. That's configured courtesy of the Simple Authentication and Security Layer (SASL). As implemented in RHEL 7, it's based on the cyrus-sasl package, configured in the /etc/sasl2 directory. The configuration file for Postfix (smtpd.conf) refers back to the same authentication scheme with the following directive:

```
pwcheck_method:saslauthd
```

The /etc/sysconfig/saslauthd configuration file confirms the standard mechanism for password checks with the following directive:

```
MECH=pam
```

That's a reference to the Pluggable Authentication Modules (PAM) described in Chapter 10. In other words, users who are configured on the local system are controlled by an associated file in the /etc/pam.d directory—namely, smtp.postfix and smtp.sendmail for Postfix and sendmail, respectively. However, you'll need to make a few changes to Postfix to actually make it read the authentication database.

Mail Logging

Most log messages associated with SMTP services can be found in the /var/log/maillog file. Messages that you might expect to see in this file relate to

- Restarts of Postfix
- Successful and failed user connections
- Sent and rejected e-mail messages

Common Security Issues

By default, the SMTP service uses port 25. If you open port 25 on the firewall, outside users may have access to that server. You can open that port on the default zone with the following commands:

```
# firewall-cmd --permanent --add-service=smtp
# firewall-cmd --reload
```

To create a custom rule that supports access only from systems on the 192.168.122.0/24 network, you can add a rich rule with the following command:

```
# firewall-cmd --permanent --add-rich-rule='rule family=ipv4↵
source address=192.168.122.0/24 service name=smtp accept'
```

In general, SELinux is not an issue for SMTP services. Only one SELinux boolean applies to the Postfix service, allow_postfix_local_write_mail_spool. It's active by default. As suggested by the name, it allows the Postfix service to write e-mail files to local spools in the /var/spool/postfix directory.

Testing an E-Mail Server

Besides the **telnet** command described later in this chapter, the appropriate way to test an e-mail server is with an e-mail client. Of course, it would be convenient to have a GUI e-mail client available; however, as discussed in Chapter 2, only text clients such as **mutt** might be available.

EXERCISE 13-3

Create Users Just for E-Mail

In this exercise, you will create three users on the local system, just so they can access the local SMTP server. It is understood that additional configuration is required to set up access or limits for these users on the Postfix SMTP server. The users are mailer1, mailer2, and mailer3.

1. Review the **useradd** command. Identify the switch associated with the default login shell.
2. Review the contents of the /etc/passwd file. Find a shell that does not allow logins:

```
/sbin/nologin
```

3. Run commands such as **useradd mailer1 -s /sbin/nologin** to add a new user. Make sure to assign that user a password.

4. Review the result in /etc/shadow.

5. Repeat Step 3 for the mailer2 and mailer3 users.

6. Try logging in to one of the new accounts as a regular user. It should fail. Review associated messages in the /var/log/secure file.

7. Keep the new users.

CERTIFICATION OBJECTIVE 13.04

The Configuration of Postfix

The Postfix mail server is one way to manage the flow of e-mail on a system and for a network. Standard configuration files are stored in the /etc/postfix directory. The **postconf** command can be used to test the configuration. As installed, Postfix accepts e-mail from only the local system. The configuration changes required to set up Postfix to accept incoming e-mail and to forward e-mail through a smart host are relatively simple.

For the purpose of this chapter, Postfix was installed on the physical host system. Another Postfix server was installed on server1.example.com and configured to forward e-mails to the central mail server running on the physical host. Access tests were performed from the VMs configured in Chapters 1 and 2, representing different external networks.

The details of Postfix configuration files include options for user- and host-based security. If you already know how to configure Postfix for basic operation and just want to know what's required to meet the SMTP objectives for Postfix, jump ahead to the section associated with configuring Postfix as a null client.

Configuration Files

The configuration files are stored in the /etc/postfix directory. The main configuration file, main.cf, is somewhat simpler than the sendmail alternative, sendmail.cf. It's still complex, as it includes nearly 700 lines.

Except for the .cf files, any changes must first be processed into a database with the **postmap** command. For example, if you've added limits to the access file, it can be processed into a binary access.db file with the following command:

```
# postmap /etc/postfix/access
```

In many cases, the content of files in the /etc/postfix directory is a commented version of the associated man page. The following sections do not cover the main.cf and master.cf files, as those are explained later. They also do not cover the header_checks file, as that's more of a message filter.

After any changes are made to Postfix configuration files, it's normally best to reload them into the daemon with the following command:

```
# systemctl reload postfix
```

The Postfix access File

The access file may be configured with limits on users, hosts, and more. It includes a commented copy of the associated man page, which can also be called with the **man 5 access** command. When limits are included in that file, they're configured in the following form:

```
pattern action
```

Patterns can be set up in a number of ways. As suggested by the **man 5 access** man page, you can limit users with patterns such as

```
username@example.com
```

Patterns can be configured with individual IP addresses, network addresses, and domains, such as in the following examples. Pay attention to the syntax, specifically the lack of a dot at the end of the 192.168.100 and at the beginning of the example.org expressions. These expressions are inclusive of all systems on the 192.168.100.0/24 network and the *.example. org domain.

```
192.168.122.50
server1.example.com
192.168.100
example.org
```

Of course, such patterns have no meaning without an action. Typical actions include **REJECT** and **OK**. The following examples of lines in the /etc/postfix/access file follow the pattern action format:

```
192.168.122.50 OK
server1.example.com OK
192.168.100 REJECT
example.org REJECT
```

The Postfix canonical and generic Files

The files named canonical and generic in the /etc/postfix directory work like an alias file. In other words, when users move from place to place, or if a company moves from one domain to another, the canonical file can ease that transition. Whereas the canonical file applies to incoming e-mail from other systems, the generic file applies to e-mail being sent to other systems.

Similar to the access file, options in these files follow a pattern:

```
pattern result
```

The simplest iteration is the following, which forwards e-mail sent to a local user to a regular e-mail address:

```
michael michael@example.com
```

For companies that use different domains, the following line would forward e-mail directed to michael@example.org to michael@example.com. It would forward other example.org e-mail addresses in a similar fashion.

```
@example.org @example.com
```

Don't forget to process the resulting files into databases with the **postmap canonical** and **postmap generic** commands. If you modify the relocated, transport, or virtual files in the /etc/postfix directory, apply the **postmap** command to those files as well.

The Postfix relocated File

The /etc/postfix/relocated file is designed to contain information for users who are now on external networks, such as users who have left a current organization. The format is similar to the aforementioned canonical and generic files in the same directory. For example, the following entry might reflect forwarding from a local corporate network to a personal e-mail address:

```
john.doe@example.com    john.doe@example.net
```

The Postfix transport File

The /etc/postfix/transport file may be useful in some situations where mail is forwarded, such as from a smart host. For example, the following entry forwards e-mail directed to the example.com domain to an SMTP server such as Postfix on the server1.example.com system:

```
example.com   smtp:server1.example.com
```

The Postfix virtual File

The /etc/postfix/virtual file can forward e-mail addressed in a normal fashion, such as to elizabeth@example.com, to the user account on a local system. For example, if user elizabeth is actually the administrator on a system, the following entry forwards mail sent to the noted e-mail address to the root administrative user:

```
elizabeth@example.com root
```

The main.cf Configuration File

Back up the main.cf configuration file and open it in a text editor. There are several things that you should configure in this file to get it working. When the service is properly configured, the changes should limit access to the local system and network. This section also describes the function of other active directives, based on the default version of the file.

First, Postfix queues include either e-mail that has yet to be sent or e-mail that has been received. They can be found in the queue_directory:

```
queue_directory = /var/spool/postfix
```

The following directory is a standard. It describes the location of most Postfix commands.

```
command_directory = /usr/sbin
```

Postfix includes a substantial number of executable files for configuration in the master.cf file. The daemon_directory directive specifies their location:

```
daemon_directory = /usr/libexec/postfix
```

Postfix includes writable data files in the following directory; it normally includes a master.lock file with the PID of the Postfix daemon:

```
data_directory = /var/lib/postfix
```

As defined in the comments of the main.cf file, some files and directories should be owned by the root administrative user; others should be owned by the specified mail_owner. In the /etc/groups file, you can confirm a dedicated group named postfix, as well as a group named mail that contains the postfix user:

```
mail_owner = postfix
```

While Postfix works for the local system "out of the box," you need to do more to get it running on a network. To that end, you may need to activate and modify the following **myhostname** directive to point to the fully qualified domain name of the local system, as returned by the **hostname** command. Unless this differs from the Internet hostname of the system, there's no need to change the entry

```
#myhostname = host.domain.tld
```

to the fully qualified domain name, such as

```
myhostname = server1.example.com
```

on the **job** **An MX record can be configured on the authoritative DNS server for a domain to specify the hostname of the SMTP server that accepts e-mails for that domain.**

You need to configure an SMTP server for an entire domain name with the **mydomain** directive. To that end, change the comment

```
#mydomain = domain.tld
```

to reflect the domain name of the local network:

```
mydomain = example.com
```

Normally, you'd just uncomment the following **myorigin** directive to label e-mail addresses coming from this Postfix server with an origination domain. In this case, the origination domain is example.com:

```
myorigin = $mydomain
```

By default, the following active directive limits the scope of the Postfix service to the local system:

```
#inet_interfaces = all
inet_interfaces = localhost
```

For an e-mail server that handles incoming e-mails for an entire domain, you'd normally change the active directive so that Postfix listens on all active network interfaces:

```
inet_interfaces = all
#inet_interfaces = localhost
```

Normally, Postfix listens on both IPv4 and IPv6 networks, based on the following **inet_protocols** directive:

```
inet_protocols = all
```

The **mydestination** directive specifies the systems served by this Postfix server. Based on the previous settings, the following default directive means that accepted mail may be sent to the local system's FQDN (server1.example.com), the localhost address on the example .com network, and the localhost system:

```
mydestination = $myhostname, localhost.$mydomain, localhost
```

For a Postfix server configured for the local network, you should add the name of the local domain, already assigned to the **mydomain** directive:

```
mydestination = $mydomain, $myhostname, localhost.$mydomain,
localhost
```

The RHCE objectives require you to configure a null client—that is, a system that forwards all e-mails to a central mail server. In that case, you should leave the **mydestination** directive empty to indicate that the local Postfix system is not the final destination for any e-mail domains:

```
mydestination =
```

In addition, you'll want to set up the **mynetworks** directive to point to the client IP address to be trusted by this Postfix server. The default commented directive does not point to the example.com network defined for this book:

```
#mynetworks = 168.100.189.0/28, 127.0.0.0/8
```

So for systems like server1.example.com, this directive may be changed to

```
mynetworks = 192.168.122.0/24, 127.0.0.0/8
```

If you are configuring a null client, this directive should instead be set to the localhost IP address:

```
mynetworks = 127.0.0.0/8
```

Once the changes made to the main.cf file (and any other files in the /etc/postfix directory) are complete and saved, you may want to review the current Postfix parameters. To do so, run the following command:

```
# postconf
```

Of course, most of these parameters are defaults. To review the parameters defined by the main.cf file, run the following command:

```
# postconf -n
```

| FIGURE 13-5 | Custom Postfix settings, based on /etc/posfix/main.cf |

```
[root@Maui postfix]# postconf -n
alias_database = hash:/etc/aliases
alias_maps = hash:/etc/aliases
command_directory = /usr/sbin
config_directory = /etc/postfix
daemon_directory = /usr/libexec/postfix
data_directory = /var/lib/postfix
debug_peer_level = 2
debugger_command = PATH=/bin:/usr/bin:/usr/local/bin:/usr/X11R6/bin ddd $daemon_
directory/$process_name $process_id & sleep 5
html_directory = no
inet_interfaces = localhost
inet_protocols = all
mail_owner = postfix
mailq_path = /usr/bin/mailq.postfix
manpage_directory = /usr/share/man
mydestination = $myhostname, localhost.$mydomain, localhost
mydomain = example.com
myhostname = maui.example.com
mynetworks = 192.168.122.0/24, 127.0.0.0/8
newaliases_path = /usr/bin/newaliases.postfix
queue_directory = /var/spool/postfix
readme_directory = /usr/share/doc/postfix-2.10.1/README_FILES
sample_directory = /usr/share/doc/postfix-2.10.1/samples
sendmail_path = /usr/sbin/sendmail.postfix
setgid_group = postdrop
unknown_local_recipient_reject_code = 550
[root@Maui postfix]#
```

The output is shown in Figure 13-5.

One setting from the **postconf -n** output is important to authentication. Specifically, when the following directive is added to the main.cf file, Postfix requires authorized usernames and passwords for access:

```
smtpd_sender_restrictions = permit_sasl_authenticated, reject
```

In addition, Postfix includes a syntax checker in the basic daemon. Run the following command to see if there are any fatal errors in the main.cf file:

```
# postfix check
```

The /etc/aliases Configuration File

Another directive from the /etc/postfix/main.cf file includes the database hash from the /etc/aliases file, which is processed into the /etc/aliases.db file when the Postfix system is restarted:

```
alias_maps = hash:/etc/aliases
```

The /etc/aliases file is normally configured to redirect e-mail sent to system accounts, such as to the root administrative user. As you might see at the end of that file, e-mail messages sent to root can be redirected to a regular user account:

```
# root    marc
```

While there are a number of additional directives available in this file, they're beyond the basic configuration associated with the RHCE objectives. When changes are complete, you can and should process this file into an appropriate database with the **newaliases** command.

Test the Current Postfix Configuration

As noted in previous chapters, the **telnet** command is an excellent way to review the current status of a service on a local system. Based on the default configuration of Postfix, an active version of this service should be listening on port 25. In that case, a **telnet localhost 25** command should return messages similar to the following:

```
Trying 127.0.0.1...
Connected to localhost.
Escape character is '^]'.
220 server1.example.com ESMTP Postfix
```

If IPv6 networking is enabled on the local system, the IPv4 loopback address (127.0.0.1) would be replaced by the regular IPv6 loopback address (::1). The **quit** command can be used to exit from this connection. But don't quit yet. Type the **EHLO localhost** command and press ENTER; the **EHLO** is the enhanced **HELO** command, which returns the basic parameters of an SMTP server.

```
EHLO localhost
250-maui.example.com
250-PIPELINING
250-SIZE 10240000
250-VRFY
250-ETRN
250-ENHANCEDSTATUSCODES
250-8BITMIME
250 DSN
```

For our purposes, the most important information is what's missing. No authentication is required on this server. When authentication is properly configured on Postfix, you'll also see the following line in the output:

```
250-AUTH GSSAPI
```

FIGURE 13-6

Directions to
set up Postfix
authentication

```
Quick Start to Authenticate with SASL and PAM:
-----------------------------------------------

If you don't need the details and are an experienced system
administrator you can just do this, otherwise read on.

1) Edit /etc/postfix/main.cf and set this:

smtpd_sasl_auth_enable = yes
smtpd_sasl_security_options = noanonymous
broken_sasl_auth_clients = yes

smtpd_recipient_restrictions =
  permit_sasl_authenticated,
  permit_mynetworks,
  reject_unauth_destination

2) Turn on saslauthd:

   /sbin/chkconfig --level 345 saslauthd on
   /sbin/service saslauthd start

3) Edit /etc/sysconfig/saslauthd and set this:

   MECH=pam

4) Restart Postfix:

   /sbin/service postfix restart
```

Configure Postfix Authentication

When authentication is configured in Postfix, user limits can apply. However, as there are no hints in the standard main.cf configuration file, you'll have to refer to Postfix documentation for clues. As suggested in Chapter 3, most packages include some level of documentation in the /usr/share/doc directory. Fortunately, Postfix documentation in that directory is rather extensive. In RHEL 7, you'll be able to find that documentation in the postfix-2.10.1/ subdirectory.

The directives that you need to add to the main.cf file to set up authentication are shown in the README-Postfix-SASL-RedHat.txt file in that directory. The key excerpt is shown in Figure 13-6.

For the first step listed, it's sufficient to copy the four directives indicated to the end of the main.cf file. The first enables SASL authentication for Postfix connections:

```
smtpd_sasl_auth_enable = yes
```

Next, the following disables anonymous authentication:

```
smtpd_sasl_security_options = noanonymous
```

The directive that follows allows authentication from nonstandard and deprecated clients such as Microsoft Outlook Express:

```
broken_sasl_auth_clients = yes
```

The next line allows authenticated users, grants access from networks configured with the **mynetworks** directive, and rejects destinations other than the Postfix server:

```
smtpd_recipient_restrictions = permit_sasl_authenticated,
    permit_mynetworks, reject_unauth_destination
```

Configure Postfix as an SMTP Server for a Domain

The directives required to set up Postfix to accept incoming e-mail from other systems have been previously shown in the description of the main.cf file. However, that discussion was a more comprehensive description of that file. This section just summarizes the minimum requirements to configure Postfix to accept inbound e-mails from other systems. Given a Postfix server configured on the maui.example.com system, on the 192.168.122.0/24 network, you'd make the changes shown in Table 13-5 to the main.cf file in the /etc/postfix directory.

Each of these options replaces either a comment or an active directive in the default /etc/postfix/main.cf file. For example, you should at least comment out the following directive:

```
#inet_interfaces = localhost
```

Configure Postfix as a Null Client

This section covers the minimum requirements to configure Postfix, in the words of the RHCE objectives, "to forward all email to a central mail server." A smart host provides this

| **TABLE 13-5** | Postfix Configuration as an SMTP Server for example.com |

Postfix Parameter	Description
myhostname = maui.example.com	Specifies the hostname of the system
mydomain = example.com	Sets the local domain name
myorigin = $mydomain	Specifies the domain that local e-mails will appear to be sent from
mydestination = $myhostname, localhost .$mydomain, localhost, $mydomain	Lists the domain that this machine is a destination for
inet_interfaces = all	Tells Postfix to listen on all interfaces
mynetworks = 192.168.122.0/24, 127.0.0.0/8	Lists the IP range of trusted SMTP clients

| TABLE 13-6 | Postfix Configuration as a Null Client |

Postfix Parameter	Description
myhostname = server1.example.com	Specifies the hostname of the system
mydomain = example.com	Sets the local Internet domain name
myorigin = server1.example.com	Tells Postfix that e-mails must appear to be sent from the server1.example.com domain
mydestination =	Configures the system as a null client (in other words, as a machine that is not a destination for any domain)
local_transport = error: local mail delivery is disabled	Disables e-mail delivery to the local system
inet_interfaces = localhost	Directs Postfix to listen only to the localhost interface
relayhost = maui.example.com	Forwards all e-mails to the host maui.example.com
mynetworks = 127.0.0.0/8	Lists the IP range of the trusted SMTP clients

functionality and works as a regular SMTP server, except for the forwarding of all e-mail through a second SMTP server. The location of the smart host can be specified with the **relayhost** directive. For example, if the remote smart host is outsider1.example.org, you'd add the following directive to the /etc/postfix/main.cf file:

```
relayhost = outsider1.example.org
```

A null client configuration is even more restrictive than a smart host. Similarly to a smart host configuration, all e-mails are forwarded to a central mail server. In addition, no e-mail message is accepted for local delivery. The corresponding configuration settings are shown in Table 13-6.

CERTIFICATION OBJECTIVE 13.05

iSCSI Targets and Initiators

The relevant RHCE objective of this section is to "configure a system as either an iSCSI target or initiator that persistently mounts an iSCSI target." The iSCSI initiator is a client. The iSCSI target is the shared storage on the server, which communicates with the client over TCP port 3260.

The iSCSI protocol encapsulates and delivers SCSI commands over an IP network. Once the server and the client are configured, you'll have access to the storage LUN on the iSCSI target; that LUN will look like just another SCSI hard drive on the client.

Set Up an iSCSI Target

Today, many storage arrays support the iSCSI protocol. However, for the purpose of the RHCE exam, you need to learn how to configure a Linux server as an iSCSI target (that is, an iSCSI storage server). Of course, the latency and response time will probably be slower than on an enterprise-class iSCSI storage array, but that depends on many factors, including the type of disks and throughput of the network.

**on the !
Job**

In a production iSCSI deployment, you may consider enabling "jumbo frames" on all targets, initiators, and Ethernet switches in the iSCSI fabric. Jumbo frames are Ethernet frames with a larger MTU size (typically 9,000 bytes), and as such they usually provide better throughput than the default 1,500 bytes MTU. To enable Jumbo frames on a network card on RHEL 7, add the MTU=9000 **directive to the corresponding ifcfg-* configuration file in the /etc/sysconfig/network-scripts directory.**

One way you can set up an iSCSI target is with the targetcli package. Install it as shown:

```
# yum install targetcli
```

The package includes the **targetcli** command, which starts a user-friendly configuration shell that guides you through all the steps to deploy an iSCSI target. After starting the **targetcli** shell, type the **ls** command. You will see the output displayed in Figure 13-7.

From the **targetcli** shell, you can navigate to different configuration sections using the **cd** command, like in a filesystem. The **ls** command displays the content of the current section,

FIGURE 13-7

The targetcli administrative shell

```
[root@server1 ~]# targetcli
targetcli shell version 2.1.fb34
Copyright 2011-2013 by Datera, Inc and others.
For help on commands, type 'help'.

/> ls
o- / ......................................................... [...]
  o- backstores ............................................. [...]
  | o- block ................................... [Storage Objects: 0]
  | o- fileio .................................. [Storage Objects: 0]
  | o- pscsi ................................... [Storage Objects: 0]
  | o- ramdisk ................................. [Storage Objects: 0]
  o- iscsi ........................................... [Targets: 0]
  o- loopback ........................................ [Targets: 0]
/> █
```

while **help** provides a useful contextual help screen. Like in a normal shell, you can use TAB completion to fill partially typed commands or arguments.

Configure a Backstore

As suggested by Figure 13-7, the first step consists of configuring a backstore—that is, a backing store device that will be later exported to iSCSI clients. If you have set up the virtual machines as suggested in Chapter 1, you should have enough free space on the local drive to create a new logical volume to be dedicated to an iSCSI backstore area.

As an example, log in to server1.example.com and create a new logical volume that's 1GB in size on the default rhel_server1 volume group that was created during the operating system installation (substitute accordingly if the name of your volume group is different):

```
# lvcreate -L 1G -n backstore rhel_server1
  Logical volume "backstore" created
```

For the backstore device, you can use any block device, such as a logical volume, a disk partition, or even an entire disk drive. But there's more. As shown in Figure 13-7, **targetcli** not only supports block devices as backing storage, but also image files (**fileio**), physical SCSI disks in pass-through mode (**pscsi**), and temporary in-memory filesystems (**ramdisk**). For the purpose of this section, we'll be using a block device.

Once you have a block device ready to be configured, go back to the **targetcli** shell and create a block storage object:

```
/> cd backstores/block
/backstores/block> create disk1 /dev/rhel_server1/backstore
Created block storage object device1 using /dev/rhel_server1/backstore
```

This **create** command tells **targetcli** to use the /dev/rhel_server1/backstore volume as a block storage object, with a name of disk1.

Set Up an iSCSI Qualified Name

From the **targetcli** shell, navigate to the /iscsi path:

```
/backstores/block> cd /iscsi
/iscsi>
```

Type the **help** command to display a list of available options. The next step consists of creating an iSCSI Qualified Name (IQN). This is a unique string that identifies an iSCSI initiator or target, for example:

```
iqn.2015-01.com.example:server1-disk1
```

The IQN must follow a specific format. It must start with the "iqn." string, followed by the year and month (YYYY-MM) in which an organization registered its public domain.

Next, there is the domain of the organization in reverse order, followed by a column-separated optional string.

Back to the **targetcli** shell, let's create the IQN:

```
/iscsi> create iqn.2015-01.com.example:server1-disk1
Created target iqn.2015-01.com.example:server1-disk1.
Created TPG 1.
/iscsi>
```

As indicated by the output of the preceding command, **targetcli** created the IQN for the target and a new entity, TPG 1. A TPG is a target portal group. Its purpose is to link together several parts of the configuration, as you will see in the next section.

Configure a Target Portal Group

If you have completed the configuration steps illustrated so far, type the **ls** command from the **targetcli** shell. You will see the output illustrated in Figure 13-8.

As you can see in the figure, the **targetcli** shell includes new menu entries underneath the IQN and TPG lines. Following the order shown in Figure 13-8, we will perform the following steps:

1. We will configure an access control list (ACL) to allow access to the target only from a specific client.
2. We will create a logical unit number (LUN) for the current backstore device.
3. We will define a portal—that is, an IP address and optionally a custom port that the iSCSI target will listen on for connections.

To configure an ACL and restrict access to the IQN of a specific iSCSI initiator, type the following commands:

```
/iscsi> cd iqn.2015-01.com.example:server1-disk1/tpg1/acls
/iscsi/iqn.20...sk1/tpg1/acls> create iqn.2015-01.com.example:tester1
Created Node ACL for iqn.2015-01.com.example:tester1
/iscsi/iqn.20...sk1/tpg1/acls>
```

FIGURE 13-8

Configuring a TPG
from the targetcli
shell

```
/iscsi> ls
o- iscsi ..................................................... [Targets: 1]
  o- iqn.2015-01.com.example:server1-disk1 .......................... [TPGs: 1]
    o- tpg1 .......................................... [no-gen-acls, no-auth]
      o- acls ..................................................... [ACLs: 0]
      o- luns ..................................................... [LUNs: 0]
      o- portals .............................................. [Portals: 0]
/iscsi> █
```

Next, navigate to the LUNs section and associate a LUN number to the backstore device previously created:

```
/iscsi/iqn.20...sk1/tpg1/acls> cd ../luns
/iscsi/iqn.20...sk1/tpg1/luns> create /backstores/block/disk1 0
Created LUN 0.
Created LUN 0->0 mapping in node ACL iqn.2015-01.com.example:tester1
/iscsi/iqn.20...sk1/tpg1/luns>
```

Finally, navigate to the portal section and create a new iSCSI portal to listen to the local IP address (192.168.122.50 in this example). If you don't specify a TCP port, by default **targetcli** will be using TCP port 3260:

```
/iscsi/iqn.20...sk1/tpg1/luns> cd ../portals
/iscsi/iqn.20...tpg1/portals> create 192.168.122.50
Using default IP port 3260
Created network portal 192.168.122.50:3260
/iscsi/iqn.20...tpg1/portals>
```

This completes the configuration of the TPG. Type **ls /** to show the full configuration of the iSCSI target, as illustrated in Figure 13-9. Then, type **exit** to close the **targetcli** shell. The configuration is saved automatically.

All system services must be configured to start at boot. There's no exception for the iSCSI target service, so you must ensure that it is configured to start the next time that the machine is powered on. This can be done by running the following commands:

```
# systemctl enable target
# systemctl start target
```

FIGURE 13-9

The configuration of an iSCSI target

```
/iscsi/iqn.20.../tpg1/portals> ls /
o- / ....................................................................... [...]
  o- backstores ........................................................... [...]
  | o- block ................................................. [Storage Objects: 1]
  | | o- disk1 ..... [/dev/rhel_server1/backstore (1.0GiB) write-thru activated]
  | o- fileio ............................................... [Storage Objects: 0]
  | o- pscsi ................................................ [Storage Objects: 0]
  | o- ramdisk .............................................. [Storage Objects: 0]
  o- iscsi ....................................................... [Targets: 1]
  | o- iqn.2015-01.com.example:server1-disk1 ........................ [TPGs: 1]
  |   o- tpg1 ................................................ [no-gen-acls, no-auth]
  |     o- acls ..................................................... [ACLs: 1]
  |     | o- iqn.2015-01.com.example:tester1 ................. [Mapped LUNs: 1]
  |     |   o- mapped_lun0 ........................... [lun0 block/disk1 (rw)]
  |     o- luns ..................................................... [LUNs: 1]
  |     | o- lun0 ................. [block/disk1 (/dev/rhel_server1/backstore)]
  |     o- portals ............................................... [Portals: 1]
  |       o- 192.168.122.50:3260 ........................................ [OK]
  o- loopback ................................................... [Targets: 0]
/iscsi/iqn.20.../tpg1/portals> █
```

Don't forget to allow connections through the local firewall. By default, the iSCSI target service uses TCP port 3260:

```
# firewall-cmd --permanent --add-port=3260/tcp
# firewall-cmd --reload
```

Connect to Remote iSCSI Storage

In this section we will configure the tester1.example.com virtual machine to mount the LUN exported by the iSCSI target defined in the previous section. To set up an iSCSI client, you'll need the iscsi-initiator-utils packages, along with any dependencies:

```
# yum install iscsi-initiator-utils
```

on the

Ĵob

The iscsi-initiator-utils package implements a software iSCSI initiator. However, today most network adapters provide iSCSI initiator functionalities in hardware. The configuration of a hardware iSCSI initiator depends on the manufacturer of the card, and as such it varies between different card vendors and models.

Next, configure an IQN for the initiator. This is defined in the /etc/iscsi/initiatorname .iscsi file. Edit the content and type a custom IQN:

```
InitiatorName=iqn.2015-01.com.example:tester1
```

If you have configured an ACL on the iSCSI target, the IQN of the client must match the IQN defined on the ACL; otherwise, the client will not be granted access to the target.

Next, enable the iscsi service on the client and ensure that it starts at the next boot:

```
# systemctl start iscsi
# systemctl enable iscsi
```

You'd use the **iscsiadm** utility to discover available iSCSI targets. One method is with the following command:

```
# iscsiadm -m discoverydb -t st -p 192.168.122.50 -D
```

To interpret, this **iscsiadm** command queries iSCSI targets. It works in discovery database (**discoverydb**) mode (**-m**), where the discovery type (**-t**) requests that the **sendtargets** (or **st**) command is sent to the iSCSI target, defined on a portal (**-p**) listening on the noted IP address, to discover (**-D**) shared storage LUNs.

If successful, you'll see output similar to the following:

```
192.168.122.50:3260,1 iqn.2015-01.com.example:server1-disk1
```

To use the target you have just discovered, you need to run the following command:

```
# iscsiadm -m node -T iqn.2015-01.com.example:server1-disk1 -l
```

This command works in node mode (**-m**) to log in to (**-l**) the target IQN (**-T**) iqn.2015-01 .com.example:server1-disk1. If successful, you'll be able to see an additional disk storage device by running the **fdisk -l** command

You should then be able to manage the shared storage as if it were a new hard drive on the local system. The hard drive device file will show up in the /var/log/messages file with information such as the following, which points to device file /dev/sdc:

```
Sep 25 20:22:15 tester1 kernel sd 6:0:0:0: [sdc] Attached SCSI disk
```

Then, you can create partitions and more on the new /dev/sdc drive, just as if it were a local drive, based on the techniques discussed in Chapter 6. Of course, a "persistent mount" as described in the relevant RHCE objective requires that you make sure the iSCSI service starts the next time the system is rebooted.

To make sure there's an actual mount, you may also need to set up a partition that's actually mounted in the /etc/fstab file. In practice, the actual device file for the iSCSI drive may vary on each reboot. Therefore, such mounts should be configured with the Universally Unique Identifier (UUID) numbers described in Chapter 6.

CERTIFICATION OBJECTIVE 13.06

The Network Time Service

The configuration of NTP as a client and a default server is covered in Chapter 5. In contrast, the configuration of NTP as a server that synchronizes time using NTP peers is covered here. Nevertheless, you need to know how to secure NTP just as you secure other network services such as Samba and NFS.

To allow NTP to work as a server, you need to allow access through UDP port 123. This can be achieved by adding the ntp service to the relevant firewalld zone.

The NTP Server Configuration File

As discussed in Chapter 5, the time configuration depends on the time zone that the /etc/localtime symbolic link points to, as well as the NTP servers configured in the /etc/ntp.conf file (or /etc/chrony.conf file, if chronyd is in use). Now it's time to configure one of those NTP servers. We'll focus on ntpd, as this is the standard NTP daemon for systems that are always connected to the network.

The default /etc/ntp.conf configuration file starts with the **driftfile** directive, which monitors the error drift in the local system clock:

```
driftfile /var/lib/ntp/drift
```

There are also **restrict** directives that can help protect an NTP server. This directive works with IPv4 and with IPv6 networking, as shown here:

```
restrict default nomodify notrap nopeer noquery
restrict 127.0.0.1
restrict ::1
```

The options to the **restrict** directive can be described as follows:

- **default**   Refers to default connections from other systems; may be further limited by other **restrict** directives.
- **nomodify**   Denies queries that attempt to change the local NTP server configuration.
- **notrap**   Denies the control message trap service; you might remove this option to enable remote logging.
- **nopeer**   Stops access from potential peer NTP servers.
- **noquery**   Ignores queries.

However, these restrictions, when combined, are good only for an NTP client. To set up an NTP server, specifically one that "synchronizes time using other NTP peers," you should remove at least the **nopeer** directive from the **restrict** list. Some NTP servers may need to synchronize with yours, which is possible if you remove the **noquery** from the list as well.

The next two restrict directives limit access to the local NTP server to the local system. You should recognize the default IPv4 and IPv6 loopback addresses here:

```
restrict 127.0.0.1
restrict ::1
```

Of course, when setting up an NTP server for other clients, you'll want to loosen that restriction. The comment that follows includes a network address in the required format. So to set up an NTP server for the 192.168.122.0/24 network, you'd change the **restrict** directive to

```
restrict 192.168.122.0 mask 255.255.255.0 notrap nomodify
```

For a basic "default configuration NTP server," no additional changes should be required. Of course, the local NTP server should also be configured as a client to master NTP servers. Substitute the hostname for the actual NTP servers on your network for the following:

```
server 0.rhel.pool.ntp.org iburst
server 1.rhel.pool.ntp.org iburst
server 2.rhel.pool.ntp.org iburst
server 3.rhel.pool.ntp.org iburst
```

And to repeat the reference from the RHCE objectives, the other reference is to peers. The relevant directive is **peer**.

To test the directive on one NTP server, you could set this machine to **peer** with another host, as shown here:

```
peer server1.example.com
```

Alternatively, you could be given the hostname to an NTP peer server, perhaps on a corporate network, perhaps on a network that has been configured during the exam.

Security Limits on NTP

As just described, the **restrict** directive from the /etc/ntp.conf configuration file can be used to limit access to a local NTP server, but that assumes an open port 123. Security limits can also refer to configured firewalls. Just be aware that an appropriate firewall rule for NTP opens up UDP (not TCP) port 123. This can be configured by adding the ntp service to the appropriate firewall zone, like so:

```
# firewall-cmd --permanent --add-service=ntp
# firewall-cmd --reload
```

To test a connection to an NTP server, the **ntpq -p** *hostname* command can help. That command looks for the peers listed in the /etc/ntp.conf file. If the server is operational, you'll see something similar to the following output to the **ntpq -p localhost** command shown in Figure 13-10.

The * sign in front of a hostname or IP address indicates the current NTP peer or server is used as a primary reference, whereas the + sign identifies additional peers designated as acceptable for synchronization. Of course, if the **ntpq** command works from a remote system, using the local hostname or IP address, you've verified that the remote NTP server is operational.

FIGURE 13-10

```
[root@server1 ~]# ntpq -p
     remote           refid      st t when poll reach   delay   offset  jitter
==============================================================================
+time2.mediainve 131.188.3.220    2 u   21   64    3   26.719    1.814  12.969
+stz-bg.com      192.53.103.104   2 u   19   64    3   54.418    6.646  28.389
*ntp2.litnet.lt  .GPS.            1 u   18   64    3   48.583    2.647  22.977
+betelgeuse.retr 193.62.22.90     2 u   17   64    3    2.299    0.548  25.659
[root@server1 ~]# █
```

NTP server status, verified with the ntpq -p command

SCENARIO & SOLUTION

You need to configure a caching-only DNS server for the local network.	Use the default named.conf file; modify the **listen-on** and **allow-query** directives.
You need to configure a caching-only DNS server to forward requests elsewhere.	Use the named.conf file, configured as a caching-only name server; add a **forwarders** directive to point to a desired DNS server.
You're told to configure an SMTP server for the 192.168.0.0/24 network.	Use the default Postfix server; modify the **myhostname**, **mydomain**, **myorigin**, **mydestination**, **inet_interfaces**, and **mynetworks** directives in /etc/postfix/main.cf.
You're asked to configure Postfix as a null client.	Set **relayhost** to the remote server to forward e-mails to; modify **mydestination** and **local_transport**; and limit access to the server with the **inet_interfaces** and **mynetworks** directives.
You're told to allow access just to the SMTP server for user1, user2, and user3.	Create the noted users with a /sbin/nologin default shell.
You need to set up an NTP server as a peer.	Modify the ntp.conf file to specify the host or IP address of a peer NTP server with the **peer** directive. Add a **restrict** directive without the **nopeer** option to allow access to the desired host.

CERTIFICATION SUMMARY

DNS provides a database of domain names and IP addresses that help hosts translate hostnames to IP addresses on various networks, including the Internet. It's a distributed database where each administrator is responsible for his or her own zone of authority, such as mheducation.com. The default DNS server uses the **named** daemon, based on the Berkeley Internet Name Domain (BIND). Other alternatives, such as the Unbound resolver, are also available.

There are four basic types of DNS servers: master, slave (or secondary), caching-only, and forwarding-only. The RHCE objectives specifically exclude master and slave name servers. The default /etc/named.conf file is built for a caching-only DNS server configuration. A forwarding-only name server uses the **forward only** and **forwarders** directives in the named.conf file. In either case, you should configure the **listen-on** and **allow-query** directives to support access from the local system and desired network(s). To test a DNS server, use commands such as **rndc status**, **dig**, and **host**.

Red Hat includes two servers associated with the SMTP protocol: Postfix and sendmail. Postfix is the default and is somewhat easier to configure than sendmail. Different Postfix configuration files can be found in the /etc/postfix directory. User and host limits can be configured in the access file. Several other files relate to redirected or renamed e-mail accounts or domains. You'll need to modify Postfix configuration directives in the /etc/postfix/main.cf file, including **myhostname**, **mydomain**, **myorigin**, **mydestination**, **inet_interfaces**, and **mynetworks**. The **relayhost** directive can help configure forwarding to a smart host. If you need to configure a null client, you also need to set the **local_transport** directive to avoid e-mails being delivered to the local system.

The iSCSI protocol emulates a SCSI bus over an IP network. With the **targetcli** command shell, you can configure interactively a Linux host as an iSCSI target to export local storage to remote iSCSI initiators. The iSCSI initiators can discover and log in to remote targets using the **iscsiadm** command.

Finally, to configure an NTP server for a network, you need to modify the /etc/ntp.conf file. The **restrict** directive should be changed to specify the network address. To support the peers suggested in the RHCE objectives, you also need a **restrict** directive without the **noquery** and (most important) **nopeer** options. Then to set up other systems as peers, you'd use the **peer** *hostname* format.

✓ TWO-MINUTE DRILL

Here are some of the key points from the certification objectives in Chapter 13.

An Introduction to Domain Name Services

❑ DNS is based on the Berkeley Internet Name Domain (BIND), using the **named** daemon.

❑ Key packages include bind-chroot, which adds security by supporting DNS in a chroot jail, and bind-utils, which includes command utilities such as **dig** and **host**.

❑ Four basic types of DNS servers are master, slave (secondary), caching-only, and forwarding-only. The RHCE objectives specifically require coverage of just caching-only DNS services.

Minimal DNS Server Configurations

❑ Critical BIND configuration files include /etc/named.conf and the files in the /var/named directory.

❑ The default /etc/named.conf file is set up for a caching-only name server, limited to the local system. Changes to the **listen-on** and **allow-query** directives can enable access from DNS clients on a network.

❑ A forwarding name server requires a **forward only** and **forwarders** directive that specifies the IP addresses of the remote DNS servers.

❑ Unbound provides an alternative to BIND for setting up a secure caching-only and forwarding name server.

A Variety of E-Mail Agents

❑ Postfix is the default mail transfer agent in RHEL 7.

❑ Mail server information is logged in the /var/log/maillog file.

The Configuration of Postfix

❑ The Postfix server can be configured through configuration files in the /etc/postfix directory. The main configuration file is main.cf file.

❑ You can configure e-mail aliases in /etc/aliases.

❑ You can set up various kinds of e-mail forwarding in files such as canonical, generic, and relocated, all in the /etc/postfix directory.

❑ The **relayhost** directive can be used to set up a connection to a smart host.

❑ To set up Postfix as a null client, you need to prevent e-mails from being delivered to the local system with the **local_transport** directive.

❑ You can test a standard Postfix configuration from the local system with the **telnet localhost 25** command.

iSCSI Targets and Initiators

❑ You can configure an iSCSI target by activating the target service and running the **targetcli** administrative shell.

❑ To set up an iSCSI target, you need to define a backstore device, set an IQN, define a LUN, create a portal, and (optionally) define ACLs.

❑ To configure an iSCSI client, you need the iscsi-initiator-utils package, which can be used to discover and log in to iSCSI targets with the **iscsiadm** command.

❑ To make sure the iSCSI connection survives a reboot, you'll need to activate the iscsi service.

The Network Time Service

❑ The default NTP configuration file, /etc/ntp.conf, sets up a client with access limited to the local system.

❑ A standard **restrict** directive in the default ntp.conf file is available to open access to systems on a specified network. You'll also need to allow NTP traffic through the local firewall.

❑ The RHCE objectives suggest connections to peers; such connections can be configured with the **peer** directive.

SELF TEST

The following questions will help measure your understanding of the material presented in this chapter. As no multiple choice questions appear on the Red Hat exams, no multiple choice questions appear in this book. These questions exclusively test your understanding of the chapter. It is okay if you have another way of performing a task. Getting results, not memorizing trivia, is what counts on the Red Hat exams. There may be more than one answer to many of the questions.

An Introduction to Domain Name Services

1. Name two packages that provide DNS services on RHEL 7.

   _____

Minimal DNS Server Configurations

2. To configure DNS communication on port 53, what changes would you make to a firewall to support access by other clients to the local DNS server?

   _____

3. What file includes a basic template for a BIND DNS caching-only name server?

   _____

4. What command makes sure that the BIND DNS service starts the next time you boot Linux in the default target?

   _____

A Variety of E-Mail Agents

5. List two examples of an MTA available on RHEL 7.

   _____

6. What command can be used to switch between the installed Postfix and sendmail services?

   _____

The Configuration of Postfix

7. How would you change the following directive in /etc/postfix/main.cf to open Postfix to all systems?

```
inet_interfaces = localhost
```

_____

8. If you use /etc/aliases for forwarding e-mail, what command processes these files into an appropriate database file for Postfix?

_____

9. What directive in the main.cf file is used to specify the domain served by the Postfix server?

_____

iSCSI Targets and Initiators

10. What service should be running on reboot on a properly configured iSCSI target?

_____

11. What command utility can be used to configure an iSCSI target?

_____

The Network Time Service

12. Enter a directive, suitable for /etc/ntp.conf, that limits access to the 192.168.0.0/24 network.

_____

LAB QUESTIONS

Several of these labs involve configuration exercises. You should do these exercises on test machines only. It's assumed that you're running these exercises on KVM-based virtual machines. For this chapter, it's also assumed that you may be changing the configuration of a physical host system for such virtual machines.

Red Hat presents its exams electronically. For that reason, the labs in this and future chapters are available from the media that accompanies the book. Labs for this chapter are in the Chapter13/ subdirectory. In case you haven't yet set up RHEL 7 on a system, refer to Chapter 1 for installation instructions.

The answers for each lab follow the Self Test answers for the fill-in-the-blank questions.

SELF TEST ANSWERS

An Introduction to Domain Name Services

1. The BIND and Unbound software packages provide DNS services on RHEL 7.

Minimal DNS Server Configurations

2. To support access by other clients to the local DNS server, make sure TCP and UDP traffic is supported through the firewall on port 53 by enabling the dns service on the required firewalld zone.

3. The default /etc/named.conf file includes a basic template for a DNS caching name server.

4. The command that makes sure that the BIND DNS service starts the next time you boot Linux is

```
# systemctl enable named
```

A Variety of E-Mail Agents

5. Two examples of MTAs supported on RHEL 7 are Postfix and sendmail.

6. The command that can be used to help switch between the Postfix and sendmail MTAs is **alternatives --config mta**.

The Configuration of Postfix

7. The simplest solution is to change the directive to

```
inet_interfaces = all
```

8. Forwarding e-mail addresses are normally stored in /etc/aliases. Make sure to process these files into appropriate databases; for /etc/aliases, the database is updated with the **newaliases** command.

9. The directive in the main.cf file that is used to specify the domain served by the Postfix server is **mydestination**.

iSCSI Targets and Initiators

10. The target service should be running on reboot on a properly configured iSCSI target.

11. The **targetcli** command shell can be used to configure an iSCSI target.

The Network Time Service

12. One directive in the /etc/ntp.conf file that limits access based on the noted conditions is

```
restrict 192.168.122.0 mask 255.255.255.0
```

LAB ANSWERS

Lab 1

In this lab, you can use the existing configuration in the /etc/named.conf configuration. All you need to do is follow these steps:

1. Install the bind RPM package.

2. Modify the **listen-on port 53** directive to include the local IP address; for example, if the local IP address is 192.168.122.150, the directive will look like

```
listen-on port 53 { 127.0.0.1; 192.168.122.150; };
```

3. Modify the **allow-query** directive to include the local IP network address:

```
allow-query { localhost; 192.168.122.0/24; };
```

4. Save your changes to /etc/named.conf.

5. Start the **named** service:

```
# systemctl start named
```

6. Change the local client to point to the local DNS caching name server; replace any **nameserver** directives in /etc/resolv.conf with the IP address of the local system. For example, if the local computer is on 192.168.122.150, the directive is

```
nameserver 192.168.122.50
```

7. Test out the new local DNS server. Try commands such as **dig www.mheducation.com**.

8. Point client systems to the DNS server. Add the aforementioned **nameserver** directive to /etc/resolv.conf on those remote client systems:

```
nameserver 192.168.122.50
```

9. To make sure the DNS service starts the next time Linux is booted, run the following command:

```
# systemctl enable named
```

10. Open up TCP and UDP ports 53 in the firewall on the local system. The simplest method is with the firewall-cmd utility:

```
# firewall-cmd --permanent --add-service=dns
# firewall-cmd --reload
```

Lab 2

As with Lab 1, the focus in this lab is on the configuration of the /etc/named.conf file. Nominally, the default caching-only DNS server already includes forwarding features. However, to set up a specific forwarding server, you should add a **forwarders** entry such as the following in the **options** stanza:

```
forwarders { 192.168.122.1; };
```

As for the other requirements of the lab, you can clear the current cache with the **rndc flush** command and reload the configuration file with the **rndc reload** command.

Lab 3

For Labs 3, 4, and 5, you may be using an e-mail client such as **mutt**. To send an e-mail to user michael@localhost, take the following steps:

1. Run the **mutt michael@localhost** command. The **To: michael@localhost** message should appear.
2. Press ENTER. At the **Subject:** prompt, enter an appropriate test subject name and press ENTER.
3. You're taken to a blank screen in the vi editor. Use commands appropriate to that editor in a screen similar to that shown in Figure 13-11.
4. From the screen shown in Figure 13-11, press Y to send the noted message.

In addition, you may be verifying e-mail receipt in a username file in the /var/spool/mail directory. Normally, such e-mail can be reviewed from within a user account with the **mail** or **mutt** command.

FIGURE 13-11

The mutt e-mail client

```
y:Send  q:Abort  t:To  c:CC  s:Subj  a:Attach file  d:Descrip  ?:Help
      From:  root <root@>
        To:  michael@localhost
        Cc:
       Bcc:
   Subject:  this is a test
  Reply-To:
       Fcc:  ~/sent
  Security:  Clear


-- Attachments
-  I    1 /tmp/mutt-Maui-0-607-0              [text/plain, 7bit, us-ascii, 0.1K]


-- Mutt: Compose  [Approx. msg size: 0.1K   Atts: 1]--------------------------
```

In Postfix, to disable local-only access in the /etc/postfix/main.cf file, change the **inet_interfaces** directive to accept all connections:

```
inet_interfaces = all
```

However, to meet the requirements of the lab, you'll want to retain the default value of that directive:

```
inet_interfaces = localhost
```

In general, to verify authentication on an SMTP server, connect from the local system with the **telnet localhost 25** command. When you see a message similar to

```
220 maui.example.com ESMTP Postfix
```

type in the following command:

```
EHLO localhost
```

To verify receipt of e-mail in a user account, log in to that account, or at least verify the timestamp associated with the username in the /var/mail directory. To make sure e-mail directed to the root user is redirected to a regular user account, you'd add a line like the following to the /etc/aliases file:

```
root:  michael
```

Given the wording for the question, any standard user account would be acceptable. Of course, to implement this change, you'll have to run the **newaliases** command, which processes this file into the /etc/aliases.db file.

Lab 4

To enable access from more than just the localhost, you'll need to modify the inet_interfaces directive in /etc/postfix/main.cf to

```
inet_interfaces = all
```

The next job is to limit access to a specific network (in this case, example.com). While there are options in /etc/postfix files, perhaps the most efficient way to limit access to a specific network is with an appropriate firewalld rich rule. For example, the following custom rule would limit access to TCP port 25 to systems on the given IP address network. The network shown is based on the originally defined configuration for example.com, the 192.168.122.0/24 network:

```
# firewall-cmd --permanent --add-rich-rule='rule family=ipv4↵
  source address=192.168.122.0/24 service name=smtp accept'
```

In addition, you can set up this network in the /etc/postfix/access file with a rule like the following:

```
192.168.122 OK
```

Once Postfix is running, you should be able to confirm the result with an appropriate **telnet** command from a remote system. For example, if Postfix is configured on a system with a 192.168.122.50 IP address, the command would be

```
# telnet 192.168.122.50 25
```

The configuration of a smart host in Postfix is based on the **relayhost** directive. For the parameters given in the lab, if the physical host is located on the system maui.example.com, the directive in the main.cf file would be

```
relayhost = maui.example.com
```

If Postfix on the server1.example.com system is properly configured as a smart host, e-mails to the forwarded host should be reliably delivered and logged in to the appropriate /var/log/maillog file.

Lab 5

The configuration of Postfix as a null client is straightforward and is summarized in Table 13-6.

At a minimum, you should configure the **myorigin**, **mydestination**, **local_transport**, and **relayhost** directives. Other directives such as **myhostname**, **mydomain**, and **mynetworks** should already have appropriate default values.

Confirm your settings with the **postconf -n** command and start the service. Don't forget to configure Postfix to start automatically the next time the machine is powered on.

Lab 6

This is a long lab, but it is very similar to the configuration example described in the "iSCSI Targets and Initiators" section of this chapter. Please refer to that section for an in-depth discussion.

Lab 7

In this lab, you'll set up one NTP server as a peer to another. That's possible with the **peer** directive, configured in the /etc/ntp.conf configuration file. For example, if a regular NTP server is configured on IP address 192.168.122.50, you can set up a peer on the 192.168.122.150 server with the following directive:

```
peer 192.168.122.50
```

Just remember, an NTP peer doesn't work unless the **nopeer** option has been removed from the **restrict** directive in the ntp.conf file.

Chapter 14

The Apache Web Server

U nix was developed by AT&T in the late 1960s and early 1970s, and it was freely distributed among a number of major universities during those years. When AT&T started charging for Unix, a number of university developers tried to create clones of this operating system. One of these clones, Linux, was developed and released in the early 1990s.

Many of these same universities were also developing the network that evolved into the Internet. With current refinements, this makes Linux perhaps the most Internet-friendly network operating system available. The extensive network services available with Linux are not only the tops in their field, but they create one of the most powerful and useful Internet-ready platforms available today at any price.

Currently, Apache is the most popular web server on the Internet. According to a Netcraft survey (http://www.netcraft.com), Apache is currently used by nearly 50 percent of all Internet active websites. Apache is included with RHEL 7.

This chapter deals with the concepts surrounding the use the Apache web server at a basic level of configuration.

INSIDE THE EXAM

Inside the Exam

This chapter directly addresses five RHCE objectives. While the objectives specify the HTTP (Hypertext Transfer Protocol) and HTTPS (HTTP, secure) protocols, that is an implicit reference to the Apache web server. It's the only web server currently supported on RHEL 7. The objectives are to

■ Configure a virtual host

Virtual hosts are the bread and butter of Apache. They support the configuration of multiple websites on the same server.

■ Configure private directories

Private directories on an Apache web server restrict access to a group of users or hosts.

■ Configure group-managed content

Sometimes groups of users have to maintain the content of a website jointly. As private directories can be configured for individual users in their home directories, directories can be configured for groups of users in a shared directory.

■ Deploy a basic CGI application

Don't worry if you don't know the Common Gateway Interface (CGI), but dynamic content on web pages often depends on scripts such as those associated with CGI.

■ Configure TLS security

We have already encountered TLS in the previous chapters. TLS (and its predecessor, SSL) is a suite of protocols used to encrypt network communications. It was originally developed in the mid-1990s to provide certificate-based authentication and secure communications for the Netscape Navigator web browser. Therefore, it's no surprise that today TLS still plays an important role in securing communications on an Apache web server.

In addition, there are the standard requirements for all network services, discussed in Chapters 10 and 11. To summarize, you need to install the service, make it work with SELinux, make sure it starts on boot, configure the service for basic operation, and set up user- and host-based security.

The Apache Web Server

Based on the HTTP daemon (**httpd**), Apache provides simple and secure access to all types of content using the regular HTTP protocol, as well as its secure cousin, HTTPS.

Apache was developed from the server code created by the National Center for Supercomputing Applications (NCSA). It included so many patches that it became known as "a patchy" server. The Apache web server continues to advance the art of the Web and provides one of the most stable, secure, robust, and reliable web servers available. This server is under constant development by the Apache Software Foundation (http://www.apache.org).

For a full copy of Apache documentation, make sure to include the httpd-manual RPM during the installation process. It'll provide a full HTML copy of the Apache manual in the /usr/share/httpd/manual directory, which can be navigated from the local server by pointing a browser to http://localhost/manual.

Apache 2.4

As befits its reliability and stability, RHEL 7 includes an updated version of Apache 2.4. RHEL 6 included an older version of Apache 2.2. However, Apache 2.4 included with RHEL 7 has all the updates needed to support the latest features, with the best possible security from the risks associated with the Internet.

The LAMP Stack

One of the powers of Apache as a web server is the way it can be easily integrated with other software components. The most common set is known as the LAMP stack, which refers to its components: Linux, Apache, MySQL, and one of three scripting languages (Perl, Python, or PHP).

In the RHCE objectives for RHEL 7, you are expected to install MariaDB, a community-developed fork of the MySQL database management system. We will discuss the installation and configuration of MariaDB in Chapter 17.

Installation

The RPM packages required by Apache are included in the Web Server package group. The simplest way to install Apache is with the following command:

```
# yum install httpd
```

However, additional packages are required. It may be simpler to install the mandatory and default packages associated with the Web Server package group with the following command:

```
# yum group install "Web Server"
```

There is also an environment group, named Basic Web Server, that installs the Web server group by default, but also includes some optional groups, such as a MariaDB and PostgreSQL client, Perl and PHP extensions, Java, and so on. If you don't remember the names of available groups, run the **yum group list** command.

The standard method to start Linux services is via the **systemctl** utility. However, you can stop and start Apache, as well as reload the configuration file gracefully, with the following commands:

```
# apachectl stop
# apachectl start
# apachectl graceful
```

The default Red Hat Apache package supports basic operation, without additional configuration. Once Apache is running, start a web browser and enter a URL of **http://localhost**. For example, Figure 14-1 displays the default home page for Apache, based on the default configuration, in the **elinks** web browser.

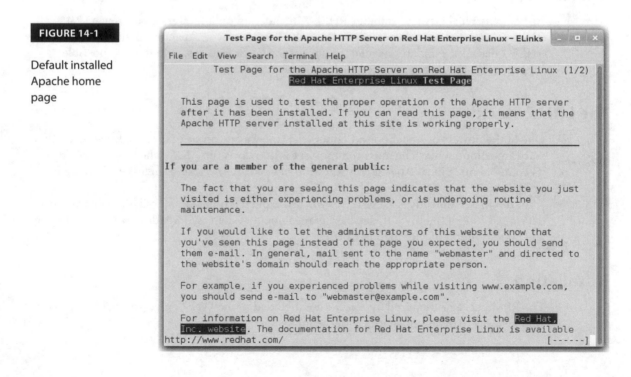

FIGURE 14-1

Default installed Apache home page

The web page is based on the contents of the /etc/httpd/conf.d/welcome.conf file, which displays the /usr/share/httpd/noindex/index.html file if there is no index.html file for the default website.

EXERCISE 14-1

Install the Apache Server

In this exercise, you'll install all the packages generally associated with the Apache server. Then you'll configure the system so Apache is active the next time Linux is booted. The twist here is that you'll do it all from the command-line interface. This assumes you've already taken the steps discussed in Chapter 7 to either register with the Red Hat Portal or connect the system to the RHEL 7 (or rebuild DVD) media as a repository.

1. If you're in the GUI, open a command-line console. Press ALT-F2 and log in as the root user.

2. Run the following command to review available groups. You should see "Basic Web Server" in the list of available environment groups.

   ```
   # yum group info
   ```

3. Check which groups are included within the "Basic Web Server" environment group. You should see web-server in the list of mandatory groups.

   ```
   # yum group info "Basic Web Server"
   ```

4. Display the packages included in the web-server group with the following command:

   ```
   # yum group info web-server
   ```

5. You can install all default packages in the web-server package group with the following command:

   ```
   # yum group install web-server
   ```

   If you just install the httpd RPM package, other important packages may not get installed, including mod_ssl, for the secure websites cited in the RHCE objectives.

6. Run the following command to see if Apache is already configured to start at boot:

   ```
   # systemctl is-enabled httpd
   ```

7. Now use the following command to make sure Apache starts in the default target the next time Linux boots normally:

   ```
   # systemctl enable httpd
   ```

8. Start the Apache service with the following command:

   ```
   # systemctl start httpd
   ```

9. If you haven't already done so in Chapter 2, install a text-based web browser. The RHEL 7 standard is **elinks**, which you can install with the following command:

```
# yum install elinks
```

10. Now start the ELinks browser, pointing to the local system, with the following command:

```
# elinks http://localhost
```

11. Review the result. Do you see the Apache test page?

12. Exit from the ELinks browser. Press Q, and when the Exit ELinks text menu appears, press Y.

13. Back up the default httpd.conf configuration file; a logical location is your home directory.

14. Run the **rpm -q httpd-manual** command to confirm the installation of Apache documentation. Since that package is a default part of the Web Server package group, you shouldn't get a package "not installed" message. However, if you do get that message, install that package with the **yum install httpd-manual** command.

15. Browse the documentation by pointing the ELinks browser to the following URL:

```
# elinks http://localhost/manual
```

The Apache Configuration Files

The two key configuration files for the Apache web server are httpd.conf in the /etc/httpd/conf directory and ssl.conf in the /etc/httpd/conf.d directory. The default versions of these files create a generic web server service. All the configuration files are located in three directories: /etc/httpd/conf, /etc/httpd/conf.d, and /etc/httpd/conf.modules.d. They're illustrated in Figure 14-2.

Apache can work with a lot of other software, such as Python, PHP, the Squid Proxy server, and more. If installed, associated configuration files can generally be found in the /etc/httpd/conf. d/ directory.

FIGURE 14-2

Apache
configuration files

```
[root@server1 ~]# ls /etc/httpd/conf
httpd.conf  magic
[root@server1 ~]# ls /etc/httpd/conf.d
autoindex.conf  manual.conf  ssl.conf     welcome.conf
fcgid.conf      README       userdir.conf
[root@server1 ~]# ls /etc/httpd/conf.modules.d
00-base.conf  00-lua.conf  00-proxy.conf  00-systemd.conf  10-fcgid.conf
00-dav.conf   00-mpm.conf  00-ssl.conf    01-cgi.conf
[root@server1 ~]#
```

To configure a regular and a secure web server, you'll need to understand the httpd.conf and ssl.conf configuration files in some detail.

Analyze the Default Apache Configuration

Apache comes with a well-commented set of default configuration files. In this section, you'll examine some key directives in the httpd.conf configuration file. Browse through this file in your favorite text editor or using a command pager such as **less**. Before beginning this analysis, remember that the main Apache configuration file incorporates the files in the /etc/httpd/conf.d directory with the following directive:

```
IncludeOptional conf.d/*.conf
```

The httpd.conf file also includes the configuration for external modules with the following directive:

```
Include conf.modules.d/*.conf
```

The difference between **IncludeOptional** and **Include** is that the former does not generate errors if the path specified does not match any file.

There are a couple of basic constructs in httpd.conf. First, directories, files, and modules are configured in "containers." The beginning of the container starts with the name of the directory, file, or module to be configured, inside directional brackets (< >). Examples of this include

```
<Directory "/var/www/html">
<Files "^\.ht*">
<IfModule mime_magic_module>
```

The end of the container is also an expression inside brackets (<>), which starts with a forward slash (/). For the same examples, the ends of the containers would look like

```
</Directory>
</Files>
</IfModule>
```

Next, Apache includes a substantial number of directives—commands that Apache can understand that have some resemblance to English. For example, the **ExecCGI** directive supports executable CGI scripts.

While this provides an overview, the devil is often in the details, which are analyzed (briefly) in the next section. If you've installed the httpd-manual RPM, get the Apache server going and navigate to http://localhost/manual.

The Main Apache Configuration File

This section examines the default Apache configuration file, httpd.conf. We recommend that you follow along on a test system such as server1.example.com. Only the default active directives in that file are discussed here. Read the comments; they include more information and options.

Once Apache and the httpd-manual RPMs are installed per Exercise 14-1, refer to http://localhost/manual/mod/quickreference.html. It provides detailed information on each directive. The default directives are summarized in the following tables. Table 14-1 specifies directives shown near the beginning of the file.

In Tables 14-1 and 14-2, directives are listed in the order shown in the default version of httpd.conf. If you want to experiment with different values for each directive, save the change and then use **systemctl restart httpd** to restart the Apache daemon or **systemctl reload httpd** to just reread the Apache configuration files.

Table 14-2 specifies directives associated with the Main Server Configuration section.

Basic Apache Configuration for a Simple Web Server

As described in Table 14-2, Apache looks for web pages in the directory specified by the **DocumentRoot** directive. In the default httpd.conf file, this directive points to the /var/www/html directory. In other words, all you need to get your web server up and running is to transfer web pages to the /var/www/html directory.

The default **DirectoryIndex** directive looks for an index.html web page file in this directory. A standard RHEL 7 index.html page is available in the /usr/share/doc/HTML/en-US directory. Copy that file to the /var/www/html directory and then navigate to http://localhost with a browser such as ELinks.

TABLE 14-1	Global Environment Directives

Directive	Description
ServerRoot	Sets the default directory for configuration files; any relative path referenced in the configuration is a relative path to the ServerRoot directory.
Listen	Specifies a port and possibly an IP address (for multihomed systems) to listen for requests.
Include	Adds the content of other configuration files.
User	Specifies the username that Apache runs as on the local system.
Group	Specifies the group name that Apache runs as on the local system.

TABLE 14-2 Main Server Configuration Directives

Directive	Description
ServerAdmin	Sets the administrative e-mail address; may be shown (or linked to) on default error pages.
AllowOverride	Supports overriding of previous directives from .htaccess files.
Require	Grants or denies access to a directory for all users or specific users/groups.
DocumentRoot	Assigns the root directory for website files.
Options	Specifies features associated with web directories, such as ExecCGI, FollowSymLinks, Includes, Indexes, MultiViews, and SymLinksIfOwnerMatch.
DirectoryIndex	Specifies files to look for when navigating to a directory; set to index.html by default.
ErrorLog	Locates the error log file, relative to **ServerRoot**.
LogLevel	Specifies the level of log messages.
LogFormat	Sets the information included in log files.
CustomLog	Creates a customized log file, using an existing log format, with a location relative to **ServerRoot**.
ScriptAlias	Similar to **Alias**, maps a web path into a filesystem location outside of **DocumentRoot**; in addition to **Alias**, it tells Apache that the noted directory contains CGI scripts.
TypesConfig	Locates mime.types, which specifies file types associated with extensions.
AddType	Maps filename extensions to a specified content type.
AddOutputFilter	Maps filename extensions to a specified filter.
AddDefaultCharset	Sets a default character encoding.
MIMEMagicFile	Normally uses the file /etc/httpd/conf/magic to determine the MIME type of a file.
EnableSendfile	Uses the sendfile system call to send static files to clients for better performance.

The base location of configuration and log files is determined by the **ServerRoot** directive. The default value from httpd.conf is

```
ServerRoot "/etc/httpd"
```

Figure 14-2 confirms that the main Apache configuration files are stored in the conf/, conf.d/, and conf.d.modules/ subdirectories of **ServerRoot**. Run the **ls -l /etc/httpd** command. Note the soft-linked directories. You should see a link from the /etc/httpd/logs directory to the directory with the actual log files, /var/log/httpd.

Apache Log Files

As suggested earlier, while Apache log files are configured to be saved in the /etc/httpd/logs directory, they're actually stored in the /var/log/httpd directory. In fact, /etc/httpd/logs is a symbolic link to /var/log/httpd. Standard logging information from Apache is stored in two baseline log files. Custom log files may also be configured. Such log files may have different names, depending on how virtual hosts are set up, how secure websites are configured, and how logs are rotated.

Based on the standard Apache configuration files, access attempts are logged in the access_log file and errors are recorded in the error_log file. Standard secure log files include ssl_access_log, ssl_error_log, and ssl_request_log.

In general, it's helpful to configure different sets of log files for different websites. To that end, you should also set up different log files for the secure versions of a website. The traffic on a website is important when choosing a log-rotation frequency.

There are standard Apache log file formats. For more information, take a look at the **LogFormat** directive in Figure 14-3. Three different formats are shown: common, combined (similar to common, but also includes the web page used to get to your site and the user's web browser type and version), and combinedio (same as the combined format, plus a log of the bytes received and sent by the server and client). The **LogFormat** lines include a number of percent signs followed by lowercase letters. These directives determine what goes into the log.

FIGURE 14-3

Specific log formats

```
# LogLevel: Control the number of messages logged to the error_log.
# Possible values include: debug, info, notice, warn, error, crit,
# alert, emerg.
#
LogLevel warn

<IfModule log_config_module>
    #
    # The following directives define some format nicknames for use with
    # a CustomLog directive (see below).
    #
    LogFormat "%h %l %u %t \"%r\" %>s %b \"%{Referer}i\" \"%{User-Agent}i\"" combined
    LogFormat "%h %l %u %t \"%r\" %>s %b" common

    <IfModule logio_module>
        # You need to enable mod_logio.c to use %I and %O
        LogFormat "%h %l %u %t \"%r\" %>s %b \"%{Referer}i\" \"%{User-Agent}i\" %I %O" com
binedio
    </IfModule>

    #
    # The location and format of the access logfile (Common Logfile Format).
    # If you do not define any access logfiles within a <VirtualHost>
    # container, they will be logged here.  Contrariwise, if you *do*
    # define per-<VirtualHost> access logfiles, transactions will be
    # logged therein and *not* in this file.
    #
    #CustomLog "logs/access_log" common
```

You can then use the **CustomLog** directive to select a location for the log file, such as logs/special_access_log, and the desired log file format, such as common. For more information on log files and formats, refer to http://localhost/manual/logs.html.

on the Job

Some web log analyzers have specific requirements for log file formats. For example, the popular open-source tool AWStats (Advanced Web Statistics) uses the combined log format. AWStats is a great tool for graphically displaying site activity. You can install it from the EPEL (Extra Packages for Enterprise Linux) repository.

CERTIFICATION OBJECTIVE 14.02

Standard Apache Security Configuration

You can configure several layers of security for the Apache web server. Firewalls based on the **firewall-cmd** command can limit access to specific hosts. Security options based on rules in Apache configuration files can also be used to limit access to specific users, groups, and hosts. Of course, secure Apache websites can encrypt communication. If there is a problem, SELinux can limit the risks.

Ports and Firewalls

With the **Listen** and **VirtualHost** directives, the Apache web server specifies the standard communication ports associated with both the HTTP and HTTPS protocols, 80 and 443. To allow external communication through the noted ports, you can set up both ports as trusted services in the Firewall Configuration tool.

Of course, for systems where HTTP and HTTPS are configured on nonstandard ports, you'll have to adjust the associated **firewall-cmd** rules accordingly.

If you just open these ports indiscriminately, the firewall allows traffic from all systems. It may be appropriate to set up a rich rule to limit access to one or more systems or networks. For example, the following custom rich rule allows access to every system except the one with IP address 192.168.122.150, over port 80:

```
firewall-cmd --permanent --add-rich-rule='rule family=ipv4 source \
address=192.168.122.150 service name=http reject'
firewall-cmd --reload
```

Similar rules may be required for port 443. Of course, that depends on the requirements of the job and possibly the RHCE exam.

Apache and SELinux

Take a look at the SELinux settings associated with Apache. To review, SELinux settings mostly fall into two categories: boolean settings and file labels. Start with the file labels.

Apache and SELinux File Labels

The default file labels for Apache configuration files are consistent, as shown in the output to the **ls -Z /etc/httpd** and **ls -Z /var/www** commands. Individual files use the same contexts as their directory. The differences in the file contexts are shown in Table 14-3.

The first five are just the default SELinux contexts for standard directories. For websites where scripts read and/or append data to web forms, you'd consider the last two contexts, which support read/write (rw) and read/append (ra) access.

The contexts listed in Table 14-3 are the most common ones. For a full list of all file contexts related to the Apache web server and their corresponding SELinux labeling rules, run the following command:

```
# semanage fcontext -l | grep httpd_
```

Create a Special Web Directory

In many cases, you'll create dedicated directories for each virtual website. It's better to segregate the files for each website in their own directory tree. But with SELinux, you can't just create a special web directory. You'll want to make sure that new directory at least matches the SELinux contexts of the default /var/www directory.

Run the **ls -Z /var/www** command. Note the SELinux contexts. For most subdirectories of /var/www, the default type is http_sys_content_t. For a newly created /www directory, you could just create a new SELinux rule and change the file contexts with the following

TABLE 14-3   SELinux File Contexts for the Apache Web Server

Directory	SELinux Context Type
/etc/httpd, /etc/httpd/conf, /etc/httpd/conf.d, /etc/httpd/conf.modules.d, /etc/httpd/run	httpd_config_t
/usr/lib64/httpd/modules	httpd_modules_t
/var/log/httpd	httpd_log_t
/var/www, /var/www/html	httpd_sys_content_t
/var/www/cgi-bin	httpd_sys_script_exec_t
n/a	httpd_sys_rw_content_t
n/a	httpd_sys_ra_content_t

commands. The **-R** applies the changes recursively, so the new contexts are applied to all files and subdirectories.

```
# semanage fcontext -a -t httpd_sys_content_t '/www(/.*)?'
# restorecon -R /www
```

The first command creates a file_contexts.local file in the /etc/selinux/targeted/contexts/files directory. If there's also a cgi-bin/ subdirectory, you'll want to set up appropriate contexts for that subdirectory as well with the following command:

```
# semanage fcontext -a -t httpd_sys_script_exec_t '/www/cgi-bin(/.*)?'
```

Apache and SELinux Boolean Settings

Boolean settings are more extensive. For display purposes, we've isolated them in the SELinux Administration tool, as shown in Figure 14-4. Only a few SELinux boolean settings are enabled by default, and they're described in Table 14-4.

FIGURE 14-4 Apache-related SELinux boolean settings

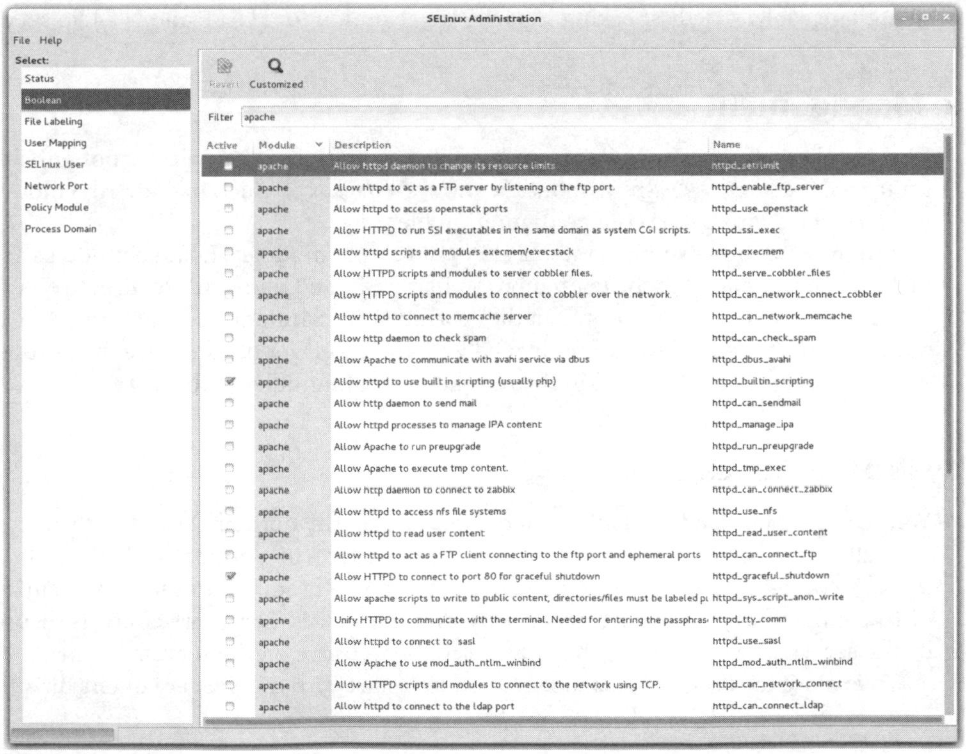

| TABLE 14-4 | Default Active Apache-Related SELinux Boolean Settings |

Active Boolean	Description
httpd_builtin_scripting	Supports the use of scripts (such as PHP)
httpd_enable_cgi	Allows HTTP services to execute CGI scripts, labeled with the httpd_sys_script_exec_t type
httpd_graceful_shutdown	Allows Apache to connect to port 80 for graceful shutdown

Out of the many other SELinux options, pay attention to httpd_enable_homedirs, which supports access to files on user home directories. Other scripts of potential interest relate to interactions with other services, specifically httpd_enable_ftp_server, httpd_use_cifs, and httpd_use_nfs. These options allow Apache to act as an FTP server, as well as to read shared Samba/NFS directories.

The uses of these and the other disabled SELinux Apache-related options from Figure 14-4 are summarized in Table 14-5. All descriptions are based on the perspective "What would happen if the boolean were enabled?" For variety, the terms HTTP and Apache are used interchangeably; strictly speaking, Apache is one option for HTTP and HTTPS services.

Module Management

The Apache web server includes many modular features. For example, it's not possible to set up SSL-secured websites without the mod_ssl package, which includes the mod_ssl.so module along with the ssl.conf configuration file.

A number of other similar systems are organized in modules. Loaded modules are included in standard Apache configuration files with the **LoadModule** directive. A full list of available modules is located in the /usr/lib64/httpd/modules directory, but available modules aren't used unless they're loaded with the LoadModule directive in appropriate Apache configuration files within the /etc/httpd/conf.modules.d directory.

Security Within Apache

You've read about (and hopefully tested) Apache security options related to the zone-based firewall as well as SELinux. Now you'll examine the security options available in the main Apache configuration file, httpd.conf. That file can be modified to secure the entire server or to configure security on a directory-by-directory basis. Directory controls secure access by the server, as well as users who connect to the websites on the server.

To explore the basics of Apache security, let's start with the **ServerTokens** directive:

```
ServerTokens OS
```

TABLE 14-5   Default Inactive Apache-Related SELinux Boolean Settings

Inactive Boolean	Description
httpd_anon_write	Allows the web server to write to files labeled with the public_content_rw_t file type.
httpd_can_check_spam	Works with web-based e-mail applications to check for spam.
httpd_can_network_connect	Allows Apache scripts/modules to establish TCP network connections.
httpd_can_network_connect_cobbler	Enables Apache scripts/modules to connect to Cobbler over the network.
httpd_can_network_connect_db	Allows Apache scripts/modules to connect to a database server over the network.
httpd_can_network_memcache	Enables Apache to connect to a memcache server.
httpd_can_network_relay	Supports the use of the HTTP service as a forward or reverse proxy.
httpd_can_sendmail	Allows Apache to send mail.
httpd_enable_homedirs	Grants Apache permission to access files in user home directories; the files must be labeled with the httpd_sys_content_t SELinux type.
httpd_execmem	Supports access from HTTP modules to executable memory regions; some Java applications may require this permission.
httpd_mod_auth_ntlm_winbind	Supports authentication to Microsoft Active Directory if the mod_auth_ntlm_winbind module is loaded.
httpd_mod_auth_pam	Enables access to PAM authentication modules if the mod_auth_pam module is loaded.
httpd_setrlimit	Allows Apache to modify its resource limits, such as the maximum number of file descriptors.
httpd_ssi_exec	Allows Apache to execute Server Side Include (SSI) scripts in a page.
httpd_tmp_exec	Supports the execution of scripts in the /tmp directory.
httpd_tty_comm	Supports access to a terminal; needed by Apache to prompt for a password if the private key of a TLS certificate is password-protected.
httpd_use_cifs	Enables Apache access to shared Samba directories when labeled with the cifs_t file type.
httpd_use_fuse	Allows Apache to access FUSE file systems, such as GlusterFS volumes.
httpd_use_gpg	Grants Apache permissions to run gpg.
httpd_use_nfs	Enables Apache access to shared NFS directories when labeled with the nfs_t file type.
httpd_use_openstack	Allows Apache to access OpenStack ports.
httpd_sys_script_anon_write	Configures write access by scripts to files labeled with the public_content_rw_t file type.

This line looks deceptively simple; it limits the information that Apache sends in its "Server" response header. This information is sometimes displayed if you navigate to a nonexistent page, but you can also fetch the HTTP headers that Apache sends to clients using the following command:

```
$ curl --head http://localhost
```

Edit the httpd.conf file and add a **ServerTokens OS** line at the top. Then, reload the server configuration by running **systemctl reload httpd** and open the default web page in a browser. You should see the following Server header:

```
Server: Apache/2.4.6 (Red Hat Enterprise Linux)
```

Contrast that output with what happens if you change that line to **ServerTokens Full**:

```
Server: Apache/2.4.6 (Red Hat) OpenSSL/1.0.1e-fips mod_auth_kerb/5.4
mod_fcgid/2.3.9 mod_wsgi/3.4 Python/2.7.5
```

In other words, with one option, outsiders can see whether modules such as FastCGI have been loaded, along with their version numbers. As not everyone updates their software in a perfectly timely manner, imagine what happens when a black hat hacker sees a version that has been compromised. For this reason, we recommend that you set **ServerTokens Prod** to limit the amount of information about the server that is sent to clients.

Next, look at the default access settings for all files and directories in the root filesystem:

```
<Directory />
    AllowOverride None
    Require all denied
</Directory>
```

This configures a very restrictive set of permissions. The **Require all denied** line denies access to all content within the root filesystem for all users. The **AllowOverride None** line disables any .htaccess files. A .htaccess file is placed inside a web directory and contains directives that can override the default web server settings.

However, there's an appropriate use for .htaccess files. For example, in a shared hosting environment, when placed in a subdirectory such as /www/html/customer023, an .htaccess file can override the default server settings and permit access to authenticated users, and such changes would apply only to that directory and its subdirectories.

You can also limit access to all but explicitly allowed domains or IP addresses by adding the following commands to the desired **<Directory>** container:

```
Order Allow,Deny
Allow from example.com
Deny from all
```

The next <**Directory**> container limits access to /var/www, the default location for website files and CGI scripts:

```
<Directory "/var/www">
    AllowOverride None
    # Allow open access:
    Require all granted
</Directory>
```

The **Require all granted** directive grants access to the content of /var/www unconditionally. The next <**Directory**> block regulates access to the /var/www/html directory, which corresponds to the same path referenced by the **DocumentRoot** directive (while the following directives are divided by numerous comments, they are all in the same container):

```
<Directory "/var/www/html">
    Options Indexes FollowSymLinks
    AllowOverride None
    Require all granted
</Directory>
```

The **Options** directive enables two features: the **Indexes** setting allows readers to see a list of files on the web server if no index.html file is present in the specified directory, and the **FollowSymLinks** option supports the use of symbolic links.

But wait a second! By default, there are no files in the /var/www/html directory. Based on the description, you should navigate to the system in question and see the screen shown in Figure 14-5. As there are no files in the /var/www/html directory, no files are shown in the output.

However, when you navigate to the default website associated with the Apache server, the page shown in Figure 14-6 appears. For more information on how that works, see Exercise 14-2.

FIGURE 14-5   Browse to an index of files.

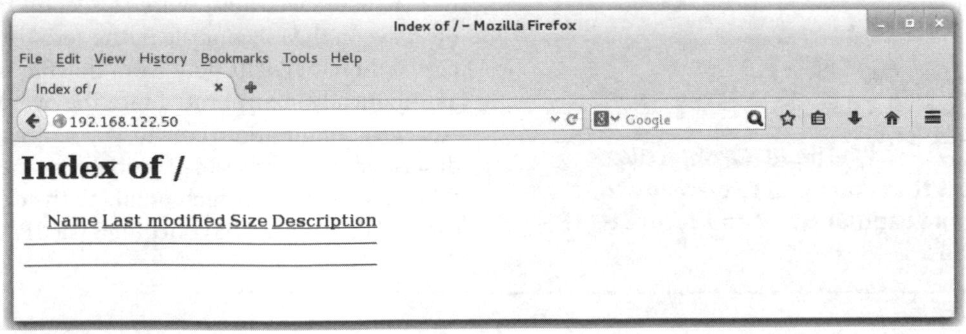

FIGURE 14-6 Browse to the default Apache test page.

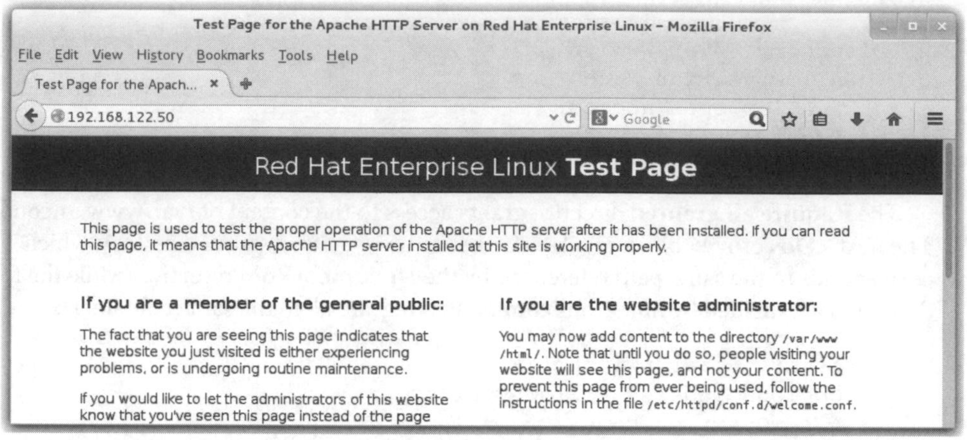

Finally, the **Listen** directive defines the IP address and TCP/IP port for this server. For example, the default shown next means that this server will work with every client that requests a web page from any of the IP addresses of your server on the standard TCP/IP port, 80:

```
Listen 80
```

If more than one IP address is available on the local system, the **Listen** directive can be used to limit access to one specific IP address. For example, if a system has two network cards with IP addresses 192.168.0.200/24 and 192.168.122.1/24, the following directive can help limit access to systems on the 192.168.122.0/24 network:

```
Listen 192.168.122.1:80
```

exam watch

The RHCE objectives suggest that you need to be ready to configure regular HTTP and secure HTTPS websites.

For secure websites, there's a second **Listen** directive in the ssl.conf file in the /etc/httpd/conf.d directory. The data from this file is automatically incorporated into the overall Apache configuration, courtesy of a directive described in Exercise 14-2. It includes the following directive, which points to the default secure HTTP (HTTPS) port for TCP/IP, 443:

```
Listen 443 https
```

███ **EXERCISE 14-2** ███

The Apache Welcome and the noindex.html Story

In this exercise, you'll trace the story behind the standard test page associated with the Apache web server, like that shown in Figure 14-6. This exercise assumes the httpd package is already installed and the Apache service is running. You'll also see what happens when the path to that web page is broken, with an index of a bunch of test files in the /var/www/html directory.

1. Open the httpd.conf file in the /etc/httpd/conf directory. Find the following line:

   ```
   IncludeOptional conf.d/*.conf
   ```

   The **IncludeOptional conf.d/*.conf** directive includes the contents of *.conf files from the /etc/httpd/conf.d directory in the Apache configuration. Exit from the httpd.conf file.

2. Navigate to the /etc/httpd/conf.d directory. Open the welcome.conf file.

3. Identify and make a note of the parameters of the **Alias** directive.

4. Note the **ErrorDocument** page. While it points to the /.noindex.html file, that's based on the aforementioned **Alias** directive. In other words, you should be able to find the index.html file in the /usr/share/httpd/noindex directory.

5. Take a look at the /usr/share/httpd/noindex/index.html file. To open it up in the ELinks browser, run the **elinks /usr/share/httpd/noindex/index.html** command. The web page that appears should now be familiar.

6. Exit from the browser. Move the welcome.conf file from the /etc/httpd/conf.d directory to a backup location.

7. Reload the Apache configuration with the **systemctl reload httpd** command.

8. Navigate to the localhost system with the **elinks http://127.0.0.1** command. What do you see?

9. Open a second terminal, navigate to the /var/www/html directory, and run the **touch test{1,2,3,4}** command.

10. Reload the browser in the original terminal. In ELinks, CTRL-R reloads the browser. What do you see?

11. Exit from the browser. Restore the welcome.conf file to the /etc/httpd/conf.d directory.

EXERCISE 14-3

Create a List of Files

In this exercise, you'll be setting up a list of files to share with others who access your web server. The process is fairly simple; you'll configure an appropriate firewall rule, create a subdirectory of **DocumentRoot**, fill it with several files, set up the appropriate security contexts, and activate Apache.

1. Make sure the firewall does not block access to ports 80 and 443. One way to do so is with the **firewall-cmd --list-all** command, which displays all services enabled in the default zone. Alternatively, you could use the **firewall-config** GUI tool.

2. Create a subdirectory of **DocumentRoot**, which is /var/www/html by default. For this exercise, we've created the /var/www/html/help directory.

3. Copy the files from the /var/www/manual directory:

   ```
   # cp -a /usr/share/httpd/manual/* /var/www/html/help/
   ```

4. Ensure that the Apache service is running with the following command:

   ```
   # systemctl status httpd
   ```

5. Make sure Apache starts the next time you boot:

   ```
   # systemctl enable httpd
   ```

6. Use the **ls -Zd /var/www/html** and **ls -Z /var/www/html/help** commands to review the security context for the sharing directory and copied files. If the security context doesn't already correspond to the contexts shown here, set them up with the following command:

   ```
   # restorecon -R /var/www/html/help
   ```

7. Start the ELinks browser on the local server, directed at the help/ subdirectory:

   ```
   # elinks http://127.0.0.1/help
   ```

8. Go to a remote system and try accessing the same web directory. For example, if the IP address of the local system is 192.168.122.50, navigate to http://192.168.122.50/help. If possible, try this a second time from a conventional GUI browser.

Host-Based Security

You can add the **Order, allow,** and **deny** directives to regulate access based on hostnames or IP addresses. The following standard command sequence allows access by default. It reads the **deny** directive first:

```
Order deny,allow
```

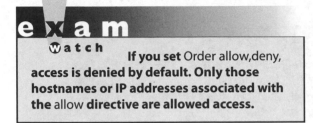

You can **deny** or **allow** from various forms of hostnames or IP addresses. For example, the following directive denies access from all computers in the mheducation.com domain:

```
Deny from mheducation.com
```

If you don't want to rely on the DNS service, you may prefer to use IP addresses. The first of the following sample directives uses a single IP address; alternatively, you can set up the 192.168.122.0 subnet in partial, netmask, or CIDR (Classless InterDomain Routing) notation, as shown here:

```
Deny from 192.168.122.66
Allow from 192.168.122
Deny from 192.168.122.0/255.255.255.0
Allow from 192.168.122.0/24
```

User-Based Security

You can limit access to websites configured on the Apache server to authorized users with passwords. As described shortly, these passwords can be different from the system authentication database.

For example, to configure user-based security for the website described in Exercise 14-3, you'll need to set up a **<Directory>** container on the /var/www/html/help directory. You'll want several commands in the **<Directory>** container:

- To set up basic authentication, you'll need an **AuthType Basic** directive.
- To describe the site to requesting users, you can include an **AuthName "*some comment*"** directive.
- To refer to a web server password database named /etc/httpd/webpass, you'll need a **AuthUserFile /etc/httpd/webpass** directive.
- To limit the site to a single user named engineer1, you could add a **Require user engineer1** directive.
- Alternatively, to limit the site to a group as defined in /etc/httpd/webgroups, you'd add the **AuthGroupFile /etc/httpd/webgroups** directive. You would also need a directive such as **Require group *design***, where *design* is the name of the group specified in webgroups.

FIGURE 14-7 Password protection for a website

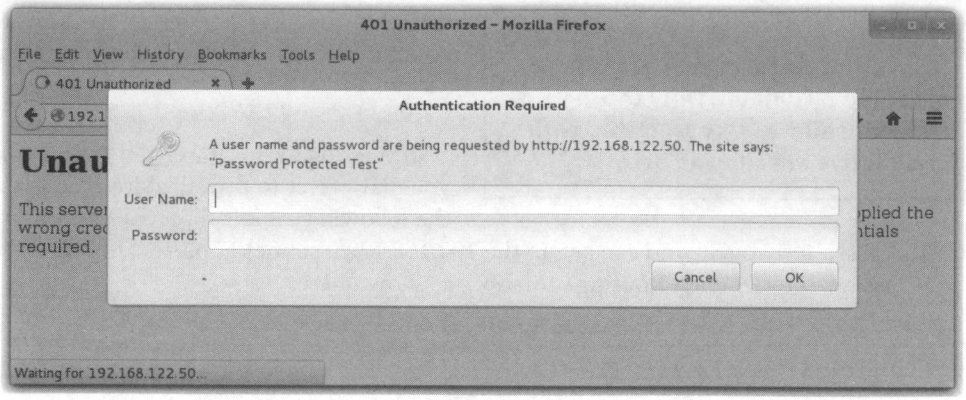

Here's an example of code that we've added after the **<Virtual Host>** container:

```
<Directory "/var/www/html/help">
    AuthType Basic
    AuthName "Password Protected Test"
    AuthUserFile /etc/httpd/webpass
    Require user engineer1
</Directory>
```

With this configuration in place, Figure 14-7 illustrates the username/password prompt that appears when you access the http://server1.example.com/help website in a regular web browser. To authenticate, you will also need to create a local password database for Apache. We'll cover this topic in the next section and in Exercise 14-4.

CERTIFICATION OBJECTIVE 14.03

Specialized Apache Directories

In this section, you'll explore several options for specialized Apache directories. It may be appropriate to set up specialized security for some of these directories with the .htaccess file. As suggested earlier, you can set up password protection based on users and groups, which corresponds to the "private directories" cited in the RHCE objectives. One example preconfigured for a private home directory is shown in the conf.d/userdir.conf file. With the right options, such directories can also be managed by members of a group.

Once any changes are made to the Apache configuration files, you may want to test the result. To do so you could run the **systemctl restart httpd** command. Alternatively, to make Apache reload the configuration file without kicking off any currently connected users, run the **systemctl reload httpd** command, which is functionally equivalent to **apachectl graceful**.

Control Through the .htaccess File

With all of the complexity associated with the httpd.conf file, you might look at the .htaccess file and think, "Great, one more complication." But used correctly, the .htaccess file can simplify the list of directives applied to a directory, or a virtual host, because it can be used to override inherited permissions. To do so, you'll need to include the following command in targeted **<Directory>** containers:

```
AllowOverride Options
```

Then you can configure .htaccess files to override previously set directory options. The .htaccess file can be stored in any web directory, labeled with the httpd_sys_content_t SELinux type.

Password-Protected Access

To configure passwords for a website, you need to create a separate database of usernames and passwords. Just as the **useradd** and **passwd** commands are used for regular users, the **htpasswd** command is used to set up usernames and passwords for Apache.

For example, to create a database file named webpass in the /etc/httpd directory, start with the following command:

```
# htpasswd -c /etc/httpd/webpass engineer1
```

The **-c** switch creates the specified file, and the first user is engineer1. You're prompted to enter a password for engineer1. Users in the webpass database do not need to have a regular Linux account. Note the use of the **ServerRoot** directory (/etc/httpd). It's also helpful when configuring virtual hosts.

If you want to add more users to this authentication database, leave out the **-c** switch. For example, the following command sets up a second account for user drafter1:

```
# htpasswd /etc/httpd/webpass drafter1
```

To set up access for more than one user, you may also want to create a group file. For example, to set up the engineer1 and drafter1 users as a group named design, you could add the following line to the /etc/httpd/grouppass file:

```
design: engineer1 drafter1
```

In this case, the AuthUserFile directive would be associated with the /etc/httpd/webpass authentication database, and the AuthGroupFile directive would be associated with the group database.

Home Directory Access

The default /etc/httpd/conf.d/userdir.conf file includes commented suggestions that can enable access to user home directories. One useful option is access to a user's home directory. You can start to set up access to user home directories by changing the following directives from

```
UserDir disabled
#UserDir public_html
```

to

```
#UserDir disabled
UserDir public_html
```

Then anyone will have access to web pages that a user puts in his or her ~/public_html directory. For example, a user named michael can create a /home/michael/public_html directory and add the web pages of his choice.

However, this requires a bit of a security compromise; you need to make michael's home directory executable for all users. This is also known as *701 permissions,* which can be configured with the following command:

```
# chmod 701 /home/michael
```

You'll also need to make the public_html subdirectory executable by all users in the same way with the following command:

```
# chmod 701 /home/michael/public_html
```

But that entails some security risks. Even though a malicious hacker might not be able to directly read the contents of the noted directories, if he sees a script through the resulting website, he'd be able to execute that script as any logged-in user.

There is one alternative for filesystems with Access Control List (ACL) support (see Chapter 4). You could create ACLs on the noted directories specifically for the user named apache. For user michael and his home directory, you could run the following commands:

```
# setfacl -m u:apache:x /home/michael
# setfacl -m u:apache:x /home/michael/public_html
```

Whether permissions are set directly or through ACLs, the logical next step as a web server is to add an index.html file to this directory. For our purposes, it can be a text file.

FIGURE 14-8

View the index .html file for user Michael.

The commented container that follows is one excellent way to help keep home directories thus shared a bit more secure.

In addition, SELinux must be configured to "Allow HTTPD To Read Home Directories," associated with the httpd_enable_homedirs boolean. You can activate that option either with the SELinux Administration tool or with the **setsebool -P httpd_enable_homedirs 1** command.

At that point, a web server that's directed to user michael's directory can read an index .html file in the public_html subdirectory. Figure 14-8 illustrates the result, where the noted text is the only content of index.html. Note that users' public_html directories are accessible at the URL http://servername/~*user*, where *user* is the corresponding username.

Of course, additional settings are included in the userdir.conf file. The container that starts with the following line supports additional levels of access to the public_html subdirectory of all users' home directories:

```
<Directory "/home/*/public_html">
```

The AllowOverride directive allows users to set an .htaccess file to override the default server settings related to document types (FileInfo); access associated with authorization directives (AuthConfig); access secured by directives such as Allow, Deny, and Order; and to override the default directory indexing settings.

```
AllowOverride FileInfo AuthConfig Limit Indexes
```

The Options directive configures what can be seen in a specific directory, based on content negotiation (MultiViews), a list of files in the current directory (Indexes), an option that allows symbolic links only if associated with the same owner (SymLinksIfOwnerMatch), and also activates an option that does not allow scripts (IncludesNoExec). While it may be a bad security practice to allow a script in a user directory, it may be appropriate for users who are developers on test systems, and possibly during a Red Hat exam. In that case, you would remove the IncludesNoExec option:

```
Options MultiViews Indexes SymLinksIfOwnerMatch IncludesNoExec
```

The Require directive limits access only to the listed HTTP methods:

```
Require method GET POST OPTIONS
```

You could combine these directives with password protection. One straightforward possibility is to require the username and password of the user whose home directory is being shared. But as noted earlier, the authentication database generated by **htpasswd** is unrelated to the shadow password suite. You can use the Apache module mod_authnz_ldap if you want to implement authentication and authorization against an LDAP directory. However, this is outside the scope of the RHCE exam.

Group-Managed Directories

You can combine the features of group directories discussed in Chapter 8 with the public_html/ subdirectory just described. However, the steps required to set up a group to manage shared web content are somewhat different. Specifically, to set up a group-managed directory, it's best to start that group as a user. The standard Apache configuration directives for a private user can apply to private groups. Conceptually, you'd take the following steps:

1. Create a regular user.
2. Set up that user with a higher UID and GID number, beyond those associated with existing local and network users.
3. Configure the home directory of that user with the user nobody as the owner. Set up the login shell of that user as /sbin/nologin.
4. Create the public_html subdirectory.
5. Change permissions for the group home directory, with associated subdirectories, to be consistent with the group requirements described in Chapter 8, along with the requirements of the Apache web server. For example, if the new group directory is /home/design, you'd run the following command:

```
# chmod -R 2771 /home/design
```

Of course, as discussed in Chapter 8, you could substitute an executable ACL restricted to the user named apache for the execute bit for all users. In that case, you'd run the following commands:

```
# chmod -R 2770 /home/design
# setfacl -m u:apache:x /home/design
# setfacl -m u:apache:x /home/design/public_html
```

6. Log in as a user member of the new group. Create a new file in the public_html subdirectory. Check the ownership of that file; with the Super Group ID (SGID) bit included in the **chmod** command, the group owner should be the owner of all files created in the public_html subdirectory.

7. Make the changes described earlier in this chapter in the httpd.conf file associated with the **UserDir** directive.

8. Make the Apache web server reread the file.

You will have a chance to set this up in one of the chapter labs.

EXERCISE 14-4

Password Protection for a Web Directory

In this exercise, you'll configure password protection for your regular user account on a subdirectory of **DocumentRoot**. This involves the use of the **AuthType Basic**, **AuthName**, and **AuthUserFile** directives. This will be done with the standard Apache website; virtual hosts are covered in the next major section.

1. Back up the main configuration file, httpd.conf, from the /etc/httpd/conf directory. Then open up that file in a text editor.

2. Navigate below the line **<Directory "/var/www/html">**. Create a new container for a **DocumentRoot** subdirectory. One option is the /var/www/html/chapter directory. The first and last directives in the stanza would look like this:

```
<Directory "/var/www/html/chapter">
</Directory>
```

3. Add the following directives: **AuthType Basic** to set up basic authentication, the **AuthName "Password Protected Test"** directive to configure a comment that you should see shortly, and the **AuthUserFile /etc/httpd/testpass** directive to point to a password file. Substitute your regular username for *testuser* in **Require user *testuser***.

```
<Directory "/var/www/html/chapter">
    AuthType Basic
    AuthName "Password Protected Test"
    AuthUserFile /etc/httpd/testpass
    Require user testuser
</Directory>
```

4. Check the syntax of your changes with either of the following commands:

```
# httpd -t
# httpd -S
```

5. Assuming the syntax checks out, make Apache reread the configuration files:

```
# systemctl reload httpd
```

6. Add an appropriate index.html file to the /var/www/html/chapter directory. It's okay to use a text editor to enter a simple line such as "test was successful." No HTML coding is required.

7. Create the /etc/httpd/testpass file with an appropriate password. On our systems, we created a web password for users michael and alex in the noted file with the following commands:

```
# htpasswd -c /etc/httpd/testpass michael
# htpasswd /etc/httpd/testpass alex
```

If you're adding another user, leave out the **-c** switch.

8. Test the result, preferably from another system. (In other words, make sure the firewall allows access from at least one remote system.)

9. You should now see a request for a username and password, with the comment associated with the **AuthName** directive. Enter the username and password just added to /etc/httpd/testpass and observe the result.

10. Close the browser, and restore any earlier configuration.

CERTIFICATION OBJECTIVE 14.04

Regular and Secure Virtual Hosts

Perhaps the most useful feature of Apache is its ability to handle multiple websites on a single IP address. In a world where there are virtually no more new IPv4 addresses available, this can be useful. To do so, you can configure virtual hosts for regular websites as separate configuration files in the /etc/httpd/conf.d directory. In that way, you can configure multiple domain names such as www.example.com and www.mheducation .com on the same IP address on the same Apache server. This is referred as "name-based" virtual hosting.

Conversely, you can configure a different IP address for each virtual host. This is known as "IP-based" virtual hosting. Both approaches are valid, although name-based virtual hosting is usually preferred because it can significantly reduce your public IP requirements.

on the
job

The example.com, example.org, and example.net domain names cannot be registered and are officially reserved by the Internet Engineering Task Force (IETF) for documentation. Many other example.* domains are also reserved by appropriate authorities.

In the same fashion, you can create multiple secure websites accessible through the HTTPS protocol. While the details vary, the basic directives associated with both regular and secure virtual hosts are the same.

If you use the ELinks text-based browser to test the connection to the regular and secure virtual websites created in this chapter, there are several things to keep in mind:

- Make sure the /etc/hosts file of the client systems includes the IP address with the specified fully qualified domain names (FQDNs). IP addresses with different FQDNs are normal. (If there's a DNS server for the local network, you can skip this step.)
- Open the /etc/elinks.conf configuration file, and set the first directive in that file to 0, to disable certificate verification.
- To access a regular website, make sure to include the protocol in front of the FQDN, such as http://vhost1.example.com or https://vhost2.example.com.

The beauty of **VirtualHost** is that you can copy virtually the same container to create as many websites on an Apache server, limited only by the capabilities of the hardware. All that's required is one IP address. The next virtual host can be set up with a copy of the original **VirtualHost** container. All that you absolutely have to change for name-based virtual hosts is the **ServerName**. Most administrators will also change the **DocumentRoot**, but even that's not absolutely necessary. You'll see how that works for regular and secure virtual hosts in the following sections.

e**x**a**m**
watch　　　**Be prepared to create multiple websites on an Apache web server using virtual hosts. It's best to create separate** VirtualHost **containers in different configuration files for this purpose.**

The Standard Virtual Host

In RHEL 6, the default httpd.conf included sample directives that could be used to create one or more virtual hosts. This is not the case anymore, so if you forget the syntax to create a new virtual host, you may look at the Apache documentation at http://localhost/manual/vhosts.

As noted earlier, the **IncludeOptional conf.d/*.conf** directive automatically includes information from *.conf files in that directory. With that in mind, create and edit a vhost-dummy.conf file in the /etc/httpd/conf.d directory.

Then, add a **<Directory>** container to grant access to the content files of the website. The following example assumes that the new host is named dummy-host.example.com and that the website content is located in the directory /srv/dummy-host/www:

```
<Directory "/srv/dummy-host/www">
    Require all granted
</Directory>
```

Next, add a container for the virtual host configuration:

```
<VirtualHost *:80>
    ServerAdmin webmaster@dummy-host.example.com
    DocumentRoot /srv/dummy-host/www
    ServerName dummy-host.example.com
    ServerAlias www.dummy-host.example.com
    ErrorLog logs/dummy-host.example.com-error_log
    CustomLog logs/dummy-host.example.com-access_log common
</VirtualHost>
```

Port 80 is the default for serving web pages. You could also substitute **<VirtualHost 192.168.122.50:80>**, but in general you can leave that directive as is to support the use of the same IP address for different websites.

If you've read the descriptions of the first two sections of the main part of the httpd .conf file, you should recognize most of these directives. However, each directive points to nonstandard files and directories. To review:

- The e-mail address defined by **ServerAdmin** is included in all error messages that are returned to clients.

- The web pages can be stored in the **DocumentRoot** directory. Make sure the SELinux security contexts of any **DocumentRoot** directory you create are consistent with the contexts of the default /var/www directory (and subdirectories). Apply the **restorecon** and **semanage fcontext -a** commands, as required, to make the security contexts match. Note that by default the SELinux policy already marks the files in /srv/*/www with the httpd_sys_content_t type.

- Based on the **ServerName** directive, Apache knows that requests to http://dummy-host.example.com must use the configuration declared in this <VirtualHost> block.

- **ServerAlias** specifies additional names that the virtual host can be reached as.

- The **ErrorLog** and **CustomLog** directives specify a *relative* log directory, relative to the **ServerRoot**. These files can be found in the /etc/httpd/logs directory. Normally, that directory is soft linked to /var/logs/httpd.

You can add more directives to each virtual host container, to customize the settings for the virtual host relative to the main configuration file. You'll set up a CGI script in a virtual host later in this chapter, with some custom directives.

It's easy to configure a virtual host website. Substitute the IP domain names, directories, files, and e-mail addresses of your choice. Create the **DocumentRoot** directory if it doesn't already exist. To that end, we've set up two virtual hosts with the following containers:

```
<Directory "/srv/vhost1.example.com/www">
    Require all granted
</Directory>
<VirtualHost *:80>
    ServerAdmin webmaster@vhost1.example.com
    DocumentRoot /srv/vhost1.example.com/www
    ServerName vhost1.example.com
    ErrorLog logs/vhost1.example.com-error_log
    CustomLog logs/vhost1.example.com-access_log common
</VirtualHost>

<Directory "/srv/vhost2.example.com/www">
    Require all granted
</Directory>
<VirtualHost *:80>
    ServerAdmin webmaster@vhost2.example.com
    DocumentRoot /srv/vhost2.example.com/www
    ServerName vhost2.example.com
    ErrorLog logs/vhost2.example.com-error_log
    CustomLog logs/vhost2.example.com-access_log common
</VirtualHost>
```

Don't forget to set up the /etc/hosts file, or a DNS server for the local network, with the IP addresses for the virtual host domain names described so far (dummy-host.example.com, vhost1.example.com, and vhost2.example.com).

You should also make sure the SELinux contexts are appropriate. You can test the syntax of any configuration changes with the following command:

```
# httpd -t
```

Apache will verify your configuration or identify specific problems. When you run this command on the default configuration, you'll get the following message:

```
Syntax OK
```

If you've created multiple virtual hosts, you can check them as well with either of the following commands:

```
# httpd -S
# httpd -D DUMP_VHOSTS
```

The output should list the default and individual virtual hosts. For example, we see the following output from our server1.example.com RHEL 7 system:

```
VirtualHost configuration:
*:443                is a NameVirtualHost
  default server server1.example.com (/etc/httpd/conf.d/ssl.conf:56)
  port 443 namevhost server1.example.com (/etc/httpd/conf.d/ssl.conf:56)
wildcard NameVirtualHosts and _default_ servers:
*:80                 is a NameVirtualHost
  default server vhost1.example.com (/etc/httpd/conf.d/vhost1.conf:1)
  port 80 namevhost vhost1.example.com (/etc/httpd/conf.d/vhost1.conf:1)
  port 80 namevhost vhost2.example.com (/etc/httpd/conf.d/vhost2.conf:1)
```

Secure Virtual Hosts

If you're configuring a secure web server that conforms to the HTTPS protocol, Red Hat provides a different configuration file for this purpose: ssl.conf in the /etc/httpd/conf.d directory. If this file isn't available, you need to install the mod_ssl package. Before editing this file, back it up.

The first directive in ssl.conf ensures that the server listens on TCP port 443:

```
Listen 443 https
```

As suggested by the title, this configuration file includes a number of other SSL/TLS directives. Generally, no changes are required to the following lines:

```
SSLPassPhraseDialog exec:/usr/libexec/httpd-ssl-pass-dialog
SSLSessionCache         shmcb:/run/httpd/sslcache(512000)
SSLSessionCacheTimeout  300
SSLRandomSeed startup file:/dev/urandom  256
SSLRandomSeed connect builtin
SSLCryptoDevice builtin
```

Now you can set up virtual hosts with the directives that follow. The default ssl.conf file also has a default virtual host container, but it is a bit difficult to read with all of the comments. Therefore, a sample of the revised configuration file, focused on the virtual host container for the vhost1.example.com system, is shown in Figure 14-9. You can edit directly the ssl.conf file, although as a best practice it is recommended to use a separate configuration file in /etc/httpd/conf.d for each virtual host.

In the default version of the ssl.conf file, examine the **<VirtualHost _default_:443>** container. Compare it to the **<VirtualHost *:80>** container in the previous standard virtual hosts configuration. Some changes are required. First, you should replace **_default_** in the **VirtualHost** container with an asterisk (*):

```
<VirtualHost *:443>
```

FIGURE 14-9

Secure virtual
host container for
vhost1.example.com

```
<VirtualHost *:443>
        ServerAdmin webmaster@vhost1.example.com
        DocumentRoot /srv/vhost1.example.com/www
        ServerName vhost1.example.com

        ErrorLog logs/vhost1_ssl_error_log
        TransferLog logs/vhost1_ssl_access_log
        LogLevel warn

        SSLEngine on
        SSLProtocol all -SSLv2
        SSLCipherSuite HIGH:MEDIUM:!aNULL:!MD5
        SSLCertificateFile /etc/pki/tls/certs/localhost.crt
        SSLCertificateKeyFile /etc/pki/tls/private/localhost.key

        <Files ~ "\.(cgi|shtml|phtml|php3?)$">
            SSLOptions +StdEnvVars
        </Files>
        <Directory "/var/www/cgi-bin">
            SSLOptions +StdEnvVars
        </Directory>

        BrowserMatch "MSIE [2-5]" \
                nokeepalive ssl-unclean-shutdown \
                downgrade-1.0 force-response-1.0

        CustomLog logs/ssl_request_log \
                "%t %h %{SSL_PROTOCOL}x %{SSL_CIPHER}x \"%r\" %b"

</VirtualHost>
```

Don't forget to add the https service to the default zone on the firewall:

```
# firewall-cmd --permanent --add-service=https
# firewall-cmd --reload
```

In the ssl.conf file, you should also include **ServerAdmin**, **DocumentRoot**, and **ServerName** directives. Examples of directives that would be consistent with the virtual hosts created in the preceding section include the following:

```
ServerAdmin webmaster@vhost1.example.com
DocumentRoot /srv/vhost1.example.com/www
ServerName vhost1.example.com
```

While the **DocumentRoot** directive can be set to any directory, it's appropriate for organizational purposes to keep the files associated with each virtual host in a dedicated directory.

The standard error log directives can be changed. In fact, if you want log information for each secure website to be set up in different files, they should be changed, as shown next.

Based on the **ServerRoot** directive from the httpd.conf file, these log files can be found in the /var/log/httpd directory.

```
ErrorLog logs/vhost1_ssl_error_log
TransferLog logs/vhost1_ssl_access_log
LogLevel warn
CustomLog logs/vhost1_ssl_request_log \
         "%t %h %{SSL_PROTOCOL}x %{SSL_CIPHER}x \"%r\" %b"
```

The TLS directives in the file are based on the default certificates for the localhost system. Shortly, you'll see how to configure a new TLS certificate. The following five directives, in order, activate SSL/TLS, disable the insecure SSL version 2, support a variety of encryption ciphers, and point to the default TLS certificate as well as the TLS key file:

```
SSLEngine on
SSLProtocol all -SSLv2
SSLCipherSuite HIGH:MEDIUM:!aNULL:!MD5
SSLCertificateFile /etc/pki/tls/certs/localhost.crt
SSLCertificateKeyFile /etc/pki/tls/private/localhost.key
```

The container that follows relates to files with extensions associated with dynamic content. For such files, along with any files in the standard CGI directory, standard SSL environment variables are used:

```
<Files ~ "\.(cgi|shtml|phtml|php3?)$">
    SSLOptions +StdEnvVars
</Files>
<Directory "/var/www/cgi-bin">
    SSLOptions +StdEnvVars
</Directory>
```

The following container deals with situations associated with clients running legacy versions of the Microsoft Internet Explorer browser:

```
BrowserMatch "MSIE [2-5]" \
         nokeepalive ssl-unclean-shutdown \
         downgrade-1.0 force-response-1.0
```

Of course, the virtual host container ends with the following directive:

```
</VirtualHost>
```

You do not need to apply all the directives just listed to a new TLS-based virtual host. A minimal configuration is shown next. This includes **DocumentRoot**, **ServerName**, and the directives that enable TLS and configure the certificate path:

```
<VirtualHost *:443>
    DocumentRoot /srv/vhost1.example.com/www
    ServerName vhost1.example.com
```

```
        SSLEngine on
        SSLCertificateFile /etc/pki/tls/certs/vhost1.example.com.crt
        SSLCertificateKeyFile /etc/pki/tls/private/vhost1.example.com.key
    </VirtualHost>
```

When Apache is configured with an untrusted certificate, regular clients that access that site get a warning about the secure web host, as shown in Figure 14-10. In the next session you will see how to generate a certificate request to be signed by a certificate authority.

Create a New TLS Certificate

While the default TLS certificate listed in the ssl.conf configuration file can work for basic configuration, you may want to either create a customized self-signed certificate or otherwise use an actual certificate signed from a reputable certificate authority (CA) such as VeriSign or Thawte. Navigate to the /etc/pki/tls/certs directory. Note the file named

FIGURE 14-10 A warning about secure hosts

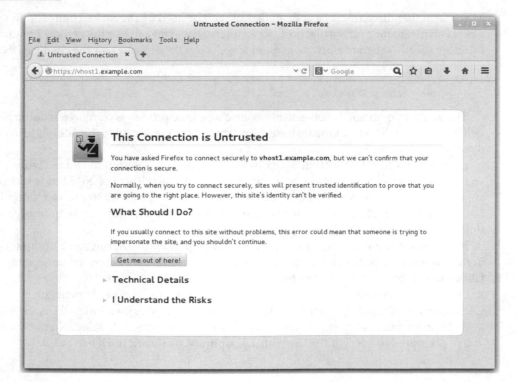

FIGURE 14-11

Generate a self-signed certificate.

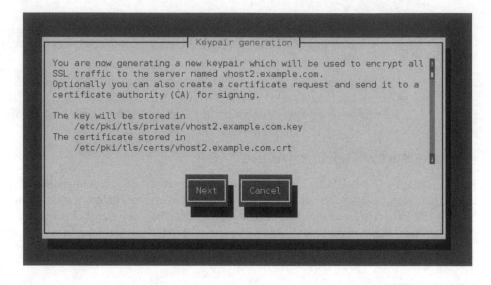

```
┤ Keypair generation ├
You are now generating a new keypair which will be used to encrypt all
SSL traffic to the server named vhost2.example.com.
Optionally you can also create a certificate request and send it to a
certificate authority (CA) for signing.

The key will be stored in
    /etc/pki/tls/private/vhost2.example.com.key
The certificate stored in
    /etc/pki/tls/certs/vhost2.example.com.crt


                    Next        Cancel
```

Makefile in that directory. The code in that file can be used by the **make** command to create a new certificate for each virtual host. As an alternative, you can use the **genkey** command to automatically generate a private key and a "self-signed certificate" for the cited FQDN, as shown in Figure 14-11.

```
# genkey vhost2.example.com
```

The **genkey** command is convenient because when the process is complete, it automatically writes the key to the /etc/pki/tls/private directory and the certificate to the /etc/pki/tls/certs directory.

For the purpose of this section, select Next to continue. In the step shown in Figure 14-12, you'd select a key size. In a production environment, the default size of 2048 bits is usually appropriate. But in an exam context, you may want to select a smaller size to save time. The Linux random number generator may require additional activity; this may be an excellent time to put the process aside and do something else.

If you have nothing else to do and need to speed up the process, run some of the scripts in the /etc/cron.daily directory. Run some of the **find** commands described in Chapter 3. Click a bunch of times in an open terminal.

Once a key is generated, you're prompted with a question: whether to generate a Certificate Request (CSR) to send to a CA. Unless you run your own internal CA or you're actually preparing to purchase a signed certificate from a public CA, select No to continue. You're prompted to encrypt the key with a passphrase, as shown in Figure 14-13.

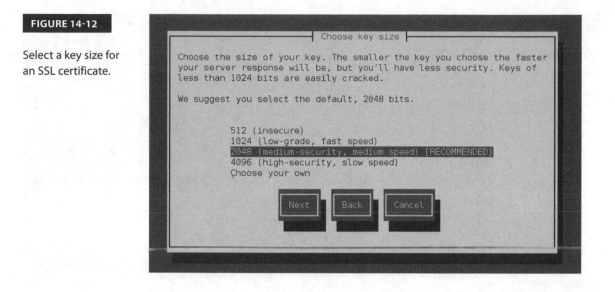

FIGURE 14-12

Select a key size for
an SSL certificate.

If security is most important, you should select the Encrypt the Private Key option. If
speed is important, avoid the option. Make a choice and select Next to continue. If you did
not select the Encrypt the Private Key option, you'll be taken immediately to the certificate
details shown in Figure 14-14. Make any appropriate changes and select Next to continue.
If successful, you'll see output similar to that shown in Figure 14-15.

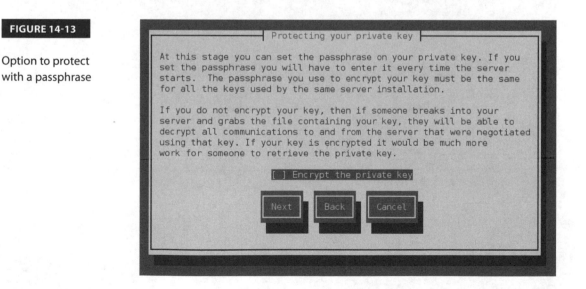

FIGURE 14-13

Option to protect
with a passphrase

FIGURE 14-14

SSL certificate details

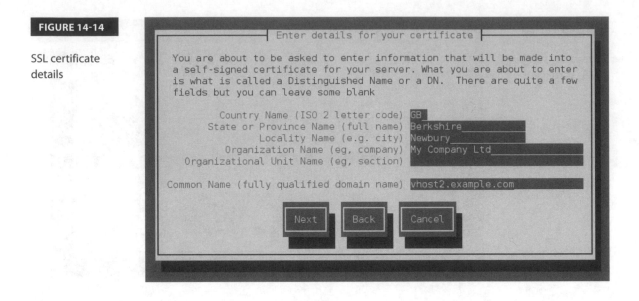

```
┌──────────────┤ Enter details for your certificate ├──────────────┐

   You are about to be asked to enter information that will be made into
   a self-signed certificate for your server. What you are about to enter
   is what is called a Distinguished Name or a DN.  There are quite a few
   fields but you can leave some blank


               Country Name (ISO 2 letter code) GB
             State or Province Name (full name) Berkshire
                      Locality Name (e.g. city) Newbury
                  Organization Name (eg, company) My Company Ltd
          Organizational Unit Name (eg, section)

      Common Name (fully qualified domain name) vhost2.example.com


                   ┌─────┐      ┌─────┐      ┌──────┐
                   │Next │      │Back │      │Cancel│
                   └─────┘      └─────┘      └──────┘
```

FIGURE 14-15

SSL certificate command output

```
[root@server1 conf.d]# genkey vhost2.example.com
/usr/bin/keyutil -c makecert -g 2048 -s "CN=vhost2.example.com, O=My Company Ltd, L=Newb
ury, ST=Berkshire, C=GB" -v 1 -a -z /etc/pki/tls/.rand.23390 -o /etc/pki/tls/certs/vhost
2.example.com.crt -k /etc/pki/tls/private/vhost2.example.com.key
cmdstr: makecert

cmd_CreateNewCert
command:  makecert
keysize = 2048 bits
subject = CN=vhost2.example.com, O=My Company Ltd, L=Newbury, ST=Berkshire, C=GB
valid for 1 months
random seed from /etc/pki/tls/.rand.23390
output will be written to /etc/pki/tls/certs/vhost2.example.com.crt
output key written to /etc/pki/tls/private/vhost2.example.com.key


Generating key. This may take a few moments...

Made a key
Opened tmprequest for writing
/usr/bin/keyutil Copying the cert pointer
Created a certificate
Wrote 1682 bytes of encoded data to /etc/pki/tls/private/vhost2.example.com.key
Wrote the key to:
/etc/pki/tls/private/vhost2.example.com.key
[root@server1 conf.d]# ▮
```

Test Pages

You may need to create some index.html files to test virtual hosts in various situations, in various pre-production configurations, or even during an exam. Fortunately, the Red Hat exams don't test knowledge of HTML. You could use Apache's default web page. You can change this or any other web page with a text- or HTML-specific editor.

You can even save a simple text file as index.html. For the purpose of this chapter, all we put into the index.html file for the regular vhost1.example.com website is the following text:

```
Test web page for Virtual Host 1
```

Once appropriate changes were made to Apache configuration files, we restarted the service. When we then ran the **elinks http://vhost1.example.com** command, the screen shown in Figure 14-16 appeared.

Syntax Checkers

In many cases, the **apachectl restart** and the **systemctl restart httpd** commands will reveal syntax problems. But that's just in many cases. In some cases, you might try to restart Apache, proceed to test the result with a client browser, and get frustrated, only to find that Apache did not start because of a syntax error. To minimize the risk of that issue, the following command checks the work that you've done to edit Apache configuration files:

```
# httpd -S
```

You can also check the log messages captured by the systemd journal:

```
# journalctl -u httpd
```

If no problems are found, you should be able to start the local web server and connect from a client with a browser request.

FIGURE 14-16

A test web page

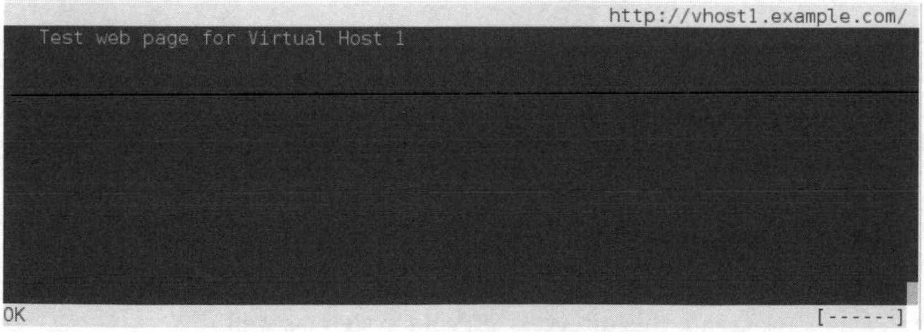

Apache Troubleshooting

When the right Apache packages are installed, the default configuration normally creates a running system. You can check basic syntax with the **httpd -t** command. But if you're setting up a real website, you probably want more than just the test page. Before making changes, back up the Apache configuration files. If something goes wrong, you can always start over.

Some Apache errors fall into the following categories:

- **Error message about an inability to bind to an address**   Another network process may already be using the default http port (80). Alternatively, Apache is configured to listen to the wrong IP address.

- **Network addressing or routing errors**   Double-check network settings. For more information on network configuration, see Chapter 3's section on network configuration and troubleshooting.

- **Apache not running**   Run **systemctl status httpd**. Check the error_log in the /var/log/httpd directory.

- **Apache not running after a reboot**   Run **systemctl is-enabled httpd**. Make sure Apache (httpd) is set to start at the appropriate target during the boot process with the command

  ```
  # systemctl enable httpd
  ```

on the **Job**

Apache administration is a necessary skill for any Linux system engineer. You should develop the ability to install, configure, and troubleshoot Apache quickly. You should also be able to set up and customize virtual websites.

EXERCISE 14-5

Set Up a Virtual Web Server

In this exercise, you'll set up a web server with a virtual website. You can use this technique with different directories to set up additional virtual websites on the same Apache server.

1. Add a virtual website for the fictional company LuvLinex, with a URL of www.example .com. Use the sample configurations from http://localhost/manual/vhosts for hints as needed. Save the configuration in the vhost-luvlinex.conf file inside the /etc/httpd/conf.d directory.

2. Assign the **DocumentRoot** directive to the /luvlinex directory. (Don't forget to create this directory on your system as well.)

3. Grant access to the files to be served using a **Require all granted** directive inside a **<Directory>** block.

4. Open the /luvlinex/index.html file in a text editor. Add a simple line in text format such as

    ```
    This is the placeholder for the LuvLinex Website.
    ```

5. Save this file.

6. If you've enabled SELinux on this system, you'll have to modify the context type and apply the **restorecon** command to the DocumentRoot directory:

    ```
    # semanage fcontext -a -t httpd_sys_content_t "/luvlinex(/.*)?"
    # restorecon -R /luvlinex
    ```

7. If you're running a DNS service, update the associated database. Otherwise, update /etc/hosts with www.example.com and the appropriate IP address.

8. If you want to check the syntax, run the **httpd -t** and **httpd -D DUMP_VHOSTS** commands.

9. Remember to restart the Apache service; the proper way is with the **systemctl restart httpd** command.

10. Ensure that the local firewall is configured to grant access to connections to the HTTP service:

    ```
    # firewall-cmd --list-all
    # firewall-cmd --permanent --add-service=http
    # firewall-cmd --reload
    ```

11. Navigate to a remote system. Update the remote /etc/hosts if appropriate. Open the browser of your choice. Test the access to the configured website (www.example.com).

12. Close the browser on the remote system. Restore the original httpd.conf configuration file.

CERTIFICATION OBJECTIVE 14.05

Deploy a Basic CGI Application

When you see the RHCE objective to "deploy a basic CGI application," the requirement is easier than it looks. In fact, the steps required can be read from the Apache documentation, available from the httpd-manual package. When the application is installed, navigate to http://localhost/manual page. Apache documentation should appear. Select CGI: Dynamic Content for detailed directions, as explained in the following sections.

Apache Configuration Changes for CGI Files

To allow Apache to read CGI files, the conf.modules.d/00-cgi.conf file includes the **LoadModule cgi_module** directive. To control which directories include scripts, Apache includes the **ScriptAlias** directive. For example, the following **ScriptAlias** directive links the /cgi-bin/ URL path to the default /var/www/cgi-bin directory:

```
ScriptAlias /cgi-bin/ "/var/www/cgi-bin"
```

With this **ScriptAlias** directive, if the website is server1.example.com, scripts can be found in the http://server1.example.com/cgi-bin/ URL.

Alternatively, you can set up CGI scripts in a directory other than /var/www/cgi-bin and change the reference accordingly. The default **<Directory>** block configuration for /var/www/cgi-bin is shown next:

```
<Directory "/var/www/cgi-bin">
    AllowOverride None
    Options None
    Require all granted
</Directory>
```

As suggested in the Apache web server documentation available from the httpd-manual package, you'd need to make changes to allow CGI scripts outside a **ScriptAlias** directory to actually be executable by the Apache server:

```
<Directory "/home/*/public_html">
    AllowOverride None
    Options ExecCGI
    AddHandler cgi-script .pl
    Require all granted
</Directory>
```

As a security measure, the **AllowOverride None** command prevents regular users from changing configuration settings in that directory using an .htaccess file. The **Options ExecCGI** line supports executable scripts in the noted directory. The **AddHandler** directive associates CGI scripts with files with the .pl extension. The **Require all granted** line grants access to the directory from all users.

If CGI scripts are required for one of the previously configured virtual hosts, you can set up a different **ScriptAlias** and a corresponding **<Directory>** container. For the vhost1.example.com site described previously, we add the following directives:

```
ScriptAlias /cgi-bin/ /srv/vhost1.example.com/cgi-bin/
<Directory "/srv/vhost1.example.com/cgi-bin">
    Options none
    Require all granted
</Directory>
```

Set Up a Simple CGI Script in Perl

The Apache documentation includes instructions on how to set up a simple CGI script in the Perl programming language. Make sure that the httpd-manual package is installed and the local httpd service is active. In a browser, navigate to http://localhost/manual. Under the "How-To / Tutorials" section, click CGI: Dynamic Content. Scroll down to the "Writing a CGI Program" section.

In this section, the Apache documentation suggests a simple Perl script, called first.pl, based on the following code:

```
#!/usr/bin/perl
print "Content-type: text/html\n\n";
print "Hello, World!";
```

Create this file in the /srv/vhost1.example.com/cgi-bin directory. The first line is similar to the **#!/bin/bash** shebang; in this case, **perl** is the command interpreter. The content type is declared, followed by two newlines (as symbolized by the **\n**). The final line prints the expression commonly used for introductory program scripts. CGI scripts need to be executable by the apache user, and are usually assigned 755 permissions. In other words, once the first.pl file is saved, you'd apply the noted permissions with the following command:

```
# chmod 755 first.pl
```

Run the **ls -Z** command on the script. In the /var/www/cgi-bin directory, it should inherit the httpd_sys_script_exec_t SELinux file type associated with the directory. If necessary, you can apply the context type to the file and directory with the **restorecon** command. If the script directory is set up in a custom directory other than /var/www/cgi-bin, make sure the file type stays applied after a SELinux relabel with the **semanage fcontext -a** command:

```
# semanage fcontext -a -t httpd_sys_script_exec_t \
'/srv/vhost1.example.com/cgi-bin(/.*)?'
```

Connections to a Website

Once a CGI script is configured, you should be able to access that script from a client browser. For the purpose of this exercise, assume the first.pl Perl script has been configured on the server1.example.com system. You should then be able to review the result from a remote system with the **elinks http://vhost1.example.com/cgi-bin/first.pl** command. If successful, the following words should show up in the body of the browser:

```
Hello, world!
```

On occasion, you may see an error message such as "Internal Server Error." The most likely cause is a Perl script that does not have executable permissions for the user named apache. To repeat, that's normally addressed by giving that Perl script 755 permissions.

SCENARIO & SOLUTION

You need to configure one website.	Install Apache; configure appropriate files in the /var/www/html directory.
You need to configure multiple websites.	With Apache, use <**VirtualHost**> containers configured in separate files within the /etc/httpd/conf.d directory.
You need to configure a secure website.	Configure a virtual host in the ssl.conf file in the /etc/httpd/conf.d directory.
You need a dedicated SSL certificate for the www.example.org website.	Run the **genkey www.example.org** command.
The Apache service is not running after a reboot.	Make sure the httpd service starts in the default target with the **systemctl enable httpd** command. If that's okay, check the contents of the error_log in the /var/log/httpd directory.
CGI scripts in Apache are not running.	In the Apache configuration file, make sure the **ScriptAlias** is pointing to the appropriate directory; if no **ScriptAlias** is configured, ensure that the **ExecCGI** option is active for the script directory and that a **AddHandler** directive specifies the proper script extension; make sure the script is executable by Apache and matches default SELinux contexts in the /var/www/cgi-bin directory.

CERTIFICATION SUMMARY

Apache is the most popular web server in use today. Key packages can be installed from the "Web Server" package group. The httpd-manual package includes a locally browsable manual that can help with other Apache configuration tasks, even during an exam. Key configuration files include httpd.conf in the /etc/httpd/conf directory and ssl.conf in the /etc/httpd/conf.d directory. With the help of sample containers in both noted configuration files, you can create regular and secure virtual hosts for multiple websites on one system, even if only one IP address is available. Related log files are stored in the /var/log/httpd directory.

You can allow access to Apache through ports 80 and 443 to some or all systems with **firewall-cmd**. Apache files and directories are associated with several different SELinux contexts. Different Apache functions may be regulated by a variety of different SELinux boolean settings.

The **Listen VirtualHost** directives direct traffic to the Apache web server to ports such as 80 and 443, along with specified virtual hosts. Host- and user-based security can also be set up within Apache configuration files with commands such as **htpasswd** and directives such as **Require, Allow**, and **Deny**.

With the right security options, user- and group-managed directories are possible. In fact, there's a commented container that can enable content in user home directories. Group-managed directories are somewhat more complex, combining aspects of Apache-based user directories and shared group directories discussed in Chapter 8. Also in security, new certificates can be created for a specific host such as www.example.org with a command like **genkey www.example.org**.

The configuration of CGI content on an Apache website is easier than it looks. In fact, detailed information on the process is provided with Apache documentation, including a Perl script that you can use to confirm that the resulting configuration works.

✔ TWO-MINUTE DRILL

Here are some of the key points from the certification objectives in Chapter 14.

The Apache Web Server

❑   Red Hat Enterprise Linux includes the Apache web server, which is currently used by more Internet websites than all other web servers combined.

❑   You can install Apache and associated packages as part of the "Web Server" package group.

❑   Apache configuration files include httpd.conf in the /etc/httpd/conf directory and ssl.conf in the /etc/httpd/conf.d directory.

❑   Log information for Apache is available in the /var/log/httpd directory.

Standard Apache Security Configuration

❑   Apache can be secured through **firewall-cmd** rules and various SELinux booleans and contexts.

❑ Apache supports security by specifying active ports through the **Listen** and **VirtualHost** directives.

❑ Apache supports host-based security by IP address or domain name.

❑ Apache supports user-based security by password, with the help of the **htpasswd** command.

Specialized Apache Directories

❑ Apache makes it easy to set up access to user home directories in their public_html/ subdirectories.

❑ Group-managed directories can be configured in a fashion similar to user home directories.

Regular and Secure Virtual Hosts

❑ You can configure multiple websites on your server, even with only one IP address. This is possible through the use of virtual hosts.

❑ The RHEL configuration supports virtual hosts for regular and secure websites, usually set up in their own configuration files within the /etc/httpd/conf.d directory.

❑ The RHEL configuration includes a default secure virtual host in the /etc/httpd/conf.d/ssl.conf file.

❑ SSL certificates can be created with the **genkey** command.

Deploy a Basic CGI Application

❑ The use of CGI content depends on configuration options such as **ScriptAlias**, **ExecCGI**, and **AddHandler cgi-script**.

❑ Standard CGI scripts need to be executable by the Apache user. If needed, sample instructions are provided in the Apache manual available from the httpd-manual package.

Q

SELF TEST

The following questions will help measure your understanding of the material presented in this chapter. As no multiple choice questions appear on the Red Hat exams, no multiple choice questions appear in this book. These questions exclusively test your understanding of the chapter. It is okay if you have another way of performing a task. Getting results, not memorizing trivia, is what counts on the Red Hat exams. There may be more than one answer to many of these questions.

The Apache Web Server

1. What is the Apache directive that specifies the base directory for configuration and log files?

    _____

2. Once you've modified httpd.conf, what command would make Apache reread this file, without kicking off currently connected users?

    _____

3. What directive specifies the TCP/IP port associated with Apache?

    _____

Standard Apache Security Configuration

4. What command creates the /etc/httpd/passwords file and configures a password for user elizabeth?

    _____

5. If you see the following directives limiting access within the container for a virtual host, what computers are allowed access?

    ```
    Order Allow,Deny
    Allow from 192.168.0.0/24
    ```

    _____

6. What standard services do you need to open in FirewallD to allow access to a regular website and a secure one?

    _____

Specialized Apache Directories

7. What regular permissions would work with a home directory that's shared via Apache?

   _____

8. What regular permissions would work with a shared group directory that's also shared via Apache?

   _____

Regular and Secure Virtual Hosts

9. What file does RHEL provide to help configure a virtual host as a secure server?

   _____

10. If you're creating a name-based virtual host, how many IP addresses would be required for three virtual servers?

   _____

11. To verify the configuration of one or more virtual hosts, what switch can you use with the **httpd** command?

   _____

Deploy a Basic CGI Application

12. What option with the **Options** directive supports dynamic CGI content in an Apache configuration file?

   _____

LAB QUESTIONS

Several of these labs involve configuration exercises. You should do these exercises on test machines only. It's assumed that you're running these exercises on virtual machines such as KVM. For this chapter, it's also assumed that you may be changing the configuration of a physical host system for such virtual machines.

Red Hat presents its exams electronically. For that reason, the labs in this and future chapters are available from the media that accompanies the book, in the Chapter14/ subdirectory. In case you haven't yet set up RHEL 7 on a system, refer to Chapter 1 for installation instructions.

The answers for each lab follow the Self Test answers for the fill-in-the-blank questions.

SELF TEST ANSWERS

The Apache Web Server

1. The **ServerRoot** directive sets the default directory for the Apache server. Any files and directories not otherwise configured—or configured as a relative directory—are set relative to **ServerRoot**.

2. There are two basic ways to make Apache reread the configuration file without restarting the service. You can keep Apache running and make it reread the file with a command such as **apachectl graceful** or **systemctl reload httpd**. The **kill -HUP $(cat /run/httpd/httpd.pid)** command is also an acceptable answer.

3. The **Listen** directive specifies the TCP port associated with Apache.

Standard Apache Security Configuration

4. The command that creates the /etc/httpd/passwords file and configures a password for user elizabeth is **htpasswd -c /etc/httpd/passwords elizabeth**. If /etc/httpd/passwords already exists, all that's required is **htpasswd /etc/httpd/passwords elizabeth**.

5. As described in the chapter, the **Order Allow,Deny** directive denies access to all systems by default, except those explicitly allowed access. Therefore, access is limited to computers on the 192.168.0.0/24 network.

6. The standard services you need to open in FirewallD to allow access to regular and secure websites are http and https.

Specialized Apache Directories

7. The associated permissions are 701, executable permissions for other users. As "regular permissions" are specified, ACLs are not an option.

8. The associated permissions are 2771, which combine SGID permissions, rwx permissions for a shared group directory, and executable permissions for other users. As "regular permissions" are specified, ACLs are not an option.

Regular and Secure Virtual Hosts

9.   The file associated with secure servers for virtual hosts is ssl.conf in the /etc/httpd/conf.d directory.

10. One IP address is required for a name-based virtual server, no matter how many virtual sites are configured.

11. To check your configuration of virtual hosts, you can use one of two switches with the **httpd** command: **httpd -S** checks the configuration file, including virtual host settings. Alternatively, **httpd -D DUMP_VHOSTS** focuses on the virtual host configuration, and is therefore also an acceptable answer.

Deploy a Basic CGI Application

12. The **Options ExecCGI** directive is commonly used in Apache-configured directories that contain CGI scripts such as Perl programs.

LAB ANSWERS

Lab 1

First, make sure the Apache web server is installed. If an **rpm -q httpd** command tells you that it is missing, the Web Server package group has not yet been installed. The most efficient way to do so is with the **yum group install "Web Server"** command. (To find appropriate package group names, run the **yum group list hidden** command.) This assumes a proper connection to a repository, as discussed in Chapter 7.

To start Apache, run the **systemctl start httpd** command. To make sure it starts the next time the system is booted, run the **systemctl enable httpd** command.

Once Apache is installed, you should be able to access it from a browser via http://localhost. From the default Apache configuration file, you can verify that the **DocumentRoot** points to the /var/www/html directory. You can then copy the index.html file from the /usr/share/doc/HTML/en-US directory to the /var/www/html directory. Then you can test the result by navigating once again to http://localhost. If you did not copy the other files associated with the default home page, the display will be missing some icons, but that's not an issue for this lab.

Lab 2

This is an informational lab. When it is complete, you should be able to refer to these Apache configuration hints in situations where this book and the Internet are not available, such as during a Red Hat exam.

Of course, you should study these tips in advance. If you forget the syntax of one or two commands, these files can be a lifesaver.

Lab 3

This lab requires that you create two virtual hosts. While there are certainly other methods to set up different virtual hosts, the description in this lab answer is one method—and it is important that you know at least one method to create a virtual host. One way to make this happen is with the following steps:

1. The **ServerRoot** directive for the system sets the default directory for the Apache server. Any files and directories not otherwise configured—or configured as relative paths—are set relative to **ServerRoot**. Don't change this setting.

2. In the /etc/httpd/conf.d directory, create two files named vhost-big.conf and vhost-small.conf for the configuration of the two virtual hosts.

3. Add a separate **VirtualHost** containers with settings appropriate for the big.example.com virtual host.

4. Assign the **ServerAdmin** to the e-mail address of this website's administrator.

5. Configure a unique **DocumentRoot** directory for big.example.com.

6. Set the first **ServerName** to big.example.com.

7. Add **ErrorLog** and **CustomLog** directives and set them to unique filenames in the /etc/httpd/logs directory (which is linked to the /var/logs/httpd directory). With the default **ServerRoot**, you can use a relative path such as the following:

```
ErrorLog logs/big.example.com-error.log
CustomLog logs/big.example.com-access.log combined
```

8. Make sure to close the **VirtualHost** container (with a **</VirtualHost>** directive at the end of the container).

9. Add a **<Directory>** container to grant access to the directory that you have configured as the **DocumentRoot**:

```
<Directory "/srv/vhost-big/www">
    Require all granted
</Directory>
```

10. Repeat the process for the second website, making sure to set the second **ServerName** to **small.example.com**.

11. Close and save the configuration files with your changes.

12. Create any new directories that you configured with the **DocumentRoot** directives.

13. Create index.html text files in each directory defined by the associated new **DocumentRoot** directives. Don't worry about HTML code; a text file is fine for the purpose of this lab.

14. Make sure these domain names are configured in a local DNS server or in the /etc/hosts file. For example, if the Apache server is on a system with IP address 192.168.122.150 (such as tester1 .example.com), you could add the following lines to /etc/hosts:

```
192.168.122.150 big.example.com
192.168.122.150 small.example.com
```

The same data should be included in the /etc/hosts file of a remote client system.

15. Use the **firewall-cmd** utility to allow HTTP data through the firewall:

    ```
    # firewall-cmd --permanent --add-service=http
    # firewall-cmd --reload
    ```

16. You may need to configure appropriate SELinux file contexts on the directory associated with the **DocumentRoot**. For example, if that directory is /vhost-big, one way to do so is with the following commands:

    ```
    # semanage fcontext -a -t httpd_sys_content_t '/vhost-big(/.*)?'
    # restorecon -R /vhost-big
    ```

    Note that the first command is not required if you have set the **DocumentRoot** to a directory that the SELinux policy marks with the httpd_sys_content_t type by default, such as /srv/vhost-big/www. In fact, the /srv/*/www directories have their default context type already set to httpd_sys_content_t. If in doubt, check the settings of the SELinux policy by running **semanage fcontext -l | grep httpd_sys_content_t**.

17. Make sure to run the **systemctl reload httpd** command to make Apache reread its configuration files, with the changes you've made.

18. Now you can test the results. Navigate to a remote system and try to access the newly created websites in the browser of your choice. If it works, the big.example.com and small.example.com domain names should display the index.html files created for each website.

19. If there are problems, check the syntax with the **httpd -t** and **httpd -S** commands. Check the log files in the /var/log/httpd directory.

Lab 4

This lab should be straightforward; when it is complete, you should find the following two files, which can be used to support a virtual host for a secure version of the big.example.com website:

```
/etc/pki/tls/certs/big.example.com.crt
/etc/pki/tls/private/big.example.com.key
```

Corresponding files for the small.example.com system should also now exist in these directories. The process is based on standard responses to the questions generated by the **genkey big.example.com** and **genkey small.example.com** commands.

Lab 5

The basics of this lab are straightforward. You'll need to repeat the same steps that you performed in Lab 3 and use the certificate and key files created in Lab 4. You can use the contents of the /etc/httpd/conf.d/ssl.conf file as a template. In addition, you should be concerned about the following:

1. While not absolutely required, you may want to set up the **DocumentRoot** in a directory different from a regular web server. Otherwise, the same web page will appear for both the regular and secure versions of a website.

2. It's a good practice to configure the **ErrorLog** and **CustomLog** with appropriate filenames to help identify that information is from the secure version of a given website.

3. It's helpful to copy the SSL directives from the template SSL virtual host in the ssl.conf file. All directives can apply to the secure versions of the big.example.com and small.example.com websites. You need at the minimum to set a **ServerName** directive, turn on **SSLEngine**, and set proper paths to **SSLCertificateFile** and **SSLCertificateKeyFile**:

```
ServerName big.example.com
SSLEngine On
SSLCertificateFile /etc/pki/tls/certs/big.example.com.crt
SSLCertificateKeyFile /etc/pki/tls/private/big.example.com.key
```

Of course, you'd substitute small.example.com for big.example.com for the noted directives in the secure virtual host container for that website. Don't forget to add the https service to the default zone on the firewall:

```
# firewall-cmd --permanent --add-service=https
# firewall-cmd --reload
```

Lab 6

In the default conf.d/userdir.conf file, the configuration of user home directories requires that you enable the **UserDir** directive. You can then customize the commented container associated with user home directories. If successful, only one user is allowed access to his home directory through the Apache web server from a client browser. In general, you may see directives such as the following within the container for the given home page:

```
AuthType Basic
AuthName "Just for one user"
AuthUserFile /etc/httpd/oneuser
Require user michael
```

As suggested in the chapter, the home directory should have regular executable permissions for other users, or at least for the user named apache, through ACLs. In addition, access won't be allowed unless you've set the httpd_enable_homedirs SELinux boolean. You'll also need to set up user michael in the authentication database for this directory with the **htpasswd -c /etc/httpd/oneuser michael** command.

Lab 7

The process required to set up a group-managed directory is a hybrid. The overall basic steps are as follows:

1. Create a regular user and group named techsupport. While not required, it can be helpful to configure that user with a higher UID and GID to avoid interfering with other future users and groups.

2. Make the other users a member of that group named techsupport.

3. Create a public_html/ subdirectory of the new user's home directory.

4. Set up appropriate permissions to support access by members of the techsupport group, normally 2770 permissions. The new techsupport's home and public_html directories should have either regular executable permissions by other users or executable permissions by the user named apache configured in an ACL.

5. Set up an index.html file in the public_html directory. It should be set with ownership by the techsupport group.

6. You will need to configure basic authentication for the group in Apache. Don't forget to set up the group in the authentication database for this directory with the **htpasswd** command.

Lab 8

The specified hello.pl script should include something like the following entries:

```
#!/usr/bin/perl
print "Content-type: text/html\n\n";
print "Hello World";
```

That script should be located in the directory specified by a **ScriptAlias /cgi-bin/** directive in the big.example.com virtual host container.

As an alternative configuration, you can create a new **<Directory>** block for the CGI directory. That container should include the **Options ExecCGI** and **AddHandler cgi-script .pl** directives. You may also need to disable the default **ScriptAlias** directive in httpd.conf. Although it's normally best to have scripts in a different directory than the **DirectoryRoot** tree configured for a virtual host, it's not required.

In addition, the permissions on the hello.pl file should be set to 755, and the SELinux contexts on the file (and directory) should be of the httpd_sys_script_exec_t file type. Of course, you'll have run an appropriate **semanage fcontext -a** command to make the change permanent. In any case, a successful result is as suggested in the lab question.

Chapter 15

The Samba File Server

S amba is the Linux implementation of the networking protocols used to connect Microsoft operating systems. In a network of Microsoft Windows computers, file sharing is based on the Common Internet File System (CIFS), which was developed from the Server Message Block (SMB) protocol. Samba was developed as a freely available SMB server for all Unix-related operating systems, including Linux, and has been upgraded to support CIFS.

Samba interacts with CIFS so transparently that Microsoft clients cannot tell your Linux server from a genuine Windows server. With Samba running only on Linux machines, there are no server, client, or client access licenses to purchase. If you can learn to edit the main Samba configuration file from the command-line interface, you can configure Samba quickly.

Learn to test network services such as Samba. These are services that you might configure and/or troubleshoot on the Red Hat exams. Take some time to understand the configuration files associated with each of these services, and practice making them work on different Linux systems. In some cases, two or more systems running Linux will be useful to practice what you learn in this chapter.

INSIDE THE EXAM

Inside the Exam

This chapter directly addresses two RHCE objectives related to Samba File System services. When you're finished with this chapter, you'll know how to

■ Provide network shares to specific clients

■ Provide network shares suitable for group collaboration

With Samba, communications are seamless with Microsoft clients. However, because you might not have access to Microsoft Windows during the Red Hat exams, you'll see how

Samba communications are also seamless with other Linux clients. Shares can be limited to specific clients with Samba and other security options.

Samba also provides support for group collaboration, as does Apache in Chapter 14. The principles are the same as the way group directories were configured on Linux in Chapter 8.

Do not forget the standard requirements for all network services, discussed in Chapters 10 and 11. To review, you need to install the service, make it work with SELinux, make sure it starts on boot, configure the service for basic operation, and set up user- and host-based security.

CERTIFICATION OBJECTIVE 15.01

Samba Services

Microsoft's CIFS was built on the Server Message Block (SMB) protocol. SMB was developed in the 1980s by IBM, Microsoft, and Intel as a way to share files and printers over a network.

As Microsoft developed SMB into CIFS, the Samba developers have upgraded Samba accordingly. Samba services provide a stable, reliable, fast, and highly compatible file and print sharing service that allows your computer to act as a client, a member server, a Primary Domain Controller (PDC), or a member of an Active Directory (AD) service on Microsoft-based networks.

on the
job

With the release of Samba version 4.0, you can now configure Samba to act as an AD Domain Controller (DC) on a Microsoft-based network. Although the configuration of a DC is outside the scope of the RHCE exam, it is an important skill for many systems administrators.

It is easy to configure Samba to do a number of things on a Microsoft-based network. Here are some examples:

- Participate in a Microsoft Windows Workgroup or a domain as a client, member server, or even a PDC.
- Provide user/password and share directory databases locally, either from another Samba server or from a Windows PDC.
- Configure local directories as shared SMB filesystems.

Samba can do more, but you get the idea. Samba features are configured through one very big file, smb.conf, in the /etc/samba directory. Although this file may intimidate some users, read the comments therein. You might be surprised at what you can do with Samba!

exam
watch

In RHEL7, Red Hat no longer includes GUI tools for Samba configuration. You'll have to edit the Samba configuration file directly.	**Fortunately, the default /etc/samba/smb .conf configuration file includes many useful comments and suggested directives.**

Install Samba Services

The process of installing Samba differs from other servers. Samba packages are not organized in a single package group. While all you need to set up a Samba server is the Samba RPM package (and dependencies), you'll find other helpful Samba packages. Important Samba packages are described in Table 15-1.

Some Samba Background

Samba services provide interoperability between Microsoft Windows and Linux/Unix systems. Before configuring Samba, you need a basic understanding of how Microsoft Windows networking works with TCP/IP.

| TABLE 15-1 | Samba Packages |

RPM Package	Description
samba	Includes the basic SMB server software for sharing files and printers.
samba-client	Provides the utilities needed to connect to SMB/CIFS shares and printers.
samba-common	Contains common Samba files used by both the client and the server.
samba-dc	Included in the RHEL Server Optional repository; provides integration with Active Directory.
samba-libs	Contains the libraries needed by the other Samba software packages.
samba-python	Contains the Python modules needed by the other Samba software packages.
samba-winbind	Provides the Winbind daemon, which enables Samba to be a member server on Microsoft-based domains and supports Windows users on Linux servers.
samba-winbind-krb5-locator	Included in the RHEL Server Optional repository; allows the local Kerberos library to use the same KDC as Samba.
samba-winbind-modules	Provides a client connection to the Winbind daemon via PAM and the Network Service Switch (NSS).

The original Microsoft Windows networks were configured with computer hostnames, known as NetBIOS names, limited to 15 characters. These unique hostnames provided a simple, flat hostname system for the computers on a LAN.

All computer identification requests were made through broadcasts. This overall network transport system was known as the NetBIOS Extended User Interface (NetBEUI), and was not "routable." In other words, it did not allow communication between different networks. As a result, administrators could configure only 100–200 nodes on the original Microsoft-based PC networks.

Microsoft needed a solution to route information between networks. They could have used the Novell IPX/SPX protocol stack, but that was not good enough. As the Internet grew, Microsoft needed a standard compatible with TCP/IP. Microsoft adapted its NetBIOS system to TCP/IP with SMB. Since Microsoft published SMB as an industry-wide standard, anyone could set up their own service to work with it. As Microsoft has moved toward CIFS, Samba developers have adapted to the changes.

One of the features of Windows networks is the browser service. All computers register their NetBIOS names with one "elected" master browser, the keeper of the database of network-wide services. In fact, a browse database is maintained by some elected host for every protocol running on the Microsoft-based network. For instance, if the NetBEUI and TCP/IP protocols were installed on a host, then two duplicate browse databases were required—one per protocol—because the services available might differ between protocols.

Ports, Firewalls, and Samba

Samba as a service and a client requires access through multiple network ports. To enable communications through the local firewall for a Samba server, run the following commands:

```
# firewall-cmd --permanent --add-service=samba
# firewall-cmd --reload
```

For Samba clients, you need to enable the following firewalld service:

```
# firewall-cmd --permanent --add-service=samba-client
# firewall-cmd --reload
```

The configuration of the corresponding firewalld services is defined in the files samba.xml and samba-client.xml, located in the /usr/lib/firewalld/services directory. As shown in Figure 15-1 and Figure 15-2, the Samba server requires four open ports, whereas the Samba Client service requires only two open ports.

You'll note that two of the open ports are associated with the User Datagram Protocol (UDP), which is not connection based. Therefore, to track locally originating NetBIOS requests and allow packets matching the corresponding returning traffic through the firewall, both the Samba and the Samba Client services use the firewalld helper module **ns_conntrack_netbios_ns**.

FIGURE 15-1

Configuration file for the Samba firewalld service

```
[root@server1 ~]# cat /usr/lib/firewalld/services/samba.xml
<?xml version="1.0" encoding="utf-8"?>
<service>
  <short>Samba</short>
  <description>This option allows you to access and participate in Windows file
and printer sharing networks. You need the samba package installed for this opti
on to be useful.</description>
  <port protocol="udp" port="137"/>
  <port protocol="udp" port="138"/>
  <port protocol="tcp" port="139"/>
  <port protocol="tcp" port="445"/>
  <module name="nf_conntrack_netbios_ns"/>
</service>
[root@server1 ~]# ▌
```

FIGURE 15-2

Configuration file for the Samba Client firewalld service

```
[root@server1 ~]# cat /usr/lib/firewalld/services/samba-client.xml
<?xml version="1.0" encoding="utf-8"?>
<service>
  <short>Samba Client</short>
  <description>This option allows you to access Windows file and printer sharing
 networks. You need the samba-client package installed for this option to be use
ful.</description>
  <port protocol="udp" port="137"/>
  <port protocol="udp" port="138"/>
  <module name="nf_conntrack_netbios_ns"/>
</service>
[root@server1 ~]# ▌
```

Port/Protocol	Description
137/UDP	NetBIOS name service
138/UDP	NetBIOS datagram service
139/TCP	NetBIOS session service
445/TCP	Samba over TCP/IP

The TCP and UDP ports needed for the Samba client are shown in Table 15-2. Collectively, the services that listen on ports 137–139 are associated with NetBIOS communication over TCP/IP (NBT).

Configure SELinux Booleans for Samba

Several directives are associated with making a Samba server work with SELinux in targeted mode, as described in Table 15-3. You may have to activate one or more booleans to support different Samba functions. While this may seem repetitive for some readers, SELinux is not well understood even by many Linux experts.

If you want to allow Samba to share local home directories with others on the network, run the following command:

```
# setsebool -P samba_enable_home_dirs 1
```

The **-P** makes sure the change survives a reboot.

If you need to configure directories to be shared through other services, it's appropriate to enable the samba_export_all_ro or samba_export_all_rw boolean. For example, files that are shared via an Apache web server must be labeled with the httpd_sys_content_t file context. However, Samba requires a different SELinux context for files and directories, samba_share_t. To allow Samba to access files that don't have the samba_share_t label, you must enable the samba_export_all_ro or samba_export_all_rw boolean.

Configure SELinux File Contexts for Samba

Normally, Samba can only share those files and directories labeled with the samba_share_t file type. However, the samba_share_t file type is not required if the samba_export_all_ro or samba_export_all_rw booleans is enabled. It is also not required if the files are labeled with public_content_rw_t or public_content_t and the smbd_anon_write boolean is enabled.

However, enabling samba_export_all_rw may be a security risk because it would allow all directories to be shared by Samba, regardless of their SELinux context. So in most cases, you'll want to label directories (and the files therein) with the samba_share_t SELinux context by running a command such as the following:

```
# chcon -R -t samba_share_t /share
```

TABLE 15-3   Samba SELinux Booleans

Boolean	Description
cdrecord_read_content	Allows the **cdrecord** command to read shared Samba (and other network) directories
ksmtuned_use_cifs	Allows KSM (a service that reduces identical memory pages into a single page) to access CIFS filesystems
samba_create_home_dirs	Supports the creation of home directories, normally via the pam_mkhomedir.so PAM module
samba_domain_controller	Allows Samba to act as a Domain Controller for authentication management
samba_enable_home_dirs	Enables the sharing of user home directories
samba_export_all_ro	Sets up read-only access to any directory, even those without the samba_share_t file type label
samba_export_all_rw	Sets up read/write access to any directory, even those without the samba_share_t file type label
samba_portmapper	Allows Samba to act as a portmapper
samba_run_unconfined	Supports the execution of unconfined scripts from the /var/lib/samba/scripts directory
samba_share_fusefs	Allows Samba to share filesystems mounted via fusefs, such as GlusterFS filesystems
samba_share_nfs	Enables sharing of NFS filesystems from Samba
smbd_anon_write	Allows Samba to modify files on public directories configured with the **public_content_rw_t** and **public_content_r_t** SELinux contexts
sanlock_use_samba	Allows sanlock (a shared storage lock manager) to access CIFS filesystems
use_samba_home_dirs	Supports the use of a remote Samba server for local home directories
virt_sandbox_use_samba	Allows sandbox containers to access CIFS filesystems
virt_use_samba	Allows a VM to access files mounted to the CIFS filesystem

In addition, to make sure the changes survive a relabel of SELinux, you'll want to change the default file context policy defined in the file_contexts.local file in the /etc/selinux/targeted/contexts/files directory. This can be achieved with a command such as the following:

```
# semanage fcontext -a -t samba_share_t '/share(/.*)?'
```

Samba Daemons

The sharing of directories and printers on a Microsoft-style network requires several daemons and a number of related commands. Working together, the commands can help configure Samba, and the daemons help it communicate through the different communication ports described earlier in this chapter.

Samba includes commands that run the service, as well as aid in configuration. The most important of these commands are the binary files in the /usr/sbin directory that start the various Samba services.

You need two daemons to run Samba: the main Samba service (**smbd**) and the NetBIOS name service (**nmbd**). In addition, some administrators may want to run the Winbind service (**winbindd**) for user and hostname resolution. This is provided by the samba-winbind RPM package. All three daemons are configured through the /etc/samba/smb.conf configuration file.

If you want to make sure the services are running the next time Linux is booted, execute the following command:

```
# systemctl enable smb nmb winbind
```

You can start the associated **smbd**, **nmbd**, and **winbindd** daemons with the following command:

```
# systemctl start smb nmb winbind
```

The **systemctl** command can help you confirm the way a daemon is running. For example, the command listed in Figure 15-3 confirms that the Samba service is running with main PID 14691.

Samba Server Global Configuration

You can configure a Samba server through the main Samba configuration file, /etc/samba/smb.conf. This file is long and includes a number of directives that require some understanding of

---

FIGURE 15-3	

Showing status information about the smb service unit

```
[root@server1 rhel7]# systemctl status smb
smb.service - Samba SMB Daemon
   Loaded: loaded (/usr/lib/systemd/system/smb.service; disabled)
   Active: active (running) since Mon 2015-05-04 11:29:46 BST; 1min 20s ago
 Main PID: 14691 (smbd)
   Status: "smbd: ready to serve connections..."
   CGroup: /system.slice/smb.service
           ├─14691 /usr/sbin/smbd
           └─14692 /usr/sbin/smbd

May 04 11:29:46 server1.example.net systemd[1]: Starting Samba SMB Daemon...
May 04 11:29:46 server1.example.net smbd[14691]: [2015/05/04 11:29:46.609245...)
May 04 11:29:46 server1.example.net systemd[1]: Started Samba SMB Daemon.
Hint: Some lines were ellipsized, use -l to show in full.
[root@server1 rhel7]# ▊
```

the concepts associated with Microsoft Windows networking. Fortunately, the default version of this file also includes helpful documentation with suggestions and useful options.

The default Samba configuration file includes a number of non-default commented directives. You can find the default value of such directives in the man page for the smb.conf file.

Before editing this file, study its contents. Once you understand how the file is structured, back it up and then try editing the file directly. Check the syntax of smb.conf using the **testparm** command. Test the result of your changes by reloading the Samba server with the following command:

```
# systemctl reload smb
```

To help you with this process, we'll analyze the default RHEL 7 version of this file. The excerpts shown next are essentially a complete view of this file. In some cases, we've replaced the comments in the file with our own explanations. You might want to browse your own /etc/samba/smb.conf file as well.

The smb.conf file includes two types of comment lines. The hash symbol (#) is used as a general text comment. This is typically verbiage that describes a feature. The second comment symbol is the semicolon (;), used to comment out Samba directives (which you may later wish to uncomment to enable a feature).

(Note that the physical dimensions of this book limit the lengths of lines of code. In a few cases, we've modified the code lines slightly to meet this limitation without changing the intent of any command in this configuration file.)

```
# This is the main Samba configuration file. For detailed information
# about the options listed here, refer to the smb.conf(5) manual page.
# Samba has a huge number of configurable options, most of which are
# not shown in this example.

# Note: Run the "testparm" command after modifying this file to check
# for basic syntax errors.
```

While you need to know what can be done with different global settings, you should change as little as possible. The less you change, the less can go wrong. Perfect configuration files are not required. Configuration files that meet the specific requirements of an exam or a job are.

The smb.conf file can be split into different sections. After the first set of comments, there is another commented block with a description of the most important SELinux booleans and file contexts related to Samba. Due to lack of

exam

w a t c h   **As stated in the Red Hat Exam Prep guide, RHCEs must be able to configure various services, including Samba, for basic operation. Some of the details of the default version of the main Samba configuration go beyond basic operation.**

space, we only show the first lines of this section. Do read through all the comments of the smb.conf file, because they are a very useful source of information:

```
# Security-Enhanced Linux (SELinux) Notes:
#
# Turn the samba_enable_home_dirs Boolean on if you want to share home
# directories via Samba. Run the following command as the root user to turn
# this boolean on:
# setsebool -P samba_enable_home_dirs on
#
# If you create a new directory, such as a new top-level directory, label it
# with samba_share_t so that SELinux allows Samba to read and write to it. Do
# not label system directories, such as /etc/ and /home/, with samba_share_t,
# as such directories should already have an SELinux label.
```

Then, there is a global settings section that defines the overall attributes of a server. This section starts with the following two lines:

```
#======================= Global Settings==========================
[global]
```

Now examine the global settings that follow. First, if you see the line

```
#--authconfig--start-line--
```

this means the configuration file has been modified by the **authconfig** or the **system-config-authentication** tool.

Network-Related Options

Scroll down to the subsection entitled

```
#----------- Network Related Options ---------------
```

Examine each of the directives in this part of the Global Settings section. Despite the name, the **workgroup** variable may specify the name of a workgroup or, more commonly, a domain. However, because peer-to-peer workgroups were developed first, the default Samba **workgroup** is **WORKGROUP**, which happens to be the default peer-to-peer workgroup on older Microsoft Windows systems. On RHEL 7, it's now set to the following value:

```
workgroup = MYGROUP
```

The **server string** directive that follows becomes the comment shown with the NetBIOS name of the system in the visible browse list, where Samba substitutes the version number for the **%v** variable:

```
server string = Samba Server Version %v
```

It's a good idea to add a NetBIOS name for the local system to this file. While limited to 15 characters, it can be the same as the hostname used for the system. This becomes what other clients see in network browse lists, such as those shown from a Microsoft **net view** command or a Linux **smbclient** command.

```
;    netbios name = MYSERVER
```

If the local system is connected to more than one network, you can specify the interfaces Samba should listen to with the **interfaces** directive, as shown here. Of course, the devices and network addresses should be changed appropriately.

```
;    interfaces = lo eth0 192.168.12.2/24 192.168.13.2/24
```

If you activate the **hosts allow** directive, that action can limit access to the specified network(s). The following default would limit access to the hosts within the 192.168.12.0/24 and 192.168.13.0/24 networks, as well as the local computer (127.):

```
;    hosts allow = 127. 192.168.12. 192.168.13.
```

It's possible to configure a **hosts deny** directive in a similar fashion. With such directives, you can set up host-based security for Samba. In the global section, such security would apply server-wide. You can also use the **hosts allow** and **hosts deny** directives in the definitions for individual shared directories, as described later in this chapter.

Next, the **max protocol** directive specifies the highest protocol level that the Samba server will support. By default, this is set to the Windows 7 SMB2 version:

```
;    max protocol = SMB2
```

Logging Options

The next section sets up logging options, as indicated by the following line:

```
#----------- Logging Options ---------------
```

The **log file** directive, as shown, sets up separate log files for every machine that connects to this Samba server, based on its machine name (**%m**). By default, the log file is limited to 50KB. As suggested by the comment, log files that exceed the given size are rotated. If logs exceed that size, you'll still see them in the /var/log/samba directory with the .old extension.

```
# log files split per-machine
log file = /var/log/samba/log.%m
# maximum size of 50KB per log file, then rotate:
max log size = 50
```

Standalone Server Options

The following section sets up security options, based on configuration as a standalone server:

```
#----------- Standalone Server Options --------------
```

The **security** directive may be a bit confusing. The standard value of the directive, as shown here, means that connections check the local password database. It is appropriate when configuring this computer as a Domain Controller (DC), specifically a Primary Domain Controller (PDC).

```
security = user
```

Alternatively, you can configure this computer as a member server on a domain to use a password database from a DC. In that case, you would substitute the following command:

```
security = domain
```

on the **Job**

To set up a Linux system as a workstation that happens to share directories on a Microsoft domain, you'll need to set up the computer as a member server on that domain.

Alternatively, to configure a system as a domain member on an Active Directory Services realm, substitute the following command:

```
security = ads
```

Finally, note that the **server** and **share** values are deprecated. To summarize, there are three basic authentication options: **user**, **domain**, and **ads**.

Now, refocus this directive on the authentication database. The default is **security = user**; in this case, make sure to create Samba usernames and passwords to populate the user database. If the database is local, it could be either

```
passdb backend = smbpasswd
```

or

```
passdb backend = tdbsam
```

The smbpasswd database is stored in the local /etc/samba directory. The tdbsam option, short for the Trivial Database Security Accounts Manager, is the recommended database format and is stored in the /var/lib/samba/private directory.

Alternatively, for a remote database such as LDAP, you could activate the following directive. If the LDAP server is located on a remote system, that Uniform Resource Identifier (URI) address can be included here.

```
passdb backend = ldapsam
```

If you've set up **security = ads**, you'll also want to activate the following directive to specify the Active Directory (AD) realm, substituting the actual AD realm for *MY_REALM:*

```
;    realm = MY_REALM
```

Domain Controller Options

The following section supports the configuration of a system as a Domain Controller, starting with the following comment:

```
#----------- Domain Controller Options -------------
```

Additional configuration is required for a Samba server configured as a Domain Controller. In brief, these options specify the role of the system as the domain master and as the system that receives requests for logins to the domain:

```
;    domain master = yes
;    domain logons = yes
```

The next directive sets up Microsoft command-line logon scripts by computer and user. The directive afterward stores Microsoft user profiles on the local Samba server:

```
# the following login script name is determined by the machine name
# (%m):
;    logon script = %m.bat
# the following login script name is determined by the UNIX user
# used:
;    logon script = %u.bat
;    logon path = \\%L\Profiles\%u
```

The remaining configuration options are fairly self-explanatory as scripts that add and delete users, groups, and machine accounts:

```
;    add user script = /usr/sbin/useradd "%u" -n -g users
;    add group script = /usr/sbin/groupadd "%g"
;    add machine script = /usr/sbin/adduser -n -c ↵
        "Workstation (%u)" -M -d /nohome -s /bin/false "%u"
;    delete user script = /usr/sbin/userdel "%u"
;    delete user from group script = /usr/sbin/userdel "%u" "%g"
;    delete group script = /usr/sbin/groupdel "%g"
```

Browse Control Options

The following section controls whether and how a system may be configured as a browse master, which maintains a list of resources on the network. Related directives start with the following comment:

```
#----------- Browser Control Options -------------
```

If the **local master** option is enabled, Samba participates in browser elections like any other Microsoft Windows computer, using the specified **os level** priority:

```
;   local master = no
;   os level = 33
```

You can force a local browser election when **nmbd** starts, using the **preferred master** directive:

```
;   preferred master = yes
```

Name Resolution

The following section allows you to set up a Samba server with a database of NetBIOS names and IP addresses. The section starts with the following comment:

```
#----------- Name Resolution --------------
```

The Windows Internet Name Service (WINS) is functionally similar to DNS on Microsoft-based networks. If you activate the following configuration option, the **nmbd** daemon will enable a WINS server on the local computer:

```
;   wins support = yes
```

Alternatively, you can point the local computer to a remote WINS server on the network; of course, you'd have to substitute the IP address for *w.x.y.z*. Do not activate both the **wins support** and **wins server** directives on the same system, as they are mutually exclusive.

```
;   wins server = w.x.y.z
```

WINS may not be supported on some clients. In that case, you could enable the following directive to allow Samba to answer resolution queries on behalf of those clients:

```
;   wins proxy = yes
```

If Samba is acting as a WINS server and a NetBIOS name has not been registered, the following directive would enable a DNS name lookup through the locally configured DNS servers:

```
;   dns proxy = yes
```

Printing Options

Printers were included in the RHCT exam objectives for RHEL 5. However, they are not listed in either the RHCSA or the RHCE objectives for RHEL 6 and RHEL 7. Nevertheless, printing is part of the default Samba server configuration, so you should at least scan the corresponding section in the Samba configuration file, starting with the following comment:

```
#----------- Printing Options --------------
```

These default printer settings are required to share printers from this Samba server. The following three directives load printers as defined by **printcap name** = **/etc/printcap**. The **cups options** = **raw** directive means that CUPS sends data to the printer in "raw" mode—that is, without any additional filtering. This setting is used when the printer driver is installed on the Windows clients so that no additional data processing is required by CUPS:

```
load printers = yes
cups options = raw
printcap name = /etc/printcap
```

Alternatively, it's possible to configure a different print server. The following option obtains information from printers configured on System V hosts, which rely on the **lpstat** command to list available printers:

```
printcap name = lpstat
```

Filesystem Options

The following section configures how Microsoft Disk Operating System (DOS) filesystem attributes are stored. The best option to provide support for DOS attributes is to store the Samba shares on a filesystem that supports extended attributes, such as XFS. Alternatively, Samba can create maps between DOS attributes and Unix permissions bits. The following directives define defaults for all shared directories:

```
#----------- File System Options --------------
```

First, the **map archive** directive can control whether the DOS file archive attribute is mapped to the local file owner execute bit, if supported by the **create mask** directive:

```
;   map archive = no
```

The **map hidden** directive can control whether DOS hidden files are mapped to the local file world execute bit:

```
;   map hidden = no
```

The **map read only** directive, also known as **map readonly** in Samba documentation, controls how the DOS read-only attribute is mapped on Linux:

```
;   map read only = no
```

The **map system** directive, if set to yes, supports the mapping of DOS-style system files to the file group execute bit:

```
;   map system = no
```

Finally, the **store dos attributes** directive, if active, tells Samba to attempt to read DOS attributes from the filesystem-extended attributes, rather than mapping DOS attributes to permission bits. This is the default setting:

```
;        store dos attributes = yes
```

Shared Samba Directories

The second part of the main Samba configuration file, /etc/samba/smb.conf, is used to set up shared directories and printers via Samba. This section includes an analysis of the default version of the file.

In Samba, settings for shared directories are organized into *stanzas,* which are groups of commands associated with a share name. (*Stanza* doesn't seem like a technical term, but some believe that well-constructed configuration code is like good poetry.)

Shared Home Directories

The first four lines in this section define the **[homes]** share, which automatically shares the users' home directories. The **browseable = no** command prevents the share from being shown when a client searches the servers for available shares.

The "homes" section is a special one, as there is no default /homes directory. It's just a label. You don't need to supply a home directory because Samba will read the user's account record in /etc/passwd to determine the directory to be shared.

By default, this does not allow access to unknown users (**guest ok = no**). In addition, you can limit the systems that can use this share with directives such as **hosts allow** and **hosts deny**, described earlier. The effects of the **hosts allow** and **hosts deny** directives are limited to the share stanza where they are used.

```
#============================ Share Definitions =============
[homes]
   comment = Home Directories
   browseable = no
   writable = yes
```

on the
ⓘob

There are a number of directives in smb.conf **that are not spelled correctly, such as browseable. In some cases, the correct spelling (browsable) also works. Even if misspelled, they are still accepted Samba variables. Check the spelling in the man page of** smb.conf **if in doubt.**

Shared Printers

The [**printers**] stanza normally works as is to allow access by all users with accounts on a computer or domain. Even though the spool directory (/var/spool/samba) is not browsable, the associated printers are browsable by their NetBIOS names. While changes are straightforward, the standard options mean that guest users aren't allowed to print, related print spools are not writable, and **printable = yes** is a prerequisite for loading associated configuration files, such as for CUPS.

```
# NOTE: If you have a BSD-style print system there is no need to
# specifically define each individual printer
[printers]
    comment = All Printers
    path = /var/spool/samba
    browseable = no
# Set guest ok = yes to allow users to connect without a password
    guest ok = no
    writable = no
    printable = yes
```

Domain Logons

The commands in the following stanza support the configuration of a [**netlogon**] share for Microsoft Windows workstations. As there are no [**netlogon**] shares, even for Samba-enabled Linux workstations, this section requires a Microsoft Windows computer to verify functionality. If you believe that you'll have access to a Microsoft Windows computer during the Red Hat exams, study this section carefully.

```
# Un-comment the following and create the netlogon directory for
# Domain Logons
; [netlogon]
;    comment = Network Logon Service
;    path = /var/lib/samba/netlogon
;    guest ok = yes
;    writable = no
;    share modes = no
```

Workstation Profiles

This next stanza configures a specific roaming profile share for Microsoft Windows workstations. As these profiles are used by Windows workstations, you're unlikely to configure this section in a network of Linux-only computers. Make your own judgment on whether this section might apply during an RHCE exam.

```
# Un-comment the following to provide a specific roving profile
# share. The default is to use the user's home directory:
;[Profiles]
;    path = /var/lib/samba/profiles
;    browseable = no
;    guest ok = yes
```

Group Directories

The following stanza, as suggested by the comment, configures the /home/samba directory to be shared by the group named staff. You can configure this common group of users to share this directory. To configure special ownership and permissions for /home/samba, you'll need also to configure appropriate permissions. Both processes are described in Chapter 8.

```
# A publicly accessible directory that is read only, except for
# users in the "staff" group (which have write permissions):
;[public]
;    comment = Public Stuff
;    path = /home/samba
;    public = yes
;    writable = yes
;    printable = no
;    write list = +staff
```

The staff group can be labeled +staff or @staff. To set up appropriate permissions on the shared directory, you might also want to include the following directives for creating files and directories:

```
create mask = 0770
directory mask = 2770
```

Then, create a unique group name, preferably with a higher GID number, with the **groupadd** command. Make sure appropriate users are members of that Linux group, and that those users are also present in the Samba user database, as described later. In addition, the /home/samba directory, along with any files contained in that directory, normally must have the proper SELinux file context, something made possible with the following command:

```
# chcon -R -t samba_share_t /home/samba
```

Of course, you'll want to make sure such a change survives a SELinux relabel, and that can be configured for the noted directory with the following command:

```
# semanage fcontext -a -t samba_share_t '/home/samba(/.*)?'
```

Other Sample Stanzas

To learn more about Samba, it may be helpful to examine other stanzas for shared directories. The following examples were included in earlier Red Hat releases of Samba. While they're not included in the comments for Samba, they still can be included in the smb.conf configuration file, and therefore are still useful at least for learning purposes.

The RHCE objectives specify a requirement to "provide network shares suitable for group collaboration."

For example, the following share of the /tmp directory can provide a common location where users share downloaded files. If it's activated, all users (**public = yes**) get write access (**read only = no**) to this share.

```
# This one is useful for people to share files
;[tmp]
;     comment = Temporary file space
;     path = /tmp
;     read only = no
;     public = yes
```

This stanza configures a directory for Fred's exclusive use. It allows that user exclusive access to his home directory via Samba. A better location for the **path** would be within the /home directory.

```
# A private directory, usable only by fred. Note that fred
# requires write access to the directory.
;[fredsdir]
;     comment = Fred's Service
;     path = /usr/somewhere/private
;     valid users = fred
;     public = no
;     writable = yes
;     printable = no
```

Some parameters in smb.conf **are inverted synonyms, such as** writable = yes **and** read only = no. **You can specify either one form or the other because they have exactly the same effect.**

The following stanza is slightly different from the **[tmp]** share. The only user that is allowed to connect is a guest, without authentication. Unless you've configured a guest user in Samba, this defaults to the user named nobody.

```
# A publicly accessible directory, read/write to all users. Note
# that all files created in the directory by users will be owned
# by the default guest user, so any user with access can delete
# other user's files. Obviously this directory must be writable
# by the default user. Another user could of course be specified,
# in which case all files would be owned by that user instead.
;[public]
;   path = /usr/somewhere/else/public
;   public = yes
;   only guest = yes
;   writable = yes
;   printable = no
```

Finally, this is another variation on the User Private Group scheme, which creates a group directory. Unlike the **[public]** stanza, this share is private.

```
# The following two entries demonstrate how to share a directory so
# that two users can place files there that will be owned by the
# specific users. In this setup, the directory should be writable
# by both users and should have the sticky bit set on it to prevent
# abuse. Obviously this could be extended to as many users as
required.
;[myshare]
;   comment = Mary's and Fred's stuff
;   path = /usr/somewhere/shared
;   valid users = mary fred
;   public = no
;   writable = yes
;   printable = no
;   create mask = 0765
```

Let Samba Join a Domain

If you've configured a Samba server and it's not the DC for the network, you may need to configure it as a member of the domain. To do so, you can configure an account on the DC for the network. As long as there's one domain on this network, you can join a domain with the following command:

```
# net rpc join -U Administrator
```

If there is more than one domain available, substitute the name of the controller for *DC* in the **net rpc join -S** *DC* **-U root** command. This assumes that the user named Administrator is the administrative user on the DC. If the command is successful, it prompts for that user's password on the remote DC. The result adds an account for the local computer to the DC's user database.

The Samba User Database

You could set up identical usernames and passwords for both the Microsoft Windows and Samba-enabled Linux computers on a network. However, this is not always possible, especially when there are preexisting databases. In that case, you can set up a database of Samba users and passwords that correspond to current Microsoft usernames and passwords on your network.

The quickest way to set up Samba users is with the **smbpasswd** command, which is provided by the **samba-client** RPM package. Remember that you can create a new Samba user only from valid accounts on a Linux computer.

However, you can configure such an account without login privileges on the Linux system. For example, the following command adds the noted user without a valid login shell:

```
# useradd winuser1 -s /sbin/nologin
```

You can then configure that user with a Samba password with the **smbpasswd -a winuser1** command. The **smbpasswd** command is powerful; it includes a number of useful switches, as described in Table 15-4.

The location of the authentication database depends on the value of the **passdb backend** directive. If it's set to the old **smbpasswd** format, you'll find it in the /etc/samba/smbpasswd file. If it's set to **tdbsam**, you'll find it in the passwd.tdb file in the /var/lib/samba/private directory. To read the list of current users, run the following command:

```
# pdbedit -L
```

TABLE 15-4	smbpasswd Switch	Description
Various smbpasswd Command Options	-a *username*	Adds the specified *username* to the database.
	-d *username*	Disables the specified *username*, thus preventing that account from authenticating with SMB.
	-e *username*	Enables the specified *username*; opposite of **-d**.
	-r *computername*	Allows changes to a Windows or Samba password on a remote computer. Normally goes with **-U**.
	-U *username*	Normally changes the *username* on a remote computer, if specified with the **-r** switch.
	-x *username*	Deletes the specified *username* from the database.

Create a Public Share

With this information, you should now know how to create a public access share for use with the entire network. For the purpose of this example, create the /publicshare directory. The following sample stanza in the /etc/samba/smb.conf configuration file reflects a directory available to all users:

```
[PublicShare]
    comment = Shared Public Directory
    path = /publicshare
    writeable = yes
    browseable = yes
    guest ok = yes
```

But that kind of security might not be appropriate. For example, assume the following limits are desirable:

- Access to the **[PublicShare]** should be limited to users with a regular local Linux account (or a user who can log in locally based on a remote authentication database such as LDAP).
- Denied access to guest users and others.
- Access to all users in the local example.com domain.
- Denied access to all users from a suspect computer such as evil.example.com.

To make this happen, change the last directive in this stanza. As **guest ok** = **no** is the default, you can just erase the **guest ok** = **yes** directive. To provide access to all users in the given domain, add the following command:

```
hosts allow = .example.com
```

Then, to deny access to one specific computer on that network, you could add **EXCEPT**; for example, the following line specifically excludes the noted **evil.example.com** system from the list:

```
hosts allow = .example.com EXCEPT evil.example.com
```

Alternatively, if this domain is on the 192.168.122.0 network, either of the following directives supports access to all systems on that network:

```
hosts allow = 192.168.122.
hosts allow = 192.168.122.0/255.255.255.0
```

You could specifically deny access to computers with a command such as the following:

```
hosts deny = evil.example.com
```

Alternatively, you could substitute the IP addresses for evil.example.com.

You've defined the share attributes in the Samba smb.conf configuration file, but you need to modify the directory associated with the share with the following command:

```
# chmod 1777 /publicshare
```

The digit (1) in front of the 777 directory permission string is known as the "sticky bit." While 777 permissions allow read, write, and execute permissions to all users, the sticky bit restricts the ability to delete or rename a file only to the owner.

Alternatively, you can limit directory permissions to members of a group, with the SGID bit. For example, take a directory with 2770 permissions. The digit (2) in front of user read/write/execute permissions (770) ensures that all files created inherit the group ownership of the directory.

Finally, don't forget to set the appropriate SELinux context on the shared directory:

```
# chcon -R -t samba_share_t /publicshare
# semanage fcontext -a -t samba_share_t '/publicshare(/.*)?'
```

Test Changes to /etc/samba/smb.conf

Before putting a new version of the /etc/samba/smb.conf file in production, test those changes. The first step in such a test is a syntax check. For that purpose, you can use the **testparm** utility, shown in Figure 15-4. A syntax utility does not check functionality; it only checks the syntax of the configuration file.

The directives shown in the output are share stanzas, along with associated directives. In this output, the [**homes**] share is not read-only and is not browsable by all clients.

FIGURE 15-4

Review the Samba configuration with testparm.

```
[root@server1 ~]# testparm
Load smb config files from /etc/samba/smb.conf
rlimit_max: increasing rlimit_max (1024) to minimum Windows limit (16384)
Processing section "[homes]"
Processing section "[printers]"
Loaded services file OK.
Server role: ROLE_STANDALONE
Press enter to see a dump of your service definitions

[global]
        workgroup = MYGROUP
        server string = Samba Server Version %v
        log file = /var/log/samba/log.%m
        max log size = 50
        idmap config * : backend = tdb
        cups options = raw

[homes]
        comment = Home Directories
        read only = No
        browseable = No

[printers]
        comment = All Printers
        path = /var/spool/samba
        printable = Yes
        print ok = Yes
        browseable = No
[root@server1 ~]# ▮
```

Configure a Samba Home Directory Share

In this exercise, you'll learn about the basic home directory share. You'll need at least two computers, one of which should be a Samba server. The other can be a Linux or Microsoft Windows client. You'll connect to the Samba server from the client and access the files in your home directory on the Samba server. These steps assume that the user account is michael; substitute your regular user account name as appropriate.

1. Install and configure Samba to start at boot using the methods described earlier in this chapter.

2. Open the /etc/samba/smb.conf configuration file. Look for the current value of **workgroup**.

3. Make sure that the computers on the local network have the same value for **workgroup**. If the local network is a Windows-style domain, set **workgroup** to the name of the domain.

4. Run the **testparm** command.

5. Read and address any problems that appear in the output from the **testparm** command. Fix any smb.conf syntax problems defined in the output.

6. Activate the samba_enable_home_dirs boolean on the Samba server with the following command:

```
# setsebool -P samba_enable_home_dirs on
```

7. Set up a user account on the Samba server in the authentication database with the following command. Note that a corresponding account must already exist in /etc/passwd; otherwise, the command will fail (enter an appropriate password when prompted):

```
# smbpasswd -a michael
```

8. Start the Samba services with the following command:

```
# systemctl start smb nmb
```

Alternatively, if Samba is already running, reload the configuration in the smb.conf file with the following command:

```
# systemctl reload smb nmb
```

9. Open appropriate ports in the firewall for the Samba server:

```
# firewall-cmd --permanent --add-service=samba
# firewall-cmd --reload
```

On clients, the following commands open the required ports in firewalld:

```
# firewall-cmd --permanent --add-service=samba-client
# firewall-cmd --reload
```

10. Go to a remote Linux or Microsoft Windows workstation on the same domain or workgroup. On a Linux machine, ensure that the **samba-client** RPM is installed.

11. If you can browse the list of computers from the Samba server with the following command, browsing is working. Substitute the name of the configured Samba server host for *sambaserver.*

```
# smbclient -L sambaserver -U michael
```

12. Log in as the root user on the remote RHEL 7 client. Ensure that the **cifs-utils** RPM is installed.

13. From that remote RHEL 7 client, use the **mount.cifs** command to configure the remote [**homes**] directory share on an empty local directory. For example, as the root user, you could mount on the local /share directory (create it if required) with the following command:

```
# mount //sambaserver/michael /share -o username=michael
```

14. Test the result. Can you browse the home directory on the remote computer?

15. Bonus: disable the **samba_enable_home_dirs** boolean and try again. What happens?

CERTIFICATION OBJECTIVE 15.02

Samba as a Client

You can configure two types of clients through Samba. One is an FTP-like client that can browse and access directories and printers, shared from Microsoft Windows servers or Samba servers on Linux/Unix. The second adds support to the **mount** command for the SMB and CIFS protocols. The Samba client commands are available from the **samba-client** and **cifs-utils** RPMs.

Command-Line Tools

To browse shared directories from a Linux computer, you should know how to use the **smbclient** command. This can test connectivity to any SMB host on a Windows- or

Samba-based Linux/Unix computer. Assuming it's allowed through a firewall, you can use **smbclient** to check the shared directories and printers from other systems on at least the local network. For example, the following **smbclient** command checks shared directories and printers:

```
# smbclient -L server1.example.com -U donna
```

We've specified two arguments with the **smbclient** command: the **-L** argument tells the name of the Samba server, and the **-U** argument specifies a username on the remote computer. When the command reaches the Samba server, you're prompted for the appropriate password.

A list of shares will appear; for example, the following output reveals shares named public and donna, as well as a printer named OfficePrinter on a remote system named Maui:

```
Domain=[MYGROUP] OS=[Unix] Server=[Samba 4.1.1]
     Sharename       Type        Comment
     ---------       ----        -------
     public          Disk        Public Stuff
     IPC$            IPC         IPC Service (Samba Server Version 4.1.1)
     OfficePrinter   Printer     Printer in the office
     donna           Disk        Home Directories
```

From the displayed output, there's a share available named **public**. You can also use the **smbclient** command to browse and copy files, in a similar way to an FTP client. The required command to make a connection is shown next:

```
$ smbclient //server1.example.com/public -U michael
```

Of course, most administrators would prefer to mount that share on a local directory. That's where options to the **mount** command are helpful.

Mount Options

Shares can be mounted by the root administrative user. The standard is with the **mount.cifs** command, functionally equivalent to the **mount -t cifs** command. For example, the following command mounts the share named "public" on the local /home/shared directory:

```
# mount.cifs //server1.example.com/public /home/shared -o username=donna
```

This command prompts for user donna's password on the remote server. That password should be part of the Samba user authentication database on the server1.example.com system, normally different from the standard Linux authentication database.

While there is no longer an **umount.cifs** command for shared Samba directories, you can still use the **umount** command to unmount such directories.

Automated Samba Mounts

As it takes a few extra steps to set up a shared directory, you may want to automate the process. One way to automate mounts is through the /etc/fstab configuration file discussed in Chapter 6. To review the essential elements of that chapter, you could set up the public share in /etc/fstab by adding the following line (which can be wrapped in that file):

```
//server1.example.com/public /home/shared cifs username=donna,password=pass,↵
  0 0
```

However, that can be a risk, as the /etc/fstab file is world-readable. To that end, you can configure a dedicated credentials file with the username and password, as follows:

```
//server1.example.com/public /home/share cifs credentials=/etc/smbdonna 0 0
```

As suggested in Chapter 6, you can then set up the username and password in a file with a name such as /etc/smbdonna:

```
username=donna
password=donnaspassword
```

While the contents of that file must still exist in clear text, you can configure the /etc/smbdonna file as readable only by the root administrative user. It's also possible to configure the automounter with similar information. However, because the automounter is an RHCSA skill, you'll have to refer to Chapter 6 for that information.

EXERCISE 15-2

Configuring a Samba Share for Group Collaboration

In this exercise, you'll configure Samba to share a directory for collaboration so that only users in the "editors" group have write access to the share.

1. Create the Samba-only users michael and alex, and add them to the "editors" group:

```
# groupadd editors
# useradd -s /sbin/nologin -G editors michael
# useradd -s /sbin/nologin -G editors alex
# smbpasswd -a michael
# smbpasswd -a alex
```

2. Create the /editors directory and assign appropriate ownership and permissions for collaboration (2770):

```
# mkdir /editors
# chgrp editors /editors
# chmod 2770 /editors
```

3. Make sure to set the appropriate SELinux context for the directory with the following command:

```
# chcon -R -t samba_share_t /editors
```

In addition, to make sure the changes survive a relabel of SELinux, you'll want to update the SELinux policy with a command such as the following:

```
# semanage fcontext -a -t samba_share_t '/editors(/.*)?'
```

4. Open the /etc/samba/smb.conf file in a text editor.

5. Configure Samba to share the /editors directory to users who belong to the "editors" group. In the Share Definitions section, you could add the following commands:

```
[Editors]
    comment = shared directory for McGraw-Hill editors
    path = /editors
    valid users = @editors
    writable = yes
```

6. Write and save changes to the smb.conf file.

7. Ensure that the firewall grants access to the Samba service. If you don't remember how to allow this traffic through the firewall, review Exercise 15-1.

```
# firewall-cmd --list-all
```

8. You can see if Samba is already running with the **systemctl status smb nmb** command. If it's stopped, you can start it with the **systemctl start smb nmb** command. If it's running, you can make Samba reread your configuration file with the following command:

```
# systemctl reload smb nmb
```

This option allows you to change your Samba configuration without disconnecting users from the Samba server.

9. On a different machine, browse the share using the smbclient and michael's credentials:

```
# smbclient //server1.example.com/Editors -U michael
```

10. Mount the share to a directory, using alex's credentials, and verify that you can create a file:

```
# mkdir /mnt/alex
# mount -t cifs -o username=alex //server1/Editors /mnt/alex
# touch /mnt/alex/testfile
```

11. As a bonus, create another Samba user named "evil." Try remounting the share as user evil. What happens?

Multiuser Samba Mounts

When mounting a Samba share via the **mount.cifs** command as root, you need to specify the credentials of a valid Samba account that has access permissions to the share. Those credentials are required to validate the mount, as well as file and directory permissions. In a multiuser environment, this solution is not ideal. That's because whenever a file is created on the Samba share, that file is owned by the user specified with the **mount** command.

To address this problem, the **mount.cifs** command includes a **multiuser** option. As an example, you can modify the **mount** command from Exercise 15-2 as shown:

```
# mount.cifs -o multiuser,username=alex //server1/Editors /mnt/editors
```

You can see how this works when you go through Lab 6 at the end of the chapter. Unless Samba is configured with Kerberos authentication (which is outside the scope of the RHCE exam), users must enter their SMB credentials to access the mounted share. The **cifscreds** tool, included with the **cifs-utils** RPM package, serves this purpose. The command adds a user's credentials to the kernel keyring, as shown here:

```
$ cifscreds add server1.example.com
```

Credentials are only stored for the current user's session. When a new session is established, they must be reentered by running the preceding command again.

CERTIFICATION OBJECTIVE 15.03

Samba Troubleshooting

Samba is complex. With a complex service, simple mistakes may be difficult to diagnose. Fortunately, Samba includes excellent tools for troubleshooting. The basic **testparm** command tests syntax, but log files can tell you more. Of course, unless appropriate changes are made in local firewalls, Samba might not even be accessible from remote systems.

Samba Problem Identification

Samba is a forgiving service. It includes synonyms for a number of parameters. But beyond those parameters, the **testparm** command, which we have already discussed, can help identify problems. For example, Figure 15-5 illustrates a number of problems. Unrecognized parameters are highlighted with the "unknown parameter" message.

Some parameters don't work with each other. For example, the following message in the **testparm** output highlights two incompatible directives:

```
ERROR: both 'wins support = true' and 'wins server = <server list>' cannot
be set in the smb.conf file. nmbd will abort with this setting.
```

FIGURE 15-5

Some syntax
problems
identified by
testparm

```
[root@server1 ~]# testparm
Load smb config files from /etc/samba/smb.conf
rlimit_max: increasing rlimit_max (1024) to minimum Windows limit (16384)
Unknown parameter encountered: "ecurity"
Ignoring unknown parameter "ecurity"
Unknown parameter encountered: "assdb backend"
Ignoring unknown parameter "assdb backend"
Processing section "[homes]"
Processing section "[printers]"
Processing section "[public]"
Unknown parameter encountered: "rite list"
Ignoring unknown parameter "rite list"
Loaded services file OK.
ERROR: both 'wins support = true' and 'wins server = <server list>' cannot be se
t in the smb.conf file. nmbd will abort with this setting.
Server role: ROLE_STANDALONE
Press enter to see a dump of your service definitions
```

Sometimes, troubleshooting commands come in the output to other commands. For example, often the output message is straightforward, such as the following output to a specific **mount.cifs** command, associated with an incorrect share name. It also suggests that the case of share names is less important on networks associated with Microsoft operating systems.

```
Retrying with upper case share name
```

Sometimes, messages may appear to be more straightforward, such as

```
mount error(13): Permission denied
```

But that message could refer to an incorrect password or a user who has not been configured in the Samba database.

Sometimes problems may seem more annoying. For example, if you mount a remote home directory and no files show up in that directory, it could mean that the SELinux **samba_enable_home_dirs** boolean has not been enabled. If you mount a remote directory other than a user home directory, it could mean that the directory and associated files are not properly labeled with the **samba_share_t** file context type.

Local Log File Checks

Problems associated with Samba may appear in the /var/log/messages file, or they may appear in different files in the /var/log/samba directory. First, syntax errors revealed in the output to the **testparm** command may also appear in the /var/log/messages file. As the Samba services are started, errors in the configuration file are problems worth reporting in the standard system log file.

In addition, when an attempted mount of a shared Samba directory fails, associated messages also appear in the /var/log/messages file. Sometimes the messages are straightforward, such as "cifs_mount failed" or NT_STATUS_LOGON_FAILURE.

The systemd journal is a very useful resource for searching and browsing Samba log entries. All messages specific to the **smb** and **nmb** systemd units can be displayed by the following command:

```
# journalctl -u smb -u nmb
```

Samba server log files are stored in the /var/log/samba directory. The log files are classified by the host or IP address of the client that connects to the server. By default, Samba is not very verbose. You may want to set the **log level** entry to 1 or 2 in /etc/samba/smb.conf, and look at how the detail of the log messages has changed. As an example, a connection to a localhost system, useful for troubleshooting, may include the following message in the log.127.0.0.1 log file:

```
127.0.0.1 (ipv4:127.0.0.1:44218) connect to service michael initially ↵
 as user michael (uid=1001, gid=1001) (pid 23800)
```

The connected user is identified by UID, GID, and PID numbers. If an unauthorized user connects, these numbers can help identify a problem user and/or a compromised account, along with an associated process ID number.

Most of the other files in this directory relate to various services as named; for example, the log.smbd, log.nmbd, and log.winbindd files collect messages associated with the daemons named in each respective log file.

SCENARIO & SOLUTION	
You need to set up sharing on a network with Microsoft computers.	Install Samba and configure shared directories in /etc/samba/smb.conf. Make sure shared directories (except for user home directories) have the appropriate **samba_share_t** SELinux context type.
You want to set up sharing of user home directories via Samba.	Activate the [**homes**] stanza, set up appropriate users in the Samba authentication database, and turn on the **samba_enable_home_dirs** boolean.
You want to set up host-based security for Samba.	Set up appropriate **hosts allow** and **hosts deny** directives in smb.conf or configure firewalld to limit access.
You want to set up user-based security for Samba.	Set up appropriate **valid users** and/or **invalid users** directives in smb.conf.
You need to set up a share for group collaboration.	Set up a share stanza with **valid users** set to a specific group, along with **writeable = yes** and appropriate permissions for group collaboration on the shared directory. Make sure the shared directory and its content have the **samba_share_t** SELinux context type.
You have mounted a CIFS share in /etc/fstab and want users to access the content using their own Samba credentials, rather than those specified by the **mount** command.	Mount the Samba share with the **multiuser** option. Instruct users to run the **cifscreds** command and provide their SMB credentials before accessing the contents of the share.

CERTIFICATION SUMMARY

Samba allows a Linux computer to appear like any other Microsoft computer on a Microsoft Windows–based network. Samba is based on the Server Message Block protocol, which allows Microsoft computers to communicate on a TCP/IP network. It has evolved as Microsoft has adapted SMB to the Common Internet File System. Network communication to Samba works through UDP ports 137 and 138, as well as TCP ports 139 and 445. The key SELinux boolean is **samba_enable_home_dirs**. Shared directories should be set to the **samba_share_t** file context type.

The main Samba configuration file, /etc/samba/smb.conf, includes separate sections for global settings and share definitions. The **smbpasswd** command can be used to set up existing Linux users in a local Samba authentication database. The **multiuser** mount option and the **cifscreds** command authenticate with the corresponding user's credentials when accessing a share.

As for troubleshooting, changes to smb.conf can be easily tested with the **testparm** utility. Samba includes a number of synonyms for directives; some proper directives are based on spelling mistakes. While basic Samba service log messages can be found in the /var/log/messages file, most Samba log information can be found in the /var/log/samba directory. Many of the files in that directory include the client name or IP address.

TWO-MINUTE DRILL

Here are some of the key points from the certification objectives in Chapter 15.

Samba Services

❑ Samba allows Microsoft Windows computers to share files and printers across networks, using the Server Message Block (SMB) protocol and NetBIOS over the TCP/IP protocol stack.

❑ Samba includes a client and a server. Variations on the **mount -t cifs** and **mount.cifs** commands support mounting of a shared Samba folder or even joining a Microsoft domain.

❑ The main Samba configuration file is /etc/samba/smb.conf.

❑ Samba supports configuration of a Linux computer as a Microsoft Windows server. It can also provide Microsoft browsing, WINS, and Domain Controller services, even on an Active Directory network.

Samba as a Client

❑ The **smbclient** command can display shared directories and printers from specified remote Samba and Microsoft servers, using an FTP-like interface.

❑ The **mount.cifs** command can mount directories shared from a Samba or Microsoft server.

❑ Samba shares can be mounted during the boot process with the help of the /etc/fstab configuration file.

❑ The **multiuser** mount option and the **cifscreds** command regulate access and permissions to a share using the credentials of each user, rather than those specified by the **mount** command.

Samba Troubleshooting

❑ The **testparm** command performs a syntax check on the main Samba configuration file, /etc/samba/smb.conf.

❑ Logs of Samba daemons may be written to the /var/log/messages file.

❑ Most Samba log files can be found in the /var/log/samba directory. Different log files can be found by client and by daemon.

SELF TEST

The following questions will help measure your understanding of the material presented in this chapter. As no multiple choice questions appear on the Red Hat exams, no multiple choice questions appear in this book. These questions exclusively test your understanding of the chapter. It is okay if you have another way of performing a task. Getting results, not memorizing trivia, is what counts on the Red Hat exams. There may be more than one answer to many of these questions.

Samba Services

1. An IT department that runs Microsoft servers has set up a Windows Server to handle file and print sharing services. This server correctly refers to a WINS server on 192.168.55.3 for name resolution and configures all user logins through the DC on 192.168.55.8. If you're configuring the

local Linux system as a DC, what directive, at a minimum, do you have to configure in the local Samba configuration file?

_____

2. You've recently revised the Samba configuration file and do not want to disconnect any current users. What command forces the Samba and NetBIOS services to reread the configuration file—without having to disconnect Microsoft users or restart the service?

_____

3. What ports must be open for a Samba server to work with remote systems?

_____

4. What SELinux setting is appropriate for sharing home directories over Samba?

_____

5. What SELinux file context type is appropriate for shared directories on Samba?

_____

6. What Samba directive limits access to systems on the example.org network?

_____

7. What Samba directive limits access to users tim and stephanie?

_____

8. What Samba directive limits access in a shared stanza to a configured group named ilovelinux?

_____

9. What Samba directive supports access to all users in a shared directory?

_____

10. What command adds user elizabeth to a tdbsam Samba authentication database?

_____

Samba as a Client

11. What command can be used to mount remotely shared Microsoft directories?

_____

Samba Troubleshooting

12. You made a couple of quick changes to a Samba configuration file and need to test it quickly for syntax errors. What command tests smb.conf for syntax errors?

_____

LAB QUESTIONS

Several of these labs involve configuration exercises. You should do these exercises on test machines only. It's assumed that you're running these exercises on virtual machines such as KVM. For this chapter, it's also assumed that you may be changing the configuration of a physical host system for such virtual machines.

Red Hat presents its exams electronically. For that reason, the labs in this and future chapters are available from the media that accompanies the book, in the Chapter15/ subdirectory. In case you haven't yet set up RHEL 7 on a system, refer to Chapter 1 for installation instructions.

The answers for each lab follow the Self Test answers for the fill-in-the-blank questions.

SELF TEST ANSWERS

Samba Services

1. At a minimum, to configure a Linux system as a DC, you need to change the **security = user** directive. If it's on an Active Directory system, you should use the **security = ads** directive.

2. The command that forces the Samba and NetBIOS services to reread the configuration file—without disconnecting Microsoft users or restarting the service—is **systemctl reload smb nmb**.

3. Open ports associated with communication to a Samba server are UDP ports 137 and 138, as well as TCP 139 and 445.

4. The SELinux boolean associated with the sharing of home directories on Samba is **samba_enable_home_dirs**.

5. The SELinux file type appropriate for shared Samba directories is **samba_share_t**.

6. The Samba directive that limits access to systems on the example.org network is

   ```
   hosts allow = .example.org
   ```

   The following directive is also an acceptable answer:

   ```
   allow hosts = .example.org
   ```

7. One Samba directive that limits access to the noted users is

   ```
   valid users = tim stephanie
   ```

8. One Samba directive that limits access to the noted group is

   ```
   valid users = @ilovelinux
   ```

   The **+ilovelinux** group would also be acceptable.

9. One Samba directive that supports access to all users in a shared directory is

   ```
   guest ok = yes
   ```

10. The command that adds user elizabeth to a tdbsam Samba authentication database is

   ```
   # smbpasswd -a elizabeth
   ```

Samba as a Client

11. The command that can be used to mount remotely shared Microsoft directories is **mount.cifs**. The **mount -t cifs** command is also an acceptable answer.

Samba Troubleshooting

12. The command that can test a Samba configuration file for errors is **testparm**.

LAB ANSWERS

Lab 1

The chapter lab on Samba is designed to be easy to follow. However, you'll need explicit Linux knowledge to complete several steps.

1. You've installed the "File and Print Server" environment group, or as an alternative the "File and Storage Server" group, which includes one Samba-related RPM, samba. Dependent packages, such as samba-common and samba-libs, will also be installed.

2. One way to find all related Samba packages is with the **yum search samba** command. You can then install noted packages with the **yum install** *packagename* command.

3. To support communications to a local Samba server, run the following:

   ```
   # firewall-cmd --permanent --add-service=samba
   # firewall-cmd --reload
   ```

On clients, run this:

```
# firewall-cmd --permanent --add-service=samba-client
# firewall-cmd --reload
```

4. You can use the **systemctl enable smb nmb** command to make sure that Samba and NetBIOS start the next time you boot Linux.

5. Use the **systemctl start smb nmb** command to begin the Samba and NetBIOS services.

6. One way to verify that Samba is running is to look for the existence of the **smbd** and **nmbd** processes in the process table. Use **ps aux | grep mbd** to see if these processes are present. Another way is with a systemd command such as the **systemctl status smb nmb** command.

Lab 2

This lab should familiarize you with the available documentation for the Samba file server. When you run the **man smb.conf** command, it will open the manual for the main Samba configuration file. You should be able to search through the file with vi-style commands. For example, to search for the **hosts allow** directive, going forward in the file, type in

```
/hosts allow
```

and press N to see the next instance of that directive. Alternatively, to search backward, type in

```
?hosts allow
```

and press N to see the previous instance of that directive in the man page.

From the command line, browse around other Samba man pages. Learn what you need as a reference for the job, or for an exam.

Lab 3

This lab assumes that you've backed up the smb.conf file from the /etc/samba directory.

1. Some administrators stick with the standard Microsoft Windows **workgroup** name of **WORKGROUP**. You can find it in the output from the **smbclient -L //***clientname* command.

2. To limit access to a Samba server, you can do so in the global section, with the **hosts allow** directive.

3. To limit access from a specific computer, you can do so in the global section, with the **hosts deny** directive.

4. You can make Samba read the changes with the **systemctl reload smb** command. Before committing the changes, you can test them with the **testparm** command.

5. When testing the connection from another system, use the **smbclient** command. You'll need to allow access through UDP ports 137 and 138 for that purpose, something possible by enabling the samba-client service with the Firewall Configuration tool.

6. If you need a fresh version of the smb.conf file, delete or move the existing version of the file from the /etc/samba directory and run the **yum reinstall samba-common** command.

Lab 4

If successful, only one remote user will get access to his home directory via Samba, something that you can test with appropriate **smbclient** and **mount.cifs** commands. One way to implement the requirements of this lab is with the following steps.

1. Open the main Samba configuration file, /etc/samba/smb.conf, in a text editor.

2. Navigate to the [**homes**] share in the last part of this file.

3. Unless there is already an appropriate limitation in the [**global**] section in this file, you can limit the [**homes**] share with the **hosts allow** = **.example.com**.

4. Add a **valid users** = *username* directive with the name of the desired user in the [**homes**] stanza.

5. Add the desired user to the Samba authentication database with the **smbpasswd -a** *username* command.

6. Restart or reload the Samba service with the appropriate **systemctl** command.

7. Save the changes made so far.

8. Test the result from a remote system with the **smbclient** command. You should also be able to use the **mount.cifs** command from a client root account, with the **-o username=***username* switch, to mount the shared user home directory.

Lab 5

This lab can be a continuation of Lab 4. You're just adding another stanza to the main Samba configuration file.

1. At the end of the file, start a [**public**] stanza. Add an appropriate comment for the stanza.

2. Set **path** = **/home/public**.

3. Make sure to set **hosts allow** = **.example.com**. Save your changes to the smb.conf file.

4. Set permissions for the public share with the following commands:

```
# mkdir /home/public
# chmod 1777 /home/public
```

The 777 setting for permissions grant read, write, and execute/search permissions to all users (root, root's group, and everyone else). The 1 at the beginning of the permission value sets the sticky bit. This bit, when set on directories, keeps users from deleting or renaming files they don't own.

5. Commit the changes to the currently running Samba service with the **systemctl reload smb** command.

6. When testing the result from a remote system, any username in the local Samba database should work.

Lab 6

This lab may take a significant amount of work. You'll need to set up a group of users, with group ownership of a dedicated directory. Because that discussion in Chapter 8 was based on an RHCSA requirement, you may have to repeat that process in this lab.

Set up a user account for mounting the Samba share:

```
# useradd -M -s /sbin/nologin sambashare
# smbpasswd -a sambashare
```

Add the credentials of this user account in a file (for example, /etc/sambashare). The content of the file should include the following directives:

```
username=sambashare
password=sambasharepssword
```

Then, add a line like the following to /etc/fstab:

```
//server1.example.com/public /home/share cifs multiuser,↵
credentials=/etc/sambashare 0 0
```

Note that the mount options include the **multiuser** directive. Once the filesystem is mounted, users must run the following command to store their credentials into the system keyring and access the contents of the share:

```
$ cifscreds add server1.example.com
```

Lab 7

It's important to make sure that the configured service actually runs after a reboot. In fact, it's best to make sure the configured service works after a SELinux relabel, but that process can take several minutes or more. Also, it's quite possible that you won't have that kind of time during an exam.

1. To complete many Linux configuration changes, you need to make sure that the service will start automatically when you reboot your computer. In general, the key command is **systemctl**. In this case, the **systemctl enable smb nmb** command sets up the **smbd** and **nmbd** daemons to become active when you boot Linux in the default target.

2. You can use various commands to perform an orderly shutdown, such as **shutdown**, **halt**, and more.

3. After the reboot, you should verify at least one appropriate change to the Samba SELinux settings with the following command:

   ```
   # getsebool samba_enable_home_dirs
   ```

4. In addition, you should confirm appropriate directories are configured with the samba_share_t file context type, not only with the **ls -Z** command in the noted directories, but also in the file_contexts.local file, in the /etc/selinux/targeted/contexts/files directory.

Chapter 16

NFS Secured with Kerberos

L inux is designed for networking. It allows you to share files in two major ways: Samba, covered in Chapter 15, and the Network File System (NFS). RHEL 7 does not include GUI tools for NFS, but that is not a problem because NFS configuration files are relatively simple.

This chapter starts with a description of NFS, a powerful and versatile way of sharing data between servers and workstations. A default installation of RHEL 7 includes an NFS client, which supports connections to NFS servers.

An NFS server can limit access to clients based on their hostnames or IP addresses. In addition, NFS trusts the UIDs sent by clients to verify file permissions. This provides only a basic level of security, which may not be adequate for some organizations. But if used in conjunction with Kerberos, NFS can authenticate access to network shares and provide data encryption. This chapter will explain how to set up such configuration.

Take the time you need to understand the configuration files associated with the NFS service and Kerberos, and practice making them work on a Linux computer. In some cases, two or three computers (such as the KVM virtual machines discussed in Chapters 1 and 2) running Linux can help you practice the lessons of this chapter.

INSIDE THE EXAM

Inside the Exam

As shown here, the RHCE objectives for NFS are essentially the same as for Samba. Of course, what you do to configure NFS is different.

- Provide network shares to specific clients
- Provide network shares suitable for group collaboration

The process for limiting NFS access to specific clients is straightforward. In addition, the way to set up group collaboration for an NFS network share is based on techniques that we have already discussed in Chapter 8.

The integration between NFS and Kerberos is a new requirement for the RHCE exam on RHEL 7. The objective is to

- Use Kerberos to control access to NFS network shares

In addition, you will configure firewalld and SELinux to work with NFS.

CERTIFICATION OBJECTIVE 16.01

The Network File System (NFS) Server

NFS is the standard for sharing files with Linux and Unix computers. It was originally developed by Sun Microsystems in the mid-1980s. Linux has supported NFS (both as a client and a server) for years, and NFS continues to be popular in organizations with Unix- or Linux-based networks.

You can create NFS shares by editing the /etc/exports configuration file, or by creating a new file in the /etc/exports.d directory. In that way, you can set up NFS for basic operation. To set up more advanced configurations, it can be helpful to understand the way NFS works and how it communicates over a network.

You can enhance NFS security in a number of ways, including the following:

- A properly configured firewall
- TCP Wrappers
- SELinux
- Kerberos authentication and encryption

NFS Options for RHEL 7

While NFS version 4 (NFSv4) is the default, RHEL 7 also supports NFS 3 (NFSv3). The differences between NFSv3 and NFSv4 include the way clients and servers communicate, the maximum file sizes, and support for Windows-style access control lists (ACLs).

If you use NFSv4, you do not need to set up Remote Procedure Call (RPC) communication with the **rpcbind** package. However, RPC is required for NFSv3.

NFSv3 introduced support for 64-bit file sizes to handle files larger than 2GB. NFSv4 extends NFSv3 and provides several performance improvements. It also supports better security, through integration with Kerberos. Whereas NFSv3 relies on a separate protocol for file locking known as "NLM" (the Network Lock Manager), NFSv4 includes file locking natively.

on the Job

NFS version 4.1 supports clustered deployments through the pNFS (parallel NFS) extension. pNFS allows NFS to scale by distributing data across multiple servers and by retrieving that data in parallel from clients. For more information, see the websites http://www.pnfs.org and https://github.com/nfs-ganesha/nfs-ganesha.

Basic NFS Installation

The primary group associated with NFS software is the "File and Storage Server" group. In other words, if you run the following command, **yum** installs the mandatory packages from that group:

```
# yum group install "File and Storage Server"
```

However, this group also includes packages for Samba, CIFS, and iSCSI target support. The only package required to set up an NFS server or client is **nfs-utils**:

```
# yum -y install nfs-utils
```

You may want to install additional packages, including the following:

■ **nfs4-acl-tools**   Provides command-line utilities to retrieve and edit access lists on NFS shares.

■ **portreserve**   Supports the **portreserve** service, the successor to **portmap** for NFS communication. Prevents NFS from taking ports needed by other services.

■ **quota**   Provides quota support for shared NFS directories.

■ **rpcbind**   Includes RPC communication support for different NFS channels.

Basic NFS Server Configuration

NFS servers are relatively easy to configure. All you need to do is export a filesystem and then mount that filesystem from a remote client.

Of course, that assumes you have opened up the right ports in the firewall and modified appropriate SELinux options. NFS is controlled by a series of systemd service units. It also comes with a broad array of control commands.

NFS Services

Once the appropriate packages are installed, they are controlled by several different systemd service units:

■ **nfs-server.service**   Service unit for the NFS server; refers to /etc/sysconfig/nfs for basic configuration.

■ **nfs-secure-server.service**   Starts the **rpc.svcgssd** daemon, which provides Kerberos authentication and encryption support for the NFS server.

■ **nfs-secure.service**   Starts the **rpc.gssd** daemon, which negotiates Kerberos authentication and encryption between an NFS client and server.

■ **nfs-idmap.service**   Runs the **rpc.idmapd** daemon, which translates user and group IDs into names. Automatically started by the **nfs-server** systemd unit.

■ **nfs-lock.service**   Required by NFSv3. Starts the **rpc.statd** daemon, which provides locks and the status for files currently in use.

■ **nfs-mountd.service**   Runs the **rpc.mountd** NFS mount daemon. Required by NFSv3.

■ **nfs-rquotad.service**   Starts the **rpc.rquotad** daemon, which provides filesystem quota services to NFS shares. Automatically started by the **nfs-server** systemd unit.

■ **rpcbind.service**   Executes the **rpcbind** daemon, which converts RPC program numbers into addresses. Used by NFSv3. Automatically started by the **nfs-server** systemd unit.

To bring up an NFS server, you don't have to memorize all the service units just listed. Given the default dependencies between service units, all you need to do is run the following commands on the NFS server machine:

```
# systemctl start nfs-server
# systemctl enable nfs-server
```

To enable Kerberos support for NFS, you also need to activate the **nfs-secure-server** and **nfs-secure** services on the server and client machines, respectively. This will be covered in more detail in the next sections.

NFS Control Commands and Files

NFS includes a wide variety of commands to set up exports, to show what's available, to see what's mounted, to review statistics, and more. Except for specialized **mount** commands, these commands can be found in the /usr/sbin directory.

The NFS **mount** commands are **mount.nfs** and **umount.nfs**. There are also two symbolic links, **mount.nfs4** and **umount.nfs4**. Functionally, they work like regular **mount** and **umount** commands. As suggested by the extensions, they apply to filesystems shared via NFSv4 and other NFS versions. Like other **mount.*** commands, they have functional equivalents. For example, the **mount.nfs4** command is functionally equivalent to the **mount -t nfs4** command.

If you're mounting a share via the **mount.nfs** and **mount -t nfs** commands, NFS tries to mount the share using NFSv4 and fails back to NFSv3 if version 4 is not supported by the server.

The packages associated with NFS include a substantial number of commands in the /usr/sbin directory. The list of commands shown here are just the ones most commonly used to configure and test NFS:

- **exportfs** The **exportfs** command can be used to manage directories shared through and configured in the /etc/exports file.

- **nfsiostat** A statistics command for input/output rates based on an existing mount point. Uses information from the /proc/self/mountstats file.

- **nfsstat** A statistics command for client/server activity based on an existing mount point. Uses information from the /proc/self/mountstats file.

- **showmount** The command most closely associated with a display of shared NFS directories, locally and remotely.

You can use ACL-related commands from the nfs4-acl-tools RPM. You can run these commands against filesystems mounted locally with the **acl** option, as discussed in Chapter 6. The commands themselves are straightforward, as they set (**nfs4_setfacl**), edit (**nfs4_editfacl**), and list (**nfs4_getfacl**) the current ACLs of specified files. While these commands go beyond the basic operation of NFS, they are briefly discussed here and in Chapter 4.

Assume you have mounted a /home directory with the **acl** option. You've shared that directory via NFS. When you apply the **nfs4_getfacl** command on a file on that shared directory, you may see the following output:

```
A::OWNER@:rwatTcCy
A::GROUP@:tcy
A::EVERYONE@:tcy
```

The ACLs are set to either Allow (A) or Deny (D) access to the file owner (OWNER, GROUP, or EVERYONE). The permissions that follow are finer-grained than regular rwx permissions. For example, to represent Linux write permissions, ACLs enable both write (w) and append (a) permissions.

Perhaps the simplest way to modify these ACLs is with the **nfs4_setfacl -e *filename*** command, which allows you to edit current permissions in a text editor. As an example, to edit a file ACL on a share mounted via NFSv4 from a remote system, run the following command:

```
$ nfs4_setfacl -e /tmp/michael/filename.txt
```

This command opens the given NFSv4 ACLs in the default text editor for the user (normally **vi**). When we deleted the append permissions for the owner of the file and then saved the changes, this action actually removed both append and write permissions for the file. To review the result, run the **nfs4_getfacl** command again:

```
D::OWNER@:wa
A::OWNER@:rtTcCy
A::GROUP@:rwatcy
A::EVERYONE@:rtcy
```

If you try the **ls -l** command on the same file, you will note that the file owner no longer has write permissions.

Configure NFS for Basic Operation

The NFS share configuration file, /etc/exports, is fairly simple. Once it's configured, you can export the directories configured in that file with the **exportfs -a** command.

Each line in /etc/exports lists the directory to be exported, the hosts to which it will be exported, and the options that apply to this export. While you can set multiple conditions, you can export a particular directory only once. Take the following examples from an /etc/exports file:

```
/pub    tester1.example.com(rw,sync) *(ro,sync)
/home   *.example.com(rw,async) 172.16.10.0/24(ro)
/tftp   nodisk.example.net(rw,no_root_squash,sync)
```

In this example, the /pub directory is exported to the tester1.example.com client with read/write permissions. It is also exported to all other clients with read-only permissions. The /home directory is exported with read/write permissions to all clients on the example .com network, and read-only to clients on the 172.16.10.0/24 subnet. Finally, the /tftp directory is exported with full read/write permissions (even for root users) to the nodisk .example.net computer.

While these options are fairly straightforward, the /etc/exports file is somewhat picky. A space at the end of a line could lead to a syntax error. A space between a hostname and the conditions in parentheses would open access to all hosts.

All of these options include the **sync** flag. This requires write operations to be committed to disk before returning the status to the client. Before NFSv4, many such options included the **insecure** flag, which allows access on ports above 1024. More options will be discussed in the following sections.

You can also split the NFS configuration in multiple files with a .exports extension, within the /etc/exports.d directory. For instance, you could take the three configuration lines in the previous /etc/exports file and move them into separate files named pub.exports, home.exports, and tftp.exports within the /etc/exports.d directory.

e x a m

ⓦ a t c h   **Be careful with the /etc/exports file. For example, an extra space after either comma in (ro,no_root_ squash,sync) means that the specified directory won't get exported.**

Wildcards and Globbing

In Linux network configuration files, you can specify a group of computers with the right wildcard, which in Linux is also known as *globbing*. What can be used as a wildcard depends on the configuration file. The NFS /etc/exports file uses "conventional" wildcards: for example, *.example.net specifies all computers within the example.net domain. In contrast, in the /etc/hosts.deny file, .example.net, with the leading dot, specifies all computers in that same domain.

For IPv4 networks, wildcards often specify an implicit subnet mask. For example, 192.168.0.* is equivalent to 192.168.0.0/255.255.255.0, which specifies the 192.168.0.0 network of computers with IP addresses that range from 192.168.0.1 to 192.168.0.254. Some services, including NFS, support the use of CIDR (Classless Inter-Domain Routing) notation. In CIDR, since 255.255.255.0 masks 24 bits, CIDR represents this with the number *24*. When configuring a network in CIDR notation, you can represent this network as 192.168.0.0/24.

More NFS Server Options

With /etc/exports, it's possible to use a number of different parameters. The parameters described in Tables 16-1 and 16-2 fall into two categories: general and security options.

TABLE 16-1	NFS /etc/exports General Options

Parameter	Description
async	Write operations are performed asynchronously. Provides better throughput, at the risk of losing data if the NFS server crashes.
hide	Hides filesystems; if you export a directory and subdirectory such as /mnt and /mnt/inst, shares to /mnt/inst must be explicitly mounted.
mp	Exports a directory only if it was successfully mounted; requires the export point to also be a mount point on the server.
ro	Exports a volume read-only.
rw	Exports a volume read-write.
sync	Commits write operations to disk before replying to the client. Active by default.

Other parameters relate to security settings of NFS shared directories. As shown in Table 16-2, the options are associated with the root administrative user, anonymous-only users, and Kerberos authentication.

Activate the List of Exports

After you configure the /etc/exports file, make those directories available to clients with the **exportfs -a** command. The next time RHEL 7 is booted, if the right services are activated, the nfs-server systemd unit runs the **exportfs -r** command, which re-exports directories configured in /etc/exports.

However, if you're modifying, moving, or deleting NFS shares, you should temporarily un-export all directories first with the **exportfs -ua** command. You can make desired

TABLE 16-2	NFS /etc/exports Security Options

Parameter	Description
all_squash	Maps all local and remote accounts to the anonymous user.
anongid=*groupid*	Specifies a group ID for the anonymous user account.
anonuid=*userid*	Specifies a user ID for the anonymous user account.
insecure	Supports communications above port 1024, primarily for NFS versions 2 and 3.
no_root_squash	Treats the remote root user as local root; if this parameter is not set, by default the root user will be mapped to the nfsnobody user.
sec=*value*	Specifies a list of colon-separated security options. The default value is **sys**, which instructs the NFS server to rely on UIDs/GIDs for file access. Kerberos-related values are **krb5**, **krb5i**, and **krb5p**.

changes and then export the shares with the **exportfs -a** or **exportfs -r** command. The difference between **-a** and **-r** is subtle but important: whereas **-a** exports (or un-exports, in combination with **-u**) all directories, **-r** re-exports all directories by synchronizing the list of shares and removing those that have been deleted from the /etc/exports configuration file.

Once exports are active, you can review their status with the **showmount -e** *servername* command. For example, the **showmount -e server1.example.com** command looks for the list of exported NFS directories from the server1.example.com system. If this command is not successful, communication may be blocked by a firewall.

Fixed Ports in /etc/sysconfig/nfs

NFSv4 is easier to configure, especially with respect to firewalls. To enable communication with an NFSv4 server, the only port you need to open is TCP port 2049. This port is part of the nfs service in firewalld, so you should run the following commands on an NFS server to allow inbound connections:

```
# firewall-cmd --permanent --add-service=nfs
# firewall-cmd --reload
```

While NFSv4 is the default, RHEL 7 also supports NFSv3. So given the publicly available information on the RHCE exam, you might also need to know how to handle this version of NFS. NFSv3 uses dynamic port numbers through the RPC service, which listens on UDP port 111, and is associated to the rpc-bind firewalld service. You also need to grant access to the mountd service, so in total you need to allow the following services to support NFSv3 through firewalld:

```
# firewall-cmd --permanent --add-service=nfs --add-service=rpc-bind \
> --add-service=mountd
# firewall-cmd --reload
```

Once the NFS service is started with the **systemctl start nfs-server** command, if successful you'll see the associated ports in the output to the **rpcinfo** command, which lists all communication channels associated with RPC. The following command is more precise because it isolates actual port numbers:

```
# rpcinfo -p
```

Sample output is shown in Figure 16-1. At first glance, the lines may appear repetitive; however, every line has a purpose. Unless another RPC-related service such as the Network Information Service (NIS) is running, all of the lines shown here are required for NFS communications. Examine the first line shown here:

```
program vers proto   port  service
 100000    4   tcp    111  portmapper
```

FIGURE 16-1

Sample rpcinfo -p
output with NFS-
related ports

```
[root@server1 ~]# rpcinfo -p
   program vers proto   port  service
    100000    4   tcp    111  portmapper
    100000    3   tcp    111  portmapper
    100000    2   tcp    111  portmapper
    100000    4   udp    111  portmapper
    100000    3   udp    111  portmapper
    100000    2   udp    111  portmapper
    100024    1   udp  35364  status
    100024    1   tcp  50967  status
    100005    1   udp  20048  mountd
    100005    1   tcp  20048  mountd
    100005    2   udp  20048  mountd
    100005    2   tcp  20048  mountd
    100005    3   udp  20048  mountd
    100005    3   tcp  20048  mountd
    100003    3   tcp   2049  nfs
    100003    4   tcp   2049  nfs
    100227    3   tcp   2049  nfs_acl
    100003    3   udp   2049  nfs
    100003    4   udp   2049  nfs
    100227    3   udp   2049  nfs_acl
    100021    1   udp  41077  nlockmgr
    100021    3   udp  41077  nlockmgr
    100021    4   udp  41077  nlockmgr
    100021    1   tcp  46344  nlockmgr
    100021    3   tcp  46344  nlockmgr
    100021    4   tcp  46344  nlockmgr
    100011    1   udp    875  rquotad
    100011    2   udp    875  rquotad
    100011    1   tcp    875  rquotad
    100011    2   tcp    875  rquotad
[root@server1 ~]#
```

The first line represents the arbitrary RPC program number, the NFS version, and the use of TCP as a communications protocol, over port 111, with the portmapper service. Note the availability of the portmapper service to NFS versions 2, 3, and 4, communicating over the TCP and UDP protocols.

Communication through selected ports should also be allowed through any configured firewall. For example, Figure 16-2 shows that the firewalld configuration supports remote access to a local NFS server through protocol versions 3 and 4.

You can set up these firewall rules with the graphical **firewall-config** tool discussed in Chapter 4.

Make NFS Work with SELinux

Of course, you need to configure more than a firewall. SELinux is an integral part of the security landscape, with respect to both boolean options and files. First, be aware of the following NFS SELinux file types:

- **nfs_t** Associated with NFS shares that are exported read-only or read-write.
- **public_content_ro_t** Associated with NFS shares that are exported read-only.

FIGURE 16-2

Firewall rules
for NFS

```
[root@server1 ~]# firewall-cmd --permanent --add-service=nfs \
> --add-service=rpc-bind --add-service=mountd
success
[root@server1 ~]# firewall-cmd --reload
success
[root@server1 ~]# firewall-cmd --list-all
public (default, active)
  interfaces: eth0
  sources:
  services: dhcpv6-client mountd nfs rpc-bind ssh
  ports:
  masquerade: no
  forward-ports:
  icmp-blocks:
  rich rules:

[root@server1 ~]# █
```

- **public_content_rw_t**   Associated with NFS shares that are exported read-write. Requires the **nfsd_anon_write** boolean to be set.
- **var_lib_nfs_t**   Associated with dynamic files in the /var/lib/nfs directory. Files in this directory are updated as shares are exported and mounted by clients.
- **nfsd_exec_t**   Assigned to system executable files such as **rpc.mountd** and **rpc.nfsd** in the /usr/sbin directory. Closely related are the rpcd_exec_t and gssd_exec_t file types for services associated with RPCs and communications with Kerberos servers.

In general, you won't have to assign a new file type to a shared NFS directory. In fact, the SELinux file types that are related to file shares (nfs_t, public_content_ro_t, and public_content_rw_t) are effective only when the nfs_exports_all_ro and nfs_exports_all_rw booleans are disabled. So for most administrators, these file types are shown for reference.

For SELinux, the boolean directives are most important. The options are shown in the Booleans section of the SELinux Administration tool, with the nfs filter, as shown in Figure 16-3. The figure reflects the default configuration; as you can see, two of the options in the global module are enabled by default.

The following directives are associated with making NFS work with SELinux in targeted mode. While most of these options were already listed in Chapter 10, they're worth repeating, if only to help those who fear SELinux. The options are described in the order shown in the figure.

- **httpd_use_nfs**   Supports access by the Apache web server to shared NFS shares.
- **cdrecord_read_content**   Enables access to mounted NFS shares by the **cdrecord** command.
- **cobbler_use_nfs**   Allows Cobbler to access NFS filesystems.
- **ftpd_use_nfs**   Allows the use of shared NFS directories by FTP servers.

FIGURE 16-3 NFS-related SELinux boolean options

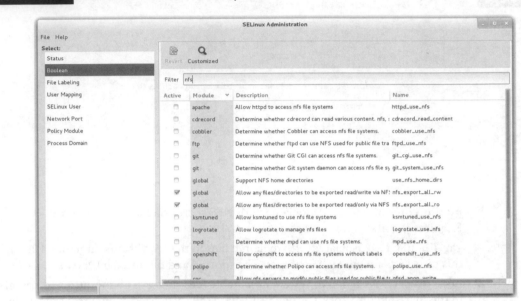

- **git_cgi_use_nfs** Supports access to NFS shares by the git revision control system service in CGI scripts.
- **git_system_use_nfs** Supports access to NFS shares by the git revision control system service.
- **use_nfs_home_dirs** Enables the mounting of /home from a remote NFS server.
- **nfs_export_all_rw** Supports read-write access to shared NFS directories.
- **nfs_export_all_ro** Supports read-only access to shared NFS directories.
- **ksmtuned_use_nfs** Allows ksmtuned to access NFS shares.
- **logrotate_use_nfs** Allows logrotate to access NFS files.
- **mpd_use_nfs** Allows the Music Player Daemon to access content from NFS shares.
- **openshift_use_nfs** Allows OpenShift to access NFS filesystems.
- **polipo_use_nfs** Allows access by the Polipo web proxy to NFS-mounted filesystems.
- **nfsd_anon_write** Allows NFS servers to modify public files. Files must labeled with the public_content_rw_t type.
- **samba_share_nfs** Allows Samba to export NFS-mounted filesystems.
- **sanlock_use_nfs** Enables the SANlock lock manager daemon to access NFS files.

- **sge_use_nfs** Allows the Sun Grid Engine to access NFS files.
- **virt_use_nfs** Enables access by VMs to NFS-mounted filesystems.
- **virt_sandbox_use_nfs** Allows sandbox containers to access NFS filesystems.
- **xen_use_nfs** Allows access by the Xen hypervisor to NFS-mounted filesystems.

To set these directives, use the **setsebool** command. For example, to activate access to NFS filesystems by an FTP server, in a way that survives a reboot, run the following command:

```
# setsebool -P ftpd_use_nfs 1
```

Quirks and Limitations of NFS

NFS does have its limitations. Any administrator who controls shared NFS directories would be wise to take note of these limitations.

Statelessness

NFSv3 is a "stateless" protocol. In other words, you don't need to log in separately to access a shared NFS directory. Instead, the NFS client normally contacts **rpc.mountd** on the server. The **rpc.mountd** daemon handles mount requests. It checks the request against currently exported filesystems. If the request is valid, **rpc.mountd** provides an NFS *file handle* (a "magic cookie"), which is then used for further client/server communication for this share.

The stateless protocol allows the NFS client to wait if the NFS server ever has to be rebooted. The software waits, and waits, and waits. This can cause the NFS client to hang. The client may even have to reboot or even power-cycle the system.

This can also lead to problems with insecure single-user clients. When a file is opened through a share, it may be "locked out" from other users. When an NFS server is rebooted, handling the locked file can be difficult.

The changes that led to the development of NFSv4 introduced a stateful protocol to make the locking mechanism more robust, and should help address this problem.

Root Squash

By default, NFS is set up to **root_squash**, which prevents root users on an NFS client from gaining root access to a share on an NFS server. Specifically, the root user on a client (with a user ID of 0) is mapped to the *nfsnobody* unprivileged account (if in doubt, check the local /etc/passwd file).

This behavior can be disabled via the **no_root_squash** server export option in /etc/exports. For exported directories with the **no_root_squash** option, remote root users can use their root privileges on the shared NFS directory. While it can be useful, it is also a security risk, especially from "black hat" hackers who use their own Linux systems to take advantage of those root privileges.

NFS Hangs

Because NFSv3 is stateless, NFS clients may wait up to several minutes for a server. In some cases, an NFS client may wait indefinitely if a server goes down. During the wait, any process that looks for a file on the mounted NFS share will hang. Once this happens, it is generally difficult to unmount the offending filesystems, unless you pass the "lazy" option to the **umount** command (**umount -l**). This may still leave some processes in an uninterruptible sleep state, waiting for I/O. You can do several things to reduce the impact of this problem:

- Take great care to ensure the reliability of NFS servers and the network.
- Mount infrequently used NFS exports only when needed. NFS clients should unmount these shares after use.
- Don't use **async**, and set up NFS shares with the **sync** option (the default), which should at least reduce the incidence of lost data.
- Keep NFS-mounted directories out of the search path for users, especially that of root.
- Keep NFS-mounted directories out of the root (/) directory; instead, segregate them to a less frequently used filesystem, if possible, on a separate partition.

Inverse DNS Pointers

An NFS server daemon checks mount requests. First, it looks at the current list of exports, based on /etc/exports. Then it looks up the client's IP address to find its hostname. This requires a reverse DNS lookup.

This hostname is then finally checked against the list of exports. If NFS can't find a hostname, **rpc.mountd** will deny access to that client. For security reasons, it also adds a "request from unknown host" entry in /var/log/messages.

File Locking

Multiple NFS clients can be set up to mount the same exported directory from the same server. It's quite possible that people on different computers end up trying to use the same shared file. This is addressed by the file-locking daemon service.

While mandatory locks are supported by NFSv4, NFS has historically had serious problems with file locks. If you have an application that depends on file locking over NFS, test it thoroughly before putting it into production.

In addition, you should never share the same directory with NFS and Samba simultaneously because the different locking mechanisms used by these services can cause data corruption.

Performance Tips

You take several steps to keep NFS running in a stable and reliable manner. As you gain experience with NFS, you might monitor or even experiment with the following factors:

- Eight NFS processes, which is the default, is generally sufficient for good performance, even under fairly heavy loads. To increase the capacity of the service, you can add more NFS processes through the **RPCNFSDCOUNT** directive in the /etc/sysconfig/nfs configuration file. Just keep in mind that the extra processes consume additional system resources.

- NFS write performance can be slow. In applications where data loss is not a big concern, you may try the **async** option. This makes NFS faster because the server immediately returns the state of a write operation to the client, without waiting for the data to be written to disk. However, a loss of power or network connectivity can result in a loss of data.

- Hostname lookups are performed frequently by the NFS server; you can start the Name Switch Cache Daemon (**nscd**) to speed lookup performance.

NFS Security Directives

NFS includes a number of potential security problems and should never be used in hostile environments (such as on a server directly exposed to the Internet), at least not without strong precautions.

Shortcomings and Risks

NFS is an easy-to-use yet powerful file-sharing system. However, it is not without its limitations. The following are a few security issues to keep in mind:

- **Authentication**   NFS relies on the host to report user and group IDs. However, this can be a security risk if root users on other computers access your NFS shares. In other words, data that is accessible via NFS to *any user* can potentially be accessed by *any other* user. This risk is addressed by NFSv4 if Kerberos is used for authentication.

- **Privacy**   Before NFSv4, NFS did not support encryption. NFSv4 with the support of Kerberos can provide encrypted communications.

- **rpcbind infrastructure**   Both the NFSv3 client and server depend on the RPC portmap daemon. The earlier versions of the daemon had historically a number of serious security holes. For this reason, RHEL 7 has replaced it with the rpcbind service.

Security Tips

If NFS *must* be used in or near a hostile environment, you can reduce the security risks:

- Educate yourself in detail about NFS security. If possible, set up encrypted NFSv4 communications with the help of Kerberos. Otherwise, restrict NFS to friendly, internal networks protected with a good firewall.
- Export as little data as possible, and export filesystems as read-only if possible.
- Unless absolutely necessary, don't supersede the **root_squash** option. Otherwise, "black hat" hackers on allowed clients may grant root-level access to exported filesystems.
- Use appropriate firewall settings to deny access to the portmapper and nfsd ports, except from explicitly trusted hosts or networks. If you're using NFSv4, it's good enough to open only the following port via the nfs firewalld service:

```
2049     TCP           nfsd            (server)
```

Options for Host-Based Security

To review, host-based security on NFS systems is based primarily on the systems allowed to access a share in the /etc/exports file. Of course, host-based security can also include limits based on firewall rules.

e x a m

w a t c h As long as there's a common user database, such as LDAP, the permissions associated with a common group directory carry over to a mount shared via NFS.

Options for User-Based Security

As NFS mounts should reflect the security associated with a common user database, the standard user-based security options should apply. That includes the configuration of a common group, as discussed in Chapter 8.

EXERCISE 16-1

NFS

This exercise requires two systems: one set up as an NFS server, the other as an NFS client. Then, on the NFS server, take the following steps:

1. Set up a group named IT for the Information Technology group in /etc/group.
2. Create the /MIS directory. Assign ownership to the MIS group with the **chgrp** command.

3. Set the SGID bit on this directory to enforce group ownership.
4. Ensure that the **nfs-utils** RPM package is installed.
5. On the server, start and enable the NFS service to run at boot:

```
# systemctl start nfs-server
# systemctl enable nfs-server
```

6. Update the /etc/exports file to allow read and write permissions to the share for the local network. Run the following command to apply the change:

```
# exportfs -a
```

7. Make sure the SELinux booleans are set appropriately; specifically, make sure the nfs_export_all_ro and nfs_export_all_rw booleans are both enabled. This is the default setting. You can do so either with the **getsebool** command or the SELinux Management tool.

8. Open the required ports on the firewall. For NFSv4, the following commands are required:

```
# firewall-cmd --permanent --add-service=nfs
# firewall-cmd --reload
```

Then, on an NFS client, take the following steps:

9. Ensure that the **nfs-utils** RPM package is installed.
10. Create a directory for the server share called /mnt/MIS.
11. Mount the shared NFS directory on /mnt/MIS.
12. List all exported shares from the server and save this output in the shares.list file in the /mnt/MIS directory.
13. Make this a permanent mount in the /etc/fstab file. Assume that the connection might be troublesome, and add the appropriate options, such as **soft** mounting.
14. Run the **mount -a** command to reread /etc/fstab. Check to see if the share is properly remounted.
15. Test the NFS connection. Stop the NFS service on the server and then try copying a file to the /mnt/MIS directory. While the attempt to copy will fail, it should not hang the client.
16. Restart the NFS service on the server.
17. Edit /etc/fstab again. This time, assume that NFS is reliable and remove the special options added in Step 13.
18. Now shut down the server and test what happens. The mounted NFS directory on the client should hang when you try to access the service.
19. The client computer may lock. If so, you can boot into the rescue target, as described in Chapter 5, to avoid the pain of a reboot. Restore the original configuration.

Test an NFS Client

Now you can mount a shared NFS directory from a client computer. The commands and configuration files are similar to those used for any local filesystem. In the preceding section, you configured an NFS server. For now, stay on the NFS server system, as the first client test can be run directly from this machine.

NFS Mount Options

Before doing anything elaborate, you should check for the list of shared NFS directories. Then you can mount a shared NFS volume from a second Linux system, presumably a RHEL 7 system (or equivalent). To that end, the **showmount** command displays the available shared volumes.

Run the **showmount** command with the **-e** option; when coupled with the hostname or IP address of the NFS server, the command displays the export list, possibly including the host limits of the share. For example, given a simple share of the /mnt and /home directories on a given NFS server, the **showmount -e server1.example.com** command provides the following result:

```
Export list for server1.example.com:
/mnt  192.168.100.0/24
/home 192.168.122.0/24
```

If you don't see a list of shared directories, log in to the NFS server system. Repeat the **showmount** command, substituting localhost or 127.0.0.1 for the hostname or IP address. If there's still no output, review the steps described earlier in this chapter. Make sure the /etc/exports file is configured properly. Remember to export the shared directories. Use the command

```
# systemctl status nfs-server
```

to confirm that the NFS services are running.

Now to mount this directory locally, you'll need an empty local directory. Create a directory such as /remotemnt. You can then mount the shared directory from a system such as 192.168.122.50 with the following command:

```
# mount.nfs 192.168.122.50:/share /remotemnt
```

This command mounts the NFS /share directory from the computer on the noted IP address. If desired, you could substitute the **mount -t nfs** command for **mount.nfs**. When it works, you'll be able to access files from the remote /share directory as if it were a local directory. If the local mount works but the remote mount does not, check the firewall settings and ensure that the service is running.

Configure NFS in /etc/fstab

You can also configure an NFS client to mount a remote NFS directory during the boot process, as defined in /etc/fstab. For example, the following entry in a client /etc/fstab mounts the /homenfs share from the computer named nfsserv on the local /nfs/home directory, using the default version 4 of the protocol:

```
nfsserv:/homenfs   /nfs/home  nfs  soft,timeo=100  0  0
```

The **soft** and **timeo** options are two specialized NFS mount options. Such options, as shown here, can also be used to customize how mounts are done during the boot process in the /etc/fstab file.

Consider using the **soft** option when mounting NFS filesystems. When an NFS server fails, a soft-mounted NFS filesystem will fail rather than hang. However, this can cause data corruption in case of a temporary network outage. Use this option only when the responsiveness of a client is more important than data integrity. In addition, you can use the **timeo** option to set a timeout interval, in tenths of a second.

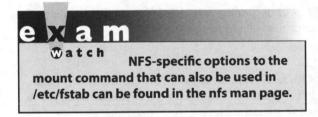

For more information on these and related options, see the nfs man page, available with the **man nfs** command.

Alternatively, an automounter can be used to mount NFS filesystems dynamically as required by the client computer. The automounter can also unmount these remote filesystems after a period of inactivity. For more information on the governing autofs service, see Chapter 6.

Diskless Clients

NFS supports diskless clients, which are computers that do not store the operating system locally. A diskless client may use a flash memory chip to get started. Then embedded commands can mount the appropriate root (/) directory, set up swap space, set the /usr directory as read-only, and configure other shared directories such as /home in read/write mode. If your computer is set up as a diskless client, you'll also need access to DHCP and TFTP servers to boot the system from a network boot server.

Red Hat Enterprise Linux includes features that support diskless clients. While they are not listed as part of the current Red Hat exam requirements or related course outlines, we would not be surprised to see such requirements in the future.

Current NFS Status

The current status of NFS services is documented in two directories: /var/lib/nfs and /proc/fs/nfsd. If there's a problem with NFS, look at some of the files in these directories. Take these directories one at a time. First, there are two key files in the /var/lib/nfs directory:

- **etab**   Includes a full description of exported directories, including default options
- **rmtab**   Specifies the state of shared directories currently mounted

Take a look at the contents of the /proc/fs/nfsd directory. As this is a virtual directory, files in the /proc directory tree have a size of zero. However, as dynamic files, they can contain valuable information. Perhaps the key option for basic operation is the file /proc/fs/nfsd/versions. The content of that file specifies the currently recognized versions of NFS.

The normal content of this file is just a little cryptic, which suggests that the current NFS server can communicate using NFSv3, NFSv4, and NFSv4.1, but not with NFSv4.2 and NFSv2:

```
-2 +3 +4 +4.1 -4.2
```

If you set the **RPCNFSDARGS="-V 4.2"** option in the /etc/sysconfig/nfs file and restart the NFS service, the contents of the versions file will change to

```
-2 +3 +4 +4.1 +4.2
```

The difference is subtle but important. In fact, NFSv4.2 provides an experimental feature that allows you to keep the original SELinux context of each file in the shared directory. You may want to switch to NFSv4.2 if you need this feature.

CERTIFICATION OBJECTIVE 16.03

NFS with Kerberos

For several years, NFS was considered an insecure protocol. One reason is that NFS, by default, trusts the UID and GID sent by a client. A "black hat" hacker that has access to an NFS share can easily impersonate the identity of another user and pass her UID/GID credentials, because NFS is based on trust.

NFSv4 security issues have been addressed with Kerberos, which can provide strong authentication, integrity, and encryption services. If you need security with NFS, protect NFS exports with Kerberos.

This section is focused on the configuration of NFS with a Kerberos server. It assumes that you have set up a Kerberos KDC and that clients have joined the Kerberos realm, as described in Chapter 12.

Kerberos-Enabled NFS Services

To set up a simple NFS service as you did in Exercise 16-1, you need to activate the nfs-server systemd unit on the NFS server host. If you want to integrate NFS with Kerberos, you need to enable two additional services, nfs-secure-server and nfs-secure, as illustrated in Tables 16-3 and 16-4.

Therefore, the simplest way to set up all the required services on an NFS server is with the following commands:

```
# systemctl start nfs-server
# systemctl start nfs-secure-server
# systemctl enable nfs-server
# systemctl enable nfs-secure-server
```

It's also important to enable the following service unit on all NFS clients:

```
# systemctl start nfs-secure
# systemctl enable nfs-secure
```

As noted in Chapter 11, these commands start the noted service units and make sure the services start the next time the system is rebooted.

TABLE 16-3   The systemd Service Units on a Kerberos-Enabled NFS Server

systemd Service Unit	Description
nfs-server	The main service unit for the NFS server. It activates other service units, such as nfs-idmap, nfs-rquotad, and rpcbind.service. It uses /etc/sysconfig/nfs for basic configuration.
nfs-secure-server	Provides Kerberos-based authentication and encryption for an NFS server through the **rpc.svcgssd** daemon.

TABLE 16-4   The systemd Service Units on a Kerberos-Enabled NFS Client

systemd Service Unit	Description
nfs-secure	Provides Kerberos authentication and encryption services to an NFS client via the **rpc.gssd** daemon

Configure NFS Exports with Kerberos

The configuration of a Kerberos-enabled NFS export is straightforward and is based on the **sec** security option of /etc/exports, which we have already encountered in Table 16-2.

The **sec** option is followed by a colon-separated list of security flavors that an NFS server provides to its client. As an example, examine the following line from an /etc/exports file:

```
/nfs-share *.example.com(rw,sec=sys:krb5:krb5p)
```

This configuration exports the directory /nfs-share via NFS to clients in the example.com domain, with read-write access. Clients can mount the NFS share using one of the following security options: sys, krb5, or krb5p.

These options are illustrated in Table 16-5. From the information in the table, the most secure export method is **krb5p** because it provides Kerberos authentication, data integrity, and encryption. However, this comes at a cost, as data encryption requires CPU resources and may significantly affect performance.

The **krb5** and **krb5i** security options provide authentication and integrity services, and are a good compromise between security and throughput. Finally, the **sys** security method corresponds to the UID/GID trust model of NFS, which is always assumed as the default security method when the **sec** security option is not specified in /etc/exports.

If you want to force NFS clients to mount an NFS share using a specific security option, include that option as part of the **sec** parameter. For example, the following line in /etc/exports ensures that clients in the example.com domain mount the nfs-share directory with Kerberos authentication, integrity, and encryption:

```
/nfs-share *.example.com(rw,sec=krb5p)
```

Do remember to run **exportfs -r** on the NFS server to apply the change and refresh the list of exported directories.

TABLE 16-5 NFS Security Options

Security Option	Description
sys	Trusts the UID/GID provided by clients to determine file access permission. Enabled by default when no **sec=** option is specified.
krb5	Verifies the UID/GID provided by clients using Kerberos authentication.
krb5i	Has the same effect as the **krb5** option, but in addition provides strong communication integrity.
krb5p	Has the same effect as the **krb5i** option, but in addition provides encryption services.

Configure NFS Clients with Kerberos

NFS clients can easily mount an NFS share with Kerberos authentication, integrity, and encryption services using the **sec** option with the values listed in Table 16-5. To do so, include the **sec** option either with the **mount** command or in the /etc/fstab file.

For example, the following command mounts the nfs-share directory from the host 192.168.122.50 using Kerberos authentication:

```
mount -t nfs -o sec=krb5 192.168.122.50:/nfs-share /mnt
```

Similarly, the following line in /etc/fstab instructs the system to mount the nfs-share directory during the boot process using Kerberos authentication, encryption, and strong integrity:

```
192.168.122.50:/nfs-share   /mnt   nfs   soft,sec=krb5p 0   0
```

EXERCISE 16-2

Prepare a System for NFS Secured with Kerberos

To prepare a system to export shared directories via NFS secured with Kerberos, you need to complete a few configuration steps. We assume that you have installed a Kerberos KDC and configured server1.example.com for Kerberos authentication, as illustrated in Exercise 12-5.

Then on the KDC, take the following steps:

1. Create host principals for the NFS server (server1.example.com) and all clients (such as tester1.example.com):

```
# kadmin.local
Authenticating as principal root/admin@WAMPLE.COM with password
kadmin.local:  addprinc -randkey host/server1.example.com
WARNING: no policy specified for host/server1.example.com@EXAMPLE.COM;
defaulting to no policy
Principal "host/server1.example.com@EXAMPLE.COM" created.
kadmin.local: addprinc -randkey host/tester1.example.com
WARNING: no policy specified for host/tester1.example.com@EXAMPLE.COM;
defaulting to no policy
Principal "host/tester1.example.com@EXAMPLE.COM" created.
kadmin.local:
```

2. Add NFS service principals for the server and client machines:

```
kadmin.local: addprinc -randkey nfs/server1.example.com
WARNING: no policy specified for nfs/server1.example.com@EXAMPLE.COM;
defaulting to no policy
Principal "nfs/server1.example.com@EXAMPLE.COM" created.
kadmin.local: addprinc -randkey nfs/tester1.example.com
WARNING: no policy specified for nfs/tester1.example.com@EXAMPLE.COM;
defaulting to no policy
Principal "nfs/tester1.example.com@EXAMPLE.COM" created.
kadmin.local:
```

3. Generate the keytab files for the NFS server and client machines:

```
# kadmin.local: ktadd -k /tmp/server1.keytab nfs/server1.example.com
[output truncated]
# kadmin.local: ktadd -k /tmp/tester1.keytab nfs/server1.example.com
[output truncated]
```

4. Copy the keytab files to the /etc/krb5.keytab file on the remote systems:

```
# scp /tmp/server1.keytab server1.example.com:/etc/krb5.keytab
# scp /tmp/tester1.keytab tester1.example.com:/etc/krb5.keytab
```

5. Copy the /etc/krb5.conf file from the KDC to all NFS servers and clients:

```
# scp /etc/krb5.conf server1.example.com:/etc/krb5.conf
# scp /etc/krb5.conf tester1.example.com:/etc/krb5.conf
```

EXERCISE 16-3

Configure a Kerberos-Enabled NFS Share

In this exercise, you'll install an NFS server on a RHEL system and export a share with Kerberos authentication and encryption. This exercise assumes that you've set up a Kerberos Key Distribution Center and configured your server1.example.com and tester1.example.com virtual machines as described in Exercises 12-5 and 16-2.

1. Make sure the NFS server is installed on server1.example.com. The easiest way is with the following command:

```
# rpm -q nfs-utils
```

2. If it isn't already installed, use the techniques discussed earlier to install the nfs-utils RPM package.

3. Start the NFS service and its secure component to provide Kerberos authentication and encryption services:

```
# systemctl start nfs-server nfs-secure-server
```

4. Make sure the services are automatically activated the next time the system boots with the following command:

```
# systemctl enable nfs-server nfs-secure-server
```

5. Create a directory named nfs-secure:

```
# mkdir /nfs-secure
```

6. Configure the share in the /etc/exports file to allow read and write permissions to all clients with Kerberos authentication and encryption:

```
# echo "/nfs-secure *(rw,sec=krb5p)" >> /etc/exports
```

7. Apply the change:

```
# exportfs -r
```

8. Ensure that the nfs service is enabled on the firewall default zone:

```
# firewall-cmd --list-all
```

9. If it isn't enabled, add the service to the default zone:

```
# firewall-cmd --permanent --add-service=nfs
# firewall-cmd --reload
```

10. On the tester1.example.com client, ensure that the **nfs-utils** RPM package is installed.

11. Start the nfs-secure service and activate the service at boot:

```
# systemctl start nfs-secure
# systemctl enable nfs-secure
```

12. Create a directory for the server share called /mnt/nfs:

```
# mkdir /mnt/nfs
```

13. Add the following line to /etc/fstab:

```
192.168.122.50:/nfs-secure   /mnt/nfs  nfs  sec=krb5p 0  0
```

14. Run the **mount -a** command to mount the share.

SCENARIO & SOLUTION

You're having trouble configuring a firewall for NFS.	Enable the nfs service by running **firewall-cmd --add-service=nfs**.
You want to prohibit read/write access to shared NFS directories.	Make sure shares are configured with the **ro** parameter in /etc/exports.
You need to set up automatic mounts of a shared NFS directory.	Configure the shared directory in /etc/fstab.
You want to export an NFS share with Kerberos authentication and encryption.	Export and mount the share with the **sec=krb5p** option. Ensure that your systems are set up for Kerberos authentication, as described in Appendix A.
You need to start NFS services to export an NFS share with Kerberos authentication.	Enable the services **nfs-server** and **nfs-secure-server** on the NFS server, and **nfs-secure** on the clients.

CERTIFICATION SUMMARY

NFS allows you to share filesystems between Linux and Unix computers. It is an efficient way to share files between such systems, and it can be secured with Kerberos authentication and encryption.

While RHEL 7 supports NFSv4, it also supports access by NFSv3 clients. It's controlled by a group of systemd units. The service unit **nfs-server** is required to start the NFS daemon. Kerberos-based authentication and encryption are controlled by the **rpcsvcgssd** and **rpcgssd** daemons, which depend, respectively, on the **nfs-secure-server** service unit (on the server) and **nfs-secure** (on the client). The global options for the NFS service are set up primarily in the /etc/sysconfig/nfs file. Related commands include **exportfs** and **showmount**.

In most cases, you can set up a basic configuration of NFS via a straightforward one-line directive in the /etc/exports file. Once the NFS service is running, such exports are activated through the **exportfs** command. Firewalls should be configured by enabling the nfs service through the appropriate zone. Active ports and services can be confirmed with the **rpcinfo -p** command.

Generally, the default configuration of SELinux supports basic NFS operation. You can configure security for mounted NFS directories as if the mounted filesystems were local. You can also automate NFS mounts in /etc/fstab or through the automounter. The current status of NFS is documented in various files in the /var/lib/nfs and /proc/fs/nfsd directories.

TWO-MINUTE DRILL

Here are some of the key points from the certification objectives in Chapter 16.

The Network File System (NFS) Server

❑ NFS is the standard for sharing files between Linux and Unix computers. RHEL 7 supports NFS versions 3 and 4; NFSv4 is the default.

❑ Key NFS daemons are **rpc.mountd** for mount requests, **rpc.rquotad** for quota requests, and the **nfsd** daemon.

❑ You can find configuration options for these processes in the /etc/sysconfig/nfs file.

❑ NFS shares are configured in /etc/exports and activated with the **exportfs -r** command.

❑ Firewalls can be set by enabling the nfs service through the appropriate zone in firewalld.

❑ In most cases, required booleans for SELinux are already active.

❑ To disallow read/write access in SELinux, disable the nfs_export_all_rw boolean.

❑ When NFS directories are mounted, they should appear seamless. User permissions work in the same way as with a local directory.

Test an NFS Client

❑ Clients can mount permanent NFS shares through /etc/fstab.

❑ You can review shared directories on a client with the **showmount** command.

❑ The **mount** command is designed to mount directories shared via NFSv4 and NFSv3.

❑ If an NFS server fails, it can "hang" an NFS client. The **soft** and **timeo** options to the **mount** command can help prevent such hangs. However, using them would risk compromising the integrity of the data if a system crashes.

NFS with Kerberos

❑ By default, NFS is insecure because it trusts the UID/GID sent by clients.

❑ When integrated with Kerberos, NFS can provide strong authentication (**sec=krb5**), communication integrity (**sec=krb5i**), and encryption (**sec=krb5p**).

❑ To configure Kerberos-based NFS shares, specify the appropriate security parameter via the **sec=** option on the NFS clients and server.

❑ The **nfs-secure-server** service must be running on the NFS server to provide Kerberos services.

❑ The **nfs-secure** service must be running on the NFS clients to support Kerberos-authenticated mounts.

❑ NFS with Kerberos requires you to set up a KDC, as explained in Chapter 12.

SELF TEST

The following questions will help you measure your understanding of the material presented in this chapter. As no multiple choice questions appear on the Red Hat exams, no multiple choice questions appear in this book. These questions exclusively test your understanding of the chapter. It is okay if you have another way of performing a task. Getting results, not memorizing trivia, is what counts on the Red Hat exams. There may be more than one answer to many of these questions.

The Network File System (NFS) Server

1. In the /etc/exports file, you want to export the /data directory as read-only to all hosts and grant read and write permission to the hostname superv in the example.com domain. What directive would you enter in that file?

   _____

2. Once you've configured /etc/exports, what command exports these shares?

   _____

3. What port number is associated with the portmapper?

   _____

4. What port number is associated with NFSv4?

   _____

5. What is the NFS configuration option that supports access by the root administrative user?

   _____

Test an NFS Client

6. You're experiencing problems with NFS clients for various reasons, including frequent downtime on the NFS server and network disconnections between NFS clients and servers. What type of mounting can prevent NFS clients from hanging and retrying NFS requests indefinitely?

   _____

7. What is the command that can display NFS shared directories from the outsider1.example.org system?

   _____

NFS with Kerberos

8. Which service should you start on an NFS client to support Kerberos-based authentication via the **rpcgssd** daemon?

   _____

9. What directive should you include to mount an NFS share with Kerberos authentication and encryption?

   _____

10. What directive should you add to /etc/exports to export an NFS share with standard file access permissions and optionally with Kerberos authentication?

   _____

LAB QUESTIONS

Several of these labs involve configuration exercises. You should do these exercises on test machines only. It's assumed that you're running these exercises on virtual machines such as KVM. For this chapter, it's also assumed that you may be changing the configuration of a physical host system for such virtual machines.

Red Hat presents its exams electronically. For that reason, the labs in this chapter are available in the Chapter 16/ subdirectory from the media that accompanies the book. In case you haven't yet set up RHEL 7 on a system, refer to Chapters 1 and 2 for installation instructions.

The answers for each lab follow the Self Test answers for the fill-in-the-blank questions.

SELF TEST ANSWERS

The Network File System (NFS) Server

1. The following entry in /etc/exports would export the /data directory as read-only to all hosts and grant read and write permission to the host superv in the example.com domain:

   ```
   /data superv.example.com(rw,sync) (ro,sync)
   ```

2. Once you've revised /etc/exports, the **exportfs -a** command exports all filesystems. Yes, you can also re-export filesystems with the **exportfs -r** command.

3. The port number associated with the portmapper is UDP port 111.

4. The port number associated with NFSv4 is TCP port 2049.

5. The NFS configuration option that supports access by the root administrative user is **no_root_squash**.

Test an NFS Client

6. Soft mounting and timeouts associated with the **soft** and **timeo** options can prevent clients from hanging and retrying NFS requests indefinitely.

7. The command that can display NFS shared directories from the named remote system is **showmount -e outsider1.example.org**.

NFS with Kerberos

8. You should start the **nfs-secure** server to provide support for Kerberos-based authentication on a client via the **rpcgssd** daemon.

9. The directive that you should include to mount an NFS share with Kerberos authentication and encryption is **sec=krb5p**.

10. You can export the share with the **sec=sys:krb5p** security option.

LAB ANSWERS

Lab 1

When this lab is complete, you'll see the following features on the system with the NFS server:

- The nfs-utils RPM in the list of installed packages.
- An active NFS service, which can be confirmed in the output to the **systemctl status nfs-server** command.
- A zone-based firewall that supports access to the nfs service. It should also be limited by IP address network.

In addition, you'll be able to perform the following tasks from the NFS client:

- You can run the **showmount -e server1.example.com** command, where server1.example.com is the name of the NFS server system (substitute if and as needed).
- You can mount the shared directory as the root user with the **mount -t nfs server1.example .com:/shared /testing** command.
- The first time the share is mounted, you should be able to copy local files as the root user to the /testing directory.
- The second time the share is mounted, with the **no_root_squash** directive in effect, such copying should not work, at least from the client root user account.

Lab 2

This lab is the first step toward creating a single /home directory for your network. Once you get it working on a single client/server combination, you can set it up on all clients and servers. You can then use an LDAP server to set up a single Linux/Unix database of usernames and passwords for the network. Alternatively, matching usernames (with matching UID and GID numbers) on different local systems should also work. On the NFS server, take the following steps:

1. Set up a couple of users and identifying files such as user1 and user1.txt on the system being used as the NFS server.

2. Share the /home directory in /etc/exports on the server1.example.com client. You can do this in this file with the following command:

   ```
   /home *.example.com(rw,sync)
   ```

3. Export this directory with the following command:

   ```
   # exportfs -a
   ```

4. Make sure that the exported /home directory shows in the export list. On the local server, you can do this with the following command:

```
# showmount -e server1.example.com
```

5. If problems appear during this process, check the /etc/exports file carefully. Make sure there aren't extra spaces in /etc/exports, even at the end of a code line. Make sure the NFS service is actually running with the **systemctl status nfs-server** command.

6. You may also want to check your firewall and make sure the appropriate services described in this chapter are running with the **rpcinfo -p** command.

7. Remember to make sure that the NFS server starts automatically the next time the system is booted. One way to do so is with the following command:

```
# systemctl enable nfs-server
```

Now on the NFS client, take the following steps to connect to the shared /home directory:

1. Make sure you can see the shared /home directory. You can substitute the IP address of the server1.example.com system:

```
# showmount -e server1.example.com
```

2. Now mount the share that is offered on the local /remote directory:

```
# mount -t nfs server1.example.com:/home /remote
```

3. Run the **mount** command. If you see the NFS mount, all is well.

4. Examine the mounted /home directory. Look for the *.txt files created earlier in this lab. If you find those files, you've successfully created and connected to the /home directory share.

5. To make the mount permanent, add it to the /etc/fstab file on the client. Once you've added a line such as the following to that file, the Linux client automatically mounts the shared /home directory from the NFS server the next time the client is booted, with the soft option and a timeout of 100 seconds, which can help prevent a "hang":

```
server1.example.com:/home    /remote nfs soft,timeout=100  0  0
```

Lab 3

The reference to SELinux is deliberate and should provide an important hint. You may not have enough time to modify every directory shared and configured in the /etc/exports file on each NFS server. One simple way to prevent writes to shared NFS directories is to deactivate the associated SELinux boolean, with the following command:

```
# setsebool -P nfs_export_all_rw off
```

You should then be able to test the result with the next mounting of a shared NFS directory.

Lab 4

This lab is an extension of Exercise 16-2 and tries to familiarize you with some of the common problems when configuring NFS shares with Kerberos.

Export the share with the **sec=sys:krb5:krb5i:krb5p** security option to provide optional Kerberos authentication, communication integrity, and encryption. See if the tester1.example.com client can mount the NFS share using any of the available security methods. Reproduce the troubleshooting scenarios described in the lab and take note of the error messages you encounter.

Chapter 17

The MariaDB Server

R elational databases, commonly referred to as relational database management systems (RDBMSs), provide a standardized method to organize persistent data in a structured way. They use tables to store data, rules to ensure uniqueness and consistency between tables, and indexes to support rapid access. In addition, most relational database systems support the Structured Query Language (SQL), a standard tool to retrieve data and perform many other tasks.

MySQL is the most popular open-source RDBMS, and it's a key part of the "LAMP" stack (Linux, Apache, MySQL, and Perl/Python/PHP) commonly used to support web applications. It is also extremely easy to install, configure, and use.

Before RHEL 7, MySQL was the default RDBMS in Red Hat Enterprise Linux. After MySQL was acquired by Oracle, Red Hat moved to MariaDB, a community-developed fork of MySQL, licensed under the GPL. MariaDB contains additional community-developed features and optimizations. It is not the only database that comes with RHEL. Others (most obviously including PostgreSQL) are also available but not covered by the RHCE exam.

INSIDE THE EXAM

The ability to install and configure MariaDB (and its equivalent MySQL) is a common requirement for system administrators, although it is new to the RHCE exam in RHEL7. This chapter directly addresses the exam objectives related to MariaDB:

- Install and configure MariaDB
- Back up and restore a database

- Create a simple database schema
- Perform simple SQL queries against a database

In addition, this chapter covers the common network service requirements discussed in Chapter 11.

CERTIFICATION OBJECTIVE 17.01

Introduction to MariaDB

MySQL AB, a Swedish company, first released MySQL in 1995 as a free implementation of an earlier database known as mSQL. The first releases were based on the existing ISAM indexing method from IBM, which eventually turned into DB2. MySQL was included by Red Hat in its first RHEL release and rapidly acquired popularity. RHEL 6 included MySQL version 5.1.

In 2008 MySQL was purchased by Sun Microsystems, and in 2009 Oracle acquired Sun Microsystems. As Oracle sells an alternative RDBMS to MySQL, this acquisition triggered a substantial backlash both by regulatory authorities and the open-source community.

Eventually, the European Union allowed Oracle to acquire Sun in 2010. To satisfy governmental regulatory concerns, Oracle committed to continue to develop MySQL under the existing "dual-source" license model.

One of the original founders of MySQL, Michael "Monty" Widenius, chose to fork MySQL in 2009. He called it *MariaDB*, after his youngest daughter, Maria. Previously, he had named MySQL after his eldest daughter. MariaDB obtained funding, and a substantial number of developers started moving their work from MySQL to the new MariaDB project.

MariaDB was initially released with the same version numbers as MySQL to suggest complete compatibility. After MariaDB 5.5 was released, developers changed the version number to 10, in part to move away from full compatibility with MySQL. For our purposes, MariaDB 5.5 is fully compatible with MySQL 5.5. In other words, clients and libraries compiled against MySQL 5.5 will just work on a MariaDB 5.5 server.

MariaDB Installation

The RPM package mariadb-server installs mariadb-libs and mariadb as dependencies. These packages include all files that you need to get a working MariaDB installation, such as the server itself (**mysqld**), the MariaDB client (**mysql**), and all the Perl libraries required for associated helper scripts.

If you want to develop applications that use MariaDB, you may need the mariadb-devel and MySQL-python packages. However, these are beyond the scope of the RHCE exam.

For the purpose of this chapter, install the MariaDB server with the following command:

```
# yum -y install mariadb-server
```

This command installs the MariaDB server, the client, and over 30 Perl modules. On client machines, you can install the MariaDB client with the mariadb RPM package.

No configuration is required for basic operation. You can start and ensure that the service survives a reboot with the following commands:

```
# systemctl start mariadb
# systemctl enable mariadb
```

The first time MariaDB starts, it writes some standard tables to the internal "mysql" database by calling the **mysql_install_db** script. Any problems with this process should appear in the file mariadb.log, located in the /var/log/mariadb directory.

on the job
The MariaDB systemd unit in /lib/systemd/system/mariadb.service includes the directive TimeoutSec=300, **which limits the amount of time for the server to start up to 300 seconds. While sufficient for a small test database, such a small value for** TimeoutSec **would lead to problems for a large, real-world database server. Without sufficient time, a transaction recovery may result in an endless cycle of failed starts. Fortunately, this is not an exam concern.**

```
[root@server1 ~]# ss -tpna | grep 3306
LISTEN     0      50                          *:3306                    *:*
users:(("mysqld",3584,13))
[root@server1 ~]# █
```

MariaDB listens to
TCP port 3306.

As MariaDB is a "fork" of MySQL, it retains many filenames and commands associated with MySQL. For example, the MariaDB client command is **mysql** and the server daemon is **mysqld**. Among others, the Python module is **MySQLdb** and it works with both MySQL and MariaDB servers.

Now that the service is running, verify that it is listening on the default TCP port 3306 with the **ss** command. The result is shown in Figure 17-1. Note from the output of the command that by default MariaDB listens on all interfaces available on the server.

To confirm that MariaDB is operational, connect with the **mysql** client. The result is illustrated in Figure 17-2. Type **quit** or **exit** to close the session.

The **mysql** command has various command options, which will be explained in detail in the following sections. The most common ones are described in Table 17-1.

```
[root@server1 ~]# mysql
Welcome to the MariaDB monitor.  Commands end with ; or \g.
Your MariaDB connection id is 10
Server version: 5.5.35-MariaDB MariaDB Server

Copyright (c) 2000, 2013, Oracle, Monty Program Ab and others.

Type 'help;' or '\h' for help. Type '\c' to clear the current input statement.

MariaDB [(none)]> █
```

The mysql client

mysql Command Options

mysql Command Option	Description	Default Value
-h	Hostname/FQDN of the MariaDB server	localhost
-p	Password	Try passwordless authentication
-P	Custom TCP port number (see Exercise 17-2)	3306
-u	MariaDB username	Current Linux username

FIGURE 17-3

The /etc/my.cnf
configuration file

```
[root@server1 ~]# cat /etc/my.cnf
[mysqld]
datadir=/var/lib/mysql
socket=/var/lib/mysql/mysql.sock
# Disabling symbolic-links is recommended to prevent assorted security risks
symbolic-links=0
# Settings user and group are ignored when systemd is used.
# If you need to run mysqld under a different user or group,
# customize your systemd unit file for mariadb according to the
# instructions in http://fedoraproject.org/wiki/Systemd

[mysqld_safe]
log-error=/var/log/mariadb/mariadb.log
pid-file=/var/run/mariadb/mariadb.pid

#
# include all files from the config directory
#
!includedir /etc/my.cnf.d

[root@server1 ~]# 
```

Initial Configuration

Although you can do more, RHEL 7 includes a working configuration of MariaDB "out of the box." On the job, the additional changes you make to the MariaDB configuration relate to performance tuning.

Examine the MariaDB configuration file /etc/my.cnf shown in Figure 17-3. By default, it contains two sections: [mysqld] and [mysqld_safe]. The [mysqld_safe] section defines the locations of the log and process identifier (PID) files for **mysqld_safe**, a wrapper script that monitors the health of the **mysqld** process and restarts it in the event of a hard crash.

The [mysqld] section begins with the **datadir** directive, which specifies the location of the data. Next, the **socket** directive points to the location of the socket file. In a typical installation, you don't have to change these settings. The last setting in this section is the **symbolic-links** directive, which prevents MariaDB from following symbolic links for security reasons.

Note the **includedir** directive at the end of the my.cnf file. It loads the content of a few other configuration files from the /etc/my.cnf.d directory.

on the
job

The includedir **directive in the default my.cnf file includes the contents of every file in the /etc/my.cnf.d directory. By default, the files in this location only affect MariaDB clients, but it is worth ensuring that no other packages have put a file down in here when you are troubleshooting.**

MariaDB ships with a script, **mysql_secure_installation**, to improve the security of the default configuration. After you start the MariaDB service for the first time, run this script as the Linux root user. It will ask a series of security-related questions interactively.

Exercise 17-1 guides you through the installation of MariaDB and the execution of the **mysql_secure_installation** script.

Install and Secure MariaDB

In this exercise you will install MariaDB and run the **mysql_secure_installation** script to secure the installation. The script prompts you with a series of interactive questions to set a password for the root user (different from the Linux root superuser!), disable remote logins, remove anonymous users, and delete the default test database.

1. Install MariaDB:

   ```
   # yum -y install mariadb-server
   ```

2. Start the service and ensure that it is enabled at the next system boot:

   ```
   # systemctl start mariadb
   # systemctl enable mariadb
   ```

3. Run the **mysql_secure_installation** script. When you see the following prompt, simply press ENTER, as there is no password for the MariaDB root user:

   ```
   # mysql_secure_installation
   [...]
   Enter current password for root (enter for none):
   OK, successfully used password, moving on...
   ```

4. Set a new MariaDB root password. As you can see here, we have set ours to "changeme" but you should select a real password in a production server:

   ```
   Set root password? [Y/n] y
   New password: changeme
   Re-enter new password: changeme
   Password updated successfully!
   Reloading privilege tables..
    ... Success!
   ```

5. By default, MySQL supports connections from anonymous users. This should be disabled, as shown here:

   ```
   Remove anonymous users? [Y/n] y
    ... Success!
   ```

6. To further discourage black hat hackers, you should disable remote root access to MariaDB:

   ```
   Disallow root login remotely? [Y/n] y
    ... Success!
   ```

7. The MariaDB installation includes a default database named test. While the **mysql_secure_installation** script recommends deleting it, you can keep it for testing purposes:

```
Remove test database and access to it? [Y/n] n
 ... skipping.
```

8. Finally, when you flush the privilege tables, MariaDB implements your changes:

```
Reload privilege tables now? [Y/n] y
 ... Success!
```

Run MariaDB on a Nonstandard TCP Port

By default, MariaDB listens to TCP port 3306. If you want to change the default port, you need to complete the following steps:

1. Open the my.cnf configuration file and add a **port=*num*** directive.
2. Open the noted port in your firewall.
3. Modify the default MariaDB port defined in the SELinux policy.

This process is relatively simple and is illustrated in Exercise 17-2.

EXERCISE 17-2

Run MariaDB on a Nonstandard TCP Port

There are three parts to this exercise: editing the MariaDB configuration file, modifying the firewall, and changing SELinux port labeling. We assume that you want to run MariaDB on TCP port 3307, rather than on the default 3306.

1. Add a **port=3307** line to the [mysqld] section in /etc/my.cnf:

```
[mysqld]
port=3307
```

2. Allow connections to the new port in the firewall configuration of the default zone:

```
# firewall-cmd --permanent --add-port=3307/tcp
# firewall-cmd --reload
```

3. Add the new port to the list of permitted ports for MySQL in the SELinux policy:

```
# semanage port -a -t mysqld_port_t -p tcp 3307
```

4. You can now show the ports that SELinux allows MySQL and MariaDB to use. From the following command, verify that it includes your new port:

```
# semanage port -l | grep mysqld
mysqld_port_t                  tcp      3307, 1186, 3306, 63132-63164
```

5. Restart MariaDB:

```
# systemctl restart mariadb
```

6. Connect to the server on the new port:

```
# mysql -u root -h 127.0.0.1 -P 3307 -p
Enter password:
Welcome to the MariaDB monitor.  Commands end with ; or \g.
Your MariaDB connection id is 4
Server version: 5.5.35-MariaDB MariaDB Server

Copyright (c) 2000, 2013, Oracle, Monty Program Ab and others.


Type 'help;' or '\h' for help. Type '\c' to clear the current
  input statement.
MariaDB [(none)]>
```

The previous command connects to the MariaDB server running on the specified IP address (**-h**) and port (**-P**), as user root (**-u**), identified by a password (**-p**). Note that if you specify the host to connect to as "localhost," the MariaDB client communicates to the local server via Unix sockets rather than on a TCP connection.

7. Close the session by typing **quit** or **exit**.

8. Remove the line that you added to /etc/my.cnf and restart MariaDB to run the service on its default port.

If you don't modify the SELinux policy to account for the custom port, you would see the following error when you try to start MariaDB:

```
[root@server1 ~]# systemctl start mariadb.service
Job for mariadb.service failed. See 'systemctl status mariadb.service'
and 'journalctl -xn' for details.
```

You should also see this corresponding error in the /var/log/mariadb/mariadb.log file:

```
150124  8:21:27 [ERROR] Can't start server: Bind on TCP/IP port.
Got error: 13: Permission denied
```

CERTIFICATION OBJECTIVE 17.02

Database Management

Relational database management systems such as MariaDB store information in a very structured way. At the highest level, there are databases, which serve as containers for related data. Within databases, data is stored in tables, with each column representing an attribute of the data, and each row representing a record.

Database Concepts

If you have never used a RDBMS before but have worked with spreadsheet software such as LibreOffice Calc or Microsoft Excel, you may notice similarities with the concepts of worksheets, columns, and rows. In fact, tables in a database can, in some ways, be considered a giant spreadsheet, with rows and columns containing data. The structure and organization of a database into different tables and columns is referred to as the schema.

Columns can handle various different types of data, and this is defined for each column when it is created. For example, a column may be able to store numbers up to a certain size or up to a certain amount of text characters. Columns can be mandatory or not, and some have a default value. When defining the schema, you can also express constraints. For example, you can specify that a row in one table must have a unique identifier, or "link," to a record in another table. These rules are enforced when users attempt to insert or change any data in the database.

Users interact with the database by means of SQL commands: some of those commands create databases, create tables, and adjust the schema of tables; others insert data into those tables, and still others obtain data from the database. We cover the basic operation of many of these queries in this chapter. Table 17-2 summarizes the most important concepts of an RDBMS.

TABLE 17-2	Database Terminology

Term	Explanation
Database	A collection of related tables
Table	A data structure in which data is organized in columns and rows
Row or record	A single item inside a table, containing the data required for that schema
Column	An attribute of a record, belonging to a certain data type
Schema	A specification of the properties of all data in a database
SQL command	A human-readable command to manage databases, as well as add, remove, or retrieve data, in one or more tables

FIGURE 17-4

Listing all the
databases

```
MariaDB [(none)]> SHOW DATABASES;
+--------------------+
| Database           |
+--------------------+
| information_schema |
| mysql              |
| performance_schema |
| test               |
+--------------------+
4 rows in set (0.00 sec)

MariaDB [(none)]> ▮
```

Working with Databases

The default MariaDB installation includes a few databases. To list the currently installed databases, connect to MariaDB using the **mysql** client:

```
# mysql -p
```

Then run the **SHOW DATABASES** SQL command:

```
MariaDB [(none)]> SHOW DATABASES;
```

The output is shown in Figure 17-4. Note that four databases are available (three if you deleted the test database in Exercise 17-1):

■ **mysql**   An internal database for MariaDB to manage users and permissions
■ **information _schema** and **performance_schema**   Specialized databases used by MariaDB to inspect metadata and query execution at run time
■ **test**   A test database

on the
job

You can write SQL commands such as SHOW DATABASES **in uppercase or lowercase characters. By convention, documentation specifies SQL keywords in uppercase.**

You can create a new database from the **mysql** client with the **CREATE DATABASE** *db_name* command, as shown next. The new database contains no data until you create a table and add some data to it:

```
MariaDB [(none)]> CREATE DATABASE myapp;
```

For pretty much every command in the MariaDB shell other than the ones for creating users and databases, you should first tell the MariaDB client that you are working in a given database with the **USE** command. In MariaDB, by default, the shell prompt tells you what database you are in (none and mysql in the following examples):

```
MariaDB [(none)]> USE mysql;
Database changed
MariaDB [mysql]>
```

TABLE 17-3	Data Type	Description
	INT	32-bit integer
MariaDB Data	FLOAT	Single-precision floating-point number
Types	VARCHAR	Variable-length string
	TEXT	Large string
	BLOB	Binary object
	DATETIME	Date and time

Similarly, a database can be removed with the **DROP DATABASE** *db_name* command:

```
MariaDB [(none)]> DROP DATABASE test;
```

Working with Tables

A database is not much of a utility without one or more tables. For the RHCE exam, you are required to "create a simple database schema." If you want to know more about this topic, refer to the MariaDB website (https://mariadb.com/kb/en/mariadb/create-table).

MariaDB tables consist of columns that you can configure as different data types. These data types determine what data can be stored inside a column. You can represent most of the different data formats with the data types listed in Table 17-3.

You should also add indexes to a table to retrieve data without having to read every row (called a "table scan"). This is critical for performance for larger tables. Generally, these involve two types of indexes: unique indexes and secondary indexes.

A unique index should specify something unique about a row, such as an ID number. A special type of unique index is one created with the **PRIMARY KEY** keyword, which is used internally by MariaDB to identify a given row. If you don't specify a primary key, the default storage engine in MariaDB will automatically create a primary key on a commonly used column.

Conversely, secondary indexes don't specify a unique element in a row and are used to speed up queries that rely on a key other than the primary key and avoid table scans.

To create a new table, use the **CREATE TABLE** command. Here is the syntax of this command in its simplest form:

```
CREATE TABLE table_name (
  col_name1 INT|FLOAT|VARCHAR|TEXT|BLOB|DATETIME [NOT NULL|AUTO_INCREMENT],
  col_name2 INT|FLOAT|VARCHAR|TEXT|BLOB|DATETIME [NOT NULL|AUTO_INCREMENT],
  ...
  PRIMARY KEY (col_name1)
);
```

| TABLE 17-4 | SQL Database and Table Commands |

SQL Command	Description
CREATE DATABASE *db_name*	Creates the database *db_name*
DROP DATABASE *db_name*	Deletes the database *db_name*
SHOW DATABASES	Lists all databases
USE *db_name*	The next SQL commands will have an effect on the *db_name* database
CREATE TABLE *table_name* (...)	Creates the table *table_name*
DROP TABLE *table_name*	Deletes the table *table_name*
SHOW TABLES	Lists all tables in the current database
DESCRIBE *table_name*	Displays the schema of the table *table_name*

The command defines each column in the table, identified by a name and a type, and an optional constraint such as **NOT NULL**, which prevents entries in the column from taking an undefined value, or **AUTO_INCREMENT**, which automatically inserts a new unique number when a new record is added to the table.

The **PRIMARY KEY** constraint tells MariaDB that the specified column is a primary key. In other words, the given column must contain only unique non-null values.

Table 17-4 summarizes the commands related to database and table management. Each command must be terminated by a semicolon character. Some of these commands will be explored in Exercise 17-3.

EXERCISE 17-3

Create a Table

In this exercise you will create a simple table. Start by connecting to MariaDB with the **mysql** client.

1. Create a database named "myapp":

   ```
   CREATE DATABASE myapp;
   ```

2. Tell MariaDB that the next commands will affect the myapp database:

   ```
   USE myapp;
   ```

FIGURE 17-5

Display the
schema of an
existing table.

```
MariaDB [myapp]> DESCRIBE widgets;
+--------+--------------+------+-----+---------+----------------+
| Field  | Type         | Null | Key | Default | Extra          |
+--------+--------------+------+-----+---------+----------------+
| id     | int(11)      | NO   | PRI | NULL    | auto_increment |
| name   | varchar(255) | YES  |     | NULL    |                |
+--------+--------------+------+-----+---------+----------------+
2 rows in set (0.00 sec)

MariaDB [myapp]> ▌
```

3. Create a simple table: a list of widgets, each with an automatically generated ID. To
    do so, use a **CREATE TABLE** statement:

```
CREATE TABLE widgets (
  id INT AUTO_INCREMENT,
  name VARCHAR(255),
  PRIMARY KEY (id)
);
```

Note that the "id" column is marked as a primary key. There is also a second column
("name") that can contain a string of variable length, up to 255 characters.

4. Display the newly created table with **SHOW TABLES**:

```
SHOW TABLES;
+------------------+
| Tables_in_myapp  |
+------------------+
| widgets          |
+------------------+
```

5. You can show the full schema of the table with the **DESCRIBE** *tablename*
    command. It will print out the schema you entered earlier. The output is shown in
    Figure 17-5.

CERTIFICATION OBJECTIVE 17.03

Simple SQL Queries

SQL is a special-purpose programming language that operates both as a data manipulation
language, to modify data or the schema in a database, and as a query language, to retrieve
data from a database.

In the previous section, we have shown how you can use SQL commands to manage databases and tables. In this section, we provide a brief introduction to several SQL commands to retrieve and insert data.

After creating a database and a table, you can make changes to the data with the SQL statements **INSERT**, **SELECT**, **UPDATE**, and **DELETE**. These are the basic SQL commands required by the RHCE exam.

on the
!
①ob

In computer programming, the SQL INSERT, SELECT, UPDATE, **and** DELETE **statements are also referred as "CRUD" operations, where the letters of the acronym stand for "Create, Read, Update, and Delete."**

The INSERT SQL Command

The **INSERT** statement adds a record into a table. The syntax of the command is as follows:

```
INSERT INTO table_name (field1, field2) VALUES ('a', 'b');
```

For example, you can insert a new record into the widgets table with the following command:

```
MariaDB [myapp]> INSERT INTO widgets (id, name) VALUES (1, "widget A");
Query OK, 1 row affected (0.01 sec)
```

This command adds a new record to the table widgets with the integer value "1" in the id column and the string "widget A" in the name column.

Since we defined the id column as **AUTO_INCREMENT** in Exercise 17-3, MariaDB automatically gives a unique and incrementing ID to the next row you insert. Hence, you don't even need to specify the id field when you add a row:

```
MariaDB [myapp]> INSERT INTO widgets (name) VALUES ("widget B");
Query OK, 1 row affected (0.01 sec)
```

This SQL statement adds a new record to the table widgets with the string "widget B" in the name column. MariaDB will automatically assign the value "2" to the id field.

As we defined the id column to be a **PRIMARY KEY**, this means that each value in the column must be unique. If you create a new row with the same ID as the previous one, MariaDB will return an error:

```
MariaDB [myapp]> INSERT INTO widgets (id, name) VALUES (2, "widget C");
ERROR 1062 (23000): Duplicate entry '2' for key 'PRIMARY'
```

The SELECT SQL Command

As you have some records stored in the widget table, you can now use the **SELECT** statement to retrieve the data from the table. In its simplest form, the command syntax is as follows:

```
SELECT field1, field2 FROM table_name [WHERE field2 = "value"];
```

For example, the next command lists all rows in the table named widgets:

```
MariaDB [myapp]> SELECT id, name FROM widgets;
+----+----------+
| id | name     |
+----+----------+
|  1 | widget A |
|  2 | widget B |
|  3 | widget C |
+----+----------+
3 rows in set (0.00 sec)
```

You can also use the star wildcard to specify all the columns in a table. The following SQL statement is equivalent to the last command:

```
MariaDB [myapp]> SELECT * FROM widgets;
```

To filter results, pass the **WHERE** clause to the command. The next example shows how to retrieve a column from a row with a specific ID:

```
MariaDB [myapp]> SELECT name FROM widgets WHERE id=2;
+----------+
| name     |
+----------+
| widget B |
+----------+
1 row in set (0.00 sec)
```

MariaDB supports numerous operators you can include in a **WHERE** clause. For example, the <> operator matches all the entries that are not equal to a given value.

As an example, the following statement returns all records from the widgets table, whose ID is not equal to the value "2":

```
MariaDB [myapp]> SELECT * FROM widgets WHERE id<>2;
+----+----------+
| id | name     |
+----+----------+
|  1 | widget A |
|  3 | widget C |
+----+----------+
2 rows in set (0.00 sec)
```

Table 17-5 lists the most commonly used operators.

MariaDB Operator	Description
=	Equal
<>	Not equal
>	Greater than
<	Less than
>=	Greater or equal than
<=	Less or equal than
LIKE	Searches for a pattern—for example, **WHERE name LIKE "pattern"**
IN	Lists all possible values for a field—for example, **WHERE id IN (1,2,4)**

The DELETE SQL Command

The **DELETE** statement works in a similar fashion to **SELECT**, except it deletes the records matched. The syntax is illustrated in the next line:

```
DELETE FROM tablename WHERE field1 = "value";
```

For example, if you want to remove the row from the widgets table that has a value of "1" in the id column, run the following:

```
MariaDB [myapp]> DELETE FROM widgets WHERE id=1;
Query OK, 1 row affected (0.01 sec)
```

The following **SELECT** query confirms that the corresponding row has been removed from the table:

```
MariaDB [myapp]> SELECT * widgets;
+----+----------+
| id | name     |
+----+----------+
|  2 | widget B |
|  3 | widget C |
+----+----------+
2 rows in set (0.00 sec)
```

The UPDATE SQL Command

Finally, the **UPDATE** SQL statement allows you to update one or more rows. This command is slightly more complicated—you have to include the table you are modifying, the change you want to make, and the affected rows:

```
UPDATE table_name SET field1="value" WHERE field2="value";
```

TABLE 17-6	Summary of Common SQL Queries
SQL Statement	**Example**
INSERT	INSERT INTO table_name (field1, field2) VALUES ("value1", "value2");
SELECT	SELECT field1, field2 FROM table_name WHERE field1="value"
UPDATE	UPDATE table_name SET field1="value" WHERE field2="value"
DELETE	DELETE FROM table_name WHERE field="value";

For example, the next command sets the value in the name column to a new value, for the record whose ID is equal to "2":

```
MariaDB [myapp]> UPDATE widgets SET name='Widget with a new name' WHERE id=2;
Query OK, 1 row affected (0.01 sec)
Rows matched: 1  Changed: 1  Warnings: 0
```

The following **SELECT** statement confirms that the change has been applied:

```
MariaDB [myapp]> SELECT * from widgets;
+----+------------------------+
| id | name                   |
+----+------------------------+
|  2 | Widget with a new name |
|  3 | Widget C               |
+----+------------------------+
2 rows in set (0.00 sec)
```

Table 17-6 summarizes the SQL queries we have described so far.

EXERCISE 17-4

Practice with Simple SQL Queries

In this exercise, you will import a freely available test database to provide sufficient data to be able to explore some slightly more challenging SQL queries.

1. Connect to the MySQL client as root:

   ```
   # mysql -u root -p
   ```

2. Create a new database named "employees":

   ```
   MariaDB [(none)]> CREATE DATABASE employees;
   ```

3. Return to the shell (with the **quit** command). We will use a standard test database that is available from the media that accompanies this book. Insert the media, navigate to the Chapter17/ subdirectory, and copy the employees_db-full-1.0.6.tar.bz2 file to the local drive.

4. Extract and import the database using the following commands:

```
# tar xvfj employees_db-full-1.0.6.tar.bz2
# cd employees_db
# cat employees.sql | mysql -u root -p employees
```

5. Wait for the files to load and verify that the new tables exists, as shown next:

```
# mysql -u root -p
MariaDB [(none)]> USE employees;
```

```
MariaDB [employees]> SHOW TABLES;
+---------------------+
| Tables_in_employees |
+---------------------+
| departments         |
| dept_emp            |
| dept_manager        |
| employees           |
| salaries            |
| titles              |
+---------------------+
6 rows in set (0.00 sec)

MariaDB [employees]> █
```

6. Find the schema of the departments table:

```
MariaDB [employees]> DESCRIBE departments;
+-----------+-------------+------+-----+---------+-------+
| Field     | Type        | Null | Key | Default | Extra |
+-----------+-------------+------+-----+---------+-------+
| dept_no   | char(4)     | NO   | PRI | NULL    |       |
| dept_name | varchar(40) | NO   | UNI | NULL    |       |
+-----------+-------------+------+-----+---------+-------+
2 rows in set (0.00 sec)

MariaDB [employees]> █
```

7. Display all the content of the departments table:

```
MariaDB [employees]> SELECT * FROM departments;
+---------+---------------------+
| dept_no | dept_name           |
+---------+---------------------+
| d009    | Customer Service    |
| d005    | Development         |
| d002    | Finance             |
| d003    | Human Resources     |
| d001    | Marketing           |
| d004    | Production          |
| d006    | Quality Management  |
| d008    | Research            |
| d007    | Sales               |
+---------+---------------------+
9 rows in set (0.00 sec)

MariaDB [employees]> █
```

Now, try a slightly more difficult example. You will search for the employee with the highest salary. First, display the schema of the "salaries" table:

```
MariaDB [employees]> DESCRIBE salaries;
+-----------+---------+------+-----+---------+-------+
| Field     | Type    | Null | Key | Default | Extra |
+-----------+---------+------+-----+---------+-------+
| emp_no    | int(11) | NO   | PRI | NULL    |       |
| salary    | int(11) | NO   |     | NULL    |       |
| from_date | date    | NO   | PRI | NULL    |       |
| to_date   | date    | NO   |     | NULL    |       |
+-----------+---------+------+-----+---------+-------+
4 rows in set (0.00 sec)

MariaDB [employees]> █
```

8. Identify the employee with the highest salary. To do so, we introduce a new clause, **ORDER BY** *field*, which orders the results of a **SELECT** query based on the values of a specified column. The optional **DESC** keyword sorts the results in descendent order. In addition, the number of records returned by the query can be limited to a maximum amount with the **LIMIT** *num* clause.

9. The result is shown here:

```
MariaDB [employees]> SELECT * FROM salaries ORDER BY salary DESC LIMIT 5;
+--------+--------+------------+------------+
| emp_no | salary | from_date  | to_date    |
+--------+--------+------------+------------+
|  43624 | 158220 | 2002-03-22 | 9999-01-01 |
|  43624 | 157821 | 2001-03-22 | 2002-03-22 |
| 254466 | 156286 | 2001-08-04 | 9999-01-01 |
|  47978 | 155709 | 2002-07-14 | 9999-01-01 |
| 253939 | 155513 | 2002-04-11 | 9999-01-01 |
+--------+--------+------------+------------+
5 rows in set (1.16 sec)

MariaDB [employees]> █
```

10. From the output of the last query, you can see that the employee with ID 43624 has a salary of $158,220.

11. The next step is to find the details of such employee in the corresponding "employee" table. To do so, run a **SELECT** query with a **WHERE** clause to display the record for the employee with ID 43624:

```
MariaDB [employees]> SELECT * FROM employees WHERE emp_no=43624;
+--------+------------+------------+-----------+--------+------------+
| emp_no | birth_date | first_name | last_name | gender | hire_date  |
+--------+------------+------------+-----------+--------+------------+
|  43624 | 1953-11-14 | Tokuyasu   | Pesch     | M      | 1985-03-26 |
+--------+------------+------------+-----------+--------+------------+
1 row in set (0.00 sec)

MariaDB [employees]> █
```

on the **!** **j o b**   **To combine data from multiple tables, you can use a SQL join clause, rather than the step-by-step procedure illustrated in Exercise 17-4. As an example, the final result in Exercise 17-4 can be retrieved with a single query:**
SELECT * FROM employees NATURAL JOIN salaries ORDER BY salary DESC LIMIT 1;
However, this is beyond the scope of the RHCE exam.

CERTIFICATION OBJECTIVE 17.04

Secure MariaDB

In a default installation, MariaDB accepts connections from any system on the network. Access is granted to the root user without a password.

Clearly, this is not a secure configuration. In a previous section, we explained how to secure a MariaDB installation with the **mysql_secure_installation** script. However, there's more to do to set up a secure installation.

You may have applications that need to connect to MariaDB. For example, a web service may need access. While you can support remote access by some systems, you should ensure that access is prohibited to all other hosts. MariaDB provides a flexible permission scheme that allows you to specify all the types of commands a user can run on the system.

Host-Based Security

You should start by prohibiting remote access to MariaDB, if possible. Alternatively, you can limit access only to the systems that should be entitled to connect to it. There are two key directives available to this regard in /etc/my.cnf:

- **skip-networking**   Prevents MariaDB from listening on any TCP connection. This does not limit access from the local system via Unix sockets.
- **bind-address**   Allows MariaDB to listen to a specific IP address. If you set this directive to 0.0.0.0, MariaDB listens for connections on all local IPv4 addresses. This is the default setting. If you set it to ::, MariaDB listens for traffic on all IPv4 and IPv6 addresses. On systems with multiple interfaces and IP addresses, you may want MariaDB to listen on one specific IP address only.

Of course, you can also use **firewall-cmd** to restrict access to MariaDB. The following example sets a firewall rich rule that allows connections only from the host with IP address 192.168.122.1:

```
# firewall-cmd --permanent --add-rich-rule='rule family=ipv4 source ↵
address=192.168.122.1 service name=mysql accept'
# firewall-cmd --reload
```

If you need to enable remote access to MariaDB for all hosts, run the following:

```
# firewall-cmd --permanent --add-service=mysql
# firewall-cmd --reload
```

User-Based Security

Access to MariaDB is maintained via an internal user database and privileges known as "grants."
From the MariaDB **mysql** client, the default username is the username you are logged on with. So, if you are logged on the server as root, this is the default username. You can connect as a specific user with the **-u** command switch. You can pass **-p** to ask the MariaDB client to prompt you for a password, and **-P** to pass a custom TCP port. The last argument, which is optional, specifies a database name to connect to.

For example, to connect to the myapp database on server 192.168.122.1 on port 3307 with username myuser and password changeme, run this command:

```
# mysql -u myuser -pchangeme -P 3307 -h 192.168.122.1 myapp
```

Note that there must be no space between the **-p** switch and the password.

Managing MariaDB Users

MariaDB uses the internal **mysql** database to manage users and permissions. To list the current users, run these SQL statements:

```
MariaDB [(none)]> USE mysql;
MariaDB [mysql]> SELECT user, host from mysql.user;
```

You can create a new user with the **CREATE USER** command. The syntax is illustrated in the following example:

```
CREATE USER appuser@'192.168.122.1' IDENTIFIED BY 'changeme';
```

This SQL command creates a user named "appuser" that can connect only from the host with IP address 192.168.122.1, with the password "changeme." New users are not assigned any privileges, so you must specifically assign the permissions that a user should be entitled to.

Managing User Privileges

Each user can be assigned a list of permissions ("grants") that you can display with the SQL command **SHOW GRANTS [FOR *username*]**. A sample output is shown in Figure 17-6.

Focus on the first line of the output. This tells us that the root user connecting from the localhost is granted **ALL PRIVILEGES**, on all databases and all tables (***.***), with an additional permission known as **GRANT OPTION** that allows that user to create new users and assign them grant privileges.

FIGURE 17-6

Default grants for the MariaDB root user

```
MariaDB [(none)]> SHOW GRANTS;
+---------------------------------------------------------------------------+
| Grants for root@localhost                                                 |
+---------------------------------------------------------------------------+
| GRANT ALL PRIVILEGES ON *.* TO 'root'@'localhost' WITH GRANT OPTION |
| GRANT PROXY ON ''@'' TO 'root'@'localhost' WITH GRANT OPTION        |
+---------------------------------------------------------------------------+
2 rows in set (0.00 sec)

MariaDB [(none)]> █
```

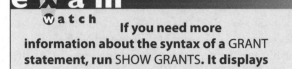

If you need more information about the syntax of a GRANT **statement, run** SHOW GRANTS. **It displays** the grants of the currently connected user, which you can use as a template to modify the grants of other user accounts.

A list of the most common privileges is shown in Table 17-7.

Each **GRANT** statement is applied either globally (***.***), to a given database (**db_name.***), or to a given table (**db_name.table_name**). **GRANT** statements add more privileges; to revoke a privilege, use the **REVOKE** command.

To put this into practice, we will create a user named "appowner" that can log in to MariaDB from any host (**'%'**), with full privileges on the myapp database and "password123" as a password:

```
MariaDB [(none)]> CREATE USER appowner@'%' IDENTIFIED BY 'password123';
MariaDB [(none)]> GRANT ALL PRIVILEGES ON myapp.* TO appowner@'%';
```

The previous commands can be merged into a single **GRANT** command. In other words, the next statement has the same effect as the previous ones:

```
MariaDB [(none)]> GRANT ALL PRIVILEGES ON myapp.* TO appowner@'%'
    > IDENTIFIED BY 'password123';
```

TABLE 17-7   Grant Privileges

Grant Privilege	Description
ALL PRIVILEGES	Grants all privileges, with the exception of **GRANT OPTION**.
WITH GRANT OPTION	Allows for creating a new user and assigning permissions up to the level of the current user.
CREATE	Gives the permission to create new databases and tables.
DROP	Allows for deleting databases and tables.
ALTER	Used to modify a table, such as to add or remove columns.
DELETE	Use the SQL **DELETE** statement to delete rows from a table.
INSERT	Use the SQL **INSERT** statement to create rows in a table.
SELECT	Use the SQL **SELECT** statement to retrieve data from a table.
UPDATE	Use the SQL **UPDATE** statement to modify rows in a table.

If you want a user to be able to log in to MariaDB from the localhost via both TCP and Unix socket connections, you should run the **GRANT** command twice and specify the host as 127.0.0.1 and localhost. An example of this syntax is provided in Exercise 17-5.

MariaDB stores privileges internally in a database called "mysql." When you make changes to user permissions, these are reflected in a database table. However, MariaDB does not implement these changes until you "flush" these privileges (or restart the service). At the MariaDB prompt, the required command is **FLUSH PRIVILEGES**:

```
MariaDB [(none)]> FLUSH PRIVILEGES;
Query OK, 0 rows affected (0.00 sec)
```

Next, you can verify that the new user account works by connecting to the **mysql** client and listing the current user's grants.

Don't forget to run FLUSH PRIVILEGES **after modifying a user's grants.**

Deleting MariaDB Users

To delete a MariaDB user, run the **DROP USER** statement. An example is shown here:

```
MariaDB [(none)]> DROP USER appowner;
```

This command has an immediate effect and does not require you to flush the user's privileges.

EXERCISE 17-5

Practice MariaDB User's Permissions

In this exercise, we assume that you have completed Exercise 17-3 and created a "myapp" database. You will create two MariaDB users:

- **apprw**   This user is identified by the password "pass123" and has read, write, update, and delete permissions to all the tables in the myapp database. The user can log in from any host.
- **appro**   This user is identified by the password "pass456" and has read permissions to all the tables of the myapp database. The user can log in only from the localhost.

1. Connect to the MySQL client as root:

   ```
   # mysql -u root -p
   ```

2. Create the apprw user with the following command:

   ```
   MariaDB [(none)]> GRANT SELECT, INSERT, UPDATE, DELETE ON myapp.*
       -> TO apprw@'%' IDENTIFIED BY 'pass123';
   ```

3. Create the appro user:

```
MariaDB [(none)]> GRANT SELECT ON myapp.* TO appro@'127.0.0.1' IDENTIFIED
    -> BY 'pass456';
MariaDB [(none)]> GRANT SELECT ON myapp.* TO appro@'localhost';
```

4. Apply the new privileges:

```
MariaDB [(none)]> FLUSH PRIVILEGES;
```

5. Open a new terminal window and check that the new users can connect to MariaDB using the **mysql** client. For example, to connect as the appro user, run the following:

```
# mysql -u appro -h localhost -ppass456 myapp
```

6. Run a simple **SELECT** query, such as the following:

```
MariaDB [myapp]> SELECT * from widgets;
```

Does this command work for the appro and apprw users?

7. Run an **INSERT** query:

```
MariaDB [myapp]> INSERT INTO widgets (name) VALUES ("test widget");
```

Does this command work for the appro and apprw users?

8. Exit the **mysql** client with the **quit** command.

CERTIFICATION OBJECTIVE 17.05

Database Backup and Recovery

MariaDB ships with the **mysqldump** backup program, which converts the entire contents of one or more tables or databases into SQL statements that would be required to re-create them.

Data can also be exported by redirecting the result of a **SELECT** query into a file. This can be done through the **SELECT INTO OUTFILE** statement, or by executing a query from the **mysql** command and redirecting the output to a file.

Back Up and Restore with mysqldump

The **mysqldump** command outputs SQL statements to the standard output. To make that output useful, you can redirect the output to a .sql file, or capture any errors that are sent

```
[root@server1 ~]# cat /tmp/widgets.sql
--
-- Table structure for table `widgets`
--

DROP TABLE IF EXISTS `widgets`;
CREATE TABLE `widgets` (
  `id` int(11) NOT NULL AUTO_INCREMENT,
  `name` varchar(255) DEFAULT NULL,
  PRIMARY KEY (`id`)
) ENGINE=InnoDB AUTO_INCREMENT=4 DEFAULT CHARSET=latin1;

--
-- Dumping data for table `widgets`
--

LOCK TABLES `widgets` WRITE;
INSERT INTO `widgets` VALUES (1,'widget A'),(2,'widget B'),(3,'widget C');
UNLOCK TABLES;
[root@server1 ~]# █
```

to stderr. For example, you can save the content of the widgets table created earlier with the following command:

```
[root@server1 ~]# mysqldump -u appowner -p myapp widgets > /tmp/widgets.sql
```

If **mysqldump** returns any errors, make sure that the database and table exist, and that the user has permissions to access the database and retrieve its contents.

Figure 17-7 shows the contents of the file generated by the previous command after some of the comment lines have been removed.

The first command is a **DROP TABLE IF EXISTS** statement. This line removes the widgets table only if it already exists to avoid any error messages if the table is not present.

Next, you will see a **CREATE TABLE** command, which should resemble the one from Exercise 17-3.

The **LOCK** and **UNLOCK** statements that follow prevent other commands from modifying the contents of the table while its contents are restored with the **INSERT** command.

With a backup file generated by **mysqldump**, you can re-create every entry in your database from this file. For example, if you want to import this backup into a database called myapp_restored, take the following three steps:

1. Create a new database:

   ```
   MariaDB [(none)]> CREATE DATABASE myapp_restored;
   ```

2. Add a grant for the owner account:

   ```
   MariaDB [(none)]> GRANT ALL PRIVILEGES ON myapp_restored.* TO
   appowner@'%';
   ```

3. Execute the contents of the dump file from the **mysql** client:

```
MariaDB [(none)]> USE myapp_restored;
MariaDB [(none)]> SOURCE /tmp/widgets.sql
```

As an alternative, the last step can be executed from a Bash shell with the following command:

```
# cat /tmp/widgets.sql | mysql -u appowner -p myapp_restored
```

So far, we have backed up and restored a single table. However, **mysqldump** can also back up an entire database. For example, the following command creates a full backup of the employee database:

```
# mysqldump -u root -p employees > /tmp/employees.sql
```

If you want to back up all databases in your MariaDB system, substitute the **--all-databases** flag for the database name.

```
# mysqldump --all-databases -u root -p > /tmp/full-backup.sql
```

Back Up with a Dump of the Data to a Text File

If you have a large amount of data, you can create a dump of the data in a text file (for example, to be imported by another application). There are two ways to create a file with specific rows in it: using the **SELECT INTO OUTFILE** statement and the **-e** flag to the **mysql** command.

SELECT INTO OUTFILE creates a file on the server that contains the requested table rows. For example, the following command selects all the employee IDs and names and saves the result in the /tmp/employees.data file:

```
MariaDB [employees]> SELECT emp_no, first_name, last_name FROM employees
    -> INTO OUTFILE '/tmp/employees.data';
Query OK, 300024 rows affected (0.12 sec)
```

As another option, you can use standard output redirection and the **-e** flag to the **mysql** command:

```
# mysql employees -e "SELECT emp_no, first_name, last_name \
FROM employees" > /tmp/employees.data
```

You should be aware that while the **mysqldump** command can back up and restore the data and schema of a database, the commands illustrated in this section cannot back up the schema. In addition, there isn't a standard and easy procedure for restoring the data generated by a **SELECT INTO OUTFILE** statement into a database or table.

CERTIFICATION SUMMARY

MariaDB is a very popular relational database management system, derived from and fully compatible with MySQL. The mariadb-server RPM package installs the server components, whereas the client and libraries are included with the mariadb and mariadb-libs packages.

The default configuration in RHEL 7 works "out of the box," and no changes are required to the /etc/my.cnf configuration file. However, at a minimum you should secure the installation by running the **mysql_secure_installation** script.

Like in many other relational database management systems, a MariaDB database is organized into different tables. Each table consists of columns of various data types and rows (or records). The specification of the properties of all data in a database is known as the schema. Databases and tables can be created with the **CREATE DATABASE** and **CREATE TABLE** statements. Other SQL statements perform the most common "CRUD" (create, read, update, delete) operations. These are **INSERT**, **SELECT**, **DELETE**, and **UPDATE**.

MariaDB supports some host-based security directives in the /etc/my.cnf configuration file, such as **skip-networking** to disable TCP connectivity, and **bind-address**, to listen for connections on a specific IP address. Access to the server can also be restricted on the local zone-based firewall.

User access is managed with the **GRANT** statement. This command can assign a specific set of permissions to each user, either on a per-database or per-table basis. After modifying user permissions, you must apply the changes with the **FLUSH PRIVILEGES** command.

The **mysqldump** command can perform a full backup of the contents and schema of a single table, a database, or all the databases on a system. The backup can be saved into a file, which can be passed to the **mysql** client as a script to restore the backup into MariaDB.

✓ TWO-MINUTE DRILL

Here are some of the key points from the certification objectives in Chapter 17.

Introduction to MariaDB

❏ MariaDB is an RDBMS included in the base RHEL7 repositories. It is a community-developed fork of MySQL released under the GPL license.

❏ The server package is provided by the mariadb-server RPM, whereas the client is in the mariadb RPM.

❏ The main MariaDB configuration file is /etc/my.cnf.

❏ The **port=***num* directive in /etc/my.cnf can be used to run the service on a different port.

❑ The **mysql_secure_installation** script can be used to secure a MariaDB server installation by assigning a password to the MariaDB root user, disabling remote logins, removing anonymous users, and deleting the default test database.

Database Management

❑ Databases store data in tables.

❑ Tables are a sort of giant spreadsheet, with rows and columns containing data.

❑ The schema defines how data is organized and structured into a database.

❑ The **CREATE DATABASE** and **CREATE TABLE** SQL commands create a new database and table, respectively.

Simple SQL Queries

❑ Data can be retrieved, inserted, edited, and modified with the SQL **SELECT**, **INSERT**, **UPDATE**, and **DELETE** statements.

❑ The **WHERE** clause filters the results or applies a condition to a SQL statement.

❑ The **ORDER BY** clause sorts the records of a query in ascending or descending (with the **DESC** keyword) order.

❑ The **LIMIT** clause restricts the amount of records returned by a query.

Secure MariaDB

❑ The **skip-networking** directive in /etc/my.cnf disables TCP connections to the database and allows access only via Unix sockets.

❑ The **bind-address** directive specifies the IP address that MariaDB should listen to for connections.

❑ MariaDB users can be assigned a list of permissions ("grants") with the **GRANT** command.

❑ Permissions must be applied with the **FLUSH PRIVILEGES** command.

Database Backup and Recovery

❑ Backups of an entire database or specific tables can be taken with the **mysqldump** command.

❑ Databases can be restored from a SQL file (such as one created by **mysqldump**) by redirecting its contents to the **mysql** command.

❑ Data can be saved into a file with the **SELECT INTO OUTFILE** statement.

SELF TEST

The following questions will help measure your understanding of the material presented in this chapter. As no multiple choice questions appear on the Red Hat exams, no multiple choice questions appear in this book. These questions exclusively test your understanding of the chapter. It is okay if you have another way of performing a task. Getting results, not memorizing trivia, is what counts on the Red Hat exams. There may be more than one answer to many of these questions.

Introduction to MariaDB

1. Which RPM package provides the MariaDB server?

   _____

2. Which four actions are performed by the **mysql_secure_installation** script?

   _____

3. Which configuration directive runs MariaDB on TCP port 33066?

   _____

Database Management

4. What SQL command would you use to create a database named foo?

   _____

5. What SQL command would you use to create a table named person, containing two columns to store the first and last name?

   _____

Simple SQL Queries

6. What SQL command would you run to print all the records in the table salaries, where the value in the column salary is greater than or equal to 10,000?

   _____

7. What SQL command would you run to insert the values 7 and "finance" in the column id and department of the departments table?

_____

8. What SQL command would you run to delete all the records in the employees table where the last_name column is equal to "Smith"?

_____

9. What SQL command would you run to change the value of the first_name column to "Adam" in the employees table where the id column is equal to 5?

_____

Secure MariaDB

10. To disable all TCP connections, what directive would you include in /etc/my.cnf?

_____

11. What command would you use to set up a user named "redhat" with password "redhat"? Also, give that user read-only access to a table named bar on the database foo, and grant access only from the IP address 192.168.1.1.

_____

12. How do you display what privileges you have as a user logged in to a MariaDB client?

_____

Database Backup and Recovery

13. What is the command to back up the entire database foo to a text file /tmp/foo.sql?

_____

LAB QUESTIONS

Several of these labs involve configuration exercises. You should do these exercises on test machines only. It's assumed that you're running these exercises on virtual machines such as KVM. For this chapter, it's also assumed that you may be changing the configuration of a physical host system for such virtual machines.

Red Hat presents its exams electronically. For that reason, the labs in this chapter are available in the Chapter17/ subdirectory from the media that accompanies the book. In case you haven't yet set up RHEL 7 on a system, refer to Chapter 1 for installation instructions.

The answers for each lab follow the Self Test answers for the fill-in-the-blank questions.

SELF TEST ANSWERS

Introduction to MariaDB

1. The mariadb-server RPM package installs the MariaDB server.

2. The **mysql_secure_installation** script sets a password for the MariaDB root user, disables remote logins, removes anonymous users, and deletes the default test database.

3. The directive **port=33066** in /etc/my.cnf runs MariaDB on TCP port 33066. You would also need to configure the local firewall and customize the default SELinux policy to allow MariaDB to accept connections on that port.

Database Management

4. The following SQL command creates a database named foo:

   ```
   CREATE DATABASE foo;
   ```

5. The following command creates a table named person, with two columns to store the first and last name:

   ```
   CREATE TABLE person (
     first_name VARCHAR(255),
     last_name VARCHAR(255)
   );
   ```

Simple SQL Queries

6. The following SQL statement prints all the records in the table salaries, where the value in the column salary is greater than or equal to 10,000:

   ```
   SELECT * FROM salaries WHERE salary >=10000;
   ```

7. The following SQL statement adds a record with the values 7 and "finance" in the columns id and department of the departments table:

   ```
   INSERT INTO departments (id, department) VALUES (7, "finance");
   ```

8. The following SQL statement deletes all the records in the employees table where the last_name column is equal to "Smith":

   ```
   DELETE FROM employees WHERE last_name="Smith";
   ```

9. The following SQL statement modifies the value of the first_name column to "Adam" in the employees table where the id column is equal to 5:

```
UPDATE employees SET first_name="Adam" WHERE id=5;
```

Secure MariaDB

10. To disable all remote TCP connections, add the **skip-networking** directive in the [mysqld] section of /etc/my.cnf.

11. The following command sets up a user named "redhat" with password "redhat" and read-only access to a table named bar on the database foo from the IP address 192.168.1.1:

```
GRANT SELECT ON foo.bar TO redhat@192.168.1.1 IDENTIFIED BY 'redhat';
```

Don't forget to run **FLUSH PRIVILEGES** to make the change effective.

12. To list the privileges of the current user, run the **SHOW GRANTS** command.

Database Backup and Recovery

13. The following command backs up the entire database foo to a text file /tmp/foo.sql:

```
# mysqldump -uuser -ppass foo > /tmp/foo.sql
```

LAB ANSWERS

Lab 1

This lab is a skill drill—practice it until you can do it without thinking. Install the mariadb-server package, start and enable the MariaDB service, run **mysql_secure_installation**, and ensure that the local firewall allows MySQL connections.

Then, connect as the MariaDB root user with the **mysql** client from the localhost, and run the following commands:

```
GRANT ALL PRIVILEGES ON *.* TO 'root'@'%' IDENTIFIED BY 'letmein'↵
WITH GRANT OPTION;
FLUSH PRIVILEGES;
```

To test, connect to the database server from a remote host:

```
# mysql -h 192.168.122.50 -uroot -pletmein
```

Lab 2

The first part of this lab was covered in Exercise 17-4.

To create the new user and assign the required permissions, execute the following SQL commands:

```
GRANT SELECT ON employees.departments TO labuser@'%' IDENTIFIED BY↵
'changeme';
GRANT SELECT ON employees.dept_emp TO labuser@'%';
GRANT SELECT ON employees.dept_manager TO labuser@'%;
GRANT SELECT ON employees.employees TO labuser@'%';
GRANT SELECT ON employees.titles TO labuser@'%';
FLUSH PRIVILEGES;
```

Lab 3

The queries in question 4 of this lab can be solved using a single SQL join query. However, SQL join clauses are beyond the scope of the Red Hat exam. Hence, we have provided the answers using simple **SELECT** statements.

To explore the structure of the employees database, use the **SHOW TABLES** and **DESCRIBE** *table_name* commands.

1. Execute the following query to retrieve all employees born on the 31st of October 1963:

   ```
   SELECT * FROM employees WHERE birth_date='1963-10-31';
   ```

   This query should return 61 records.

2. The second question is similar to the previous, but requires a second condition in the **WHERE** clause:

   ```
   SELECT * FROM employees WHERE birth_date='1963-10-20' AND gender='F';
   ```

   The query should return 25 records.

3. To find the youngest employee, retrieve all the first few records from the employee table, sorted by birth data in descending order:

   ```
   SELECT * FROM employees ORDER BY birth_date DESC LIMIT 5;
   ```

   The youngest employees were born on the 1st of February 1965.

4. This question requires multiple queries to be answered. First, find the relevant record for Eran Fiebach in the employee table:

   ```
   SELECT * FROM employees WHERE first_name="Eran" AND last_name="Fiebach";
   ```

This query should return the employee number of 50714 for Eran Fiebach. Next, retrieve the job title using this information:

```
SELECT * FROM titles WHERE emp_no='50714';
```

The job title returned by the query is Technique Leader. The last step is to find the salary information for this employee number:

```
SELECT * FROM salaries WHERE emp_no='50714';
```

This query should return 14 salaries for Eran Fiebach. You should find that her starting salary was $40,000, while the current salary is $57,744.

Lab 4

As discussed in the answers to Lab 3, you may need to study the structure of the database using the **SHOW TABLES** and **DESCRIBE** *table_name* commands.

Then, add a record for the new employee in the employees table:

```
INSERT INTO employees (emp_no, birth_date, first_name, last_name, gender,
hire_date) VALUES ('500000', '1990-06-09', 'Julia', 'Chan', 'F',
'2015-06-01');
```

Then, add the job title:

```
INSERT INTO titles (emp_no, title, from_date, to_date) VALUES ('500000',
'Senior Engineer', '2015-06-01', '9999-01-01');
```

Note the special date 9999-01-01 to indicate that this is a current entry for the employee.

To assign the new employee to the Development department, we need the department code. The following query tells us that this is d005:

```
SELECT * FROM departments;
```

With this information, we assign the employee to the Development department:

```
INSERT INTO dep_emp (emp_no, dept_no, from_date, to_date) VALUES ('500000',
'd005', '2015-06-01', '9999-01-01');
```

The last step consists of adding the salary information:

```
INSERT INTO salaries (emp_no, salary, from_date, to_date) VALUES ('500000',
'60000', '2015-06-01', '9999-01-01');
```

Lab 5

Create the backup with the following command:

```
# mysqldump -p employees employees | gzip >> /root/emp.sql.gz
```

It is also perfectly acceptable to save the raw SQL file and then run **gzip** to compress the file. To verify that the backup is valid, explore the contents of the file:

```
# less /root/emp.sql.gz
```

Ensure that you have backed up only the contents of the employees table from the employees database. To restore the backup, first create the new database:

```
CREATE DATABASE emp_restored;
```

Then import the contents of the backup:

```
# gunzip /root/emp.sql.gz
# cat emp.sql | mysql -p emp_restored
```

As a final check, verify that the data looks the same by running the SQL query that you used to answer part 1 of Lab 3.

Appendix A

Prepare a System for the Sample Exams

Randy Russell, Red Hat's Director of Certification, stated in a 2009 blog entry that the Red Hat exams no longer require "a bare-metal installation." In other words, when you sit down for a Red Hat exam today, a preinstalled system will be provided for you. In this appendix, you'll set up a preinstalled system that will work for the sample exams included in electronic format on the DVD in the Exams/ subdirectory. Each exam is described on the first page of Appendixes B through E, and the answers follow.

If you're just studying for the RHCSA, read the following section. If you're also studying for the RHCE, read the section after that as well.

Basic Sample Exam System Requirements

A test system for RHEL 7 requires more. There is no requirement for a *physical* "bare-metal" installation in the objectives for either the RHCSA or the RHCE exam. However, for the RHCSA, you do need to "configure a physical machine to host virtual guests." You can also expect to "install Red Hat Enterprise Linux systems as virtual guests."

The default RHEL 7 virtual machine solution (KVM) requires a CPU that supports hardware-enabled virtualization, as discussed in Chapter 1. You may need to enable hardware virtualization support in your BIOS.

With those objectives in mind, you can set up a test system based on the following criteria:

- Installation on physical 64-bit hardware
  - A dual-boot configuration with another operating system is acceptable.
  - Enable hardware virtualization support in the BIOS.
- Sufficient hard drive space
  - A total of 60–70GB should be sufficient (though more would be helpful).
  - Also, 16GB each for two or three virtual machine systems should be sufficient.

In some cases, it is possible to install a virtual machine within a virtual machine. While we did not test such a configuration for this book, virtual machine solutions such as VMware Workstations can in turn host a guest hypervisor running other virtual machines. If this is too expensive or complex, just install RHEL 7 on a physical 64-bit system.

Since one of the objectives is to "configure a physical machine to host virtual guests," you'll need to set up a physical system without installing KVM software. (Of course, you should be prepared to install KVM during an exam.) As discussed in Chapter 1, it's ideal if you have a genuine release of RHEL 7 for this purpose. Rebuild distributions such as Scientific Linux 7, CentOS 7, and even Oracle Linux 7 should work equally well, as they are based on the publicly available RHEL 7 source code.

However, you should not use Fedora Linux to study for the Red Hat exams. Although RHEL 7 is based on Fedora Linux, RHEL 7 has a different look and feel. In some cases, it has a different functionality from the most similar Fedora releases, Fedora 19 and Fedora 20.

With those provisos in mind, you should prepare a 64-bit physical test system per the requirements described in Chapter 1. As suggested in that chapter, you should configure a Virtualization Host installation, as shown in Figure A-1.

You may also set up a GUI, as also discussed in Chapter 1. For that purpose, you should select the Server with GUI base environment during the installation process. This includes the following optional package groups:

- **Virtualization Client** Includes clients for installing and managing virtualization instances
- **Virtualization Hypervisor** Installs the smallest possible virtualization host installation
- **Virtualization Tools** Includes tools for offline virtual image management

But to meet the implied requirements of a test system for the RHCSA, you'll need to make sure that virtual machine software is not installed during the installation process, as shown in Figure A-2.

FIGURE A-1 RHEL 7 Virtualization Host installation

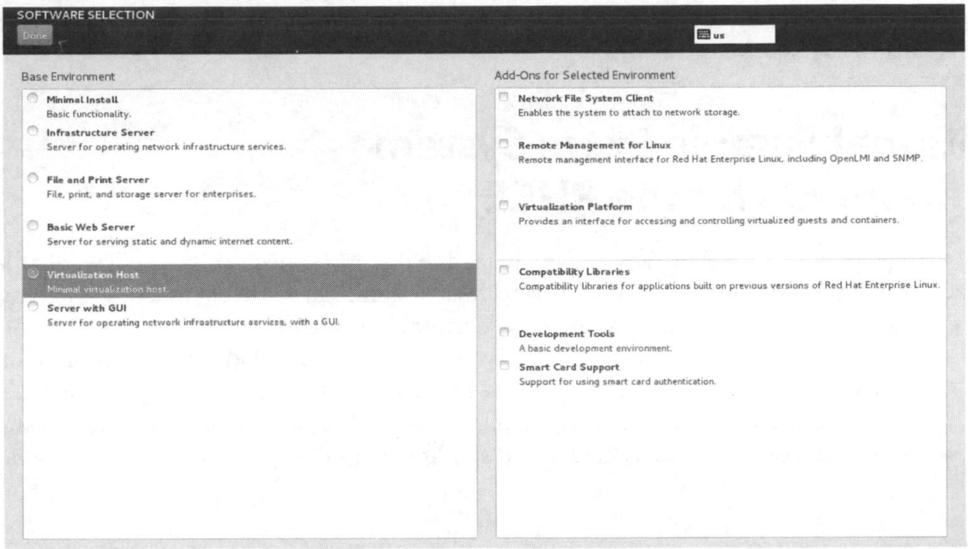

FIGURE A-2 RHEL 7 Server with GUI installation, no virtual machine software

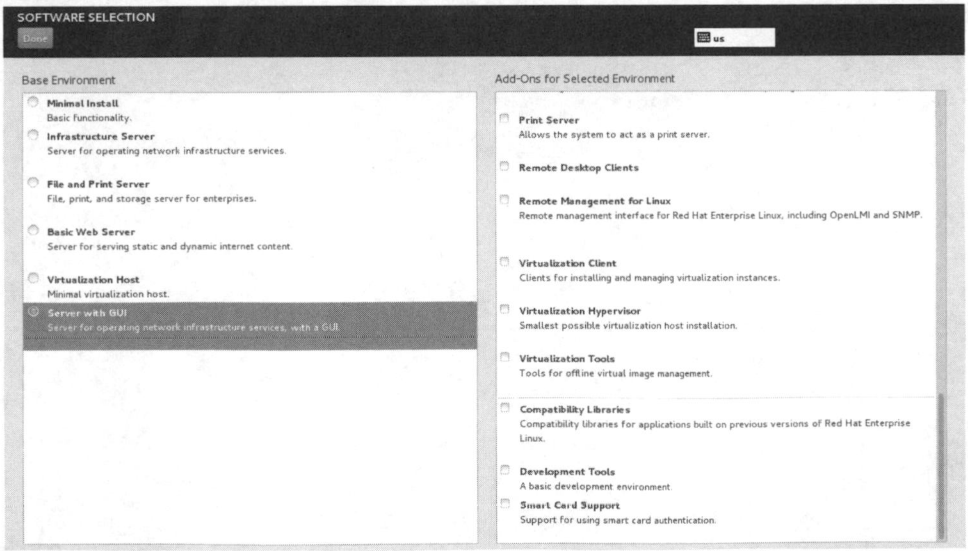

Once installation is complete, the system will be ready for the RHCSA exam. But there is one more step required. You'll need to set up an installation repository for the local network. It's okay to do so on the physical host system. One method is described in Chapter 1, Lab 2.

Additional Sample Exam System Requirements for the RHCE

To be ready for the RHCE exam, you'll need to do more. Specifically, you'll want at least two virtual machine systems on the physical host system. Three virtual machine systems, plus a spare, were configured on two different networks in Chapter 1.

If you're just studying for the RHCE, you can choose to include virtual machine software in the installation process for the physical host system. You should set up the virtual systems per the requirements discussed in Chapters 1 and 2. Kickstart files ks.cfg, ks1.cfg, and ks2.cfg are available on the DVD, in the Exams/ subdirectory, to help create those virtual systems.

Appendix B

Sample Exam 1: RHCSA

The following questions will help measure your understanding of the material presented in this book. As discussed in the introduction, you should be prepared to complete the RHCSA exam in 2.5 hours.

The RHCSA exam is "closed book." However, you are allowed to use any documentation that can be found on the Red Hat Enterprise Linux computer. While test facilities allow you to make notes, you won't be allowed to take these notes from the testing room.

The RHCSA is entirely separate from the RHCE. Although both exams cover some of the same services, the objectives for those services are different.

In most cases, there is no one solution, no single method to solve a problem or install a service. There is a nearly infinite number of options with Linux, so we can't cover all possible scenarios.

Even for the following exercises, *do not use a production computer*. A small error in some or all of these exercises may make Linux unbootable. If you're unable to recover from the steps documented in these exercises, you may need to reinstall Red Hat Enterprise Linux. Saving any data that you have on the local system may then not be possible.

Red Hat presents its exams electronically. For that reason, the exams in this book are available from the companion DVD, in the Exams/ subdirectory. This exam is in the file named RHCSAsampleexam1 and is available in .txt, .doc, and .html formats. For details on how to set up RHEL 7 as a system suitable for a practice exam, refer to Appendix A. Be very sure to set up the repository configured in Chapter 1, Lab 2.

Don't turn the page until you're finished with the sample exam!

RHCSA Sample Exam 1 Discussion

In this discussion, we'll describe one way to check your work to meet the requirements listed for the Sample 1 RHCSA exam.

1. One way to see if SELinux is set in enforcing mode is to run the **sestatus** command.

2. If the virtualization software is installed on the local system, you'll have access to the Virtual Machine Manager in the GUI, or at least the **virt-install** and **virsh** commands from the command line.

3. If successful, you should be able to access the new server2.example.com system, via ssh or with the Virtual Machine Manager.

4. One way to set the noted system to start automatically the next time the host is booted is with the **virsh autostart server2.example.com** command. One way to confirm this is in the output to the **virsh dominfo server2.example.com** command.

5. If you don't know how to recover a root password, review Exercise 5-2.

6. To review current volume groups, run the **vgdisplay** command. Check the PE size. To list all logical volumes, run the **lvdisplay** command. The size of the new volume should be 32 logical extents, equivalent to 256MB.

7. To make sure that volume is automatically mounted the next time the system is booted, it should be configured in /etc/fstab to the appropriate format, with the UUID associated with the volume, as provided by the **blkid** command. Here's an example:

   ```
   UUID=d055418f-1ff6-46bf-8476-b391e82a6f51 /project xfs defaults 1 2
   ```

8. The following command shows one method to complete this task:

   ```
   # find /etc -type f -name "*.conf" >/root/configfiles.txt 2>/dev/null
   ```

9. Run the **file /tmp/etc.tar.bz2** command to confirm that the file you have created is bzip-compressed. Uncompress the archive to verify its content, or check its content with the following command:

   ```
   # cat /tmp/etc.tar.bz2 | bunzip2 | tar -t
   ```

10. The /home/friends directory should be owned by the group friends. As long as users donna and mike are not part of that group, and other users don't have permissions (or ACLs) on that directory, access should be limited to members of the friends group. The directory should also have SGID permissions:

    ```
    # ls -ld /home/friends
    drwxrws---. 2 root friends 6 Nov 18 10:54 /home/friends
    # getent group friends
    friends:x:2000:nancy,randy
    ```

11. If you've modified user mike's account to make his account expire in seven days, the right expiration date should appear in the output to the **chage -l mike** command.

12. There are a number of ways to set up a cron job; it could be configured in the /etc/cron.monthly directory or as a cron job for the user root or mike with the **crontab -u mike -e** command. In any of these cases, the command would be associated with an appropriate timestamp, with a line such as this:

```
50 3 2 * * /bin/find /home/mike/tmp -type f -exec /bin/rm {} \;
```

13. Run the **getfacl /home/mike/project.test** command. If user donna has read permissions in the ACLs, you'll see it in the output to that command. You should also set an ACL on the /home/mike directory and grant user donna the execute permission in order to access files within the directory.

14. Run the **authconfig-gtk** command to review the current settings. "Use LDAP" must be enabled in the User Information settings, along with "Use LDAP Authentication." The server URL should be set to ldap://192.168.122.1, with TLS enabled.

Appendix C

Sample Exam 2: RHCSA

The following questions will help measure your understanding of the material presented in this book. As discussed in the introduction, you should be prepared to complete the RHCSA exam in 2.5 hours.

The RHCSA exam is "closed book." However, you are allowed to use any documentation that can be found on the Red Hat Enterprise Linux computer. While test facilities allow you to make notes, you won't be allowed to take these notes from the testing room.

The RHCSA is entirely separate from the RHCE. Although both exams cover some of the same services, the objectives for those services are different.

In most cases, there is no one solution, no single method to solve a problem or install a service. There is a nearly infinite number of options with Linux, so we can't cover all possible scenarios.

Even for the following exercises, *do not use a production computer*. A small error in some or all of these exercises may make Linux unbootable. If you're unable to recover from the steps documented in these exercises, you may need to reinstall Red Hat Enterprise Linux. Saving any data that you have on the local system may then not be possible.

Red Hat presents its exams electronically. For that reason, the exams in this book are available from the companion DVD, in the Exams/ subdirectory. This exam is in the file named RHCSAsampleexam2 and is available in .txt, .doc, and .html formats. For details on how to set up RHEL 7 as a system suitable for a practice exam, refer to Appendix A. Be very sure to set up the repository configured in Chapter 1, Lab 2.

Don't turn the page until you're finished with the sample exam!

RHCSA Sample Exam 2 Discussion

In this discussion, we'll describe one way to check your work to meet the requirements listed for the Sample 2 RHCSA exam.

1. If the virtualization software is installed on the local system, you'll have access to the Virtual Machine Manager in the GUI, or at least the **virt-install** and **virsh** commands from the command line.

2. If the newly Kickstarted installation is successful, you should be able to access the new outsider2.example.org system, either via ssh or with the Virtual Machine Manager.

3. Anyone with access to the administrative account on the VM can review ssh-based logins in the /var/log/secure file. It's an easy way to verify that you've used the **ssh** command to connect to the new system. If you don't know how to recover a root password, review Exercise 5-2.

4. All partitions (the new 500MB partition, additional swap space) should be shown in the output to the **fdisk -l** command.

5. When properly configured, the new filesystem should be shown in the output to the **mount** command, marked as "type xfs."

6. When additional swap space is created, it should be shown in the contents of the /proc/swaps file. Alternatively, the total amount of swap space should be shown in the output to the **free** command.

7. Run the **blkid** command to retrieve the UUID of the new volumes to be set in /etc/fstab. The type of the filesystem must be specified as swap in the /etc/fstab file. Here's an example:

   ```
   UUID=a110ef54-caed-42b2-a5bb-e3086792d168 swap swap defaults 0 0
   ```

8. The following command shows one method to complete this task:

   ```
   # grep -rl redhat /etc/* >/root/etc-redhat.txt 2>/dev/null
   ```

   Another method is listed next:

   ```
   # find /etc -type f -exec grep -l redhat {} \;↵
   >/root/etc-redhat.txt 2>/dev/null
   ```

9. New local users should be listed in /etc/passwd and/etc/shadow. To specifically deny regular users access to a directory, it's easiest to use ACLs. You should be able to confirm that users bill and richard don't have access to the /cooks directory with the **getfacl /cooks** command. Try to create a file as user bill or richard with the **touch** command.

```
# getfacl /cooks
getfacl: removing leading '/' from absolute path names
# file: cooks
# owner: root
# group: root
user::rwx
user:bill:---
user:richard:---
group::r-x
mask::rwx
other::rwx
```

10. To confirm, you should be able to insert a DVD into the appropriate drive. (Alternatively, you can set up an ISO file on a virtual machine.) Then when you run the **ls /misc/dvd** command, the automounter will mount the DVD and provide file information on that drive. This should be an easy configuration, based on a slight change to the default /etc/auto.misc file. If unsure, review Chapter 6, Certification Objective 6.06. Of course, you'll need to make sure the autofs service runs after a reboot, which can be confirmed with the **systemctl is-enabled autofs** command.

11. When new kernels are installed, they should include a new stanza in the bootloader configuration file, /boot/grub2/grub.conf. The default stanza is based on the **saved_entry** directive in the /boot/grub2/grubenv file; just remember, **saved_entry=0** points to the first stanza, **saved_entry=1** points to the second stanza, and so on. Use the **grub2-set-default** command to boot a different default kernel.

12. Default targets are configured with the **systemctl set-default** command.

13. Edit the /etc/ntp.conf file. The **server** directive in that file should point to the desired system (in this case, the physical host). Of course, a test on that system with the **ntpq -p** command won't work unless the physical host is configured as an NTP server. In a real-world configuration, that second host would be an actual NTP server. Once again, you'll need to make sure the ntpd service runs after a reboot, which can be confirmed with the **systemctl is-enabled ntpd** command.

14. To make sure SELinux is set in permissive mode, run the **sestatus** command.

Appendix D

Sample Exam 3:
RHCE Sample Exam 1

T he following questions will help measure your understanding of the material presented in this book. As discussed in the introduction, you should be prepared to complete the RHCE exam in 3.5 hours.

Like the RHCSA, the RHCE exam is "closed book." However, you are allowed to use any documentation that can be found on the Red Hat Enterprise Linux computer. While test facilities allow you to make notes, you won't be allowed to take these notes from the testing room.

Although the RHCE exam is entirely separate from the RHCSA, you need to pass both exams to receive the RHCE certificate. Nevertheless, you can take the RHCE exam first. While both exams cover some of the same services, the objectives for those services are different.

In most cases, there is no one solution, no single method to solve a problem or install a service. There is a nearly infinite number of options with Linux, so we can't cover all possible scenarios.

Even for these exercises, *do not use a production computer*. A small error in some or all of these exercises may make Linux unbootable. If you're unable to recover from the steps documented in these exercises, you may need to reinstall Red Hat Enterprise Linux. Saving any data that you have on the local system may then not be possible.

Red Hat presents its exams electronically. For that reason, the exams in this book are available from the companion DVD, in the Exams/ subdirectory. This exam is in the file named RHCEsampleexam1 and is available in .txt, .doc, and .html formats. For details on how to set up RHEL 7 as a system suitable for a practice exam, refer to Appendix A. Be very sure to set up the repository configured in Chapter 1, Lab 2.

Don't turn the page until you're finished with the sample exam!

RHCE Sample Exam 1 Discussion

In this discussion, we'll describe one way to check your work to meet the requirements listed for the Sample 1 RHCE exam. Since there is no one way to set up a Red Hat Enterprise Linux configuration, there is no one right answer for the listed requirements. However, there are some general things to remember. You need to make sure your changes work after a reboot. For the RHCE, you'll need to make sure that the services you set up are configured to start automatically at boot.

1. The first task should be straightforward. Users katie and dickens should have accounts on the SSH server. While it's possible to limit user access to SSH via TCP Wrappers, the most straightforward way to do so is with the following directive in the main SSH server configuration file:

   ```
   AllowUsers katie
   ```

   Of course, the "proof of the pudding" is the ability for user katie to log in from a remote system on the local network and for user dickens to be refused such access. In addition, limited access to the local network requires an appropriate limit via a zone-based firewall rule, or an appropriate line in the TCP Wrappers configuration files, /etc/hosts.allow and /etc/hosts.deny.

2. The Samba server will be configured with two different shared directories. The system can be configured with the samba_export_all_rw SELinux boolean, or alternatively, the directories should be set with the samba_share_t type label. In addition, the most straightforward way to limit access to the given users is with the **allow users** directive in the smb.conf configuration file in the appropriate stanzas. The given users should exist in the separate Samba password database. Of course, success is based on the ability of users dickens, tim, and stephanie to access the given directories from a remote system.

3. NTP servers are limited to the local system by default. Expanding access to the local network requires a change to the /etc/ntp.conf file, in the **restrict** directive, as well as appropriate open ports in the firewall. You can test the connection remotely with the **ntpdate** *ntpserver* command. (Of course, you're welcome to substitute the IP address for the hostname of the NTP server.) Remember, NTP communicates over UDP port 123.

4. Although other methods are available, you can limit access in the main NFS configuration file (/etc/exports) to a single host, with a directive such as the following:

   ```
   /home maui.example.com(rw)
   ```

You should substitute the hostname or IP address of your physical exam system. In addition, you may run into different requirements, such as read-only (ro), no root access (root_squash), and more. Access should be confirmed from the physical host system by mounting the shared NFS directory.

5. The most straightforward way to configure a secure virtual website is with the help of the standard configuration defined in the ssl.conf file in the /etc/httpd/conf.d directory. If successful, you'll be able to access the secure websites https://shost1 .example.com and https://shost2.example.com. Since these certificates aren't from an official authority, you should not be concerned about the "invalid security certificate" message that appears in a browser, assuming the SSL key names are shown in the message.

6. Add the https service to the default zone on the local zone-based firewall of server .example.com. To limit HTTP access from outstider1.example.net, you can set up a rich rule. Alternatively, add the IP address of outsider1 to the drop zone on the firewall. Before testing, ensure that DNS resolution for the hostnames shost1.example .com and shost2.example.com works by adding the IP and host entries to the /etc/hosts files of every machine.

7. The typical location for a daily cron job is the /etc/cron.d directory. The backup.sh script must be run from the local directory where the backup files need to be saved. Hence, you should change to the /tmp directory before running the script. The cron line should look like this:

```
0 2 * * * root (cd /tmp; /usr/local/bin/backup.sh /home)
```

8. To configure IP forwarding for both IPv4 and IPv6 addressing, you'll need to add the following directives in /etc/sysctl.conf:

```
net.ipv4.ip_forward=1
net.ipv6.conf.all.forwarding=1
```

9. Success on this task can be verified by "pinging" the two IPv6 addresses from the two hosts, with the commands **ping6 2001:db8:1::1/64** and **ping6 2001:db8:1::2/64**.

10. Use the **targetcli** shell to set up the iSCSI target. Upon completion, the **targetcli ls** command should display all the required configuration parameters. Review Chapter 13, Certification Objective 13.06, for more information on how to use the **targetcli** shell.

11. On the client, run the **iscsiadm** command in discovery database mode to see the remote target. If no targets are displayed, review the configuration, including the iSCSI access list, the IQN names, and firewall rules. Ensure that the iscsi and target services are running on the client machine and the storage server, respectively. If the discovery phase is successful, log in to the target and create a filesystem. You would need an entry in /etc/fstab to automatically mount the volume at boot.

12. The default time period when the system accounting tool is run is 10 minutes, as shown in the default /etc/cron.d/sysstat file. It's easy to change that to one minute in the noted file.

13. Connect with the **mysql -u root** command to the database and issue the following commands:

```
USE exam;
SELECT * from mark;
```

The SELECT query should return the three records listed in the exercise.

14. If successful, you should be able to log in to the MariaDB database by running **mysql -u examuser -p** and typing **pass123**. The user must have full access to the exam database, which you can confirm with the **SHOW GRANTS** command. The root user must not be able to access MariaDB without a password. You can confirm that this is the case with the **mysql -u root** command.

Appendix E

Sample Exam 4:
RHCE Sample Exam 2

Т he following questions will help measure your understanding of the material presented in this book. As discussed in the introduction, you should be prepared to complete the RHCE exam in 3.5 hours.

Like the RHCSA, the RHCE exam is "closed book." However, you are allowed to use any documentation that can be found on the Red Hat Enterprise Linux computer. While test facilities allow you to make notes, you won't be allowed to take these notes from the testing room.

Although the RHCE exam is entirely separate from the RHCSA, you need to pass both exams to receive the RHCE certificate. Nevertheless, you can take the RHCE exam first. While both exams cover some of the same services, the objectives for those services are different.

In most cases, there is no one solution, no single method to solve a problem or install a service. There is a nearly infinite number of options with Linux, so we can't cover all possible scenarios.

Even for these exercises, *do not use a production computer*. A small error in some or all of these exercises may make Linux unbootable. If you're unable to recover from the steps documented in these exercises, you may need to reinstall Red Hat Enterprise Linux. Saving any data that you have on the local system may then not be possible.

Red Hat presents its exams electronically. For that reason, the exams in this book are available from the companion DVD, in the Exams/ subdirectory. This exam is in the file named RHCEsampleexam2 and is available in .txt, .doc, and .html formats. For details on how to set up RHEL 7 as a system suitable for a practice exam, refer to Appendix A. Be very sure to set up the repository configured in Chapter 1, Lab 2.

Don't turn the page until you're finished with the sample exam!

RHCE Sample Exam 2 Discussion

In this discussion, we'll describe one way to check your work to meet the requirements listed for the Sample 2 RHCE exam. Since there is no one way to set up a Red Hat Enterprise Linux configuration, there is no one right answer for the listed requirements. However, there are some general things to remember. You need to make sure your changes work after a reboot. For the RHCE, you'll need to make sure that the services you set up are configured to start automatically at boot.

1. This task is essentially identical to Exercises 12-5 and 12-6. To verify the configuration, ensure that Kerberos principals exist on the KDC for each user. After you open an SSH session on server1, the **klist** command should confirm that a TGT has been granted. In case of issues, review the configuration. Based on the question, the client should include the following directives in /etc/krb5.conf:

   ```
   default_realm = EXAMPLE.COM
   ```

   In addition, the kdc and admin_server directives in the /etc/krb5.con file should be set to the FQDN of the physical host system.

2. The first part of this task requires the following configuration line in /etc/exports:

   ```
   /nfsshare tester1.example.com(rw)
   ```

   The configuration of an NFS share secured with Kerberos is explained in Exercises 16-2 and 16-3. Verify that you have created and installed Kerberos host and service principals for all your machines. On the server, the nfs-server and nfs-secure-server services must be running. The NFS share must be exported with the **sec=krb5p** option.

3. This exercise is the continuation of the previous task. If the client can automatically mount the NFS share at boot with the **sec=krb5p** option, you have successfully completed this task. If you face any issues, check that the nfs-secure service is enabled on the client and review your firewall rules. Run the **mount** command in verbose mode (**-v**) and analyze the output and the logs for error messages.

4. If successful, you should see the contents of the noted index.html files for each website. You should also change the default SELinux context of the /web directory to match that of the /var/www/html directory. Review Chapter 14, Certification Objective 14.04, for more information on secure virtual hosts.

5. If you are successful, users elizabeth and fred, and no others, will have access to the cubs subdirectory of the main directory. Both users will have access only from systems on the local network. If your configuration does not work as expected, review your setup. You must have a **<Directory>** block container for the cubs subdirectory in the Apache configuration files, with **AuthType Basic** and **Require user** directives. You will also need an **AuthUserFile** line pointing to a password file. You can restrict access to the local network with an **Allow from** directive.

6. The CGI application should be accessible from the following URL:
   http://test1.example.com/cgi-bin/good.pl
   When you navigate to that URL, the browser should print the string "Good Job!"

7. If you use BIND, the default named.conf configuration file is itself sufficient for a caching-only DNS server. To that file, you'll need to add a **forwarders** directive, with the IP address of the physical host system, which presumably has a DNS server.

8. Configure Postfix and review your configuration with the **postconf -n** command. At a minimum, you need to configure the **myorigin**, **mydestination**, **local_transport**, and **relayhost** directives. Test the configuration with an e-mail client such as mutt. The server should accept e-mails from the local system only and deliver them to your physical host. Verify in /var/log/maillog that this is the case.

9. When user mike attempts to connect from a given client, the system should prompt for and accept the passphrase defined in the exam question: **Linux rocks, Windows does not.** (Note that the passphrase includes a comma and period.) SSH key-based authentication is a requirement for both the RHCSA and RHCE exams and was covered in in Chapter 4, Certification Objective 4.04.

10. When masquerading is configured, connections from internal systems in the 192.168.122.0/24 network such as server1.example.com to outsider1.example.net appear as if they come from the physical host system. That can be confirmed by attempting a SSH connection and looking at log messages in /var/log/secure.

11. If the configuration works, you should still have IP connectivity after disabling one of the interfaces with the **ifdown** command. Verify that round-robin mode is in use with the **cat /proc/net/bonding/bond0** command (if you configured bonding) or with the **teamdctl team state** command (if you configured teaming). For more information on interface teaming and bonding, review Chapter 12, Certification Objective 12.06.

12. Users with an account on the Samba server should be able to connect to their home directories on that server. However, the files on that directory won't be accessible unless the samba_enable_home_dirs boolean is enabled.

13. Peers on an NTP server can be enabled in the /etc/ntp.conf file, in place of the **server** directive. Just remember, NTP communicates over UDP port 123. One way to check if UDP port 123 is open is with the following command: **nmap -sU server1 -p 123**.

14. To avoid responding to the **ping** command, which works over IPv4, the **icmp_echo_ignore_all** option must be active. You can set that up permanently in the /etc/sysctl .conf file with the **net.ipv4.icmp_echo_ignore_all = 1** directive.

Appendix F

About the DVD

T he DVD-ROM included with this book comes complete with the lab files, as explained in each chapter, and also includes a digital copy of the book. To access the lab files and e-book, insert the DVD. Unless you're running a GUI where automounting has been enabled, you'll have to mount the DVD with a command such as the following:

```
# mount /dev/cdrom /media
```

System Requirements

The electronic book requires either Adobe Reader or an equivalent Linux PDF reader such as Evince. As discussed in Chapter 1, the RHCSA exam includes KVM, which Red Hat supports only on 64-bit systems.

Electronic Book

The contents of the Study Guide are provided in PDF format. If you've mounted the DVD as suggested earlier, you'll find the chapter labs and sample exams as PDF files in the /media directory. When the DVD is mounted in that way, you can access files for each chapter in the directories /media/Chapter1, /media/Chapter2, /media/Chapter3, and so on. Besides the PDF files for individual chapters, you'll also find different files for chapter labs, some scripts, and sample exams, as explained in the body of the book.

In addition, a complete book PDF has been provided to allow you to search across the entire book and to give you access to the front matter, which contains important information on the book and DVD. The book PDF can be found in the directory /media/BookPDF.

Many excellent PDF readers are available for Linux. In RHEL 7, Evince is the default document viewer for PDF, PostScript, and other common document file formats.

To start Evince, in the GNOME Desktop Environment, click Applications | Utilities | Document Viewer. Alternatively, from a GNOME terminal, run the **evince** command.

If Evince is not available in your system, you can install it with the following command:

```
# yum install evince
```

Technical Support

For questions regarding the PDF copy of the book or the lab files, e-mail techsolutions@mhedu .com or visit http://mhp.softwareassist.com.

For questions regarding book content, e-mail customer.service@mheducation.com.
For customers outside the United States, e-mail international_cs@mheducation.com.

Glossary

Access control list (ACL) Access control lists (ACLs) provide an additional layer of access control to files and directories stored in extended attributes on the filesystem. These ACLs are set and verified with the **setfacl** and **getfacl** commands.

Address Resolution Protocol (ARP) A protocol that maps an IP address to the hardware (MAC) address of a network interface.

anacron The anacron service is designed to run **cron** jobs that could not run while a server was powered down; this is now integrated into periodic job management through the /etc/anacrontab file.

Apache web server The Apache web server provides both normal and secure web services via the **httpd** daemon.

apachectl   The **apachectl** command is a method to start, stop, and reload an Apache server; the **apachectl graceful** command reloads a revised configuration file without resetting existing connections.

arp   The **arp** command is used to view or modify the kernel's ARP table. Using **arp**, you can detect problems such as duplicate addresses on the network. Alternatively, you can use **arp** to manually add the required entries from your LAN.

at   The **at** command is similar to **cron**, but it allows you to run a job on a one-time basis.

automounter   The automounter can be configured to mount local and network directories on an as-needed basis. It's configured in the auto.master, auto.net, auto.misc, and auto.smb files in the /etc directory.

bash   The default shell for Linux users is bash, also known as the Bourne-Again Shell.

BIND (Berkeley Internet Name Domain)   BIND is the software that is used to set up a Domain Name System (DNS) service. The associated daemon is **named**.

BIOS   The BIOS is the Basic Input/Output System. It initializes hardware resources when you power up your computer. On most modern systems, the BIOS has been replaced by the UEFI. The BIOS menu allows you to customize many options, including the sequence of boot media.

/boot   The directory with the main files required to boot Linux, including the Linux kernel and initial RAM disk. By default, /boot is mounted on a separate partition.

Caching-only name server   A caching-only name server performs many of the functions of a DNS server. It stores the DNS records associated with recent name searches for use by other computers on your LAN.

CentOS   The Community Enterprise Operating System is a "rebuild" of RHEL based on Red Hat source code.

chage   The **chage** command manages the expiration date of a password.

chattr   The **chattr** command allows you to change file attributes.

chgrp   The **chgrp** command changes the group that owns a file.

chmod   The **chmod** command changes the permissions on a file.

chown   The **chown** command changes ownership on a file.

CIFS (Common Internet File System)   CIFS is a file-sharing protocol widely used on Microsoft Windows systems. It's also supported by the version of Samba included with RHEL 7.

cron   A service that runs jobs on a periodic basis. It's configured in /etc/crontab; by default, it executes jobs in the /etc/cron.d, /etc/cron.hourly, /etc/cron.daily, /etc/cron .weekly, and /etc/cron.monthly directories.

crontab   Individual users can run the **crontab** command to configure jobs that are run periodically.

/dev   This directory includes device files, used to represent hardware and software components.

DHCP (Dynamic Host Configuration Protocol)   DHCP clients lease IP addresses for a fixed period of time from a DHCP server on a local network.

dmesg   The **dmesg** command lists the kernel ring buffer and the initial boot messages. If your system successfully boots, /var/log/dmesg is one place to look for messages.

DNS (Domain Name System)   The DNS service maintains a database of IP addresses and fully qualified domain names, such as www.mheducation.com. If the domain name is not in the local database, DNS is normally configured to forward the query to another DNS server.

dumpe2fs   The **dumpe2fs** command provides various information about an ext2/ext3/ ext4 filesystem.

e2label   The **e2label** command associates a label to an ext2/ext3/ext4 filesystem.

Environment   Each user's environment specifies default variables that define the login prompt, terminal, the PATH, mail directory, and more.

/etc/fstab   The /etc/fstab configuration file defines the filesystems to be mounted at boot.

/etc/ntp.conf   The main NTP server configuration file.

exportfs   The **exportfs** command allows directories to be shared as NFS volumes on a network.

ext2/ext3/ext4   The second, third, and fourth extended filesystems (ext2, ext3, ext4). The ext3 and ext4 filesystems include journaling. The ext4 filesystem can handle a maximum size of 1 exabyte (1,000,000 terabytes).

fdisk   A standard disk partition command utility that allows you to modify the physical and logical disk MBR partition layout.

Fedora Linux   The successor to the freely available version of Red Hat Linux; more information on this Linux distribution is available online at https://fedoraproject.org.

Filesystem   Filesystem has multiple meanings in Linux. It refers to mounted storage volumes; the root directory (/) filesystem is mounted on its own filesystem. It also refers to filesystem formats; RHEL 7 volumes are typically formatted to the XFS filesystem.

Firewall   A hardware or software system that prevents unauthorized access to and from a network.

firewall-cmd   A command-line tool to administer firewalld.

firewalld   A zone-based firewall that is activated by default on RHEL 7.

fsck   The **fsck** command checks a filesystem on a Linux partition for consistency. Variations on this command are available for specific filesystems, such as fsck.ext3, fsck.ext4, and fsck.xfs.

FTP (File Transfer Protocol)   The FTP protocol is a TCP/IP protocol designed to transfer files on a network.

Gateway   The word *gateway* has multiple meanings in Linux. A default gateway address is the IP address of a computer or router that connects two network segments, such as a local subnet to the Internet. A gateway can also be a router between networks.

gdisk   A disk partition command utility that allows you to modify partitions created with the GPT partitioning scheme.

genkey   The **genkey** command supports the generation of SSL keys for secure websites.

getfacl   The **getfacl** command lets you read access control lists (ACLs) on files and directories.

getsebool   The **getsebool** command lets you read the current status of an SELinux boolean.

GNOME (GNU Network Object Model Environment)   GNOME is the default GUI desktop for Red Hat Enterprise Linux.

GPG (GNU Privacy Guard)   GPG is an implementation of the OpenPGP standard. On RHEL 7, GPG is available with the **gpg2** command.

GPL   The GPL is the General Public License, under which most Linux software is released.

Group ID   Every Linux group has a group ID, usually defined in /etc/group.

GRUB 2 (Grand Unified Bootloader version 2)   The default boot loader for RHEL 7.

grub2-install   The **grub2-install** command installs the GRUB 2 bootloader on a device, such as /boot/grub/grub.

GUID Partition Table (GPT)   A disk-partitioning scheme that supports up to 128 partitions.

Home directory   The home directory is the default login directory for Linux users. Normally, this is /home/*user*, where user is the user's login name. It's also represented by the tilde (~) in the bash shell.

htpasswd   The **htpasswd** command creates a password database that can be used with an Apache web server for HTTP authentication.

Hypervisor   A virtual machine manager that allows a guest operating system to run on a host computer.

ICMP (Internet Control Message Protocol)   A protocol for sending error control messages on a network. ICMP is associated with the **ping** command.

ifconfig   The **ifconfig** command is considered obsolete. It is replaced by the **ip** command.

Initial RAM disk   RHEL uses an initial RAM disk in the boot process; it's stored as an initramfs-`uname -r`.img file in the /boot directory.

ip   The **ip** command is used to configure and display network devices.

IP forwarding   IP forwarding is a kernel parameter that allows you to route packets between two different network interfaces on a system.

iptables   The **iptables** command is the basic command to configure firewall rules and network address translation (NAT).

IPv4, IPv6   IPv4 and IPv6 are different versions of the IP protocol. Version 4 is based on 32-bit addresses; version 6 is meant to replace version 4 and is based on 128-bit addresses.

iSCSI (Internet SCSI)   Internet SCSI is a protocol that allows clients (iSCSI initiators) to send SCSI commands to storage devices (iSCSI targets) over an IP-based network.

iscsiadm   The **iscsiadm** command allows you to set up connections to remote iSCSI targets from an iSCSI initiator.

journalctl   The **journalctl** command displays the content of the systemd journal.

Kdump   Kdump is a kernel crash dump service for Linux.

Kerberos   Kerberos is a protocol that provides authentication services over an insecure network for users, hosts, and services.

Kernel   The kernel is the heart of any operating system. The Linux kernel is monolithic and can load some of its code as separate modules at run time.

Kernel module   Kernel modules are object files that can be loaded and unloaded into the kernel as needed. Loaded kernel modules are shown with the **lsmod** command.

Kickstart   Kickstart is the Red Hat automated installation system, where answers to installation questions can be supplied from a single text file.

KVM   KVM, the Kernel-based Virtual Machine, is the default virtualization technology for RHEL 7.

lftp   The **lftp** command starts a flexible FTP command-line client.

Lightweight Directory Access Protocol (LDAP)   The Lightweight Directory Access Protocol provides a central user authentication database.

Live CD   Used in reference to a complete Linux operating system that can be booted directly from CD/DVD media.

locate   The **locate** command searches through a default database of files and directories. The database is refreshed daily with the **mlocate** cron script in the /etc/cron.daily directory.

Logical extent (LE)   A logical extent (LE) is a chunk of disk space that corresponds to a physical extent (PE).

Logical volume (LV)   A logical volume (LV) is composed of a group of logical extents (LEs).

Logical Volume Management (LVM)   Logical Volume Management (LVM) allows you to set up a filesystem on multiple partitions. Also known as the Logical Volume Manager.

logrotate   The **logrotate** command utility supports automated log file maintenance. With the help of cron, it rotates, compresses, and removes various log files.

lsattr   The **lsattr** command lists file attributes.

lvcreate   The **lvcreate** command creates a logical volume (LV) from a specified number of available logical extents (LEs).

lvdisplay   The **lvdisplay** command specifies current configuration information for logical volumes (LVs).

lvextend   The **lvextend** command allows you to increase the size of a logical volume (LV).

lvremove   The **lvremove** command deletes a logical volume (LV).

Masquerading   Masquerading is a form of network address translation (NAT). It allows you to provide Internet access to all of the computers on a LAN with a single public IP address.

MBR (Master Boot Record)   The MBR is a type of boot sector and partitioning format. Once the BIOS cycle is complete, it looks for a pointer on the boot disk's MBR, which then looks at a boot loader configuration file such as grub.conf for directions on how to start an operating system.

MD5 (Message Digest 5)   A hashing algorithm. Although it's no longer the default hashing scheme for Linux user passwords, it is still used for other passwords such as those in the GRUB 2 configuration file.

mkfs   The **mkfs** command can help you format a newly configured volume. Variations are available, including mkfs.xfs, which formats to the default XFS filesystem.

mkswap   The **mkswap** command can help you set up a newly configured volume as swap space.

modprobe   You can use the **modprobe** command to add and remove kernel modules.

mount   You can use the **mount** command to list mounted partitions, or attach local or network partitions to specified directories. Variations are available for different network mounts, such as mount.nfs, mount.nfs4, and mount.cifs.

NAT (Network Address Translation)   NAT allows you to map an IP address into another one on a different network segment. It can be used to make computers inside a LAN visible to an external network such as the Internet, while disguising their true IP addresses.

netstat   The **netstat** command is considered obsolete and is replaced by the **ss** command.

Network Manager   Network Manager (sometimes shown as one word) is a service to monitor and manage network settings. It is associated with commands such as **nmcli**, **nmtui**, and **nm-connection-editor**.

Network Time Protocol (NTP)   The Network Time Protocol supports time synchronization between the local computer and a central timeserver.

NFS (Network File System)   NFS is a file-sharing protocol originally developed by the company once known as Sun Microsystems; it is the networked filesystem most commonly used for networks of Linux and Unix computers.

nmap   A port scanner that can review the open and available status of TCP/IP ports.

PAM (Pluggable Authentication Modules)   PAM separates the authentication process from individual applications. PAM consists of a set of dynamically loadable library modules that provide various authentication and authorization mechanisms.

parted   A standard disk partition command utility that allows you to modify the physical and logical disk partition layout. Be careful when using **parted** because changes are immediately written to the partition table.

PATH   A shell variable that specifies which directories (and in what order) the shell automatically searches for commands.

PGP (Pretty Good Privacy)   A technique for encrypting messages, often used for e-mail. It includes a secure private- and public-key system similar to RSA. The Linux version of PGP is known as GPG (GNU Privacy Guard).

Physical extent (PE)   A chunk of disk space created from a physical volume (PV) for the Logical Volume Manager (LVM).

Physical volume (PV)   An area of space for the Logical Volume Manager (LVM) that usually corresponds to a partition or a hard drive.

PolicyKit   The PolicyKit is a security framework used primarily for administrative configuration tools when working from a GNOME desktop environment.

Postfix   A standard e-mail server application used by many Internet e-mail servers. The default Red Hat solution for RHEL 7.

Parallel ATA (PATA)   Parallel ATA is an old interface standard associated with older IDE drives, also known as ATA (Advanced Technology Attachment).

/proc   /proc is a Linux virtual filesystem. *Virtual* means that it doesn't occupy real disk space. /proc files are used to provide information on kernel configuration and device status.

Public/private key   Encryption standards such as PGP, GPG, and RSA are based on public/private key pairs. The private key is kept on the local computer; others can decrypt messages with the public key.

pvcreate   The **pvcreate** command allows you to create physical volumes (PVs) from a partition or disk drive.

pvdisplay   The **pvdisplay** command specifies current configuration information for physical volumes (PVs).

QEMU   The hypervisor used with the Red Hat implementation of KVM. It is sometimes known by its former acronym, the quick emulator.

Red Hat Certified Engineer (RHCE)   An elite certification available for Linux professionals. It qualifies Linux administrators with significant experience in Linux services on Red Hat Enterprise Linux. Although the RHCE exam can be taken first, a candidate must pass both the RHCSA and RHCE exams before Red Hat awards that person the RHCE credential.

Red Hat Certified System Administrator (RHCSA)   Another certification available for Linux systems administrators. It's designed to qualify Linux professionals with significant experience in systems administration.

Red Hat Package Manager (RPM)   The Red Hat Package Manager is a package management system that allows software to be distributed in special RPM files. The associated **rpm** command allows you to add, remove, upgrade, and erase packages and more.

Red Hat Subscription Management (RHSM)   Red Hat Subscription Management (RHSM) replaces the Red Hat Network (RHN). It supports remote administration of systems and of their subscriptions.

relayhost   The **relayhost** directive in Postfix supports a connection to a smart host.

resize2fs   The **resize2fs** command allows you to extend the size of an ext filesystem.

Rescue target   When RHEL starts in rescue target mode, it provides a rescue shell to troubleshoot system boot problems.

root   This word has multiple meanings in Linux. The root user is the default administrative user. The root directory (/) is the top-level directory in Linux. The root user's home directory, /root, is a subdirectory of the root directory (/).

Router   A host that forwards packets between network segments. Computers that are connected to multiple networks often serve as routers.

rpc.mountd   The rpc.mountd daemon supports mount requests for shared NFS directories.

rwx/ugo   A reference to basic Linux permissions and ownership on a file; rwx/ugo stands for read, write, execute, user, group, other.

Samba   The Linux and Unix implementation of the Server Message Block protocol and the Common Internet File System (CIFS). Samba allows computers that run Linux and Unix to communicate with computers that run Microsoft Windows operating systems.

Scientific Linux   A "rebuild" of RHEL developed by scientists associated with Fermilab and CERN. That rebuild is based on Red Hat source code.

sealert   The **sealert** command, with audit log files in the /var/log/audit directory, supports detailed analysis of SELinux problems.

Secure virtual host   An Apache virtual host with support for secure HTTP (HTTPS). You can configure multiple secure virtual hosts on a single Apache server.

Security Enhanced Linux (SELinux)   An implementation of mandatory access control integrated into the Linux kernel; in essence, SELinux provides a different way of layering security within Linux and enforcing a security policy by the Linux kernel.

SELinux Troubleshooter   A GUI tool for troubleshooting SELinux log messages.

Sendmail   A standard e-mail server application used by most Internet e-mail. Sendmail was the default Red Hat solution until RHEL 5; it is still supported by Red Hat on RHEL 7.

Serial ATA (SATA)   A standard protocol on hard drives that replaced the Parallel ATA (PATA) standard.

Serial Attached SCSI (SAS)   A protocol compatible with SATA that replaced the old Parallel SCSI bus technology.

Server   A computer that controls centralized resources such as web services, or shared files and printers. Servers can share these resources with client computers on a network.

setfacl   The **setfacl** command lets you set access control lists (ACLs) on files and directories.

setsebool   The **setsebool** command lets you change the status of an SELinux boolean.

SGID   The SGID bit sets the set-group permissions bit on a file or directory. It allows the file to be executed with the effective GID of the group owner. If it is set on a directory, files created within the directory will belong to its group owner.

SHA2, SHA256, SHA512   A series of secure hash algorithms created by the NSA, now in more common use on RHEL 7. SHA512 is the default hashing algorithm for user passwords.

Shadow Password Suite   The Shadow Password Suite creates an additional layer of protection for Linux users and groups in the /etc/shadow and /etc/gshadow files.

showmount   The **showmount** command lists the shared directories from an NFS server.

smbpasswd   The **smbpasswd** command helps you create usernames and passwords for a Samba network.

SMTP (Simple Mail Transfer Protocol)   SMTP is a TCP/IP protocol for sending mail; used by sendmail.

ss   The **ss** command displays network connections on the local system. For example, the **ss -tupa** command is used to display all active TCP and UDP sockets.

ssh-copy-id   The **ssh-copy-id** command can help you copy a public SSH key to the appropriate location on a remote system to set up secure connections without regular passwords.

ssh-keygen   The **ssh-keygen** command can help you create a public-private keypair for SSH-based authentication.

SUID   The SUID bit is the set-user identification bit on a file. It allows the file to be executed with the effective UID of the file owner.

Superuser   The superuser represents a regular user who has taken root user privileges. It is closely associated with the **su** and **sudo** commands.

Swap space   Linux uses swap space as an extension of physical RAM. It is normally configured in Linux in a swap partition.

systemctl   The **systemctl** command manages various functionalities of systemd. It can activate or deactivate service units, modify the default target, and automatically activate service units at boot time.

system-config-*   Red Hat has created a series of GUI configuration tools to help configure a number of different systems and services. You can start them with a number of different commands that begin with **system-config-***. Although it's usually faster to configure a file directly, not every experienced administrator knows every detail of every major configuration file.

systemd   systemd is the first process that is started at boot. It initializes the system and activates appropriate system units. It replaces the traditional init daemon found on RHEL 6.

systemd journal   The logging system of systemd.

Target unit   A group of systemd units that a system can activate at boot. Common targets are the multi-user and graphical targets.

targetcli   An interactive command-line tool to create and administer iSCSI targets.

telnet   A terminal emulation program that allows you to connect to remote computers. The **telnet** command can be used to test the availability of services on specified port numbers.

testparm   The **testparm** command is a syntax checker for the main Samba configuration file, smb.conf.

UEFI   The UEFI is the Unified Extensible Firmware Interface that initializes hardware devices when you power up your computer. On most modern systems, it has replaced the BIOS. The UEFI menu allows you to customize many options, including the sequence of boot media.

umask   The **umask** command defines default permissions for newly created files and directories.

Unbound   Unbound can be used in place of BIND to set up a recursive and caching name server.

Universally Unique Identifier (UUID)   A UUID is a unique 128-bit number, often associated with formatted storage volumes. A current list is available in the output to the **blkid** command. It's used to identify volumes to be mounted in the /etc/fstab file.

User ID (UID)   Every Linux user has a user ID, usually defined in /etc/passwd.

useradd   The **useradd** command creates a new user account.

usermod   The **usermod** command modifies different user account settings, such as the account expiration date and group membership.

Very Secure FTP (vsFTP)   The Very Secure FTP service is the default FTP server for RHEL.

vgcreate   The **vgcreate** command creates a volume group (VG) from one or more physical volumes (PVs) for the Logical Volume Manager (LVM).

vgdisplay   The **vgdisplay** command specifies current configuration information for volume groups (VGs).

vgextend   The **vgextend** command allows you to increase the extents or space allocated to a volume group (VG).

vi   The vi editor is a basic Linux text editor. While other editors are more popular, vi (or vi improved, also known as vim) may be the only editor you have available in certain rescue environments.

virsh   The **virsh** command supports the management of virtual machines on RHEL 7.

virt-clone   The **virt-clone** command supports the copying of an existing virtual machine on RHEL 7.

virt-install   The **virt-install** command supports the creation of a virtual machine on RHEL 7.

Virtual hosts   You can configure multiple websites on a single Apache server by configuring a number of virtual hosts for the Apache configuration file.

Virtual machine (VM)   A system where an application or an entire operating system is run with the help of a hypervisor such as QEMU and a virtualization solution such as KVM.

Virtualization   Virtualization is an abstraction of computer resources. It is most often associated with hardware virtualization, in which you can run one or more virtual machines on a physical system. The default RHEL 7 virtualization solution is KVM.

Volume group (VG)   A collection of physical volumes (PVs) in the Logical Volume Manager (LVM).

WINS (Windows Internet Name Service)   WINS provides name resolution on Microsoft networks; it can be activated on Samba.

XFS   The default filesystem on RHEL 7. It supports journaling and a maximum filesystem size of 8 exabytes (EB).

xfs_growfs   The **xfs_growfs** command allows you to extend the size of an XFS filesystem.

INDEX

D

H

Q

T

LICENSE AGREEMENT

THIS PRODUCT (THE "PRODUCT") CONTAINS PROPRIETARY SOFTWARE, DATA AND INFORMATION (INCLUDING DOCUMENTATION) OWNED BY McGRAW-HILL EDUCATION AND ITS LICENSORS. YOUR RIGHT TO USE THE PRODUCT IS GOVERNED BY THE TERMS AND CONDITIONS OF THIS AGREEMENT.

LICENSE: Throughout this License Agreement, "you" shall mean either the individual or the entity whose agent opens this package. You are granted a non-exclusive and non-transferable license to use the Product subject to the following terms:

(i) If you have licensed a single user version of the Product, the Product may only be used on a single computer (i.e., a single CPU). If you licensed and paid the fee applicable to a local area network or wide area network version of the Product, you are subject to the terms of the following subparagraph (ii).

(ii) If you have licensed a local area network version, you may use the Product on unlimited workstations located in one single building selected by you that is served by such local area network. If you have licensed a wide area network version, you may use the Product on unlimited workstations located in multiple buildings on the same site selected by you that is served by such wide area network; provided, however, that any building will not be considered located in the same site if it is more than five (5) miles away from any building included in such site. In addition, you may only use a local area or wide area network version of the Product on one single server. If you wish to use the Product on more than one server, you must obtain written authorization from McGraw-Hill Education and pay additional fees.

(iii) You may make one copy of the Product for back-up purposes only and you must maintain an accurate record as to the location of the back-up at all times.

COPYRIGHT; RESTRICTIONS ON USE AND TRANSFER: All rights (including copyright) in and to the Product are owned by McGraw-Hill Education and its licensors. You are the owner of the enclosed disc on which the Product is recorded. You may not use, copy, decompile, disassemble, reverse engineer, modify, reproduce, create derivative works, transmit, distribute, sublicense, store in a database or retrieval system of any kind, rent or transfer the Product, or any portion thereof, in any form or by any means (including electronically or otherwise) except as expressly provided for in this License Agreement. You must reproduce the copyright notices, trademark notices, legends and logos of McGraw-Hill Education and its licensors that appear on the Product on the back-up copy of the Product which you are permitted to make hereunder. All rights in the Product not expressly granted herein are reserved by McGraw-Hill Education and its licensors.

TERM: This License Agreement is effective until terminated. It will terminate if you fail to comply with any term or condition of this License Agreement. Upon termination, you are obligated to return to McGraw-Hill Education the Product together with all copies thereof and to purge all copies of the Product included in any and all servers and computer facilities.

DISCLAIMER OF WARRANTY: THE PRODUCT AND THE BACK-UP COPY ARE LICENSED "AS IS." McGRAW-HILL EDUCATION, ITS LICENSORS AND THE AUTHORS MAKE NO WARRANTIES, EXPRESS OR IMPLIED, AS TO THE RESULTS TO BE OBTAINED BY ANY PERSON OR ENTITY FROM USE OF THE PRODUCT, ANY INFORMATION OR DATA INCLUDED THEREIN AND/OR ANY TECHNICAL SUPPORT SERVICES PROVIDED HEREUNDER, IF ANY ("TECHNICAL SUPPORT SERVICES"). McGRAW-HILL EDUCATION, ITS LICENSORS AND THE AUTHORS MAKE NO EXPRESS OR IMPLIED WARRANTIES OF MERCHANTABILITY OR FITNESS FOR A PARTICULAR PURPOSE OR USE WITH RESPECT TO THE PRODUCT. McGRAW-HILL EDUCATION, ITS LICENSORS, AND THE AUTHORS MAKE NO GUARANTEE THAT YOU WILL PASS ANY CERTIFICATION EXAM WHATSOEVER BY USING THIS PRODUCT. NEITHER McGRAW-HILL EDUCATION, ANY OF ITS LICENSORS NOR THE AUTHORS WARRANT THAT THE FUNCTIONS CONTAINED IN THE PRODUCT WILL MEET YOUR REQUIREMENTS OR THAT THE OPERATION OF THE PRODUCT WILL BE UNINTERRUPTED OR ERROR FREE. YOU ASSUME THE ENTIRE RISK WITH RESPECT TO THE QUALITY AND PERFORMANCE OF THE PRODUCT.

LIMITED WARRANTY FOR DISC: To the original licensee only, McGraw-Hill Education warrants that the enclosed disc on which the Product is recorded is free from defects in materials and workmanship under normal use and service for a period of ninety (90) days from the date of purchase. In the event of a defect in the disc covered by the foregoing warranty, McGraw-Hill Education will replace the disc.

LIMITATION OF LIABILITY: NEITHER McGRAW-HILL EDUCATION, ITS LICENSORS NOR THE AUTHORS SHALL BE LIABLE FOR ANY INDIRECT, SPECIAL OR CONSEQUENTIAL DAMAGES, SUCH AS BUT NOT LIMITED TO, LOSS OF ANTICIPATED PROFITS OR BENEFITS, RESULTING FROM THE USE OR INABILITY TO USE THE PRODUCT EVEN IF ANY OF THEM HAS BEEN ADVISED OF THE POSSIBILITY OF SUCH DAMAGES. THIS LIMITATION OF LIABILITY SHALL APPLY TO ANY CLAIM OR CAUSE WHATSOEVER WHETHER SUCH CLAIM OR CAUSE ARISES IN CONTRACT, TORT, OR OTHERWISE. Some states do not allow the exclusion or limitation of indirect, special or consequential damages, so the above limitation may not apply to you.

U.S. GOVERNMENT RESTRICTED RIGHTS: Any software included in the Product is provided with restricted rights subject to subparagraphs (c), (1) and (2) of the Commercial Computer Software-Restricted Rights clause at 48 C.F.R. 52.227-19. The terms of this Agreement applicable to the use of the data in the Product are those under which the data are generally made available to the general public by McGraw-Hill Education. Except as provided herein, no reproduction, use, or disclosure rights are granted with respect to the data included in the Product and no right to modify or create derivative works from any such data is hereby granted.

GENERAL: This License Agreement constitutes the entire agreement between the parties relating to the Product. The terms of any Purchase Order shall have no effect on the terms of this License Agreement. Failure of McGraw-Hill Education to insist at any time on strict compliance with this License Agreement shall not constitute a waiver of any rights under this License Agreement. This License Agreement shall be construed and governed in accordance with the laws of the State of New York. If any provision of this License Agreement is held to be contrary to law, that provision will be enforced to the maximum extent permissible and the remaining provisions will remain in full force and effect.

31901059491565